AFRICAN-AMERICAN BLUES, RHYTHM AND BLUES, GOSPEL AND ZYDECO ON FILM AND VIDEO, 1926-1997

For Matthew, who grew up with all of this.

African-American Blues, Rhythm and Blues, Gospel and Zydeco on Film and Video, 1926–1997

Paul Vernon

Ashgate

Aldershot • Brookfield USA • Singapore • Sydney

Published by

Ashgate Publishing Limited
Gower House
Croft Road
Aldershot
Hants
GU11 3HR
England

Ashgate Publishing Company
Old Post Road
Brookfield
Vermont 05036–9704
USA

British Library Cataloguing-in-Publication data
Vernon, Paul
African-American blues, rhythm and blues, gospel and zydeco on film and video, 1926–1997
1.Motion picture, music – History 2. Afro-American – Music
I.Title
781.5'42

Library of Congress Cataloging-in-Publication data
Vernon, Paul
African-American blues, rhythm and blues, gospel and zydeco on film and video, 1926–1997 / by Paul Vernon.
Includes bibliographical references.
1. Afro-Americans – Music– Filmography. 2. Blues (Music) – Filmography. 3. Rhythm and blues music – Filmography. 4. Gospel music – Filmography. 5. Zydeco music – Filmography. I. Title.
ML158.6.A35V47 1999
016.781643'089'96073–DC21 98–48218
CIP
MN

ISBN 1 84014 294 4

Typeset in Times by Pat FitzGerald and printed on acid-free paper and bound in Great Britain

CONTENTS

PREFACE

The early history of African-American vernacular music on film is essentially one of random attention and accident. That we have evidence of Whistler's Jug Band but not the Memphis Jug Band, that Elder Michaux received media attention while the Reverend J M Gates did not, is due to the general lack of interest displayed by contemporary film-makers.

The earliest footage, from 1926, made by Dr Milton Metfessel, depicts un-named amateur artists and was made for research purposes. Newsreels filmed by Fox Movietone, beginning some two years later, feature more unnamed amateurs, and it was not until Dudley Murphy's flawed 1929 classic *St. Louis Blues* that the first conscious effort to record some form of blues on film was made at all. In the same year an unknown filmmaker captured a few moments by the Excelsior Quartette, but not until 1931, when Hearst Metrotone filmed Whistler's Jug Band, was anything approaching a fully-formed non-urban style given any attention; yet that film was never used at the time, and has survived only through benign neglect.

Little else happened in the ensuing decade; Leadbelly appeared in front of cameras in 1935 for the *March Of Time* series, and Fox Movietone filmed the gospel radio star Elder Michaux in his Washington church that same year. The rise of independent African-American film-makers did little to remedy this lack of attention. The first use of any hardcore blues was in Spencer Williams' 1941 film *The Blood Of Jesus* when he employed a partial sound track recording by Texas guitarist Black Ace. The first serious attention paid to African-American vernacular music in any meaningful sense was that accorded it by the Soundies corporation, who from 1941 to 1946 produced three minute monochrome film shorts designed to be played in coin-operated machines installed in public places. These 'Soundies' represent the first significant body of filmed African-American vernacular music and are especially crucial today since they are the only animate evidence from an era of huge and culturally important change in this music. Prime examples of the music of Louis Jordan, Lucky Millinder, Roy Milton, Rosetta Tharpe and other early Rhythm & Blues artists exist only because of Soundies.

Following the demise of the Soundies corporation, in 1946, attention again largely fell away until 1955, when the TV series 'Harlem Variety Review' popularly known as 'Showtime At The Apollo', was filmed for US TV syndication. Backed by the Paul Williams band, Joe Turner, Dinah Washington, the Larks, Ruth Brown, Amos Milburn, the Clovers and others performed live versions of their current hits. In the following two years cheap, quickly made films produced in response to the Rock & Roll craze brought Chuck Berry, The Moonglows, The Flamingos, Fats Domino, Lavern Baker, Little Richard and others to a wider – that is, white – audience for the first time with any real measure of impact.

As Rock & Roll abated, to a degree giving way to the so-called 'Folk Boom' that began in the late 1950s, rural blues styles began to receive some belated attention. Working alone, Pete Seeger had filmed Big Bill Broonzy in 1957, and Sonny Terry and J C Burris in 1958, but these privately made shorts were not available to the public at the time. In Europe and America, beginning in 1960, enthusiasts slowly began the documentation of traditional blues styles. PBS TV in America filmed the 1960 Newport Jazz Festival, recording for posterity the Muddy Waters band in something close to its prime, while in Europe Yannick Bruynoghe, who had helped Jean Delire make the 1956 Belgian short *Big Bill Blues* was able to film Roosevelt Sykes on a visit to Brussels. Two years later, while Sam Charters was editing his documentary *The Blues*, Horst Lipmann and Fritz Rau brought the first American Folk Blues Festival package to Europe, where German Sudwestfunk TV filmed them and broadcast the results.

These events occurred at the very beginning of an extraordinary era in Europe, when blues and Rhythm & Blues suddenly became massively popular. The 1963 Folk Blues Festival package that toured several European countries appeared on both German and British TV, and the period to 1966 was a busy one for blues musicians in TV studios. British programmes including 'Ready Steady Go', 'Beat Room' and 'Jazz 625', the work of producer John Hamp and director Phil Casson at Granada TV, and the continuing interest by German Sudwestfunk, all contributed to a body of recordings that we can be grateful for today, even if a few individual performances are somewhat lacklustre. Several key artists, including Sonny Boy Williamson, J B Lenoir and Little Walter would have gone completely unfilmed had it not been for these efforts. On a technical level, this activity coincided with the increased use of videotape, allowing producers and directors greater flexibility in editing, and providing television with its own medium, rather than borrowing from the cinematic world.

In the spring of 1963 German film-maker Dietrich Wawzyn, accompanied by Arhoolie Records owner Chris Strachwitz, conducted a tour of North America, visiting several major cities and filming powerful performances by a number of traditional musicians. These were initially made for the German television programme 'Die Blues', but the bulk of footage shot by Wawzyn has survived to this day.

In the meantime, within the United States, significant events were occurring. From 1963 gospel music was the subject of two long running TV shows, 'Jubilee Showcase' and 'TV Gospel Time', both of which have fortunately been reasonably well archived and provide a large number of very important musical performances. Simultaneously, a few Rhythm & Blues acts were beginning to appear elsewhere on US TV, as series like 'Shindig' and specials such as the 'TAMI Show', designed to appeal to a white teen market, began using more and more African-American vernacular music acts. The Dallas-based network show 'The Beat', while only surviving one season in the spring and summer of 1966, provided many excellent examples of contemporary blues and Rhythm & Blues, and every episode survives intact. Canada's most interesting contribution was the 1966 show entitled 'Festival Presents The Blues', the result of a marathon three day recording session in Toronto involving Muddy Waters and his band, Sunnyland Slim, Willie Dixon, Mable Hillery, Bukka White, Brownie McGhee and Sonny Terry, Big Joe Williams and Jesse Fuller.

By the mid 1960s a few serious folklorists were documenting older traditions for posterity. John Ullman of the Seattle Folklore Society filmed older country blues musicians. Les Blank's career began with a film – *The Blues According to Lightnin' Hopkins* – that remains today one of the few truly classic blues documentaries, and sporadic filming of the annual Newport summer folk festival was ongoing, the most important footage being made in 1966 by veteran folklorist Alan Lomax. As the 1960s progressed, and turned into the 1970s, a significant number of individual documentaries were made that attempted to trace one or other aspect of African-American vernacular music and offer some historical perspective. The University of Mississippi, beginning in 1969, Harley Cokliss in 1970, and Robert Manthoulis in 1971 all produced worthy documentaries.

From 1972, the Montreux Jazz Festival was routinely videotaped, providing an increasingly important archive of performances, and from the mid 1970s onwards a large number of documentaries have been made both by European production companies and US Public Broadcasting System TV stations covering different aspects of the music. The 1976 BBC field trip that produced *The Devil's Music* is especially important, as is the continuing work of independent film makers such as Les Blank and Robert Mugge. Feature films, intended for general public consumption, have only infrequently employed African-American vernacular music but directors such as Elia Kazan and John Landis clearly marked themselves as fans by their continued use of it.

The body of work that all these efforts have produced is little enough when viewed within the context of other media, especially sound recordings, and one can only regret the many lost opportunities that have, over the decades, left us without film of Memphis Minnie in 1931, Roy Byrd in 1949 or the Five Blind Boys in 1954. However, what has survived is often good, sometimes great and always, at least, historically interesting. These film recordings serve as a useful adjunct to the vast body of sound recordings, photographs and collected text on African-American vernacular music, adding a dimension that allows us to see an artist's body language, facial expressions and instrumental techniques. This collected evidence will take on new importance as the world draws a line under the twentieth century and reflects, as it surely must, upon its own recent history.

Paul Vernon

ACKNOWLEDGEMENTS

The contents of this book are the sum total of twenty years of interest and research. During that time very many people and organisations have contributed, in different measure, to the work presented here. My thanks are due especially to:

Sherwin Dunner for supplying much useful information and good feedback;

Raymond R Funk for much of the detailed gospel information that appears in this work, and also for other useful and generous assistance;

Bill Greensmith for a vast array of useful information unavailable elsewhere, and for his counsel, freely and willingly given;

Stefan Grossman for supplying much useful information;

Robert Laughton for most of the gospel personnel details;

Robert Mugge for assistance above and beyond the call of duty;

Howard Rye for generously providing pre-publication information from *Blues & Gospel Records 1890–1943*, most of the information in the Louis Jordan entry, and for much of the detailed information concerning Soundies and commercially issued videotapes;

Chris Smith for expert and detailed proofreading, for many relevant suggestions and for much additional information;

and also to the following, who all assisted in various ways:

Archive Films, London and New York; Arlington County Library, Ballston, Virginia; Bruce Bastin; Terry Bedford; Chris Bentley; Alasdair Blaazer; Les Blank; Borders Books and Music, Bailey's Crossroads, Virginia; British Film Institute, London; Tony Brown; Viv Broughton; Centre For Southern Culture; Dave Clarke; the late David J Colebeck; Christine Collozo; Gil Cook; Malcolm Crewe; Norman Darwen; Nicola Ebenau; Judy Rolph Ebner; George Edick; Alan Empson; Flower Films; Tom Freeland; Mike Gavin; Mel Geeves; Steve Goldfield; Goldhawk Television Productions, London; Gina and John Goldman; Peter Goldsmith; Granada Television, Manchester; Brian Griffiths; Nick Heath; Joseph C Hickerson; Historic Footage, NYC; Derek Howe; Cilla Huggins; Bruce Iglauer; International Broadcasting Trust, London; International Creative Exchange of Los Angeles; Interstate Music Ltd, Bexhill, England; Richard Johnson; Richard and Maggie Kay [K-Jazz]; Joe Lauro; Robert Laughton; Alan Lewens; Library of Congress, Washington, DC; Dr. Kip Lornell; Dr. Rainer Lotz; The Mississippi Dept of Archives and History; Dave Moore; Ken Morse; Multicultural Media,

Vermont; Conrad Novakowski; Opal Louis Nations; Giles Oakley; Offstage Theatre and Film Bookshop, London; Steve Outram; Judy Peiser; Dave Penny; Jim Potts; Julian Purser; Ray's Jazz Shop, London; Red Lick Records, Wales; Rhino Records, Los Angeles; Mike Rowe; Shanachie Entertainment, New York; Peter Shertser; Brian Smith; Ken Smith; Smithsonian Institute, Washington DC; Leo St. Clair; Glen Stapleton; the late Ian Stewart; Chris Strachwitz; Angus Trowbridge; TCB Releasing; Cornelius Lee Vernon-Boas; Vestapol Videos; Dietrich Wawzyn; Del White; Francis Wilford-Smith; Dave Williams; Windows To The World Telecommunications Inc; Yazoo Videos

Finally, a vote of thanks to Rachel Lynch, my editor, whose calm expertise has guided me through many a technical minefield.

Paul Vernon

INTRODUCTION

This book is principally designed as a reference work to assist film directors, producers and researchers to establish what material exists within the parameters of the title and where it may be found. In addition, historians, writers, collectors and enthusiasts may also find the contents useful and so it has been compiled with all these potential readers in mind.

For the film-maker, it is hoped that this volume will drastically cut research time and therefore enable any research budgets – often minimal – to be used more effectively. For this reason all known announcements, monologues, dialogues, conversations and interviews have also been recorded here, to allow a full exploration of existing material.

For the collector or enthusiast it may be especially frustrating to realize that she or he will be denied access to much of this material unless it is used by a film-maker and then released for public consumption. Particular attention, therefore, has been paid to the material available on commercially released videotape aimed at the domestic consumer market. Appendix 5 will provide most home consumers with more than enough excellent footage to satisfy their desires. Most of these tapes, especially those on K-Jazz, Rhapsody, Vestapol and Yazoo, are of excellent quality, both artistically and technically. Vestapol tapes have the added benefit of lengthy and informative notes to accompany each issue. Furthermore, feature films available to the home video market are flagged in the List of Programme and Film Titles, and Production Companies.

For the historian and researcher, combining the material presented here with existing biographical and discographical information can often prove to be an enlightening endeavour. The careers of Memphis Slim, Willie Dixon and the Stars of Faith, for instance, take on an added dimension with the inclusion of their visually recorded performances.

The parameters of this work are defined largely by the title, but it may be useful to expand upon them here. All traditional African-American blues, non-blues secular vernacular music, rhythm and blues, rock and roll, gospel, zydeco, and the few extant examples of African-American Cajun are included. The definition of Rhythm and Blues includes populist styles of the 1940s, mainstream R&B and Rock & Roll of the 1950s and regional material up to the 1960s. Some of this arguably strays into jazz but has been included here both for the sake of completeness and because it allows a fuller context to be explored. Artists whose careers began during any of the above mentioned time frames are included up to their last known recording unless, as in the case of the Staple Singers or Ike Turner, their style altered radically enough to put them outside the scope of this work.

Not included here are jazz singers, rock singers and blues style material performed by people other than African-Americans. This has meant the exclusion of artists like Lou Rawls, Jimi Hendrix, Odetta, Paul Butterfield, John Hammond Jr, Aretha Franklin and Billie Holiday, although where such artists play a supporting role, their contributions have been documented. Further, 1960s soul music, and post-1970 gospel except that which is very clearly traditional, have also been excluded. All these areas of musical endeavour require similar documentation, and it is to be hoped that they will soon receive the attention they deserve. Those wishing to research jazz in visually recorded performances are earnestly recommended to consult David Meeker's *Jazz In The Movies* which is due for republication in a much revised edition before the turn of the century.

Performed songs are listed in the order in which they appear in the production and may be assumed to be complete unless otherwise noted in parenthesis after the title. The term 'part only' indicates that the performance, while not complete, is generally long enough to be relevant to both the student and the film-maker searching for archive footage. The term 'fragment only' generally indicates a performance of under 15 seconds duration. In some cases partially used titles may still exist in full in the archives that hold them, but it has not been possible to conduct an exhaustive search. Often, in feature films, music will be used as a background to the plot, and many performances will therefore include cutaway shots to dialogue or action. This can often include audience reaction scenes in clubs, bars and theatres, which does not therefore render the performance totally unusable.

Soundtrack material is only included if it was specifically written for a production. No attempt has been made to catalogue the frequent use of previously recorded performances on soundtrack; thus, for instance, the Chess recording of Muddy Waters 'Hoochie Coochie Man', employed in *Give My Poor Heart Ease*, or the use of Blind Willie Johnson's 'Dark Was The Night, Cold Was The Ground' in Pasolini's *The Gospel According To St. Matthew* have not been documented here.

It has also been necessary to omit any privately made video recordings of an amateur nature. While the advent of home video recording has bestowed a great freedom upon the individual enthusiast, those efforts potentially relevant to this work cannot be included for two reasons. First, the technical standard of both sound and vision, in most cases, renders them virtually unbroadcastable and second, the copyright is often too difficult to negotiate. Readers should remain aware, however, that such material is in circulation and often available from sources known to collectors. That said, the inclusion of material in this volume is no guarantee of quality. A few broad guidelines, filtered through the compiler's sensibilities, are offered in the accompanying short essay.

The main section of this work has been organized alphabetically, by artist name, and then chronologically under each artist name. Artists who changed their names will be found under the first letter of their professional surname. Thus, William George Tucker, who changed his name to John Henry Barbee, will be found under B. Artists who employed a pseudonym not including a surname will be found under the first letter of the first word of the pseudonym, thus Lightnin' Slim (Otis Hicks) will be found under L and Bo Diddley (Ellas Otha Bates McDaniel) will be found under B. Artists who used a pseudonym or nickname for the first part of their name coupled with their given surname will be found under the first letter of the given surname. Thus, T-Bone Walker will be found under W. All group names will be found under the first letter of the first name of the group, so that while the Larks appear under L, the Voices of Triumph will be found under V. Where an alternative name is known it is given in parenthesis, as this will often be an aid to copyright research.

Where more than one artist shares equal credit in creating a performance, the entry will be found under all the artists' names. Jam sessions, for example, are thoroughly cross-referenced. However, where an artist takes a clear leading role, even in a duet, the entry will be found under the leading artist's name, although those artists who are associated with each other are cross-referenced.[1] Further information on associated performances may be gathered by studying the accompanists index.

In the cases of large, mostly jazz-oriented bands and orchestras, neither the known nor the likely personnel has been listed. To list every musician in the entries for Jimmy Rushing or Joe Williams, for example, would be to duplicate large quantities of information readily accessible elsewhere. However, a very real attempt has been made to list personnel for those entries where such information is not readily available.

The fact that an artist appeared on record within a few weeks of making a film or TV appearance is no guarantee that the accompanying personnel will be the same. In some cases, such as Muddy Waters, enough corroborative evidence exists in many instances to be reasonably certain who accompanied him, but in the cases of, for example, performances by Fats Domino or B.B. King that have not been viewed by the compiler, no assumptions have been made. The use of the words 'probably' and 'possibly' indicate, in the first instance, strong circumstantial evidence leading to the suggested information and, in the second, an informed guess. All other information has been verified by either viewing the production or working from other original material, including production shot-lists, catalogues and other archive sources.

The use of the word 'guitar' indicates a standard 6-string acoustic instrument played without amplification. The term 'electric guitar' indicates either a solid-bodied amplified 6-string instrument or an acoustic 6-string instrument amplified by a pick-up. The use of 12-string guitars, where known, is noted. The use of the term 'steel guitar' indicates a steel-bodied acoustic instrument often, but not exclusively, a National brand Resonator, played without amplification. In the rare cases where a pedal-steel guitar is used, it is duly noted.

'Harmonica' indicates the wind instrument also known as the mouth-organ. Generally, but not exclusively, these are played without amplification in rural musics, and through a microphone and amplifier in urban musics. The pan-European term 'harmonica', as applied to a keyboard-operated accordion, is not used here. Accordions, where they appear, are mentioned specifically.

'Piano' indicates an unamplified standard 88-key instrument, either upright, baby grand or full grand. 'Keyboards' indicates electric or electronic instruments equipped with keyboard systems. These may be electric pianos, organs or synthesizers. Where specific instruments are known, they are noted.

'Bass' indicates an acoustic, upright four string wooden-bodied instrument. The use of the term 'electric bass' indicates an amplified four string bass guitar.

Wherever possible, the use of alto, baritone, soprano and tenor saxophones has been noted. If an entry reads simply 'saxophone' then the pitch of the instrument is unknown and should not be assumed. Other wind instruments are mentioned, where they occur, in as much detail as possible.

The use of the word 'drums' generally indicates a full standard drum kit. Where specific percussion appears it, too, is mentioned in as much detail as possible.

Where unique instruments are featured, such as the 9-string guitar, the fotdella and the razor strop, they are all specifically noted.

A standard entry may be read thus:

ARTIST[S] NAME[S] (given or alternate name in parenthesis)
details of personnel and instrumentation. In cases where the instrumentation varies from one performance to another, the differences are indicated by the use of numerics (see example below). If the artist is miming, then the original catalogue number of the record to which the mime is being performed is given.

Location: Place and date of recording. The appearance of a full day/date may be read as verified correct information. In cases where the location alters the differences are indicated by the use of letters [A] and [B]. See example below. All locations outside the USA are specifically noted. If no country is given, the reader may assume a North American location.

Title[s] performed:

Full title as it appears in either the credit to the programme, or from an announcement within the programme. In some cases it has been necessary to reference the title from another source. In a few cases, where the title is clearly in error, a more likely alternative has also been suggested. Details of announcements, monologues, dialogues and conversations are also recorded here.

Commercially available video tape company name[s] and catalogue number[s], in those cases where the material has been commercially released. Each individual title is accorded, where relevant, a separate release number since in several complex cases the catalogue numbers will vary from title to title, and some titles remain unissued.

Source: The film or programme name, details of which will be found in the Production Index

Any other notes relevant to the artists or songs will appear here. This includes cross referencing to associated artists. The use of the term 'unconfirmed' indicates that the information has been derived from a single unsupported source and may be rightly regarded as hearsay awaiting confirmation.

Thus:

ALPHONSE [BOIS-SEC] ARDOIN

Vocal and accordion accompaniment: Canray Fontenot (violin): Isom Fontenot (triangle)–1
Canray Fontenot, violin and vocal accompaniment: Ardoin (accordion)–2

Location: Newport, Rhode Island. July 1966
[A] On stairwell
[B] In open air

Titles performed:

Two Step De Eunice [A]–1	Vestapol 13050
La Valse De La Prison [A]–2	Vestapol 13050
[interview] [A]	
Laccasine Breakdown [B]–1	Vestapol 13050
untitled 2-step [B]–1	Vestapol 13050
Bon Soir Moreau [B]–2	Vestapol 13050

Source: *Alan Lomax film collection*
See also Canray Fontenot.

This may then be cross-referenced to the following appendices:

1. The List of Programme and Film Titles, and Production Companies, which contains details of the production itself, including, where known, the director, production company and production year[s]; whether it is a documentary, film, film short, TV series or animated feature; whether it is in colour or monochrome. There then follows an alphabetical list of all artists appearing in the production and any relevant footnotes pertaining to the production itself and information on its commercial availability.

2. The List of Accompanists which gives, alphabetically, all known accompanying musicians together with alphabetical lists of those whom they accompanied.

3. The List of Directors which gives all known directors alphabetically, and all films they directed, listed alphabetically under each directorial name.

4. Useful Resources, which furnishes information on how to obtain material found in this book. The term 'commercial only' means that the company in question supplies material at trade rates only to film makers, and will not deal on an individual basis with private enquiries.

5. Commercially Available Videotapes, which lists, alphabetically by company name, and then numerically by issue number, all commercially available videotapes for domestic consumption. This list excludes feature films, which may be found in the List of Programme and Film Titles, and Production Companies, duly flagged.

6. Commercially Available Laser Discs, which lists alphabetically by company name, and then numerically by issue number, all commercially available laser discs for domestic consumption.

7. Non-performing Interviewees, which lists those people interviewed in productions who do not make any musical contributions, together with the subjects upon which they speak and the productions in which they may be found.

8. Soundtracks, which lists CD and vinyl issues of material directly related to visual recordings.

Abbreviations used in all these appendices will be found in the key to abbreviations on page xvii.

The reader's attention is drawn to the following numbering systems allocated to specific series by the archives that hold them. Time and energy can be saved by using these numbering systems when enquiring about or ordering any programme:

JUBILEE SHOWCASE. Shown either after each entry, or in 'source' in the main section, e.g. [Prog # 17-2]

SOUNDIES. Shown before each individual title, in parenthesis, e.g. [17M1]

TV GOSPEL TIME. Shown after each entry or in 'source' in the main section, e.g. TV Gospel Time #8

It will quickly become clear which performances listed in this work have been studied in depth and which have not. Access to some of this material is currently difficult, and in some cases it is far from certain that it has even survived. Early TV performances are especially problematic, and many may have been lost. Nevertheless, so much has been rescued within the last decade that almost nothing is beyond the realms of possibility. The practice of using the kinescope system to distribute early American TV productions may well have secured, in some obscure archive, a programme long thought to have been irretrievable. Material on videotape leased from one company to another, often overseas, may still lie forgotten in company archives. The discovery of a huge cache of early African-American independent films in Tyler, Texas during the late 1980s is evidence that little can ever be considered completely lost.

No claim is made for the completeness of this work, an impossible concept in an undertaking of this nature. But the author is reasonably confident that it represents the great bulk of extant material. If there are areas of weakness, they are probably within the realms of early North American local TV broadcasts, Japanese and East European TV broadcasts and material made within twelve months prior to the publication of this book. I would welcome any additions and amendments to this work.

I hope that readers will find this book entertaining as well as useful. There are many splendidly bizarre cultural encounters recorded here, and ultimately the sum total of information presented within these pages provides some evidence of just how far-reaching and influential this wonderful music is.

Note

1 However, the case of Brownie McGhee and Sonny Terry is especially complex and therefore all their duet work, together with McGhee's solo work, is to be found under McGhee's name. Only those sessions by Terry where McGhee is not present are listed under Terry's name.

LIST OF ABBREVIATIONS

[AF]	Animated film
aka	also known as
ATV	Associated Television Company [UK]
BBC	British Broadcasting Corporation [UK]
[C]	colour film/video
[D]	documentary
[F]	film
[FS]	film short
[G]	group of musicians; often rock-orientated
ITV	Independent Televison [UK]
LWT	London Weekend Television [UK]
[M]	monochrome film/kinescope/video
NTSC	National Television System Committee
[orch]	orchestra
PAL	Phase Alternation Line
PBS	Public Broadcasting System [USA]
[prog #]	specifically for Jubilee Showcase, the allocated programme number by which material may be found
SECAM	Séquential Couleur A Mémoire
[ST]	sound-track
TV	television

Works on Film and Video: Alphabetical Entries by Artist

A

THE ACES
Louis Myers (vocal and electric guitar); David Myers (electric bass); Fred Below (drums)

Location: Chicago, Illinois. Wednesday 28 January 1976

Titles performed:
'Take A Little Walk With Me'
'Blue Shadows' [unbroadcast]

Source: *The Devil's Music*.
See also Louis and David Myers.

FAYE ADAMS
Vocal accompaniment: Paul Williams (baritone saxophone); Jimmy Brown (trumpet); unknown (tenor saxophone, piano, bass and drums)

Location: New York City. 1955

Titles performed:

[introduction by Willie Bryant and Faye Adams] Storyville SV6016
'Everyday' Storyville SV6016, Video Images 73R
'Someday, Somewhere' Storyville SV6016

Source: *Showtime At The Apollo*

JOHNNY ADAMS
Vocal accompaniment: unknown

Location: Germany. Mid-1980s

Titles performed:
'Garbage Man'
'Road Block'

Source: *Ohne Filter Blues*

MARIE ADAMS AND THE THREE TONS OF JOY
See Johnny Otis.

ALABAMA IKE
See William Greaves.

LYNN ALBRITTON
Piano solos, with appearances by the following dancers: Lou Ellen–1; The Six Knobs–2; Billy and Ann–3; The Harlem Cuties–4

Location: probably New York City. Spring 1943

Titles performed:
[11802] 'Block Party Revels' –2, –4 Charly #2
[11905] 'Backstage Blues' –1, –3 Charly #2, Storyville SV6013, Virgin VVD-762
[12408] 'Dispossessed Blues'–2

Source: *Soundies*
11802 copyrighted 17 May 1943; 11905 1 June 1943;12408 5 July 1943

ERNESTINE [ANISTEEN] ALLEN
Vocal accompaniment: the Lucky Millinder orchestra

Location: New York City. Early–mid-1946

Title performed:
[24M4] 'I Want A Man'

Source: *Soundie*
Copyrighted 19 August 1946. See Rosetta Tharpe for likely personnel

Vocal accompaniment: the Lucky Millinder orchestra

Location: New York City. 1948

Title performed:
'Let It Roll' Timeless Video 5603

Source: *Boarding House Blues*

DAVE ALEXANDER

Vocal and piano accompaniment, if any: unknown

Location: Los Angles, California. 1975

Titles performed:
unknown

Source: *Perspective* [unconfirmed]
Alexander is now known as Omar Sharriff.

LUTHER ALLISON

Vocal and electric guitar accompaniment: unknown

Location: Chicago, Illinois. 1976

Title performed:
'Luther's Blues' [ST]

Source: *Cooley High*

Vocal and electric guitar accompaniment: unknown

Location: Chicago, Illinois. 1978

Titles performed:
unknown

Source: *Soundstage*

Vocal, harmonica and electric guitar accompaniment: Michael Carras (keyboards); Mike Morrison (electric bass); Jay Mattes (drums)

Location: Montreux, Switzerland. Friday 15 July 1983

Titles performed:
'Hot Shot'
'Life Is A Bitch'
'Should I Wait'
'Just My Guitar And Me'
'Show Me A Reason'
'I Gave It All'
'Bad News'
'Back Pack'
'Serious As A Heart Attack'
'Confusion In The Parking Lot'
'Let Me Love You Baby'
'The Sky Is Crying'

Source: *Montreux Jazz*

Vocal and electric guitar accompaniment: unknown

Location: Montreux, Switzerland. 1985

Title performed:
'I Just Can't Turn You Loose' and other, unknown, titles

Source: *Montreux Jazz*

Vocal and electric guitar accompaniment: unknown

Location: Hamburg, Germany. Tuesday 28 October 1986

Titles performed:
'Back Track'
'I'm On The Road Again'
'Got To Get You Into My Life'
'Show Me A Reason To Stay'
'I Got My Guitar And Me'

Source: *German TV broadcast* [C]

Vocal and electric guitar accompaniment: Bernard Allison (second electric guitar); Sulaiman Hakim (tenor saxophone and clarinet); Michael Carras (keyboards); Peter Giron (electric bass); Vincent Duane (drums)–1
as above, Allison, vocal and harmonica–2
as above, instrumental, without Luther Allison–3

Location: Tokyo, Japan. Saturday 23 May 1993

Titles performed:
'Compromise'–1
'Hoochie Coochie Man'–2
'Life Is A Bitch'–1
'Serious'–1
'Just Memories'–1
'Freedom'–3

Source: *Japanese TV broadcast* [C]

RICH AMERSON
Vocal, unaccompanied

Location: Livingston, Alabama. c. 31 October 1940

Titles performed:
unknown

Source: *Library Of Congress*

RUTH AMES
Vocal accompaniment: Lightnin' Hopkins (guitar)

Location: Centerville, Texas. 1967

Title performed:
'I'm Walkin'' Flower 1, K-Jazz 053
[dialogue with Hopkins] Flower 1, K-Jazz 053

Source: *The Blues According To Lightnin' Hopkins*

ALBERT AMMONS AND PETE JOHNSON
Pete Johnson, piano solo–1
Lena Horne, vocal accompaniment: Pete Johnson, piano–2
Ammons and Johnson, piano duet accompaniment: J C Heard (drums)–3
Lena Horne, vocal accompaniment: Johnson (piano) and Teddy Wilson and his orchestra: Emmett Berry (trumpet); Benny Morton (trombone); Jimmy Hamilton (clarinet); Teddy Wilson (piano); Johnny Williams (bass); J C Heard (drums)–4

Location: possibly Astoria Studios, Long Island City, New York City. c. 16 September–20 October 1941

Titles performed:
piano tuning–1 Jazz Classics 108, JVC 111, Parkfield MKJ0007, Proserpine 811, Storyville SV6013, Virgin VVD662
[dialogue between Ammons, Johnson and Horne leading to;]
[21M1] 'My New Gown'–2 Jazz Classics 108, JVC 111, Parkfield MKJ0008, Proserpine 811, Storyville SV6013 Virgin VVD662
[leading to;]
short instrumental solo–1 Jazz Classics 108, JVC 111, Parkfield MKJ0008, Proserpine 811, Storyville SV6013, Virgin VVD662
[introduction by Lena Horne, leading to;]
[20008] 'Boogie Woogie Dream'–3 Jazz Classics 108, JVC 111, Parkfield MKJ0008, Proserpine 666, 811, Storyville SV6013, Virgin VVD662
[19208] 'Unlucky Woman'–4 Jazz Classics 108, JVC 111, Parkfield MKJ0008, Proserpine 611, 811, Storyville SV6013, View Video 1313, Virgin VVD662

Source: *Boogie Woogie Dream*
The numbers in parenthesis are the issue numbers allocated each piece when they were distributed as Soundies.

The entire film, including dialogue, is available on Jazz Classics 108; JVC 111; Parkfield MKJ0008; Proserpine 811; Storyville SV6013; and Virgin VVD662. Proserpine 611, 666 and View Video 1313 offer extracts only.

ERNESTINE ANDERSON
Vocal accompaniment: the Johnny Otis band

Location: Monterey, California. 1987

Title performed:
'See See Rider'

Source: *Monterey Jazz Festival*

PINKNEY [PINK] ANDERSON

Vocal and guitar accompaniment: his son, Alvin 'Little Pink' Anderson, vocal–1

Location: Spartanburg, South Carolina. Summer 1962

Titles performed:
'Weeping Willow Blues'
'Old Cotton Fields Of Home'–1

Source: *The Blues* [1]

Vocal and guitar

Location: South Carolina. 1970

Titles performed:
'She Knows How To Stretch it' Vestapol 13037
'Ain't Nobody Home But Me' Vestapol 13037
'Crow Jane' Vestapol 13037
'You Don't Know What The Lord Told Me' Vestapol 13037

Source: *uncredited* [M]

ROBERT ANDERSON

Vocal accompaniment: unknown

Location: Chicago, Illinois. Saturday 10 October 1964

Titles performed:
'It's In My Heart' [A]
'Just A Closer Walk With Thee' [A]
'I've Got Jesus In My Soul' [B]
'O Lord, Is It I?' [B]

Source: *TV Gospel Time* #37[A], #39[B]

Vocal accompaniment: unknown

Location: Chicago, Illinois. Sunday 10 September 1972

Titles performed:
unknown

Source: *Jubilee Showcase* [M] [prog #2–1]

INEZ ANDREWS AND THE ANDREWETTES

Vocal group accompaniment, if any: unknown

Location: Chicago, Illinois. Saturday 10 October 1964

Titles performed:
'There Must Be A God Somewhere'
'What Love'
'Let The Church Roll On'

Source: *TV Gospel Time* #37

Inez Andrews, Elaine Davis, Mildred Span, Elizabeth Dargan (vocals), unaccompanied

Location: Free Trade Hall, Manchester, England. January 1965

Titles performed:
unknown

Source: *They Sing Like Someone's Happy*

As above

Location: Alpirsbach Monastery, Schwarzwald, Germany. Late January 1965

Titles performed:
'There Must Be A God Somewhere' Praise 3012
'What Love' Praise 3012
'Mary Don't You Weep' Praise 3012

Source: *German TV broadcas*t [M]

Vocal group accompaniment, if any: unknown

Location: Chicago, Illinois.

The following appearances are known:
1966
Sunday 23 January [prog #6-2]
1967
Sunday 5 March [prog #17-1]
1969
Saturday 5 July [prog #12-2]
Saturday 1 November [prog #8-3]
1972
Saturday 12 August [prog #4-3]
1973

Saturday 24 November [prog #32-1]
1975
Thursday 13 March [prog #19-2]

Titles performed:
unknown

Source: *Jubilee Showcase*

Vocal group accompaniment, if any: unknown

Location: Chicago, Illinois. 1976

Titles performed:
unknown

Source: *Here Comes Gospel*

Vocal group accompaniment: unknown

Location: Chicago, Illinois. Monday 20 September 1982

Titles performed:
unknown

Source: *Jubilee Showcase* [prog #33–3]

Vocal group accompaniment: unknown

Location: unknown {USA}. 1980s

Titles performed:
unknown — Savoy 9500

Source: *Down Memory Lane*

ANGELIC CHOIR OF NEWARK, NEW JERSEY
Mixed vocal choir, accompaniment: unknown

Location: probably New York City. 1965–66

Titles performed:
unknown

Source: *TV Gospel Time* #49

ANTIOCH BAPTIST CHURCH CONGREGATION
Vocals, unaccompanied

Location: Antioch, Mississippi. August 1995

Title performed:
untitled lining out hymn [part only]

Source: *Too Close To Heaven*

ANTIOCH GOSPEL CHOIR [*sic*]
Three males, one female, vocals
accompaniment: unknown (two electric guitars, electric bass, drums)

Location: Antioch Spiritual Church, New Orleans, Louisiana. 1990

Title performed:
unknown song (part only)

Source: *Big World*

ALPHONSE [BOIS-SEC] ARDOIN
Vocal and accordion accompaniment: Canray Fontenot (violin); Isom Fontenot (triangle)–1
Canray Fontenot, violin and vocal accompaniment: Ardoin (accordion)–2

Location: Newport, Rhode Island. July 1966
[A] On stairwell
[B] In open air

Titles performed:

'Two Step De Eunice' [A]–1	Vestapol 13050
'La Valse De La Prison' [A]–2	Vestapol 13050
[interview] [A]	
'Laccasine Breakdown' [B]–1	Vestapol 13050
untitled 2-step [B]–1	Vestapol 13050
'Bon Soir Moreau' [B]–2	Vestapol 13050

Source: *Alan Lomax film collection*

[27] Male step-dancer accompanied by Clark Kessinger (violin); Gene Meade (guitar); Wayne Hauser (banjo)

Location: Newport, Rhode Island. Summer 1966

Titles performed:

'Billy In The Lowgrounds'	Vestapol 13051
'Leather Britches'	Vestapol 13051

Source: *Alan Lomax film collection*

Vocal and accordion accompaniment: Bud, Morris and Black Ardoin (percussion); Canray Fontenot (violin)

Location: Eunice, Louisiana. 1973

Titles performed:
'Mardi Gras Song' Flower 4
'Home Sweet Home' Flower 4
untitled song Flower 4

Source: *Dry Wood*

Vocal and accordion accompaniment: Canray Fontenot (violin); Ronald Ardoin (drums); Ralph Thomas (triangle)

Location: Opelousas, Louisiana. 1983

Title performed:
'Jongle Moi Une Foise Par Jove'

Source: *Zydeco*

Vocal and accordion accompaniment: two of Ardoin's sons (percussion [2 forks and a cardboard box] and violin).

Location: Welch, Louisiana. 1987–88

Title performed:
'Lake Charles Two-Step' Flower 7

Source: *J'ai Eté Au Bal*

Ardoin, vocal and accordion, Fontenot, vocal and violin–1
as above accompaniment: unknown (guitar, triangle, rub-board)–2

Location: Louisiana. 1990

Titles performed:
'Pensez A Moi Une Fois Par Jour'–1 Channel 5 083 258-3, Island 083 258-3
'J'Etais Au Bal Le Dernier Soir' Channel 5 083 258-3, Island 083 258-3

Source: *Zydeco Nite 'N' Day*
Ardoin appears very briefly in *Cajun Country* [1], filmed in 1983.

ARGO SINGERS
Probably Lorenza Brown Porter, Minnie Colbert, Shirley Walls, Dora Jones, Rebecca Nixon and Estherline Smith (vocals) accompaniment: unknown

Location: Chicago, Illinois.

The following appearances are known:
1963
Sunday 17 November [prog #27–3]
1964
Saturday 8 February [prog #26–2]

Titles performed:
unknown

Source: *Jubilee Showcase*

HOWARD ARMSTRONG
Mandolin solo accompaniment: Ted Bogan (guitar)–1
Violin solo accompaniment: Bob Coxe (piano); Willie Sievers (guitar)–2
Vocal and mandolin accompaniment: Mary Shepherd (vocals and piano); Elsie Loweroy (vocals); a third sister (vocals)–3
Violin and mandolin accompaniment: Ted Bogan (guitar); Banjo Ikey Robinson (banjo); Tom Armstrong (bowed bass)–4

Locations: Chicago, Illinois [A]
La Follette, Tennessee [B]
Maxwell Street, Chicago, Illinois [C]. 1985

Titles performed:
'New State Street Rag' [A] –1
'Cacklin' Hen' [B] –2
'When He Calls Me I Will Answer' [B] –3
'Vine Street Drag' [A] –4
'Wrap Your Troubles In Dreams' [C] –4
'Railroad Blues' [C] –4
[interviews]
[conversations with Bogan, Rachell and Robinson]

Source: *Louie Bluie*
See also Ted Bogan, Yank Rachell and Banjo Ikey Robinson.

WILLIAM [BILLY BOY] ARNOLD
Vocal and harmonica accompaniment: Louis Myers (electric guitar); David Myers (electric bass); Fred Below (drums)

Location: Chicago, Illinois. Wednesday 28 January 1976

Titles performed:
'She Fooled Me'
'Think It Over'
'Somebody Help Me' [unbroadcast]

Source: *The Devil's Music series 2*

B

BABY DOO
See Leonard (Baby Doo) Caston

TREVOR BACON
Vocal accompaniment: the Lucky Millinder orchestra

Location: New York City. Mid-1941

Title performed:
[3807] 'Big Fat Mama' Storyville SV6000, Virgin VDD865

Source: *Soundie*
Bacon was the guitarist in the Millinder orchestra.
See Rosetta Tharpe for the likely accompanying personnel.

HAROLD BAILEY SINGERS OF CHICAGO
Probably Harold Bailey, Dorothy Moore, Alice Kirk, Lottie Woods, Barbara White and Dora James (vocals) accompaniment: unknown

Location: Chicago, Illinois

The following appearances are known:

1964
Sunday 12 July [prog #15–1]
1966
Sunday 8 May [prog #23–1]
1969
Saturday 22 February [prog #19–3]

Titles performed:
unknown

Source: *Jubilee Showcase*

ETTA BAKER
Guitar solos

Location: North Carolina. 1988

Titles performed:
untitled instrumental rag
untitled instrumental blues
[interview]

Source: *Step It Up And Go*
See also Cora Phillips.

LAVERN BAKER
Vocal accompaniment: unknown

Location: New York City. November 1955

Title performed:
'Tweedley-dee'

Source: *The Ed Sullivan Show*

Vocal accompaniment: unknown orchestra

Location: unknown {USA}. 1956

Title performed:
'Tra-La-La' Gold Star BSG203

Source: *Rock, Rock, Rock*

Vocal accompaniment: unknown orchestra

Location: unknown {USA}. 1957

Titles performed:
'Humpty Dumpty Heart'
'Love Me Right'
'Early In The Morning'

Source: *Mister Rock And Roll*

Vocal accompaninent: unknown

Location: unknown {USA}. 1990

Titles performed:
unknown [ST only]

Source: *Dick Tracey*

JOHN HENRY BARBEE (William George Tucker)
Vocal and guitar accompaniment: John Estes (guitar); Hammie Nixon (briefly harmonica, then blown jug)

Location: Baden-Baden, Germany. October 1964

Title performed:
[introduction by Hammie Nixon;]
'We Sure Can't Agree'

Source: *American Folk Blues Festival 1964*
Barbee was too ill to continue with the American Folk Blues Festival and therefore did not appear in *The Blues Came Walking* (the UK ATV programme of the 1964 AFBF). He died on 4 November 1964 of a heart attack.

ROOSEVELT [BOOBA] BARNES
Vocal and electric guitar accompaniment: The Blues Cohorts

Location: probably Greenville, Mississippi. 1984

Titles performed:
unknown

Source: *In The Delta of Mississippi*

Vocal and electric guitar accompaniment: The Playboys, unknown (electric bass, drums)

Location: Playboy Club, Nelson Street, Greenville, Mississippi. Autumn 1990

Titles performed:

'Ain't Gonna Worry About Tomorrow'	Anxious 45099-29643, BMG un-numbered
'Heart Broken Man'	Anxious 45099-29643, BMG un-numbered
[interview]	Anxious 45099-29643, BMG un-numbered

Source: *Deep Blues*

[SWEET] EMMA BARRETT
Vocal and piano accompaniment: unknowns (bass and drums)

Location: Preservation Hall, New Orleans, Louisiana. Spring 1963

Title performed:
'I Ain't Gonna Give Nobody None Of My Jelly Roll' [part only]

Source: *Dietrich Wawzyn film collection.* She appears in *The Cincinatti Kid.*

Vocal and piano

Location: as above. Early 1960s

Title performed:
'Bill Bailey, Won't You Please Come Home'

Source: *unknown* [M]. This film is played on a public TV monitor at Preservation Hall in New Orleans.

BARRETT SISTERS
Probably Deloris Barrett Campbell, Billie Greenbey, Rhodessa Porter (vocals) accompaniment: unknown

Location: Chicago, Illinois

The following appearances are known:

1964
Sunday 8 March [prog #17–3]
1966
Friday 13 May [prog #34–2]
Sunday 11 December [prog #15–3]
1968
Sunday 1 September [prog #28–2]
1969
Sunday 1 June [prog #24–3]
Saturday 4 October [prog #27–1]
1971
Saturday 14 August [prog #1–2]

1972
Sunday 10 September [prog #2–1]
1974
Sunday 20 January [prog #6–3]
Sunday 11 August [prog #3–1]
1976
Saturday 9 October [prog #9–1]
1982
Monday 20 September [prog #14]

Titles performed:
unknown

Source: *Jubilee Showcase*

Also the following;

Probably as last accompaniment: Roberta Martin (piano)–1
as last accompaniment: the Five Blind Boys of Mississippi, probably Henry Johnson, Jimmy Carter, Reverend Willie Mincey, Lawrence Abrams, Lloyd Woodard, Jay T Clinkscales (vocals)–2

Location: Chicago, Illinois. Saturday 10 October 1964

Titles performed:
'Out Of Nowhere'–1
'Yes, Jesus Loves You'–1
'Come On Up To Bright Glory'–2

Source: *TV Gospel Time* #40, #43

Probably as last accompaniment: unknown

Location: unknown {USA}. 1970s

Titles performed:
unknown Savoy 9500

Source: *Down Memory Lane*

Vocal group accompaniment: organ and congregational vocal

Location: Antioch Baptist church, St. Louis, Missouri. 1982

Titles performed:
'Hallelujah' FRF un-numbered
'I Won't Turn Around' FRF un-numbered
'We Are Blessed' FRF un-numbered
'Trust Him Now' FRF un-numbered
[interviews and conversation] FRF un-numbered

Source: *Say Amen Somebody!*

Vocal group accompaniment: unknown

Location: Denver, Colorado. 1985

Titles performed:
unknown

Source: *probably US PBS TV*

Vocal group accompaniment: unknown

Location: Beersheba Baptist Church, Chicago, Illinois. Sunday 25 November 1990

Title performed:
'I'll Fly Away'
'We Are Blessed'

Source: *Soundstage*
See also Deloris Barrett Campbell.

DALLAS BARTLEY AND HIS BAND

Unknown (vocal, tenor saxophone, alto saxophone, piano, drums); Dallas Bartley (bass)

Location: New York City. Early 1945

Titles performed:
[88208] 'Cryin' And Singin' The Blues' Charly #5
[88608] 'Ya Fine And Healthy Thing' Charly #5
[88908] 'All Ruzzit Buzzit' Charly #5
[12M2] 'Sandin' Joe' Charly #5
[17M3] 'We Pitched A Boogie Woogie'

Source: *Soundies*
88208 and 88908 copyrighted 16 July 1945; 12M2 and 88608 10 September 1945; 17M3 18 March 1946. See also Louis Jordan.

FONTELLA BASS

Vocal accompaniment: unknown, possibly miming to Checker 1120

Location: London. Friday 14 February 1966

Title performed:
'Rescue Me'

Source: *Ready Steady Go*

Vocal accompaniment: unknown

Location: St. Louis, Missouri. 1989

Titles performed:
'Soul Of A Man'
'Rescue Me'
'Mama, He Treats Your Daughter Mean'
'Gee Whiz'

Source: *St. Soul-Soul of St. Louis R&B*

BEAU JOCQUE (Andrus Espre)
Vocal and accordion accompaniment: unknown (electric guitar, rub-board, electric bass, drums)

Location: Lafayette, Louisiana. 1994

Titles performed:

'Damballah' [A]	BMG un-numbered
'Zydeco Boogie' [A]	BMG un-numbered
'Give Him Cornbread' [A]	BMG un-numbered
unnnamed song[B]	BMG un-numbered
[interview][A]	BMG un-numbered

Source: *The Kingdom Of Zydeco* [A]; *True Believers – The Story Of Rounder Records* [B]. See also Zydeco Straits.

CAREY BELL (Carey Bell Harrington)
Vocal and harmonica accompaniment: unknown

Location: Chicago, Illinois. 1970

Titles performed:
unknown

Source: *Made In Chicago*

Vocal and harmonica accompaniment: unknown

Location: unknown {USA}. 1975

Titles performed:
unknown

Source: *Sincerely The Blues*

Vocal and harmonica accompaniment: Hubert Sumlin and Eddie Taylor (electric guitars); Bob Stroger (electric bass); Odie Payne (drums)

Location: Germany. 1980

Titles performed:
'One Day'
'What Do The Poor Boy Do'

Source: *American Folk Blues Festival 1980*

Vocal and harmonica accompaniment: unknown

Location: Belgium. 1981

Title performed:
'A Man And His Blues'

Source: *American Folk Blues Festival 1981*

Vocal and harmonica accompaniment: Lurrie Bell (electric guitar); unknown (electric bass and drums)

Location: unknown {Europe}. 1982

Titles performed:
'Blue Harp Blues'
'Goin' To Main Street'
'Easy To Love'
'Break It Up'
'I Want You To Love Me'

Source: *German TV broadcast* [C]

BELLS OF JOY
Vocal quintet, including A C Littlefield accompaniment: two of them (electric guitars)

Location: Texas. Friday 10 July 1987

Titles performed:
'Let's Talk About Jesus'
'Kneel Down And Pray'
'Leaning On The Everlasting Arm'
two untitled songs
[interviews]

Source: *Texas Music Museum*

CHARLES EDWARD ANDERSON [CHUCK] BERRY
Vocal and electric guitar, miming to Chess 1645

Location: unknown {USA}. c.1956

Title performed:

'You Can't Catch Me'	Gold Star BGS203

Source: *Rock, Rock, Rock*

Vocal and electric guitar, miming to Chess 1664

Location: unknown {USA}. 1957

Title performed:
Oh Baby Doll

Source: *Mister Rock And Roll*

Vocal and electric guitar accompaniment: the Alan Freed Orchestra; Big Al Sears and Sam 'The Man' Taylor (tenor saxophones) and others, unknown

Location: New York City. July–August 1957

Titles performed:
unknown

Source: *The Big Beat* [2]

Vocal and electric guitar, miming to Chess 1866 [A]; 1722 [B] Alan Freed (miming as a drummer)–1

Location: unknown {USA}. 1958

Titles performed:
'Memphis, Tennessee' [A]
'Little Queenie' [part only] [B]–1

Source: *Go Johnny Go*

Vocal and electric guitar accompaniment; unknown

Location: Philadelphia, Pennsylvania. 1958

Titles performed:
'Sweet Little Sixteen'

Source: *Dick Clark's American Bandstand*

Vocal and electric guitar accompaniment: The Count Basie Orchestra

Location: Newport, Rhode Island. Summer 1958

Title performed:
Sweet Little Sixteen Castle Hendring 2.239

Source: *Jazz On A Summer's Day*

Vocal and electric guitar accompaniment: unknown

Location: Philadelphia, Pennsylvania. 1959

Titles performed:
unknown

Source: *Dick Clark's Saturday Night Beechnut Show*

Vocal and electric guitar accompaniment; unknown (electric bass, drums, brass)

Location: Civic Auditorium, Santa Monica, California. 1964

Titles performed:
'Johnny B. Goode'
'Maybelline'
'Sweet Little Sixteen'
'Nadine'

Source: *The TAMI Show*

Vocal and electric guitar accompaniment; unknown

Location: Brussels, Belgium. 1965

Titles performed:
'Maybelline'
'Things I Used To Do'
'Roll Over Beethoven'
'Memphis'
'No Particular Place To Go'
'Promised Land'
'Johnny B. Goode'

Source: *Face Au Public*

Vocal and electric guitar accompaniment; unknown

Location: Los Angeles, California. 1965

Titles performed:
unknown

Source: *Hollywood A Go-Go*

Vocal and electric guitar accompaniment: unknown

Location: Los Angeles, California. 1965

Title performed:
'Back In The USA' Rhino R3 1453

Source: *Shindig* [1]

Vocal and electric guitar accompaniment; unknown

Location: unknown 1965–66

Title performed:
'Johnny B. Goode' Rhino R3 90701

Source: *Hullabaloo!* [1]

Vocal and electric guitar accompaniment; unknown

Location: Greenwich Village, New York City. 1968

Titles performed:
unknown

Source: *Live From The Bitter End*

Vocal and electric guitar accompaniment: unknown

Location: unknown {USA}. 1968

Titles performed:
unknown

Source: *Upbeat*

Vocal and electric guitar accompaniment: unknown

Location: New York City. 1970

Titles performed:
unknown

Source: *The Dick Cavett Show*

Vocal and electric guitar accompaniment: unknown

Location: Los Angeles, California. 1971

Titles performed:
unknown

Source: *The Mike Douglas Show*

Vocal and electric guitar accompaniment: Rocking Horse [G] (piano, electric guitar, electric bass, drums)

Location: London, England. Late February 1972

Titles performed:
'Roll Over Beethoven'
'Sweet Little Sixteen'
'Memphis, Tennessee'
'South Of Her Border'
'Beer Drinkin' Woman'
'Let It Rock'
'Mean Old World'
'Oh Carol'
'Liverpool Drive'
'Nadine'
'Johnny B. Goode'

Source: *Sounds For Saturday*

Vocal and electric guitar accompaniment: Louis Myers (electric guitar); David Myers (electric bass); Fred Below (drums)

Location: Montreux, Switzerland. June–July 1972

Titles performed:
'Maybelline'
'Wee Wee Hours'
'Rock And Roll Music'
and other, unknown, titles

Source: *Montreux* Jazz

Vocal and electric guitar accompaniment: unknown

Location: Toronto, Canada. Summer 1972

Titles performed:
'Rock And Roll Music' BMG 791150
'No Particular Place To Go' BMG 791150
'Johnny B. Goode' [2 versions] BMG 791150
'Hoochie Coochie Man' BMG 791150
'Sweet Little Sixteen' BMG 791150

Source: *Keep On Rockin'*

Vocal and electric guitar accompaniment: unknown

Location: Wembley Stadium, Middlesex, England. August 1972

Titles performed:

'No Particular Place To Go'	MMGV-015
'Memphis, Tennessee'	MMGV-015
'Sweet Little Sixteen'	MMGV-015
'Mean Ole Frisco'	MMGV-015
'Beer Drinkin' Woman'	MMGV-015
'Wee Wee Hours'	MMGV-015
'Johnny B. Goode'	MMGV-015
'Oh Carol'	MMGV-015
'Little Queenie'	MMGV-015
'Reelin' And Rockin''	MMGV-015

Source: *The London Rock And Roll Show*

Vocal and electric guitar accompaniment: unknown

Location: Madison Square Garden, New York City. 1973

Titles performed:
'Reelin' And Rockin''
'School Days'
'Sweet Little Sixteen'

Source: *Let The Good Times Roll* [1]

Vocal and electric guitar accompaniment: unknown

Location: Civic Auditorium, Santa Monica, California. 1973

Titles performed:
unknown

Source: *Dick Clark Presents The Rock and Roll Years*

Vocal and electric guitar accompaniment: unknown

Location: probably Los Angeles, California. 1973

Titles performed:
unknown

Source: *Sonny And Cher Comedy Hour*

Vocal and electric guitar accompaniment: unknown

Location: probably New York City. c.1974

Titles performed:
'Sweet Little Sixteen'
'Maybelline'

Source: *Midnight Special*

Vocal and electric guitar accompaniment: unknown

Location: probably New York City. 1975

Titles performed:
unknown

Source: *The Midnight Special*

Vocal and electric guitar accompaniment: unknown

Location: probably Las Vegas, Nevada. 1975

Titles performed:
unknown

Source: *Sammy And Company*

Vocal and electric guitar accompaniment: unknown

Location: New York City. 1975

Titles performed:
unknown

Source: *Saturday Night Live*

Vocal and electric guitar accompaniment: unknown

Location: unknown {USA}. 1976

Titles performed:
unknown

Source: *Dinah And Her New Best Friends*

Vocal and electric guitar accompaniment: unknown

Location: unknown {USA}. 1977

Titles performed:
'Reelin' And Rockin''
'Roll Over Beethoven'
'Sweet Litle Sixteen'
[dialogue]

Source: *American Hot Wax*

Vocal and electric guitar accompaniment:
unknown

Location: Los Angeles, California. 1977

Titles performed:
unknown

Source: *Dick Clark's American Bandstand 25th Anniversary*

Vocal and electric guitar accompaniment:
unknown

Location: Los Angeles, California. 1977

Titles performed:
unknown

Source: *Donny And Marie*

Vocal and electric guitar accompaniment:
unknown

Location: unknown {USA}. 1977

Title performed:
'Roll Over Beethoven'

Source: *Sha Na Na*

Vocal and electric guitar accompaniment:
unknown

Location: New York City. 1977

Titles performed:
unknown

Source: *Saturday Night Live*

Vocal and electric guitar accompaniment:
unknown

Location: unknown {USA}. 1977–78

Titles performed:
unknown

Source: *The Merv Griffin Show* [probably more than one appearance]

Vocal and electric guitar accompaniment:
unknown

Location: probably Los Angeles, California. 1978

Titles performed:
unknown

Source: *American Music Award*s [C]

Vocal and electric guitar accompaniment:
unknown

Location: unknown {USA}. February–April 1978

Titles performed:
unknown

Source: *The Chuck Barris Rah Rah Show*

Vocal and electric guitar accompaniment:
unknown

Location: unknown {USA}. 1978

Titles performed:
unknown

Source: *The Today Show*

Vocal and electric guitar accompaniment:
unknown

Location: Nice, France. Between Thursday 5 and Sunday 15 July 1979

Titles performed:
'Roll Over Beethoven'
'Long Live Rock And Roll'
'Sweet Little Sixteen'
'Maybelline'
'Nadine'
'Shuffle In E'
'Memphis'
'Down In St. Louis'
'Baby, What You Want Me To Do'
'Wee Wee Hours'

Source: *French TV broadcast* [C]

Vocal and electric guitar accompaniment: unknown

Location: probably Las Vegas, Nevada. 1980

Titles performed:
'The Promised Land'
'Reelin' And Rockin''

Source: *The Sammy Davis Jr. Show*

Vocal and electric guitar accompaniment: unknown as above, in duet with Ingrid Berry–1, Tina Turner–2

Location: Los Angeles, Calfornia. 1982

Titles performed:

'Roll Over Beethoven'	Old Gold 0001
'Hail Hail Rock And Roll'	Old Gold 0001
'Sweet Little Sixteen'	Old Gold 0001
'Nadine'	Old Gold 0001
'Let It Rock'	Old Gold 0001
'The Promised Land'	Old Gold 0001
'Memphis'	Old Gold 0001
'Johnny B. Goode'	Old Gold 0001
'Brown Eyed Handsome Man'	Old Gold 0001
'Too Much Monkey Business'	Old Gold 0001
'Oh Carol'	Old Gold 0001
'Little Queenie'	Old Gold 0001
'Reelin' And Rockin''–1	Old Gold 0001
'Rock And Roll Music'–2	Old Gold 0001

Source: *Live At The Roxy*

Vocal and electric guitar accompaniment: unknown in duet with Ingrid Berry–1

Location: Covo di Nord Est, S Margherita Ligure, Italy. 1983

Titles performed:
'Go Johnny Go'
'Wee Wee Hours'
'Brown Eyed Handsome Man'
'Kingston Town'
'Rambling Rose'
'Nadine'
'Everyday I Have The Blues'
'Johnny B. Goode'
'Key To The Highway'–1
'Gone Gone Gone'–1
'Reelin' And Rockin''

Source: *Italian TV broadcast* [C]

Vocal and electric guitar accompaniment: the Doc Severinson orchestra

Location: Los Angeles, California. 1987

Titles performed:
unknown
[interview]

Source: *Tonight Show Starring Johnny Carson*

Vocal and electric guitar accompaniment:
Johnny Johnson (piano); unknown (electric bass and drums)–1
as –1 including Eric Clapton (electric guitar)–2
Vocal and electric guitar accompaniment: Keith Richards (electric guitar) and others, unknown–3
Guest appearances by: Linda Ronstadt–4; Julian Lennon–5; Robert Cray–6; Eric Clapton–7; Etta James–8

Locations: [A] Como Club, St. Louis, Missouri. 1987.
[B] Concert stage, St. Louis, Missouri. 1987

Titles performed:
'Maybelline'–1 [A]
untitled instrumental blues–1 [A]
'I'm Through With Love'–2 [A]
'Roll Over Beethoven'–3 [B]
'Almost Grown'–3 [B]
'Sweet Little Sixteen'–3 [B]
'No Money Down'–3 [B]
'Nadine'–3 [B]
'Memphis, Tennessee'–3 [B]
'Little Queenie'–3 [B]
'Too Much Monkey Business'–3 [B]
'No Particular Place To Go'–3 [B]
'Hail Hail Rock And Roll'–3 [B]
'Cottage For Sale'–3 [B]
'Back In The USA'–3,4 [B]
'Johnny B. Goode'–3, 5 [B]
'Brown Eyed Handsome Man'–3, 6 [B]
'Wee Wee Hours'–3, 7 [B]
'Rock And Roll Music'–3, 8 [B]

Source: *Hail, Hail, Rock And Roll*

Vocal and electric guitar accompaniment: unknown

Location: London, England. 1988

Memphis
[interview]

Source: *Aspel And Company*

Speech

Location: St. Louis, Missouri. 1995

[interview]

Source: *Rock And Roll – Part 1*

The following film biography of the artist is also relevant: *Johnny B. Goode* [this includes lengthy interviews and amateur colour film made by Berry in the 1950s].

BETHEL BAPTIST CHOIR
Mixed vocal choir accompaniment: unknown

Location: probably New York City. 1965–66

Titles performed:
unknown

Source: *TV Gospel Time* #50

NATHAN BEAUREGARD
Vocal and electric guitar

Location: Tutwiler, Mississippi. 1968

Title performed:
''bout A Spoonful' [part only] K-Jazz 030, Yazoo 505

Source: *Good Morning Blues*
Beauregard was reportedly 97 years old when this performance was filmed.

BIBLEWAY JOYBELL CHOIR OF WASHINGTON DC
Mixed vocal choir accompaniment: unknown

Location: New York City or Washington DC. 1965–66

Titles performed:
unknown

Source: *TV Gospel Time* #53

BIG AMOS (Patton)
Vocal and harmonica accompaniment: the Willie Mitchell band; Mitchell (trumpet); Fred Ford (tenor saxophone); unknown (piano, electric guitar, electric bass, drums). Miming to Hi 2108

Location: WFAA-TV studios, Dallas, Texas. Late summer 1966

Title performed:
'He Won't Bite Me Twice'

Source: *The Beat*

BIG MACEO (Major Merriweather)
Vocal and piano accompaniment, if any: unknown

Location: probably Chicago, Illinois. Late 1940s

Titles performed:
unknown

Source: *I Come For To Sing* [unconfirmed]

BIG MAYBELLE (Maybelle Louise Smith)
Vocal accompaniment: unknown

Location: Newport, Rhode Island. Summer 1958

Title performed:
'Rockhouse' Castle Hendring 2 239

Source: *Jazz On A Summer's Day*

BIG MEMPHIS MA RAINEY (Lillian Glover)
Vocal accompaniment: Big Sam Clark (piano); unknown (drums)

Location: Blues Alley club, Memphis, Tennessee. 1978

Title performed:
'I Love You Daddy' K-Jazz 030, Yazoo 505

Source: *Good Morning Blues*

BIG TWIST (Lawrence Nolan) AND THE MELLOW FELLOWS
Twist, vocal accompanient: The Mellow Fellows: (brass, electric guitar, piano, electric bass, drums)

Location: Chicago, Illinois. c. 1979

Title performed:
'I Brought The Blues On Myself'

Source: *Chicago On The Good Foot*

THOMAS BIRD
Vocal and electric guitar

Location: Atlanta, Georgia. October 1984

Title performed:
'Hey Lord'

Source: *National Down Home Blues Festival*

BIRMINGHAM JUBILEES
Vocal group accompaniment, if any: unknown

Location: Hollywood, California. 1931

Titles performed:
unknown

Source: *Pardon Us*

BIRMINGHAM SUNLIGHTS
Vocal quartet, unaccompanied

Location: [A] Birmingham or Bessemer, Alabama. Early 1984
[B] Friendship Baptist Church, Brighton, Alabama. Early 1984

Titles performed:
[rehearsing 'When I Was A Singer' and 'My Home is Over in Canaan' with the Sterling Jubilee Singers] [A]
'Take it to the Lord' [B]

Source: *On The Battlefield*

BIVENS SPECIALS
Probably Louise Elizabeth Bivens, Jackie Robinson, Lucious Larkins, Lillie Roth Jenkins, Charlotte Vanessa Brown, Rosa Marylin Roberts (vocals) accompaniment: unknown

Location: Chicago, Illinois. Saturday 14 June, 1969

Titles peformed:
unknown

Source: *Jubilee Showcase* [prog # 19–1]

WILLIAM [BILLY] BIZOR
Vocal and harmonica accompaniment: Lightnin' Hopkins (guitar)

Location: Centerville, Texas. 1967

Titles performed:
'It Hurts Me So Bad (Morning Train)' Flower 1, K-Jazz 053
untitled harmonica blues instrumental Flower 1, K-Jazz 053

Source: *Blues According To Lightnin' Hopkins*
See also Lightnin' Hopkins and Mance Lipscomb.

BLACK ACE (Babe Kyro Lemon Turner)
Vocal and steel guitar

Location: radio station KFJZ, Fort Worth, Texas. 1941

Title performed:
'Truck 'Em On Down' [part only; ST] Hollywood Select 50543

Source: *The Blood Of Jesus*
This song is used as background for scenes in a juke joint, shot on location in either Don's Keyhole in San Antonio or the Rose Room in Dallas. 'Truck 'em On Down' is the same song as 'Golden Slipper', which this artist recorded in 1960 for Arhoolie records.

Vocal and steel guitar

Location: the Turner residence, Fort Worth, Texas. Spring 1963

Title performed:
'I Am The Black Ace' [part only] Yazoo 520

Source: *Die Blues*

SONNY BLAKE
Vocal and harmonica accompaniment: Joe Willie Wilkins (electric guitar); Mose Vinson (piano); L T Lewis (drums)

Location: Memphis, Tennessee. Monday 19 January 1976

Titles performed:
'One Room Country Shack'
'Bring It On Home'

Source: *The Devil's Music series 2*

ROBERT [BOBBY] BLAND
Vocal accompaniment: unknown

Location: probably New York City. 1967

Titles performed:
unknown

Source: *Harlem Cultural Festival* [unconfirmed]

Vocal accompaniment: unknown

Location: unknown {USA}. 1969

Titles performed:
unknown

Source: *Weequahic Park Love Festival* [unconfirmed]

Vocal accompaniment: unknown

Location: unknown {USA}. 1975

Titles performed:
unknown

Source: *The Midnight Special*

Vocal accompaniment: unknown

Location: unknown {USA}. 1975

Titles performed:
unknown

Source: *Soul Train*

Vocal accompaniment: unknown

Location: Chicago, Illinois. Monday 10 January 1977

Titles performed:
'Ain't That Lovin' You'
'Driftin' Blues'
'Stormy Monday'
'The Feeling Is Gone'

Source: *Soundstage*
See also Riley [BB] King

Speech

Location: Memphis, Tennessee. 1978

[interview]

Source: *Beale Street*

Location: Chicago, Illinois. 1981

Titles performed:
unknown

Source: *Chicago Blues Festival* [1]

Vocal accompaniment: unknown

Location: Olympia theatre, Paris, France. Monday 10 July 1989

Titles performed:
'So Doggone Lonesome'
'That's The Way Love Is'
'Reap What You Sow'
'Bad Luck And Trouble'
'I Want To Take Your Place'
'Share Your Love'
'Things Have Changed'
'Today I Started Loving You Again'
'Sunday Morning Love'
'St. James Infirmary'
'Stormy Monday Blues'

Source: *French TV broadcast* [C]

BLIND BOYS OF ALABAMA and BLIND BOYS OF MISSISSIPPI
See Five Blind Boys of Alabama and Five Blind Boys of Mississippi.

BO DIDDLEY (Ellas Otha Bates McDaniel)
Vocal and electric guitar accompaniment: Jerome Green (maracas); Frank Kirkland (drums)

Location: New York City. November 1955

Title performed:
'Bo Diddley'

Source: *The Ed Sullivan Show*

Vocal and electric guitar, miming to Checker 827

Location: London, England. Saturday 28 September 1963

Title performed:
'Pretty Thing'

Source: *Thank Your Lucky Stars*

Vocal and electric guitar accompaniment: unknown (electric bass and drums); the Ronettes (erotic dancing)

Location: Civic Auditorium, Santa Monica, California. 1964

Titles performed:
'Hey Bo Diddley'
'Bo Diddley'
'Roadrunner'

Source: *The TAMI show*

Vocal and electric guitar accompaniment: unknown

Location: New York City. 1965

Titles performed:
'You Can't Judge A Book By Looking At The Cover' MMGV–010
'Road Runner' MMGV–010
'Hey Bo Diddley' MMGV–010
'Can Your Monkey Do The Dog' MMGV–010

Source: *The Clay Cole Show*

Vocal and electric guitar accompaniment: unknown

Location: Los Angeles, California. 1965

Titles performed:
unknown

Source: *Shindig*

Vocal and guitar accompaniment: Jerome Green (maracas); 'the Duchess' (electric bass); probably miming

Location: London, England. Saturday 2 October 1965

Title performed:
unknown

Source: *Thank Your Lucky Stars*

Vocal and electric guitar accompaniment: unknown

Location: Chicago, Illinois. 1966–67

Titles performed:
'500 Per Cent More Man'
'Bo Diddley'
'We're Gonna Get Married'
and other, unknown, titles

Source: *The Legend Of Bo Diddley*

Vocal and electric guitar accompaniment: unknown

Location: unknown {USA}. 1970

Titles performed:
unknown

Source: *The Midnight Special*

Vocal and electric guitar accompaniment: unknown

Location: unknown {USA}. 1970

Titles performed:
unknown

Source: *Music Scene*

Vocal and electric guitar accompaniment: unknown

Location: unknown {USA}. 1971

Titles performed:
unknown [ST only]

Source: *Fritz The Cat*

Vocal and electric guitar accompaniment: unknown

Location: Los Angeles, California. 1971

Titles performed:
unknown

Source: *The Mike Douglas Show*

Vocal and electric guitar accompaniment: unknown

Location: Toronto, Canada. Summer 1972

Titles performed:
'Hey Bo Diddley' BMG 791150
'Bo Diddley' BMG 791150

Source: *Keep On Rockin'*

Vocal and electric guitar accompaniment: unknown (second electric guitar, electric bass, drums)

Location: Montreux, Switzerland. July 1972

Titles performed:
'Bo Diddley'
'I'm A Man'
'Shut Up Woman'
'Diddley Daddy'
[monologue on his career]
'Mona'
'Lyin' Woman'
'It Must Be Love'
untitled instrumental

Source: *Montreux Jazz*

Vocal and electric guitar accompaniment: unknown

Location: Wembley Stadium, Middlesex, England. August 1972

Titles performed:
'Road Runner' MMG-015
'Bring It To Jerome' MMG-015
'Mona' MMG-015

Source: *The London Rock And Roll Show*

Vocal and electric guitar accompaniment: unknown

Location: Los Angeles, California. 1973

Titles performed:
unknown

Source: *Dick Clark Presents The Rock and Roll Years*

Vocal and electric guitar accompaniment: unknown (electric bass, drums); Cookie Vee (vocals and tambourine)

Location: Montreux, Switzerland. July 1975

Titles performed:
unknown

Source: *Montreux Jazz*

Vocal and electric guitar accompaniment: unknown

Location: Los Angeles, California. 1976

Titles performed:
unknown

Source: *Donny And Marie*

Vocal and electric guitar accompaniment: unknown

Location: Los Angeles, California. 1977

Titles performed:
unknown

Source: *Dick Clark's Good Old Days*

Vocal and guitar accompaniment: unknown

Location: New York City. c.1977–78

Titles performed:
unknown

Source: *Sha Na Na*

Vocal and electric guitar accompaniment:
unknown

Location: Hollywood, California. 1978

Titles performed:
unknown

Source: *Dick Clark's Live Wednesday*

Vocal and electric guitar accompaniment:
unknown

Location: Australia. October 1981

Title performed:
'Mona'
[interview]

Source: *Australian TV broadcast* [C]

Vocal and electric guitar accompaniment:
unknown

Location: London, England. 1984

Titles performed:
'Bo Diddley'
'I'm A Man'
'Bo Diddley Put The Rock In Rock And Roll'
[interview]

Source: *The Tube*

Vocal and electric guitar accompaniment: Ron Wood, Carl Wilson, John Hammond, Carmine Grillo (electric guitars); Kenny Jones, Mick Fleetwood, Mitch Mitchell, Carmine Appice (drums): Bill Champlin, John Mayall, John Lodge (keyboards); Phil Chen, Rudy Sarzo (electric basses)

Location: Irvine Meadows Amphitheatre, unknown US location. Friday 25 October 1985

Titles performed:
'Bo Diddley' Rhino R3.2222
'I'm A Man' Rhino R3.2222
'Bo Diddley Put The Rock In Rock And Roll' Rhino R3.2222
'Who Do You Love' Rhino R3.2222
'Bo Diddley Is A Gunslinger' Rhino R3.2222
'Hey Bo Diddley' Rhino R3.2222

Source: *Bo Diddley's 30th Anniversary Of Rock And Roll*

Speech

Location: unknown {USA}. 1986

[interview]

Source: *Remembering Black Music*

Vocal and electric guitar accompaniment:
unknown

Location: probably Hollywood, California. 1987

Title performed:
'Bo Diddley'
[interview]

Source: *Late Night With Joan Rivers*

Speech

Location: unknown {USA}. 1987

[interview]

Source: *Ain't Nothin' But The Blues*

Vocal and electric guitar accompaniment:
unknown–1;
same, duet with Ron Wood–2

Location: Japan. 1988

Titles performed:
'Bo Diddley'–1
'Road Runner'–1
'Who Do You Love'–2
'I'm A Man'–1
'You Can't Judge A Book'–1
'Hey Bo Diddley'–1

Source: *Japanese TV broadcast* [C]

Vocal and electric guitar accompaniment: unknown

Location: Rome, Italy. Thursday 17 November 1988

Titles performed:
'Bo Diddley'
'I'm A Man'
'Who Do You Love'

Source: *The Giants Of Rock And Roll*

Vocal and electric guitar accompaniment: unknown

Location: Australia. 1989

Titles performed:
'Hey Bo Diddley'
'I'm A Man'
'Who Do You Love'
[interview]

Source: *Australian TV broadcast* [C]

Vocal and electric guitar accompaniment: unknown

Location: unknown {USA}. 1989

Title performed:
'Bo Diddley'

Source: *Nike sports shoes TV advert*
This advert, originally made for the American market and featuring Bo Diddley interacting with athlete Bo Jackson, was re-edited for British TV replacing Jackson with English cricketer Ian Botham.

Vocal and guitar accompaniment: unknown

Location: Expo '92, Seville, Spain. 1992

Titles performed:
'Bo Diddley'
'I'm A Man'
'Who Do You Love'

Source: *Guitar Legends*

Vocal and electric guitar accompaniment: G E Smith's band

Location: Washington DC. Saturday 11 October 1997

Title performed:
'I'm A Man'

Source: *A Tribute To Muddy Waters*

Speech

Location: unknown {USA}. 1995

[interview]

Source: *Rock and Roll Part 1*

Speech

Location: unknown {USA}. 1997

[interview]

Source: *Record Row*
Bo Diddley has a dramatic cameo role in the 1983 film *Trading Places.*

TED BOGAN

Vocal and guitar accompaniment: Howard Armstrong (mandolin)

Location: Chicago, Illinois. 1985

Titles performed:
'That Will Never Happen No More'
'Du, Du Liegst Mir Im Herzen'
[conversations with Armstrong and Yank Rachell]

Source: *Louie Bluie*
See also Howard Armstrong, Martin Bogan and Armstrong, Yank Rachell and Banjo Ikey Robinson.

WELDON [JUKE BOY] BONNER

Vocal, guitar and harmonica

Location: London, England. Monday 3 November 1969

Title performed:
'Sad Sad Sound'

Source: *Late Night Line Up*

Vocal, guitar and harmonica

Location: Montreux, Switzerland. Saturday 12 July 1975

Titles performed:
'I'm Going To Louisiana'
'Rock Me Mama'
'I'm A Blues Man'

Source: *Montreux Jazz*

BOOGIE WOOGIE RED (Vernon Harrison)

Vocal and piano or piano only

Location: Brighton Polytechnic, Sussex, England. Friday 16 February 1973

Titles performed:
unknown

Source: *Blues Legends 73*

JAMES BOOKER

Vocal and piano

Location: Nice, France. July 1978

Titles performed:
'Make A Better World'
'Please Send Me Someone To Love'
'Classified'
'Let Them Talk'
'Put Out That Light'
'Malaguena'
'I'm True'

Source: *French TV broadcast* [C]

Vocal and piano

Location: Montreux, Switzerland. July 1978

Titles performed:
'Pixie'
'Papa Was A Rascal'

Source: *Montreux Jazz*

Vocal and piano

Location: New Orleans, Louisiana. 1985

Titles performed:
'Kind Hearted Woman'
'Little And Low'
'Seagram's Jam'

Source: *New Orleans Now – All Alone With The Blues*

[MEMPHIS] WILLIE BORUM

Vocal and guitar–1
Vocal, guitar and harmonica accompaniment: Gus Cannon (jug)–2

Location: Memphis, Tennessee. Summer 1962

Titles performed:
'Alone In The Evening Hours'–1
'Sittin' Here Thinkin''–2

Source: *The Blues* [1]

LEONARD BOWLES AND IRVIN COOK

Leonard Bowles (vocal and banjo), Irvin Cook (vocal and violin)

Location: WDBJ-TV studios, Roanoke, Virginia. Spring/Summer 1987

Titles performed:
'Take This Ring I Give You' [part only]
untitled instrumental [part only]

Source: *Black Music Traditions Of Virginia: Non-blues Secular Music*

EDWARD RILEY [EDDIE] BOYD

Vocal and piano accompaniment: Buddy Guy (electric guitar); Jimmy Lee Robinson (electric bass); Fred Below (drums)

Location: Baden-Baden, Germany. October 1965

Title performed:
[introduction by Fred Below;]
'Five Long Years'

Source: *American Folk Blues Festival 1965*

[PROFESSOR] HORACE BOYER
speech, piano, vocal, descriptive body language and occasional dancing

Location: Tindley United Methodist Church, Philadelphia, Pennsylvania. August 1995

[interview concerning the origins and history of Gospel music]

Source: *Too Close To Heaven*

MAGGIE BRACEY
Vocal accompaniment: unknown

Location: Chicago, Illinois. Tuesday 11 June 1966

Titles performed:
unknown

Source: *Jubilee Showcase* [prog # 23–2]

ALEX BRADFORD
Vocal accompaniment: unknown

Location: London, England. c. October 1962

Titles performed:
unknown

Source: *Black Nativity*

Bradford, vocal accompaniment: The Bradford Singers: probably Madeleine Bell, Robert Pinkston, Kenneth Washington and Bernie Durand Jr (vocals)

Location: Chicago, Illinois

The following appearances are known:
1963
Sunday 15 December [prog #11–1]
1964
Sunday 2 February [prog #20–1]
1965
Sunday 25 April [prog #21–2]
1966
Friday 13 May [prog #34–2]

Titles performed:
unknown

Source: *Jubilee Showcase*

Also the following;

probably as last accompaniment: unknown

Location: probably New York City. c.1966

Titles performed:
unknown

Source: *TV Gospel Time* #55

ROBERT J BRADLEY
Vocal accompaniment: unknown

Location: probably New York City. c. April 1965

Titles performed:
'You've Got To Love Everybody' [A]
'He Lives' [A]
'It's Me, Oh Lord' [B]
'Amazing Grace' [B]

Source: *TV Gospel Time* #42[A], 44[B]

[SISTER] EMILY BRAM
Vocal accompaniment: unknown

Location: Charlotte, North Carolina. Saturday 1 August 1964

Titles performed:
'Bye and Bye'
'I Want Jesus To Walk With Me'
'I'm Thine'

Source: *TV Gospel Time* #29

WILLIAM EARL (BILLY) BRANCH
Harmonica solo–1;
as above accompaniment: unknown (electric guitar)–2;
as –1 accompaniment: unknown (electric guitar, electric bass, drums)–3;

Location: Chicago, Illinois. 1980
In school assembly hall [A]
In unnamed café [B]

Titles performed:
untitled instrumental–1[A] K-Jazz 075, Rhapsody 8020
'Juke'–2 [A] K-Jazz 075, Rhapsody 8020
[monologue on the history of the blues] [A] K-Jazz 075, Rhapsody 8020
'Got My Mojo Working'–2 [A] K-Jazz 075, Rhapsody 8020
'Hoochie Coochie Man'–3 [B] K-Jazz 075, Rhapsody 8020
[interview] K-Jazz 075, Rhapsody 8020

Source: *Big City Blues*

Vocal and harmonica accompaniment: unknown

Location: Chicago, Illinois. 1983

Titles performed:
unknown

Source: *Sweet Home Chicago* [1]

Vocal and harmonica accompaniment: unknown

Location: Chicago, Illinois. 1991

Titles performed:
unknown

Source: *Blues And The Alligator*

[BLIND] JAMES BREWER
Speech

Location: Chicago, Illinois. Monday 11 July 1960

monologue [ST only] K-Jazz 014, Rhapsody 8022

Source: *Blues Like Showers Of Rain*

Vocal and electric guitar accompaniment: Carrie Robertson (vocal); unknown (second electric guitar and tambourines)

Location: Maxwell Street, Chicago, Illinois. 1964

Title performed:
'I'll Fly Away' [part only] Shanachie 1403

Source: *And This Is Free*

Vocal and guitar accompaniment, if any, unknown

Location: Chicago, Illinois. c. 1965

Titles performed:
unknown

Source: *The Songmakers*

Vocal and guitar accompaniment, if any, unknown

Location: Chicago, Illinois. 1970

Titles performed:
unknown

Source: *Made In Chicago*

Vocal and guitar

Location: Chicago, Illinois. 1980

Titles performed:
'My Home Ain't Here' K-Jazz 075, Rhapsody 8020
[interview] K-Jazz 075, Rhapsody 8020

Source: *Big City Blues*

Vocal and electric guitar accompaniment: Albert Holland (electric bass)–1; Vocal and guitar–2

Locations: Chicago, Illinois. Summer 1980
Maxwell Street [A]
the Arvella Gray residence [B]

Titles performed:
'I'll Fly Away' [A]–1 K-Jazz 031, Rhapsody 8045
'Farther Along' [A]–1 K-Jazz 031, Rhapsody 8045
'Sweet Home Chicago' [B] [ST]–2 K-Jazz 031, Rhapsody 8045
'I'd Rather Drink Muddy Water'–2 [B] K-Jazz 031, Rhapsody 8045
'You Don't Treat Me Right' [B]–2 K-Jazz 031, Rhapsody 8045
[interview] [B] K-Jazz 031, Rhapsody 8045

Source: *Maxwell Street Blues*
See also Arvella Gray and Carrie Robertson.

REVEREND HERBERT BREWSTER AND HIS CONGREGATION

Choir, unaccompanied vocal, with solos

Location: Memphis, Tennessee. 1984

Titles performed:
'Deep River' Arrow AV015
'He Is Worthy' Arrow AV015
'Pay Day' Arrow AV015

Source: *Saturday Blues*
See also Dorothy Ford.

ETHEL BROOKS

Vocal accompaniment: unknown

Location: Chicago, Illinois. Sunday 31 May 1964

Titles performed:
unknown

Source: *Jubilee Showcase* [prog # 29–2]

HADDA BROOKS

Probably vocal and piano

Location: probably Los Angeles, California. 1947

Titles performed;
unknown

Source: *Queen Of The Boogie*

Vocal and piano

Location: probably Los Angeles. California. 1948

Titles performed:
'Don't Take Your Love From Me'
'I'm Tired Of Everything But You'
'Don't You Think I Ought To Know'

Source: *Boogie Woogie Blues*

Probably vocal and piano

Location: probably Los Angeles, California. 1948

Titles performed:
'The Joint Is Jumpin''
and probably other, unknown, titles

Source: *The Joint Is Jumpin'*

Probably vocal and piano

Location: Hollywood, California. 1950

Titles performed:
'I Hadn't Anyone Till You'

Source: *In A Lonely Place*

Speech

Location: Los Angeles, California. 1986

[interview]

Source: *Remembering Black Music*
This artist relocated to Australia during the 1960s where she reportedly hosted her own TV show. Details remain unknown.

JOHNNY BROOKS

Vocal, unaccompanied

Location: Juke joint, unknown location, Mississippi. Between 11 August and 9 September 1978

Title performed:
'The Signifying Monkey' Vestapol 13078

Source: *Land Where The Blues Began*

LONNIE BROOKS (Lee Baker Jr.)
Vocal and guitar accompaniment: unknown

Location: Ames, Iowa. 1979

Titles performed:
unknown

Source: *Maintenance Shop Blues*

Vocal and electric guitar accompaniment: Tom Giplin (keyboards); O C Anderson (second electric guitar); Lafayette Lyle (electric bass); Jim Shootie (drums)

Location: probably Louisville, Kentucky. c.1987

Titles performed:
'Boomerang'
'Jealous Man'
'Cold Lonely Nights'
'I Want All My Money Back'
'I Want To Know'
'Brand New Mojo Hand'
'Watchdog'
Freddy King medley[instrumental]
[interview]

Source: *Kentucky Educational Television*

Vocal and electric guitar accompaniment: unknown

Location: Chicago, Illinois. 1991

Titles performed:
unknown

Source: *Blues And The Alligator*

Vocal and electric guitar accompaniment: Ronnie Brooks (electric guitar); Tom Gablin (keyboards); Augustus Taylor (electric bass); Kevin McRonie (drums)

Location: Chestnut Cabaret, Philadelphia, Pennsylvania. Thursday 12 March 1992

Titles performed:

'Wife For Tonight'	BMG 80046-3
'I Want All My Money Back'	BMG 80046-3
[interview]	BMG 80046-3

Source: *Pride And Joy – The Story Of Alligator Records*
See also Koko Taylor.

Vocal and guitar accompaniment: Harmonica Fats (harmonica and dialogue)

Location: unknown, probably {USA}. c.1992

untitled blues

Source: *Heineken beer advert No. 1*

As above

Location: unknown, probably {USA}. c. 1993

untitled blues

Source: *Heineken beer advert No. 2*

LUCIUS [DUSTY] BROOKS
See the Four Tones.

WILLIAM LEE CONLEY [BIG BILL] BROONZY
Unknown contribution (possibly vocal and guitar accompaniment: the Chicago Five)

Location: unknown {USA}. c. 1939

Titles performed:
unknown

Source: *Swingin' The Dream* [unconfirmed]

Vocal and guitar

Location: probably Chicago, Illinois. c. early 1950s

Titles performed:
unknown

Source: *I Come For To Sing* [unconfirmed]

Vocal and guitar

Location: Brussels, Belgium. c. late 1955–early 1956

Titles performed:
'When Did You Leave Heaven' Jazz & Jazz Vidjazz 13, Yazoo 518
'Just A Dream' Jazz & Jazz Vidjazz 13, Yazoo 518
'House Rent Stomp' Jazz & Jazz Vidjazz 13, Yazoo 518
'In The Evening (Saturday Evening Blues)' Jazz & Jazz Vidjazz 13, Yazoo 518

Source: *Big Bill Blues – Low Lights And Blue Smoke*

Vocal and guitar

Location: Milan or Rome, Italy. c. June 1956

Titles performed:
'In The Evening'
and one other, unknown, title

Source: *RAI, Italian TV broadcast.*

Vocal and guitar

Location: London, England. Friday 1 March 1957

Title performed:
'Black Brown And White'

Source: *Six-Five Special*

Vocal and guitar–1
guitar solo–2

Location: Circle Pines Camp, Western Michigan. Summer/autumn, 1957

Titles performed:
'Worried Man Blues'–1 Storyville SV6032, Vestapol 13003,13042, Yazoo 518
'How You Want It Done'–1 Storyville SV6032, Vestapol 13003,13042, Yazoo 518
'John Henry'–1 Storyville SV6032, Vestapol 13003,13042, Yazoo 518
'Stump Blues'–1 Storyville SV–6032, Vestapol 13003,13042, Yazoo 518
'Guitar Boogie' [aka 'Guitar Shuffle' aka 'Hey Hey']–2 Storyville SV6032, Vestapol 13003, 13042, Rhino R3.2101, Yazoo 518
'Blues in E'–2 Storyville SV6032, Vestapol 13003, 13042, Yazoo 518

Source: *Pete Seeger film collection* [M]
The original footage of the above was made in the following order: REEL 1; 'How You Want It Done': 'John Henry' (incomplete); REEL 2: 'Stump Blues' (incomplete); REEL 3: 'Worried Man Blues'; REEL 4: 'Blues in E': 'Guitar Boogie' [aka 'Hey Hey' aka 'House Rent Stomp'] (incomplete).

Amateur silent film, made in England during 1957 by Graeme Bell, is known to exist. Extracts appear in both *Jazz Scrapbook* and *Graeme Bell*, UK TV broadcasts, shown during the early 1980s. The [FS] entitled *This Train*, often credited as a Broonzy film, is simply a montage of railway images employing a 1950s Broonzy recording of the title song (probably from July 12/13 1957).

The following is also of interest: *Rhythms Of The World* [D] [C], UK TV broadcast. 1993. A short documentary on Big Bill Broonzy in Britain, including interviews with people who met him.

ADA BROWN

Vocal accompaniment: Fats Waller (piano), unknown (trumpet, trombone, bass, drums)

Location: unknown {USA}. 1943

Titles performed:
'That Ain't Right'
[dialogue]

Source: *Stormy Weather*

CHARLES BROWN

Vocal and piano accompaniment: unknown

Location: probably Los Angeles, California. 1970

Titles performed:
unknown

Source: *The Homewood Show* [unconfirmed]

Vocal and piano accompaniment: unknown Swedish musicians, (electric guitar, electric bass, drums)

Location: Stockholm, Sweden. 1979

Titles performed:
'Money's Getting Cheaper'
'Teardrops From My Eyes'
'Merry Christmas Baby'
'Please Don't Drive Me Away'
'Trouble Blues'
'I Don't Know'
'Please Come Home For Christmas'
'Bad Bad Whiskey'
'I'm Gonna Push On'
[interview]

Source: *Swedish TV broadcast* [C]

Vocal and piano accompaniment: unknown Swedish musicians, probably as above.

Location: Stockholm, Sweden. October 1980

Titles performed:
'Watching And Waiting For You'
'Drifting Blues'
'Don't Go Changing'

Source: *Swedish TV broadcast* [C]

Vocal and piano accompaniment: probably The Honeydrippers

Location: Los Angeles, California. 1984

Titles performed:
'Driftin' Blues'
'Merry Christmas Baby'

Source: *Legends Of Rhythm And Blues*

Vocal and piano accompaniment: unknown

Location: probably Los Angeles, California. 1988

Titles performed:
unknown

Source: *That Rhythm, Those Blues*

Vocal and piano accompaniment: unknown

Location: Memphis, Tennessee. 1990

Titles performed:

'Driftin' Blues'	BMG 791.151, Rhino R91226
'All My Life'	BMG 791.151, Rhino R91226

Source: *Blues Alive*

CLARENCE [GATEMOUTH] BROWN

Electric guitar–1, electric violin–2, vocal and electric guitar–3 accompaniment: The Blue Beats; Johnny Johnson (electric guitar); Dave 'Fathead' Newman and one unknown (trumpets) Harrison Calloway and one unknown (tenor saxophones): 'Skip'[possibly Skippy Brooks] (piano) Finis Tasby (electric bass); Freeman Brown (drums). Dave 'Fathead' Newman (vocal)–4

Location: WFAA-TV studios, Dallas, Texas. February–August 1966

Titles performed
'Okie Dokie Stomp'–1
'Walkin' Delirium'–1
untitled instrumental #1–2
untitled instrumental #2–1
'Summertime'–1
'Jamaica Farewell'–1
untitled instrumental #3–1
'Have You Ever Been Mistreated'–3
untitled instrumental #4–1
'When My Blue Moon Turns To Gold'–2
'Orange Blossom Special'–2
untitled instrumental #5–1
'Twelfth Street Rag'–1
untitled instrumental #6–1
'Polk Salad'–1
'Cleaver's Tune'–1
'Soft Shoe'–1
'Jose'–1
'A Hard Day's Night'–1
'When The Saints Go Marching In'–4
'Milestone'–1
untitled instrumental #7–1
'Don't Bother Me'–1
'Take Five'–1
'Teddy Bear'–1
'Blues For Cochise'–1
'Battle At The KO Coral' [*sic*]–1
'Moon River'–1
'One O'Clock Jump'–1

'Chicken Fat'–1
'Pickin' Up Chips'–1
'I'll Remember April'–1
untitled instrumental #8–1

Source: *The Beat*
Gatemouth Brown was the leader of the houseband known as the Blue Beats throughout this show's one season run. The recordings were made on several occasions during the period indicated, and generally two performances per show were used. See also Freddy King for a guitar duet with that artist.

Vocal and electric guitar–1; harmonica solo–2 accompaniment: Henry Vestine (electric guitar); James Shane (electric bass); Fito De La Parra (drums)

Location: Montreux, Switzerland. July 1973

Titles performed:
'Please Mr Nixon'–1
untitled instrumental–2

Source: *Montreux Jazz*

Vocal, electric guitar and violin accompaniment: unknown

Location: Austin, Texas. 1977–78

Titles performed:
unknown

Source: *Austin City Limits*

Vocal accompaniment: unknown

Location: Ames, Iowa. c.1979

Titles performed:
unknown

Source: *Maintenance Shop Blues*

Vocal and violin in duet with Roy Clark (violin) accompaniment: unknown

Location: probably Nashville, Tennessee. c.1979

Titles performed:
unknown

Source: *Hee Haw*

Vocal, electric guitar and violin accompaniment: Homer Brown, Bill Samuels, Joe Sunseri, Craig Wroten, Miles Wright, Robert Shipley (individual instrumentation unknown)

Location: Hamburg, Germany. 1983

Titles performed:
'Sometimes I Feel Myself Slippin''
'Dollar Got The Blues'
'Song For Rene'
'Up Jumped The Devil'
'Sunrise, Cajun Style'

Source: *German TV broadcast* [C]

Vocal and electric guitar accompaniment: Lloyd Glenn (piano); unknown (trumpet, tenor saxophone, electric bass, drums)–1
Violin solo accompaniment: unknown (piano, electric bass, drums)–2

Location: San Francisco. 1983

Titles performed:
'Sometimes I Feel Myself Slipping'–1
'Goofus'–2
[interview]

Source: *San Francisco Blues Festival*

Vocal and electric guitar accompaniment: unknown (keyboards, electric bass, drums)

Location: Sacramento, California. September 1987

Titles performed:
'Do The Zydeco'

Source: *Sacramento Blues Festival 1987*

Brown also appears in an untitled 58 minute concert with Gate's Express [G], date and other details currently unknown, available from Phoenix.

GEORGE WASHINGTON BROWN

Vocal accompaniment: unknown

Location: unknown {USA}. c.1942–44

Titles performed:
[12008] 'Keep Waitin''
[12607] 'God's Heaven' (probably: 'I'm Gonna Shout all Over God's Heaven')

Source: *Soundies*

HENRY BROWN
Piano solo accompaniment: Henry Townsend (guitar)

Location: St. Louis, Missouri. Probably 23 January 1976

short instrumental blues [unbroadcast]

Source: filmed for *The Devil's Music*, but unused in the final edit.

JIMMY BROWN
Vocal and trumpet accompaniment: Paul Williams (baritone saxophone); unknown (tenor saxophone, piano, bass, drums)

Location: New York City. 1955

Title performed:
[introduction by Willie Bryant and Jimmy Brown leading to;]
My Love Is True — Storyville SV6016, Video Images 74

Source: *Showtime At The Apollo*

[REVEREND] PEARLY BROWN
Monologue, leading to conversation with Bukka White and Howlin' Wolf–1
Vocal and guitar accompaniment: Christine Brown, (second vocal)–2

Location: Newport, Rhode Island. July 1966

Titles performed:
[monologue/conversation]–1
'Keep Your Lamp Trimmed And Burning' [incomplete]–2
'Keep Your Lamp Trimmed And Burning'–2 — Vestapol 13049
'Pure Religion'–2 — Vestapol 13049
'It's A Mean Old World'–2 — Vestapol 13049

Source: *Alan Lomax film collection*

Brown can also be seen in the background during performances by hillbilly artists Kilby Snow and Jimmy Driftwood, recorded at the same time as the above, available on Vestapol video 13051.

Vocal and guitar

Location: KCTS-TV, Seattle, Washington. c.1967–69

Titles performed:
unknown

Source: *Seattle Folklore Society*. Videotape only, currently unavailable.

Vocal and guitar

Location: Atlanta, Georgia, 1977

Titles performed:
'It's A Mean Old World' — Shanachie 1401
'How Long Has It Been Since You Been Home' — Shanachie 1401
'Not Uneasy, My Lord' — Shanachie 1401
'You Got To Move' — Shanachie 1401
'Another Child Of God Gone Home' — Shanachie 1401
'Will The Circle Be Unbroken' — Shanachie 1401
'Please Stay Home With Me' — Shanachie 1401
'If I Never See You Anymore' — Shanachie 1401
'Great Speckled Bird' — Shanachie 1401

Source: *It's a Mean World*

RUTH BROWN (Ruth Weston)
Vocal accompaniment: Paul Williams (baritone saxophone); Jimmy Brown (trumpet); unknown (tenor saxophone, piano, bass, drums)

Location: New York City. 1955

Titles performed:
'Tears Keep Tumblin' Down' — Bavaria 12177
[dialogue with Willie Bryant, leading to;] — Storyville SV6016
'Oh What a Dream' — Fil A Film 2023, Storyville SV6016
'Teardrops From My Eyes' — Storyville SV6016
'Mama, He Treats Your Daughter Mean' — Storyville SV6016
'Have A Good Time' — Video View 1313

Source: *Showtime At The Apollo*

Vocal accompaniment: unknown (electric organ)

Location: Baltimore, Maryland. Saturday, 16 February 1963

Titles performed:
'I'm Going Home On The Morning Train'
'Deep River'

Source: *TV Gospel Time* #26

Vocal accompaniment: unknown Swedish musicians

Location: Stockholm, Sweden. October 1980

Titles performed:
'Business Makes The World Go Round'
'Everybody Rock'
'5-10-15 Hours'

Source: *Swedish TV broadcast* [C]

Vocal accompaniment: unknown

Location: unknown {USA}. 1988

Titles performed:
unknown

Source: *That Rhythm, Those Blues*

Vocal accompaniment: unknown

Location: New York City. 1989

Title performed:
'Teardrops From My Eyes'

Source: *Late Night With David Letterman*

Vocal accompaniment: unknown

Location: Memphis, Tennessee. 1990

Titles performed:
'If I Can't Sell It' Rhino R91226
'Just A Lucky So And So' Rhino R91226

Source: *Blues Alive*

Ruth Brown also appeared in the US TV sitcom *Hello Larry* [NBC, 1979–1980], and had a cameo role in the 1985 film *Hairspray*.

THOMAS BROWN

Vocal accompaniment: unknown

Location: Baltimore, Maryland. Saturday 16 February 1963

Titles performed:
'After It's All Over'
'Near The Cross'

Source: *TV Gospel Time* #25

WALTER BROWN

Vocal, unaccompanied

Location: Greenville, Mississippi. Between 11 August and 9 September 1978

Titles performed:
demonstration of roustabout songs
[interview] Vestapol 13078

Source: *Land Where The Blues Began*
See also Joe Savage.

WILLIE BROWN JR

Vocal accompaniment: unknown

Location: Chicago, Illinois

The following appearances are known:

1966
Tuesday 1 February [prog #31–1]
1969
Thursday 27 March [prog #25–1]

Titles performed:
unknown

Source: *Jubilee Showcase*

[REVEREND] MILTON BRUNSON

Vocal accompaniment: unknown

Location: Chicago, Illinois.

The following appearances are known:
1964
Sunday 12 April [prog #10–1]
1966

Sunday 11 December [prog #15–3]
1969
Saturday 5 July [prog #12–2]
1974
Sunday 14 July [prog #6–1]

Titles performed:
unknown

Source: *Jubilee Showcase*

GLADYS BRYANT
Vocal accompaniment: studio orchestra

Location: Los Angeles, California. c. 1952–53

Title performed:
[conversation with Groucho Marx, leading to short, untitled song followed by dance steps and subsequent participation in programme game]

Source: *You Bet Your Life*

PRECIOUS BRYANT (female artist)
Vocal and guitar

Location: Atlanta, Georgia. October 1984

Title performed:
'Black Rat Swing'

Source: *National Down Home Blues Festival*

BUCKWHEAT ZYDECO
Stanley Dural (vocal, accordion); Melvin Veazie (electric guitar); Lee Allen Zeno (electric bass); Herman 'Rat' Brown (drums); Patrick Landry (rub-board)

Location: The Mean Fiddler club, Harlesden, London, England. 1989

Titles performed:
'There's Good Rockin' Tonight' Channel 5 083-368-3
'Takin' It Home' Channel 5 083-368-3
'On A Night Like This' Channel 5 083-368-3
'Let The Good Times Roll' Channel 5 083-368-3
'Rock Me Baby' Channel 5 083-368-3
'Ya Ya' Channel 5 083-368-3
'Why Does Love Got To Be So Bad?' Channel 5 083-368-3
'Make a Change' Channel 5 083-368-3

Source: *Taking It Home Live In Concert*

Vocal and accordion accompaniment: unknown (tenor saxophone, alto saxophone, electric bass, rub-board, drums)

Location: Louisiana. 1990

Titles performed:
'Make A Change' Channel 5 083 258–3, Island 083 258–3
'Baby Do Right' Channel 5 083 258–3, Island 083 258–3

Source: *Zydeco Nite'N'Day*

Probably as above

Location: New Orleans, Louisiana. 1991

Titles performed:
unknown

Source: *Let The Good Times Roll* [2]

BOBBY BUFORD
Vocal and guitar

Location: WDBJ-TV Studios, Roanake, Virginia. Spring/Summer 1987

Titles performed:
'Step It Up And Go' [A] [part only]
'Long Gone Lonesome Blues' [A] [part only]
'John Henry' [B] [part only]

Source: *Black Musical Traditions In Virginia: Blues* [A] *Black Musical Traditions In Virginia: Non-blues Secular Music* [B]

ALDEN BUNN
See Tarheel Slim.

DAN BURLEY

Piano solos accompaniment: Johnny Taylor (electric organ)

Location: unknown {USA}. 1947

Titles performed:

'Boogie In D'	Jazz Classics JCVC115, Storyville SV6035
'Boogie In C'	Jazz Classics JCVC115, Storyville SV6035
untitled instrumental	Jazz Classics JCVC115, Storyville SV6035

Source: *Jivin' In Be-Bop*

R L BURNSIDE

Vocal and electric guitar

Location: Holly Springs, Mississippi. Between 11 August and 9 September 1978

Title performed:
'Poor Boy, Long Ways From Home' [part only] Vestapol 13078

Source: *Land Where The Blues Began*

Vocal and electric guitar–1
Vocal and electric guitar accompaniment: Dave Stewart (guitar)–2

Location: Holly Springs, Mississippi. Autumn 1990

Titles performed:

'Jumper On The Line'–1	Anxious 45099-29643, BMG un-numbered
'Long Haired Doney'–2	Anxious 45099-29643, BMG un-numbered

Source: *Deep Blues*

J C BURRIS

Vocal and bones, accompanying Sonny Terry, vocal and harmonica–1; dancing–2; dancing and body slapping–3

Location: New York City or the Pete Seeger residence, New York. 1958

Titles performed:

'Crazy 'bout You Baby'–1	Vestapol 13042, 13057
'Buck Dance'–2	Vestapol 13042, 13057
'Hand Jive'–3	Vestapol 13042, 13057

Source: *Pete Seeger film collection*

Vocal and harmonica accompaniment, if any: unknown

Location: San Francisco, California. 1975

Titles performed:
unknown

Source: *Open Studio*

Vocal and harmonica accompaniment, if any: unknown

Location: San Francisco, California. 1975

Titles performed:
unknown

Source: *AM San Francisco*

Vocal and harmonica accompaniment, if any: unknown

Location: San Francisco, California. 1976

Titles performed:
unknown

Source: *San Francisco Blues*

Vocal and harmonica

Location: unknown {USA}. 1976

Titles performed:
unknown [ST only]

Source: *Leadbelly* [unconfirmed]

Vocal and harmonica accompaniment, if any: unknown

Location: unknown {USA}. 1976

Titles performed:
unknown

Source: *Showboat 1988 – The remake*

Vocal and harmonica accompaniment, if any: unknown

Location: San Francisco, California. 1977

Titles performed:
unknown

Source: *Evening Show*

Vocal and harmonica–1
Vocal and body slapping–2

Location: Veterans Hall, Albany, California. November 1985

Titles performed:
[introduction by Chris Strachwitz;] Arhoolie ARV 402
'Blues All Around My Bed'–1 Arhoolie ARV 402
'Down On The Farm'–1 Arhoolie ARV 402
'The Educated Hand Jive'–2 Arhoolie ARV 402

Source: *It's Got To Be Rough To Be Sweet*

CHARLIE BURSE
See Will Shade.

THOMAS BURT
Vocal and guitar–1
as above, in duet with Moses Rascoe (vocal and guitar)–2

Location: North Carolina. 1988

Titles performed:
'Can't Live Here No More'–1
'Step It Up And Go'–2
[interview]

Source: *Step It Up And Go*
See also Moses Rascoe.

CAROLYN BUSH
Vocal accompaniment: unknown

Location: New York City. Sunday 2 December 1962

Title performed:
'Precious Lord, Take My Hand'

Source: *TV Gospel Time* #4

HENRY BUTLER
Vocal and piano

Location: unknown {USA}. 1980

Title performed:
'Somebody Else Is Taking My Place'

Source: *Dreamland*

ROY BYRD
See Professor Longhair.

C

CABIN KIDS
Three male and two female juveniles (vocal), unaccompanied

Location: probably New York City. 1936

Titles performed:
unknown

Source: *Gifts Of Rhythm*

As above.

Location: probably New York City. 1938

Titles performed:
'Pink Lemonade'
'Rhythm Saves The Day'
'Way Down Yonder In New Orleans'
and possibly two other, unknown, titles

Source: *All's Fair*

CADILLACS
Probably Earl Carroll, Robert Phillips, Laverne Drake, Gus Willingham, Papa Clark, vocals accompaniment: unknown

Location: Philadelphia, Pennsylvania. c.1956.

Titles performed:
unknown [probably 'Speedoo']

Source: *Dick Clark's American Bandstand*

Probably Earl Carroll, Robert Phillips, Laverne Drake, Charles Brooks, Earl Wade, vocals accompaniment: unknown (tenor saxophone, electric guitar, bass, drums)

Location: unknown {USA}. 1958

Titles performed:
'Jay Walker'
'Please Mister Johnson'

Source: *Go Johnny, Go*

SHIRLEY CAESAR
Vocal accompaniment: unknown

Location: Chicago, Illinois.

The following appearances are known;
1964
Sunday 26 January [prog #73]
1966
Sunday 23 January [prog #6–2]
1972
Friday 4 August 1972 [prog #11–2]
1975
Sunday 13th April [prog # 11–2] [*sic*]

Titles performed;
unknown

Source: *Jubilee Showcase*

Also, the following:

vocal accompaniment: unknown

Location: unknown {USA}. c. 1969

Titles performed:
'He's Got It All In Control'
'The World Didn't Give It To Me'
'No Charge'

Source: *Soul Set Free*

Vocal accompaniment: unknown (keyboards, electric guitar, electric bass, drums)

Location: London, England. 1984

Titles performed:
'Lost'
'Jesus Won't Let Go'

Source: *Rock Gospel*

Speech

Location: Raleigh, North Carolina. August 1995

[interview]

Source: *Too Close To Heaven*

Vocal accompaniment: unknown (electric organ)

Location: QVC TV studios, Lancaster, Pennsylvania. Tuesday 28 October 1997

Title performed:
'Someone, Somewhere'
[interview]
[monologue advising the immediate purchase of a CD]

Source: *QVC*

Vocal accompaniment: unknown orchestra

Location: The Kennedy Centre, Washington DC. Sunday 7 December 1997

Title performed:
'You Got To Serve Somebody'

Source: *Kennedy Centre Awards Ceremony 1997*

The following documentary on the artist is also of interest: *Hold My Mule* [1993] [D] [C] Mercury Films.
See also the Caravans.

JAMES [BUTCH] CAGE
Speech

Location: Zachary, Louisiana. Sunday 7 August 1960

Monologue [ST only] K-Jazz 014, Rhapsody 8022

Source: *Blues Like Showers Of Rain*
See also Willie Thomas.

CALVIN AND THE MAJESTICS
Vocal group, including Dionne Warwick, accompaniment: unknown

Location: New York City. Sunday 9 December 1962

Titles performed:
'Jesus Said, "If You Go"' [*sic*]
'To Those That Wait'

Source: *TV Gospel Time* #7 [M]

CAMP MEETING GOSPEL CHORUS
Mixed vocal choir, accompaniment: unknown
Soloist: William James–1

Location: Brooklyn, New York City. Sunday 14 October 1962

Titles performed:
'I've Made My Vows To The Lord'
'Rock Of Ages'
'Over My Head'
'I Adore Him'–1

Source: *TV Gospel Time* #11

As above: soloists: Irene Coston–1; William James–2

Location: Brooklyn, New York City. Sunday 18 November 1962

Titles performed:
'Ezekiel Saw The Wheel'
'I Want Jesus To Walk With Me'–1
'It Means So Much'
'Climbing Up The Mountain'–2

Source: *TV Gospel Time* #10 [*sic*]

DELORIS BARRETT CAMPBELL
Vocal accompaniment: unknown

Location: Chicago, Illinois.

The following appearances are known:

1964
Sunday 8 March [prog #17–3]
Sunday 26 April [prog #9–3]
1966
Wednesday 13 April [prog #34–2]
Saturday 11 June [prog #23–2]
Sunday 11 December [prog #15–3]
1968
Saturday 21 September [prog #28–2]
1969
Saturday 15 February [prog #18–2]
Thursday 27 March [prog #5–2]
Saturday 21 June [prog #24–3]
Saturday 4 October [prog #27–1]
1971
Saturday 14 August [prog #1–2]
1972
Sunday 10 September [prog #2–1]
1974
Sunday 20 January [prog #6–3]
Sunday 11 August [prog #3–1]
1976
Saturday 9 October [prog #9–1]

Titles performed:
unknown

Source: *Jubilee Showcase*

Also, the following;

vocal accompaniment: the Raymond Raspberry Singers (vocal group)

Location: probably New York City. c. April 1965

'He's So Divine' [A]
'Oh Say So' [A]
'I Hear God' [B]
'What A Blessing In Jesus I Found' [B]

Source: *TV Gospel Time* #41 [A], 43 [B]
See also the Barrett Sisters and Roberta Martin.

EDDIE C CAMPBELL
Vocal and electric guitar accompaniment: unknown (electric bass, drums)

Location: Willesden, London, England. Early 1985

Titles performed:
'Don't Throw Your Love On Me So Strong'
'Look What Santa Did'

Source: *The Blues And Beyond*

Vocal and electric guitar accompaniment: unknown (second electric guitar, harmonica, piano, electric bass, drums)

Location: Germany. 1989

Titles performed:
'Summertime' [instrumental]
'If You Don't Slow Down'
'All Your Love'
'Mellow Down Easy'
'All Your Love, I Miss Lovin'' [instrumental]
'She Moves Me'
'Nineteen Years Old'
'Don't Know Where I'm Going'
'Santa's Messin' With The Kid'
[interview]

Source: *German TV broadcast* [C]

BLIND JAMES CAMPBELL AND HIS NASHVILLE STRING BAND

Campbell, vocal and guitar accompaniment: Bell Ray (guitar); Beauford Clay (violin); Ralph Robinson (tuba)

Location: Nashville, Tennessee. Spring 1963

Titles performed:
'Goin' To Chicago' [part only] Yazoo 520
'John Henry' [part only] Yazoo 520

Source: *Dietrich Wawyzn film collection*

MILTON CAMPBELL

See Little Milton.

CANNON TEMPLE CHURCH OF GOD IN CHRIST CHOIR

Mixed vocal choir accompaniment: unknown
Soloists: Archie Dennis Jr.–1; Carolyn McClurkin–2; Pauline Jones–3

Location: Charlotte, North Carolina. Sunday 20 September 1964

Titles performed:
'Oh, Didn't It Rain'–1
'Have Faith In God'
'What A Friend We Have In Jesus'–1
'Jesus Said If You Go'–2, –3
'Lower Down The Chariot'–1

Source: *TV Gospel Time* #28

GUS CANNON

Vocal and 4-string banjo

Location: Memphis, Tennessee. Summer 1960

Title performed:
'My Money Never Runs Out'
[ST only] K-Jazz 014, Rhapsody 8022

Source: *Blues Like Showers Of Rain*

Vocal and 4 string banjo

Location: Memphis, Tennessee. January–February 1976

Title performed:
'Walk Right In' [part only]
[interview]

Source: *The Devil's Music series 1*

Vocal and 4 string banjo

Location: Memphis, Tennessee. 1978

demonstration of the medicine show style K-Jazz 030, Yazoo 505

Source: *Good Morning Blues*
Cannon is listed in some reference works as appearing, with his Jug Stompers, in the 1929 film *Hallelujah*, but there is no evidence in any inspected print of the film itself to support this. See also [Memphis] Willie Borum.

CARAVANS

Albertina Walker, Cassietta George, Shirley Caesar, Delores Washington, Johneron Davis (vocals) accompaniment, if any: unknown

Location: Chicago, Illinois

The following appearances are known;

1964
Sunday 26 January [prog #7–3]
1966
Sunday 23 January [prog #6–2]
1967
Sunday 5 March [prog #17–1]

1969
Thursday 24 April [prog #18–3]
1975
Sunday 13 April [prog #2–3]

Titles performed:
unknown

Source: *Jubilee Showcase*

Also, the following;

Albertina Walker, Shirley Caesar, Cassietta George and one other (vocals) accompaniment: Caesar (tambourine) and unknown (piano)

Location: Memphis, Tennessee. Saturday 19 January 1963

'Just Like Jesus' [A]
'I'm Ready To Serve The Lord' [A]
'Until I Meet The Lord' [A]
'To Whom Shall I Turn?' [B]
'That's Why I Call Him Mine' [B]
'No Coward Soldier' [B]

Source: *TV Gospel Time* #20 [A], #21 [B]
See also Shirley Caesar, Cassietta George and Albertina Walker.

UNA MAE CARLISLE
Vocal accompaniment: Garland Wilson (piano)

Location: Paris, France. 1938

Title performed:
'Darling, Je Vous Aime Beaucoup'

Source: *Carrefour*

Vocal and piano

Location: unknown {USA}. 1944

Titles performed:
[introduction by Louis Jordan to;]
[17608] 'I'm A Good, Good Woman' Jazz Classics JCVC-105
[8M2] ''Taint Yours' Jazz Classics JCVC-105

Source: *Soundies*
17608 copyrighted 7 August 1944, 8M2 28 August 1944. One of the above probably appears in *Hep Cat Serenade*.

Vocal accompaniment: Lucky Millinder and his band

Location: probably New York City. 1948

Titles performed:
'Throw It Out Your Mind' Timeless Video 5603
'It Ain't Like That' Timeless Video 5603

Source: *Boarding House Blues*

ROY [CHUBBY] CARRIER
Vocal and accordion accompaniment: unknown (electric guitar, electric bass, rub-board, drums)

Location: New Orleans, Louisiana. 1990

Title performed:
'Bernadette'

Source: *Big World*

CONNIE CARROLL
Vocal accompaniment: unknown

Location: unknown {USA}. 1956

Titles performed:
'Rock And Roll Is The Latest Fad'
'Fast Movin' Mama'
'TV Is The Thing'

Source: *Rockin' The Blues*

JOE CARTER
Vocal and electric guitar accompaniment: Louis Myers (electric guitar); David Myers (electric bass); Fred Below (drums)

Location: Chicago, Illinois. Wednesday 28 January 1976

Title performed:
'It Hurts Me Too' [part only]

Source: *The Devil's Music series 1*

LAVADA CARTER
Vocal, unaccompanied

Location: New York City. 1948

Title performed:
'John Saw The Number' Hollywood Select 97803

Source: *Miracle In Harlem*

ELAINE CASTON
Vocal accompaniment: unknown

Location: Chicago, Illinois. Sunday 2 October 1966

Titles performed:
unknown

Source: *Jubilee Showcase* [prog #15–2]

LEONARD [BABY DOO] CASTON
Vocal and keyboards accompaniment: The Minnesota Barking Ducks [G] unknown (2 electric guitars, harmonica, electric bass, drums)

Location: Wilibeski's Blues Saloon, St. Paul, Minnesota. Wednesday 14 March 1984

Title performed:
'Pie In The Sky'

Source: *Survivors: The Blues Today*

Vocal and piano accompaniment: the Chicago Blues All Stars
John Watkins (electric guitar); Arthur Dixon (piano); Carey Bell (harmonica); Mike Morrison (electric bass); Clifton James (drums)

Location: Denver, Colorado. 1984

Titles performed:
'I Just Want To Make Love To You'
'I Got The Blues'
'All Night Long'

Source: *I Am The Blues*

Vocal accompaniment: Mark Naftalin's band

Location: Fairfax, California. 1986

Title performed:
'Low Down Dog'

Source: *US PBS TV broadcast* [C]. Origin unknown

CAT-IRON (William Carradine)
Vocal and guitar

Location: Buckner's Alley Natchez, Mississipi. c. 1956

Titles performed:
unknown

Source: *Seven Lively Arts: They Took A Blue Note*

CATS AND THE FIDDLE
Vocal group, accompaniment: own guitar, ukelele, tiple, bass: single member of group, guitar solo–1

Location: probably New York City. 1938

Title performed:
'Killin' Jive' Jazz Classics JCVC112, Timeless Video 5044
untitled instrumental–1 Jazz Classics JCVC112, Timeless Video 5044

Source: *The Duke Is Tops*

Probably as above

Location: probably Hollywood, California. 1938

Titles performed:
unknown

Source: *Two Gun Man From Harlem*

CEDAR STREET BAPTIST CHURCH CHOIR OF COLUMBUS, OHIO
Mixed vocal choir, accompaniment: unknown

Location: probably New York City. 1966

Titles performed:
unknown

Source: *TV Gospel Time* # 64

CELESTIAL CHOIR OF WASHINGTON TEMPLE

Mixed vocal choir, accompaniment: unknown

Location: probably New York City. 1966

Titles performed:
unknown

Source: *TV Gospel Time* #66
See also the Washington Temple groups.

CELESTIAL ECHOES

Vocal quartet accompaniment, if any: unknown

Location: New York City. Monday 23 December 1962

Titles performed:
'Yes, Jesus Loves Me'
'When Was Jesus Born'?

Source: *TV Gospel Time* #9 [M]

JOHN CEPHAS AND PHIL WIGGINS

Cephas (vocal and guitar), Wiggins (vocal and harmonica)

Location: Belgium. 1981

Titles performed:
'Burning Bridges'
'Worried Man Blues'

Source: *American Folk Blues Festival 1981*

As above

Location: Atlanta, Georgia. October 1984

Title performed:
'Baby What You Want Me To Do'

Source: *National Down Home Blues Festival*

As above

Location: Fairfax Station, Virginia. 1985

Title performed:

'Richmond Blues'	Blues Houseparty BH–01, JVC V–225

Source: *Houseparty Productions* [C]

As above–1
Cephas, (vocal and guitar) in duet with Larry Johnson (vocal and guitar)–2

Location: New York City. Saturday 25 January 1986

Titles performed:

'No Special Rider'–1	K-Jazz 076, Rhapsody 8013
'Let us Pray Together'–2	K-Jazz 076, Rhapsody 8013

Source: *John Jackson – An American Songster*

Cephas (vocal and guitar); Wiggins (harmonica)

Location: Bowling Green, Virginia. Summer 1988

Titles performed:
'Death Don't Have No Mercy' [fragment only]
'Black Rat Swing' [part only]
'John Henry' [part only]
[demonstrations of different blues styles]
[interview]

Source: *WETA TV*

As above

Location: Smithsonian Festival of Folklife, Washington, DC. Late June–early July 1988

Title performed:
'John Henry'

Source: *WETA TV*

CHALLENGERS
Vocal group accompaniment: unknown

Location: probably New York City. c. April 1965

Titles performed:
'The Storm Is Passing Over'
'Right Now Is The Needed Time'

Source: *TV Gospel Time* #42
See also the Combined Harvest Metropolitan And Christian Choirs.

CHANSONETTES
Female vocal group accompaniment: unknown

Location: Chicago, Illinois. Sunday 19 December 1965

Titles performed:
unknown

Source: *Jubilee Showcase* [prog # 29–1]

CHANTICLEERS
Vocal group accompaniment: unknown

Location: unknown. c.1941–44

Titles performed:
[12808] 'Lovin' Up A Solid Breeze'
[13908] 'Jumpin' Jack From Hackensack'
[14408] 'Ain't My Sugar Sweet'
[14608] 'If You Treat Me To A Hug'

Source: *Soundies*
One, at least, of the above probably appears in *Hep Cat Serenade*.

FANNIE BELL CHAPMAN
Vocal, unaccompanied

Location: Centreville, Mississippi. 1975

Titles performed:
unknown CFSC 1066

Source: *Fannie Bell Chapman: Gospel Singer*

RAY CHARLES (Ray Charles Robinson)
Vocal and piano accompaniment: probably Gosady McGee (electric guitar) and Milton Garred (bass)

Location: probably Seattle, Washington. c. late 1940s–early 1950s

Titles performed:
unknown

Source: *local TV broadcasts*

Vocal and piano accompaniment: the Ray Charles orchestra and the Raelettes

Location: Newport, Rhode Island. July 1960

Titles performed:
'My Baby'
'Drown In My Own Tears'
'What'd I Say'
'Let The Good Times Roll'
'I Believe'

Source: *Jazz–USA*

Vocal and keyboards accompaniment: unknown

Location: unknown {USA}. 1962

Titles performed:
unknown

Source: *The Dinah Shore Chevy Show*

Vocal and keyboards accompaniment: unknown

Location: unknown {USA}. 1963

Titles performed:
unknown

Source: *Scorpio Rising*

Vocal and piano accompaniment: probably the Ray Charles orchestra and the Raelettes

Location: possibly Dublin, Ireland. 1964

Titles performed:
'Let The Good Times Roll'
'Hit The Road Jack'
'That Lucky Old Sun'
'Unchain My Heart'
'Hallelujah I Just Love Her So'
'Don't Tell Me Your Troubles'

'I Got A Woman'
'Busted'
'Nobody But You'
'Light Out Of Darkness'
'What'd I Say'

Source: *Ballad In Blue*
Although this film, in which Charles has a substantial dramatic role, was made in Ireland, it is unclear if the above listed concert footage was also filmed there or elsewhere.

Vocal and piano accompaniment: the Ray Charles orchestra and the Raelettes

Location: London, England. c. August 1964

Titles performed:
'Busted'
'Margie'
'You Don't Know Me'
'Hallelujah, I Just Love Her So'
'Georgia'
'Don't Set Me Free'
'Hit The Road Jack'
'Take These Chains From My Heart'
'What'd I Say'

Source: *The Man They Call The Genius*

Vocal and piano accompaniment: the Ray Charles orchestra and the Raelettes

Location: Civic Auditorium, Santa Monica, California. 1964

Titles performed:
[introduced by Chuck Berry]
'Georgia'
'Let The Good Times Roll'

Source: *The TAMI Show*

Vocal and keyboards accompaniment: unknown

Location: unknown {USA}. 1965

Titles performed
unknown [probably ST only]

Source: *The Cincinatti Kid*

Vocal and keyboards accompaniment: unknown

Location: Hollywood, California. 1965

Titles performed:
unknown

Source: *Shindig*

Vocal and keyboards accompaniment: unknown

Location: probably Hollywood, California. 1967

Titles performed:
uknown

Source: *The Andy Williams Show*

Vocal and keyboards accompaniment: the Ray Charles orchestra and the Raelettes

Location: probably New York City. 1967

Title performed:
'In The Heat Of The Night' [ST only]

Source: *In The Heat Of The Night*

Vocal and keyboards accompaniment: unknown

Location: Hollywood, California. 1967

Titles performed:
unknown

Source: *The Kraft Music Hall*

Vocal and keyboards accompaniment: possibly Lou Brown and his orchestra

Location: Hollywood, California. 1968

Titles performed:
unknown

Source: *The Jerry Lewis Show*

Vocal and keyboards accompaniment: unknown

Location: unknown {USA}. 1968

Titles performed:
unknown

Source: *The Joey Bishop Show*

Vocal and keyboards accompaniment: unknown

Location: unknown {USA}. 1968

Titles performed:
unknown

Source: *Operation Entertainment*

Vocal and keyboards accompaniment: the Ray Charles orchestra and the Raelettes

Location: London, England. c. February 1969

Titles performed:
unknown

Source: *Soul Man*

Vocal and keyboards accompaniment: unknown

Location: unknown {USA}. 1969

Titles performed:
unknown

Source: *Della*

Vocal and keyboards accompaniment: unknown

Location: unknown {USA}. 1969

Titles performed:
unknown

Source: *The Joey Bishop Show*

Vocal and keyboards accompaniment: probably the Mort Lindsay orchestra

Location: unknown {USA}. 1969

Titles performed:
unknown

Source: *The Merv Griffin Show*

Vocal and keyboards accompaniment: unknown

Location: Hollywood, California. 1969

Titles performed:
unknown

Source: *The Smothers Brothers Comedy Hour*

Vocal and keyboards accompaniment: unknown

Location: London, England. 1970

Titles performed:
unknown

Source: *The Engelbert Humperdinck Show*

Vocal and keyboards accompaniment: unknown

Location: unknown {USA}. 1970

Titles performed:
unknown

Source: *The Glen Campbell Good Time Hour*

Vocal and keyboards accompaniment: unknown

Location: unknown {USA}. 1970

Titles performed:
unknown

Source: *Hee Haw*

Speech

Location: Hollywood, California. 1970

Guest appearance as participant in game show

Source: *Hollywood Squares*

Vocal and keyboards accompaniment: unknown

Location: Nashville, Tennessee. 1970

Titles performed:
unknown

Source: *The Johnny Cash Show*

Vocal and keyboards accompaniment: unknown

Location: London, England or Hollywood, California. 1970

Titles performed:
unknown

Source: *This Is Tom Jones*
Either location is possible, since production of this show alternated between the two cities.

Vocal and keyboards accompaniment: unknown

Location: unknown {Europe}. 1970

Titles performed:
unknown

Source: *Warnung Vor Einer Heiligen Nutte*

Vocal and keyboards accompaniment: unknown

Location: Los Angeles, California. 1971

Titles performed:
unknown

Source: *The Cosby Show*

Vocal and piano, in duet with Flip Wilson (in the persona of 'Geraldine'), accompaniment: unknown studio orchestra

Location: Los Angeles, California. 1971

Titles performed:
'Unchain My Heart'
'Your Cheatin' Heart'
'Hey Good Lookin''
[dialogue]

Source: *The Flip Wilson Show*

Vocal and piano accompaniment: unknown studio orchestra

Title performed:
'Look What They Done To My Song, Ma'

Source: *The Flip Wilson Show*

Vocal and keyboards accompaniment: unknown

Location: unknown {USA}. 1972

Titles performed:
unknown

Source: *Black Rodeo*

Vocal and keyboards accompaniment: probably the Peter Matz orchestra

Location: unknown {USA}. 1972

Titles performed:
unknown

Source: *The Carol Burnett Show*

Vocal and keyboards accompaniment: unknown

Location: New York City. 1972

Titles performed:
unknown
[probably interview]

Source: *The Dick Cavett Show*

Vocal and keyboards accompaniment: unknown

Location: New York City. 1972

Titles performed:
unknown

Source: *The Ed Sullivan Show*

Vocal and keyboards accompaniment: unknown

Location: Los Angeles, California. 1972

Titles performed:
unknown
[probably interview]

Source: *The Mike Douglas Show*

Vocal and keyboards accompaniment: probably the Doc Severinson orchestra

Location: New York City. 1972

Titles performed:
unknown
[probably interview]

Source: *The Tonight Show Starring Johnny Carson*

Vocal and keyboards accompaniment: the Duke Ellington orchestra

Location: unknown {USA}. 1973

Titles performed:
unknown

Source: *Duke Ellington Special*

Vocal and keyboards accompaniment: unknown

Location: probably Hollywood, California. 1973

Titles performed:
unknown

Source: *NBC Follies*

Vocal and keyboards

Location: New York City. c. 1973–74

Titles performed:
'The Alphabet Song'
'It's Not Easy Being Green'

Source: *Sesame Street*
[these are probably two separate broadcasts]

Vocal and keyboards accompaniment: unknown

Location: unknown {USA}. 1974

Titles performed:
unknown

Source: *Cotton Club*

Vocal and keyboards accompaniment: unknown

Location: unknown {USA}. 1975

Titles performed:
unknown

Source: *Cher*

Vocal and keyboards accompaniment: unknown

Location: unknown {USA}. 1975

Titles performed:
unknown

Source: *Cotton Club*

Vocal and keyboards accompaniment: unknown

Location: unknown {USA}. 1975

Titles performed:
unknown

Source: *Ebony Readers' Music Poll Award Show*

Vocal and keyboards accompaniment: unknown

Location: unknown. 1975

Titles performed:
unknown

Source: *Salute To The American Imagination*

Vocal and keyboards accompaniment: probably the George Rhodes orchestra

Location: Las Vegas, Nevada. 1975

Titles performed:
unknown

Source: *Sammy And Company*

Vocal and keyboards accompaniment: unknown

Location: unknown {USA}. 1976

Titles performed:
unknown

Source: *Celebration: The American Spirit*

Unknown contribution

Location: unknown {USA}. 1976

Titles performed:
unknown [or] unknown contribution

Source: *Comedy In America*

Vocal and piano accompaniment: probably the Ray Charles orchestra and the Raelettes

Location: unknown {USA}. 1976

Titles performed:
unknown

Source: *The Midnight Special*

Vocal and keyboards accompaniment: unknown

Location: Opryland USA, Nashville, Tennessee. 1976

Titles performed:
unknown

Source: *Music Hall America*

Vocal and keyboards accompaniment: unknown

Location: unknown {USA} or Canada. 1976

Titles performed:
unknown

Source: *Oscar Peterson: Very Special*

Vocal and keyboards accompaniment: probably the Doc Severinsen orchestra

Location: Los Angeles, California. 1976

Titles performed:
unknown
[probably interview]

Source: *The Tonight Show Starring Johnny Carson*

Vocal and keyboards accompaniment: unknown

Location: unknown {USA}. 1977

Title performed:
'Eleanor Rigby'

Source: *Beatles Forever*

Vocal and keyboards accompaniment: unknown

Location: Los Angeles, California. 1977

Titles performed:
unknown
[probably interview]

Source: *The Mike Douglas Show*

Vocal and keyboards accompaniment: studio orchestra

Location: New York City. 1977

Titles performed:
unknown

Source: *Saturday Night Live*

Vocal and keyboards accompaniment: unknown

Location: unknown {USA}. Early 1978

Titles performed:
unknown

Source: *Johnny Cash – Spring Fever*

Location: Los Angeles, California. 1978

Titles performed:
unknown

Source: *The Chuck Barris Rah Rah Show*

Vocal and keyboards accompaniment: unknown

Location: probably Nashville, Tennessee. 1978

Titles performed:
unknown

Source: *Fifty Years Of Country Music*

Vocal and keyboards accompaniment: unknown

Location: New York City. 1978

Titles performed:
unknown

Source: *Saturday Night Live*

Vocal and keyboards accompaniment: unknown

Location: Los Angeles, California. 1978

Titles performed:
unknown

Source: *The Second Barry Manilow Special*

Vocal and keyboards accompaniment: unknown

Location: unknown {USA}. 1978

Titles performed:
unknown

Source: *Thank You Rock And Roll*

Vocal and keyboards accompaniment; probably the Ray Charles orchestra and the Raelettes

Location: Antibes, France. Tuesday 17–Wednesday 18 July 1979

Titles performed:
'Georgia'
'Some Enchanted Evening'
'I Want Your Love'
'I Can't Stop Loving You'
'Sunshine Day'

Source: *International Festival Of Jazz*

Vocal and keyboards accompaniment: the Munich Gospel Choir

Location: Munich, Germany. December 1979

Titles performed:
'Angels Keep Watching'
'There'll Be No Peace'
'Santa Claus Blues'
'Heaven Help Us All'
'Amen'

Source: *Noel Avec Ray Charles* [M]. European TV. Origin unknown

Vocal and electric organ accompaniment: unidentified pre-recorded soundtrack

Location: Chicago, Illinois. 1980

Title performed:
'Shake A Tail Feather'

Source: *The Blues Brothers*
Charles also has a dramatic cameo role in this film.

Vocal and keyboards accompaniment: the Ray Charles orchestra and the Raelettes

Location: Jubilee Auditorium, Edmonton, Canada. 1981

Titles performed:
'Busted'
'Georgia'
'Oh What A Beautiful Morning'
'Some Enchanted Evening'
'Hit The Road Jack'
'I'm Still A Fool For You'
'I Can't Stop Loving You'
'I Can See Clearly Now'
'Keep On Singing'
'What'd I Say'

Source: *probably Canadian TV broadcast* [C]

Vocal and keyboards accompaniment: unknown

Location: Rome, Italy. Monday 21 September 1981

Titles performed:
'Busted'
'Georgia'
'Some Enchanted Evening'
'Rock Steady'
'I Can't Stop Loving You'
'Crying Time'
'Baby Please Don't Go'
'What'd I Say'
[interview]

Source: *Italian TV broadcast* [C]

Vocal and keyboards accompaniment: unknown

Location: Teatro Tenda Bussoladomani, Lido di Camaiore, Italy. c. September 1981

Titles performed:
'Let The Good Times Roll'
'One Day Soon'
'Yesterday'
'Some Enchanted Evening'
'Georgia'
'She Knows'
'Hit The Road Jack'
'I Can't Stop Loving You'
'I Can See Clearly Now'
'Knock On Wood'
'What'd I Say'

Source: *Italian TV broadcast* [C]

Vocal and keyboards accompaniment: unknown

Location: Netherlands. Tuesday 17 November 1981

Titles performed:
'Your Cheatin' Heart'
[interview]

Source: *Dutch TV broadcast* [C]

Vocal and keyboards

Location: London, England. 1982

Titles performed:
[interview and short examples of musical styles]

Source: *B A In Music*

Vocal and keyboards accompaniment: unknown

Location: Capitol Jazz Festival, Knebworth, England. 1982

Titles performed:
'Busted'
'Georgia'
'Oh What A Beautiful Morning'
'Dream On'

'Some Enchanted Evening'
'Love Is What We Need'
'I Can't Stop Loving You'
'Hit The Road Jack'
'Knock On Wood'
'Baby Please Don't Go'
'What'd I Say'

Source: *In The Spotlight*

Vocal and piano accompaniment: the Munich Gospel Choir

Location: Munich, Germany. December 1983

Titles performed:
'Go Tell It On The Mountain'
'I Saw Three Ships'
'All Night, All Day'
'God Bless The Child'
'Amazing Grace'
'Take My Hand, Precious Lord'
'Merry Christmas Baby'
'Lord Help Us All'
'Amen'

Source: *German TV broadcast* [C]

Vocal and keyboards accompaniment; unknown

Location: Austin, Texas. 1984

Titles performed:
'Let's Get It On'
'Georgia'
'Busted'
'I Can't Stop Loving You'
'In Three-quarter Time'
'Born To Love Me'
'What'd I Say'

Source: *Austin City Limits*

Speech and piano

Location: unknown {USA}. 1986

monologue on behalf of the National Organisation For Disabilties

Source: *US PBS TV advert*

Vocal and alto saxophone

Location: unknown {USA}. 1989

Titles performed:
unknown

Source: *Limit Up*
Charles plays the part of a street busker in this film, playing a great deal of unaccompanied saxophone, as well as some accompanied by unknown rock bands.

SAM CHATMON
Vocal and guitar

Location: Festival of American Folklife, Washington, DC. Summer 1974

Title performed:
'Stir It Girl'

Source: *Oh Happy Day*

Vocal and guitar

Location: probably New York City. 1976

Titles performed:
unknown

Source: *The Today Show*

Vocal and guitar

Location: Hollandale, Mississippi. Tuesday 20 January 1976

Titles performed:
'Big Road Blues' Vestapol 13016
'That's All Right' Vestapol 13016
'Sam's Rag' Vestapol 13016
'Liza Jane'
'Stop And Listen'
[unbroadcast interview]

Source: *The Devil's Music series 2*

Vocal and guitar

Location: probably Hollandale, Mississippi. 1978

Titles performed:
'St. Louis Blues' K-Jazz 030, Yazoo 505
'Sitting On Top Of The World' K-Jazz 030, Yazoo 505

Source: *Good Morning Blues*

Vocal and guitar

Location: Hollandale, Mississippi. Between 11 August and 9 September 1978

Title performed:
'Shaking In The Bed With You' [A]
'Snatch It Back' [fragment only] [A]
[interview] [A]
'How Long Blues' [fragment only] [B]
'Sugar Blues' [fragment only] [B]
'Bumble Bee' [fragment only] [B]
[interview] [B]

Source: *Land Where The Blues Began* [A] Vestapol 13078; *Dreams And Songs of The Noble Old* [B] Vestapol 13081
'Shaking In The Bed With You' contains verses from Charlie Patton's 'Shake It And Break It' and Joe Calicott's Fare Thee Well'.

Vocal and guitar, in duet with Eugene [Sonny Boy Nelson] Powell, vocal and guitar

Location: Freedom Village, Greenville, Mississippi. Saturday 8 September 1979

Titles performed:
'We Going Round The Mountain' K-Jazz 081
How Long That Evening Train Been Gone?' K-Jazz 081

Source: *Mississippi Blues*

BOOZOO CHAVIS
Vocal and accordion

Location: Louisiana. 1987–88

Title performed:
'Johnny Ain't No Goat' Flower 7

Source: *J'ai Eté Au Bal*

Vocal and accordion accompaniment: The Magic Sound [G], personnel unknown

Location: Louisiana. 1988

Titles performed:
'Sassy One-step'
'Paper In My Shoe'

Source: *Aly Meets The Cajuns*
See also *Cajun Country*, which includes re-edited material from the above broadcast.

Vocal and accordion accompaniment: as above

Location: Plaisance, Louisiana. 1988

Titles performed:
'Oh My My' [fragment] K-Jazz 098, Rhapsody 8062

Source: *Zydeco Gumbo*

Vocal and accordion–1; rub-board and vocal–2 accompaniment: The Magic Sounds (electric guitar, electric bass, rub-board, drums)

Location: Louisiana. 1990

Titles performed:
'Make It To Me'–1 Channel 5 083 258–3, Island 083 258–3
'Dog Hill'–2 Channel 5 083 258–3, Island 083 258–3
'Bye Bye Jolie' Channel 5 083 258–3, Island 083 258–3

Source: *Zydeco Nite'N'Day*

Vocal and accordion accompaniment: Charles Chavis (rub-board); unknown (electric guitar, electric bass, drums)

Location: Lafayette, Louisiana. 1994

Titles performed:
'Gilton' BMG un-numbered
'Motor Dude Special' BMG un-numbered
'Gone A La Maison' BMG un-numbered
'Forty One Days' BMG un-numbered
[interview] BMG un-numbered

Source: *The Kingdom Of Zydeco*

[REVEREND] JULIUS CHEEKS
Vocal accompaniment: The Four Knights (vocal group)–1
Vocal duet with Jesse Mae Renfro accompaniment: The Four Knights–2
Vocal accompaniment: the Four Knights and Marianne Cheeks (piano)–3

Location: Baltimore, Maryland. Saturday 5 September 1964

Titles performed:
'Mother Sang These Songs'–1
'Great Change In Me'–1
'That's Worrying Me'–2
'Morning Train'–3

Source: *TV Gospel Time* #33

C J CHENIER
Speech

Location: Louisiana. 1988

[interview]

Source: *Zydeco Gumbo*

Vocal and accordion accompaniment: unknown

Location: New Orleans, Louisiana. 1990

Titles performed:
'Check Out The Zydeco'
'Caldonia'

Source: *New Orleans Jazz And Heritage Festival 1990*

Speech

Location: Louisiana. 1990

[interview] Channel 5 083 258–3, Island 083 258–3

Source: *Zydeco Nite'N'Day*

Vocal and accordion accompaniment: unknown

Location: Austin, Texas. 1992

Titles performed:
'Just Like A Woman'
'I'm Comin' Home'
'Bow Legged Woman'
'Hey Ma-Ma'
'She's My Woman'
'Rockin' Accordeon'

Source: *Austin City Limits*
This artist is the son of Clifton Chenier

CLEVELAND CHENIER
Speech

Location: Louisiana. 1987–88

[interview] Flower 7

Source: *J'ai Eté Au Bal*
This artist is Clifton Chenier's brother.

CLIFTON CHENIER
Vocal and accordion accompaniment: unknown

Location: Opelousas, Breaux Bridge and Lafayette, Louisiana. 1973

Titles performed:
'Zydeco Two-Step' Flower 5, K-Jazz 066
'Big Mamou' Flower 5, K-Jazz 066
'Hot Rod' Flower 5, K-Jazz 066
'Baby, Please Don't Go' Flower 5, K-Jazz 066
'Johnny Can't Dance' Flower 5, K-Jazz 066

Source: *Hot Pepper*

Vocal and accordion accompaniment: unknown

Location: unknown {USA}. 1974

Titles performed:
unknown

Source: *Gettin' Back*

Vocal and accordion accompaniment: unknown

Location: Louisiana. 1974

Titles performed:
unknown

Source: *Within Southern Lousiana*

Vocal and accordion accompaniment: Cleveland Chenier (rub-board); Paul Staneger (electric guitar); Joseph Bruckner (electric bass); Robert Peter (drums)

Location: Montreux, Switzerland. Saturday 12 July 1975

Titles performed:
'Walkin' The Floor'
'Pinetop's Boogie Woogie'
untitled blues

Source: *Montreux Jazz*

Vocal and accordion accompaniment: unknown

Location: Austin, Texas. 1976

Titles performed:
unknown

Source: *Austin City Limits*

Vocal and accordion accompaniment: unknown (tenor saxophone, electric piano, electric bass, drums)

Location: New Orleans, Louisiana. 1978

Title performed:
'I'm A Hog For You Baby' Flower 7

Source: *J'ai Eté Au Bal*

Vocal and accordion accompaniment: Cleveland Chenier (rub-board); unknown (tenor saxophone, keyboards, electric bass, drums)

Location: San Francisco, California. 1983

Titles performed:
'Oh My My'
'What'd I Say'
'Colinda'
[interview]

Source: *San Francisco Blues Festival*

Vocal and accordion accompaniment: unknown

Location: unknown {USA}. 1987

Titles performed:
unknown

Source: *Clifton Chenier – The King Of The Zydeco*

Vocal and accordion accompaniment: unknown (trumpet, tenor saxophone, keyboards, electric guitar, electric bass, drums)

Location: Louisiana. 1987

Titles performed:
'I'm A Hog For You, Baby' K-Jazz 098, Rhapsody 8062
'Comin' Home' K-Jazz 098, Rhapsody 8062

Source: *Zydeco Gumbo*

Vocal and accordion accompaniment: unknown

Location:. Louisiana, 1987

Titles performed:
'Black Gal' [fragment only] Channel 5 083 258-3, Island 083 258-3
'Let The Good Times Roll' [fragment only] Channel 5 083 2358-3, Island 083 258-3

Source: *Zydeco Nite'N'Day*

CHICAGO COMMUNITY CHOIR

Mixed vocal choir, unaccompanied. Soloist; Verlene Moore–1

Location: Chicago, Illinois. Tuesday 15 November 1964

Titles performed:
'He Won't Turn His Back On Me'–1
'The Failure Is Not In God, It's In Me'
'I'm Taking Him Home'

Source: *TV Gospel Time* #40

[LITTLE] JOHNNY CHRISTIAN

Vocal and electric guitar accompaniment: unknown

Location: Chicago, Illinois. Late 1970s

Titles performed:
'I'm Gonna Leave'
untitled blues

Source: *Chicago Melodie*

CHURCH USHERS CHORUS

Mixed vocal choir, accompaniment: unknown

Location: Baltimore, Maryland. Saturday 16 February 1963

Titles performed:
'Keep Trusting'
'In The Garden'
'No Condemnation'

Source: *TV Gospel Time* # 25

SAVANNAH CHURCHILL

Vocal accompaniment: the Les Hite orchestra

Location: Hollywood, California. April 1942

Titles performed:
[6408] 'The Devil Sat Down And Cried'
[6601] 'What To Do (What's Cookin')'
[7006] 'That Ol' Ghost Train'

Source: *Soundies*
6408 copyrighted 20 April 1942; 6601 4 May 1942; 7006 1 June 1942

Vocal accompaniment: Lynn Proctor trio: Proctor (piano); unknown (bass, drums)

Location: New York City. 1948

Title performed:
'I Want To Be Loved'

Source: *Miracle In Harlem*

Vocal accompaniment: unknown orchestra

Location: probabably New York City. 1949

Titles performed:
'The Things You Do To Me'

Source: *Souls Of Sin*

Vocal and piano accompaniment; John Kirby and his band

Location: unknown {USA} 1950

Titles performed:
unknown

Source: *Harlem Follies*

CORTELIA CLARK

A short piece of silent monochrome film, made by Dietrich Wawzyn in 1963, almost certainly shows this Nashville street singer and guitarist.

EDDIE CLEARWATER (Edward Harrington)

Vocal and electric guitar accompaniment: unknown

Location: Philadelphia, Pennsylvania. 1959

Title performed:
[probably] 'Hillbilly Blues'

Source: *Dick Clark's American Bandstand*
If, indeed, the title performed on the above was 'Hillbilly Blues', then the likliehood is that Clearwater was performing as 'Clear Waters', under which soubriquet he recorded 'Hillbilly Blues' for Atomic-H records (Chicago) in 1959.

Vocal and electric guitar accompaniment: Carey Bell (harmonica) and others, unknown

Location: Chicago, Illinois. Late 1970s

Titles performed:
'Two Times Nice'
'Sweet Home Chicago'

Source: *Good Morning*

Vocal and electric guitar accompaniment: unknown

Location: Den Haag, Netherlands. 1979

Titles performed:
'Everything Gonna Be Allright'
'Johnny B. Goode'

Source: *Dutch TV broadcast* [C]

Vocal and electric guitar accompaniment: Jimmy Johnson (electric guitar); David Myers (electric bass); Odie Payne (drums)

Location: Montreux, Switzerland. July 1979

Titles performed:
'Johnny B. Goode'
'Couldn't Lay My Guitar Down'

Source: *Montreux Jazz*

Vocal and electric guitar accompaniment: unknown

Location: Chicago, Illinois. c.1979

Titles performed:
unknown

Source: *I Call It Murder*

CLEFS OF FAITH

Vocal group accompaniment: unknown

Location: Chicago, Illinois. Sunday 8 March 1964

Titles performed:
unknown

Source: *Jubilee Showcase* [prog #26–3]

CLEVELAND COLOURED QUARTET

There are reportedly several silent films, lasting approximately fifteen minutes, featuring this quartet. These are believed to predate sound film, and are therefore assumed to have been made prior to 1928. No further details are available.

[REVEREND] JAMES CLEVELAND

Vocal accompaniment: the Tears of Music (vocal group)–1
Vocal accompaniment: the Refuge Temple Voices (choir)–2
Vocal accompaniment: the Mount Olive Baptist Church Choir–3
Vocal accompaniment: unknown (electric organ)–4
Vocal accompaniment: the Mitchell Gospel Choral Ensemble–5

Location: New York City. Sunday 15 December 1962

Titles performed:
'He's So Good'–1 [A]
'He's Coming Back Again'–2 [B]
'Deep Down In My Heart'–3 [C]
'It's In My Heart'–4 [D]
'Couldn't Keep It To Myself'–5 [E]

Source: *TV Gospel Time* [M] #14 [A], #15 [B], #16 [C], #17 [D], #18 [E]. Cleveland can be seen glaring off camera during the performance of 'It's In My Heart' when the organist plays a short series of wrong notes.

Vocal accompaniment: unknown

Location: Chicago, Illinois. Sunday 5 April 1964

Titles performed:
unknown

Source: *Jubilee Showcase* [prog #4–1]

As above

Location: Chicago, Illinois. Wednesday 20 August 1969

Titles performed:
unknown

Source: *Jubilee Showcase* [prog #4–1] [*sic*]

Vocal accompaniment: unknown

Location: Chicago, Illinois. 1976

Titles performed:
unknown

Source: *Here Comes Gospel*

Vocal accompaniment: the Southern California Community Choir

Location: All Saints Church, Northampton, England. 1984

Titles performed:
unknown

Source: *In The Spirit*

Vocal accompaniment: unknown

Location: unknown {USA}. 1984

Titles performed:
unknown

Source: *Gospel*

Vocal accompaniment: unknown

Location: Jerusalem. 1985

Titles performed:
unknown

Source: *Gospel In The Holy Land*
See also Gospel All-Stars

CLOUDS OF JOY
See the Mighty Clouds Of Joy.

CLOVERS
Probably Billy Mitchell, Matthew McQuater, Harold Lucas Jr, Harold Winley, vocals and Willie Harris (electric guitar) accompaniment: Paul Williams (baritone saxophone); Jimmy Brown (trumpet); unknown (tenor saxophone, piano, bass, drums)

Location: New York City. 1955

Titles performed:
'Fool Fool Fool' Fil A Film 2023, Storyville SV6016
'Your Cash Ain't Nothin' But Trash' Bavaria 12177
'Hey Miss Fannie' Storyville SV6016, Video Images 73R
'Lovey Dovey' Storyville SV6017

Source: *Showtime At The Apollo*

COASTERS
Probably Carl Gardner, Will 'Dub' Jones, Bill Guy, Earl Carroll, vocals accompaniment: unknown orchestra

Location: Los Angeles, California. 1965

Titles performed:
'What Is The Secret Of Your Success?'
'Searchin''
'Along Came Jones'

Source: *Shindig*
Later performances by groups under this name, with significantly different personnel, are excluded.

DOROTHY LOVE COATES
Vocal accompaniment: unknown

Location: Chicago, Illinois. Saturday 3 May 1969

Titles performed:
unknown

Source: *Jubilee Showcase* [prog #33–2]

As above

Location: Chicago, Illinois. Saturday 4 October 1969

Titles performed:
unknown

Source: *Jubilee Showcase* [prog #27–1]

Speech

Location: Birmingham, Alabama. August 1995

[interview]

Source: *Too Close To Heaven*
See also the Gospel Harmonettes.

WILLIE COBBS
Vocal and harmonica

Location: Greenwood, Mississippi. 1991

Title performed:
untitled instrumental blues

Source: *Mississippi Masala*

FRANCIS COLE
Vocal accompaniment: unknown

Location: probably Washington, DC. 1966

Titles performed:
unknown [A]
unknown [B]

Source: *TV Gospel Time* #55 [A], 56 [B]

NAT [KING] COLE (Nathaniel Adams Coles)
King Cole Trio: Nathaniel 'King' Cole (vocal and piano); Oscar Moore (electric guitar); Wesley Prince (bass); Ida James (vocal)–1

Location: probably Hollywood, California. Mid-late 1943

Title performed:
[15408] 'Is You Is Or Is You Ain't My Baby?'–1
Channel 5 CFV10552,
Jazz Classics JCVC-105

Source: *Soundie*
Copyrighted 21 February 1944

As above

Location: Hollywood, California. Late 1945

Titles performed:
[16M2] 'I'm A Shy Guy'
[16M4] 'Come To Baby, Do'
Jazz Classics JCVC106,
Storyville SV6003,
Virgin VVD868
[18M5] 'Got A Penny, Benny?'
Storyville SV6003,
Virgin VVD-868
[19M3] 'Errand Boy For Rhythm'
Storyville SV6003,
Jazz Classics JCVC-106, 111
Virgin VVD-868
[87408] 'Frim Fram Sauce'

Source: *Soundies*
16M2 copyrighted 11 February 1946; 16M4 15 February 1946; 18M5 22 April 1946; 19M3 27 May 1946.
The bulk of this artist's output clearly falls outside the scope of this work, but the above, among his earliest visually recorded performances, are of some interest to aficionados of Rhythm and Blues.

JOE COLLIER
Vocal and guitar accompaniment: Wendy Smith (tambourine)

Location: New York City. c.1970

Titles performed:
'I Want To Be Somebody'
'Burn, Baby, Burn'

Source: *Black Roots*

ALBERT COLLINS
Vocal and electric guitar accompaniment: unknown

Location: Chicago, Illinois. c.1979

Title performed:
'When A Guitar Plays The Blues'

Source: *Chicago Melodie*

Vocal and electric guitar accompaniment: Barrelhouse[G]

Location: Boerenhafstede, Netherlands. c. 1979–80

Titles performed:
'Frosty'
'Conversation With Collins'
'Sweet Home Chicago'
and other, unknown, titles

Source: *Dutch TV broadcast* [C]

Vocal and electric guitar accompaniment: the Icebreakers, personnel unknown, but probably including A C Reed (tenor saxophone)

Location: Dortmund, Germany. December 1980

Titles performed:
'The Things I Used To Do'
'Cold Cold Feeling'
'I've Got A Mind To Travel'
'Frosty'
untitled instrumental

Source: *German TV broadcast* [C]

Vocal and electric guitar accompaniment: the Icebreakers; A C Reed (tenor saxophone); and others, unknown

Location: Montreux, Switzerland. July 1981

Titles performed:
'Cold Cold Feeling'
'Cold Cut'
untitled instrumental

Source: *Montreux Jazz*

Vocal and electric guitar accompaniment: unknown (tenor saxophone, second electric guitar, piano, electric bass, drums)

Location: San Francisco, California. 1983

Titles performed:
'Cold, Cold Feeling'
untitled instrumental
[interview]

Source: *San Francisco Blues Festival*

Vocal and electric guitar accompaniment: The Icebreakers

Location: Tokyo, Japan. 1984

Titles performed:
unknown

Source: *Japanese TV broadcast*

Vocal and electric guitar accompaniment: unknown

Location: Dingwall's, Camden Town, London, England. Tuesday 26 February 1985

Title performed:
'Frosty'
[interview]

Source: *The Old Grey Whistle Test*

Vocal and electric guitar accompaniment: George Thorogood and the Destroyers: Thorogood (electric guitar); Hank Carter (tenor saxophone); Micahel Lenn (electric bass); Jeff Simon (drums)

Location: Philadelphia, Pennsylvania. Saturday 13 July 1985

Title performed:
'Madison Blues'

Source: *Live Aid*

Vocal and electric guitar accompaniment: unknown

Location: Carnegie Hall, New York City. c. 1985–6

Titles performed:
'If Trouble Was Money'
unknown title

Source: *Further Down The Road*

Vocal and electric guitar accompaniment: unknown

Location: Australia. 1986

Titles performed:
'Frosty'
untitled instrumental
[interview]

Source: *Australian TV broadcast* [C]

Vocal and electric guitar accompaniment: unknown

Location: Austin, Texas. c. 1987

Titles performed:
'Tired Man'
'Honey Hush'
untitled instrumental
'Black Cat Bone'
'You're Accusing Me Baby'

Source: *Austin City Limits*

Vocal and electric guitar accompaniment: the Icebreakers, personel unknown, but probably including A C Reed (tenor saxophone)

Location: Antone's Blues Club, Austin, Texas. 1987

Titles performed:
band instrumental
'Honey Hush'
untitled instrumental
'Black Cat Bone'
'You're Accusing Me Baby'
[interview]

Source: *Ain't Nothin' But The Blues*

Vocal and electric guitar accompaniment: unknown

Location: probably Chicago, Illinois. 1987

Titles performed:
unknown

Source: *Adventures in Babysitting*

Vocal and electric guitar accompaniment; Paul Shaffer (keyboards); unknown (trumpet, tenor saxophone, second electric guitar, electric bass, drums)

Location: New York City. c.1989

Titles performed:
'A Good Fool Is Hard To Find'

Source: *Late Night with David Letterman*

Vocal and electric guitar accompaniment: unknown

Location: London, England. Friday 22 June 1990

Titles performed:
'Too Tired'
'Further On Up The Road'

Source: *Wired*

Vocal and electric guitar in duet with Buddy Guy, vocal and electric guitar, accompaniment: unknown

Location: Checkerboard Lounge, Chicago, Illinois. 1990

Titles performed:
untitled instrumental–1 BMG 791.151, Rhino R91226
'I Ain't Drunk'–2 BMG 791.151, Rhino R91226
'Black Cat Bone'–2 BMG 791.151, Rhino R91226

Source: *Blues Alive*

Vocal and electric guitar accompaniment: unknown (2 tenor saxophones, trombone, trumpet, second electric guitar, electric organ, electric bass, drums)

Location: Austin, Texas. 1991

Titles performed:
'Iceman' Vestapol 13041
'Head Rag' Vestapol 13041
'The Lights Are On But Nobody's Home' Vestapol 13041

Source: *Austin City Limits*

Vocal and electric guitar accompaniment: unknown

Location: Austin, Texas. 1992

Titles performed:
'Ice Man'
'Accusing Me'
'Broke And Hungry'
untitled instrumental

Source: *Austin City Limits*
Collins also appears in a tutorial video (REH 18446) and a Seagrams Wine Cooler US TV advert in the company of Bruce Willis, date unknown, but probably early 1990s. He also appears in *Jump The Blues Away* with Etta James, details unknown. See also A C Reed.

COMBINED HARVEST, METROPOLITAN AND CHRISTIAN TABERNACLE CHOIRS

Large mixed vocal choir accompaniment: unknown, but including the Challengers (vocal group)–1
As above without the Challengers, soloists: Reverend William T Sawyer–2; Gwendolyn Gabriel–3;
Frank Davis and Robert Bradley–4

Location: probably New York City. c. 1965

Titles performed:
'Noah'–1
'I'll Let Nothing Separate Me From The Love Of God'–2
'Spread The News'–3
'Come, Ye Disconsolate'–4

Source: *TV Gospel Time* #42
See also Frank Davis.

GENE CONNORS
See Mighty Flea.

CONSOLERS
Sullivan Pugh (vocal and Hawaiian guitar), Iola Pugh (vocal)

Location: Jacksonville, Florida. 1966

Titles performed:
unknown

Source: *TV Gospel Time* #58

As last

Location: unknown {USA}. 1970s

Titles performed:
unknown

Source: *Look Up And Sing Out*

EDNA GALLMON COOKE
Vocal accompaniment: the Sons Of Faith (vocal group)

Location: Baltimore, Maryland. Saturday 5 September 1964

Titles performed:
'Pray Sometime'
'Come On, Let's Run'

Source: *TV Gospel Time* #35

JOE COOPER
Vocal accompaniment: unknown

Location: Mississippi. 1984

Titles performed:
unknown

Source: *In The Delta of Mississippi*

JOHNNY COPELAND
Vocal and electric guitar accompaniment: unknown

Location: Montreux, Switzerland. Saturday 16 July 1983

Titles performed:
'Boogie Woogie Nighthawk'
'Natural Born Believer'
'Honky Tonkin''
'Everybody Wants A Piece Of Me'
'Early In The Morning'
'Texas Blues'

Source: *Montreux Jazz*

Vocal and electric guitar accompaniment: unknown

Location: Paris, France. 1984

Titles performed:
'Just One More Time'
'Devil's Hand'
'Honky Tonkin''

Source: *French TV broadcast* [C]

Vocal and electric guitar accompaniment: unknown

Location: Germany. 1984

Titles performed:
'Boogie Woogie Nighthawk'
'Natural Born Believer'
'Well, Well, Baby-la'
'Cold Outside'
'Excuses'
'Houston, Let Me Come Home'
untitled instrumental
'Early In The Morning'
'Devil's Hand'
'Midnight Fantasy'
'Rock And Roll Lily'

Source: *Ohne Filter*

As above

Location: Germany. 1984

Titles performed:
'Houston, Let Me Come Home'
'Love Utopia'
'Boogie Woogie Nighthawk'
'Natural Born Believer'
'Well, Well, Baby-la'
'Cold Outside'
'Excuses'
'Early In The Morning'
'Devil's Hand'
'Midnight Fantasy'
'Rock And Roll Lily'

Source: *Ohne Filter* [different broadcast to above]

Vocal and electric guitar accompaniment: Kenny Peno (electric guitar); Theo Layasmyer (keyboards); Michael Merritt (electric bass); Damon DuWhite (drums)

Location: London, England. 1988

Titles performed:

'Track Him Down'	Magnum 7991
'Shuffle Incorporated'	Magnum 7991
'Cut Off My Right Arm'	Magnum 7991
'You Got Me Singing A Love Song'	Magnum 7991
'Texas Party'	Magnum 7991
'Down On Bending Knee'	Magnum 7991
'Johnny's Gone'	Magnum 7991
'Nobody But You'	Magnum 7991
'Daily Bread'	Magnum 7991
'My Woman Has A Black Cat Bone'	Magnum 7991
'Railroad Bill'	Magnum 7991
'Learned My Lesson'	Magnum 7991
[interview]	Magnum 7991

Source: *The Three Sides Of Johnny Copeland*

Vocal and guitar accompaniment: unknown

Location: unknown {USA}. 1995

Titles performed:
unknown
[interview]

Source: *Good Morning America*

Vocal and guitar accompaniment: unknown

Location: unknown {USA}. 1995

Titles performed:
unknown
[interview]

Source: *CNN*

CORNERSTONE BAPTIST CHOIR

Mixed vocal choir accompaniment: unknown–1 as above, combined with the New Shiloh Baptist Choir–2
Soloists: Thomas Faust–3; Earl Chainey–4

Location: Baltimore, Maryland. Saturday 16 February 1963

Titles performed:
'Hold Out' [A]–1
'I Shall Not Be Moved' [A]–2
'Down By The Riverside' [B]–3
'How I Got Over' [B]–1
'I'm Saved' [B]–4

Source: *TV Gospel Time* #26 [A], 27 [B]

CORNERSTONE CHOIR OF JERSEY CITY, NEW JERSEY

Mixed vocal choir accompaniment; unknown

Location: probably New York City. c. 1965–66

Titles performed:
unknown

Source: *TV Gospel Time* #51
This is believed to be a different group from the Cornerstone Baptist Choir.

ELIZABETH COTTEN

Vocal and guitar

Location: probably New York City. 1966

Titles performed:

'Goin' Down The Road'	Vestapol 13004
'Mama, Your Papa Loves You'	Vestapol 13004

Source: *Pete Seeger's Rainbow Quest*

Vocal and guitar; guitar solo–1

Location: unknown {USA}. 1969

Titles performed:
'Freight Train' Vestapol 13004, 13019
'What A Friend We Have In Jesus' Vestapol 13004, 13019
'Ruben'–1 Vestapol 13019
'Vestapol'–1 Vestapol 13019
'Washington Blues' Vestapol 13019
'A Jig'–1 Vestapol 13019
[interviews] Vestapol 13019

Source: *Laura Weber's Guitar, Guitar*

Vocal and guitar; guitar solo–1

Location: KCTS-TV Studios, Seattle, Washington. c. 1970

Titles performed:
'Freight Train' Yazoo 503
'Sweet Bye And Bye' Yazoo 503
'Vestapol'–1 Yazoo 503
'Georgia Buck'–1 Yazoo 503
'Washington Blues' Yazoo 503
'I'm Going Away' Yazoo 503

Source: *Masters Of American Traditional Music*

Vocal and guitar

Location: unknown {USA}. 1974

Titles performed:
unknown

Source: *Grass Roots Series* #1 – *Old Time Music*

Vocal and guitar; guitar solo–1
4 string banjo solo–2

Location: unknown {USA}. c. 1978

Titles performed:
'Freight Train' Vestapol 13019
'Wilson Rag'–1 Vestapol 13019
'Georgia Buck'–2 Vestapol 13019
'Rattler'–2 Vestapol 13019
'Spanish Flang Dang'–1 Vestapol 13019
'Judy's Got A Ramblin' Mind' Vestapol 13019
'Mama, Your Son's Done Gone' Vestapol 13019
'Wreck Of The Old 97' Vestapol 13019
'Jesus Is Tenderly Calling Today' Vestapol 13019
'Vestapol'–1 Vestapol 13019
'Buck Dance'–1 Vestapol 13019
'Oh Babe, It Aint No Lie' Vestapol 13019
'Ontario Blues' Vestapol 13019
'Mama, Where's The Baby' Vestapol 13019
untitled instrumental–1 Vestapol 13019
[interviews throughout with Mike Seeger] Vestapol 13019

Source: *uncredited; probably US PBS TV broadcast* [C]

Vocal and guitar

Location: Washington DC. 1979

Title performed:
'Freight Train Blues'

Source: *Homemade American Music*

Vocal and 12 string guitar

Location: Ohio University, c. 1979–80

Titles performed:
'Graduation March' Ramblin' 804
'Freight Train' Ramblin' 804
'Spanish Flangdang' Ramblin' 804
'Shake Sugaree' Ramblin' 804

Source: *Ohio University Telecommunications* Centre.

Cotton also appears in *Me And Stella* [D], details unknown. Available from Phoenix.

JAMES COTTON

Vocal and harmonica accompaniment: unknown

Location: unknown {USA}. 1969

Titles performed:
unknown

Source: *Playboy After Dark* [unconfirmed]

Vocal and harmonica accompaniment: unknown

Location: unknown {USA}. 1970

Titles performed:
unknown

Source: *Dial M For Music* [unconfirmed]

Vocal and harmonica accompaniment: unknown

Location: unknown {USA}. 1972

Titles performed:
unknown

Source: *Playing That Thing* [unconfirmed]

Vocal and harmonica accompaniment: unknown (electric guitar, tenor saxophone, electric bass, drums)

Location: Chicago, Illinois. c. 1979

Titles performed:
'Rocket Eighty-Eight'
[interview]

Source: *Chicago On The Good Foot*

Location: Ames, Iowa. c.1979

Titles performed:
unknown

Source: *Maintenance Shop Blues*

Vocal and harmonica accompaniment: unknown

Location: Montreux, Switzerland. July 1981

Titles performed:
'A Funky Good Time'
'Take A Little Walk With Me'
untitled instrumental
and other, unknown, titles

Source: *Living Legends Of The Blues*

Vocal and harmonica accompaniment: unknown

Location: Chicago, Illinois. 1983

Titles performed:
unknown

Source: *Sweet Home Chicago* [1]

Harmonica solo

Location: Chicago, Illinois. 1993

Title performed:
demonstration of Little Walter's 'Juke' MCA V10944
[interview] MCA V10944

Source: *Sweet Home Chicago* [2]
See also Muddy Waters.

TOM [TOMCAT] COURTNEY

Vocal and electric guitar accompaniment: unknown (keyboards, electric bass, drums)

Location: San Diego, California. July 1987

Titles performed:
'All Night Long' [instrumental]
'Sweet Little Angel'
'It's My Own Fault'
[monologue on Lightnin' Hopkins and Big Bill Broonzy, leading to;]
'Key To The Highway'
[interview]

Source: *Tom Coppin Productions*

COUSIN JOE

See [Cousin] Joe Pleasants

BISHOP A COWARD

Preaching

Location: New Haven, Connecticut. 1977

Titles performed:
unknown

Source: *Two Black Churches*

IDA COX

Vocal accompaniment: Jesse Crump (piano)

Location: probably New York City. 1947

Title performed:
'Worried Blues' ['Kentucky Man Blues'] Storyville SV6032, Video View 1313
''fore Day Creep' Storyville SV6032, Rhino R3.2102

Source: *A Woman's A Fool*

WILLIE [COWBOY] CRAIG

This artist appears in *Afro-American Worksongs In A Texas Prison* leading one or more songs, but titles are not known. Some may be represented by titles listed under Unidentified Artists [B] (26).

ROBERT CRAY

Electric guitar

Location: Eugene, Oregon. 1978

As a member of the fictitious group 'Otis Day And The Knights', Cray appears playing guitar in a club scene.

Titles performed:
'Shout'
'Rama-Lama-Ding-Dong'

Source: *National Lampoon's Animal House*
The part of Otis Day was played by DeWayne Jessie.

Vocal and electric guitar accompaniment: Mike Vannice (keyboards); Richard Cousins (electric bass); David Olson (drums)

Location: San Francisco, California. 1983

Titles performed:
'Too Many Cooks'
'Let's Have A Natural Ball'
'Run Here Mama'
[interview]

Source: *San Francisco Blues Festival*

Vocal and electric guitar accompaniment: as above

Location: Dingwall's, Camden Town, London, England. Tuesday 2 April 1985

Titles performed:
'Bad Influence'
'Phone Booth'
[interview]

Source: *The Old Grey Whistle Test*

Vocal and electric guitar accompaniment: probably Peter Boe (keyboards); Richard Cousins (electric bass); David Olson (drums)

Location: Sacramento, California. September 1985

Title performed:
'The Porch Light's On'

Source: *Sacramento Blues Festival*
This song appears in the 1987 Sacramento Blues Festival programme even though it was recorded in 1985.

Vocal and electric guitar accompaniment: probably as above

Location: London, England. November 1985

Titles performed:
'Change Of Heart'
'The Last Time I Get Burned Like This'

Source: *The Old Grey Whistle Test*

Vocal and electric guitar accompaniment: probably as above

Location: Germany. c. late 1985–early 1986

Titles performed:
'Foul Play'
'T-Bone Shuffle'
'Smoking Gun'

Source: *Ohne Filter*

Vocal and electric guitar accompaniment: probably as above

Location: Montreux, Switzerland. Sunday 9 November 1986

Titles performed:
'Hit That Highway'
'Because Of Me'
'Tell Me What's The Reason'
'Bad Influence'
'I'm In A Phone Booth'

Source: *Montreux Jazz*

Vocal and electric guitar accompaniment: probably as above

Location: London, England. March 1987

Titles performed:
'Right Next Door'
'Smoking Gun'
'Still Around'
'Further On Up The Road'
'Breaking All The Rules'
[interview]

Source: *The Tube*

Vocal and electric guitar accompaniment: unknown

Location: unknown {USA}. 1987

Title performed:
'I Don't Have A Wife'
[interview]

Source: *Ain't Nothin' But The Blues*

Vocal and electric guitar accompaniment: unknown

Location: San Diego, California. 1987

Titles performed:
unknown

Source: *Three Generations Of The Blues part 2*

Vocal and electric guitar accompaniment: unknown

Location: London, England. Friday 5 August 1988

Titles performed:
'Don't Be Afraid Of The Dark'
'A Change Is Gonna Come'

Source: *Wired*

Vocal and electric guitar accompaniment: Peter Boe (keyboards); Tim Kaihatsu (second electric guitar); Richard Cousins (electric bass); David Olson (drums); and The Memphis Horns (brass)

Location: Hammersmith Odeon, London, England. January 1989

Titles performed:
'I Guess I Showed Her'
'Foul Play'
'Don't Be Afraid Of The Dark'
'The Last Time'
'Acting This Way'
'Night Patrol'
'I Can't Go Home'
'Smokin' Gun'
'Playin' In The Dirt'
[interview]

Source: *Rhythms Of The World*

Vocal and electric guitar accompaniment: The Sunday Night Band: unknown (second electric guitar, alto saxophone, keyboards, electric bass, drums

Location: New York City. 1989

Titles performed:
'All Your Love, I Miss Loving'
'Something Is Wrong With My Baby'
'Don't You Even Care'

Source: *Sunday Night*

Vocal and electric guitar accompanimnent: Eric Clapton (electric guitar); Johnny Johnson (piano); Richard Cousins (electric bass); David Olson (drums)
As above, including Clapton (vocal) and Buddy Guy (vocal and electric guitar)–1

Location: Royal Albert Hall, London, England. 1990

Titles performed:
'Cry For Me'
'Worried Life Blues'–1

Source: *Rock Steady*

Vocal and electric guitar accompaniment: unknown–1
Vocal and electric guitar accompaniment Double Trouble [G]–2

Location: Austin, Texas. 1991

Titles performed:
'The Forecast Calls For Pain'–1
'I'm Finding Out For Myself'–1
'Consquences'–1
'Because Of Me'–1
'Walk Around'–1
'Sweet Home Chicago'–2
'Leave My Girl Alone'–2

Source: *Austin City Limits*

Vocal and electric guitar in duet with John Lee Hooker, vocal and electric guitar

Location: unknown {USA}. 1991

Title performed:
'Mister Lucky'

Source: *promotional video*

Vocal and electric guitar accompaniment: Dave Edmunds and Steve Cropper (electric guitars); and others, unknown.

Location: Expo '92, Seville, Spain. 1992

Titles performed:
'Phone Booth'
'Just Like The Devil'
'Dock Of The Bay'
'Green Onions'

Source: *Guitar Legends*

Speech

Location: unknown. 1993

[interview]

Source: *John Lee Hooker*
This artist is also known to have appeared on *The Tonight Show Starring Johnny Carson* sometime during the late 1980s, but details are unknown.

CONNIE CURTIS [PEE WEE] CRAYTON

Electric guitar solo accompaniment: the Gerald Wiggins orchestra

Location: unknown {USA}. 1982

Title performed:
'Blues After Hours' Magnum MMGV–035

Source: *America's Music–Blues Volume 1*

Vocal and electric guitar accompaniment: unknown

Location: Tokyo, Japan. 1983

Titles performed:
unknown

Source: *Japanese TV broadcast* [C]

JOYCE CRAYTON

Vocal accompaniment: her mother, Handsome Crayton (piano)–1; church group–2

Location: Boston, MA. 1980

Titles performed:
'He'll Understand'–1
'All My Life'–2

Source: *Dreamland*

ARTHUR [BIG BOY] CRUDUP

Vocal and guitar accompaniment, if any: unknown

Location: London, England. Tuesday 24 February 1970

Title performed:
'I Almost Lost My Mind'

Source: *Late Night Line Up*

As above

Location: London, England. Tuesday 10 March 1970

Title performed:
'That's All Right'

Source: *Late Night Line Up*

Vocal and guitar accompaniment: his four sons (two guitars, bass, drums)

Location: Franktown, Virginia. c. 1971

Title performed:
'Greyhound Bus Blues' [part only] K-Jazz 020, Yazoo 507

Source: *Out Of The Blacks, Into The Blues part 2*

Vocal and electric guitar

Location: Franktown, Virginia. 1973

Titles performed:
'So Cold In Chicago' Shanachie 1401
'If I Get Lucky' Shanachie 1401
'Rock Me Mama' Shanachie 1401
'My Baby Left Me' Shanachie 1401
'So Glad You're Mine' Shanachie 1401
'Getting Old And Grey' Shanachie 1401
[interviews] Shanachie 1401

Source: *Arthur Crudup; Born With The Blues*
There is a possibility that this artist appeared on Australian television during his 1972 tour.

D

DOROTHY DANDRIDGE

Unknown contribution

Location: probably New York City. 1940

Titles performed:
unknown

Source: *Four Shall Die*

Vocal accompaniment: Cee Pee Johnson and his band–1
Vocal accompaniment: Paul White and Ted Fio Rito–2
Vocal duet with Billy Mitchell accompaniment: Mitchell (piano)–3
Vocal accompaniment: unknown (piano and harmonica); Dudley Dickerson, spoken interjections–4

Location: Hollywood, California. Mid-1942

Titles performed:
[1406] 'Swing For Your Supper'–1
[1802] 'Jungle Jig'–1 Storyville SV6003, Jazz Classics JCVC-110, Virgin VVD-868
[5801] 'A Zoot Suit'–2 Storyville SV6003, Virgin VVD-868
[8302] 'Blackbird Fantasy'–3
[9104] 'Cow Cow Boogie'–4 Channel 5 CFV10542, Charly #2, Jazz Classics JCVC-107

Source: *Soundies*
9104 copyrighted 26 October 1942
See also the Spirits of Rhythm.

Vocal accompaniment: Tiny Grimes and his orchestra

Location: probably Hollywood, California. c. 1945

Titles performed:
'Cow Cow Boogie'
and other, unknown, titles

Source: *Cow Cow Boogie*

Unknown contribution

Location: probably New York City. 1947

Titles performed:
unknown

Source: *Flamingo*
Dandridge also appears in *Ebony Parade*. It is believed that the title[s] in that film are drawn from *Soundies* listed above, although it is not known which. She also had a small, uncredited role as a crowd member in the Marx Brothers' *A Day At The Races* (Sam Wood, 1937) and appeared as a tap dancer and singer in *Sun Valley Serenade* (Bruce Humberstone, 1941). Later films by this artist, including *Carmen Jones* and *Island In The Sun* fall outside the parameters of this work and are therefore excluded.

LARRY DARNELL

Vocal accompaniment: Paul Williams (baritone saxophone); Jimmy Brown (trumpet); unknown (tenor saxophone, piano, bass, drums)

Location: New York City. c. 1955

Titles performed:
'Be Good To Me' Fil A Film 2023
'Don't Go' Video Images 73R
'(I Guess I'd) Better Be On My Way'
'What More Do You Want Me To Do' Bavaria 12177

Source: *Showtime At The Apollo*

ETHEL DAVENPORT
Vocal accompaniment: Pleasant Green Baptist Choir–1
Vocal duet with Georgia Lewis accompaniment: unknown–2
Vocal accompaniment: unknown–3

Location: probably New York City. c. April 1965

Titles performed:
'The Great Big Jubilee'–1
'Briny Tears'–2
'Leave It There'–3

Source: *TV Gospel Time* #48

LESTER DAVENPORT
Vocal and harmonica accompaniment: Eddie C. Campbell (electric guitar); Nolan Struck (electric bass); Chico Chism (drums)

Location: South Bank Arts Centre, London, England. Tuesday 27 November 1979

Title performed:
'I Got A Woman'

Source: *Mainstream*

[BIG] CeDELL DAVIS
Vocal and electric guitar accompaniment: unknown (drums)

Location: Clarksdale, Mississippi. 1984
the Davis residence [A]
unnamed juke joint [B]

Titles performed:

'Chicken And The Hawk' [A]	Arrow AV015
'Stoop Down Baby' [A]	Arrow AV015
'Cummins Farm Prison' [A]	Arrow AV015
'Gone To Main Street' [B]	Arrow AV015

Source: *Saturday Blues*
Material by this artist was filmed in autumn 1990 by Robert Mugge for the documentary *Deep Blues*, but was not used in the final edit.

[FAMOUS] DAVIS SISTERS
Alfreda Davis, Audrey Davis, Jackie Verdell, Lela Dargan (vocals) accompaniment: unknown (piano). Shouted interruption by Brother Joe May–1

Location: Baltimore, Maryland. Saturday 5 September 1964

Titles performed:
'We Need Power'–1
'I'll Go Back Home'
'On The Right Road'
'Bye And Bye'

Source: *TV Gospel Time* #34
See also Brother Joe May and Jackie Verdell.

FRANK DAVIS
Vocal accompaniment: unknown–1
Vocal accompaniment: the Helen Thompson youth orchestra–2

Location: Chicago, Illinois. Saturday 10 October 1964

Titles performed:
'I Asked The Lord'–1
'I've Been In The Storm Too Long'–1
'Come And Go With Me'–2

Source: *TV Gospel Time* #38

Vocal accompaniment: unknown

Location: probably New York City. 1965–66

Titles performed:
unknown

Source: *TV Gospel Time* #53, #54, #65
See also the Combined Harvest, Metropolitan And Christian Tabernacle Choir.

[REVEREND] GARY DAVIS
Vocal and 12-string guitar

Location: New York City. 1964

Titles performed:
'I Feel Like Going Home' [part only]
'Death Don't Have No Mercy' [part only]

Source: *Blind Gary Davis*

Vocal and 12-string guitar accompaniment: Pete Seeger (banjo)

Location: probably New York City. 1966

Titles performed:
'Children Of Zion' Vestapol 13003
'Oh Glory, How Happy I Am' Vestapol 13037

Source: *Pete Seeger's Rainbow Quest*
Vestapol gives a date of 1969 for 'Oh Glory, How Happy I Am', but the above is more likely. Certainly, both performances were made on the same day.

Vocal and 12-string guitar

Location: KCTS-TV studios, Seattle, Washington. 1966

Titles performed:
'What A Beautiful City' Yazoo 501
'If I Had My Way' Yazoo 501
'Old Man Peter' Yazoo 501
'She Wouldn't Say Quit' Yazoo 501
'Glory Hallelujah' Yazoo 501
'Heard The Angels Singing' Yazoo 501
'Buck Dance' Vestapol 13016, Yazoo 501
'Hard Walking Blues' Vestapol 13016
'Make Believe Stunt' Vestapol 13016
'Keep Your Lamp Trimmed and Burning' Vestapol 13016

Source: *Masters Of American Traditional Music*

Vocal and 12-string guitar–1
Vocal and 12-string guitar accompaniment: Larry Johnson (harmonica); Wendy Smith (tambourine)–2

Location: New York City. 1970

Titles performed:
'Death Don't Have No Mercy'–1 Vestapol 13003
'I Belong To The Band'–2 Vestapol 13004

Source: *Black Roots*

Vocal and 12-string guitar

Location: unknown {USA}. 1970

Titles performed:
unknown

Source: *Like It Is*

IDA MAE DAVIS

Vocal accompaniment: unknown

Location: Chicago, Illinois. Sunday 2 August 1964

Titles performed:
unknown

Source: *Jubilee Showcase* [prog # 26–2]

[BLIND] JOHN DAVIS

Vocal and piano accompaniment: unknown

Location: Chicago, Illinois. 1977

Titles performed:
unknown

Source: *Made In Chicago*

Vocal and piano accompaniment: unknown

Location: Montreux, Switzerland. 1981

Titles performed:
'You're Gonna Cry Someday'
'Anybody Seen My Cat'
'Summertime'
'You're Bound To Look Like A Monkey'
'Walking Ground Hog'
'Basin Street Blues'
'Boogie'

Source: *Living Legends Of The Blues*

Vocal and piano

Location: Chicago, Illinois. c.1981–2

Titles performed:
'Born To Lose'
'How Long Blues'
'No Mail Today'
'Pinetop's Boogie Woogie'
unknown title
[interview with Studs Terkel]

Source: *probably US PBS TV broadcast* [C]

Vocal and piano accompaniment, if any, unknown

Location: Chicago, Illinois. 1983

Titles performed:
unknown

Source: *Sweet Home Chicago* [1]

Vocal and piano

Location: Chicago, Illinois. c.1984–5

Titles performed:
unknown
[interview with Studs Terkel]

Source: *Studs Terkel Talks To Blind John Davis*

JOHN HENRY DAVIS
Vocal and electric guitar accompaniment: L V Banks (electric bass); Willie Monroe (drums)

Location: Maxwell Street, Chicago, Illinois. Summer 1980

Titles performed:
'Dust My Broom' K-Jazz 031, Rhapsody 8045

Source: *Maxwell Street Blues*

LARRY DAVIS
See A C Reed.

MARTHA DAVIS AND SPOUSE
Martha Davis (vocal and piano) accompaniment: Calvin Ponder (bass)

Location: New York City. Early 1950s

Titles performed:
unknown

Source: *The Garry Moore Show*

As above

Location: New York City. 1955

Titles performed:
'We Just Couldn't Say Goodbye' Fil A Film 2023, Storyville SV6016, Video Images 74
'Vipity-Vop' Bavaria 12177, Storyville SV6016
'Martha's Boogie' Storyville SV6013
'Goodbye'

Source: *Showtime At The Apollo*

WALTER DAVIS
Speech

Location: Albany Hotel, St. Louis, Missouri. Summer 1960

monologue [ST only] K-Jazz 014, Rhapsody 8022

Source: *Blues Like Showers Of Rain*

JIMMY DAWKINS
Vocal and electric guitar accompaniment: unknown

Location: probably Chicago, Illinois. 1973

Titles performed:
unknown

Source: *Born In The Blues* [unconfirmed]

Vocal and electric guitar accompaniment: unknown

Location: probably Chicago, Illinois. 1973

Titles performed:
unknown

Source: *Sincerely The Blues* [unconfirmed]

Vocal and electric guitar acccompaniment: unknown

Location: probably Chicago, Illinois. 1975

Titles performed:
unknown

Source: *The Today Show*

Vocal and electric guitar accompaniment: unknown

Location: Chicago, Illinois. c.1976

Title performed:
unknown

Source: *All You Need Is Love*

DEEP RIVER BOYS
Vernon Gardner and George Lawson (tenor vocals); Harry Douglas (baritone vocal); Edward 'Mumbles' Ware (bass vocal) accompaniment: Claude Garreau and his orchestra–1
Jack Shilkret and his orchestra–2

Location: Astor Studios, New York City. Mid-1941

Titles performed:

[3903] 'Shadrack'–1	Charly #7, Storyville SV6002, Virgin VVD-867
[4102] 'Booglie Wooglie Piggy'–1	Charly #7
[4505] 'Hark, Hark, The Lark'–1	Charly #7
[4703] 'Toot That Trumpet'–2	Charly #7, Storyville SV6002, Virgin VVD-867

Source: *Soundies*
Copyright dates are; 3903, 27 November 1941: 4102, 10 November 1941: 4505, 8 December 1941: 4703 22 December 1941

Probably as above

Location: New York City. Monday 17 May 1948

Titles performed:
unknown

Source: *Broadway Jamboree*

JOHN DELAFOSE (Delaphose)
Vocal and accordion accompaniment: unknown (rub-board, electric guitar, electric bass, drums)

Location: Opelousas, Louisiana. 1988

Titles performed:

untitled instrumental	K-Jazz 098, Rhapsody 8062
[interview]	K-Jazz 098, Rhapsody 8062

Source: *Zydeco Gumbo*

Vocal and accordion accompaniment unknown: (rub-board, electric bass, drums)

Location: Louisiana. 1989

Title performed:

'Joe Pete'	Flower 7

Source: *J'ai Eté Au Bal*

Vocal and accordion accompaniment: The Eunice Playboys: unknown (electric guitar, electric bass, rub-board, drums)

Location: Louisiana. 1990

Titles performed:

'Yi Yi'	Channel 5 083 258-3, Island 083 258-3
'Hungry Man'	Channel 5 083 258-3, Island 083 258-3

Source: *Zydeco Nite'N'Day*

Vocal and accordion accompaniment: The Eunice Playboys (probably similar to above)

Location: probably Louisiana. 1993

Title performed:
'Ma Negresse'

Source: *Passion Fish*

Vocal and accordion accompaniment: Gerard Delafose (rub-board)

Location: Lafayette, Louisiana. 1994

Title performed:

'Joe Pete'	BMG un-numbered
[interview]	BMG un-numbered

Source: *The Kingdom Of Zydeco*

DELTA RHYTHM BOYS
Vocal group accompaniment: the Steve Schultz band

Location: probably New York City. 1941

Titles performed:
[3506] 'I Dreamed I Dwelt In Harlem' Storyville SV6002, Virgin VVD-867
[3803] 'Take The A Train' Proserpine 611, Storyville SV6002, Virgin VVD-867
[4005] 'Rigoletto Blues' Storyville SV6002, Virgin VVD-867
[4207] 'Jack, You're Playing The Game' Jazz Classics JCVC-106, Storyville SV6002, Verve CFV1022, Virgin VVD-867

Source: *Soundies*
3506 copyrighted 29 August 1941; 3803 20 October 1941; 4005 3 November 1941; 4207 17 November 1941

Vocal group, accompaniment, if any, unknown

Location: unknown {USA}. 1943

Title performed:
'Get On Board, Little Children'

Source: *Funzapoppin'* aka *Crazy House*

Vocal group accompaniment, if any, unknown

Location: unknown {USA}. 1944

Title performed:
unknown

Source: *Follow The Boys* aka *Three Cheers for The Boys*

Vocal group, unaccompanied

Location: unknown {USA}. 1945

Titles performed:
[20508] 'Dry Bones' Storyville SV6002, Virgin VVD-867
[21308] 'Just A Sittin' And A Rockin'' Storyville SV6002, Virgin VVD-867
[89008] 'Smoqualomie Jo Jo' Storyville SV6002, Virgin VVD-867
[26M3] 'Give Me Some Skin'
'St. Louis Blues' Parkfield MKJ-0007, Proserpine 666

Source: *Soundies.*
'Dry Bones' also appears in *Toot That Trumpet*
20508 copyrighted 30 April 1945; 21308 20 August 1945; 89008 4 June 1945; 26M3 30 December 1946

Vocal group, unaccompanied

Location: General Services Studios, Balboa Beach, California or Ryder Studios, Los Angeles, California. c. 1951

Titles performed:
'I Lied'
'Never Underestimate The Power Of A Woman'
'Fan-Tan-Fanny'
'The Gypsy In My Soul'
'Undecided'
'Is You Is Or Is You Ain't My Baby'
'Jack, You're Playing The Game'
'Little Eyes'
'Take The A Train' Bavaria 12177, Storyville SV6017
'Dry Bones' Storyville SV6017, Video Images 74

Source: *Snader Telescriptions.* 'Take The A Train' and 'Dry Bones' were included in *Showtime At The Apollo*

ARCHIE DENNIS
Vocal accompaniment: the Cannon Temple Church Of God In Christ Choir–1
Vocal accompaniment: the Gospel Harmonettes–2
Vocal accompaniment: unknown–3

Location: Charlotte, North Carolina. Saturday 1 August 1964

Titles performed:
'Oh, Didn't It Rain'–1
'What A Friend We Have In Jesus'–2
'Forgive Me Oh Lord'–3

Source: *TV Gospel Time* #28

Vocal accompaniment: unknown

Location: Jacksonville, Florida. c.1966

Titles performed:
unknown title [A]
unknown title [B]

Source: *TV Gospel Time* #59 [A], #60 [B]
See also the Cannon Temple Church of God In Christ Choir and Roberta Martin.

SUGAR PIE DESANTO (Umpeylia Marsema Balinton)
Vocal accompaniment: probably Sunnyland Slim (piano); Hubert Sumlin (electric guitar); Willie Dixon (bass); Clifton James (drums)

Location: Free Trade Hall, Manchester, England. Thursday 22 October 1964

Title performed:
[probably] 'Soulful Dress'

Source: *The Blues Came Walking*

Vocal accompaniment: probably as above

Location: London, England. Friday 30 October 1964

Title performed:
'Soulful Dress'

Source: *Ready Steady Go*

Vocal accompaniment: unknown

Location: London, England. Monday 2 November 1964

Title performed:
[probably] 'Soulful Dress'

Source: *Beat Room*
Although DeSanto was a member of the 1964 American Folk Blues Festival, but she does not appear to have performed in Germany, where her place was taken by Mae Mercer.

Speech

Location: Oakland, California. 1981

[interview]

Source: *Long Train Running*

JAMES DESHAY
Vocal and electric guitar accompaniment: 'Riley' (electric guitar); Kenneth Johnson (electric piano); Charles Jones (electric bass); Robert Cross (drums)

Location: Santa Fe Lounge, St. Louis, Missouri. Saturday 24 January 1976

Titles performed:
'Pony Blues'
'Crossroads'
'Mistake In Life'
'Evil Is Going On' [unbroadcast]
'Hold That Train, Conductor' [unbroadcast]
'Forty Four Blues' [unbroadcast]

Source: *The Devil's Music series 2*

FATHER DIVINE
Preaching, with congregational response

Location: unknown {USA}. 1940s

Titles performed:
religious monologues

Source: *US newsreel footage* [M]
Origin unknown, available from Historic.

DIXIE HUMMINGBIRDS
Beachey Thompson, Ira Tucker, James Emerdia Walker, James B Davis, Willie Bobo (vocals) accompaniment, if any, unknown

Location: Apollo Theatre, Harlem, New York City. 1959

Titles performed:
unknown

Source: *World By Night*

As last

Location: Chicago, Illinois. Sunday 14 June 1964

Titles performed:
unknown

Source: *Jubilee Showcase*

As last

Location: probably Washington DC. c. 1965–66

Titles performed:
unknown

Source: *TV Gospel Time* #53

As last accompaniment: Howard Carroll (guitar)–1
Vocal quartet accompaniment: the Gospel Harmonettes and The Swan Silvertone Singers (vocal groups)–2

Location: Newport, Rhode Island. July 1966

Titles performed:
'Christian's Automobile'–1
'The Reason I Shout'–1
'Jesus Is The Key'–2

Source: *Alan Lomax film collection*

Vocal quartet including Ira Tucker (vocals) accompaniment, if any: unknown

Location: Remus, Michigan. Sunday 7 September 1987

Titles performed:
unknown

Source: *Wheatland Music Festival* [C]. Origin unknown
There is also a documentary film about this group, made during the early 1990s, by Ashley James. Available from Searchlight Productions. See also Ira Tucker.

DIXIE JUBILEE SINGERS

This was the name given to a group of singers who appeared in the 1929 film *Hallelujah*. The content of this film, from the point of view of either blues or gospel music, is of little real value. The jazz, by Curtis Mosby and Nina Mae McKinney, is genuine and full details will be found in the book *Negro Bands On Film* by Dr. Klaus Stratemann.

FLOYD DIXON

Vocal and piano accompaniment: unknown

Location: Los Angeles, California. 1975

Titles performed:
unknown

Source: *Perspective* [unconfirmed]

JESSY DIXON

Vocal accompaniment: the Dixon Singers
Vocal accompaniment: The Chicago Community Choir–1
Vocal duet with Robert J Dixon: accompaniment the Dixon Singers–2

Location: Chicago, Illinois

The following appearances are known:
1964
Sunday 12 April [prog #18–1]
Sunday 20 September [prog #9–2]
1965
Sunday 11 July [prog #29–3]
Sunday 21 November [prog #10–1]
1966
Friday 13 May [prog #34–2]
Sunday 11 December [prog #15–3]–1
1968
Saturday 12 October [prog #16–3]
Saturday 26 October [prog #24–2]
1969
Saturday 11 January [prog # 8–3]
Saturday 8 February [prog # 34–3]–2
Saturday 15 February [prog #18–2]
Saturday 5 April [prog # 13–1]
Saturday 14 June [prog #19–1]
Saturday 28 June [prog #7–2]–2
Saturday 5 July [prog #12–2]
Saturday 16 August [prog #25–3]
Saturday 1 November [prog #12–3]
Saturday 29 November [prog #25–2]
1971
Saturday 14 August [prog #1–2]
1972
Friday 4 August [prog # 11–2]
Saturday 12 August [prog #4–3]
Saturday 26 August [prog #13–3]
1973
Tuesday 22 May [prog #5–3]
Saturday 24 November [prog # 32–1]
1974
Sunday 20 January [prog #6–3]

Sunday 14 July [prog #6–1]
Sunday 25 August [prog #1–3]
1976
Saturday 2 October [prog #3–3]
1977
Sunday 24 April [prog #22–2]
1982
Friday 20 August [prog #14]

Titles performed:
unknown

Source: *Jubilee Showcase*
See also Omega Baptist Church Choir.

WILLIE DIXON

Vocal accompaniment: unknown

Location: unknown {USA}. 1960

Titles performed:
unknown

Source: *The Today Show*

Vocal and bass accompaniment: unknown

Location: Alan Lomax residence, Greenwich Village, New York. Spring 1961

Titles performed:
unknown

Source: *Folklife Productions*

Vocal and bass accompaniment: probably Memphis Slim (piano); Clifton James (drums)

Location: Baden-Baden, Germany. c. October 1962

Titles performed:
unknown

Source: *American Folk Blues Festival 1962*
See also Memphis Slim.

Vocal and bass accompaniment: Memphis Slim (piano); Matt Murphy (electric guitar); Billie Stepney (drums)

Location: Manchester, England. October 1963

Title performed:
'Nervous'

Source: *I Hear The Blues*

Probably as above

Location: Baden-Baden, Germany. c. October 1963

Titles performed:
unknown

Source: *American Folk Blues Festival 1963*

Vocal accompaniment: unknown

Location: Chicago, Illinois. Sunday 9 February 1964

Titles performed:
unknown

Source: *Jubilee Showcase* [prog #21–1]

Vocal and guitar [*sic*]

Location: Baden-Baden, Germany. October 1964

Title performed:
[introduction by Sunnyland Slim;]
'Weak Brain, Narrow Mind'
[monologue]

Source: *American Folk Blues Festival 1964*

Vocal and bass accompaniment: probably Sunnyland Slim (piano); Hubert Sumlin (electric guitar); Clifton James (drums)

Location: Free Trade Hall, Manchester, England. Thursday 22 October 1964

Titles performed:
unknown

Source: *The Blues Came Walking*

Vocal accompaniment: unknown

Location: Chicago, Illinois. Sunday 19 December 1965

Titles performed:
unknown

Source: *Jubilee Showcase* [prog #29–1]

Vocal and bass accompaniment: Sunnyland Slim (piano); S P Leary (drums)–1
Bass solo accompaniment: as above–2
Vocal accompaniment: Muddy Waters Blues Band, with James Cotton, Jesse Fuller, Mable Hillery, Brownie McGhee, Muddy Waters, Otis Spann, Sunnyland Slim, Sonny Terry, Bukka White and Big Joe Williams (vocals)–3

Location: Toronto, Canada. Thursday 27 to Saturday 29 January 1966

Titles performed:

'Nervous'–1	Rhino R3 2313
'Crazy For My Baby'–1	Rhino R3 2313
'Bassology'–2	Rhino R3 2313
jam session–3	Rhino R3 2313

[and conversation with Barry Callaghan, Brownie McGhee, Muddy Waters and Sonny Terry]

Source: *Festival Presents The Blues*
The performance of 'Crazy For My Baby' released on Rhino R3 2313 has been digitally altered to include both the image and musical contributions of Colin James (vocal and guitar), the Canadian host of the Rhino video.

Vocal accompaniment: unknown

Location: Chicago, Illinois. 1966

The following appearances are known:
Sunday 8 May [prog #23–1]
Saturday 11 June [prog #23–2]
Sunday, 2 October [prog #15–2]
Sunday 11 December [prog #15–3]

Titles performed:
unknown

Source: *Jubilee Showcase*

Vocal accompaniment: unknown

Location: Chicago, Illinois. 1967

The following appearances are known:
Sunday 5 March [prog #17–1]
Sunday 12 March [prog #17–2]

Titles performed:
unknown

Source: *Jubilee Showcase*

Vocal accompaniment: unknown

Location: Chicago, Illinois. 1969

The following appearances are known:
Saturday 1 February [prog #25–1]
Saturday 8 March [prog #31–1]
Saturday 5 April [prog #33–2]

Titles performed:
unknown

Source: *Jubilee Showcase*

Speech

Location: Chicago, Illinois. April–May 1970

[interview and a cappella demonstration of field hollers] K-Jazz 004, Rhapsody 9012

Source: *Chicago Blues*

Vocal and bass accompaniment: Walter Horton (harmonica); Lee Jackson (electric guitar); Lafayette Leake (piano); Jerome Arnold (electric bass); Clifton James (drums)

Location: Baden-Baden, Germany. c. May 1970

Titles performed:
unknown

Source: *American Folk Blues Festival 1970*

Vocal and bass accompaniment: pre-recorded backing track and mixed kindergarten group

Location: Chicago, Illinois. 1971

Title performed:
'Jelly Jam' K-Jazz 019, Yazoo 507

Source: *Out Of The Blacks, Into The Blues part 2*

Vocal duet with Koko Taylor accompaniment: unknown

Location: Chicago, Illinois. Thursday 18 July 1974

Title performed:
'Wang Dang Doodle'

Source: *Soundstage*

Vocal and bass with 'The New Generation Of Chicago Blues' collective personnel: Billy Branch and Harmonica Hines (harmonicas); Lurrie Bell and Johnny B Moore (electric guitars); Freddie Dixon (electric bass); Vernon Harrington (electric guitar); James Kinds (electric guitar); William 'Dead Eye' Norris (electric guitar); 'Bom-Bay' [*sic*] Carter (real name William Richmond) (electric guitar and electric bass)

Location: Chicago, Illinois. 1978

Titles performed:
'Come On Back Home'
'The Thrill Is Gone'
'I Got Everything I Need'
'Hoochie Coochie Man'
'If You Leave Me Here To Cry'
'Mama Talk To Your Daughter'
'Tear Down The Berlin Wall'
and other, unknown, titles
[rehearsal footage including discussion]

Source: *I Am The Blues*

As above

Location: West Berlin, Germany. 1978

Titles performed:
'Change The Lock On The Door'
'I'm A King Bee'
'How Long'
'Everyday I Have The Blues'
'I Am The Blues'
'Can It Be Mine'
'Don't Start Me Talkin''
'All Because Of You'
'Someody Loan Me A Dime'
'I'm Ready'
'My Teardrops Fall'
'She Do Me Wrong'
'Tear Down The Berlin Wall'
'Got My Mojo Working'
and other, unknown, titles

Source: *I Am The Blues*

Speech

Location: Chicago, Illinois. c. 1979

[interview]

Source: *Chicago On The Good Foot*

Vocal and bass accompaniment: unknown

Location: Ames, Iowa. c. 1979

Titles performed:
'Seventh Son'
'Hoochie Coochie Man'
'Sweet Home Chicago'
and other, unknown, titles

Source: *Maintenance Shop Blues*

Vocal accompaniment: unknown

Location: unknown {USA}. 1980

Titles performed:
'Seventh Son'
'Hoochie Coochie Man'
'Sweet Home Chicago'
[interview with Oscar Brown]

Source: *From Jumpstreet*

Vocal accompaniment: John Watkins (electric guitar); Sugar Blue (harmonica); Arthur Dixon (piano); Freddie Dixon (electric bass); Clifton James (drums)

Location: Montreal, Canada. c. 1980–81

Titles performed:
'Flip Flop And Fly'
'Wang Dang Doodle'
'Got My Mojo Working'

Source: *Canadian TV broadcast* [C]

Vocal and bass accompaniment: Sugar Blue (harmonica); Arthur Dixon (piano); John Watkins (electric guitar); Freddy Dixon (electric bass); Clifton James (drums)

Location: Montreux, Switzerland. Friday 15 July 1983

Titles performed:
band instrumental
'Hoochie Coochie Man'
'Got My Mojo Working'

Source: *Montreux Jazz*

Vocal accompaniment: unknown

Location: Chicago, Illinois. 1983

Titles performed:
unknown

Source: *Sweet Home Chicago* [1]

Vocal and bass accompaniment: Leonard (Baby Doo) Caston (vocal, piano and electric organ); John Watkins (electric guitar); Arthur Dixon (piano); Carey Bell (harmonica); Mike Morrison (electric bass); Clifton James (drums)

Location: Centre for Performing Arts, Denver, Colorado. 1984

Titles performed:
'I Just Want To Make Love To You'
'Built For Comfort'
'The Seventh Son'
'Abyssinia My Home'
'It Don't Make No Sense'
'All Night Long'
[interview]

Source: *Probably US PBS TV broadcast* [C]

Speech

Location: Topanga Canyon, California. Saturday 25 June 1988

[interview]

Source: *Topanga Blues Festival*
There may be further, performing, footage by Dixon from this session.

Vocal accompaniment: John Sebastian (harmonica); Jools Holland (piano); unknown (alto saxophone, electric guitar, electric bass, drums)

Location: New York City. 1988

Titles performed:
'Spoonful'
'I Don't Trust Nobody'
'Wang Dang Doodle'
[interview]

Source: *Sunday Night*

Speech

Location: Chicago, Illinois. 1990

[interview] MPI 6243

Source: *Queen Of The Blues*
See also Koko Taylor.
See also the accompanists index.

ANTOINE [FATS] DOMINO

Vocal and piano accompaniment: unknown

Location: New York City. 1956

Titles performed:
'When My Dreamboat Comes Home'
'I'm In Love Again'

Source: *The Steve Allen Show*

Vocal and piano accompaniment: the Alan Freed orchestra; Big Al Sears and Sam 'The Man' Taylor (tenor saxophones) and others, unknown

Location: New York City. July–August 1957

Titles performed:
unknown

Source: *The Big Beat* [1]

Vocal and piano accompaniment: unknown

Location: Miami, Florida. 1957

Title performed:
'Blueberry Hill' MMG-010

Source: WFJH-TV, Miami

Vocal and piano, miming to Imperial 5417

Location: unknown {USA}. 1957

Title performed:
'Blue Monday' [part only]

Source: *The Girl Can't Help It*

Vocal and piano, miming to Imperial 5467

Location: unknown {USA}. 1957

Title performed:
'Wait And See'

Source: *Disk Jockey Jamboree*

Vocal and piano, miming to Imperial 5477 [A]; 5428 [B]

Location: unknown {USA}. 1957

Titles performed:
'The Big Beat' [A]
'I'm Walkin'' [B]

Source: *The Big Beat* [2]

Vocal and piano, miming to Imperial 5407 [A]; 5348 [B]; 5386 [C]

Location: unknown {USA}. c.1957

Titles performed:
'Honey Chile' [A]
'Ain't That A Shame' [B]
'I'm In Love Again' [C]

Source: *Shake Rattle And Rock*

Piano solo

Location: unknown {USA}. c.1957

short unitled instrumental
[interview]

Source: *Cinema newsreel* [M]. Origin unknown.

Vocal and piano accompaniment: unknown; as above, with Perry Como and Jo Stafford (vocals)–1

Location: New York City. 1957

Titles performed:
'Valley Of Tears' MMGV-010
'It's You I Love' MMGV-010
'I'm Walkin''–1

Source: *The Perry Como Show*

Vocal and piano accompaniment: unknown

Location: Philadelphia, Pennsylvania. 1958

Title performed:
unknown

Source: *Dick Clark's Saturday Night Beechnut Show*

Vocal and piano accompaniment: unknown

Location: Philadelphia, Pennsylvania. 1958

Title performed:
unknown

Source: *Dick Clark's American Bandstand*

Vocal and piano accompaniment: unknown

Location: New York City. c. 1958–59

Title performed:
'Blueberry Hill'

Source: *The Ed Sullivan Show*

Vocal and piano accompaniment: unknown

Location: Los Angeles, California. 1969

Titles performed:
unknown Rhino R3.2284

Source: *Thirty Three And A Third Revolutions Per Monkee*

Vocal and piano accompaniment: unknown

Location: Los Angeles, California. 1970

Titles performed:
unknown

Source: *The Mike Douglas Show*

Vocal and piano accompaniment: unknown

Location: Madison Square Garden, New York City. 1973

Titles performed:
'Blueberry Hill'
'My Blue Heaven'

Source: *Let The Good Times Roll* [1]

Vocal and piano accompaniment: unknown

Location: Los Angeles, California. 1975

Titles performed:
unknown

Source: *Dick Clark's American Bandstand 23rd Birthday*

Vocal accompaniment: unknown

Location: unknown {USA}. 1975

Titles performed:
unknown

Source: *Return To Macon County*

Vocal and piano accompaniment: unknown

Location: unknown {USA}. 1975–6

Titles performed:
unknown

Source: *The Merv Griffin Show*

Vocal and piano accompaniment: unknown

Location: New Orleans, Louisiana. 1978

Titles performed:
unknown

Source: *Captain And Tennille In New Orleans*

Vocal and piano accompaniment: unknown

Location: Vienna, Austria. 1978

Titles performed:
'I'm Walkin''
'My Girl Josephine'
'Jambalaya'
'Blue Monday'
'Let The Four Winds Blow'
'I Want To Walk You Home'
'When My Dreamboat Comes In'
'I'm In Love Again'
'Honey Chile'
'Shake Rattle And Roll'
'Blueberry Hill'
'When The Saints Go Marching In'
'Sentimental Journey'

Source: *Spotlight*

Vocal and piano accompaniment: unknown

Location: Netherlands. 1979

Titles performed:
'I'm Walkin''
'Shame On You'
'Blueberry Hill'
'When The Saints Go Marching In'

Source: *Dutch TV broadcast* [C]

Vocal and piano accompaniment: unknown

Location: Netherlands. 1979

Titles performed:
'Hello Josephine'
'I'm Gonna Be A Wheel Someday'
'I Want To Walk You Home'
'Jamabalaya'
'Blue Monday'
'Blueberry Hill'
'When The Saints Go Marching In'
'Sentimental Journey'

Source: *Dutch TV broadcast* [C]

Vocal and piano accompaniment: unknown

Location: unknown {USA}. 1980

Titles performed:
unknown

Source: *Any Which Way You Can*

Vocal and piano accompaniment: Lee Allen (tenor saxophone); Frederick Kemp, Walter Kimble, Herb Hardesty (saxophones); Thomas Johnson (trumpet); Carlton McWilliams and David Douglas (electric guitars); Teddy Royal (electric bass); Joseph Johnson (drums)

Location: Nordsee Jazz Festival, Den Haag, Netherlands. 1980

Titles performed:
'I'm Walkin''
'Blue Monday'
'I'm In Love Again'
'Honey Chile'
'I'm Ready'
'I Want To Walk You Home'

Source: *Dutch TV broadcast* [C]

Vocal and piano accompaniment: probably similar to above

Location: Montreux, Switzerland. June 1980

Titles performed:
unknown

Source: *Montreux Jazz*

Vocal and piano accompaniment: unknown, probably similar to above

Location: Montreux, Switzerland. 1983

Titles performed:
[interview]
'Blue Monday'
'I'm Ready'
'Rosalee'
'Bo Weevil'
'All By Myself'

Source: *Montreux Jazz*

Vocal and piano accompaniment: Herb Hardisty, Frederick Kemp and Walter Kimble (tenor saxophones); Thomas Johnson (trumpet); Jimmy Moliere (electric guitar); Carlton McWilliams (electric guitar); Irving Charles (electric bass); Clarence Brown and Joseph Johnson (drums) [*sic*]

Location: Perugia, Italy. Thursday 11 July 1985

Titles performed:
'I'm Walking'
'Blueberry Hill'
'Boogie Woogie'
'I Wanna Walk You Home'
'Shake, Rattle And Roll'
'I'm In Love Again'
'Jambalaya'
'After Hours'
'I'm Gonna Be A Wheel Someday'
'Ain't That A Shame'
'Blue Monday'
'I'm In The Mood For Love'
'Hello, Josephine'
'When The Saints Go Marching In'

Source: *Italian TV broadcast* [C]

Vocal and piano–1
Vocal and piano accompaniment: Jools Holland (vocal and piano)–2

Location: New Orleans, Louisiana. 1985

Titles performed:
'I'm Ready'–1
'Walking To New Orleans'–2
[interview]

Source: *Walking To New Orleans*

Vocal and piano accompaniment: unknown

Location: Los Angeles, California. 1985

Titles performed:
'Hello Josephine'
'Blue Monday'
'Blueberry Hill'
'Ain't That A Shame'
'I'm In Love Again'
'I'm Ready'
'I Wanna Walk You Home'

Source: *Live At The Universal Amphitheatre*

Vocal and piano accompaniment: Paul Shaffer (keyboards); Ron Wood (electric guitar); Sugar Blue (harmonica); and others, unknown–1; as above, with Jerry Lee Lewis and Ray Charles, vocals and pianos–2

Location: New Orleans, Louisiana. 1986

Titles performed:
'The Fat Man'–1
'Walkin' To New Orleans'–1
'Blueberry Hill'–1
'Shake Rattle And Roll'–1
'So Long'–1
'C C Rider'–1
'Sentimental Journey'–1
'Lewis Boogie'–2
'Ain't Gonna Be Your Lowdown Dog'–1
'Swanee River Rock'–1

Source: *Fats Domino And Friends*

Vocal and piano accompaniment: unknown

Location: Austin, Texas. 1987

Titles performed:
'I'm Walkin''
'Blueberry Hill'
'My Blue Heaven'
'Blue Monday'
'Hello Josephine'
'I Want To Walk You Home'
'It Keeps Raining'
'I'm Ready'
'Poor Me'
'Walking To New Orleans'
'Shake Rattle And Roll'
'I'm Gonna Be A Wheel Someday'
'Ain't That A Shame'
'I Hear You Knocking'
'Swanee River Boogie'
'Your Cheatin' Heart'
'When The Saints Go Marching In'
'Sentimental Journey'

Source: *Austin City Limits*

Vocal and piano accompaniment: unknown

Location: Bern, Switzerland. 1987

Titles performed:
'My Girl Josephine'
'The Fat Man'
'Jamabalaya'
'Blue Monday'
'When My Dreamboat Comes Home'
'I'm In Love Again'
'Shake, Rattle And Roll'
'Blueberry Hill'
'Let The Four Winds Blow'
'So Long'
'Rosalee'

Source: *Jazz-In*

Vocal and piano accompaniment: unknown

Location: Antibes, France. Friday 17 July 1987

Titles performed:
'The Fat Man'
'Jambalaya'
'Swanee River Boogie'
'Walkin' To New Orleans'
'I'm Ready'
'Blueberry Hill'
'Let The Four Winds Blow'
'I Want To Walk You Home'
'I'm Gonna Be A Wheel Someday'
'I'm In Love Again'
'My Blue Heaven'
'Valley Of Tears'
'Go To The Mardi Gras'
'Poor Me'
'Sheik Of Araby'
'Shake Rattle And Roll'
'When The Saints Go Marching In'

Source: *French TV broadcast* [C]

Vocal and piano accompaniment: unknown

Location: unknown {USA}. 1987

Titles performed:

'Blueberry Hill'	INVC-5006
'I'm Ready'	INVC-5006
'I Want To Walk You Home'	INVC-5006
'Whole Lotta Loving'	INVC-5006
'My Girl Josephine'	INVC-5006
'The Fat Man'	INVC-5006
'I'm Gonna Be A Wheel Someday'	INVC-5006
'Blue Monday'	INVC-5006
'Ain't That A Shame'	INVC-5006
'I'm In Love Again'	INVC-5006
'Walking To New Orleans'	INVC-5006
'Poor Poor Me'	INVC-5006
'Let The Four Winds Blow'	INVC-5006
'I Almost Lost My Mind'	INVC-5006

Source: *Silver Shadow Productions*

THOMAS A DORSEY
Vocal and piano accompaniment: unknown

Location: Chicago, Illinois. Sunday 9 February 1964

Titles performed:
unknown

Source: *Jubilee Showcase* [prog #12–1]

Speech

Location: Chicago, Illinois. January 1976

[unbroadcast interview]

Source: Filmed for *The Devil's Music*, unused in the final edit, but reportedly still extant

Vocal, piano accompaniment: unknown

Location: Chicago, Illinois. 1976

Titles performed:
unknown
[interview]

Source: *Here Comes Gospel*

Vocal accompaniment: unknown (piano)

Location: Chicago, Illinois. c. 1979

Title performed:
'Troubled 'bout My Soul'
[interview]

Source: *Chicago On The Good Foot*

Vocal accompaniment: unknown (piano), leading singing class–1
Fragmentary a cappella vocal, as spontaneous part of interview–2

Location: Chicago, Illinois. 1982
Pilgrim Baptist Church [A]: the Dorsey residence [B]

Titles performed:
'When I've Done The Best I Can' [A]–1
FRF un-numbered
'Take My Hand, Precious Lord' [A]–2
FRF un-numbered
'The Blues Ain't Nothing' [B]–2
FRF un-numbered
[interviews and conversation] [A] [B]
FRF un-numbered

Source: *Say Amen Somebody!*

Vocal duet with Sallie Martin accompaniment: Yazoo LP 1041 reissue of Dorsey's original 1982 recording–1
Vocal accompaniment: organ and congregation–2

Location: The Martin residence, Chicago, Illinois. 1982

Title performed:
'If You See My Saviour'–1
FRF un-numbered
'Take My Hand, Precious Lord'–2
FRF un-numbered
[interviews and conversation]
FRF un-numbered

Source: *Say Amen Somebody!*

Speech

Location: Chicago, Illinois. c.1984

[interview]

Source: *US TV broadcast, Channel 38, Chicago*[C]

WILLA DORSEY
Vocal accompaniment: unknown

Location: unknown {USA}. c.1969

Titles performed:
'His Eye Is On The Sparrow'
'I Want To See Him'

Source: *Soul Set Free*

DOSWELL TEMPLE CHURCH OF GOD IN CHRIST CHOIR
Mixed vocal choir accompaniment: unknown
Soloists: Nettie Higgins–1, Barbara Williams, Leola Owens and Barbara Byrd–2, Robert Taylor–3

Location: Baltimore, Maryland. Sunday 6 December 1964

Titles performed:
'Running, I Can't Tarry'–1
'Just To God Be True'–2
'Walking With The King'–3

Source: *TV Gospel Time* #35

[REVEREND] JOHN DOWDY
Vocal accompaniment: unknown

Location: Chicago, Illinois

The following appearances are known:
1964
Sunday 19 April [prog # 22–3]
1969
Saturday 15 March [prog #32–3]
1972
Saturday 26 August [prog # 13–3]

Titles performed:
unknown

Source: *Jubilee Showcase*

DOYLETTES
Vocal group accompaniment: unknown

Location: New York City. c. 1965–66

Titles performed:
unknown

Source: *TV Gospel Time* #52

MATTIE DOZIER
Vocal accompaniment: unknown

Location: Chicago, Illinois. Sunday 15 December 1963

Titles performed:
unknown

Source: *Jubilee Showcase* [prog #11–1]

DRINKARD SINGERS
probably Larry Drinkard, Lee Warwick, Judy Guions, Marie Epps, Emily Garland, Ann Moss (vocals) accompaniment: unknown

Location: New York City. c. 1966

Titles performed:
unknown

Source: *TV Gospel Time* #65

LAURA DUKES
Vocal and ukelele

Location: Memphis, Tennessee. Sunday 18 January 1976

Titles performed:
'Crawdad' [A][part only]
'Blues' [B]

Source: *The Devils Music series 1* [A]; *series 2* [B]

SCOTT DUNBAR
Vocal and guitar

Location: probably Lake Mary, Mississippi. 1966

Titles performed:
unknown

Source: *Anatomy of Pop: The Music Explosion*

Vocal and guitar

Location: unknown {USA}. 1972

Titles performed:
unknown

Source: *Thinking Out Loud* [unconfirmed]

[CHAMPION] JACK DUPREE

Vocal and piano accompaniment: Chris Barber's Jazz Band; Barber (trombone); Pat Halcox (trumpet); Ian Wheeler (clarinet); Eddie Smith (banjo); Dick Smith (bass); Graham Burbridge (drums)

Location: Marquee Club, London, England. Monday 3 May 1965

Titles performed:
unknown

Source: *Jazz 625*

Vocal and piano accompaniment, if any, unknown

Location: Baden-Baden, Germany. c. May 1970

Titles performed:
unknown

Source: *American Folk Blues Festival 1970*

Vocal and piano accompaniment: unknown

Location: Ronnie Scott's Jazz Club, London, England. Thursday 20 August 1970

Titles performed:
'Chicken Shack Boogie'
'What'd I Say'

Source: *Jazz Scene At Ronnie Scott's*

Vocal and piano accompaniment: King Curtis (tenor saxophone); and others, unknown

Location: Montreux, Switzerland. Thursday 17 June 1971

Titles performed:
'Junker's Blues'
'Everything's Gonna Be Alright'
'What Is Wrong With You'
'Get With It'
'Poor Boy Blues'
'I'm Having Fun'
'Sneaky Pete'

Source: *Montreux Jazz*

Vocal and piano

Location: England. 1972

Titles performed:
unknown

Source: *Twenty Four Hours*

Vocal and piano and vocal and piano accompaniment: unknown

Location(s): Halifax, Yorkshire, England and unknown European location[s]. 1973

Titles performed:
unknown
[interviews]

Source: *A Kind Of Freedom*

Vocal and piano accompaniment: unknown

Location: unknown. 1973

Titles performed:
unknown

Source: *If You Feel The Feelin' You Was Feelin'*
This may simply be a retitling of *A Kind Of Freedom.*

Vocal and piano

Location: France. 1979

Titles performed:
'Rocky Mountain'
'Low Down Dog'

Source: *French TV broadcast* [C]

Vocal and piano accompaniment: David Douglas (electric guitar); Carlton McWilliams (electric bass); Bernard Purdie (drums); as above with Lee Allen (tenor saxophone)–1

Location: Montreux, Switzerland. June 1980

Titles performed:
'Ain't That A Shame'
'One Scotch, One Bourbon, One Beer'
'I Hate To Be Alone'
'Come Back Baby'–1
'Mother In Law Blues'–1

Source: *Montreux Jazz*

Vocal and piano accompaniment, if any: unknown

Location: Germany. 1981

Titles performed:
'Chicken Shack'
'The Woman I Love'
'I Don't Know'
'Freedom'
'Pinetop's Boogie'
'I Don't Know Why'
'One Scotch, One Bourbon, One Beer'

Source: *German TV broadcast* [C]

Vocal and piano accompaniment, if any: unknown

Location: Copenhagen, Denmark. 1986

Titles performed:
unknown

Source: *Storyville productions* [C]

Vocal and piano accompaniment, if any: unknown

Location: Madrid, Spain. Sunday 8 April 1987

Titles performed:
unknown

Source: *Spanish TV broadcast* [C]
See also Magic Slim.

BIG JOE DUSKIN

Vocal and piano–1
Vocal and piano accompaniment: Axel Zwingenberger, George Green and Bob Hall (pianos); Dave Green (bass); Charlie Watts (drums)–2

Location: London, England. 1986

Titles performed:
'Pinetop's Boogie Woogie'–1
Jam session–2

Source: *Boogie Woogie*

E

FORD [SNOOKS] EAGLIN

Vocal and guitar accompaniment: unknown

Location: New Orleans, Louisiana. 1985

Titles performed:
unknown — Storyville SV6041

Source: *Jim Gabbour productions*

Vocal and guitar

Location: New Orleans, Louisiana. 1990

Title performed:
'Lipstick Traces'

Source: *Big World*

SIDNEY EASTON

Vocal duet with Babe Matthews accompaniment: possibly Easton piano); unknown (guitar)

Location: New York City. c. March–April 1940

Title performed:
'You'll Miss Me When I'm Gone Away' — Timeless Video 5048, Video Images 517

Source: *Paradise In Harlem*
See also Mamie Smith.

OBIE EATMAN

Vocal and guitar

Location: Mississippi. 1984

Titles performed:
'Motherless Children' — Arrow AV015
'Old Brown Body' ['Lonesome Valley'] — Arrow AV015

Source: *Saturday Blues*
The film identifies 'Lonesome Valley' as 'Old Brown Body' [*sic*], but it is, in fact, a largely instrumental version of 'Lonesome Valley', with a partial vocal in call-and-response form.

EBENEZER BAPTIST CHURCH CHOIR AND SOLOISTS

Vocal choir accompaniment: unknown (piano) –1;
solo female vocal accompaniment: own piano–2;
solo female vocal accompaniment previous (piano)–3

Location: Ebenezer Baptist Church, New Orleans, Lousiana. Spring 1963

Titles performed:
untitled–1
'One Day I'm Gonna Rise'–2 Yazoo 520
'Surely God Is Able'–3

Source: *Dietrich Wawzyn film collection*

Congregation, ensemble vocal, unaccompanied

Location: as above. 1997

Title performed:
unnamed

Source: *Going Places – New Orleans*
See also Lois DeJean in the index to non-performing interviewees.

EBONY TRIO

details unknown

Location: unknown {USA}. c. mid-1940s

Title performed:
'Bip Bam Boogie'

Source: *Bip Bam Boogie*

ECHOES OF HEAVEN OF AKRON, OHIO

Vocal quartette including Karen Landis accompaniment: unknown (electric organ)–1;
as above accompaniment: unknown (electric guitar, electric organ, electric bass, drums)–2

Location: North Carolina. 1985
[A] The Landis residence, Creedmoor
[B] Rock Spring Baptist Church, Rock Spring

Titles performed:
'Trouble In My Way'–1 [A] Shanachie 1402
'Bye And Bye'–2 [B] Shanachie 1402

Source: *A Singing Stream*
See also the Landis family.

ECHONEERS YOUNG PEOPLE'S CHOIR

Mixed vocal choir accompaniment: unknown
Solists: Fred Chappie, Donald Swift and Alfred Reeves–1;
Roland Smith–2

Location: Baltimore, Maryland. Saturday 5 September 1964

Titles performed:
'Jesus Is All The World To Me'–1
'Just A Little While'
'I Know The Lord'–2

Source: *TV Gospel Time* #32

ARCHIE EDWARDS

Vocal and guitar

Location: unknown {Europe}. 1982

Title performed:
'How Long Blues'

Source: *European TV broadcast.* Origin unknown [C]

Vocal and steel guitar

Location: WDBJ TV studios, Roanake, Virginia. Spring/Summer 1987

Titles performed:
'Spoonful Blues' [part only]
'Bear Cat Blues' [part only]
'Called My Baby Long Distance' [part only]

Source: *Black Musical Traditions In Virgina: Blues*

CHARLES EDWARDS
Vocal, guitar and harmonica

Location: Coahoma County, Mississippi. 1942

Title performed:
unknown

Source: *Library Of Congress*

DAVID [HONEYBOY] EDWARDS
Vocal and guitar

Location: unknown {USA}. 1978

Titles performed:
unknown

Source: *Don Kirshner's Rock Concert* [unconfirmed]

Vocal and guitar

Location: Mississippi. 1991

Title performed:
Sweet Home Chicago CMV 491132
[interview]

Source: *The Search For Robert Johnson*

ELIGIBLES
See Johnny Otis.

ROBERT [BIG MOJO] ELIM
Vocal accompaniment: Jimmy Johnson and Willie James Lyons (electric guitars); Lefty Dizz (electric bass); Odie Payne (drums); John 'Big Moose' Walker (piano)

Location: unknown {Europe}. 1978–79

Title performed:
'Mojo Boogie'

Source: *European TV broadcast* [C]. Origin unknown.

ALMA ELLISON
Vocal accompaniment: unknown

Location: New York City. Sunday 25 November 1962

Title performed:
'I Want Jesus To Walk With Me'

Source: *TV Gospel Time* #3 [M]

LORRAINE ELLISON SINGERS
Vocal group accompaniment: unknown

Location: New York City. Sunday 14 October 1962

Titles performed:
'No, I Won't Turn Back'
'My Father's World'
'When I Get Home'

Source: *TV Gospel Time* #11 [M]

Vocal group accompaniment: unknown

Location: New York City. Sunday 11 November 1962

Titles performed:
'Yes God Will'
'Oh What A Joy'
'Walk With Christ'

Source: *TV Gospel Time* #2 [*sic*]

PAULINE ELLISON
Vocal accompaniment: unknown

Location: New York City. Sunday 11 November 1962

Title performed:
'It Is No Secret What God Can Do'

Source: *TV Gospel Time* #2 [*sic*]

[QUEEN] SYLVIA EMBRY

Vocal and electric bass guitar accompaniment: John Embry (electric guitar); unknown (keyboards, drums)–1
Vocal and electric bass–2

Location: Chicago, Illinois. 1980
In unnamed club [A]
At the Embry residence [B]

Titles performed:
'I've Been Mistreated' [fragment]–1 [A] K-Jazz 075, Rhapsody 8022
'Sittin' On This Highway'–2 [B] K-Jazz 075, Rhapsody 8022
[interview] [B] K-Jazz 075, Rhapsody 8022

Source: *Big City Blues*

Vocal and electric bass guitar accompaniment Shock Treatment [G]: Lefty Dizz (electric guitar); Ralph Lapetina (organ); Woody Williams (drums); band vocal chorus

Location: Freedom Village, Greenville, Mississippi. Saturday 8 September 1979

Title performed:
'I'm Goin' To New York' K-Jazz 081

Source: *Mississippi Blues*

Vocal accompaniment: John Cephas (guitar); Phil Wiggins (harmonica)

Location: Belgium. 1981

Title performed:
'I'm Goin' To New York'

Source: *American Folk Blues Festival 1981*
See also Louisiana Red

ROOSEVELT ENGLISH

Vocal accompaniment: unknown

Location: Chicago, Illinois

The following appearances are known:
1964
Sunday 20 September [prog # 9–2]
1966
Sunday 23 January [prog #6–2]
1968
Saturday 12 October [prog #16–3]

Titles performed:
unknown

Source: *Jubilee Showcase*

[SLEEPY] JOHN ESTES (John Adam Estes)

Vocal and guitar

Location: Brownsville, Tennessee. Summer 1962

Titles performed:
'Lonesome Ground'

Source: *The Blues* [1]

Vocal and guitar accompaniment: unknown

Location: unknown {USA}. 1962

Titles performed:
unknown

Source: *Citizen South – Citizen North*

Vocal and guitar accompaniment: Hammie Nixon (harmonica); James 'Yank' Rachell (mandolin)

Location: unknown {USA}. 1964

Titles performed:
unknown

Source: *The Observer*

Vocal and guitar accompaniment: Hammie Nixon (harmonica)

Location: Baden-Baden, Germany. October 1964

Title performed:
[introduction by Willie Dixon;]
'Rats In My Kitchen'

Source: *American Folk Blues Festival 1964*
See also John Henry Barbee.

Probably as above

Location: Free Trade Hall, Manchester, England. Thursday 22 October 1964

Titles performed:
unknown

Source: *The Blues Came Walking*

Vocal and guitar accompaniment: James 'Yank' Rachell (mandolin)

Location: Studio 6, Granada TV Centre, Manchester, England. Friday 30 September 1966

Title performed:
'You Shouldn't Say That'

Source: *Nothing But The Blues*

Probably as above

Location: Baden-Baden, Germany. c. December 1966

Titles performed:
unknown

Source: *American Folk Blues Festival 1966*

Vocal and guitar accompaniment: unknown

Location: unknown {USA}. 1972

Titles performed:
unknown

Source: *Thinking Out Loud* [unconfirmed]

Vocal and guitar accompaniment: unknown

Location: unknown {USA}. 1975

Titles performed:
unknown

Source: *Born In The Blues*

Vocal and guitar accompaniment: Hammie Nixon (harmonica);

Location: unknown {USA}. 1977

Titles performed:
'Change The Lock on My Door'
'Corinna'

Source: *A Feelin' Called The Blues*

LOU DELLA EVANS

Vocal accompaniment: unknown

Location: Chicago, Illinois. Sunday 15 March 1964

Titles performed:
unknown

Source: *Jubilee Showcase* [prog # 7–1]

MARGIE EVANS

Vocal accompaniment: unknown

Location: probably Los Angeles, California. 1970

Titles performed:
unknown

Source: *The Homewood Show*

Vocal accompaniment: the Johnny Otis Band

Location: Monterey, California. 1973

Titles performed:
unknown

Source: *Monterey Jazz*

Vocal accompaniment: Lurrie Bell (electric guitar); Billy Branch (harmonica); unknown (bass and drums)–1
Vocal accompaniment: John Cephas (guitar); Phil Wiggins (harmonica)–2

Location: Belgium. 1981

Titles performed:
'Twenty Nine Ways'
'Trouble Trouble'
'That Dirty Black Rat'–1
'Margie's Boogie'–1
'Bye Bye Baby'–2

Source: *American Folk Blues Festival 1981*

Vocal accompaniment: Joe Liggins' Honeydrippers

Location: Los Angeles, California. 1984

Title performed:
'Mistreated Woman'

Source: *Legends Of Rhythm And Blues*

Vocal accompaniment: unknown

Location: Australia. c. 1986

Title performed:
'Candy'

Source: *The Midday Show*

Vocal accompaniment: unknown

Location: Australia. c. 1986

Title performed:
'This Joint Is Jumpin''

Source: *Jazz Night*

Vocal accompaniment: unknown

Location: Australia. c.1986

Title performed:
'Stormy Monday'

Source: *The Midday Show*

TERRY EVANS
This artist supplied some contributions to the soundtrack of the film *Crossroads*. See also Bobby King.

EXCELSIOR QUARTET
Vocal quartet, unaccompanied

Location: probably New York City. c.1929

Title performed:
'I Want To Cross Over'

Source: *unknown* [M]

F

FAIRFIELD FOUR
Vocal quartet, unaccompanied

Location: City Temple Church, London, England. October 1995

Titles performed:
unknown
[interview]

Source: *Too Close To Heaven*

FAITH COMMUNITY CHOIR
Mixed vocal choir, accompaniment: unknown

Location: Chicago, Illinois. Sunday 23 February 1964

Titles performed:
unknown

Source: *Jubilee Showcase* [prog # 28–1]

[FAMOUS] DAVIS SISTERS
See under 'D'.

JESSE JAMES FARLEY
Vocal accompaniment: unknown

Location: Chicago, Illinois

The following appearances are known:
1965
Sunday 25 April [prog #21–1]
1966
Sunday 27 March [prog #31–1]
Sunday 8 May [prog #23–1]
1969
Saturday 11 January [prog #8–3]
Thursday 24 April [prog #18–3]
1973
Tuesday 22 May [prog #5–3]
1975
Thursday 23 January [prog #6–2]

Titles performed:
unknown

Source: *Jubilee Showcase*
See also the Soul Stirrers.

FELLOWSHIP MISSIONARY BAPTIST CHURCH CHOIR
Mixed vocal choir, accompaniment: unknown

Location: Chicago, Illinois. Sunday 15 March 1964

Titles performed:
unknown

Source: *Jubilee Showcase* [prog # 7–1]

BETTY FIKES
Vocal accompaniment: Robert Lockwood, Johnny Shines (electric guitars); possibly Maurice Reedus (tenor saxophone); probably Eugene Schwartz (electric bass); possibly Jim 'Gator' Hoare (drums)

Location: Freedom Village, Greenville, Mississippi. Saturday 8 September 1979

Title performed:
'Rock Me Baby' K-Jazz 081

Source: *Mississippi Blues*

FIRST BAPTIST CHURCH OF FINCASTLE, VIRGINIA
Female octet accompaniment: unknown (piano)

Location: WDBJ-TV Studios, Roanoke, Virginia. Spring/Summer 1987

Titles performed:
'Gimme That Old Time Religion' [part only]
'I Must Have Jesus' [part only]

Source: *Black Musical Traditions In Virginia: Sacred Music*

FIRST COSMOPOLITAN CHURCH MALE VOICE CHOIR
Vocal quintet, unaccompanied

Location: Raleigh, North Carolina. 1995

Title performed:
'Roll Jordan, Roll'

Source: *Too Close To Heaven*

FIVE BLIND BOYS OF ALABAMA
probably George Scott, Louis Dicks, Jimmy Evans, Clarence Fountain, Olice Thomas and Johnny Fields (vocals) accompaniment: probably Scott (electric guitar)

Location: probably Chicago, Ilinois. c. April 1965

Titles performed:
'Bless Me, Jesus'
'Too Close'
'Something Got A Hold Of Me'

Source: *TV Gospel Time* #43

Clarence Fountain, Bobby Butler, J T Clinkscales, Reverend Olice Thomas, Joseph Watson (vocals) accompaniment: The Colonus Messengers

Location: unknown {USA}. 1986

Titles performed:
[See note in programme index]

Source: *The Gospel At Colonus*
Clarence Fountain played the dramatic role of Oedipus

Vocal group accompaniment: unknown

Location: New York City. February 1991

Titles performed:
unknown

Source: *South Bank Show*

Vocal group accompaniment: unknown

Location: New Orleans, Louisiana. 1991

Titles performed:
unknown Island 4973

Source: *Let The Good Times Roll* [2]
See also Cast of 'The Gospel at Colonus; and Clarence Fountain.

FIVE BLIND BOYS OF MISSISSIPPI

Probably Henry Johnson, Jimmy Carter, Reverend Willie Mincey, Lloyd Woodard, Jay T Clinkscales (vocals) accompaniment: unknown (electric guitar)–1;
as above accompaniment: The Barrett Sisters (vocal group), and unknown (electric guitar)–2

Location: Chicago, Illinois. Sunday 10 October 1964

Titles performed:
'Leaning On The Everlasting Arm'–1
'Lord, You've Been Good To Me'–1
'Come On Up To Bright Glory'–2

Source: *TV Gospel Time* #40

As above, unaccompanied

Location: Free Trade Hall, Manchester, England. January 1965

Titles performed:
unknown

Source: *They Sing Like Someone's Happy*

As above

Location: Alpirsbach Monastery, Schwarzwald, Germany. Late January 1965

Titles performed:
'O' Why' [*sic*] Praise 3012
'Jesus Rose With All Power In His Hand' Praise 3012
'Lord, You've Been Good To Me' Praise 3012

Source: *Hallelujah!*

FIVE KEYS

Vocal quintet accompaniment: unknown

Location: New York City. November 1955

Title performed:
'Ling Ting Tong'

Source: *The Ed Sullivan Show*

FIVE RED CAPS

Vocal quintet accompaniment: unknown

Location: probably New York City. 1946

Titles performed:
unknown

Source: *Mantan Messes Up*
See also the Four Toppers, from which group the Five Red Caps emerged.

FLAMINGOS

Probably Sollie McElroy, Earl Lewis, Ezekiel Carey, Jacob Carey, Johnny Carter, Paul Wilson, vocals accompaniment: unknown (electric guitar, bass, drums)

Location: unknown {USA}. 1956

Title performed:
'Would I Be Crying?' Gold Star BSG203

Source: *Rock, Rock, Rock*

Probably as above accompaniment: unknown

Location: probably Philadelphia, Pennsylvania. 1956–57

Titles performed:
unknown

Source: *Dick Clark's American Bandstand*

Probably as above accompaniment: unknown (tenor saxophone, electric guitar, bass, drums)

Location: unknown {USA}. 1958

Title performed:
'Jump Chldren'

Source: *Go Johnny Go*
See also the International Sweethearts Of Rhythm.

FLAT ROCK BAPTIST CHURCH CONGREGATION
Congregational vocal, unaccompanied

Location: Flatrock, Georgia. August 1995

Title performed:
untitled lining out hymn

Source: *Too Close To Heaven*

PAT FLOWERS
Piano solo, with Mabel Lee (dancing)

Location: probably New York City. c. 1942

Title performed:
[0002] 'Coal Mine Boogie'

Source: *Soundie*

FODDRELL FAMILY
Turner Foddrell (vocal and guitar); Lyn Foddrell (guitar); Marvin Foddrell (guitar)

Location: WDBJ TV Studios, Roanake, Virginia. Spring/Summer 1987

Titles performed:
'Flip, Flop And Fly' [part only]
'Boogie Blues' [part only]

Source: *Black Musical Traditions In Virginia: Blues*

FOLLOWERS OF CHRIST
Vocal group accompaniment. if any: unknown

Location: New Orleans, Louisiana. 1990

Title performed:
'Do You Love Everybody'

Source: *New Orleans Jazz And Heritage Festival 1990*

CANRAY FONTENOT
Vocal and violin accompaniment: Alphonse Ardoin (accordion)

Location: Newport, Rhode Island. July 1966
[A] On stairwell
[B] In Open Air

Titles performed:
'La Valse De La Prison' [A] Vestapol 13050
'Bon Soir, Moreau' [B] Vestapol 13050
[interview]

Source: *Alan Lomax collection*

Vocal and violin

Location: Eunice, Louisiana. 1973

Titles performed:
untitled instrumental #1 Flower 4, Jazz 067
untitled instrumental #2 Flower 4, Jazz 067
'Joli Blon' Flower 4, Jazz 067
'Lachez-Les' Flower 4, Jazz 067

Source: *Dry Wood*

Vocal and violin

Location: Eunice, Louisiana. 1981

Titles performed:
'Hathaway Two-step' [ST] Vestapol 13001
[interview] Vestapol 13001
'Barres De La Prison' Vestapol 13001

Source: *Cajun Visits*

Vocal and violin

Location: probably Eunice, Louisiana. Between 9 and 27 August 1983

Titles performed:
'Bon Soir, Moreau' [part only] Vestapol 13077
'La Valse De La Prison' [part only] Vestapol 13077
[interview]

Source: *Cajun Country* [1]

Vocal and violin

Location: Eunice, Louisiana. 1987–88

Titles performed:
'Lorita' Flower 7
'Bernadette' Flower 7

Source: *J'ai Eté Au Bal*

Vocal and violin accompaniment: Beausoleil [G]

Location: Eunice, Louisiana. 1992

Title performed:
'Chere Bassette' JVC 226

Source: *Motion Incorporated*, Hatfield, Connecticut.
See also Alphonse [Bois-Sec] Ardoin.

DORESSINE FONTENOT
Vocal, unaccompanied

Location: probably Eunice, Louisiana. Between 9 and 27 August 1983

Titles performed:
'Lord, Lord, Lord'
'Fare You Well'
[interview]

Source: *Cajun Country* [2]
This artist is Canray Fontenot's aunt.

DOROTHY FORD
Vocal accompaniment: Mary Smith (piano)

Location: Memphis, Tennessee. August 1995

Title performed:
'Pay Day'
[interview]

Source: *Too Close To Heaven*
See also Reverend W Herbert Brewster.

SONNY FORD
See James [Son] Thomas.

CLARENCE FOUNTAIN
Vocal accompaniment: unknown

Location: Chicago, Illinois. Saturday 14 June 1969

Titles performed:
unknown

Source: *Jubilee Showcase* [prog # 19–1]

Speech

Location: Los Angeles, California. 1986

[interview]

Source: *Remembering Black Music*

Speech

Location: Chicago, Illinois. August 1995

[interview]

Source: *Too Close To Heaven*
See also The Five Blind Boys Of Alabama.

FOUR EAGLE GOSPEL SINGERS
Vocal quartet, unaccompanied

Location: [A] Lily Grove Baptist Church, Bessemer, Alabama. Early 1984
[B] Radio Station WENN, Alabama. Early 1984
[C] Friendship Baptist Church, Brighton, Alabama. Early 1984

Titles performed:
'On the Battlefield' [A]
'The Old Landmark' [ST] (part only) [B]
'It's Getting Late in the Evening' [C]

Source: *On The Battlefield*

FOUR KNIGHTS
See Julius Cheeks and Jesse James Farley.

FOUR TONES
Lucius 'Dusty' Brooks, Rudolph Hunter, Leon Buck, Ira Hardin (vocals) accompaniment: probably Brooks (piano) and others, unknown

Location: N B Murphy Ranch, Victorville, California. 1938

Titles performed:
unknown

Source: *Harlem On The Prairie*

As above

Location: N B Murphy Ranch, Victorville, California. 1938

Titles performed:
unknown

Source: *Rhythm Rodeo*

As above

Location: Hollywood, California. 1938

Titles performed:
unknown

Source: *Two Gun Man From Harlem*

As above

Location: probably Hollywood, California. 1938

Titles performed:
unknown

Source: *Bronze Buckaroo*

As above

Location: probably New York City. 1939

Titles performed:
unknown

Source: *One Dark Night*

As above

Location: probably Hollywood, California. 1939

Titles performed:
unknown

Source: *Harlem Rides The Range*

As above

Location: probably New York City. 1940

Titles performed:
unknown

Source: *Son Of Ingagi*

As above

Location: probably New York City. 1941–44

Titles performed:
[21M4] 'Satchel Mouth Baby'
[23M3] 'Shout Brother, Shout'
Jazz Classics JCVC107

Source: *Soundies*

As above

Location: probably New York City. 1946

Titles performed:
unknown

Source: *Mantan Messes Up*

FOUR TOPPERS
Vocal quartet accompaniment, if any, unknown

Location: probably New York City. 1941

Titles performed:
unknown

Source: T*oppers Take A Bow*
See also the Five Red Caps.

[REVEREND] C L FRANKLIN
Speech

Location: New Bethel Baptist Church, Detroit, Michigan. c. 1970

Titles performed:
sermon
[interview]

Source: *Aretha*

ALAN FREED ORCHESTRA
Big Al Sears and Sam 'The Man' Taylor (tenor saxophones) and others, unknown. Freed (handclapping and incidental comments)-1

Location: unknown {USA}. 1957

Titles performed:
'Rock And Roll Boogie'–1 Gold Star BSG203
'Right Now, Right Now' Gold Star BSG203

Source: *Rock Rock Rock*
See also Accompanists index.

FRIENDLY TRAVELLERS
Vocal group accompaniment, if any, unknown

Location: New Orleans, Louisiana. 1990

Title performed:
'Search My Heart'

Source: *New Orleans Jazz And Heritage Festival 1990*

FRANK FROST
Vocal and harmonica accompaniment: Terry Evans (keyboards); Richard 'Shubby' Holmes (electric bass); John Price (drums)

Location: unknown {USA}. 1986

Titles performed:
un-named

Source: *Crossroads*
This music appears as the theme song of the film and as partial background to scenes in a juke joint. The musicians themselves do not appear on camera. See also the Jelly Roll Kings.

GERTRUDE FULLER
Vocal accompaniment: unknown

Location: Chicago, Illinois. Sunday 9 February 1964

Titles performed:
unknown

Source: *Jubilee Showcase* [prog # 12–1]

JESSE FULLER
Vocal accompaniment: presumably own guitar, harmonica, kazoo, fotdella

Location: probably Los Angeles, California. Early 1950s

Titles performed:
unknown

Source: *You're Never Too Old* [unconfirmed]

Probably as last

Location: probably Los Angeles, California. Early 1950s

Titles performed:
unknown

Source: *The Don Sherwood Show* [unconfirmed]

Probably as last

Location: Los Angeles, California. April–November 1958

Titles performed:
unknown
[interview with Bobby Troup]

Source: *Stars Of Jazz*

Vocal, 12-string electric guitar, harmonica, kazoo, fotdella

Location: San Francisco, California. Spring 1963

Title performed:
'San Francisco Bay Blues' [part only] Yazoo 520

Source: *Die Blues*

Presumably as last

Location: Hollywood, California. June–November 1965

Titles performed:
unknown

Source: *ABC's Nightlife*

Vocal, 12-string electric guitar, harmonica, kazoo, fotdella

Location: London, England. Late October 1965

Title performed:
'San Francisco Bay Blues'

Source: *Ready Steady Go*

Vocal, 12-string electric guitar, harmonica, kazoo, fotdella

Location: London, England. Late October 1965

Titles performed:
'San Francisco Bay Blues'
[interview]

Source: *Tonight*

12-string guitar solo–1
Vocal and 12-string guitar–2
Vocal, 12-string guitar, harmonica, fotdella–3
Vocal accompaniment: the Muddy Waters Blues Band, with James Cotton, Willie Dixon, Mable Hillery, Brownie McGhee, Muddy Waters, Otis Spann, Sunnyland Slim, Bukka White and Big Joe Williams (vocals)–4

Location: Toronto, Canada. Thursday 27 to Saturday 29 January 1966

Titles performed:
[interview with Barry Callaghan]
'Overture from William Tell'–1
'Stranger Blues'–2
'Take It Slow And Easy'–3
jam session–4

Source: *Festival Presents The Blues*

Vocal and 12-string electric guitar–1
Vocal and 12-string electric guitar, harmonica, fotdella–2

Location: KCTS-TV studios, Seattle, Washington. April 1968

Titles performed:

'Hark From The Tomb'–1	Vestapol 13002
'I'm Glad Salvation's Free'–1	Vestapol 13002
'John Henry'–1	Vestapol 13002
'Runnin' Wild'–2	Vestapol 13037
'The Woman I Had, She Left Me'–2	Vestapol 13037

Source: *University of Washington/Seattle Folkore Society* [C]
The first three tracks originally appeared in *Roots Of American Music.*

Vocal and 12-string guitar, harmonica, kazoo, fotdella

Location: KCTS-TV Studios, Seattle, Washington. April 1968

Titles performed:

'John Henry'	Yazoo 503
'Red River Blues'	Yazoo 503
'San Francisco Bay Blues'	Yazoo 503
[monologue, leading to;]	
'Take This Hammer'	Yazoo 503
'Oh Boys, Won't You Line 'em'	Yazoo 503
'Running Wild'	Yazoo 503
'High Sheriff Blues'	Yazoo 503

Source: *Masters Of American Traditional Music*

Vocal, 12-string electric guitar, harmonica

Location: unknown {USA}. 1970

Title performed:
'Let Me Hold You In My Arms Tonight' [ST]

Source: *The Great White Hope*
Fuller appeared as an extra in a number of silent feature films, made in Hollywood, California, during the 1920s. These dramatic appearances are documented in *Blues Who's Who* (Sheldon Harris) and are excluded from this work. The fotdella was a percussive instrument, unique to Fuller, who built it. It comprised the sawn-off top half of a double bass, re-strung with piano wire and played with foot-pedal operated hammers.

LORENZO FULLER
Vocal accompaniment: unknown

Location: New York City. c.1965–66

Titles performed:
unknown [A]
unknown [B]
unknown [C]
unknown [D]

Source: *TV Gospel Time* #50 [A], #52 [B], #63 [C], #64 [D]

LOWELL FULSON
Vocal and electric guitar accompaniment: unknown (second electric guitar, tenor saxophone, electric bass, drums)

Location: San Francisco, California. Spring 1963

Title performed:
'Be On Your Merry Way' [part only] Yazoo 520

Source: *Die Blues*

Vocal and electric guitar accompaniment: unknown

Location: probably Los Angeles, California. 1970

Titles performed:
unknown

Source: *The Homewood Show* [unconfirmed]

Vocal and electric guitar accompaniment: unknown

Location: probably Los Angeles, California. 1973

Titles performed:
unknown

Source: *All Together Now* [unconfirmed]

Vocal and electric guitar accompaniment: Mark Naftalin (piano); Henry Owen (electric bass); Fred Casey (drums)

Location: Sleeping Lady Cafe, Fairfax, California. 1981

Titles performed:
'Thing'
'You're Gonna Miss Me'
'Guitar Shuffle'
'The Right Time'

Source: *Mark Naftalin's Blue Monday Party*
These titles probably appear on K-Jazz 100.

Vocal and electric guitar accompaniment: unknown (second electric guitar, tenor saxophone, electric bass, drums)

Location: Oakland, California. 1981

Title performed:
'Reconsider Baby'
[interview]

Source: *Long Train Running*

Vocal and electric guitar accompaniment: unknown

Location: Germany. 1984

Titles performed:
'You're Gonna Miss me'
'Goin' To Chicago'
'Talkin' Woman Blues'
'Everyday I Have The Blues'
'Stoop Down Baby'

Source: *Jazz Burghausen*

Vocal and guitar–1
Vocal and electric guitar accompaniment: Lloyd Glenn (piano)–2

Location: Los Angeles, California. 1984

Titles performed:
demonstration of Texas blues guitar styles–1
'Reconsider Baby'–2

Source: *Legends Of Rhythm And Blues*

Vocal and electric guitar accompaniment: unknown (tenor saxophone, second electric guitar, electric bass, drums)

Location: Sacramento, California. September 1987

Titles performed:
'Blue Shadows Falling'

Source: *Sacramento Blues Festival 1987*

G

CASSIETTA GEORGE
Vocal accompaniment: unknown

Location: Chicago, Illinois

The following appearances are known:
1964
Sunday 26 January [prog #7–3]
1969
Saturday 14 June [prog #19–1]

Titles performed:
unknown

Source: *Jubilee Showcase*
See also the Caravans.

GEORGIA SEA ISLAND SINGERS
Mixed vocal chorus, unaccompanied

Location: KCTS-TV studios, Seattle, Washington. 1971

Titles performed:
unknown

Source: *University of Washington/Seattle Folklore Society*
See also Janie Hunter.

HIAWATHA GILES
Vocal and accordion

Location: WDBJ TV Studios, Roanoke, Virginia. Spring/Summer 1987

Titles performed:
'Who's Gonna Shoe Your Feet?' [A] [part only]
'On The Battlefield' [B] [part only]

Source: *Black Musical Traditions In Virginia: Non-blues Secular Music* [A]; *Black Musical Traditions In Virginia: Sacred Music* [B]

EARL GILMORE
Vocal and piano

Location: WDBJ TV Studios, Roanake, Virginia. Spring/Summer 1987

Titles performed:
'Going Away Blues' [A] [part only]
'Standing Here Crying' [A] [part only]
'Lift Jesus Up' [B] [part only]

Source: *Black Musical Traditions In Virginia: Blues* [A]; *Black Musical Traditions In Virginia: Sacred Music* [B]

LLOYD GLENN
Piano solo

Location: Los Angeles, California. 1984

Title performed:
Blues solo

Source: *Legends Of Rhythm And Blues*

GLORYETTE SPIRITUAL SINGERS
Vocal group accompaniment: unknown

Location: Chicago, Illinois. Sunday 7 June 1964

Titles performed:
unknown

Source: *Jubilee Showcase* [prog # unknown]

GOLDEN ECHOES
John Landis (lead vocal) accompaniment: Wilburt Malone, Luther Foster, Andrew Green, Sidney Brodie, Leonard Brodie, Ronald Perry (vocals, electric guitar, electric bass, drums; individual instrumentation unknown)

Location: Rock Spring Baptist Church, Rock Spring, North Carolina. 1985

Titles performed:
'I'm Going Up To Meet Him Bye And Bye' Shanachie 1402
'The Old Rugged Cross' Shanachie 1402

Source: *A Singing Stream*
See also the Landis family.

GOLDEN LEAF BAPTIST CHURCH CHOIR
Mixed vocal choir accompaniment: unknown

Location: Memphis, Tennessee. Tuesday 19 January 1963

Titles performed:
'Sing 'till The Power Of The Lord Comes Down'
'My Hope Is Built On Nothing Less'
'Just A Little While'

Source: *TV Gospel Time* #20

GOLDEN GATE QUARTET
Probably Henry Owens, Clyde Riddick, Willie Johnson, Orlandus Wilson (vocals), unaccompanied

Location: Los Angeles, California. 1941

Title performed:
'Take Me Off To Dreamland'

Source: *Star Spangled Rhythm*

Probably as above

Location: Los Angeles, California. 1942

Title performed:
'The General Jumped At Dawn'

Source: *Hollywood Canteen*

Probably as above

Location: Los Angeles, California. 1943

Title performed:
'Yankee-Doodle Dan'

Source: *Change Of Heart* aka *Hit Parade Of 1943*

Probably Henry Owens, Clyde Riddick, Alton Bradley, Orlandus Wilson (vocals) accompaniment: unknown (piano)

Location: Los Angeles, California. 1948

Titles performed:
'Old Blind Barnabus' [fragment only]
'Joshua Fit De Battle Of Jericho' [*sic*] [fragment only]

Source: *A Song Is Born*
Later appearances by this group on European TV, with significantly different personnel, are excluded.

GOLDEN TONES
probably Milton Oliver, Billy Shelton, Loy Oliver, Willie Jones, Dimisio Gil, James Trusk, Floyd Clinton (vocals) accompaniment: unknown

Location: Chicago, Illinois. Sunday 27 March 1966

Titles performed:
unknown

Source: *Jubilee Showcase* [prog # 31–1]

GOOD ROCKIN' CHARLES (Charles Edwards) [N.B. different man from Charles Edwards, listed under 'E']
Vocal and harmonica accompaniment: Louis Myers (electric guitar); David Myers (electric bass); Fred Below (drums)

Location: Chicago, Illinois. Wednesday 28 January 1976

Titles performed:
'Don't Start Me Talking'
'Shake Your Boogie' [unbroadcast]

Source: *The Devil's Music series 2*

ANN GOODLEY
Vocal and accordion accompaniment: unknown (rub-board, electric guitar, electric bass, drums)

Location: Opelousas, Louisiana. 1988

Title performed:
unknown [part only] K-Jazz 098, Rhapsody 8062
[interview] K-Jazz 098, Rhapsody 8062

Source: *Zydeco Gumbo*

IDA GOODSON
Vocal accompaniment: unknown

Location: unknown {USA}. 1989

Titles performed:
'Take My Hand, Precious Lord' California Newsreel 02
'Wild Women Don't Have The Blues' California Newsreel 02
[interview] California Newsreel 02

Source: *Wild Women Don't Have The Blues*

ROSCO GORDON
Gordon, vocal and piano accompaniment: The Red Tops; unknown (tenor saxophone, electric guitar, bass, drums)

Location: probably Houston, Texas. 1957

Titles performed:
'Chicken In The Rough' Rhino R3.2410
'Bop With Me Baby' Rhino R3.2410

Source: *Rock Baby, Rock It!*

Vocal and piano accompaniment: unknown (tenor saxophone, electric guitar, electric bass, drums)

Location: Sacramento, California. September 1987

Titles performed:
'No More Doggin''

Source: *Sacramento Blues Festival 1987*

GOSPEL ALL-STARS
Vocal group accompaniment: unknown

Location: New York City. Sunday 4 November 1962

Titles performed:
'I Got To Wait Till Jesus Comes'
'Trees'

Source: *TV Gospel Time* #8
This group may include James Cleveland.

GOSPELAIRES
Probably Charles McLean, Paul Arnold, Robert Lattimore, Joseph McLean, Jimmy Hawkins (vocals) accompaniment: Robert Lattimore (electric guitar) and unknown group member (electric bass)

Location: Jacksonville, Florida. 1965

Titles performed:
'Joy, Joy, Joy'
'Rest For The Weary'

Source: *TV Gospel Time* #59

Charles McLean, Paul Arnold, Robert Lattimore and Jimmy Hawkins (vocals) accompaniment: Lattimore (electric guitar)

Location: Fairfield Hall, Croydon, England. February 1966

Titles performed:
'Ride This Train'
'Rest For The Weary'

Source: *American Gospel And Spiritual Festival 1966*

GOSPEL CHIMES
Possibly Imogene Green, Claude D Timmons, Lee Charles Henry and others, (vocals) accompaniment: unknown

Location: Chicago, Illinois. Sunday 26 July 1964

Titles performed:
unknown

Source: *Jubilee Showcase* [prog # 26–1]

GOSPEL CHOICE
Vocal group accompaniment: unknown

Location: Gary, Indiana. June 1976

Titles performed:
unknown

Source: *Gospel In Gary*

GOSPEL CLEFS
Probably Leon Lumpkins, Reverend Huston, Raymond Andrews (vocals) accompaniment: unknown

Location: probably New York City. c.1965–66

Titles performed:
unknown

Source: *TV Gospel Time* #49

GOSPEL CLOUDS OF JOY
Probably William Rash, James Garland, Clarence Gertman, Morris Pollard, Walter Carrarker, John Scales (vocals) accompaniment: unknown

Location: New York City. c.1966

Titles performed:
unknown

Source: *TV Gospel Time* #64

GOSPEL HARMONETTES
Dorothy Love Coates (lead vocal), probably Mildred Miller Howard, Willie Mae Newberry, Barbara Jean Reed, Lillian McGriff (vocals), accompaniment: unknown (piano)–1;
as above accompaniment: the Cannon Temple Church Of God In Christ Choir–2

Location: Charlotte, North Carolina. Saturday 1 August 1964

Titles performed:
'I Won't Let Go'–1
'You Must Be Born Again'–1
'Right On Time'–2

Source: *TV Gospel Time* #28

As above–1, or in the company of the Dixie Hummingbirds and the Swan Silvertone Singers (vocal groups)–2

Location: Newport, Rhode Island. July 1966

Titles performed:
'Swing Down Chariot'–1
'Trouble In The Land'–1
'Jesus Is The Key'–2

Source: *Alan Lomax film collection*

Vocal quartet accompainment: unknown

Location: Chicago, Illinois. 1969

The following appearances are known:
Saturday 3 May [prog #33–2]
Saturday 4 October [prog #27–1]

Titles performed:
unknown

Source: *Jubilee Showcase*

Dorothy Love Coates, lead vocal accompaniment: unknown

Location: unknown {USA}. 1970

Titles performed:
unknown

Source: *Look Up And Sing Out*
See also Dorothy Love Coates, Archie Dennis.

GOSPEL LIGHT AND GLORY CHORUSES
Large mixed vocal choir accompaniment: unknown
Soloists: Rosa Ellison–1; Betty Armstrong–2

Location: Charlotte, North Carolina. Sunday 28 February 1965

Titles performed:
'He Rescued Me'–1
'The Way They Do'
'He's A Friend Of Mine'–2

Source: *TV Gospel Time* #31

GOSPEL REDEEMERS
Female vocal trio, including possibly Clara Walker, accompaniment: one of them (electric guitar)

Location: New York City. c.1965–66

Titles performed:
'Let's Go Down To Jordan'
'Morning Train'

Source: *TV Gospel Time* #51

GOSPEL SEEKERS
Vocal group accompaniment: unknown

Location: Baltimore, Maryland. Saturday 16 February 1963

Titles performed:
'Let Jesus Lead Me' [A]
'Come Out Of The Wilderness' [A]
'Come And Go With Me' [A]
'God Is Standing By' [B]
'I've Got Jesus' [B]
'Somehow' [B]

Source: *TV Gospel Time* #24 [A], #25 [B]

GOSPEL SONGBIRDS
Vocal group accompaniment: unknown

Location: Chicago, Illinois.

The following appearances are known:
1964
Wednesday 26 August [prog #13–3]
1965
Sunday 19 December [prog #29–1]
1969
Saturday 15 March [prog #32–2]

Titles performed:
unknown

Source: *Jubilee Showcase*
The personnel of the above group includes Otis Clay in the 1964 appearance.

GOSPEL STARLETTES
Female vocal group accompaniment: unknown

Location: New York City. Sunday 28 October 1962

Titles performed:
'He's A Mighty Good God'
'He Sets High' [*sic*]

Source: *TV Gospel Time* #5

As above

Location: New York City. Sunday 16 December 1962

Titles performed:
'I'm Leaning On His Promise'
'Lord, Hear My Prayer'

Source: *TV Gospel Time* #15

GOSPEL STARS
Vocal group, accompaniment: unknown

Location: Alabama. 1964

Titles performed:
unknown

Source: *Nothin' But A Man*

GOSPEL STIRRERS
Vocal group accompaniment: unknown

Location: Chicago, Illinois. 1976

Titles performed:
unknown

Source: *Here Comes Gospel*

[BISHOP] DADDY GRACE
Preaching, with congregational response

Location: New York City. Mid-1930s

Titles performed:
religious monologues

Source: *US Newsreel footage* [M]. Origin unknown. Available from Historic.

GRAVEL SPRINGS FIFE AND DRUM BAND
See Othar Turner.

[BLIND] ARVELLA GRAY
Speech

Location: 4403 South State Street, Chicago, Illinois. Monday 11 July 1960

monologue[ST only] K-Jazz 014, Rhapsody 8022

Source: *Blues Like Showers Of Rain*

Vocal and steel guitar

Location: Maxwell Street, Chicago, Illinois. 1964

Titles performed:
John Henry – take 1 [part only] Shanachie 1403
John Henry – take 2 [ST only] Shanachie 1403

Source: *And This Is Free*

Vocal and (probably) steel guitar

Location: Chicago, Illinois. 1965

Titles performed:
unknown

Source: *The Songmakers*

Vocal and (probably) steel guitar

Location: Chicago, Illinois. 1973

Titles performed:
unknown

Source: *Save The Children*

Vocal and guitar–1
Vocal and handclapping–2

Location: Maxwell Street, Chicago, Illinois. 1980

Titles performed:
'Good Morning Blues'–1 K-Jazz 031, Rhapsody 8045
'Tamp 'em Up Solid'–2 K-Jazz 031, Rhapsody 8045
'More Pretty Girls Than One'–1 K-Jazz 031, Rhapsody 8045
[interview] K-Jazz 031, Rhapsody 8045

Source: *Maxwell Street Blues*
Arvella Gray also appears briefly in the film *Chicago Blues* (1970, Harley Cokliss), but is not heard singing or playing.
See also Blind James Brewer.

HENRY GRAY

Vocal and piano

Location: Baton Rouge, Louisiana. 1984

Titles performed:
'Blues All Day Long'
'How Many More Years'
'Dust My Broom'
[interview]

Source: *Baton Rouge Blues*

Vocal and piano

Location: New Orleans, Louisiana. 1985

Titles performed:
'Blues Dance' [A]
'Cold Chills' [A]
unknown titles [B]

Source: Jim Gabbour Productions; titles marked [A] are included in *New Orleans Now – All Alone With the Blues*. Titles marked [A] and [B] appear in *In Concert* [3]

WILLIAM GREAVES (performing as 'Alabama Ike')

Vocal and guitar

Location: probably New York City. 1949

Titles performed:
'Lonesome Blues'
'No Good Blues'

Source: *Souls Of Sin*

AL GREEN

Vocal accompaniment: Full Gospel Tabernacle Choir

Location: Memphis, Tennessee. 1983–84

Titles performed:
'The Lord Will Make A Way'
'When The Gates Swing Open'
'Amazing Grace'
'Nearer My God To Thee'
'Pass Me Not'
'Hallelujah (I Just Want To Praise The Lord)'
'Free At Last'

'Straighten Out Your Life'
[sermons]
[interviews]

Source: *Gospel According To Al Green*
While the bulk of material by Al Green falls outside the parameters of this work, the above documentary features traditional gospel singing and preaching, and may therefore be regarded as relevant to this research.

CLARENCE GREEN

Vocal accompaniment: the Texas Houserockers [G]

Location: Houston, Texas. Friday [*sic*], 8 October 1993

Titles performed:
'Something Funny's Goin' On'
'Old And Grey Blues'

Source: *Saturday Night At Rockefeller's*

BESSIE GRIFFIN

Vocal accompaniment: unknown

Location: unknown {USA}. Early 1960s

Titles performed:
unknown

Source: *Hullabaloo* [1]

Vocal accompaniment: unknown

Location: London, England. c.1962

Titles performed:
unknown

Source: *Black Nativity*

Vocal accompaniment: unknown

Location: New York City. c. May 1963

Titles performed:
unknown

Source: *The Dinah Shore Chevy Show*

Vocal accompaniment: unknown (organ)–1
Vocal accompaniment: Omega Baptist Church Choir–2

Location: Chicago, Illinois. Saturday 10 October 1964

Titles performed:
'He Doeth All Things Well'–1 [A]
'Lord, Look Up To Me'–1 [A]
'God Will Take Care Of You'–1 [B]
'Eternity'–1 [B]
'He's Everything To Me'–2 [A]

Source: *TV Gospel Time* #36 [A], #39 [B]

Vocal accompaniment: unknown

Location: Chicago, Illinois. Saturday 19 and Saturday 26 August 1972

Titles performed:
unknown

Source: *Jubilee Showcase* [prog #13–2 & 13–3]

Vocal accompaniment: unknown

Location: Montreux, Switzerland. 1972

Titles performed:
unknown

Source: *Montreux Jazz*

DORIS GRIMES

Vocal accompaniment: unknown

Location: Chicago, Illinois

The following appearances are known:
1964
Sunday 3 May [prog #30–1]
1966
Friday 13 May [prog #34–2]
Saturday 11 June [prog #23–2]

Titles performed:
unknown

Source: *Jubilee Showcase*

LLOYD [TINY] GRIMES

Details unknown
Vocal by June Richmond–1

Location: unknown {USA}. 1944

Titles performed:
[13M1] 'Swingin' In The Groove'
Jazz Classics JCVC–110
[87508] 'Romance Without Finance'
[87708] 'TG Boogie Woogie'
Jazz Classics JCVC–107
[88808] 'Never Too Old To Swing'
'Joseph 'N' His Brudders' [*sic*]–1

Source: *Soundies*
87508 copyrighted 31 December 1945; 87708 17 December 1945; 88808 5 November 1945

[CREOLE] GEORGE GUESNON

Vocal and presumably own guitar or banjo accompaniment, if any: unknown

Location: unknown {USA} 1961

Titles performed:
unknown

Source: *David Brinkley's Journal*

As above

Location: probably New Orleans, Louisiana. 1964

Titles performed:
unknown

Source: *New Orleans Jazz*
See also Joseph [Dede] Pierce.

GUITAR SHORTY (David Kearney)

Vocal and electric guitar accompaniment: probably the Milton DeLugg orchestra.

Location: Burbank, California. c. 1978–79

Title performed:
'They Call Me Guitar Shorty'

Source: *The Gong Show*
Guitar Shorty won the first prize on the above edition of this competitive variety show by performing while balanced on his head and revolving slowly.

Electric guitar solo and acrobatics–1, vocal and electric guitar–2 accompaniment: Central Avenue [G]; unknown (second electric guitar, keyboards, electric bass, drums)

Location: Long Beach, California. c. 1989

Titles performed:
untitled instrumental–1
'The Blues Is All Right'–2
[interview]

Source: *US PBS TV broadcast*. Origin unknown [C].

GEORGE [BUDDY] GUY

Vocal and electric guitar accompaniment: probably the Soul Agents [G], (electric guitars, electric organ, electric bass, drums)

Location: ATV studios, London, England. Friday 19 February 1965

Title performed:
'Let Me Love You Baby'

Source: *Ready Steady Go*
For much of this performance Buddy Guy's vocal is largely inaudible, due to his loosely slung neck-microphone becoming entangled in his jacket collar.

Vocal and electric guitar accompaniment: unknown

Location: Chicago, Illinois. 1965

Titles performed:
unknown

Source: *The Songmakers*

Vocal and electric guitar accompaniment: Eddie Boyd (piano); Jimmie Lee Robinson (electric bass); Fred Below (drums)

Location: Baden-Baden, Germany. October 1965

Titles performed:
[introduction by John Lee Hooker;]
'Outtasight' (becoming) 'Papa's Got A Brand New Bag'

Source: *American Folk Blues Festival 1965*

Vocal and electric guitar accompaniment: unknown: (tenor saxophone, trumpet, electric bass, drums)

Location: New York City. 1968

Titles performed:
'Been Down So Long'
'Stormy Monday Blues'
'Making A Fool Outta Me'

Source: *Camera Three: Really The Country Blues*
See also Son House.

Vocal and electric guitar accompaniment: David Myers (electric bass); unknown (drums)

Location: Chicago, Illinois. April–May 1970

Titles performed:

'First Time I Met The Blues'	K-Jazz 004, Rhapsody 9012
untitled instrumental #1	K-Jazz 004, Rhapsody 9012
untitled instrumental #2 [ST only]	K-Jazz 004, Rhapsody 9012

Source: *Chicago Blues*

Vocal and electric guitar accompaniment: unknown

Location: probably Chicago, Illinois. 1970

Titles performed:
unknown

Source: *Blues Is Alive And Well In Chicago*

Vocal and electric guitar accompaniment: unknown

Location: Canada. 1970

Titles performed:
unknown

Source: *Supershow*

Vocal and electric guitar accompaniment: Bonnie Raitt (guitar) and others, unknown

Location: Chicago, Illinois. 1974

Titles performed:
unknown

Source: *Soundstage*

Vocal and electric guitar accompaniment: Junior Wells (harmonica); Terry Taylor (second electric guitar); Pinetop Perkins (piano); Bill Wyman (electric bass); Dallas Taylor (drums)

Location: Montreux, Switzerland. Friday 28 June 1974

Titles performed:

'Howlin' Wind Blues'	BMG 791051, Rhino R3.1991
[monologue on blues]	BMG 791051, Rhino R3.1991
'Ten Years Ago'	BMG791051, Rhino R3.1991

Source: *Messin' With The Blues* (Montreux Jazz)
See also Muddy Waters and Junior Wells.

Vocal and electric guitar accompaniment: Junior Wells (vocal and harmonica) and others, unknown

Location: Chicago, Illinois. 1981

Titles performed:
unknown

Source: *Chicago Blues Festival 1981*

Vocal and electric guitar accompaniment: Junior Wells (vocal and harmonica) and others, unknown–1
Vocal and electric guitar accompaniment: unknown–2

Location: Chicago, Illinois. Tuesday 20 July 1982

Titles performed:
'Little By Little'–1
'Man Of Many Words'–2
'Mystery Train'–1

Source: *Soundstage*

Vocal and electric guitar accomapniment: John Mayall's Blues Breakers; Mayall (piano); Mick Taylor (electric guitar); John McVie (electric bass); Colin Allen (drums)

Location: New Jersey. 1982

Title performed:
'My Time After Awhile' Castle Hendring

Source: *Blues Survivors*

Vocal and electric guitar in duet with Junior Wells (vocal and harmonica) accompaniment: the Gerald Wiggins orchestra

Location: unknown {USA}. 1982

Title performed:
'Who's Loving You Tonight (That's Alright)' Magnum MMGV-037

Source: *America's Music – Blues Vol. 2*

Vocal and electric guitar accompaniment: Dave Kelly (electric guitar); Richard Bailey (electric bass); Kuma Harada (drums)

Location: BBC TV studios, Shepherd's Bush, London, England. 1982

Titles performed:
'DJ Play my Blues'
untitled instrumental
'Dust my Broom' [becoming]
'Talk to Me Baby'
[interview]

Source: *B A In Music*

Vocal and electric guitar accompaniment: unknown

Location: Chicago, Illinois, 1983

Titles performed:
unknown

Source: *Sweet Home Chicag*o [1]

Vocal and electric guitar accompaniment: unknown (second electric guitar, electric bass, drums)

Location: Checkerboard Lounge, Chicago, Illinois. 1984

Titles performed:
'Five Long Years'
'Stormy Monday Blues'
[interview]

Source: *Baton Rouge Blues*

Vocal and electric guitar accompaniment: Eric Clapton (electric guitar); Chris Stainton (piano); Greg Rzab (electric bass); Gerry Porter (drums)

Location: Ronnie Scott's Club, London, England. October 1987

Titles performed:
'Stormy Monday Blues'
'Sweet Home Chicago'
jam session

Source: *The Clapton Sessions*

Vocal and electric guitar in duet with Koko Taylor (vocal) accompaniment: Willie Dixon (bass and vocals) and others, unknown

Location: Chicago, Illinois. Monday 1 January 1990

Title performed:
'Wang Dang Doodle'

Source: *Soundstage*

Vocal and electric guitar accompaniment: Eric Clapton (electric guitar); Johnny Johnson (piano) and others, unknown

Location: Royal Albert Hall, London. 1990

Title performed:
'Money (That's What I Want)'

Source: *Rock Steady*
See also Robert Cray.

Vocal and electric guitar in duet with Albert Collins, vocal and electric guitar accompaniment: unknown–1
Vocal and electric guitar accompaniment: Junior Wells (harmonica) and others, unknown–2

Location: Checkerboard Lounge, Chicago, Illinois. 1990

Titles performed:
untitled instrumental–1 BMG 791.151, Rhino R91226
'Five Long Years'–2 BMG 791.151, Rhino R91226
'Everything Gonna Be Alright'–2 BMG 791.151, Rhino R91226

Source: *Blues Alive*

Vocal and electric guitar accompaniment: Double Trouble [G] Stevie Ray Vaughn (electric guitar), and others, unknown

Location: Austin, Texas. 1991

Titles performed:
'Sweet Home Chicago'
'Leave My Girl Alone'

Source: *Austin City Limits*

Vocal and electric guitar–1
Vocal and electric guitar accompaniment: unknown (second electric guitar, electric bass, drums)–2

Location: Chicago, Illinois. 1993

Titles performed:
'The Things I Used To Do'–1 MCA V10944
demonstration of the Jimi Hendrix guitar style–1 MCA V10944
'Five Long Years'–2 MCA V10944
[interview] MCA V10944

Source: *Sweet Home Chicago* [2]

Vocal and electric guitar accompaniment: G.E. Smith and the Saturday Night Live Band

Location: New York City. 1996

Titles performed:
'I've Got My Eyes On You'
'Sweet Black Angel'
'Talk To Me Baby'
'My Time After Awhile'
'I've Got News For You'
'Damn Right I Got The Blues'
'First Time I Met The Blues'
'Let Me Love You Baby'

Source: *unknown*, see Commercially Issued Videos, under Videoplus.

Vocal and electric guitar accompaniment: G.E. Smith's band

Location: Washington, DC. Saturday 11 October 1997

Title peformed:
'She's Nineteen Years Old'

Source: *Tribute To Muddy Waters*

Speech

Location: unknown {USA}. 1997

[interview]

Source: *Record Row*
Guy also appears in a tutorial video, *Hotlicks* 22245 [C].
See also Junior Wells.

PHILLIP GUY

Vocal and electric guitar accompaniment: unknown

Location: Nice, France. 1978

Titles performed:
'Hi Heel Sneakers'

Source: *La Grande Parade Du Jazz*
This artist is Buddy Guy's brother.

SHEILA GUYSE

Vocal accompaniment: unknown

Location: probably New York City, 1948

Title performed:
'Look Down That Lonesome Road' Hollywood Select 97803

Source: *Miracle In Harlem*

H

JAMES HALL
Vocal, unaccompanied

Location: Juke joint, unknown location, Mississippi. Between 11 August and 9 September 1978

Title performed:
toast describing the events of the Second World War Vestapol 13078

Source: *Land Where The Blues Began*
A toast is a form of rhythmic poetry that some sources claim to be the root of urban rap music.

JUANITA HALL
Vocal accompaniment: unknown

Location: probably New York City. 1948

Title performed:
'Chocolate Candy Blues' Hollywood Select 97803

Source: *Miracle In Harlem*

Vocal accompaniment: probably the Vic Smalley orchestra

Location: New York City. Monday 16 August to Monday 13 September 1948

Titles performed:
unknown

Source: *Captain Billy's Showboat*

Vocal accompaniment: probably the Vic Smalley orchestra

Location: New York City. Friday 1 October to Friday 26 November 1948

Titles performed:
unknown

Source: *Captain Billy's Mississippi Music Hall*

HARMONICA FATS (Harvey Blackston)
Vocal and harmonica accompaniment: unknown (electric guitar, keyboards, electric bass, drums)

Location: probably Los Angeles, California. 1986

Title performed:
'Fannie Mae' [part only]

Source: *Remembering Black Music*
See also Lonnie Brooks

HARMONIZING FIVE
Vocal quintet, unaccompanied

Location: WDBJ-TV Studios, Roanoke, Virginia. Spring/Summer 1987

Titles performed:
'How Do You Do?' [part only] [A]
'Let The Church Roll On' [part only] [B]
'Do You Call That A Brother?' [part only] [B]

Source: *Black Music Traditions In Virginia: Non-blues Secular Music* [A]; *Black Music Traditions In Virginia: Sacred Music* [B]

HARMONIZING FOUR
Probably Thomas Johnson, Lonnie Smith, Joseph Williams, Ellis Johnson (vocals) accompaniment: unknown–1;
as above accompaniment: The Gospel Light And Glory Gospel Choruses–2

Location: Charlotte, North Carolina. Saturday 1 August 1964

Titles performed:
'I Love To Call His Name'–1
'Amazing Grace'–1
'Rock Of Ages'–1
'I Trust In God'–2

Source: *TV Gospel Time* #31

Thomas Johnson, Ellis Johnson, Lonnie Smith, 'Gospel' Joe Williams (vocals) accompaniment: Michael Rogers (electric guitar)

Location: Fairfield Halls, Croydon, England. February 1966

Titles performed:
'Old Time Religion'
'Motherless Child'
'The Lord's Prayer'

Source: *American Gospel And Spiritual Festival 1966*

Probably as last

Location: New York City. c. 1966

Titles performed:
unknown

Source: *TV Gospel Time* #61

RICHARD [HACKSAW] HARNEY
Guitar solo

Location: Memphis, Tennessee. 1978

Title performed:
'Guitar Rag' [part only] K-Jazz 030, Yazoo 505

Source: *Good Morning Blues*

HARPS OF MELODY
Female vocal group, unaccompanied

Location: Friendship Baptist Church, Brighton, Alabama. Early 1984

Title performed:
'Two Little Fishes and Five Loaves of Bread'

Source: *On The Battlefield*

HARPTONES
Vocal group accompaniment: unknown

Location: unknown {USA}. 1956

Titles performed:
'First, Last And Only Girl'
'High Flyin' Baby'
'OoWee Baby' [*sic*]
'Mambo Boogie'

Source: *Rockin' The Blues*

EDNA HARRIS
Vocal and guitar

Location: unknown {USA}. 1936

Title performed:
unknown

Source: *Green Pastures*

HI-TIDE HARRIS (William Boyd or William Gitry)
Vocal and guitar with occasional light orchestral accompaniment; Sonny Terry (harmonica–1, jew's harp–2); Brownie McGhee and David Cohen (guitars–2)

Location: probably San Francisco, California. 1975

Titles performed:
'Green Corn'–1
'Good Morning Blues'–2
untitled instrumental–2
'Rock Island Line'
'Silver City Bound'
'See That My Grave Is Kept Clean'
'Goodnight Irene'
'Fannin Street'
'Governor Pat Neff'
'Cottonfields'
'Bring A Little Water'
'The Bourgeois Blues'
'Jim Crow'
'Ella Speed'
'Midnight Special'
'Ole Rattler'

Source: these songs are sung by Harris for the film *Leadbelly*, and are mimed in the film by Roger E Mosely, who plays Leadbelly, and Art Evans, who plays Blind Lemon Jefferson. Harris also supplied soundtrack for the film *Mandingo*. There are believed to be Japanese TV broadcasts by this artist from about the same period.

REBERT HARRIS
Vocal accompaniment: the Gospel Parade (vocal group)

Location: Chicago, Illinois. Sunday 31 May 1964

Titles performed:
unknown

Source: *Jubilee Showcase* [prog # 29–2].

Speech

Location: Chicago, Illinois. c.1979

[interview]

Source: *Chicago On The Good Foot*
Harris was a founder member of the Soul Stirrers.

THERESA HARRIS
Vocal accompaniment: Curtis Mosby and his Dixieland Jug Blowers: James 'King' Porter (trumpet); unknown (trombone, alto saxophone, tenor saxophone, piano, banjo); possibly Mosby (drums)

Location: Hollywood, California. 1929

Title performed:
'Daddy, Won't You Please Come Home'

Source: *Thunderbolt*

Vocal accompaniment: Les Hite's Cotton Club Orchestra; Eddie Barefield (tenor saxophone); other personnel unknown

Location: probably New York City. 1937

Titles performed:
unknown

Source: *Bargain Wth Bullets*

Vocal accompaniment: Louis Jordan's Tympany Five, personnel unknown, and probably Dudley Dickerson, dancing

Location: probably Hollywood, California. Mid-1942

Title performed:
[9005] 'Outskirts Of Town'

Source: *Soundie*
Copyrighted 19 October 1942. Some sources spell this artist's forename Teresa.

WYNONIE HARRIS
Vocal accompaniment: unknown

Location: unknown {USA}. 1943

Titles performed:
unknown

Source: *Hit Parade Of 1943*

Vocal accompaniment: the Lionel Hampton orchestra

Location: unknown {USA}. c.1957

Title performed:
'Hey Poppa Rock' [fragment only]

Source: *Mister Rock And Roll*

HARVEY (Harvey Fuqua)
Vocal accompaniment: unknown group

Location: unknown {USA}. 1958

Title performed:
'Don't Be Afraid To Love'

Source: *Go Johnny Go*
See also Moonglows.

JALACY [SCREAMING JAY] HAWKINS
miming to Decca 32100

Location: ATV studios, London, England. Saturday 6 March 1965

Title performed:
'I Put A Spell On You'

Source: *Thank Your Lucky Stars*

Vocal accompaniment: unknown

Location: Manchester, England. c. March 1965

Titles performed:
unknown

Source: *UK Granada TV broadcast* [M]; programme title unknown.

Vocal accompaniment: unknown

Location: London, England. c. March 1965

Title performed:
unknown

Source: *Gadzooks! It's All Happening*

Vocal accompaniment: unknown

Location: unknown {USA}. 1967

Titles performed:
unknown

Source: *The Bruce Morrow Show* [unconfirmed]

Vocal accompaniment: unknown

Location: unknown {USA}. 1974

Titles performed:
unknown

Source: *The Joe Franklin Show* [unconfirmed]

Vocal accompaniment: unknown

Location: probably Los Angeles, California. 1978

Title performed:
'I Put A Spell On You'

Source: *American Hot Wax*
Despite claims to the contrary, there is no evidence of Hawkins in any inspected print of the 1957 film *Mister Rock And Roll*. Hawkins had dramatic cameo roles in the films *Mystery Train* and *A Rage In Harlem*.

HENRY HAYES
Vocal and tenor saxophone accompaniment: The Texas Houserockers [G]

Location: Houston, Texas. Friday [*sic*] 8 October 1993

Titles performed:
'Hometown Blues'
'Grinding Motion'

Source: *Saturday Night At Rockefellers*

NATHAN HAYES SEPTET
Vocal septet, accompaniment: unknown (piano)

Location: Mississippi. 1984

Title performed:
'When He Calls Me'

Source: *Saturday Blues*

GOLDIA HAYNES
Vocal accompaniment: the Mount Carmel Baptist Church Choir–1
Vocal accompaniment: the Selah Jubilee Singers–2
Vocal accompaniment: unknown (piano)–3
Vocal accompaniment: the Harmonizing Four–4

Location: Charlotte, North Carolina. Saturday 1 August 1964

Titles performed:
'This Train'–1 [A]
'Can't You Love Him?'–2 [A]
'Fire'–3 [A]
'This Old World'–3 [B]
'Beams Of Heaven'–4 [B]

Source: *TV Gospel Time* #30 [A], 31 [B]

HEAVENLY STARS
Vocal group accompaniment: unknown

Location: New Orleans, Lousiana. 1985

Title performed:
'We Need Jesus'

Source: *New Orleans Now: In The Revival Tent*

JESSE MAE HEMPHILL
Vocal and electric guitar–1
Vocal, electric guitar and foot-operated tambourine–2

Location: Senatobia, Mississippi [A]
Clarksdale, Mississippi [B]. 1984

Titles performed:
'You Can Go Back To Your Used To Be' [A]–1 Arrow AV015
'Daddy's Blues' [A]–1 Arrow AV015
'Married Man Blues' [A]–1 Arrow AV015
untitled blues [B]–2 Arrow AV015

Source: *Saturday Blues*

Vocal, electric guitar and foot-operated tambourine

Location: Atlanta, Georgia. October 1984

Title performed:
'Train, Train'

Source: *National Downhome Blues Festival*

Vocal and electric guitar–1; bass drum accompanying: Napoleon Strickland (fife) and Abe Young (snare drum)–2

Location: Holly Springs, Mississippi. Autumn 1990
[A] filmed in juke joint
[B] filmed on outdoor location

Titles performed:
'You Can Talk About Me'–1 [A] Anxious 45099-29643, BMG un-numbered
'Bouncing Ball'–2 [B] Anxious 45099-29643, BMG un-numbered
[interview] Anxious 45099-29643, BMG un-numbered

Source: *Deep Blues*
'Bouncing Ball' is performed by Jessie Mae's Fife And Drum Band [*sic*]. See also Napoleon Strickland, Othar Turner and Ed and Lonnie Young.

CLARENCE [FROGMAN] HENRY
Vocal accompaniment: unknown (tenor saxophone, piano, drums)

Location: New Orleans, Louisiana. Spring 1963

Title performed:
'Staggerlee' [fragment only]

Source: *Dietrich Wawzyn film collection*

Vocal accompaniment: The Blue Beats; Clarence 'Gatemouth' Brown and Johnnie Johnson (electric guitars); Dave 'Fathead' Newman and one unknown (trumpets); Harrison Calloway and one unknown (tenor saxophones); 'Skip' [possibly Skippy Brooks] (piano); Finis Tasby (electric bass); Freeman Brown (drums)–1
Vocal and piano, accompaniment as above but without 'Skip'–2

Location: WFAA-TV studios, Dallas, Texas. c. summer 1966

Titles performed:
'Ain't Got No Home'–1
'But I Do'–2
'Baby Ain't That Love'–1

Source: *The Beat*

Vocal accompaniment: Charles Hodges (piano); Dave Peacock (electric bass); Mick Burt (drums)

Location: London, England. 1985

Titles performed:
'But I Do'
'Blueberry Hill'
'That Old Piano'
'Ain't Got No Home'
'Your Loving's Good Enough For Me'
'Hands Off'
'What'd I Say'

Source: *UK TV broadcast* [C]. Origin unknown. Hodges and Peacock are known professionally as Chas & Dave.

Vocal accompaniment: unknown

Location: Toulouse Theatre, New Orleans, Louisiana. 1988

Titles performed:'
'Ain't Got No Home
'Little Green Frog'
'Think It Over'

Source: *Big Easy Music*

Vocal accompaniment: unknown

Location: New Orleans, Louisiana. 1990

Titles performed:
'Basin Street Blues'
'Second Line'

Source: *New Orleans Jazz And Heritage Festival 1990*

HERALDS OF CHRIST
Vocal group accompaniment: unknown

Location: New Orleans, Louisiana. 1985

Title performed:
'Answer Me Lord'

Source: *New Orleans Now: In The Revival Tent*

JAMES HERNDON SINGERS
Mixed vocal group, accompaniment: unknown

Location: Chicago, Illinois

The following appearances are known:
1964
Sunday 26 January [prog #7–3]
1966
Sunday 23 January [prog #6–2]
1967
Sunday 5 March [prog #17–1]
1969
Saturday 11 January [prog #8–3]
Saturday 8 February [prog #31–3]
Saturday 14 June [prog #15–1]
Saturday 5 July [prog #12–2]
1972
Saturday 12 August [prog #4–3]
1973
Sunday 24 November [prog #32–1]
1975
Sunday 13 April [prog #19–2]

Titles performed:
unknown

Source: *Jubilee Showcase*

HIGHWAY Q C's
Probably Ray Crume, Chris Flowers, Spencer Taylor, James Davis, Arthur Crume, James Walker (vocals) accompaniment: probably Arthur Crume (electric guitar)

Location: Memphis, Tennessee. Saturday 19 January 1963

Titles performed:
'I Heard'
'Do You Love Him?'
'I'll Be Satisfied'

Source: *TV Gospel Time* #19

Probably as above

Location: Baltimore, Maryland. Saturday 16 February 1963

Titles performed:
'Nobody Knows'
'All Men Are Made By God'
'A Man Called Jesus'

Source: *TV Gospel Time* #26

Probably as above

Location: Chicago, Illinois. Sunday 14 June 1964

Titles performed:
unknown

Source: *Jubilee Showcase* [prog # unknown]

MABLE HILLERY
Vocal accompaniment: unknown

Location: unknown {USA}. 1961

Titles performed:
unknown

Source: *Alan Lomax Folk Special* [unconfirmed]

Vocal accompaniment: Sunnyland Slim (piano); Brownie McGhee (guitar); Willie Dixon (bass); S P Leary (drums)–1
Vocal accompaniment: the Muddy Waters Blues Band with James Cotton, Willie Dixon, Jesse Fuller, Brownie McGhee, Muddy Waters, Otis Spann, Sunnyland Slim, Sonny Terry, Bukka White and Big Joe Williams (vocals)–2

Location: Toronto, Canada. Thursday 27 to Saturday 29 January 1966

Titles performed:
'How Long Has The Train Been Gone'–1
jam session–2

Source: *Festival Presents The Blues*

Location: Newport, Rhode Island. July 1966

Mable Hillery can be seen dancing during performances by Bukka White. See Vestapol 13049.

ROBERT HILLS
Vocal accompaniment: unknown

Location: New York City. Sunday 2 December 1962

Title performed:
'Nobody Knows The Trouble I've Seen'

Source: *TV Gospel Time* #4

ROSE HINES
Vocal accompaniment: unknown

Location: New York City. Sunday 4 November 1962

Title performed:
'Nobody Knows The Trouble I've Seen'

Source: *TV Gospel Time* #8

ROBERT HODGE
Vocal accompaniment: The Spiritual Ensemble (mixed vocal choir)

Location: Chicago, Illinois. Sunday 2 August 1964

Titles performed:
unknown

Source: *Jubilee Showcase* [prog #26–2]

TOMMY HODGE
Vocal accompaniment: Ike Turner's Kings of Rhythm; Ike Turner (electric guitar): Carlson Oliver (tenor saxophone): Erskine Ogelsby (baritone saxophone): Jesse Knight (electric bass): John 'Bootylip' Wings (drums)

Location: St. Louis, Missouri. 1958

Titles performed:
'I Know You Don't Love Me No More'
'Cha Cha Cha'

Source: *George Edick's Showtime*
See also Jimmy Thomas and Ike Turner.

SILAS HOGAN
Vocal and electric guitar accompaniment: Arthur [Guitar] Kelly (electric guitar)

Location: the Hogan residence, Baton Rouge, Louisiana. 1984

Titles performed:
'Hoodoo Man'
'Rats And Roaches' ('Rats In My Kitchen')
[interview]

Source: *Baton Rouge Blues*
See also Arthur [Guitar] Kelly.

JOHN DEE HOLEMAN
Unaccompanied dance steps

Location: rural North Carolina. 1983–85

[demonstration of buck dancing and shuffle rhythms] Vestapol 13079

Source: *Appalachian Journey*

Vocal and guitar

Location: North Carolina. 1988

Title performed:
'Step It Up And Go' [ST]

Source: *Step it Up And Go*
See also John Jackson.

HOLY GHOST CHURCH CHOIR
Vocals, unaccompanied

Location: Louisiana. 1991

Titles performed:

'Glory, Glory, Hallelujah'	Channel 5 083 258-3, Island 083 258-3
'He Lives'	Channel 5 083 258-3, Island 083 258–3

Source: *Zydeco Nite'N'Day*

HOMESICK JAMES (James Williamson)
Vocal and electric guitar accompaniment: probably Snooky Pryor (harmonica); Boogie Woogie Red (piano); Roger Hill (electric bass); Tom Parnell (drums)

Location: Brighton Polytechnic, Sussex, England. Friday 16 February 1973

Titles performed:
unknown

Source: *Blues Legends 73*

Vocal and electric guitar accompaniment: unknown

Location: Chicago, Illinois. c.1978

Title performed:
'The Woman I Love'

Source: *Chicago Melodie*

Speech

Location: Atlanta, Georgia. 1984

[interview]

Source: *National Downhome Blues Festival*
See also Snooky Pryor.

EARL HOOKER
This artist is reported to have appeared on *Ready Steady Go* in 1965, but current research fails to confirm this claim.

JOHN LEE HOOKER
Vocal and guitar

Location: New York City. 1960

Titles performed:

'Maudie'	Vestapol 13035
'Tupelo, Mississippi'	Vestapol 13035

Source: *Dona Marins* [M]

Vocal and guitar accompaniment: Otis Spann (piano); Pat Hare (electric guitar); Andrew Stephens (electric bass); Francis Clay (drums)

Location: Newport, Rhode Island. Sunday 3 July 1960

Titles performed:

'It's My Own Fault'	Vestapol 13035
'Come Back Baby'	Vestapol 13035

Source: *Jazz-USA*

Vocal and electric guitar or guitar accompaniment: probably Memphis Slim (piano); Willie Dixon (bass); Clifton James (drums)

Location: Baden-Baden, Germany. c. October 1962

Titles performed:
unknown

Source: *American Folk Blues Festival 1962*

Vocal and electric guitar accompaniment: unknown

Location: unknown {USA}. 1963

Titles performed:
unknown

Source: *Lyrics And Legends – Singing Styles*

Vocal and guitar, miming to Vee-Jay 205

Location: ATV studios, London, England. Saturday 4 July 1964

Title performed:
'Dimples'

Source: *Thank Your Lucky Stars*

As above

Location: London, England. July–August 1964

Title performed:
'Dimples'

Source: *Top Of The Pops*
Hooker can be seen removing his guitar from his shoulder and walking off the set as the record begins to fade.

As above

Location: ATV studios, London, England. Friday 2 October 1964

Title performed:
'Dimples'

Source: *Ready Steady Go*

Vocal and electric guitar accompaniment: unknown (electric guitar, piano, electric bass, drums)

Location: London, England. Saturday 10 October 1964

Titles performed:

'Boom Boom'	Vestapol 13035
'I'm Leavin''	Vestapol 13035

Source: *Beat Room*

Vocal and guitar

Location: London, England. May 1965

Titles performed:
'Out Of The Fold'
'Nothin' But Rainbow Gold'
'Twenty Long Years'
'Do I Dare To Fight?'
'One Summer's Day'
'The Winter Wind Is Blowing'
'I Went Upstairs'
'Looking At My Books'
'A Tempest In My Mind'
'Lord, I'm Mad'
'Measured Out My Life'
'Looked Into My Mirror'
'One Day I Went Walking'
'Lorelei (Like A Siren In The Sea)'
'Tombstones And Dry Bones'
'Endless Ebb And Flow'

Source: *Ebb*

Vocal and electric guitar

Location: Baden-Baden, Germany. October 1965

Title performed:
[introduction by Roosevelt Sykes;]
'Hobo Blues'
[short monologue]

Source: *American Folk Blues Festival 1965*

Vocal and electric guitar accompaniment: unknown

Location: unknown {USA}. 1965

Titles performed:
unknown

Source: *Kaleidoscope 4* [unconfirmed]

Vocal and electric guitar–1
Vocal and electric guitar accompaniment: Eddie Taylor (second electric guitar); T-Bone Walker (piano); Jerome Arnold (electric bass); J C Lewis (drums)–2

Location: BBC-TV studios, White City, London, England. Tuesday 22 October 1968

Titles performed
'It Serve Me Right To Suffer'–1
'Maudie'–2
'Boom Boom'–2

Source: *American Folk Blues Festival 1968* [1]

Probably as above

Location: Germany. November 1968

Titles performed:
unknown

Source: *American Folk Blues Festival 1968* [2]

Vocal and electric guitar accompaniment:
Robert Hooker (electric organ); unknown
(electric bass and drums)

Location: Detroit, Michigan. 1969

Titles performed:
'Never Get Out Of These Blues Alive'
'Maudie'
'Serves Me Right To Suffer'
'Boom Boom'
'Hobo Blues' Vestapol 13035

Source: *David Peck* [M]

Vocal and electric guitar accompaniment:
unknown

Location: New York City. 1969

Titles performed:
unknown

Source: *The Dick Cavett Show*

Vocal and electric guitar

Location: KCTS-TV studios, Seattle,
Washington. February 1970

Titles performed:
[monologue leading to;]
'I'll Never Get Out Of These Blues Alive'
Vestapol 13038,
Yazoo 519
[monologue leading to;]
'Boom Boom' Yazoo 519
[monologue leading to;]
'It Serves Me Right To Suffer' Vestapol 13038,
Yazoo 519

Source: *Masters Of American Traditional Music*

Vocal and electric guitar

Location: KCTS-TV studios, Seattle,
Washington. February 1970

Titles performed:
I'll Never Get Out Of These Blues Alive
It Serves Me Right To Suffer Vestapol 13035
Boom Boom Vestapol 13035

Source: *Roots Of American Music Part 1*

Vocal and electric guitar accompaniment:
unknown

Location: unknown, probably Los Angeles,
California. 1972

Titles performed:
unknown [ST only]

Source: *Mr. Brown*

Vocal and electric guitar accompaniment:
unknown

Location: unknown {USA}. 1972

Titles performed:
unknown

Source: *L'Aventure Du Jazz*

Vocal and electric guitar accompaniment:
unknown

Location: unknown {USA}. 1974

Titles performed:
unknown

Source: *Midnight Special, The*

Vocal and electric guitar accompaniment:
unknown

Location: unknown {USA}. 1974

Titles performed:
unknown

Source: *Gettin' Back*

Vocal and electric guitar accompaniment: Eddie
Kirkland (electric guitar) and others, unknown

Location: unknown {USA}. 1978

Titles performed:
unknown

Source: *Don Kirshner's Rock Concert*

Vocal and electric guitar accompaniment: unknown (second electric guitar, electric organ, electric bass, drums)

Location: Ames, Iowa. 1979

Titles performed:
'You're Lookin' Good Again Tonight' Vestapol 13035
'So Cold in Chicago' Vestapol 13035
and other, unknown, title[s]

Source: *Maintenance Shop Blues*

Vocal and electric guitar accompaniment: Walter Horton (harmonica); Pinetop Perkins (piano); Luther 'Guitar Jr' Johnson (electric guitar); Calvin 'Fuzz' Jones (electric bass); Willie 'Big Eyes' Smith (drums)

Location: Chicago, Illinois. 1980

Title performed:
'Boom Boom' [part only]

Source: *The Blues Brothers*

Vocal and electric guitar accompaniment: unknown

Location: Montreux, Switzerland. July 1981

Titles performed:
'One Scotch, One Bourbon, One Beer'
'I'll Never Get Out Of These Blues Alive'
'Boom Boom'
'Rock Me Baby'
'I'm In The Mood'
'Look What You Done'
'Rockin' The Boogie'

Source: *Montreux Jazz*

Vocal and electric guitar accompaniment: Mark Naftalin (piano); Charlie Musselwhite (harmonica); Luther Tucker (electric guitar); Henry Owen (electric bass); Francis Clay (drums)

Location: Sleeping Lady Cafe, Fairfax, California. 1981

Titles performed:
'So Cold In Chicago' K-Jazz 100, Rhapsody un-numbered
'Worried Life Blues' K-Jazz 100, Rhapsody un-numbered
'Voodoo Woman' K-Jazz 100, Rhapsody un-numbered

Source: *Mark Naftalin's Blue Monday Party*

Vocal and electric guitar accompaniment: unknown

Location: France. 1982

Title performed:
'Boogie On'

Source: *French TV broadcast* [C]

Vocal and electric guitar accompaniment: Melvin Jones (keyboards); Mike Osborn (electric guitar); Steve Ehrmann (electric bass); Timothy Richards (drums)

Location: Montreux, Switzerland. Friday 15 July 1983

Titles performed:
'Serve You Right To Suffer'
'I Didn't Know'
'Hi Heel Sneakers'
'Take Care Of You'
'Boom Boom'
'Worried Life Blues'

Source: *Montreux Jazz*

Vocal and electric guitar accompaniment: the Mark Naftalin band

Location: Wilibeski's Blues Salon, St. Paul, Minnesota. Thursday 15 March 1984

Title performed:
'Little Girl'

Source: *Survivors; The Blues Today*

Vocal accompaniment: unknown (second electric guitar, electric organ, electric bass, drums)

Location: Tampa, Florida. 1984

Title performed:
'One Bourbon, One Scotch, One Beer' Vestapol 13035
[short interview] Vestapol 13035

Source: *WEDU-TV, Tampa, Florida*

Vocal and electric guitar accompaniment: Mike Osborn (electric guitar); Deacon Jones (electric organ); Sue Stephens (piano); Larry Hamilton (electric bass); Tim Richards (drums)

Location: unknown {USA}. 1984

Titles performed:
'Baby Lee' Vestapol 13054
'When My First Wife Left Me' Vestapol 13054
'Maudie' Vestapol 13054

Source: *uncredited* [C]

Vocal accompaniment: Sonny Terry (harmonica); Bobby Scott (piano); Roy Gaines (electric guitar); Paul Jackson Jr (guitar)

Location: Los Angeles, California. 1985

Title performed:
'Don't Make Me No Never Mind' [ST only]

Source: *The Color Purple*

Vocal and electric guitar accompaniment: unknown

Location: San Diego, California. 1987

Titles performed:
unknown

Source: *Three Generations Of The Blues Part 2*

Vocal and electric guitar accompaniment: unknown

Location: Belly Up tavern, Salona Beach, California. 1988

Titles performed:
'Boom Boom'
'Crawlin' Kingsnake'
'Bad Like Jesse James'
'One Scotch, One Bourbon, One Beer'
[interview]

Source: *Rhythms Of The World*

Vocal and electric guitar

Location: unknown {USA}. c.1990

Title performed:
untitled instrumental

Source: *ICI advert*

Vocal and electric guitar accompaniment: probably the Paul Shaffer band

Location: New York City. 1991

Title performed:
'Boom Boom'
[interview]

Source: *Late Night With David Letterman*

Vocal and guitar accompaniment: Van Morrison (harmonica)

Location: rural Louisiana. 1991

Titles performed:
'Baby Please Don't Go'
'Wednesday Evening Blues'
'Don't Look Back'
[conversation between Hooker and Morrison]
'I Didn't Know' [originally unbroadcast]

Source: *Van Morrison – Arena Special*
The title 'I Didn't Know' was used in the UK South Bank TV special entitled *John Lee Hooker*

Vocal and electric guitar accompaniment: Keith Richards and Eric Clapton (electric guitars); Bill Wyman (electric bass); Charlie Watts (drums)

Location: unknown. 1991

Title performed:
'Boogie Chillun'

Source: *unknown*; used in *John Lee Hooker*

Vocal and guitar accompaniment: Ry Cooder (guitar)

Location: unknown {USA}. 1991

Titles performed:
'Same Old Blues' Vestapol 13054
'Just Like Jesse James' Vestapol 13054

Source: *unknown*

Vocal and electric guitar accompaniment: unknown band

Location: unknown. 1992

Title performed:
untitled blues

Source: *Levi jeans advert*

Vocal and electric guitar in duet with John Hammond (guitar)–1; Ry Cooder (guitar)–2; Bonnie Rait (guitar)–3; Robert Cray (guitar)–4; Charlie Mussewhite (harmonica) and Albert Collins (guitar)–5; all of the above–6, accompaniment: Roy Rogers (electric guitar)–7; Jim Pugh (piano)–8; Johnnie Johnson (piano)–9; Jim Cuvett (electric bass)–10; Bowen Brown (drums)–11

Location: unknown {USA}. 1992

Titles performed:
'Father Was A Jockey'–1 Vestapol 13054
'Crawlin' Kingsnake'–2 Vestapol 13054
'I'm In The Mood'–3, –7, –10, –11 Vestapol 13054
'Born For Good Luck'–4
'Mister Lucky'–4, –7, –8, –10, –11 Vestapol 13054
'The Boogie'–5, –6, –7, –9, –10, –11 Vestapol 13054

Source: *US TV broadcast* [C]. Origin unknown.

Vocal and electric guitar accompaniment: Carlos Santana (electric guitar) and pre-recorded backing track

Location: unknown {USA}. 1993

Title performed:
'The Healer'

Source: *promotional video*[C]

Vocal and guitar

Location: probably San Francisco, California. 1993

Titles performed:
'That's My Story'
'Tupelo'
'Decoration Day'
[interview]

Source: *John Lee Hooker*
See also Castle Hendring videos in the Commercially Available Videos list. This material is currently unidentified but may be detailed above.

LINDA HOPKINS

Vocal accompaniment: unknown

Location: unknown {USA}. 1956

Titles performed:
'I Can't Keep From Crying'
'They Raided The Joint'

Source: *Rockin' The Blues*

Vocal accompaniment: unknown

Location: unknown {USA}. 1982

Title performed:
'When The Blues Comes Around'

Source: *Honky Tonk Man*

Vocal accompaniment: the Gerald Wiggins orchestra–1
Vocal duet with BB King, accompaniment as above–2

Location: unknown {USA}. 1982

Titles performed:
'St. Louis Blues'–1 Magnum MMGV-035
'Unlucky Woman'–1 Magnum MMGV-035
'Everyday I Have The Blues'–2 Magnum MMGV-035

Source: *America's Music – Blues Volume 1*

Vocal accompaniment: Billy Mitchell (piano); Jimmy Woods (bass); Jimmy Smith (drums)

Location: Bern, Switzerland. Saturday 5 May 1984

Titles performed:
'Gimme A Pigfoot'
'Ain't Nobody's Business'
'You Are Nobody'
'A Good Man Is Hard To Find'
'Route Sixty-six'
'Drown In My Own Tears'
'Signed, Sealed And Delivered'
'Stormy Monday Blues'
'Amazing Grace'
'Shake A Hand'
[interview]

Source: *Jazz-In*

Vocal accompaniment: the Johnny Otis band–1
Vocal accompaniment: Delmar Evans, Barbara Morrison, Charles Williams (vocals), the Johnny Otis band–2

Location: Monterey, California. 1987

Titles performed:
'Stormy Monday'–1
'My Meat Man'–1
'Amen'–1
Gospel medley–2

Source: *Monterey Jazz Festival*
See also Riley [BB] King.

SAM [LIGHTNIN'] HOPKINS

Vocal and guitar

Location: probably New York City. c. July 1960

Titles performed:
unknown

Source: *Patterns Of Words And Music* [unconfirmed]

Vocal and guitar–1; electric guitar solo–2

Location: Houston, Texas. Spring 1963
[A] On a sidewalk
[B] In a juke joint

Titles performed:
'Lonesome Road' [A]–1 [part only] Vestapol 13022, Yazoo 520
'Lightnin's Blues' [B]–2 [part only] Vestapol 13022, Yazoo 520

Source: *Die Blues*

Vocal and electric guitar accompaniment: Willie Dixon (bass); Clifton James (drums)

Location: Baden-Baden, Germany. October 1964

Title performed:
[introduction by John Henry Barbee;]
'Mojo Hand'

Source: *American Folk Blues Festival 1964*

Vocal and guitar

Location: Free Trade Hall, Manchester, England. Thursday, 22 October 1964

Titles performed:
unknown

Source: *The Blues Came Walking*

Vocal and guitar–1
Vocal and guitar accompaniment: Ruth Ames (vocal)–2
Vocal and guitar accompaniment: Billy Bizor (harmonica)–3
Vocal and electric guitar accompaniment: Cleveland Chenier (rub–board)–4
Vocal and piano–5

Location: Houston and Centerville, Texas. 1967

Titles performed:
'I'm Walkin''–2 Flower 1, K-Jazz 053
'Good Morning Little Schoolgirl' [ST]–1 Flower 1, K-Jazz 053
'Gettin' Up In The Morning'–1 Flower 1,

K-Jazz 053
'Meet Me In The Bottom' [ST]–1 Flower 1, K-Jazz 053
untitled instrumental blues [Rodeo Music]–3 Flower 1, K-Jazz 053
'Hi-Heel Sneakers'–4 Flower 1, K-Jazz 053
'Jesus Won't You Come By Here?'–5 Flower 1, K-Jazz 053
'When Was I Sick?' [fragment]–1 Flower 1, K-Jazz 053
'How Long Has It Been Since You Been Home?'–1 Flower 1, K-Jazz 053
'She Stays Out All Night Long'–1 Flower 1, K-Jazz 053
'Bring It Home To You'–1 [ST] Flower 1, K-Jazz 053
'Woman Named Mary'–1 [ST] Flower 1, K-Jazz 053
'Trouble In Mind'–1 [ST]** K-Jazz 053
'Train Blues' [ST]** K-Jazz 053

Source: *The Blues According to Lightnin' Hopkins* and *The Sun's Gonna Shine* (**). All these titles are shown in extract only.

Vocal and guitar

Location: KCT-TV studios, Seattle, Washington. 1967

Titles performed:
'Baby Please Don't Go' Vestapol 13022
'Mojo Hand' Vestapol 13022
'Take Me Back' Vestapol 13022
[monologue leading to;]
'Hurricane Beulah Yazoo 502, Vestapol 13022
'Baby Scratch My Back' Yazoo 502, Vestapol 13022
'Come and Go With Me' Yazoo 502

Source: *Masters Of American Traditional Music*. The songs issued on Vestapol have been remastered in monochrome. There may be further titles from this session.

Vocal and guitar

Location: KCT-TV Studios, Seattle, Washington. 1967

Titles performed:
'Baby Please Don't Go Yazoo 502
'Mojo Hand' Yazoo 502
'Take Me Back' Yazoo 502

Source: *Seattle Folklore Society*

Vocal and guitar–1
Vocal and electric guitar accompaninent: unknown (washboard)–2
Vocal and guitar accompaniment: Cleveland Chenier (rub-board)–3

Location: Texas [various unnamed locations]. c.1969–70

Titles performed:
'I Fell In Love'–1 Yazoo 513
'Short Haired Woman'–2 Yazoo 513
'Walking Down 75 Highway'–3 Yazoo 513
'How Long Have It Been Since You Been Home?'–3 Yazoo 513
'Short Haired Woman'–1 Yazoo 513
'My Daddy Was A Preacher'–1 Yazoo 513
'Got A Letter This Morning'–1 Yazoo 513
'Mister Charlie'–1 Yazoo 513
'Mojo Hand'–1 Yazoo 513
'Slavery Time Blues'–1 Yazoo 513
untitled instrumental boogie–3 Yazoo 513
[interviews] Yazoo 513

Source: *untitled University of Houston system production for KUHT-TV, Houston* [D] [C]. Directed by Charles Peavey. All these titles are shown in extract only.

Vocal and guitar

Location: unknown {USA}. c.1970–71

Titles performed:
'Baby, Come And Go Home With Me' Vestapol 13041
'Goin' Down Slow' Vestapol 13041
'Bunion Stew' Vestapol 13041
'Let's Pull A Party' Vestapol 13041

Source: *A Programme Of Songs By Lightnin' Hopkins*

Vocal and guitar

Location: KCET-TV studios, Los Angeles, California. Tuesday 24 November 1970

Titles performed:

'Couldn't Be Satisfied'	Vestapol 13022
'Questionnaire Blues'	Vestapol 13022
'Ain't It Crazy'	Vestapol 13022
'Shining Moon'	Vestapol 13022
'Black And Evil'	Vestapol 13022
'Lightnin's Boogie'	Vestapol 13022
'What'd I Say'	Vestapol 13022
'How Long Has It Been Since You Been Home?'	Vestapol 13022

Source: *Boboquivari*

Vocal and electric guitar accompaniment: Ron Wilson (electric bass); Bill Gossit (drums)

Location: KLRU-TV studios, Austin, Texas. 1979

Titles performed:

'Mojo Hand'	Vestapol 13022
'Ain't No Cadillac'	Vestapol 13022
'Black And Evil'	Vestapol 13022
'Rock Me Baby'	Vestapol 13022

Source: *Austin City Limits*

Vocal and electric guitar accompaniment: William Powell (electric bass); George Green (drums)

Location: Den Haag, Netherlands. 1980

Titles performed:
'Trouble In Mind'
'Hard To Love a Woman'
untitled instrumental
'Lightnin's Suprise'
'Good Morning'

Source: *Dutch TV broadcast* [C]

JOHN [SHADRACK] HORACE

Vocal accompaniment: Johnny Moore's Three Blazers (piano, guitar, bass)

Location: Hollywood, California. 1945

Titles performed:
[21708] 'Along The Navajo Trail'
[87908] 'It's Me, Oh Lord!'

Source: *Soundies*
21708 copyrighted 15 October 1945; 87908 20 October 1945

LENA HORNE

See Albert Ammons.

[BIG] WALTER HORTON

Harmonica accompaniment: Eddie Boyd (piano); Buddy Guy (electric guitar); Jimmy Lee Robinson (electric bass); Fred Below (drums)

Location: Baden-Baden, Germany. October 1965

Title performed:
[introduction by J B Lenoir;]
'Walter's Boogie'

Source: *American Folk Blues Festival 1965*

Vocal and harmonica accompaniment: Eddie Taylor (electric guitar); T-Bone Walker (piano); Jerome Arnold (electric bass); J C Lewis (drums)

Location: BBC-TV studios, White City, London, England. Tuesday 22 October 1968

Title performed:
unknown instrumental

Source: *American Folk Blues Festival 1968* [1]

Probably as above

Location: Germany. November 1968

Titles performed:
unknown

Source: *American Folk Blues Festival 1968* [2]

Vocal and harmonica or harmonica only accompaniment: probably Lee Jackson (electric guitar); Lafayette Leake (piano); Willie Dixon (bass); Clifton James (drums)

Location: Baden-Baden Germany. c. May 1970

Titles performed:
'Walter's Shuffle'
'Chicago Boogie'

Source: *American Folk Blues Festival 1970*

Vocal and harmonica accompaniment: unknown

Location: Chicago, Illinois. 1981

Titles performed:
unknown

Source: *Chicago Blues Festival 1981* [C] [1]
See also John Lee Hooker and Johnny Shines.

EDDIE JAMES [SON] HOUSE

Vocal and steel guitar

Location: Newport, Rhode Island. July 1965

Title performed:
'Did You Ever Love A Woman' [fragment only]
[monologue]

Source: *Festival* [1]

Vocal and steel guitar–1
As above, in the company of Skip James, (vocal and guitar); Bukka White (vocal and steel guitar)–2

Location: Newport, Rhode Island. July 1966

Titles performed:
[monologue] Vestapol 13049
'You Forever On My Mind'–1 Vestapol 13049
[monologue] entitled 'Talk On The Blues' Vestapol 13050
'Did You Ever Love A Woman' Vestapol 13050
participation in 'Blues Contest';
[untitled blues]–2 Vestapol 13050

Source: *Alan Lomax film collection*
The untitled blues listed above is a random selection of standard blues verses, and cannot be said to be one specific song. Similarly, 'Did You Ever Love A Woman' also contains many verses from other songs. See also Howlin' Wolf and Bukka White.

Vocal and steel guitar–1 : vocal, unaccompanied–2

Location: KCTS-TV studios, Seattle, Washington. March 1968

Titles performed:
[monologue] leading to;
'Death Letter Blues'–1 Vestapol 13002, Yazoo 500
[monologue] leading to;
'John The Revelator'–2 Yazoo 500
[monologue] leading to;
'Preachin' The Blues'–1 Yazoo 500
[monologue] leading to;
'I Want To Live So God Can Use Me'–2 Yazoo 500
'Empire State Express'–1 Vestapol 13038
'Levee Camp Moan'–1 Rhino R3 2101, Vestapol 13038

Source: *Masters Of American Traditional Music*

Vocal and steel guitar

Location: KCTS-TV studios, Seattle, Washington. March 1968

Title performed:
'Death Letter Blues'

Source: *Roots Of American Music Part 1*

Vocal and steel guitar–1
Vocal and steel guitar accompaniment Jerry Ricks (guitar)–2
Vocal and steel guitar accompaniment: Buddy Guy (guitar)–3

Location: New York City. 1968

Titles performed:
'Government Fleet Blues [part only]–1
'Death Letter Blues'–2 Vestapol 13003
[monologue]
'Levee Camp Moan'–2 Vestapol 13002
[monologue]
'Lowdown Dirty Blues' [with closing credits running over]–3

Source: *Camera Three*
Vestapol claims the date for the above session as 1965, Sheldon Harris in *Blues Who's Who* cites 1968. Based upon Buddy Guy's hairstyle and clothes, 1968 seems more likely.

Speech–1; vocal and steel guitar–2

Location: London, England. 1970

Titles performed:
'Talk About The Blues'–1 Vestapol 13038
'I Had The Blues This Morning'–2 Vestapol 13038

Source: *Filmed privately by Pat Gavin* [C]

Vocal and steel guitar

Location: BBC-TV studios, London, England. July 1970

Titles performed:
'I Had a Woman In Hughes' Vestapol 13003
'Yonder Comes The Blues' Vestapol 13016
'Grinning In Your Face' Vestapol 13038

Source: *Late Night Line Up*

BOB HOWARD
Vocal and piano

Location: probably New York City. 1944

Title performed:
[16708] 'Hey Tojo, Count Yo' Men'

Source: *Soundie.*
Copyrighted 29 May 1944. This title was previously assigned to Louis Jordan, but that information was erroneous.

ROSETTA HOWARD
Vocal accompaniment: unknown

Location: Chicago, Illinois. Late 1940s

Titles performed:
unknown

Source: *I Come For To Sing* [unconfirmed]

HOWLIN' WOLF (Chester Arthur Burnett)
Vocal and guitar accompaniment: Sunnyland Slim (piano); Hubert Sumlin (electric guitar); Willie Dixon (bass); Clifton James (drums)

Location: Baden-Baden, Germany. October 1964

Titles performed:
[introduction by Mae Mercer;]
'Shake For Me'
'I'm Leaving'
'May I Have A Talk With You'
untitled instrumental (played over closing credits)

Source: *American Folk Blues Festival 1964*

Probably as above

Location: Free Trade Hall, Manchester, England. Thursday 22 October 1964

Title performed:
'Smokestack Lightnin''

Source: *The Blues Came Walking*

Vocal and harmonica accompaniment: Hubert Sumlin (electric guitar) and others, unknown

Location: London, England. Monday 30 November 1964

Titles performed:
unknown

Source: *Beat Room*

Speech

Location: London, England. Saturday 12 December 1964

Live guest appearance

Source: *Juke Box Jury* ·
Howlin' Wolf appeared on this programme as a mystery guest. A portion of his recording of 'Love Me Darling' (UK Pye 25283) was played, and the panel, Lonnie Donegan, Shirley Eaton, Jimmy Edwards and Polly Elwes, were asked to comment and vote it either a hit or a miss; they voted it a miss. Howlin' Wolf then appeared from behind the scenes, was introduced, one by one, to the panel and briefly interviewed by the host, David Jacobs.

Vocal and harmonica accompaniment: unknown: (electric guitar, electric bass and drums)

Location: Los Angeles, California. 1965

Title performed:
[introduction by Brian Jones and Mick Jagger]
'How Many More Years'

Source: *Shindig*

Vocal and electric guitar–1, vocal and harmonica–2 accompaniment: Hubert Sumlin (electric guitar); Eddie Shaw (tenor saxophone); unknown (electric bass and drums)

Location: Newport, Rhode Island. July 1966

Titles performed:
[conversation with Son House] Vestapol 13049
'Meet Me In The Bottom' take 1–1 Vestapol 13049
'How Many More Years'–2 Vestapol 13049
'Dust My Broom'–1 Vestapol 13049
'Meet Me In The Bottom' take 2–1 Vestapol 13049
[conversation with Pearly Brown] Vestapol 13049

Source: *Alan Lomax film collection*
Howlin' Wolf can also be seen in the background during performances by Kilby Snow and Jimmy Driftwood recorded on the same day as the above. See Vestapol 13051.
See also Pearly Brown.

Vocal accompaniment: as above

Location: Newport, Rhode Island. July 1966

Title performed:
unknown [probably 'Howling For My Darling']

Source: *Festival* [1]
This clip appears using the Chess recording of 'Howling For My Darling' (Chess 1762) dubbed onto the soundtrack.

Vocal accompaniment: unknown

Location: probably Chicago. c. 1968

Titles performed:
unknown

Source: *For Blacks Only* [unconfirmed]

Vocal accompaniment: Hubert Sumlin (electric guitar); Sunnyland Slim (piano); unknown (electric bass and drums)

Location: Chicago, Illinois. 1971

Titles performed:
'How Many More Years'
'Evil Is Going On'
'I Am The Wolf'
'Shake For Me'
'I Asked For Water'
'Goin' Down Slow'

Source: *Wolf*
There may be further titles included in a reportedly longer version of this film.
N.B. A brief silent clip of amateur colour footage by this artist, dating from c. early 1960s, appears in *Record Row*.

HELEN HUMES

Vocal accompaniment: the Dizzy Gillespie orchestra

Location: unknown {USA}. c. 1947

Titles performed:
'Hey Baba Leba' Jazz Classics JCVC115, Storyville SV6035
'Crazy 'bout A Man' Jazz Classics JCVC115, Storyville SV6035

Source: *Jivin' In Be-Bop*

Vocal accompaniment: unknown

Location: unknown {USA}. 1947

Titles performed:
unknown

Source: *Tan And Terrific*

Vocal accompaniment: unknown band

Location: probably Hollywood, California. 1950

Titles performed:
'You Ain't No Good' [ST only]

Source: *Panic In The Streets*

Vocal accompaniment: unknown

Location: unknown {USA}. 1950

Titles performed:
unknown

Source: *My Blue Heaven*

Vocal accompaniment: Count Basie and His Orchestra

Location: unknown {USA}. c.1950–52

Titles performed:
'I Cried For You' View Video 1313
'If I Could Be With You'

Source: *Count Basie and His Orchestra*

Vocal accompaniment: Count Basie and His Orchestra

Location: New York City. 1955

Titles performed:
'I Cried for You'

Source: *Showtime At The Apollo*

Vocal accompaniment: probably Memphis Slim (piano); Willie Dixon (bass); Clifton James (drums)

Location: Baden-Baden, Germany. c. October 1962

Titles performed:
unknown

Source: *American Folk Blues Festival 1962*

Vocal accompaniment: Earl Hines (piano); Buddy Tate (drums)

Location: Montreux, Switzerland. Monday 1 July 1974

Titles performed:
'I'm Satisfied'
'Blue Because Of You'
'On The Sunny Side Of The Street'
'I Got It Bad And That Ain't Good'

Source: *Montreux Jazz*

Vocal accompaniment: unknown

Location: unknown {USA}. 1975

Titles performed:
unknown

Source: *The Today Show*

Vocal accompaniment: unknown

Location: unknown {USA}. 1975

Titles performed:
unknown

Source: *The Joe Franklin Show*

Vocal accompaniment: Bill Doggett (electric organ); David 'Bubba' Brooks (tenor saxophone); Pete Mayes (electric guitar)–1
Vocal accompaniment: the Lionel Hampton orchestra–2

Location: Nice, France. Thursday 13 July 1978

Titles performed:
'Let The Good Times Roll'–1
'Basin Street Blues'–1
'I've Got It Bad'–1
'St. Louis Blues'–1
'Hey Ba Be Re Ba'–2
'Alright, OK, You Win'–2

Source: *La Grande Parade Du Jazz*

Vocal accompaniment: unknown

Location: unknown {USA}. 1978

Titles performed:
unknown

Source: *Big Band Bash*
There may be Australian TV broadcasts by this artist, who was resident in that country between 1964 and 1967.

MRS. VAN HUNT
Vocal accompaniment: Mose Vinson (piano)

Location: Memphis, Tennessee. 1978

Title performed:
'Jelly Servin' Woman' [part only] K-Jazz 030, Yazoo 505

Source: *Good Morning Blues*

ALBERTA HUNTER
Vocal accompaniment: unknown studio orchestra and choir

Location: probably Pinewood Studios, Burnham, Buckinghamshire, England. October or November 1934

Title performed:
'Black Shadows'

Source: *Radio Parade Of 1935*

Vocal accompaniment: unknown

Location: New York City. 1971

Titles performed:
unknown

Source: *Faces In Jazz*

Vocal accompaniment: unknown

Location: New York City. 1972

Titles performed:
unknown

Source: *Faces In Jazz*

Vocal accompaniment: Al Hall (brass bass); Connie Kay (drums)–1; Jackie Williams (drums)–2; Wally Richardson (guitar); Vic Dickenson (trombone); Doc Cheatham (trumpet); Budd Johnson (tenor saxophone/clarinet); Gerald Cook (piano)

Location: New York City. 27 December 1977

Titles performed:
'Workin' Man'–1
'You Reap Just What You Sow'–1
'The Love I Have For You'–1
'I've Got A Mind To Ramble'–1
'Remember My Name'–1
'My Castle's Rockin''–1
'Down Hearted Blues'–1
'Some Sweet Day'–1
'Chirpin' the Blues'–2
'I Begged and Begged You'–2

Source: *The Mike Douglas Show*

Vocal accompaniment: unknown

Location: New York City. 1977

Titles performed:
unknown

Source: *The Today Show*

Vocal accompaniment: unknown

Location: unknown {USA}. 1978

Titles performed:
unknown

Source: *The Mike Douglas Show*

Vocal accompaniment: unknown

Location: New York City. 1978

Titles performed:
unknown

Source: *Camera Three; One Hundred Years From Today*

Vocal accompaniment: unknown

Location: New York City. 1978

Titles performed:
unknown

Source: *To Tell The Truth*

Vocal accompaniment: unknown

Location: New York City. 1978

Titles performed:
unknown

Source: *The Today Show*

Vocal accompaniment: unknown

Location: The Cookery, New York City. 1978

Titles performed:
'Remember My Name'
'Workin' Man Blues'
'Downhearted Blues'
'Rough And Ready Man'
'Glory Of Love'
[interview]

Source: *Film '79*

Vocal accompaniment: unknown

Location: New York City. 1978

Titles performed:
unknown

Source: *Sixty Minutes*

Vocal accompaniment: Gerald Cook (piano); Jimmy Lewis (bass)

Location: Smithsonian Institute, Washington, DC. 1982

Titles performed:
'My Castle's Rocking' Adla 1270, Parkfield MJK0014
'Down Hearted Blues' Adla 1270, Parkfield MJK0014
'My Man's A Handy Man' Adla 1270, Parkfield MJK0014
'When You're Smiling' Adla 1270, Parkfield MJK0014
'Nobody Knows You When You're Down and Out' Adla 1270, Parkfield MJK0014
'All God's Children Got Rhythm' Adla 1270, Parkfield MJK0014
'Without A Song' Adla 1270, Parkfield MJK0014
[interview] Adla 1270, Parkfield MJK0014
'Dark Town Strutters Ball' Adla 1270, Parkfield MJK0014
'Rough And Ready Man' Adla 1270, Parkfield MJK0014
'Time Waits For No Man' Adla 1270, Parkfield MJK0014
'I've Got A Mind To Ramble' Adla 1270, Parkfield MJK0014
'You Can't Tell The Difference After Dark' Adla 1270, Parkfield MJK0014
'Remember My Name' Adla 1270, Parkfield MJK0014

Source: *Jazz At The Smithsonian*
'Time Waits For No Man' is titled 'Black Man' on the Parkfield issue.

Vocal accompaniment: unknown

Location: unknown {USA}. c.1982–83

Titles performed:
'My Castle's Rocking' Virgin VVD-771
'Two–Fisted, Double–Jointed Rough And Ready Man' Virgin VVD-771
'Darktown Strutters Ball' Virgin VVD-771
'Downhearted Blues' Virgin VVD-771
'I Got A Mind To Ramble' Virgin VVD-771
'Black Shadows' Virgin VVD-771
'I'm Having A Good Time' Virgin VVD-771
'My Handy Man' Virgin VVD-771
'You're Welcome To Come Home' Virgin VVD-771
'The Love I Have For You' Virgin VVD-771
[interviews and monologues] Virgin VVD-771

Source: *My Castle's Rockin'*

Vocal accompaniment: Eubie Blake (piano)

Location: New York City. 1983

Title performed:
Old Fashioned Love

Source: *Eubie Blake 1883–1983*

IVORY JOE HUNTER

Vocal accompaniment: possibly own piano and others, unknown

Location: New York City. Sunday August 23 1953

Title performed:
unknown

Source: *Toast Of The Town*

Vocal accompaniment: unknown

Location: New York City. 1957

Title performed:
'Since I Met You Baby' MMG 012

Source: *The Big Beat* [2]

JANIE HUNTER AND GROUP

Ensemble a cappella vocal

Location: Georgia Sea Islands. c.1983

Titles performed:
'Oh John' Vestapol 13080
'Call Eli In The Morning' Vestapol 13080
'No More Hard Times' Vestapol 13080
[interview]

Source: *Dreams And Songs Of The Noble Old*
See also the Georgia Sea Island Singers.

HURRICANES

Vocal group accompaniment: unknown

Location: unknown {USA}. 1956

Titles performed:
'Talk Talk Talk'
'Army Life'

Source: *Rockin' The Blues*

[MISSISSIPPI] JOHN HURT

Vocal and guitar

Location: New York City. 1963–64

Titles performed:
unknown

Source: *The Tonight Show Starring Johnny Carson* [unconfirmed]

Vocal and guitar

Location: Newport, Rhode Island. July 1964

Title performed:
'Candy Man' [fragment]

Source: *Festival*

Vocal and guitar

Location: unknown {USA}. 1965

Titles performed:
unknown

Source: *This Hour Has Seven Days* [unconfirmed]

Vocal and guitar

Location: New York City. 1966

Titles performed:
'Spike Driver Blues' Vestapol 13003
'You're Going To Walk That Lonesome Valley' Vestapol 13003

Source: *Pete Seeger's Rainbow Quest*

THOMAS HURT

Vocal and guitar

Location: Atlanta, Georgia. October 1984

Title performed:
'Good Girl Blues'

Source: *National Downhome Blues Festival*

JOSEPH HUTCHINSON AND THE HUTCHINSON SUNBEAMS
Vocal group accompaniment: unknown

Location: Chicago, Illinois

The following appearances are known:
1964
Sunday 19 April [prog #22–3]
1967
Sunday 12 March [prog #17–2]

Titles performed:
unknown

Source: *Jubilee Showcase*

JOSEPH BENJAMIN [J B] HUTTO
Vocal and electric guitar accompaniment: unknown (electric bass and drums)

Location: Chicago, Illinois. April–May 1970

Titles performed:
'Thank You For Your Kindness' [part only] K-Jazz 004, Rhapsody 9012
untitled instrumental blues [part only] K-Jazz 004, Rhapsody 9012
[interview] K-Jazz 004, Rhapsody 9012

Source: *Chicago Blues*

Vocal and electric guitar accompaniment: unknown

Location: Chicago, Illinois. 1970

Titles performed:
unknown

Source: *Made In Chicago*

Vocal and electric guitar accompaniment: unknown

Location: Vienna, Austria. 1975

Titles performed:
'Stranger In Your Town'
'Baby Come On Home With Me'
untitled blues
[interview]

Source: *Austrian TV broadcast* [C]

Vocal and electric guitar accompaniment: the New Hawks [G]

Location: Montreux, Switzerland. 1978 or 1979

Titles performed:
'I'm Just A Bad Boy'
'All Your Love'
'Look What You're Doin''
'Goin' Down The Highway'
'Walking The Dog'
'I Wish I Was Single'

Source: *Montreux Jazz*

Vocal and electric guitar accompaniment: unknown

Location: Hadley, Massachusetts. Sunday 12 April 1981

Titles performed:
'I Feel So Good'
'Summertime'
'Got My Mojo Working'
'Sweet Little Angel'
'You Don't Love Me No More'
'The Blues Had A Baby'

Source: *US PBS TV broadcast*. Origin unknown [C]

Vocal and electric guitar accompaniment: unknown

Location: probably Boston, Massachusetts. 1980s

Titles performed:
'Don't You Lie To Me'
'Shake Rattle And Roll'

Source: *The Club*

Vocal and electric guitar accompaniment: unknown

Location: probably Boston, Massachusetts. 1980s

Titles performed:
'Hip Shakin''
'Serves Me Right To Suffer'
'Can't Hold Out Much Longer'
[interview]

Source: *Night Life* [2]

Vocal and electric guitar accompaniment: unknown

Location: probably Boston, Massachusetts. 1980s

Titles performed:
'That's The Truth'
'Hip Shakin''
'You Don't Love Me'
[interview]

Source: *Five All Night Live*

Vocal and electric guitar accompaniment: unknown

Location: probably Chicago, Illinois. 1980s

Title performed:
'Dim Lights'

Source: *Good Morning*

I

IKETTES

Robbie Montgomery, Joshie Armstead and Frances Hodge, vocals accompaniment: unknown

Location: St. Louis, Missouri. 1989

Title performed:
'I'm Blue'

Source: *St. Soul-Soul of St. Louis R&B*
See also Ike and Tina Turner.

IMPERIAL GOSPEL SINGERS

Probably Anna Smallwood, Rosie Wallace and others accompaniment: unknown

Location: Apollo Theatre, Harlem, New York City. 1959

Titles performed:
unknown

Source: *World By Night*

Probably Anna Smallwood, Louise 'Smoke' Brown, Norma Taylor, Connie A. Noble accompaniment: unknown

Location: New York City. c. 1965

Titles performed:
'The Lord Will See You Through'
'The Fountain Of Blood'
'My Father's House'

Source: *TV Gospel Time* #44

INSPIRING VOICES OF EVANGEL TEMPLE, WASHINGTON DC

Mixed vocal choir accompaniment: unknown

Location: Washington DC. c. 1966

Titles performed:
unknown

Source: *TV Gospel Time* #56

THE INSTITUTIONAL RADIO CHOIR

Mixed vocal choir accompaniment: The Colonus Messengers

Location: Annenberg Center, Philadelphia, Pennsylvania. 1985

Titles performed:
[See note in programme index]

Source: *The Gospel at Colonus*

INTERNATIONAL SWEETHEARTS OF RHYTIIM
Probably Edna Williams or Ernestine 'Tiny' Davis (trumpet); Wille Mae Wong and Violet Burnside (saxophones); Pauline Brady (drums); unknown (piano, brass, reeds, bass)
Vocals by Anna Mae Winburn–1; Ruby Dee–2

Location: probably Los Angeles, California. 1946

Titles performed:
[22M4] 'Jump Children'–1 Storyville SV6015
[23M4] 'That Man Of Mine'–2
[25M1] 'She's Crazy With The Heat' Storyville SV6015

Source: *Soundies*
22M4 copyrighted 26 August 1946; 23M4 23 November 1946; 25M1 3 November 1946 [*sic*].
'Jump Children' is the same song as that performed by the Flamingos in the 1957 film *Go Johnny Go*

Probably similar to above

Location: unknown {USA}. 1946

Titles performed:
unidentified title Storyville SV6015
'How About That Jive' Storyville SV6015
'I Love My Man' Storyville SV6015

Source: *How About That Jive*

Probably similar to above

Location: unknown {USA}. 1946

Titles performed:
unidentified title
'Don't Get It Twisted'
'Just The Thing'

Source: *Harlem Jam Session*

Probably similar to above

Location: unknown {USA}. c. 1946–47

Titles performed:
'My Baby Rocks Me'
'I Need My Man'
'Do You Wanna Jump Children'
and other, unknown, titles

Source: *She's Crazy With The Heat*
The film *Sweethearts Of Rhythm* (1947) is believed to be a compilation of *Soundies*.

The following are also of interest: *International Sweethearts Of Rhythm*, 1986; *Tiny and Ruby : Hell Divin' Women*, 1988. Both documentaries.

J

BENJAMIN JOSEPH [BULL MOOSE] JACKSON
Vocal accompaniment: the Lucky Millinder orchestra

Location: New York City. c. 1946

Title performed:
[22M3] 'Big Fat Mamas' Storyville SV6000, Virgin VVD865

Source: *Soundies*
Copyrighted 19 August 1946.
See Rosetta Tharpe for likely personnel.

Vocal and tenor saxophone accompaniment: the Lucky Millinder orchestra

Location: New York City. 1948

Title performed:
'I Love You Yes I Do' Timeless Video 5603

Source: *Boarding House Blues*

[REVEREND] CHARLIE JACKSON
Vocal and electric guitar accompaniment: Mrs Frances Jackson (clapping); unknown female (tambourine)

Location: New Orleans, Louisiana. 1990.

Title performed:
'Fix It Jesus' (part only)

Source: *Big World*

[REVEREND] JESSE L JACKSON

Vocal accompaniment: unknown

Location: Chicago, Illinois

The following appearances are known:
1969
Thursday 27 March [prog #5–2]
1974
Saturday 7 September [prog #5–1]

Titles performed:
unknown

Source: *Jubilee Showcase*

Speech with audience response

Location: Coliseum Stadium, Los Angeles, California. Sunday 20 August 1972

Title performed:
'I Am Somebody'

Source: *Wattstax*

Speech

Location: Chicago, Illinois. August 1995

[interview]

Source: *Too Close To Heaven*
This artist is also a prominent political figure.

JIM JACKSON

Despite being listed in some reference works as appearing in the 1929 film *Hallelujah*, there is no visual or aural evidence of his presence in any inspected print of the film. It is of interest, however, that a photograph exists of Jackson with director George Cukor.

JOHN JACKSON

Vocal and guitar

Location: KCTS-TV studios, Seattle, Washington. 1970

Titles performed:
'That Will Never Happen No More' Vestapol 13037
'Rag In C' Vestapol 13037

Source: *University of Washington/Seattle Folklore Society*

Vocal and guitar

Location: the Jackson residence, Fairfax, Virginia. April 1979

Title performed:
'Key To The Highway' K-Jazz 076, Rhapsody 8013
[interview] K-Jazz 076, Rhapsody 8013

Source: *John Jackson – An American Songster*

Vocal and guitar

Location: Atlanta, Georgia. Saturday 20 October 1984

Titles performed:
'Since I Left My Baby' K-Jazz 076, Rhapsody 8013
'Rocks And Gravel'
[interview]

Source: *National Down Home Blues Festival*
'Since I Left My Baby' only appears in *John Jackson – An American Songster*; 'Rocks And Gravel' and the interview only appear in *National Down Home Blues Festival*

Vocal and guitar

Location: Fairfax Station, Virginia. 1985

Titles performed:
unknown Blues Houseparty BH-01

Source: *Houseparty Productions*

Vocal and guitar accompaniment: his three sons (two guitars and a harmonica)

Location: the Jackson residence, Fairfax, Virginia. 1985–86

Title performed:
'Ain't Nobody's Business' K-Jazz 076, Rhapsody 8013
[interview] K-Jazz 076, Rhapsody 8013

Source: *John Jackson – An American Songster*

Vocal and guitar accompaniment: John Dee Holeman (guitar)

Location: New York City. Saturday 25 January 1986

Title performed:
'Kansas City Blues' [part only] K-Jazz 076, Rhapsody 8013
[conversation with Larry Johnson] K-Jazz 076, Rhapsody 8013

Source: *John Jackson – An American Songster*

Vocal and guitar accompanied by signer for the hearing-impaired

Location: Croton Point, New York. Tuesday 24 June 1986

Titles performed:
'Kansas City Blues' [part only] K-Jazz 076, Rhapsody 8013
'Black Cat Rag (Black Rat Swing)' K-Jazz 076, Rhapsody 8013
'My Little Woman's So Sweet' K-Jazz 076, Rhapsody 8013

Source: *John Jackson – An American Songster*

Vocal and guitar–1
banjo solo–2

Location: WDBJ TV Studios, Roanake, Virginia. Spring/Summer 1987

Titles performed:
'Bad Whiskey Blues'–1 [part only] [A]
'Blind Lemon Blues'–1 [part only] [A]
untitled instrumental–2 [part only] [A]
'Railroad Bill'–1 [part only] [B]

Source: *Black Musical Traditions In Virginia: Blues* [A]; *Black Musical Traditions In Virginia: Non-blues Secular Music* [B]

Jackson also appears in the tutorial video *The Fingerpicking Blues Of John Jackson* (Homespun 3727)

LEE JACKSON

Vocal and electric guitar accompaniment: probably Walter Horton (harmonica); Lafayette Leake (piano); Willie Dixon (bass); Clifton James (drums)

Location: Baden-Baden, Germany. c. May 1970

Titles performed:
unknown

Source: *American Folk Blues Festival 1970*

MAHALIA JACKSON

Vocal accompaniment: probably the Nelson Riddle orchestra–1
Vocal duet with Nat King Cole accompaniment: probably as above–2

Location: New York City. November 1956–December 1957

Titles performed:
'Joshua Fit De Battle Of Jericho' [*sic*]–1
'Down By The Riverside'–1
'Steal Away'–2

Source: *The Nat King Cole Show*
These titles probably derive from more than one episode.

Vocal accompaniment: probably the Nelson Riddle orchestra

Location: unknown {USA}. 1958

Titles performed:
'Hide The Window' [?]
'Shall Reap In Joy' [?]
'Steal Away'

Source: *St. Louis Blues* [2]

Vocal accompaniment: Mildred Falls (piano); possibly Tom Bryant (bass)

Location: Newport, Rhode Island. Sunday 6 July 1958

Titles performed:
'Shout All Over God's Heaven' Castle Hendring 2 239, New York Video 16590
'Didn't It Rain' Castle Hendring 2 239, New York Video 16590
'Didn't It Rain' [reprise] Castle Hendring 2 239, New York Video 16590
'The Lord's Prayer' Castle Hendring 2 239, New York Video 16590

Source: *Jazz On A Summer's Day*

Vocal accompaniment: unknown

Location: New York City. c.1958–59

Titles performed:
'Old Time Religion'
'Were You There When They Crucified My Lord?'

Source: *The Milton Berle Show*

Vocal accompaniment: probably Mildred Falls (piano); unknown (drums)

Location: New York City. c.1958–59

Titles performed:
'That's Alright'

Source: *The Ed Sullivan Show*

Vocal accompaniment: unknown

Location: unknown {USA}. 1959

Titles performed:
'Troubles Of The World'

Source: *Imitation Of Life*

Vocal accompaniment: probably Mildred Falls (electric organ)

Location: New York City. December 1959 or 1960

Title performed:
'Silent Night'

Source: *The Steve Allen Show*

Vocal accompaniment: probably Mildred Falls (piano)

Location: unknown church {USA} c.1959–1961

Title performed:
'Move On Up A Little Higher'

Source: *newsreel, origin unknown* [M]. Available from Historic.

Vocal accompaniment: unknown (piano, organ, mixed vocal group)

Location: probably New York City. Early 1960s

Title performed:
'The Holy Bible'

Source: probably *The Ed Sullivan Show*. This recording was subsequently issued, probably illegally, on U.S.A. 109, a 45rpm vinyl record, and then reissued on Jewel 192, also a 45rpm vinyl record.

Vocal accompaniment: probably Mildred Falls (piano)

Location: Hamburg, Germany. Spring 1961

Titles performed:
'It Don't Cost Very Much'
'Joy To My Soul'
'How Great Thou Art'
'It's Wonderful'
'Whole World In His Hands'
'You'll Never Walk Alone'
'I Found The Answer'
'Keep Your Hands On The Plough'
'Jesus Met A Woman At The Well'
'When The Saints Go Marching In'
'Dear Lord Forgive'

Source: *German TV broadcast* [M]

Vocal, unaccompanied

Location: Washington, DC. Wednesday 28 August 1963

Title performed:
'I've Been 'buked'

Source: *Newsreel, origin unknown* [M]. Filmed at the Washington Freedom March rally, in the company of Reverend Martin Luther King. Available from Historic.

Vocal accompaniment: unknown

Location: unknown {USA}. 1963

Titles performed:
unknown

Source: *Playback*

Vocal accompaniment: probably Mildred Falls (electric organ)

Location: probably Washington, DC. 1963–64

Titles performed:
'Down By The Riverside'
and other, unknown, titles

Source: *unknown* [M]. Available from Historic.

Vocal accompaniment: unknown organ

Location: unknown {USA}. 1964

Titles performed:
'Down By The Riverside'

Source: *The Best Man*

Vocal accompaniment: Mildred Falls (piano); Edward Robinson (electric organ); Rupert Nurse (bass); Fitzroy Coleman (electric guitar)

Location: London, England. Saturday, 5 September 1964

Titles performed:
unknown

Source: *Mahalia Jackson Sings*

Vocal accompaniment: unknown

Location: unknown {USA}. 1968–69

Titles performed:
unknown

Source: *That's Life*

The following are also of interest:
i. *Got To Tell It*;
ii. *Mahalia, 1911–1972*.
[Both are documentaries about the life of the artist.]

WILLIS [GATOR TAIL] JACKSON
Vocal and tenor saxophone accompaniment: unknown

Location: New York City. November 1955

Titles performed:
unknown

Source: *The Ed Sullivan Show*

ETTA JAMES (Jamesetta Hawkins)
Vocal accompaniment: The Blue Beats; Clarence 'Gatemouth' Brown and Johnnie Johnson (electric guitars); Dave 'Fathead' Newman and one unknown (trumpets); Harrison Calloway and one unknown (tenor saxophones); 'Skip' [possibly Skippy Brooks] (piano); Finis Tasby (electric bass); Freeman Brown (drums) as above, with Esther Phillips, Roscoe Shelton and Gatemouth Brown (vocals)–1

Location: WFAA-TV Studios, Dallas, Texas. Wednesday 1 February 1966

Titles performed:
'Only Time Will Tell'
[interview with Hoss Allen]
'Something Got A Hold Of Me'
'I'm So Sorry For You'
'What'd I Say'–1

Source: *The Beat*

Vocal accompaniment: Eddie Clearwater and Jimmy Johnson (electric guitars); unknown (electric bass and drums)

Location: Montreux, Switzerland. 1979

Titles performed:
unknown

Source: *Montreux Jazz*

Vocal accompaniment: Allen Toussaint and Dr. John (pianos) and probably others, unknown

Location: Chicago, Illinois. Sunday 7 November 1982

Titles performed:
'Groove Me'
'Hey Hey What'd I Say' [*sic*]
'I'd Rather Go Blind'
'Life'
'Something's Got A Hold Of Me'
'Sugar On The Floor'
'Tell Mama'

Source: *Soundstage*

Vocal accompaniment: John Mayall's Bluesbreakers: Mayall (keyboards): Mick Taylor (electric guitar); John McVie (electric bass); Colin Allen (drums)

Location: New Jersey. 1982

Title performed:
'Baby What You Want Me To Do' Castle Hendring 6 086

Source: *Blues Survivors*

Vocal accompaniment: the Johnny Otis band

Location: Monterey, California. 1987

Title performed:
'I Just Wanna Make Love To You'

Source: *Monterey Jazz Festival*

Vocal accompaniment: unknown

Location: Silver Drome Arena, Detroit, Michigan. 1989

Titles performed:
'I'd Rather Go Blind'
'Something's Got A Hold Of Me'

Source: *This Country's Rockin'*
This artist also appears in *Etta James Live at Montreux*, Island video, and in *Jump The Blues Away* with Albert Collins. Details for both unknown.

[SISTER] JOSEPHINE JAMES

Vocal accompaniment: unknown

Location: Chicago, Illinois. Saturday 5 April 1969

Titles performed:
unknown

Source: *Jubilee Showcase* [prog #13–1]

Vocal accompaniment: The Greater Bethlehem Church Choir

Location: unknown {USA}. c. 1969

Title performed:
'I've Been Toiling'

Source: *Soul Set Free*
This artist is Reverend Cleophus Robinson's sister.

NEHEMIAH CURTIS [SKIP] JAMES

Vocal and guitar–1;
as above, in the company of Son House (vocal and steel guitar); Bukka White (vocal and steel guitar)–2

Location: Newport, Rhode Island. July 1966

Titles performed:
'Devil Got My Woman'–1 Vestapol 13049
'I'm So Glad'–1 Vestapol 13049
'Worried Blues'–1 Vestapol 13049
participation in 'Blues Contest';
'Cherry Ball Blues'–2 Vestapol 13050

Source: *Alan Lomax film collection*
See also Bukka White.

ABNER JAY

Vocal accompaniment: unknown–1
Vocal accompaniment: the Washington Temple Majestic Choir–2

Location: New York City. Sunday 9 December 1962

Titles performed:
'I Trust In God'–1
'I Want To Be Ready When He Comes'–2

Source: *TV Gospel Time* #7

Vocal accompaniment: unknown

Location: New York City. Saturday 24 February 1963

Title performed:
'He's Mine'

Source: *TV Gospel Time* #15

BETTY JEANETTE
Vocal accompaniment: Sammy Price (piano); Pat Hare (electric guitar); Andrew Stephens (electric bass); Francis Clay (drums)

Location: Newport, Rhode Island. Sunday 3 July 1960

Title performed:
'Backwater Blues'

Source: *Jazz-USA*
See also Muddy Waters.

JELLY ROLL KINGS
Frank Frost (harmonica) accompaniment: Jack Johnson (electric guitar); Sam Carr (drums)

Location: Clarksdale, Mississippi. Autumn 1990

Title performed:
'Gonna Put Her Down' [ST only] Anxious 45099-29643

Source: *Deep Blues*
See also Frank Frost.

JOHN HENRY BONES
See John Henry Nobles.

JOHNNY AND GEORGE
Vocal and piano accompaniment: unknown (bass, drums)

Location: New York City. Early 1945

Titles performed:
[88408] 'Eighty-eight Reasons Why' Charly #2
[88708] 'I Had A Dream' Charly #2
[11M2] 'Write That Letter Tonight'

Source: *Soundies*
88408 copyrighted 10 September 1945; 88708 copyrighted 16 May 1945. 11M2 4 June 1945. It is not known which artist is 'Johnny' and which is 'George'. Surnames also remain unknown.

JOHNNY AND JOE
Vocal duet accompaniment: the Alan Freed orchestra: Big Al Sears and Sam 'The Man' Taylor (tenor saxophones) and others, unknown.

Location: New York City. July–August 1957

Title performed:
'Over The Mountain'

Source: *The Big Beat* [2]

ALONZO [LONNIE] JOHNSON
Speech

Location: Chicago, Illinois. 1960

monologue [ST only] K-Jazz 014, Rhapsody 8022

Source: *Blues Like Showers Of Rain*

Vocal and guitar

Location: Manchester, England. October 1963

Title performed:
'Too Late To Cry'

Source: *I Hear The Blues*

Vocal and guitar

Location: Baden-Baden, Germany. c. October 1963

Titles performed:
unknown

Source: *American Folk Blues Festival 1963*

[ELDER] ANDERSON JOHNSON
Vocal and pedal steel guitar–1;
speech–2

Location: Newport News, Virginia. Saturday 22 July 1995

Titles performed:
'God Don't Like It' [take 1]–1
'God Don't Like It' [takes 2–3–4–5] (unbroadcast)–1
'Just A Closer Walk With Thee' [takes 1–2–3] (unbroadcast)–1
'Search Me Lord' [takes 1–2–3–4] (unbroadcast)–1
[interview] (unbroadcast)–2

Source: *Too Close To Heaven*

BETTY JOHNSON
Vocal accompaniment: unknown

Location: New York City. c. 1965–66

Titles performed:
unknown [A]
unknown [B]
unknown [C]

Source: *TV Gospel Time* #51 [A], #61[B], #66 [C]

GEORGE JOHNSON
Vocal, unaccompanied

Location: probably Natchez, Mississippi. Between 11 August and 9 September 1978

Title performed:
'Good Lord Have Mercy' Vestapol 13078

Source: *Land Where The Blues Began*

HALL JOHNSON CHOIR
Mixed vocal choir, probably unaccompanied

Location: probably New York City. 1930.

Titles performed:
unknown

Source: *Deep South*

Probably as above

Location: probably New York City. c. 1936

Titles performed:
unknown

Source: *untitled* [FS] [M]. Produced by George Randol

Probably as above

Location: unknown {USA}. 1936

Titles performed:
unknown

Source: *Green Pastures*

Probably as above

Location: probably New York City. c. 1940

Titles performed:
unknown

Source: *Mississippi Moods*

Probably as above

Location: probably Hollywood, California. 1942

Titles performed:
unknown

Source: *Cabin In The Sky*
See also Bessie Smith and unidentified artists #8.

[BIG] JACK JOHNSON
Vocal and electric guitar accompaniment: unknown (second electric guitar, electric bass, keyboards, drums)

Location: Red Top Lounge, Clarksdale, Mississippi. Autumn 1990

Titles performed:
'Catfish Blues' Anxious 45099–29643, BMG un-numbered
'Daddy, When Is Mama Comin' Home?' Anxious 45099–29643, BMG un-numbered

Source: *Deep Blues*

Speech

Location: Radio station WROX, Clarksdale, Mississippi. Autumn 1990

[interview with dj Early Wright] Anxious 45099–29643, BMG un-numbered

Source: *Deep Blues*

Vocal and electric guitar accompaniment: Frank Frost (keyboards); Terry Williams (electric guitar); David Porter (electric bass); Sam Carr (drums)

Location: Clarksdale, Mississippi. 1991

Titles performed:
'The Blues Is Alright'
'Oh Darling'
'Chinese Blues'
'Dust My Broom'
'Honey Bee'
'I'm a Big Boy Now'
'Everyday I Have The Blues'

Source: *Juke Joint Saturday Night*
See also The Jelly Roll Kings.

JAMES [STUMP] JOHNSON
speech

Location: St. Louis, Missouri. Summer 1960

monologue [ST only] K-Jazz 014, Rhapsody 8022

Source: *Blues Like Showers Of Rain*

JIMMY JOHNSON
Vocal and electric guitar accompaniment: unknown

Location: Nice, France. 1978

Titles performed:
'Paid My Dues'
'Le Blues Et Sol'

Source: *French TV broadcast* [C]

Vocal and electric guitar accompaniment: John 'Big Moose' Walker, Lefty Dizz and Willie James Lyons (electric guitars); Big Mojo Elem (electric bass); Odie Payne (drums)

Location: unknown {Europe} c. 1978–79

Titles performed:
'Every Day I Have The Blues'
'As The Years Go Passing By'

Source: *European TV broadcast*. Origin unknown [C]

Vocal and electric guitar accompaniment: Carl Snyder (piano); Larry Exum (electric bass); Ike Davis (drums)

Location: Gothenburg, Sweden. 1982

Titles performed:
'Twelve Bar Blues'
'Five Long Years'
'Long Distance Call'
'Don't Want No Woman'
'Serves Me Right'
'Breaking Up Somebody's Home'
'Ashes In My Ashtray'

Source: *Swedish TV broadcast* [C]

JOHNNIE JOHNSON
Vocal and piano

Location: St. Louis, Missouri. 1980

Titles performed:
untitled instrumental
[interview]

Source: *Johnny B. Goode*

Vocal and piano

Location: Chicago, Illinois. 1993

Title performed:
untitled instrumental
[interview]

Source: *Sweet Home Chicago* [2]

Speech, occasional piano

Location: St. Louis, Missouri. 1995

[interview]

Source: *Rock And Roll Part 1*

Vocal and piano accompaniment, if any, unknown

Location: Washington, DC. Saturday 11 October 1997

Titles performed:
unknown

Source: *A Tribute To Muddy Waters*
This artist was Chuck Berry's regular pianist.

JOSEPH [CHINAMAN] JOHNSON

This artist appears leading one or more worksongs in *Afro-American Worksongs In a Texas Prison*, but titles are not known. Some may be represented by titles listed under Unidentified Artists [B] (26).

LARRY JOHNSON

Vocal and guitar

Location: New York City. 1970

Title performed:
'How Long Blues'

Source: *Black Roots*

Vocal and guitar

Location: New York City. 1970

Titles performed:
unknown

Source: *Say Brother* [unconfirmed]

Vocal and guitar

Location: New York City. June 1971

Titles performed:
'Rag Mama Rag'
'Got The Blues, Can't Be Satisfied'
'Charlie Stone'
'Train Whistle Blues'
'Broke And Hungry'
'Honey, Where You Learn To Cook'
'If I Get Lucky'

Source: *John Hammond Presents*

Vocal and guitar

Location: Philadelphia, Pennsylvania. 1973

Titles performed:
unknown

Source: Philadelphia Folk Festival

Vocal and guitar

Location: unknown {USA}. 1976

Titles performed:
unknown

Source: *Toughing It Out*

Vocal and guitar

Location: unknown {Europe}. 1983

Titles performed:
'Midnight Hour'

Source: *European TV broadcast* [C]. Origin unknown

Vocal and guitar–1
Vocal and guitar in duet with John Cephas (vocal and guitar)–

Location: New York City. Saturday 25 January 1986

Titles performed:
'Can't You Hear The Angels Sing'–1 K-Jazz 076, Rhapsody 8022
'Charlie Stone'–1 K-Jazz 076, Rhapsody 8022

'Let Us Pray Together'–2 K-Jazz 076, Rhapsody 8022
[and conversation with John Jackson] K-Jazz 076, Rhapsody 8022

Source: *John Jackson – An American Songster*
See also Gary Davis.

LONNIE JOHNSON
See Alonzo Johnson.

MYRTLE JOHNSON
Vocal accompaniment: unknown

Location: New York City. c. 1965–66

Titles performed:
unknown [A]
unknown [B]

Source: *TV Gospel Time* #53 [A], 54 [B]

PETE JOHNSON
Piano accompaniment: orchestra

Location: unknown {USA}. c.1947

Title performed:
'Boogie Woogie On St. Louis Blues'

Source: *unknown*
See alsoAlbert Ammons.

ROBERT JOHNSON
Silent monochrome film reported possibly to feature Robert Johnson is now known to be of an unidentified artist, and will be found listed accordingly. The performer appears in front of a poster for a film released in 1941, after Johnson's death. A 'docu-drama' entitled *Can't You Hear The Wind Howl*, featuring Keb' Mo' as Johnson, was reported to have reached the final stages of production in the winter of 1997. The documentary feature *The Search For Robert Johnson* is also of interest.

JOINER'S FIVE TRUMPETS
Vocal quintet accompaniment, if any: unknown

Location: Gary, Indiana. June 1976

Titles performed:
unknown

Source: *Gospel In Gary*
It has not been possible to determine if the personnel for the above group is the same as that which recorded for J.O.B. records in 1952.

JONES BOYS SING BAND
Vocal group accompaniment, if any: unknown

Location: probably Hollywood, California. 1937

Titles performed:
unknown

Source: *Hollywood Handicap*

ARTHNEICE [GAS MAN] JONES
Vocal and harmonica accompaniment: Terry Williams (electric guitar); Howard Stovall (keyboards); Harvell Thomas (electric bass); Dione Thomas (drums)

Location: Clarksdale, Mississippi. 1991

Titles performed:
'Blue Diamond'
'Lucille'
'Annie Mae'
'Stormed Through The Door'
'Just Before The Break Of Day'
'I'll Take Care Of You'
'Saw You There'
'Turning Point'
'Stone Gas Theme Song'

Source: *Juke Joint Saturday Night*

CLINULM JONES AND GROUP

Ensemble a cappella vocals accompaniment: handclapping

Location: probably Eunice, Louisiana. Between 9 and 27 August 1983

Title performed:
'Oh, Brother Can't You Read' [part only] Vestapol 13077

Source: *Cajun Country* [1]

CURTIS JONES

Vocal and guitar–1
Vocal and piano–2

Location: BBC-TV studios, White City, London, England. Tuesday 22 October 1968

Titles performed:
unknown–1
'Cheri'–2

Source: *American Folk Blues Festival 1968* [1]

Probably as above

Location: Germany. November 1968

Titles performed:
unknown

Source: *American Folk Blues Festival 1968* [2]
There may be Belgian, French and/or Swiss TV broadcasts by this artist between 1964 and 1971 when he was resident in Europe.

FLOYD JONES

Vocal and guitar

Location: Chicago, Illinois. April-May 1970

Title performed:
Stockyard Blues [part only] K-Jazz 004, Rhapsody 9012
[interview] K-Jazz 004, Rhapsody 9012

Source: *Chicago Blues*
This song and interview are edited out of some versions of this film. The TCB/K-Jazz/ Rhapsody prints are complete.

Vocal and electric guitar accompaniment: Venson's Playboys; Adair King (electric guitar); Pat Rush (electric bass); Tenner 'Playboy' Venson (drums)

Location: Maxwell Street, Chicago, Illinois. Summer 1980

Title performed:
'Take A Little Walk With Me' K-Jazz 031, Rhapsody 8045
[interview] K-Jazz 031, Rhapsody 8045

Source: *Maxwell Street Blues*

[REVEREND] JOHNNY JONES

Vocal accompaniment: unknown

Location: Chicago, Illinois. Sunday 11 July 1965

Titles performed:
unknown

Source: *Jubilee Showcase* [prog #29–3]

Vocal accompaniment: unknown

Location: Chicago, Illinois. Saturday 24 September 1972

Titles performed:
unknown

Source: *Jubilee Showcase* [prog #2–2]

Vocal accompaniment: unknown

Location: Chicago, Illinois. 1976

Titles performed:
unknown

Source: *Here Comes Gospel*

[REVEREND] GEORGE JORDAN

Vocal accompaniment: unknown

Location: Chicago, Illinois

The following appearances are known;
1973
Saturday 26 May [prog #32–3]

1975
Saturday 13 September [prog #1–1]

Titles performed:
unknown

Source: *Jubilee Showcase*

LOUIS JORDAN
Presumably vocal accompaniment: unknown

Location: unknown {USA}. c. 1939

Titles performed:
unknown

Source: *Swingin' The Dream* [unconfirmed]

The Tympany Five: Eddie Roane (trumpet–1, vocal–2); Louis Jordan ((alto saxophone–3, tenor saxophone–4, vocal); Arnold Thomas (piano): Dallas Bartley (bass, vocal–5); Walter Martin (drums); Ruby Richards (dancing–6); Nicki O'Daniel and three others, unknown, dancing–7); ensemble vocal.

Location: New York City. Mid to late 1942

Titles performed:
[10305] 'Fuzzy Wuzzy'–1, –3, –6
BMG 80008-3,
Charly #5,
Jazz Classics JCVC-105,
Storyville SV6001,
Virgin VVD-866
[10606] 'Old Man Mose'–2 BMG 80008-3,
Charly #5
[10904] 'Down Down Down'–1, –3, –5, –7
Charly #5,
Storyville SV6001,
Virgin VVD-866
[11108] 'Five Guys Named Mo'–1, –4
BMG 80008-3,
Charly #5,
Charly SOUND-1940,
Storyville SV6001,
Vintage Jazz Classics VJC2004,
Virgin VVD-866

Source: *Soundies*
9005 copyrighted 19 October 1942; 10305, 10506, 10904, 11108 31 December 1942. 10904 and 11108 also appear in *Jumpin' At The Jubilee.*

The Tympany Five: Eddie Roane (trumpet); Louis Jordan (alto saxophone, vocal); Arnold Thomas (piano); Jessie 'Po' Simpkins (bass); Rossiere 'Shadow' Wilson (drums); The Swing Maniacs (dancing)–1

Location: probably Hollywood, California. Early 1944

Titles performed:
[15708] 'G I Jive' Storyville SV6001,
Virgin VVD-866
[15908] 'Ration Blues'
Vintage Jazz Classics VJC2004
[16208] 'Jumpin' At The Jubilee'–1
Storyville SV6001,
Vintage Jazz Classics VJC2004,
Virgin VVD-866
[16408] 'If You Can't Smile And Say Yes'
BMG 80008-3,
Storyville SV6001,
Vintage Jazz Classics VJC2004,
Virgin VVD-866
[17708] 'Jordan Jive' [instrumental]–1

Source: *Soundies*
15708 copyrighted 13 March 1944; 15908 15 March 1944; 16208 17 April 1944; 16408 8 May 1944; 17708 14 August 1944. 16208 and 16408 appear in *Jumpin' At The Jubilee.* 17708 appears in *Toot That Trumpet.*

Two film shorts, *Louis Jordan Medley #1* [3M] and *Louis Jordan Medley #2* [2M, *sic*], probably contain material from the above sessions, although exact details remain unknown. 2M was released 6 November 1944. *Hep Cat Serenade*, an anthology of performances by different artists, probably also uses material from the above sessions.

Louis Jordan And His Orchestra: Eddie Roane (trumpet); Louis Jordan (alto saxophone, vocal–1); Arnold Thomas (piano); Jessie 'Po' Simpkins (bass); Rossiere 'Shadow' Wilson (drums); George Raft (tap-dancing–2)

Location: probably Hollywood, California. Late 1943 or early 1944

Titles performed:
'Is You Is Or Is You Ain't My Baby?'–1
Vintage Jazz Classics VJC2004
'Sweet Georgia Brown'–2

Source: *Follow The Boys* aka *Three Cheers For The Boys*
Released to movie theatres 31 March 1944

The Tympany Five:
personnel unknown but probably similar to above

Location: probably Hollywood, California. Summer 1944

Title performed:
'Deacon Jones'

Source: *Meet Miss Bobbysocks*
Copyrighted 12 October 1944.

Louis Jordan And His Tympany Five:
Eddie Roane (trumpet); Louis Jordan (alto saxophone–1, tenor saxophone–2, vocal); William Austin (piano); Al Morgan (bass); Alex "Razz' Mitchell (drums); unknown female (dancing in silhouette–4); unknown couple (dancing–5)

Location: probably New York City. Late 1944

Titles performed:
[20808] 'Caldonia' BMG 80008-3, Jazz Classics JCVC-105, 111, Storyville SV6001, Verve CFV 10222, Video Images 328, Vintage Jazz Classics VJC2004, Virgin VVD866
short untitled instrumental BMG 80008-3, JCVC-105
[19808] 'Honey Chile' BMG 80008-3, Jazz Classics JCVC-105, Parkfield MJK0007, Proserpine 611, Storyville SV6001, Verve CFV 10222, Vintage Jazz Classics VJC2004, Virgin VVD866
[21108] 'Tillie' BMG 80008-3, Jazz Classics JCVC-105, Parkfield MJK0007, Proserpine 611, Storyville SV6001, Verve CFV 10222, Video Images 328, Vintage Jazz Classics VJC2004, Virgin VVD866
[20808] 'Buzz Me' BMG 80008-3, Jazz Classics JCVC-105, Parkfield MJK0008, Proserpine 611, 666, Storyville SV6001, Verve CFV 10222, Vintage Jazz Classics VJC2004, Virgin VVD866
[dialogue] BMG 80008-3, Jazz Classics JCVC-105

Source: *Caldonia*
This film short is included complete on Jazz Classics JCVC-105. The BMG issue omits some dialogue and the comedic routine by Sam Theard and George Wiltshire. The Soundies corporation released the individual songs, without dialogue, allocating the numbers indicated above. 19808 copyrighted 29 January 1945; 20308 2 April 1945; 20808 11 June 1945; 21108 23 July 1945.

Personnel unknown

Location: unknown {USA}. 1945

Titles performed:
unknown

Source: *Junior Prom*
Copyrighted 17 February 1946.

Louis Jordan's Tympany Band:
Aaron Izenhall (trumpet); Louis Jordan (alto saxophone and vocal); Joshua Jackson and one other (tenor saxophones); Carl Hogan (guitar); William Davis (piano); Jesse 'Po' Simpkins (bass); Eddie Byrd (drums)
Jordan, vocal accompaniment: William Davis (piano) only–1
Dimples Daniels (dancing)–2

Location: probably New York City. Early 1946

Titles performed:
'You Gotta Have The Beat' Storyville SV6031, Timeless 5045
'How Long Must I Wait' Storyville SV6031, Timeless 5045
'Good Morning Heartache'–1 Storyville SV6031, Timeless 5045
'Don't Worry 'bout That Mule' Storyville SV6031, Timeless 5045, Vintage Jazz Classics VJC2004

'In The Land Of The Buffalo Nickel' Storyville SV6031, Timeless 5045
'Hold On' Storyville SV6031, Timeless 5045
untitled instrumental #1 Timeless 5045
'You Gotta Have That Beat' Storyville SV6031, Timeless 5045
untitled instrumental #2 Timeless 5045
'Long Legged Lizzy'–2 Storyville SV6031, Timeless 5045
'Salt Pork, West Virginia' Storyville SV6031, Timeless 5045, Vintage Jazz Classics VJC2004
'Beware, Brother, Beware' BMG 80008–3, Storyville SV6031, Timeless 5045, Vintage Jazz Classics VJC2004
'An Old Fashioned Passion For You' Storyville SV6031, Timeless 5045
[dialogue] Timeless 5045

Source: *Beware*. Premiered Saturday 14 June 1946.

Louis Jordan And His Tympany Five: Aaron Izenhall (trumpet); Jordan (alto saxophone and vocal); unknown (tenor saxophone); Jesse 'Po' Simpkins (bass); Eddie Byrd (drums)

Location: unknown {USA}. 1946

Title performed:
'Don't Worry 'bout The Mule' BMG 80008-3
'Caldonia'

Source: *Swing Parade Of 1946*
Copyrighted 2 March 1946

Louis Jordan And His Tympany Five: Aaron Izenhall (trumpet–1, vocal–2); Louis Jordan (alto saxophone–3, vocal–4); probably James Wright (tenor saxophone–5); Bill Davis (piano); Carl Hogan (electric guitar); Jessie Simpkins (bass); Joe Morris [Christopher Columbus] (drums); June Richmond (vocal–6); unknown female (vocal–7); ensemble vocal–8); Mabel Lee (dancing–9); unknown female quartet (dancing–10); Bea Griffith (vocal–11)

Location: probably New York City. 1947

Titles performed:
'Caldonia' (theme)[fragment only]–1, –3 Jazz Classics JCVC-114, Video Images 934
'Texas And Pacific'–1, –3, –4 Jazz Classics JCVC-114, SV6031, Video Images 934
'All For The Love Of Lil'–1, –3, –4, –8 Jazz Classics JCVC-114, Video Images 934, Storyville SV6031
'Be-Bop-O-Bip' [fragment] Jazz Classics JCVC-114, Video Images 934
'Tonight Be Tender To Me' [fragment]–11 Jazz Classics JCVC-114, Video Images 934
'Tonight Be Tender To Me' [fragment]–4, –11 Jazz Classics JCVC-114, Video Images 934
'The Blues Ain't Nothin''–1, –3, –5, –7 Jazz Classics JCVC-114, Video Images 934
'Green Grass Grew All Around'–2, –4, –8 Jazz Classics JCVC-114, Storyville SV6031, Video Images 934
'I've Changed Completely'–6 Jazz Classics JCVC–114, Video Images 934
'Wham Sam'–1, –3, –4, –5, –9 Jazz Classics JCVC–114, Storyville SV6031, Video Images 934
'I Know What You're Putting Down'–1, –3, –4, –5 Jazz Classics JCVC-114, Storyville SV6031, Video Images 934
'Let The Good Times Roll'–1, –3, –4 Jazz Classics JCVC–114, Storyville SV6031, Video Images 934
'Reet-Petite and Gone'–1, –3, –4, –5, –9 Jazz Classics JCVC-114, Storyville SV6031, Video Images 934
'You Got Me Where You Want Me'–1, –3, –5, –6 Jazz Classics JCVC-114, Video Images 934
'That Chick's Too Young To Fry'–1, –3, –4, –5, –10 Jazz Classics JCVC-114, Storyville SV6031, Video Images 934

'Ain't That Just Like A Woman'–1, –3, –4, –5, –9 Jazz Classics JCVC-114, Storyville SV6031, Video Images 934
'If It's Love You Want, That's Me'–1 ,–3, –4, –5 Jazz Classics JCVC–114, Storyville SV6031, Video Images 934
[dialogue] Jazz Classics JCVC-114, Video Images 934

Source: *Reet-Petite and Gone*
The Jazz Classics and Video Images issues contain the complete film, the Storyville contains songs only. Vanita Smythe has a dramatic role in this film.

Louis Jordan's Tympany Six: Aaron Izenhall (trumpet–1); Louis Jordan (alto saxophone–2, tenor saxophone–3, vocal–4); Paul Quinichette (tenor saxophone); Bill Dogett (piano); James Jackson (electric guitar, claves–5); Bill Hadnott (bass); Joe Morris [Chris Columbus] (drums); unknown (bongos–6); ensemble vocal–7; unknown group, probably including Peggy Thomas (tap dancing–8)

Location: probably Hollywood, California. 1948

Titles performed:
'Jack You're Dead'–1, –3, –4 Storyville SV6031
'Caldonia'–1, –3, –4 Storyville SV6031
'My New Ten Gallon Hat'–1, –2, –8 Storyville SV6031
'Don't Burn The Candle At Both Ends'–1, –2, –4 Storyville SV6031
'Chicky-Mo, Craney Crow'–1, –2, –4
'We Can't Agree'–1, –4 Storyville SV6031
'Boogie In The Barnyard'–1, –4 Storyville SV6031
untitled instrumental–1, –2
'You're Much Too Fat'–1, –4 Storyville SV6031
'Roaming Blues'–1, –2 ,–4 Storyville SV–6031
'Early In The Morning'–1, –2, –4, –5, –6 Storyville SV–6031
'Look-out Sister'–1, –4, –7 Storyville SV6031
[dialogue]

Source: *Look-Out Sister*
'Jack, You're Dead' was made for the film *Reet-Petite And Gone*, but was held over and used in this production. The Storyville issue contains songs only. The entire film has not been issued commercially.

Jordan, probably alto saxophone and vocal
accompaniment: unknown

Location: New York City. c.1949

Titles performed:
unknown

Source: *Toast Of The Town*

Jordan, vocal and alto saxophone
accompaniment: unknown orchestra

Location: Apollo Theatre, Harlem, New York. Spring 1960

Titles performed:
[interview with Ronald Reagan]
'Choo Choo Ch'Boogie' Vintage Jazz Classics 2003, 2004

Source: *Those Singing, Swinging Years*

Jordan, vocal and alto saxophone
accompaniment: The Blue Beats; Clarence 'Gatemouth' Brown and Johnnie Johnson (electric guitars); Dave 'Fathead' Newman and one unknown (trumpets); Harrison Calloway and one unknown (tenor saxophones); 'Skip' [possibly Skippy Brooks] (piano); Finis Tasby (electric bass); Freeman Brown (drums)

Location: WFAA-TV Studios, Dallas, Texas. Monday 14 March 1966

Title performed:
'Saturday Night Fish Fry'
[interview with Hoss Allen]

Source: *The Beat*

Jordan, vocal and alto saxophone
accompaniment: The Tympany Five; Leo Blevins (electric guitar); Kenny Andrews (Hammond organ); Narmel Fuller (tenor saxophone); Joe Morris [Chris Colombus] (drums); 'Marsha' (vocal and dancing)–1

Location: WFAA-TV studios, Dallas, Texas. c. summer 1966

Titles performed:
'Caldonia'
[interview with Hoss Allen]
'G I Jive'

'All I Do Is Dream Of You'–1
untitled Instrumental
'Don't Let The Sun Catch You Crying'
[second interview with Hoss Allen]

Source: *The Beat*
Narmel Fuller's forename is a phonetic spelling drawn from the on screen interview.
The BMG videotape #80008-3 is a 48 minute documentary on the life of the artist. There may possibly be French TV appearances by Jordan from 1972. See also Una Mae Carlisle, Teresa Harris and June Richmond.

JUBALAIRES
J Caleb Ginyard and John Jennings (tenor vocals); Theodore Brooks, (baritone vocal); George McFadden (bass vocal) accompaniment: probably William Johnson (guitar)

Location: New York City. Early 1945

Titles performed:
[20108] 'Brother Bill' — Charly #7, Storyville SV6002, Virgin VVD-867
[20408] 'The Preacher And The Bear' — Charly #7, Storyville SV6002, Virgin VVD-867
[20708] 'Ten Thousand Years Ago' — Charly #7
[15M1] 'Noah' — Charly #7, Storyville SV6002, Virgin VVD-867

Source: *Soundies*
20108 copyrighted 5 March 1945; 20408, 16 April 1945; 20708, 28 May 1945.

As above accompaniment: unknown (piano and bass)

Location: probably Hollywood, California. 1949

Title performed:
'Let's Choo Choo Choo To Idaho'

Source: *Duchess Of Idaho, The*

Probably as above

Location: New York City. September–October 1949

Titles performed:
unknown

Source: *Sugar Hill Times*

JUBILEE FOUR
Vocal quartet accompaniment, if any, unknown

Location: unknown {USA}. 1928

Titles performed:
unknown #1
unknown #2

Source [FS]. Title unknown. Directed by William DeForest.

K

RUFUS KASEY
4-string banjo solo

Location: WDBJ TV studios, Roanoke, Virginia. Spring/Summer 1987

Title performed:
untitled instrumental [part only]

Source: *Black Musical Traditions In Virginia: Non-blues Secular Music*

ERNIE K-DOE (Ernest Kador Jr.)
Vocal accompaniment: unknown

Location: New Orleans, Louisiana. 1984

Title performed:
'Iko Iko'

Source: *Mardi Gras Funk*

Vocal accompaniment: unknown

Location: Toulouse Theatre, New Orleans, Louisiana. 1988

Titles performed:
'A Certain Girl'
'Ain't That The Truth'

Source: *Big Easy Music*

Vocal accompaniment: Milton Batiste (bass vocal); unknown (piano)

Location: New Orleans, Louisiana. 1990

Titles performed:
[disc-jockeying and interview with Andy Kershaw, leading to;]
'Mother-In-Law' (part only)

Source: *Big World*
Batiste holds a trumpet but does not play it in the broadcast extract.

KEB' MO' (Kevin Moore)
Vocal and steel guitar

Location: Washington, DC. Saturday 11 October 1997

Title performed:
'I Can't Be Satisfied'

Source: *A Tribute To Muddy Waters*
A 'docu-drama' entitled *Can't You Hear The Wind Howl*, starring Keb' Mo' as Robert Johnson, was reported to have reached the final stages of production in the winter of 1997.

[REVEREND] STANLEY KEEBLE
Vocal accompaniment: unknown

Location: Chicago, Illinois

The following appearances are known:
1964
Sunday 15 March [prog #7–1]
1965
Sunday 21 November [prog #10–1]
1969
Saturday 8 February [prog #34–3]
Wednesday 5 March [prog #33–2]

Titles performed:
unknown

Source: *Jubilee Showcase*

ARTHUR [GUITAR] KELLY
Vocal and electric guitar accompaniment: Silas Hogan (electric guitar)

Location: the Hogan residence, Baton Rouge, Louisiana. 1984

Title performed:
'One Of These Days'
'Tell Me Baby'
[interview]

Source: *Baton Rouge Blues*
See also Silas Hogan.

[BISHOP] SAMUEL KELSEY
Preaching and singing, accompaniment: Reverend John A. Little (piano)

Location: Free Trade Hall, Manchester, England. January 1965

Titles performed:
unknown

Source: *They Sing Like Someone's Happy*

As above

Location: Alpirsbach Monastery, Schwarzwald, Germany. Late January 1965

Titles performed:
'Nobody Knows The Trouble I've Seen' Praise 3012
'I Promised The Lord' Praise 3012
'I'm A Solider Of The Lord' [*sic*] Praise 3012

Source: *Hallelujah!*

Vocal duet with Reverend John I. Little, accompaniment: the Gospelaires and the Harmonising Four

Location: Fairfield Halls, Croydon, England. February 1966

Titles performed:
unknown

Source: *American Gospel And Spiritual Festival 1966*

MINNIE KENNEDY
Vocal accompaniment: unknown

Location: Chicago, Illinois. Sunday 9 February 1964

Titles performed:
unknown

Source: *Jubilee Showcase* [prog #12–1]

TROYCE KEY AND J J MALONE
Key, lead vocal and electric guitar, Malone, second vocal and electric guitar accompaniment: unknown (harmonica, electric bass, drums)

Location: Eli's Mile High Club, Oakland, California. 1981

Title performed:
'I Gotta New Car'
[interview with Key]

Source: *Long Train Running*

JUNIOR KIMBROUGH
Vocal and electric guitar accompaniment: unknown (electric bass and drums)

Location: juke joint, Holly Springs, Mississippi. Autumn 1990

Titles performed:
'Junior, I Love You' Anxious 45099-29643, BMG un-numbered

Source: *Deep Blues*

ALBERT KING (Albert Nelson)
Vocal and electric guitar accompaniment: unknown

Location: Los Angeles, California. 1968

Title performed:
unknown

Source: *Dick Clark's American Bandstand*

Vocal and electric guitar accompaniment: unknown

Location: unknown {USA}. 1968

Titles performed:
unknown

Source: *Upbeat* [unconfirmed]

Vocal and electric guitar accompaniment: unknown

Location: unknown {USA}. 1969

Titles performed:
unknown

Source: *The Merv Griffin Show*

Vocal and electric guitar accompaniment: unknown

Location: Ronnie Scott's Jazz Club, London, England. Thursday 16 July 1970

Titles performed:
'As The Years Go Passing By'
'Kansas City'

Source: *Jazz Scene At Ronnie Scott's*

Vocal and electric guitar accompaniment: unknown

Location: New York City. 1971

Titles performed:
unknown

Source: *Farewell To Fillmore East*

Vocal and electric guitar accompaniment: unknown

Location: Coliseum Stadium, Los Angeles, California. Sunday 20 August 1972

Title performed:
'I'll Play The Blues For You'

Source: *Wattstax*

Vocal and electric guitar accompaniment: unknown

Location: Montreux, Switzerland. Summer 1973

Titles performed:
'Stormy Monday'
and other, unknown, titles

Source: *Montreux Jazz*

Vocal and electric guitar accompaniment: unknown

Location: Montreux, Switzerland. July 1975

Titles performed:
'Stormy Monday Blues'
'Kansas City'
and other, unknown, titles

Source: *Montreux Jazz*

Vocal and electric guitar accompaniment: unknown

Location: Chicago, Illinois. 1978

Titles performed:
unknown

Source: *Soundstage*

Vocal and electric guitar accompaniment: unknown

Location: Sweden. c. 1978–79

Titles performed:
'Born Under A Bad Sign'
'The Sky Is Crying'
'The Very Thought Of You'
'Cadillac Assembly Line'
'Summertime'
'Cold Woman With The Warm Heart'
'As The Years Go Passing By' [two versions]
[interview]

Source: *Swedish TV broadcast* [C]

Vocal and electric guitar accompaniment: unknown (brass, electric bass, drums)

Location: Ames, Iowa. Tuesday July 28 1981

Titles performed:
'Blues Riff' K-Jazz 145, Yazoo 509
'The Grass Ain't Greener' K-Jazz 145, Yazoo 509
'Born Under A Bad Sign' K-Jazz 145, Yazoo 509
'Stormy Monday Blues' K-Jazz 145, Yazoo 509
'Kansas City' K-Jazz 145, Yazoo 509
'The Very Thought Of You' K-Jazz 145, Yazoo 509
'Let The Good Times Roll' K-Jazz 145, Yazoo 509
'Ooh Ee Baby' K-Jazz 145, Yazoo 509

Source: *Maintenance Shop Blues*

Vocal and elecric guitar accompaniment: John Mayall's Bluesbreakers; Mayall (piano); Mick Taylor (electric guitar); John McVie (electric bass); Colin Allen (drums)

Location: New Jersey. 1982

Titles performed:
'Born Under A Bad Sign' Castle Hendring 6 086
'C C Rider' Castle Hendring 6 086
'Stormy Monday Blues' Castle Hendring 6 086

Source: *Blues Survivors*

Vocal and electric guitar accompaniment: unknown

Location: Lyon, France. Friday 20 July 1984

Titles performed:
'Kansas City'
'Gonne Move To The Outskirts Of Town'
'I Done Got Wise'
'Born Under A Bad Sign'
'Stormy Monday'
untitled instrumental (1)
untitled instrumental (2)

Source: *French TV broadcast* [C]

Vocal and electric guitar accompaniment: unknown

Location: Boston, Massachusetts. c. 1990

Titles performed:
unknown

Source: *unknown, probably US TV broadcast* [C]

BB KING

See Riley [Blues Boy] King.

BOBBY KING

This artist contributed some music to the soundtrack of the film *Crossroads*. See also Terry Evans.

EARL KING (Solomon Johnson)

Vocal accompaniment: unknown

Location: Chicago, Illinois. 1974

Titles performed:
unknown

Source: *Soundstage*

Vocal accompaniment: Bobby Radcliffe (electric guitar); David Hofstra (electric bass); Dickie Dworkin (drums)

Location: town square, Lugano, Italy. Early 1980s

Titles performed:
untitled instrumental

Source: *Italian TV broadcast* [C]

FREDDY [FREDDIE] KING

Electric guitar solos–1, vocal and electric guitar–2
accompaniment: Clarence 'Gatemouth' Brown and Johnnie Johnson (electric guitars); Dave 'Fathead' Newman and one unknown (trumpets); Harison Calloway and one unknown (tenor saxophones); 'Skip' [possibly Skippy Brooks] (piano); Finis Tasby (electric bass); Freeman Brown (drums); Jimmy Church (bongo drums); three different unnamed female dancers.
King and Gatemouth Brown, electric guitar duet, accompaniment: as above–3
as –2, accompanying Jimmy Ferguson 'the six-year-old stick of dynamite' [*sic*] (vocal)–4.
Spoken introductions by Hoss Allen

Location: WFAA-TV studios, Dallas, Texas. Tuesday 15 February 1966

Titles performed:
'Hideaway'–1 Vestapol 13014
'I Love The Woman'–2 Vestapol 13014

As above

Location: as above. Wednesday 16 February 1966

Titles performed:
'Funny Bone'–1 Vestapol 13014
'I'm Tore Down'–2 Vestapol 13014

As above

Location: as above. May–August 1966

Titles performed:
'Have You Ever Loved A Woman'–2 Vestapol 13014
'San-Ho-Zay'–1 Vestapol 13014
'Papa's Got A Brand New Bag'–1 Vestapol 13014
'See See Baby'–2 Vestapol 13014
'Sitting On The Boatdock'–2 Vestapol 13014
'Shuffle'–3 Vestapol 13014
'She Put The Whammy On Me'–2 Vestapol 13014
'San-Ho-Zay' (take 2)–1 Vestapol 13014
'Funny Bone' (take 2)–1 Vestapol 13014
'Hide Away' (take 2)–1 Vestapol 13014
[interview with Hoss Allen] Vestapol 13014
'Got My Mojo Working'–4

Source: *The Beat*

Vocal and electric guitar accompaniment: unknown (second electric guitar, electric organ, electric bass, drums)

Location: Los Angeles, California. Monday 31 August 1970

Titles performed:
'What I Like About You Baby'
'Have You Ever Loved A Woman' Vestapol 13010
'Look On Yonder's Wall' Vestapol 13010
'T'aint Nobody's Business' Vestapol 13010
'Whole Lotta Lovin'' Vestapol 13010
'Hideaway'
untitled instrumental

Source: *Boboquivari*

Vocal and electric guitar accompaniment: unknown (second electric guitar, electric organ, piano, electric bass, drums)

Location: probably Los Angeles, California. c. 1972

Titles performed:
[interview with Stefan Grossman] Vestapol 13010
'Ghetto Woman' Vestapol 13010
'Blues Band Shuffle' Vestapol 13010
'Sweet Home Chicago' Vestapol 13010
'Woman Across The River' Vestapol 13010

Source: *California Community TV*

Vocal and electric guitar accompaniment: unknown (electric organ, electric bass, drums)

Location: Sweden. 1972

Titles performed:
'Big Leg Woman' Vestapol 13041
'Blues Band Shuffle' Vestapol 13041
'Goin' Down' Vestapol 13041

Source: *Swedish TV broadcast* [C]

Vocal and electric guitar accompaniment: unknown (piano, electric bass, drums)

Location: London, England. 1972

Title performed:
'Woman Across The River' Vestapol 13010

Source: *The Old Grey Whistle Test*

Vocal and electric guitar, accompaniment: unknown (second electric guitar, electric piano, electric organ, electric bass, drums)

Location: The Sugarbowl, unknown location, South Carolina. Friday 22 September 1972

Titles performed:

'Big Legged Woman' Vestapol 13072
'Ain't Nobody's Business' Vestapol 13072
'I'm In Trouble' Vestapol 13072
'Key To The Highway' Vestapol 13072
'Blues Band Shuffle' Vestapol 13072
'Have You Ever Loved a Woman' Vestapol 13072
'Goin' Down' Vestapol 13072

Source: *unknown*

Vocal and electric guitar accompaniment: David Maxwell (piano);
unknown (electric bass); Charlie Robinson (drums)

Location: TV studio, Dallas, Texas. Saturday 20 January 1973

Titles performed:
'Big Legged Woman' Vestapol 13028
'Ain't Nobody's Business' Vestapol 13028
'Look On Yonder's Wall' Vestapol 13028
'Blues Band Shuffle' Vestapol 13028
'Have You Ever Loved A Woman' Vestapol 13028
'Goin' Down' Vestapol 13028
'Hide Away' Vestapol 13028
[interview-ST only] Vestapol 13028

Source: *US KERA-TV broadcast*

Vocal and electric guitar accompaniment: unknown (electric organ, electric bass, drums)

Location: London, England. Sunday 13 May 1973

Title performed:
'Boogie Funk' ['Blues Band Shuffle']

Source: *The Old Grey Whistle Test*

Vocal and electric guitar accompaninent: unknown

Location: Montreux, Switzerland. Summer 1973

Titles performed:
'Have You Ever Loved A Woman'
'Look On Yonder Wall'
'Ain't No Sunshine'

Source: *Montreux Jazz*

Vocal and electric guitar accompaniment: David Maxwell (piano); unknown (electric organ, electric bass, drums)

Location: Sweden. 1973

Titles performed:
'Have You Ever Loved A Woman' Vestapol 13014
'Blues Band Shuffle' Vestapol 13014
'Big Leg Woman' Vestapol 13014

Source: *Swedish TV broadcast* [C]

Vocal and electric guitar accompaniment: unknown (electric organ, electric bass, drums)

Location: London, England. Tuesday, 3 December 1973

Titles performed:
'Woke Up This Morning' Vestapol 13010
'The Things I Used To Do' Vestapol 13010

Source: *The Old Grey Whistle Test*

Vocal and electric guitar accompaniment: unknown (electric organ, electric bass, drums)

Location: London, England. Tuesday 1 November 1975

Title performed:
'Boogie Funk' ['Blues Band Shuffle']

Source: *The Old Grey Whistle Test*

Vocal and electric guitar

Location: County Jail, Travis, Texas. Thursday 4 November 1976

Titles performed:
'Let The Good Times Roll'
'Sweet Home Chicago'

Source: *At Travis County Jail*
There are reportedly Australian TV broadcasts by this artist made in 1975.

[LITTLE] JIMMY KING (Manuel James Gales)

Electric guitar solo accompaniment: Ron Levy (keyboards) and pre-recorded backing supplied by The Memphis Horns–1
As above with the Memphis Horns (tenor saxophone and trumpet)–2

Location: Crosstown studio, Memphis, Tennessee. 1994

Titles performed:
'Jimmy King Song' #1 [*sic*]–1 BMG un-numbered
'Tribute To Albert King'–2 BMG un-numbered
[interview] BMG un-numbered

Source: *True Believers – The Story Of Rounder Records*

RILEY [BB] KING

This artist first toured continental Europe in the autumn of 1968. There is, therefore, the possibility of there being TV appearances by him from that period, most likely in Belgium, France and Germany. He did not appear in the United Kingdom on this tour.

Vocal and electric guitar accompaniment: LLoyd Glenn (piano), and others, unknown.
As above, in duet with T-Bone Walker–1

Location: Monterey, California. 1968

Titles performed:
'Love My Baby'
untitled instrumental–1
'What In The World's Going To Happen'–1

Source: *Monterey Jazz Festival*

Vocal and electric guitar accompaniment: unknown

Location: unknown {USA}. 1968

Title performed:
'You Put It On Me' [ST only]

Source: *For Love Of Ivy*

Vocal and electric guitar accompaniment: unknown

Location: unknown {USA}. 1968

Title performed:
unknown

Source: *NET Jazz*

Vocal and electric guitar accompaniment:
unknown

Location: unknown, {USA}. 1969

Titles performed:
unknown

Source: *The Barbara McNair Show*

Vocal and electric guitar accompaniment:
unknown

Location: unknown {USA}. 1969

Titles performed:
unknown

Source: *Upbeat* [unconfirmed]

Vocal and electric guitar accompaniment:
unknown

Location: unknown {USA}. 1969

Titles performed:
unknown

Source: *Dial M For Music* [unconfirmed]

Vocal and electric guitar accompaniment:
unknown

Location: New York City. 1969

Titles performed:
unknown

Source: *The Dick Cavett Show*

Vocal and electric guitar accompaniment:
unknown

Location: unknown {USA}. 1969

Titles performed;
unknown

Source: *The Merv Griffin Show*

Vocal and electric guitar accompaniment:
unknown

Location: unknown {USA}. 1969

Titles performed:
unknown

Source: *Soul*

Vocal and electric guitar accompaniment:
unknown

Location: New York City. 1969

Titles performed:
unknown

Source: *The Tonight Show starring Johnny Carson*

Vocal and electric guitar accompaniment:
unknown

Location: unknown {USA}. 1969

Titles performed:
unknown

Source: *Music Scene*

Vocal and electric guitar accompaniment:
unknown

Location: unknown {USA}. 1970

Titles performed:
unknown

Source: *The David Frost Show*

Vocal and electric guitar accompaniment:
unknown

Location: New York City. 1970

Titles performed:
unknown

Source: *The Ed Sullivan Show*

Vocal and electric guitar accompaniment:
unknown

Location: New York City. 1970

Title performed:
unknown

Source: *The Tonight Show starring Johnny Carson*

Vocal and electric guitar

Location: New York City. 1970

Title performed:
'The Alphabet Song'

Source: *Sesame Street*

Vocal and electric guitar accompaniment:
unknown

Location: unknown {USA}

Titles performed:
unknown

Source: *Dynamite Chicken*

Vocal and electric guitar accompaniment:
unknown

Location: New York City. 1971

Titles performed:
unknown

Source: *The Ed Sullivan Show*

Vocal and electric guitar accompaniment:
unknown

Location: unknown {USA}. 1971

Titles performed:
unknown

Source: *Fanfare* [unconfirmed]

Vocal and electric guitar accompaniment:
unknown

Location: Los Angeles, California. 1971

Titles performed:
unknown

Source: *The Flip Wilson Show*

Vocal and electric guitar accompaniment:
unknown

Location: unknown {USA}. 1971

Titles performed:
unknown [ST only]

Source: *Fritz The Cat*

Vocal and electric guitar accompaniment:
unknown

Location: unknown {USA}. 1971

Titles performed:
unknown

Source: *The Mike Douglas Show*

Vocal and electric guitar accompaniment:
unknown

Location: unknown {USA}. 1971

Titles performed:
unknown

Source: *One Night Stand*

Vocal and electric guitar accompaniment:
unknown

Location: unknown {USA}. 1971

Titles performed:
'Seven Minutes' [ST only]

Source: *Seven Minutes*

Vocal and electric guitar accompaniment:
unknown (brass,
piano, electric bass, drums)

Location: unknown {USA}. 1971

Titles performed:

'You Got Me Down' [A] [B]	K-Jazz 019, Yazoo 507
'All Of Your Affection' [A]	K-Jazz 019, Yazoo 507
'Little Bit Of Love' [A]	K-Jazz 019, Yazoo 507

'Need My Woman' [A] [B]	K-Jazz 019, Yazoo 507
[interview] [A]	K-Jazz 019, Yazoo 507
[demonstration of the 'Pepticon' radio advertising jingle] [A]	K-Jazz 019, Yazoo 507
'Togetherness' [B]	

Source: *Out Of The Blacks, Into The Blues part 2* [A]; *Le Blues Entre Les Dents* [B]
All the above performances are used in extract only.

Vocal and electric guitar accompaniment: unknown

Location: unknown {USA}. January–May 1971

Titles performed:
unknown

Source: *The Pearl Bailey Show*

Vocal and electric guitar accompaniment: unknown

Location: unknown {USA}. 1971

Titles performed:
unknown

Source: *The Virginia Graham Show*

Vocal and electric guitar accompaniment: unknown

Location: unknown {USA}. 1971

Titles performed:
'How Blue Can You Get'
'Just A Little Love'

Source: *Medicine Ball Caravan*

Vocal and electric guitar accompaniment: unknown

Location: unknown {USA}. 1972

Titles performed:
unknown

Source: *Black Rodeo*

Vocal and electric guitar accompaniment: unknown

Location: unknown {USA}. 1972

Titles performed:
unknown

Source: *Kup's Show*

Vocal and electric guitar accompaniment: unknown

Location: unknown {USA}. 1972

Titles performed:
unknown

Source: *Soul Train*

Speech, possibly vocal and electric guitar

Location: unknown. 1972

appearance as the mystery guest

Source: *What's My Line?*

Vocal and electric guitar, accompaniment: unknown (brass, piano, electric bass, drums)

Location: Sing Sing prison, Ossining, New York. Thursday 23 November 1972

Titles performed:
unknown

Source: *Sing Sing Thanksgiving*

Vocal and electric guitar accompaniment: unknown

Location: unknown {USA}. 1973

Titles performed:
unknown

Source: *All Together Now*

Vocal and electric guitar accompaniment: unknown

Location: Civic Auditorium, Santa Monica, California. 1973

Titles performed:
unknown

Source: *Dick Clark Presents The Rock And Roll Years*

Vocal and electric guitar accompaniment:
unknown

Location: unknown {USA}. 1973

Titles performed:
unknown

Source: *George Carlin Monsanto Chemical Special*

Vocal and electric guitar accompaniment:
unknown

Location: unknown {USA}. 1973

Titles performed:
unknown

Source: *The Helen Reddy Show*

Vocal and electric guitar accompaniment:
unknown

Location: unknown {USA}. 1973

Titles performed:
unknown

Source: *In Concert* [1]

Vocal and electric guitar accompaniment:
unknown

Location: unknown {USA}. 1973

Titles performed:
unknown [may be ST only]

Source: *Let The Church Say Amen*

Vocal and electric guitar accompaniment:
unknown

Location: unknown {USA}. 1973

Titles performed:
unknown

Source: *Positively Black*

Vocal and electric guitar accompaniment:
unknown

Location: unknown {USA}. 1973

Title performed:
unknown

Source: *Soul Train*

Vocal and electric guitar accompaniment:
unknown

Location: unknown {USA}. 1973

Titles performed:
unknown

Source: *Music Scene*

Vocal and electric guitar accompaniment:
unknown (brass, piano, electric-bass, drums)

Location: Cook County Jail, Chicago, Illinois. 1974

Titles performed:
'Don't Answer The Door'
'Paying The Cost To Be The Boss'
and other, unknown, titles

Source: *BB King Revisits Cook County Jail*

Vocal and electric guitar, accompaniment:
unknown (two saxophones, two trombones, trumpet, second electric guitar, electric bass, drums)

Location: Kinshasa, Zaire, Africa. 1974

Titles performed:

blues instrumental	BMG 791010, HBO 0337
'To Know You Is To Love You'	BMG 791010, HBO 0337
'I Believe'	BMG 791010, HBO 0337
'Why I Sing The Blues'	BMG 791010, HBO 0337
'Ain't Nobody Home'	BMG 791010, HBO 0337
'Sweet Sixteen'	BMG 791010, HBO 0337

'The Thrill Is Gone' BMG 791010, HBO 0337
'Guess Who' BMG 791010, HBO 0337
'I Like To Live The Love' [*sic*] BMG 791010, HBO 0337

Source: *BB King Live In Africa*
Some of this material has also been used in *When We Were Kings*. Zaire is now the Democratic Republic of Congo.

Vocal and electric guitar accompaniment: unknown

Location: unknown {USA}. 1974

Titles performed:
unknown

Source: *Feeling Good*

Vocal and electric guitar accompaniment: unknown

Location: unknown {USA}. 1974

Titles performed:
unknown

Source: *Rhythm And Blues*

Vocal and electric guitar–1
Electric guitar accompaniment: unknown (piano)–2
Vocal and electric guitar accompaniment: unknown (electric piano)–3

Location: Mississippi. 1975

Titles performed:
untitled blues–1 CFSC1077
untitled instrumental–2 CFSC1077
'The Thrill Is Gone'–3 CFSC1077
[interview] CFSC1077
[appearance as disc jockey in radio station] CFSC1077

Source: *Give My Poor Heart Ease*

Vocal and electric guitar accompaniment: unknown

Location: unknown {USA}. 1975

Titles performed:
unknown

Source: *The Merv Griffin Show*

Vocal and electric guitar accompaniment: unknown

Location: unknown {USA}. 1975

Title performed:
unknown

Source: *Soul Train*

Vocal and electric guitar accompaniment: unknown

Location: unknown {USA}. 1976

Titles performed:
unknown

Source: *Get Down*

Vocal and electric guitar accompaniment: unknown

Location: unknown {USA}. 1976

Titles performed:
unknown

Source: *The Merv Griffin Show*

Vocal and electric guitar accompaniment: unknown

Location: unknown {USA}. 1976

Titles performed:
unknown

Source: *Sammy And Company*

Vocal and electric guitar accompaniment: studio orchestra

Location: Los Angeles, California. Late 1977–early 1978

Title performed:
unknown

Source: *Captain And Tennille*

Vocal and electric guitar accompaniment: unknown–1
Vocal duet with Bobby Bland accompaniment: own electric guitar and others, unknown–2

Location: Chicago, Illinois. Monday 10 January 1977

Titles performed:
'Everybody Lies A Little'–1
'How Blue Can You Get'–1
'It's My Own Fault'–2
'Let The Good Times Roll'–2
'My Song'–1
'Outside Help'–1
'The Thrill Is Gone'–2

Source: *Soundstage*

Comedic monologue

Location: unknown {USA}. 1977

introduction to sketch entitled 'Blacks Without Soul'

Source: *Kentucky Fried Movie*

Unknown contribution

Location: unknown {USA}. 1977

Titles performed:
unknown, if any. Possibly comedic contribution

Source: *Sanford And Son*

Vocal and electric guitar accompaniment: unknown (brass, electric guitar, electric bass, drums)

Location: Nice, France. Wednesday 5–Saturday 15 July 1978

Titles performed:
band instrumental
'How Blue Can You Get'
'Caldonia'
'Outside Help'
'The Same Old Story'
'Guess Who'
'Can't Leave Your Love Alone'
'Late Hour Blues'
'The Same Old Story'–reprise
'Night Life'

Source: *La Grande Parade Du Jazz*

Vocal duet with Crystal Gayle, accompaniment: studio orchestra

Location: unknown {USA}. 1978

Titles performed:
'Same Old Story'
'Night Life'

Source: *The Crystal Gayle Show*

Vocal and electric guitar accompaniment: unknown (tenor saxophone, trumpet, electric guitar, electric bass, drums)

Location: London, England. Tuesday 17 October 1978

Titles performed:
'When It All Comes Down'
'Hold On'

Source: *The Old Grey Whistle Test*

Narration

Location: Mississippi. 1978

[on-camera narration for documentary]
K-Jazz 030,
Yazoo 505

Source: *Good Morning Blues*

Speech

Location: probably Memphis, Tennessee. 1978

[interview]

Source: *Beale Street*

Vocal and electric guitar accompaniment: unknown

Location: Montreaux, Switzerland. 1979

Titles performed:
unknown

Source: *Montreux Jazz*

Vocal and electric guitar accompaniment: unknown (brass, electric guitar, electric bass, drums)

Location: Montreux, Switzerland. July 1980

Titles performed:
'Let The Good Times Roll'
'Everyday I Have The Blues'
'How Blue Can You Get'
'Better Not Look Down'
'When It All Comes Down'
'The Thrill Is Gone'
untitled instrumental

Source: *Montreux Jazz*

Vocal and electric guitar accompaniment: unknown (brass, electric guitar, electric bass, drums)

Location: Montreux, Switzerland. July 1981

Titles performed:
band instrumental
'Let The Good Times Roll'
'Everyday I Have The Blues'
'Better Not Look Down'
'When It All Comes Down'

Source: *Montreux Jazz*

Speech

Location: unknown {USA}. 1981

[interview]

Source: *MTV*

Vocal and electric guitar accompaniment: the Gerald Wiggins orchestra–1
as above, in duet with Linda Hopkins–2

Location: unknown {USA}. 1982

Titles performed:
'Paying The Cost To Be The Boss'–1 Magnum MMGV-035
'How Blue Can You Get'–1 Magnum MMGV-035
'The Letter'–1 Magnum MMGV-035
'Everyday I Have The Blues'–2 Magnum MMGV-035

Source: *America's Music – Blues Vol. 1*

Vocal and electric guitar accompaniment: Calvin Owens, James Bolden, Edgar Synical (tenor saxophones); Joseph Carrier (keyboards); Leon Warren (electric guitar); Russell Jackson (electric bass); Herman Jackson (drums)

Location: Montreux, Switzerland. Tuesday 27 July 1982.

Titles performed:
band instrumental
'Everyday I Have The Blues'
'Sweet Little Angel'
'Let The Good Times Roll'
'Don't Answer The Door'
'In My Song'
'Guess Who'
'Love Me Tender'
untitled instrumental #1
'I Just Can't Leave Your Love Alone'
'When It All Comes Down'
'There's Gotta Be A Better World'
'Shopping For A Tombstone'
'The Thrill Is Gone'
untitled instrumental #2
'Drinkin' Woman'

Source: *Montreux Jazz*

Vocal and electric guitar accompaniment: probably as above

Location: Austin, Texas. 1983

Titles performed:
'Everyday I Have The Blues'
'Night Life'
untitled instrumental
'Since I Met You Baby'
'Love Me Tender'
'All Of Your Affection'
'When It All Comes Down'
'One Of Those Nights'
'That's The Way A Love Song Goes'
'Guess Who'
'The Thrill Is Gone'

Source: *Austin City Limits*

Vocal and electric guitar accompaniment: probably as above

Location: unknown {USA}. 1983

Titles performed:
'Every Day I Have The Blues' Castle HEN20496
'Nightlife' Castle HEN20496
'Better Not Look Down' Castle HEN20496
'Never Make Your Move Too Soon' Castle HEN20496
'Sell My Monkey' Castle HEN20496
'Love Me Tender' Castle HEN20496
'Inflation Blues' Castle HEN20496
'The Thrill Is Gone' Castle HEN20496
'There Must Be A Better World Somewhere' Castle HEN20496

Source: *Live At Nick's*

Vocal and electric guitar accompaniment: probably as above

Location: Her Majesty's Theatre, London, England. Late 1984

Titles performed:
'Everyday I Have The Blues'
'How Blue Can You Get'

Source: *Live From Her Majesty's*

Vocal and electric guitar accompaniment: probably as above

Location: London, England. Friday 28 December 1984

Titles performed:
'When It All Comes Down'
'Hummingbird'

Source: *The Tube*

Vocal and electric guitar accompaniment: probably as above

Location: Tufts University, Boston, Massachusetts. c.1984–5

Titles performed:
'Let The Good Times Roll'
'Don't Answer The Door'
'Paying The Cost To Be The Boss'
'I Need My Baby'
'Guess Who'
'The Story Of Lucille'
'The Letter'
'The Thrill Is Gone'

Source: *unknown* [C]. Broadcast as part of UK BBC-TV's *Arena Blues Night*, 27 July 1985

Vocal and electric guitar accompaniment: unknown

Location: Netherlands. Saturday 13 July 1985

Titles performed:
unknown

Source: *Live Aid*

Speech, comments, demonstration of guitar styles on electric guitar.

Location: London, England. Saturday 27 July 1985

co-host, with John Walters, of *Arena Blues Night*, a 4 hour TV special

Source: *Arena Blues Night*

Vocal and electric guitar accompaniment: Steve Watson (electric guitar); John Hobbs (keyboards); Jim Cook (synths); Ray Kreber (bass-synth); Niel Stubhausen (electric bass)

Location: Hollywood, California. March 1985

Titles performed:
'Into The Night'
'My Lucille'
'(I'm Gonna Wait Till) The Midnight Hour'

Source: *Into The Night*
Some, if not all, of the above, may be [ST] only

Vocal and electric guitar accompaniment: Walter King and Edgar Synical (tenor saxophones); James Bolden (trumpet); Jospeh Carrier (keyboards); Leon Warren (electric guitar); Michael Doster (electric bass); Caleb Emphrey Jr. (drums)

Location: Hamburg, Germany. Tuesday 28 October 1986

Titles performed:
band instrumental
'Let The Good Times Roll'
untitled instrumental
'All Of Your Affection'
'Whole Lotta Lovin''

'Night Life'
'Everyday I Have The Blues'
'Got A Mind To Give Up Living'
'Made Your Move Too Soon'
'Catfish Blues'
'Ain't Nobody's Business'
'The Thrill Is Gone'

Source: *Der Fabrik*

Vocal and electric guitar accompaniment: probably as above

Location: Barcelona, Spain. c.1986–87

Titles performed:
'All Of Your Affection'
'Night Life'
'Early In The Morning'
'Got A Good Mind To Give Up'
'One Of Those Nights'
'The Thrill Is Gone'
'Goin' Out Of My Mind'
'How Blue Can You Get'
'When The Saints Go Marchin' In'
untitled instrumental

Source: *Spanish TV broadcast* [C]

Vocal and electric guitar accompaniment: probably as above

Location: Japan. c.1986–87

Titles performed:
'Sweet Little Angel'
'Why I Sing The Blues'

Source: *5th Budweiser Annual Newport Jazz Festival*

Speech

Location: unknown {USA}. 1987

[interview]

Source: *Ain't Nothing But The Blues*

Vocal and electric guitar accompaniment: Bono (vocal, electric guitar, harmonica) and U2 [G]: The Edge (electric guitar, keyboards); Adam Clayton (electric bass); Larry Millan Jr. (drums)

Location: unknown {USA}. 1988

Titles performed:
'When Love Comes To Town'

Source: *U2: Rattle And Hum*

Vocal and electric guitar accompaniment: unknown

Location: New Orleans, Louisiana. 1991

Title performed:
unknown Island 4973

Source: *unknown*

Vocal and electric guitar accompanment: Steve Cropper, Dave Edmunds (electric guitars); and others, unknown

Location: Expo '92, Seville, Spain. 1992

Titles performed:
'Movin' On'
'Back In L.A.'
instrumental jam

Source: *Guitar Legends*

Speech

Location: unknown. c.1993

[interview]

Source: *John Lee Hooker*

Speech

Location: unknown {USA}. 1994

[interview] California Newsreel 01

Source: *Saturday Night, Sunday Morning*

Vocal and electric guitar accompaniment: unknown

Location: unknown {USA}. 1997

Titles performed:
unknown

Source: *Blues Brothers 2000*

BB King appeared, at least once, on the *Cosby Show* between 1984 and 1992. He also appears in the following tutorials:

DCI 21733 *Bluesmaster Vol. 1*;
DCI 21734 *Bluesmaster Vol. 2*;
DCI 21735 *Bluesmaster Vol. 3*;
DCI 22393/Rhino R3.90673 *Bluesmaster highlights*.

The following film biographies of the artist are also of interest:

King Of The Blues – Omnibus, UK BBC-TV broadcast, 1991;
BB King – Rockumentary/VH-1. MTV. 1997

KINGDOM CENTER ANGELIC CHOIR OF JACKSONVILLE, FLORIDA

Mixed vocal choir accompaniment: unknown

Location: Jacksonville, Florida. 1966

Titles performed:
unknown

Source: *TV Gospel Time* #59

EDDIE KIRKLAND

Speech

Location: Atlanta, Georgia. October 1984

[interview]

Source: *National Downhome Blues Festival*
Kirkland does not perform in this film, but, since he was there, the possibility exists of there being unbroadcast material by him.

Vocal and guitar accompaniment: Neal Pattman (harmonica)

Location: Macon, Georgia. 1992

Title performed:
'C C Rider' JVC V-225

Source: *Music Masters And Rhythm Kings*

Speech

Location: unknown {USA}. 1993

[interview]

Source: *John Lee Hooker*

[REVEREND] FREDERICK DOUGLASS KIRKPATRICK

Preaching and singing, accompaniment: Cook County Convention Gospel Choir (vocals)

Location: Newport, Rhode Island. July 1969

Titles performed:
unknown

Source: *Folklife* productions

MARIE KNIGHT

Vocal accompaniment: unknown (piano)–1
Vocal accompaniment: the Pentecostal Temple Choir of Memphis–2
Vocal accompaniment: the New Salem Baptist Church Choir–3

Location: Memphis, Tennessee. Saturday 19 January 1963

Titles performed:
'Poor Pilgrim'–1 [A]
'Swing Low, Sweet Chariot'–1 [C]
'very Time I Feel The Spirit'–1 [B]
'Joshua Fit De Battle Of Jericho' [*sic*]–1 [B]
'You Better Run'–2 [A]
'Jacob's Ladder'–3 [C]

Source: *TV Gospel Time* #19 [A], #20 [B], #22 [C]

L

LADIES OF HARMONY

Vocal group, accompaninent: unknown

Location: Chicago, Illinois. Sunday 15 March 1964

Titles performed:
unknown

Source: *Jubilee Showcase* [prog #7–1]

LANDIS FAMILY

Bertha–1, Claude–2, Doshie–3, Fleming–4, Jessie Mae–5, Priscilla–6, Robert–7, Tony–8, Truezell–9, Zenas–10, Bill Brasswell–11 (speech and a cappella vocals); Tony Landis (vocal) accompaniment: unknown (organ and congregation)–12

Location: North Carolina. 1985
[A] the Landis residence, Creedmoor
[B] Rock Spring Baptist Church, Rock Spring

Titles performed:
'I Belong To The Union Band' [ST] [A] Shanachie 1402
'Heaven On My Mind'–1, –2, –7, –8 [A] Shanachie 1402
'God Got Tired Of Your Wicked Ways'–2, –4, –7, –8 [A] Shanachie 1402
'When Was Jesus Born'–2, –7, –8, –11 [A] Shanachie 1402
'I'm Going Up To Meet Him Bye And Bye'–2, –4, –7, –8 [A] Shanachie 1402
'I Belong To That Union Band'–12 [B] Shanachie 1402
[interviews and conversation]–1 to 10 [A&B] Shanachie 1402

Source: *A Singing Stream*
See also the Echoes of Heaven and the Golden Echoes.

LARKS

Vocal group accompaniment: probably the Mitchell Ayres orchestra

Location: New York City. 1952

Titles performed:
unknown

Source: *The Perry Como Show*

Vocal group, including Thermon Ruth, accompaniment: Paul Williams (baritone saxophone); Jimmy Brown (trumpet); unknown (tenor saxophone, piano, bass, drums)

Location: New York City. 1955

Titles performed:
'The World Is Waiting For The Sunrise'
'Without A Song' Storyville SV6016, Video Images 73R
'Shadrack' Fil A Film 2023, Video Images 74

Source: *Showtime At The Apollo*

REESE LARUE

Vocal accompaniment: unknown

Location: unknown {USA}. 1956

Title performed:
'Don't Be That Way'

Source: *Rockin' The Blues*

BOOKER T LAURY

Vocal and piano

Location: Memphis, Tennessee. 1984

Titles performed;
'Memphis Blues' Arrow AV015
'Early In The Morning' Arrow AV015

Source: *Saturday Blues*

Vocal and piano accompaniment: unknown (bass, drums)

Location: probably Memphis, Tennessee, 1989

Title performed:
'Big Legged Woman' [part only]

Source: *Great Balls Of Fire*
Laury appears in this film as 'Piano Slim'. The above title segues into a version performed by Jerry Lee Lewis and mimed by Dennis Quaid. See also Valerie Wellington.

Vocal and piano accompaniment: unknown

Location: Blues Legends Club, Chicago, Illinois. 1990

Titles performed:
'Boogie Woogie' BMG 791.151, Rhino R91226
'Nothing But The Blues' BMG 791.151, Rhino R91226

Source: *Blues Alive*

Vocal and piano

Location: Memphis, Tennessee. Autumn 1990

Title performed:
'Memphis Blues' [44 Blues] Anxious 45099-29643, BMG un-numbered

Source: *Deep Blues*

HUDDIE WILLIAM LEDBETTER aka LEADBELLY

Vocal and 12-string guitar

Location: Taft Hotel, Wilton, Connecticut. Friday 8–Sunday 10 February 1935

Titles performed:
'Take This Hammer' take 1 Vestapol 13016
'Take This Hammer' take 2 Vestapol 13016
'Goodnight Irene' [one verse only]
[dialogue with Alan Lomax]

Source: *March of Time*
Take 2 of 'Take This Hammer' was not included in the original *March of Time* film.

Vocal and 12-string guitar

Location: Hollywood, California. c. October 1944

Titles performed:
'The Grey Goose' Vestapol 13016
'Pick A Bale Of Cotton' Rhino R3.2101, Vestapol 13016
'Take This Hammer' Vestapol 13016

Source: *Three Songs By Leadbelly*

LAFAYETTE LEAKE

Piano solo

Location: Chicago, Illinois. c. 1978

Title performed:
untitled blues instrumental

Source: *Chicago Melodie*

FRANKIE LEE

Vocal accompaniment: unknown (tenor saxophone, electric guitar, keyboards. electric bass, drums)

Location: Oakland, California. 1981

Title performed:
I Need A Lot Of Love
[interview]

Source: *Long Train Running*

JULIA LEE

Vocal and piano accompaniment: unknown

Location: probably Hollywood, California. 1957

Titles performed:
unknown

Source: *Delinquents*

MABEL LEE

Vocal and dancing accompaniment: unknown (piano, guitar, bass, drums)–1;
dance routine in the company of Nicky O'Daniel, Shim Sham and others, unknown, accompaniment: as above–2

Location: New York City. Mid 1943

Title performed:
[5M1] 'Chicken Shack Shuffle'–1 Charly #2, Jazz Classics JCVC-107, Storyville SV6003, Virgin VVD-868
[4M4] 'Dancemania'–2 Charly #2

Source: *Soundies*. Both titles copyrighted 21 September 1943.

Dancing accompaniment: Deryck Sampson (piano); unknown (guitar, bass, drums)–1 dialogue with Dewey [Pigmeat] Markham (speech), accompaniment: studio orchestra–2

Location: New York City. Late 1945

Titles Performed:
[87608] 'Cats Can't Dance'–1 Charly #2, Storyville SV6003, Virgin VVD868
[14M1] 'Pigmeat Throws The Bull'–2 Charly #2

Source: *Soundies*. Copyright dates are: 14M1, 24 Dec 1945.
Some of these titles also appear in *Ebony Parade*.

Vocal and/or dancing accompaniment: unknown

Location: probably New York City. 1947

Titles performed:
unknown

Source: *O'Voutie O'Rooney*

As above

Location: probably New York City. 1948

Titles performed:
unknown

Source: *The Dreamer*

LEFTY DIZZ (Walter Williams)

Vocal and electric bass accompaniment: Jimmy Johnson and Willie James Lyons (electric guitars); Odie Payne (drums); John 'Big Moose' Walker (piano)

Location: unknown {Europe}. c.1978–79

Title performed:
'All Your Love'

Source: *European TV broadcast* [C]. Origin unknown.

Vocal and electric guitar accompaniment: Shock Treatment [G]; Ralph Lapetine (organ); Queen Sylvia Embry (electric bass); Woody Williams (drums)

Location: Freedom Village, Greenville, Mississippi. Saturday 8 September 1979

Title performed:
'Don't Make Your Move Too Soon' K-Jazz 081

Source: *Mississippi Blues*

LEGENDARY BLUES BAND

See Joe Willie 'Pinetop' Perkins.

J B LENOIR

Vocal and guitar

Location: Chicago, Illinois. Monday 11 July 1960

Titles performed:
'Someday Baby' [ST] K-Jazz 014, Rhapsody 8022
'Stand By Me' [ST] K-Jazz 014, Rhapsody 8022

Source: *Blues Like Showers Of Rain*

Vocal and guitar–1
as above accompaniment: Fred Below (drums)–2

Location: Baden-Baden, Germany. October 1965

Titles performed:
'Alabama Blues'–1
'The Whale Has Swallowed Me'–2

Source: *American Folk Blues Festival 1965*

FURRY LEWIS

See Walter [Furry] Lewis

GEORGIA LEWIS

Vocal accompaniment: unknown–1
Vocal accompaniment: the Sanctuary Choir–2

Location: New York City. Saturday 28 July 1962

Titles performed:
'You're Not Alone'–1
'Walk All Over God's Heaven'–2

Source: *TV Gospel Time* #17

Vocal accompaniment: unknown–1
Vocal duet with Ethel Daveport, accompaniment: unknown–2

Location: New York City. c.1965

Titles performed:
'Walk With Me, God'–1
'Briny Tears'–2

Source: *TV Gospel Time* #48

Vocal accompaniment: unknown

Location: New York City. c.1965–6

Title performed:
unknown

Source: *TV Gospel Time* #58
See also Ethel Davenport.

JOHNNY LEWIS
Vocal and guitar–1
Vocal, guitar and kazoo–2

Location: Chicago, Illinois. April–May 1970

Titles performed:

'Hobo Blues'–1 [part only]	K-Jazz 004, Rhapsody 9012
untitled instrumental-2	K-Jazz 004, Rhapsody 9012
'I'm Gone'–1 [part only]	K-Jazz 004, Rhapsody 9012
[interview]	K-Jazz 004, Rhapsody 9012

Source: *Chicago Blues*

MEADE LUX LEWIS
Piano solo, with Katherine Dunham, dancing

Location: probably Hollywood, California. Mid-1942

Title performed:
[8103] 'Spirit Of Boogie Woogie'

Source: *Soundie*
Copyrighted 17 August 1942

Piano solo–1
Piano solo accompaniment: dubbed orchestra–2; piano accompaniment to Dudley Dickerson, miming to Joe Turner (vocal)–3

Location: Hollywood, California. Early 1944

Titles performed:

[16008] 'Roll 'em'–1	Charly #2, Jazz & Jazz Vidjazz 20, Storyville SV6013, Virgin VVD762
[16308] 'Boogie Woogie'–2	Charly #2, Charly SOUND-1940, Jazz & Jazz Vidjazz 20 Storyville SV6013, Virgin VVD-762
[16508] 'Low Down Dog'–3	Charly #2, Jazz & Jazz Vidjazz 20, Jazz Classics JCVC105, Storyville SV6013, Virgin VVD-762

Source: *Soundies*. Copyright dates are: 16008, 3 April 1944; 16308, 24 April 1944; 16508 15 May 1944. One, at least, of the above probably appears in *Hep Cat Serenade*.

Piano solo

Location: Hollywood, California. 1947

Title performed:
'Honky Tonk Train Blues'

Source: *New Orleans*

Piano solo

Location: Hollywood, California. 1955

Title performed:
un-named

Source: *Nightmare*
This performance is almost completely obscured by dialogue, but Lewis also appears in a dramatic role in this film. See also Joe Turner.

NATHANIEL LEWIS
Vocal accompaniment: unknown

Location: New York City. c.1966

Title performed:
unknown

Source: *TV Gospel Time* #63

NATHANIEL LEWIS SINGERS
Vocal group accompaniment: unknown; Alvin Fuller (solo vocal)–1

Location: New York City. Sunday 28 October 1962

Titles performed:
'What Will The Verdict Be'
'The Lord Raised Me'
'Somebody Touched Me'–1

Source: *TV Gospel Time* #5

SMILEY LEWIS (Amos Overton Lemon)
Vocal accompaniment: Dave Bartholomew orchestra

Location: New Orleans, Louisiana. Tuesday 2 October 1956

Title performed:
'Shame, Shame, Shame' [ST only]

Source: *Baby Doll*
This appears on the soundtrack only, is a different version to the commercially issued recording (Imperial 5418), and was included on the soundtrack vinyl LP 'Baby Doll', [US] Columbia CL958.

WALTER [FURRY] LEWIS
Vocal and guitar

Location: Memphis, Tennessee. 1962

Title performed:
'John Henry'

Source: *The Blues* [1]

Vocal and electric guitar

Location: KCTS-TV studios, Seattle, Washington. May 1968

Titles performed:
'Judge Boushe' [*sic*] Vestapol 13037
'Furry's Blues' Vestapol 13037
'See That My Grave Is Kept Clean' Vestapol 13037
'John Henry' Vestapol 13037
'Brownsville Blues' Vestapol 13004

Source: *University of Washington/Seattle Folklore Society*
'Brownsville Blues' also appears in *Roots Of American Music*

Vocal and guitar

Location: KCTS-TV studios, Seattle, Washington. Probably May 1968

Titles performed:
'Furry's Blues' Yazoo 519
'Brownsville Blues' Yazoo 519
'Kansas City' Yazoo 519
'Take Me Back Baby' Yazoo 519
'Kassie Jones' Yazoo 519
'I Will Turn Your Money Green' Yazoo 519
'Baby Won't You Please Come Home' Yazoo 519

Source: *Masters Of Traditional American Music*

Vocal and guitar

Location: Los Angeles, California. 1970

Titles performed:
unknown

Source: *The Homewood Show* [unconfirmed]

Vocal and guitar

Location: Memphis, Tennessee. 1971

Title performed:
'When I Lay My Burden Down' [part only] [A] K-Jazz 020, Yazoo 506
'Looking For My Sweet Jelly Roll' [B]

Source: *Out Of The Blacks, Into The Blues part 1* [A]; *Le Blues Entre Les Dents* [B]

Vocal and guitar

Location: unknown {USA}. 1972

Titles performed:
unknown

Source: *Thinking Out Loud* [unconfirmed]

Vocal and guitar

Location: Los Angeles, California. 1976

Title performed:
unknown

Source: *The Tonight Show Starring Johnny Carson*

Vocal and guitar

Location: unknown {USA}. 1975

Title performed:
'Shake 'em On Down' [fragment only]
'Dirty Car Blues' [fragment only]
'The Lord's Prayer' [fragment only]
incidental guitar playing [ST]

Source: *W W And The Dixie Dancekings*
Furry Lewis also had a dramatic role in the above film.

Vocal and guitar

Location: unknown {USA}. 1976

Titles performed:
unknown

Source: *The Mac Davis Show* [unconfirmed]

Vocal and electric guitar

Location: Memphis, Tennessee. 1978

Titles performed:
'Brownsville Blues' [part only] K-Jazz 030, Yazoo 505
[short monologue] K-Jazz 030, Yazoo 505

Source: *Good Morning Blues*

LI'L ED AND THE BLUES IMPERIALS (Edward Williams)
Vocal and electric guitar accompaniment: Mike Carras (electric guitar); Eddie McKinley (tenor saxophone); James Young (electric bass); Kelly Littleton (drums)

Location: recording studio, Chicago, Illinois. c. March 1992

Titles performed:
'Ed's Boogie' (take 1) BMG 80046-3
'Ed's Boogie' (take 2) BMG 80046-3
[interview] BMG 80046-3

Source: *Pride And Joy*

As above

Location: Chestnut Cabaret, Philadelphia, Pennsylvania. Thursday 12 March 1992

Title performed:
'Pride And Joy' BMG 80046-3

Source: *Pride And Joy*
See also Koko Taylor.

JOE LIGGINS
Vocal accompaniment: unknown

Location: North Carolina. 1981

Titles performed:
unknown

Source: *local TV broadcast*

Vocal accompaniment: unknown

Location: North Carolina, Sunday 25 July 1982

Titles performed:
unknown

Source: *local TV broadcast* [C]

Vocal and tenor saxophone accompaniment; the Honeydrippers, personel unknown

Location: Los Angeles, California. 1984

Titles performed:
'Honeydripper'
'Pink Champagne'
'Little Joe's Boogie'

Source: *Legends Of Rhythm And Blues*

Speech

Location: Los Angeles, California. 1986

[interview]

Source: *Remembering Black Music*

ALEXANDER [PAPA] LIGHTFOOT
presumably vocal and harmonica

Location: unknown {USA}. c.1956

Titles performed:
unknown

Source: *Spooky Loot* [unconfirmed]

LIGHTNIN' SLIM (Otis Hicks)
Vocal and electric guitar accompaniment: probably Snooky Pryor (harmonica); Boogie Woogie Red (piano); Roger Hill (electric bass); Tom Parnell (drums)

Location: Brighton Polytechnic, Sussex, England. Friday 16 February 1973

Titles performed:
unknown

Source: *Blues Legends 73*

JOE LIGON
Vocal accompaniment: unknown

Location: Chicago, Illinois. Saturday 19 October 1968

Titles performed:
unknown

Source: *Jubilee Showcase* [prog #2–3]

Speech

Location: Los Angeles, California. August 1995

[interview]

Source: *Too Close To Heaven*
See also the Mighty Clouds Of Joy.

DOROTHY LIPSCOMB
Vocal accompaniment: unknown

Location: Chicago, Illinois. Sunday 9 February 1964

Titles performed:
unknown

Source: *Jubilee Showcase* [prog #12–1]

MANCE LIPSCOMB
Vocal and guitar

Location: Navasota, Texas. Spring 1963

Title performed:
'Goin' Down Slow' [part only] Yazoo 520

Source: *Die Blues*

Vocal and guitar accompaniment: Lightnin' Hopkins (guitar); Billy Bizor (harmonica)–1
Vocal and guitar accompaniment: Lightnin' Hopkins (guitar)–2

Location: Centerville, Texas. 1967

Titles performed:
untitled–1 Flower 1, K-Jazz 053
'Goin' Away Baby'–2 Flower 1, K-Jazz 053

Source: *The Blues According To Lightnin' Hopkins*

Vocal and guitar

Location: KCTS-TV studios, Seattle, Washington. February 1968

Titles performed:
'Motherless Children Have A Hard Time' Vestapol 13002
'Run Sinner, Run' Vestapol 13004
'Captain, Captain' Vestapol 13041
'Night Time Is The Right Time' Vestapol 13041
'God Moves On The Water' Vestapol 13041
'Which Way Do The Red River Run' Vestapol 13041

Source: *University of Washington/Seattle Folklore Society*
'Motherless Children' and 'Run, Sinner Run' also appear in *Roots Of American Music.*

Vocal and guitar

Location: KCTS-TV studios, Seattle, Washington. Probably February 1968

Titles performed:
'Sugar Babe' Yazoo 502
'Ella Speed' Yazoo 502
'Want To Do Something For You' Yazoo 502
[monologue, leading to;]
'Baby, Please Don't Go' Yazoo 502
[monologue, leading to;]
'Shine On Harvest Moon' Yazoo 502
[monologue leading to;]
'You Got To See Mama Every Night' Yazoo 502
[monologue leading to;]
'Goin' Down Slow' Yazoo 502
[monologue leading to;]
'Night Time Is The Right Time' Yazoo 502
[monologue leading to;]
'Jack O'Diamonds' Yazoo 502

Source: *Masters Of Traditional American Music*

Vocal and guitar

Location: KLRU-TV, Texas. 1969

Titles performed:
'So Different Blues' Vestapol 13011
'Take Me Back' Vestapol 13011
'Going Down Slow' Vestapol 13011
'Keep On Trucking' Vestapol 13011
'Alcohol Blues' Vestapol 13011
'Angel Child' Vestapol 13011
'Silver City' Vestapol 13011
'Night Time Is The Right Time' Vestapol 13011
'Key To The Highway' Vestapol 13011
'You Got To See Mama Every Night' Vestapol 13011
'Mama Don't Allow' Vestapol 13011
'Long Way To Tipperary' Vestapol 13011
'Baby, You Don't Have To Go' Vestapol 13011
'When The Saints Go Marching In' Vestapol 13011
'Motherless Children' Vestapol 13011
'I Want To Do Something For You' Vestapol 13011

Source: *KLRU-TV, Texas* [C]

Vocal and guitar

Location: Navasota, Texas. 1970

Titles performed:
'Lonesome Bedroom Blues' Flower 2, K-Jazz 055
'Night Time Is The Right Time' Flower 2, K-Jazz 055
'Motherless Children' Flower 2, K-Jazz 055
'St. James Infirmary' Flower 2, K-Jazz 055

Source: *A Well Spent Life*
All other music heard in this film is from previously recorded material for the Arhoolie label.

Vocal and guitar

Location: probably Navasota, Texas. 1971

Titles peformed:
'Rock Me Baby' (two takes) [A] K-Jazz 020, Yazoo 506
'C C Rider' [B]
'All Night Long' [C]

Source: *Out Of The Blacks, Into The Blues Part 1* [A]; *Le Blues Entre Les Dents* [C]

Vocal and guitar

Location: KLRU-TV, Texas. 1972

Titles performed:
'Silver City' Vestapol 13003
'Angel Child' Vestapol 13003
'Take Me Back' Vestapol 13004

Source: *KLRU-TV, Texas* [C]

LITTLE CRISS
Little Criss Johnson (vocal) accompaniment: The Righteous Singers (mixed vocal group)

Location: Chicago, Illinois. Wednesday 2 August 1972

Titles performed:
unknown

Source: *Jubilee Showcase* [prog #24–1]

LITTLE DOTS
Vocal group accompaniment: unknown

Location: Gary, Indiana. June 1976

Titles performed:
unknown

Source: *Gospel In Gary*

LITTLE ED
See Li'l Ed and the Blues Imperials.

LITTLE ESTHER
See [Little] Esther Phillips.

LITTLE FOUR
Vocal quartet accompaniment: unknown

Location: unknown {USA}. c.1941–43

Titles performed:
[18808] 'Cha-Chi-Man' Charly #7
[19408] 'Love Grows On A White Oak Tree' Charly #7
[10M1] 'Chilly'n'Cold' Charly #7

Source: *Soundies*

LITTLE JEFF
Vocal and accordion accompaniment: unknown (rub-board, electric guitar, electric bass, drums)

Location: Plaisance, Louisiana. 1988

Title performed:
'Last Night' [part only] K-Jazz 098, Rhapsody 8062

Source: *Zydeco Gumbo*

LITTLE JOE BLUE (Joe Valery)
Vocal and electric guitar accompaniment: unknown (tenor saxophone, keyboards, second electric guitar, electric bass, drums)

Location: Sacramento, California. September 1987

Title performed:
'Making A Good Man Out Of Me'

Source: *Sacramento Blues Festival 1987*

LITTLE MILTON (Milton Campbell)
Vocal accompaniment: The Blue Beats; Clarence 'Gatemouth' Brown (electric guitar); Johnny Johnson (electric guitar); Dave 'Fathead' Newman and one unknown (trumpets); Harrison Calloway and one unknown (tenor saxophones); 'Skip' [possibly Skippy Brooks] (piano); Finis Tasby (electric bass); Freeman Brown (drums)

Location: WFAA-TV studios, Dallas, Texas. Monday 31 January 1966

Titles performed:
'We're Gonna Make It'
'Blind Man'
'Who's Cheating Who'
[interview with Hoss Allen]

Source: *The Beat*

As above

Location: as above, Tuesday 1 February 1966

Title performed:
'The Winning Hand'

Source: *The Beat*

As above, without Gatemouth Brown–1; miming to Checker 1138-2; Checker 1149-3

Location: as above. c. Spring 1966

Titles performed:
'I'd Rather Drink Muddy Water'–1
'When Does Heartache Begin'–2
'When A Man Loves Two'–3

Source: *The Beat*

Vocal accompaniment: unknown

Location: unknown (USA}. 1970

Titles performed:
unknown

Source: *Soul*

Vocal accompaniment: unknown

Location: Coliseum Stadium, Los Angeles, California. Sunday 20 August 1972

Title performed:
'Walking The Back Streets And Crying'

Source: *Wattstax*

LITTLE RICHARD (Richard Wayne Penniman)
Vocal and piano, miming to Specialty 572 [A]; 561 [B]; 579 [C]

Location: probably Hollywood, California. 1956

Titles performed:
'Long Tall Sally' [A]
'Tutti Frutti' [B]
'Rip It Up' [C]

Source: *Don't Knock The Rock*

Vocal accompaniment: unknown

Location: probably Philadelphia, Pennsylvania. 1956–57

Titles performed:
unknown

Source: *Dick Clark's American Bandstand*

Vocal and piano, miming to Specialty 579 [A]; 584 [B]

Location: probably Hollywood, California. 1957

Titles performed:
'Ready Teddy' [A]
'She's Got It' [B]
'The Girl Can't Help It' [ST only from Specialty 591]

Source: *The Girl Can't Help It*

Vocal and piano, miming to Specialty 598

Location: probably Hollywood, California. 1957

Title performed:
'Lucille'

Source: *Mister Rock And Roll*

Vocal and piano accompaniment: Sounds Incorporated (electric organ, electric guitar, electric bass, drums)
as above, accompaniment: the Shirelles (vocal group)–1

Location: Studio 6, Granada TV, Manchester, England. Wednesday 8 January 1964

Titles performed:
'Rip It Up'
'Lucille'
'Long Tall Sally'
'Send Me Some Loving'
'Whole Lotta Shakin' Going On'
'Hound Dog'
'Good Golly Miss Molly'
'Tutti Frutti'
'Jenny Jenny'
'Joy Joy Joy'–1

Source: *It's Little Richard!*

Vocal and piano accompaniment: unknown, possibly Sounds Incorporated.

Location: ATV Studios, London, England. Friday 8 May 1964

Titles performed:
unknown

Source: *Ready Steady Go*

Vocal accompaniment: unknown

Location: ATV studios, London, England.
Friday 25 November 1966

Titles performed;
unknown

Source: *Ready Steady Go*

Vocal accompaniment: unknown

Location: unknown {USA}. 1967

Titles performed:
unknown

Source: *Catalina Caper*

Vocal accompaniment: unknown

Location: unknown {USA}. 1967

Titles performed:
unknown

Source: *The Jerry Blavatt Show*

Vocal accompaniment: unknown

Location: New York City. 1968

Title performed:
unknown

Source: *The Tonight Show Starring Johnny Carson*

Vocal accompaniment: unknown

Location: New York City. 1969

Titles performed:
unknown title

Source: *The Tonight Show Starring Johnny Carson*

Vocal accompaniment: unknown

Location: Los Angeles, California. 1969

Titles peformed:
unknown Rhino R3.2284

Source: *Thirty Three And A Third Revolutions Per Monkee*

Vocal accompaniment: unknown

Location: New York City. 1970

Titles performed:
unknown

Source: *The Tonight Show Starring Johnny Carson*

Vocal accompaniment: unknown

Location: unknown {USA}. 1970

Titles performed:
unknown

Source: *The Mike Douglas Show*

Vocal accompaniment: unknown

Location: unknown {USA}. 1970

Titles performed:
unknown

Source: *The Smothers Brothers Comedy Hour*

Vocal accompaniment: unknown

Location: probably Los Angeles, California.
1971

Title performed:
unknown

Source: *Dick Clark's American Bandstand*

Vocal accompaniment: unknown

Location: New York City. 1971

Titles performed:
unknown

Source: *The Tonight Show Starring Johnny Carson*

Vocal accompaniment: unknown

Location: unknown {USA}. 1971

Titles performed:
unknown

Source: *The Merv Griffin Show*

Vocal accompaniment: unknown

Location: unknown {USA}. 1971

Titles performed:
unknown

Source: *The Mike Douglas Show*

Vocal accompaniment: unknown

Location: unknown {USA]. 1971

Titles performed:
unknown

Source: *The Glen Campbell Goodtime Hour*

Vocal accompaniment: unknown

Location: unknown {USA}. 1971

Titles performed;
unknown [ST]

Source: *Million Dollars*

Vocal accompaniment: unknown

Location: unknown {USA}. 1972

Titles performed:
unknown

Source: *Black Rodeo*

Vocal accompaniment: unknown

Location: unknown {USA}. 1972

Titles performed:
unknown

Source: *The Merv Griffin Show*

Vocal accompaniment: unknown

Location: London, England or Hollywood, California. 1972

Titles performed:
unknown

Source: *This Is Tom Jones*
Either location is possible, since production of this show alternated between the two cities.

Vocal and piano accompaniment: unknown [G]

Location: Toronto, Canada. Summer 1972

Titles performed:

'Lucille'	BMG 791150
'Good Golly Miss Molly'	BMG 791150
'Rip It Up'	BMG 791150
'Tutti Frutti'	BMG 791150
'Keep A Knocking'	BMG 791150
'Hound Dog'	BMG 791150
'Jenny Jenny'	BMG 791150
'Long Tall Sally'	BMG 791150

Source: *Keep On Rockin'*

Vocal and piano accompaniment: including Lee Allen (tenor saxophone), Robin Russell (drums) [G]

Location: Wembley Stadium, Middlesex, England. August 1972

Titles performed:

'Lucille'	MMG 105
'Rip It Up'	MMG 105
'Good Golly Miss Molly'	MMG 105
'Tutti Frutti'	MMG 105
'Jenny Jenny'	MMG 105

Source: *The London Rock And Roll Show*

Vocal accompaniment: unknown

Location: Madison Square Garden, New York City. 1973

Titles performed:
'Good Golly Miss Molly'
'Rip It Up'

Source: *Let The Good Times Roll* [1]

Vocal accompaniment: unknown

Location: Civic Auditorium, Santa Monica, California. 1973–74

Titles performed:
unknown

Source: *Dick Clark Presents The Rock And Roll Years*

Vocal accompaniment: unknown

Location: unknown {USA}. 1974

Titles performed:
unknown

Source: *Midnight Special*

Vocal accompaniment: unknown

Location: unknown {USA}. 1974

Titles performed:
unknown

Source: *Rock And Roll Revival*

Vocal accompaniment: unknown

Location: unknown {USA}. 1976

Titles performed:
unknown

Source: *Midnight Special*

Vocal accompaniment: unknown

Location: unknown {USA}. 1976

Titles performed:
unknown

Source: *Dinah And Her New Best Friends*

Vocal accompaniment: unknown

Location: unknown {USA}. 1976

Titles performed:
unknown

Source: *Donny And Marie*

Vocal accompaniment: unknown

Location: unknown {USA}. 1977

Titles performed:
unknown

Source: *Midnight Special*

Vocal accompaniment unknown (electric guitar, organ, electric bass, drums)

Location: Los Angeles, California. 1980

Titles performed:
unknown
[interview]

Source: *The Little Richard Story*

Speech

Location: London, England. 1985

[interview]

Source: *TV AM*

Speech

Location: London, England. 1985

[interview]

Source: *The Tube*

Speech

Location: London, England. 1985

[interview]

Source: *Ebony*

Speech

Location: Los Angeles, California. 1985

[interview]

Source: *Australian TV broadcast, via satellite* [C]

Vocal accompaniment: unknown

Location: probably Los Angeles, California. September 1985

Title performed:
'Rock Island Line'

Source: *All Star Tribute To Woody Guthrie And Leadbelly*

Vocal accompaniment: studio orchestra–1
as above, with Cannon and Ball (vocals)–2

Location: London, England. 1986

Titles performed:
'Somebody's Coming'–1
'We've Got Your Money'–2

Source: *The Cannon And Ball Show*
Cannon And Ball were a pair of comedians.

Vocal accompaniment: [G], including Dave Edmunds (electric guitar)

Location: Rome, Italy. Thursday 17 November 1988

Titles performed:
'Joy Joy Joy'
'There's No Place Like Home'
'Peace Of Mind'

Source: *The Giants Of Rock And Roll*

Speech, occasional piano and vocal

Location: unknown {USA}. 1995

[interview]

Source: *Rock And Roll Part 1*

Vocal and piano accompaniment: unknown (tenor saxophone, trumpet, electric guitar, electric bass, drums)

Location: Los Angeles, California. Wednesday 31 December 1997

Titles performed:
'Good Golly Miss Molly'
'Keep A Knockin''

Source: *The Tonight Show With Jay Leno*
The following is also of interest: *Little Richard – A Profile*. An undated, but evidently 1980s, interview with the artist about his involvment in gospel singing is available from Archive. Little Richard had a dramatic role in *Out Where The Buses Don't Run*, an episode of NBC's *Miami Vice* broadcast 18 October 1985.

LITTLE SONNY
See Aaron [Little Sonny] Willis.

LITTLE WALTER (Marion Walter Jacobs)
Vocal and harmonica, miming to Checker 811

Location: ATV studios, London, England. Friday 25 September 1964

Title performed:
'My Babe'

Source: *Ready Steady Go*

Vocal and harmonica accompaniment; unknown [G]

Location: London, England. Monday 26 October 1964

Titles performed:
'My Babe'
'Juke'

Source: *Beat Room*

JOHNNY LITTLEJOHN (John Funchess)
Vocal and guitar accompaniment; unknown

Location: Chicago, Illinois. 1970

Titles performed:
unknown

Source: *Made In Chicago*

Vocal and electric guitar accompaniment: unknown (second electric guitar, harmonica, tenor saxophone, piano, electric bass, drums)

Location: San Francisco, California. 1983

Titles performed:
'Hoochie Coochie Man'
'Bloody Tears'
[interview]

Source: *San Francisco Blues Festival*

LITTLE WILLIE LITTLEFIELD

Vocal and piano accompaniment: unknown

Location: Montreux, Switzerland. July 1980

Titles performed;
'Bad Bad Whiskey'
untitled boogie instrumental
'Happiness'
'Crying The Blues'
'Boogie Woogie'
'Blueberry Hill'

Source: *Montreux Jazz*

Vocal and piano accompaniment; unknown

Location: Montreux, Switzerland. July 1981

Titles performed:
unknown

Source: *Montreux Jazz*

Vocal and piano

Location: London. April 1985

Titles performed:
unknown

Source: *Black On Black*

Vocal and piano

Location: Baden-Baden, Germany. Thursday 7 August 1986

Titles performed:
'Take Me Back Baby'
'Kansas City'
[interview]

Source: *Ohne Filter*
See also Katie Webster.

ROBERT LOCKWOOD

Vocal and electric guitar accompaniment: Sunnyland Slim (piano)

Location: Chicago, Illinois. Wednesday 13 July 1960

Title performed:
'Take A Little Walk With Me' [ST] K-Jazz 014, Rhapsody 8022

Source: *Blues Like Showers Of Rain*

Vocal and electric guitar accompaniment: probably the Aces; Louis Myers (electric guitar); David Myers (electric bass); Fred Below (drums).

Location: Tokyo, Japan. c. 1980

Titles performed:
unknown

Source: *Japanese TV broadcast* [C]

Vocal and guitar accompaniment: Johnny Shines (vocal and guitar)

Location: Freedom Village, Greenville, Mississippi. Saturday 8 September 1979

Title performed:
'They Call Me The Little Wolf' K-Jazz 081

Source: *Mississippi Blues*

Vocal and electric guitar accompaniment: unknown (electric bass)

Location: Atlanta, Georgia. October 1984

Title performed:
'Big Legged Woman'

Source: *National Downhome Blues Festival*

Vocal and electric guitar–1, electric guitar–2 accompaniment: Sumito Amiyoshi (piano); Eugene Schwartz electric bass); Odie Payne (drums)

Location: Tokyo, Japan. Wednesday 10 July 1985

Titles performed:
'My Daily Wish'–1
'Little And Low'–1
'Driving Wheel'–1
'Everyday I Have The Blues'–1
'Take A Little Walk With Me'–1
'After Hours'–2

'Steady Rollin' Man'–1
'Ain't Nobody's Business'–1
'Sweet Home Chicago'–1
'Hear To This' [*sic*]–2
'Worst Old Feeling'–1
'Dust My Broom'–1
'Selfish Ways'–1
'In The Evening'–1
[interview]

Source: *Japanese TV broadcast* [C]
Vocal and electric guitar

Location: New Orleans, Louisiana. 1985

Titles performed:
'Driving Wheel'
'Gonna Ball Tonight'
'Kind Hearted Woman'

Source: *In Concert* [3]

Vocal and electric guitar in duet with Johnny Shines (vocal and electric guitar) accompaniment: unknown (drums)

Location: Sacramento, California. September 1987

Title performed:
'Hey Ba Ba Re Bop'

Source: *Sacramento Blues Festival*

Vocal and electric guitar accompaniment unknown

Location: Washington, DC. Saturday 11 October 1997

Titles performed
unknown

Source: *Tribute To Muddy Waters*
See also Odie Payne.

LONESOME JIMMY LEE
See Jimmy Lee Robinson.

LONESOME SUNDOWN (Cornelius Green)
Vocal and electric guitar accompaniment: unknown Swedish musicians (electric guitar, electric bass, drums)

Location: Stockholm, Sweden. 1979

Titles performed:
'My Name Is Sundown'
'Happy To Be Here'
'Lonesome Lonely Blues'
'My Home Is A Prison'
'Love Me Now'
'Just The Same'
'Woke Up This Morning'

Source: *Swedish TV broadcast* [C]

LOUISIANA RED (Iverson Minter)
Vocal and guitar

Location: New York University, New York. Tuesday 16 November 1976

Titles performed:
unknown

Source: *Library Of Congress*

Vocal and guitar accompaniment: unknown

Location: London, England. Tuesday 1 November 1977

Titles performed:
unknown

Source: *The Old Grey Whistle Test*

Vocal and guitar accompaniment: unknown

Location: Germany. 1980

Titles performed:
'New York City'
'Ma Spivey'
'Please Mr Carter'

Source: *German TV broadcast* [C]

Vocal and guitar accompaniment: Hubert Sumlin (electric guitar); unknown (electric bass and drums)

Location: Belgium. 1981

Title performed:
'Woodchopper's Blues'

Source: *American Folk Blues Festival 1981* [C]

Vocal and guitar accompaniment: Carey Bell (harmonica), and others, unknown; vocal duet with Queen Sylvia Embry, accompaniment as above–1

Location: unknown {Europe}. 1983

Titles performed:
'Future Blues'
'She's Worse'
'Reagan Is For The Rich Man'–1

Source: *European TV broadcast*. Origin unknown [C]

Vocal and guitar

Location: Germany. Mid-1980s

Titles performed:
'It Hurts Me Too'
'Freight Train'
'Take Me Home'
'The Day I Met Muddy Waters'
'The Story Of Louisiana Red'

Source: *German TV broadcast* [C]

Vocal and guitar accompaniment: unknown

Location: Bratislava, Czechoslovakia. 1989

Titles performed:
'Sleep On Muddy Waters'
'I Wonder Why'
'Don't You Want A Man Like Me'
'I'm A Man'
'Lamplight Blues'
'Two Timin' Woman'
'Shake Your Moneymaker'
'I'm In Love'

Source: *unknown, possibly Czechoslovak TV broadcast* [C].
Bratislava is now a part of the Slovakian Republic.

PRESTON LOVE
Vocal accompaniment: the Johnny Otis band

Location: Monterey, California. 1987

Title performed:
'Harlem Nocturne'

Source: *Monterey Jazz Festival*

LOVING SISTERS
Probably Gladys Williams Givens, Josephine Williams, Anna Williams, Lorraine Williams, Mary Moore, Bobbie Lewis (vocals) accompaniment; unknown (piano)

Location: Chicago, Illinois. Sunday 20 September 1964

Titles performed:
unknown

Source: *Jubilee Showcase* [prog #9–2]

As above accompaniment unknown (piano)

Location: New York City. c. 1965

Titles performed:
'That Don't Bother Me'
'Won't We Have A Time'
'John Said No'

Source: *TV Gospel Time* #46

JAMES LOWE
Vocal accompaniment: unknown

Location: New York City. Sunday 7 October 1962

Titles performed:
'Peace In The Valley'
'God Put A Rainbow In The Sky'
'His Eye Is On The Sparrow'

Source: *TV Gospel Time* #1

NELLIE LUTCHER
Vocal and piano accompaniment: unknown

Location: Los Angeles, California. 1982

Titles performed:
unknown
[probably interview]

Source: *Nellie '82*

REVEREND T E LUTCHER
Vocal accompaniment: unknown

Location: Chicago, Illinois. Saturday 22 March 1969

Titles performed:
unknown

Source: *Jubilee Showcase* [prog #34–1]

FRANKIE LYMON AND THE TEENAGERS
Lymon, lead vocal, Sherman Garnes, Joe Negroni, Herman Santiago, Jimmy Merchant (vocals) accompaniment: studio orchestra

Location: New York City. 1956

Titles performed:
'Why Do Fools Fall In Love'
[interview]

Source: *Shower Of Stars*

As above accompaniment: unknown orchestra

Location: unknown {USA}. 1956

Titles performed:
'Baby Baby' Gold Star BSG203
'I'm Not A Juvenile Delinquent' Gold Star BSG203

Source: *Rock, Rock, Rock*

As above accompaniment: unknown

Location: probably Philadelphia, Pennsylvania. 1956–57

Titles performed:
unknown

Source: *Dick Clark's American Bandstand*

As above accompaniment: probably the Val Parnell orchestra

Location: The Palladium theatre, London, England. c. Spring 1957

Titles performed:
unknown [probably 'I'm Not A Juvenile Delinquent']

Source: *Sunday Night At The London Palladium*
See also *Six-Five Special* in the Programme Index.

As above accompaniment: the Alan Freed orchestra: Big Al Sears and Sam 'The Man' Taylor (tenor saxophones) and others, unknown

Location: New York City. July–August 1957

Titles performed:
unknown

Source: *The Big Beat* [2]

As above accompaniment: unknown

Location: unknown {USA}. c. Autumn 1957

Titles performed:
'Love Put Me Out Of My Head'
'Fortunate Fella'

Source: *Mister Rock And Roll*

As above accompaniment: unknown

Location: New York City. Sunday 22 December 1957

Titles performed:
'Goody Goody'
'The Only Way To Love'
[interview with Sullivan]

Source: *The Ed Sullivan Show*

Lymon, vocal accompaniment: studio orchestra

Location: probably New York City. c.1958

Title performed:
'Goody Goody'

Source: *US TV broadcast, origin unknown*

Lymon, miming

Location: probably New York. c. 1964

Title performed:
'Why Do Fools Fall In Love'

Source: *US TV broadcast, origin unknown, possibly Shindig*

LEWIS LYMON AND THE TEEN CHORDS
Vocal group accompaniment: unknown orchestra

Location: unknown {USA}. 1957

Title performed:
[introduction by disc jockey Jocko Henderson dressed in a facsimile of a space suit;]
'Your Last Chance'

Source: *Jamboree*
This artist was Frankie Lymon's brother.

M

WILLIE MABON
Vocal and piano accompaniment: unknown

Location: Montreux, Switzerland. 1978

Title performed:
'It's A Shame'

Source: *Montreux Jazz*

Vocal and piano accompaniment: Hubert Sumlin and Eddie Taylor (electric guitars); Bob Stroger (electric bass); Odie Payne (drums)

Location: Germany. 1980

Titles performed:
'Little Red Rooster'
'I'm Mad'

Source: *American Folk Blues Festival 1980*

CASH McCALL (Morris Dollison Jr.)
Vocal and electric guitar accompaniment: unknown (harmonica, piano, electric bass, drums)

Location: Topanga Canyon, California. Saturday 25 June 1988

Titles performed:
untitled instrumental [becoming;]
'Further On Up The Road'
'I Can't Quit You Baby'

Source: *Topanga Blues Festival*

GEORGE AND ETHEL McCOY
Vocal duet accompaniment: George, guitar and Ethel, steel guitar

Location: Memphis, Tennessee. 1968

Title performed:
'Black Mary' Vestapol 13037

Source: *Adelphi Film productions* [C]

JIMMY McCRACKLIN
Vocal accompaniment: Frankie Lee Sims (guitar) and others, unknown

Location: Philadelphia, Pennsylvania. c.1957

Title performed:
'The Walk'

Source: *Dick Clark's American Bandstand*

Vocal accompaniment: unknown

Location: unknown {USA}. 1973

Titles performed:
unknown

Source: *All Together Now* [unconfirmed]

Vocal and piano accompaniment: unknown (tenor saxophone, electric guitar, electric bass, drums)

Location: Sacramento, California. September 1987

Titles performed:
'I Wonder' [part only]
'Let Me Tell You About Love'
[interview]

Source: *Sacramento Blues Festival 1987*

FRED McDOWELL

Vocal and guitar

Location: Newport, Rhode Island. July 1964

Title performed:
'61 Highway Blues' [fragment only]

Source: *Festival* [1]

Vocal and guitar

Location: probably Mississippi. c.1964–5

Title performed:
'Write Me A Few Of Your Lines'

Source: *untitled* [FS] produced by the University of Mississippi.

Vocal and guitar

Location: Baden-Baden, Germany. October 1965

Title performed:
[introduction by Doctor Ross;]
'Going Away Baby'

Source: *American Folk Blues Festival 1965*

Vocal and guitar

Location: probably Mississippi. 1968

Titles performed:
'Highway 61'
'Muleskinner Blues'

Source: *The Bluesmaker*

Vocal and electric guitar

Location: KCTS-TV studios, Seattle, Washington. c.1970

Titles performed:

'Louise'	Vestapol 13002
'Keep Your Lamps Trimmed And Burning'	Vestapol 13002
'I Heard Somebody Call'	Vestapol 13002
'Break 'em On Down'	Vestapol 13002
'My Babe'	Vestapol 13002

Source: *University of Washington/Seattle Folklore Society*

Vocal and electric guitar

Location: KCTS-TV studios, Seattle, Washington. c.1970

Titles performed:

'Shake 'em On Down'	Yazoo 504
'Good Morning, Little Schoolgirl'	Yazoo 504
'John Henry'	Yazoo 504
'Louisiana Blues'	Yazoo 504
'When I Lay My Burden Down'	Yazoo 504

Source: *Masters Of American Traditional Music*

Vocal and guitar

Location: Philadelphia, Pennsylvania. 1971

Titles performed:
unknown

Source: *Philadelphia Folk Festival*
There is believed to be earlier footage of McDowell, filmed in Mississippi during the 1960s, but no details are available. Further, the concert at the Mayfair Hotel, London (Saturday 8 March 1969) issued on Sequel CD NEBCD851 is believed to exist on videotape.

WALTER BROWN [BROWNIE] McGHEE AND SONNY TERRY (Sanders Terrell)

Because of the complex relationship between McGhee and Terry, all duet material, regardless of who takes the lead, is listed here chronologically together with McGhee's solo performances. Material by Terry only, where McGhee is not present, will be found under Terry's name.

McGhee (vocal and guitar); Terry (vocal and harmonica)

Location: unknown {USA}. c.1945

Title performed:
'Red River Blues' [part only] Vestapol 13056

Source: *March Of Time*

Woody Guthrie, vocal and guitar, accompaniment: McGhee, (vocal and guitar); Terry (harmonica)

Location: unknown {USA}. 1947

Titles performed:
'John Henry' Vestapol 13056

Source: *To Hear Your Banjo Play*

McGhee, vocal and guitar

Location: unknown {USA}. 1947

Titles performed:
unknown [ST]

Source: *The Roosevelt Story*

As above

Location: probably Los Angeles, California. Late 1956/early 1957

Title performed:
'A Face In the Crowd' [ST only]

Source: *A Face In The Crowd*
Although McGee later recorded this song for Folkways, he does not sing it on the ST LP – it is one of the two in which he accompanies Griffith. He does not appear in the film: Griffith mimes to the guitar that McGee plays. Nor does it seem likely that he sings it in the film ST.

McGhee, (vocal and guitar); Terry (vocal and harmonica) accompaniment: Chris Barber's Jazz Band: Barber (trombone); Pat Halcox (trumpet); Monty Sunshine (clarinet); Eddie Smith (banjo); Dick Smith (bass); Graham Burbridge (drums)
As above, with Otilie Patterson (vocal)–1

Location: London, England. Thursday 24 April 1958

Titles performed:
'John Henry'
'Cornbread, Peas And Black Molasses'
'Glory'–1

Source: *Jazz Session*

McGhee (vocal and guitar); Terry (vocal and harmonica)

Location: probably New York City. 1959

Titles performed:
unknown

Source: *Tonight With Belafonte*

McGhee (vocal and guitar); Terry (vocal and harmonica)

Location: Baden-Baden, Germany. c. October 1962

Titles performed:
unknown

Source: *American Folk Blues Festival 1962*

McGhee (vocal and guitar); Terry (vocal and harmonica)

Location: London, England. Sunday 18 November 1962

Titles performed:
unknown

Source: *Tempo*

McGhee (vocal and guitar); Terry (vocal and harmonica)

Location: Newport, Rhode Island. 1963 or 1964

Title performed:
'Key To the Highway' [fragment only]

Source: *Festival* [1]

Terry (vocal and harmonica) accompaniment: McGhec (guitar)–1
McGhee (vocal and guitar); Terry (vocal and harmonica)–2
as above, with Ransom Knowling(bass)–3

as above, with Muddy Waters, Cousin Joe Pleasants and Rosetta Tharpe, (vocals); Otis Spann (piano); Willie Smith (drums)–4

Location: Alexandra Park railway station, Chorlton-cum-Hardy, Manchester, England. May 1964

Titles performed:
'Whoopin' The Blues'–1 [ST only]
'Rockin' The Blues' (becoming) 'Talkin' ''Harmonica Blues'–1
'I'm a Roamin' Rambler'–2
'Walk On'–3
'Whole World In His Hands'–4

Source: *The Blues And Gospel Train*

McGhee (vocal and guitar); Terry (vocal and harmonica)

Location: unknown {USA}. 1964

Titles performed:
unknown

Source: *A La Carte*

McGhee (vocal and guitar); Terry (vocal and harmonica)

Location: unknown {USA}. 1965

Titles performed:
unknown

Source: *Roomful Of Music*

McGhee (vocal and guitar); Terry (harmonica) accompaniment: Willie Dixon (bass)–1
Terry, harmonica solo with comments accompaniment: McGhee (guitar); Dixon (bass)–2
Terry (vocal and harmonica) accompaniment McGhee (guitar) and Dixon (bass)–3
McGhee (vocal and guitar), Terry (vocal and harmonica) accompaniment: Muddy Waters Blues Band with James Cotton, Willie Dixon, Jesse Fuller, Mable Hillery, Muddy Waters, Otis Spann, Sunnyland Slim, Bukka White and Big Joe Williams (vocals)–4

Location: Toronto, Canada. Thursday 27 to Saturday 29 January 1966

Titles performed:
spoken introduction leading to;

'Living With The Blues'–1	Rhino 3.2313
'Cornbread, Peas and Molasses'–2	Rhino 3.2313
'Hooray, Hooray, These Women Is Killin' Me' –3	Rhino 3.2313
'Wholesale and Retail'–1	
'Fox Chase'–2	
jam session–4	Rhino 3.2313

[and McGhee, conversation with Barry Callaghan, Willie Dixon and Muddy Waters]

Source: *Festival Presents The Blues*

McGhee (vocal and guitar only)–1, accompaniment: Terry (vocal and harmonica)–2; Terry, vocal and harmonica accompaniment, Pete Seeger (occasional banjo), McGhee (guitar)–3
as –3, with McGhee (vocal); Seeger (12 string guitar)–4

Location: probably New York City. 1966

Titles performed:

'Don't Kid Me'–1	Vestapol 13003
'Key To The Highway'–2	Vestapol 13004
'Easy Rider'–2	Vestapol 13056
'Fighting A Losing Battle'–2	Vestapol 13056
'I Couldn't Believe My Eyes'–2	Vestapol 13056
'Burnt Child'–3	Vestapol 13057
'Rock Island Line'–4	Vestapol 13057

Source: *Pete Seeger's Rainbow Quest*

McGhee, vocal and guitar

Location: unknown {USA}. 1966

Titles performed:
unknown

Source: *The Strollin' 20's*

McGhee (vocal and guitar); Terry (vocal and harmonica)

Location: unknown {USA}. 1966

Titles performed:
unknown

Source: *World Of Music*

McGhee (vocal and guitar); Terry (harmonica)–1:
McGhee only–2

Location: KCTS-TV studios, Seattle, Washington. 1967

Titles performed:
'Roll On'–1
'In the Dead Hours of Night'–1
'Kansas City Blues'–2 Vestapol 13060
[monologue leading to];
'Me and My Dog'–2 Vestapol 13060
[monologue leading to];
'I'm Gonna Tell God How You Treat Me'–2 Vestapol 13060
[monologue leading to];
'Pawn Shop Blues'–2 Vestapol 13060
[monologue leading to];
'Born And Living With The Blues'–2 Vestapol 13060
'John Henry' Vestapol 13057

Source: *Masters Of American Traditional Music*

McGhee (vocal and guitar); Terry (vocal and harmonica);
as above, with Big Mama Thornton (vocal)–1

Location: Newport, Rhode Island. July 1969

Titles performed:
'Life Is A Gamble'
'Poor Boy, Long Way From Home'
'Rock Island Line'–1

Source: *Folklife productions*

McGhee (vocal and guitar); Terry (vocal and harmonica)

Location: Baden-Baden, Germany. c. May 1970

Titles performed:
unknown

Source: *American Folk Blues Festival 1970*

McGhee (vocal and guitar); Terry (vocal and harmonica)

Location: unknown {USA}. 1970

Titles performed:
unknown

Source: *The Hart And Lorne Terrific Hour*

McGhee (vocal and guitar); Terry (vocal and harmonica)

Location: KCTS-TV studios, Seattle, Washington. 1970

Titles performed:
'Red River Blues'/'Crow Jane' [medley] Vestapol 13056
[monologue leading to;]
'Backwater Blues' Vestapol 13056
'Life Is A Gamble' Vestapol 13056
'My Father's Words' Vestapol 13056
'Life Is A Gamble' [in colour] Vestapol 13056
'Motorcycle Blues' Vestapol 13057
'I Got My Eyes On You' Vestapol 13057
'My Baby's So Fine' Vestapol 13057
'Poor Man Blues' [becoming] 'Fighting A Losing Battle' Vestapol 13057

Source: *University of Washington/Seattle Folklore Society*
'Life Is A Gamble' probably also appears in *Roots Of American Music*

McGhee (vocal and guitar); Terry (vocal and harmonica)

Location: KCET TV, Los Angeles, California. 1970

Titles performed:
'Automobile Blues' Vestapol 13060
'My Father's Words' Vestapol 13060
'Midnight Special' Vestapol 13057
'Packin' Up' Vestapol 13057

Source: *One Of A Kind*

McGhee (vocal and guitar)

Location: unknown {USA}. 1971

Titles performed:
'John Henry' [A] [C] K-Jazz 019, Yazoo 507
'Four Word Five Letter Blues' [B] K-Jazz 020, Yazoo 506
'My Baby Done Changed The Lock' [C]

Source: *Out Of The Blacks, Into The Blues Part 2* [A] and *Part 1* [B] [*sic*]; *Le Blues Entre Les Dents* [C]

McGhee (vocal and guitar); Terry (vocal and harmonica)

Location: unknown {USA}. 1971

Titles performed:
unknown

Source: *The Virginia Graham Show*

McGhee (vocal and guitar); Terry (vocal and harmonica): accompaniment, if any, unknown

Location: unknown {USA}. 1971

Titles performed:
unknown

Source: *The Glen Campbell Goodtime Hour*

McGhee (vocal–1, speech with echo effects–2, guitar–3);
Terry (harmonica, foot-stomping–4); Al Shackman (bass)–3;
Warren Smith (drums)–3

Location: New York City. 1972

Titles performed:
'Riding To Bookers'–3
'Blue's Last Walk'–2, –3
'Eldorado'–3
'Poor Little June Bug'–4
'Cracker Cops'–4
'Blueboy's Holler'–1, –3

Source: *Book Of Numbers* [ST only]

McGhee (guitar); Terry (harmonica and probably jaw's harp)

Location: probably Hollywood, California. 1972

Titles performed:
unknown [ST only]

Source: *Buck And The Preacher*

McGhee (vocal and guitar), Terry (vocal and harmonica); Terry (harmonica) accompaniment McGhee (guitar)–1

Location: London, England. Tuesday, 5 June 1973

Titles performed:

'Walking My Blues Away'	Vestapol 13056
'Whoopin' The Blues'–1	Vestapol 13056
'Walk On, Ride On'	Vestapol 13056

Source: *The Old Grey Whistle Test*

McGhee (vocal and guitar); Terry (vocal and harmonica)

Location: Montreux, Switzerland. Friday 29 June 1973

Titles performed:
'Long Way From Home'
'When I Was Drinkin''
'Bring It On Home To Me'
'Rockin' And Whoopin'
'Wee Wee Hours'

Source: *Montreux Jazz*

McGhee (vocal and guitar); Terry (vocal and harmonica)

Location: unknown {USA}. 1973

Titles performed:
unknown

Source: *Blues For A Black Film*. May be [ST] only.

McGhee (vocal and guitar); Terry (vocal and harmonica); Terry (harmonica) accompaniment: McGhee (guitar)–1

Location: London, England. June 1974

Titles performed:

'Ride, Ride, Ride'	Vestapol 13056
'I'm A Burnt Child'	Vestapol 13056
[monologue by Terry leading to];	
'Hootin' The Blues'–1	Vestapol 13057
'I Was Born With The Blues'	Vestapol 13056
'Conversations With A River'	Vestapol 13060
'I Feel So Good'	Vestapol 13060
'Drinkin' Wine Spo-de-o-dee'	Vestapol 13060

'Rock Island Line' Vestapol 13056
'Walk On' Vestapol 13056

Source: *In Concert* [2]

McGhee (vocal and guitar); Terry (vocal and harmonica)

Location: San Francisco, California. 1975

Titles performed:
unknown

Source: *AM San Francisco*

McGhee (vocal and guitar); Terry (vocal and harmonica)

Location: unknown {USA}. 1975

Titles performed:
unknown

Source: *Sincerely The Blues*

McGhee (vocal and guitar); Terry (harmonica) accompaniment: unknown (tambourine and mixed voices)

Location: unknown {USA}. 1979

Title performed:
'Pick A Bale Of Cotton'

Source: *The Jerk*

McGhee (vocal and guitar); Terry (vocal and harmonica)

Location: Cambridge, England. Summer 1980

Titles performed:
'I Was Born With The Blues'
'I Feel So Good'
'Walk On'

Source: *Festival* [2]

McGhee (vocal and guitar); Terry (vocal and harmonica)

Location: unknown {USA}. 1980

Title performed:
'Walking My Blues Away'
[conversation with Oscar Brown]

Source: *From Jumpstreet*

McGhee, vocal duet with Glen Campbell, accompaniment: own guitar and Terry (harmonica)

Location: unknown {USA}. 1980

Title performed:
'You Bring Out The Boogie In Me'

Source: *Mississippi Days And Southern Nights*

McGhee (vocal and guitar); Terry (vocal and harmonica)

Location: Montreal, Canada. c. 1980–81

Titles performed:
'I Got The Blues'
'Hooray Hooray, These Women Is Killing Me'
'Roll Me Baby'
'Mean Woman Blues'
'Blues Had A Baby'

Source: *Canadian TV broadcast* [C]. Origin unknown

McGhee, vocal and guitar

Location: unknown {USA}. 1982

Title performed:
'Life Is A Gamble' Magnum MMGV-037

Source: *America's Music – Blues Volume 2*

McGhee (vocal and guitar) accompaniment, if any, unknown

Location: Remus, Michigan. Sunday 7 September 1986

Titles performed:
unknown

Source: *Wheatland Music Festival* [C]. Origin unknown.

McGhee (vocal and guitar)

Location: St. Paul, Minnesota. Saturday 18 April 1987

Titles performed:
[introduction by Garrison Keillor;]
'Key To The Highway'
'Good Morning Blues'

Source: *The Prairie Home Companion*

McGhee (vocal and guitar) accompaniment: Sugar Blue (harmonica); Pinetop Perkins (piano); Deacon John Moore (electric guitar); Richard Payne (electric bass); Alonzo Stewart (drums)

Location: probably Hollywood, California. 1987

Titles performed:
'Rainy Rainy Day'
'Right Key, Wrong Keyhole'

Source: *Angel Heart*. McGhee appears as 'Toots Sweet' and has a small dramatic role in this production.

McGhee (unknown contribution)

Location: probably New York City. 1987–88

Titles performed:
unknown

Source: *Family Ties*
This may have been a dramatic cameo.

McGhee (vocal and guitar) accompaniment:
Bert Jansch (guitar)–1;
McGhee, vocal and guitar only–2

Location: the McGhee residence, 688 43rd Street, Oakland, California. Summer 1992

Titles performed:

[monologue]	Vestapol 13060
'Key To The Highway'–1	Vestapol 13060
'Come On, Keep It Coming'–1	Vestapol 13060
'Death Of Blind Boy Fuller'–2	Vestapol 13060
[monologue regarding Blind Boy Fuller]	Vestapol 13060
[closing remarks]	Vestapol 13060

The following songs, from this same session, appear on Code 90 CD7 {CD} but were not used in the final production. They may still exist as visual performances.

Don't Pity Me–1
'Parcel Post Blues'–1
'Walk On'–1

Source: *Acoustic Routes*
See also Sonny Terry.

HAYES McMULLEN

Vocal and guitar

Location: probably Tutwiler, Mississippi. 1978

Title performed:

'Hurry Sundown' [part only]	K-Jazz 030, Yazoo 505

Source: *Good Morning Blues*

BIG JAY McNEELY

Tenor saxophone solos accompaniment: unknown

Location: Los Angeles, California. 1984

Title performed:
'Big Jay Shuffle'

Source: *Legends Of Rhythm And Blues*

Speech

Location: Los Angeles, California. 1986

[interview]

Source: *Remembering Black Music*

Tenor saxophone solos accompaniment: the Johnny Otis band

Location: Monterey, California. 1987

Title performed:
'Let's Work'

Source: *Monterey Jazz Festival*

Vocal and tenor saxophone, accompaniment: unknown

Location: Sydney, Australia. Monday 20 March 1989

Titles performed:
untitled instrumental
[interview]

Source: *Australian TV broadcast* [C]

ALBERT MACON
Vocal and guitar accompanying Robert Thomas, step-dancing–1
Vocal and guitar–2

Location: Atlanta, Georgia. October 1984

Titles performed:
'Got My Gal And Gone'–1
'I Can't Be Satisfied'–2
[interview]

Source: *National Downhome Blues Festival*

CLYDE McPHATTER
Vocal accompaniment: the Alan Freed orchestra: Big Al Sears and Sam 'The Man' Taylor (tenor saxophones) and others, unknown

Location: New York City. July–August 1957

Titles performed:
unknown

Source: *The Big Beat* [2]

Vocal accompaniment: unknown orchestra

Location: unknown {USA}. 1957

Titles performed:
'You'll Be There'
'Rock And Cry'

Source: *Mister Rock And Roll*

Vocal accompaniment: unknown

Location: probably Philadelphia, Pennsylvania. c.1957

Titles performed:
unknown

Source: *Dick Clark's American Bandstand*
McPhatter was the original lead singer with the Drifters. No film, telecast, video or kinescope of the original Drifters appears to have survived.

GLADYS McPHATTER
Vocal accompaniment: unknown

Location: Chicago, Illinois. Sunday 20 September 1964

Titles performed:
unknown

Source: *Jubilee Showcase* [prog #9–2]

JACK McVEA
probably vocal and tenor saxophone accompaniment: unknown

Location: Hollywood, California. 1947

Title performed:
'Open The Door, Richard!'

Source: *Sarge Goes To College*

MAGIC SAM (Samuel Maghett)
Vocal and electric guitar accompaniment: unknown

Location: unknown {USA}. 1969

Titles performed:
unknown

Source: *The Marty Faye Show* [unconfirmed]

MAGIC SLIM (Morris Holt)
Vocal and electric guitar accompaniment, presumably, the Teardrops; Nick Holt (electric bass); unknown (drums)

Location: probably Chicago, Illinois. 1975

Titles performed:
unknown

Source: *The Tilmon Tempo Show*

Vocal and electric guitar accompaniment: The Teardrops; Nick Holt (electric bass); unknown (drums)–1;
as above, but Nick Holt replaces Magic Slim as vocalist–2

Location: Sweden. 1980

Titles performed:
'Don't Want No Woman'–1
'Mustang Sally'–1
'Living In My Neighbourhood'–1
'Bad Avenue'–1
'Find Somebody New'–2
'Sweet Home Chicago'–2
'As The Years Go Passing By'–2
'If It's Too Late'–2

Source: *Swedish TV broadcast* [C]

Vocal and electric guitar accompaniment: as above

Location: Montreux, Switzerland. Wednesday 8 July 1981

Titles performed:
'Hoo Wee Baby'
'One More Time'
'Cold Cold Feeling'
'Tell Me'
'Treat My Baby Right'
'Mustang Sally'
'Hideaway'

Source: *Montreux Jazz*

Vocal and electric guitar accompaniment: as above; add Jack Dupree (vocal and piano)–1

Location: Madrid, Spain. Sunday 8 March 1987

Titles performed:
'Deep Down In Florida'
'I'm A Good Man'
'Let Me Love You Baby'
'Talk To Me Baby'
'Things I Used To Do'
'Down The Road I Go'
'Beggin' You Please'
'I'm A Man'
'The Blues Is Alright'
untitled instrumental–1

Source: *Spanish TV broadcast* [C]

Vocal and electric guitar accompaniment, presumably, as above

Location: Italy. Late 1980s

Titles performed:
unknown

Source: *Italian TV broadcast* [C]

J J MALONE
See Troyce Key.

[BISHOP] DREADY MANNING AND MOTHER MANNING
Dready Manning, vocal and unplugged electric guitar–1;
Mother Manning, vocal and tambourine accompaniment: Dready Manning (electric guitar)–2;
Dready Manning, vocal, guitar and harmonica–3

Location: Roanoke, Virgina. August 1995

Titles performed:
'The Things I Used To Do'–1
'Step It Up And Go' [unbroadcast]–1
'When I Lay My Burden Down'–2
'Hard Luck And Trouble' [takes 1–2] [unbroadcast]–2
'You Got To Move' [takes 1–2] [unbroadcast]–3
'Gospel Train' [takes 1–2] [unbroadcast]–3
[interview]

Source: *Too Close To Heaven*

MARSHALL HEIGHTS ANGELS OF BALTIMORE, MARYLAND
Mixed vocal choir accompaniment: unknown

Location: probably Baltimore, Maryland. 1966

Titles performed:
unknown

Source: *TV Gospel Time* #54

MARTIN, BOGAN AND ARMSTRONG
Carl Martin, Ted Bogan and Howard Armstrong, vocals and string instruments

Location: KCTS-TV studios, Seattle, Washington. c.1966–70

Titles performed:
unknown

Source: *University of Washington/Seattle Folklore Society*
Video only, currently unavailable.
See also Howard Armstrong and Ted Bogan.

ROBERTA MARTIN SINGERS
Probably Roberta Martin, Deloris Barrett, Norsalus McKissick, Eugene Smith, Gloria Griffin, Lucy Smith, Archie Dennis (vocals) accompaniment: unknown

Location: Chicago, Illinois.

The following appearances are known:
1964
Sunday 8 March [prog #17–3]
Sunday 26 April [prog #9–3]

Titles performed:
unknown

Source: *Jubilee Showcase*
See also Deloris Barret Campbell and Archie Dennis.

SALLIE MARTIN
Vocal accompaniment: unknown, possibly Thomas A Dorsey (piano)

Location: Chicago, Illinois. Sunday 26 April 1964

Titles performed:
unknown

Source: *Jubilee Showcase* [prog #9–3]

Vocal accompaniment: unknown

Location: New York City. c.1965–66

Title performed:
unknown

Source: *TVGT* #55

Vocal accompaniment: unknown

Location: Chicago, Illinois. 1976

Titles performed:
unknown

Source: *Here Comes Gospel*

Vocal duet with Thomas A Dorsey accompaniment: Yazoo LP1041 reissue of Dorsey's original 1932 recording.

Location: the Martin residence, Chicago, Illinois. 1982

Title performed:
'If You See My Savior' FRF un-numbered
[interviews and conversation] FRF un-numbered

Source: *Say Amen Somebody!*

SARA MARTIN
Vocal accompaniment 'Club Alabama Stompers' [Billy Fowler and his orchestra]: Jack Butler and unknown (trumpets); Dock Crawford (trombone); three unknown reeds; unknown (piano); Eddie Gibbs (banjo); Herbie Cowens (drums)

Location: New York City. 1929

Title performed:
'Cabaration Blues'

Source: [probably] *Dark Town Scandals Review*

Vocal accompaniment: unknown

Location: probably New York City. 1929

Titles performed:
unknown

Source: *Hello Bill*

AUGUSTER MAUL
Speech and vocal with congregation

Location: Friendship Baptist Church, Brighton, Alabama. early 1984

Titles performed:
[mc at gospel program, including"]
'Come And Go To That Land'

Source: *On The Battlefield*

CLYDE MAXWELL
Vocal and percussive axe-cutting

Location: Mississippi. Between 11 August and 9 September 1978

Title performed:
'Early In The Morning' Vestapol 13078

Source: *Land Where The Blues Began*

Vocal and guitar

Location: Freedom Village, Greenville, Mississippi. Saturday 8 September 1979

Title performed:
'I Left Alberta' K-Jazz 081

Source: *Mississippi Blues*

[BROTHER] JOE MAY
Vocal accompaniment: unknown (piano)–1
Vocal duet with Jackie Verdell accompaniment: unknown (organ)–2
Vocal duet with Edna Gallmon Cooke accompaniment: the Stars Of Faith (female vocal group)–3

Location: Baltimore, Maryland. Saturday 5 September 1964

Titles performed:
'Must Jesus Bear The Cross Alone?'–1 [A]
'It's A Mighty Building'–1 [A]
'Walk On And Talk On'–1 [B]
'Wake Me And Shake Me'–1 [B]
'You're Gonna Need Him'–2 [A]
'My Mother Prayed For Me'–3 [B]

Source: *TV Gospel Time* #34 [A], #35 [B]
See also the Davis Sisters and Jackie Verdell.

Vocal accompaniment: unknown

Location: unknown {USA}. 1970s

Titles performed:
unknown

Source: *Look Up And Sing Out*

PETE MAYES
Vocal and electric guitar accompaniment: The Texas Houserockers [G]

Location: Houston, Texas. Friday [*sic*] 8 October 1993

Titles performed:
'Jackson Jump'
'Society Woman'

Source: *Saturday Night At Rockefellers*

PERCY MAYFIELD
Vocal accompaniment: Mark Naftalin (piano) and others, unknown

Location: probably Los Angeles, California. c. 1980

Titles performed:
unknown K-Jazz 100

Source: *Mark Naftalin's Blue Monday Party*

MEDITATION SINGERS
Probably Ernestine Rundless, Verline Rodgers, Marie Waters and others, unknown, (vocals) accompaniment: unknown

Location: Chicago, Illinois

The following appearances are known:
1964
Friday 19 June [#23–2]
1966
Friday 13 May [#34–2]
1969
Saturday 22 Feb [#19–3]

Titles performed:
unknown

Source: *Jubilee Showcase*

Also, the following:
probably as last accompaniment: unknown

Location: Washington DC. 1966

Title performed:
unknown

Source: *TV Gospel Time* #56
See also Ernestine and Laura Rundless

MEMPHIS SLIM (Peter Chatman)
Vocal and piano accompaniment: unknown

Location: probably Chicago, Illinois. 1960

Titles performed:
unknown

Source: *The Today Show*

Vocal and piano accompaniment, if any, unknown

Location: unknown {probably USA}. 1960

Titles performed:
unknown

Source: *Memphis Slim*

Organ solo accompaniment: Willie Dixon (bass)

Location: the Alan Lomax residence, Greenwich Village, New York. Spring 1961.

Title performed:
'Honky Tonk'

Source: *Folklife Productions*

Vocal and piano accompaniment: Kansas Fields (drums)

Location: ORTF Studio, 15 rue Cognac Jay, Paris, France. Monday 30 July 1962

Titles performed:
'Sun Gonna Shine On My Back Door One Day' Jazz Averty 665031
'The Four O'Clock Blues' Jazz Averty 665031
'Cow Cow Blues' Jazz Averty 665031
'Born With The Blues' Jazz Averty 665031
'Diggin' My Potatoes' Jazz Averty 665031
'Rockin' The House' Jazz Averty 665031
'Rocking Chair Blues' Jazz Averty 665031
'Just a Dream' Jazz Averty 665031
'Baby Please Come Home' Jazz Averty 665031
'Hot Club de France Boogie' Jazz Averty 665031
'Pigalle Love' Jazz Averty 665031
'Jammin' The Boogie' Jazz Averty 665031
'Every Day I Have The Blues' Jazz Averty 665031

Source: *ORTF*

Vocal and piano accompaniment: probably Willie Dixon (bass); Clifton James (drums)

Location: Baden-Baden, Germany. c. October 1962

Titles performed:
unknown

Source: *American Folk Blues Festival 1962*

Vocal and piano accompaniment: Matt Murphy (electric guitar); Willie Dixon (bass); Billie Stepney (drums)–1
Vocal with Willie Dixon (vocal and bass); Lonnie Johnson (vocal); Matt Murphy (electric guitar); Otis Spann (vocal and piano); Billie Stepney (drums); Muddy Waters (vocal); Big Joe Williams (vocal) and Sonny Boy Williamson (vocal)–2

Location: Manchester, England. October 1963

Titles performed:
'I Found The Blues' and band introduction–1
'All By Myself'–1
'Bye Bye Baby'–2

Source: *I Hear The Blues*

Probably as above

Location: Baden-Baden, Germany. c. November 1963

Titles performed:
unknown

Source: *American Folk Blues Festival 1963*

Vocal and piano accompaniment: unknown

Location: Manchester, England. December 1963

Titles performed:
unknown

Source: *More Jazz Unlimited – A Rebirth Of The Blues*

Vocal and piano accompaniment: unknown

Location: London, England. Monday August 10 1964

Title performed:
unknown

Source: *Beat Room*

Vocal and piano accompaniment: unknown

Location: probably France. 1964

Titles performed:
unknown

Source: *Visage Des PTT*

Vocal and piano

Location: Studio de Boulonge, Paris, France. 1968

Titles performed:
unknown

Source: *The Sergeant*

Vocal and piano

Location: ORTF Studio 14, Buttes-Chaumont, Paris, France. Monday 2 February 1970

Title performed:
'Pinetop's Boogie Woogie' Jazz Averty 775031

Source: *ORTF*

Vocal and piano accompaniment: unknown

Location: France. 1970

Titles performed:
unknown

Source: *A Nous Deux, la France!*

Vocal and piano accompaniment: unknown

Location: unknown. 1970

Titles performed:
unknown

Source: *Carry It On*

Vocal and piano

Location: London, England. Sunday 2 January 1972

Title performed:
'Boogien' And Bluesin'' [*sic*]

Source: *Late Night Line Up*

Vocal and piano accompaniment: unknown

Location: France. 1972

Titles performed:
unknown

Source: *L'Aventure Du Jazz*

Vocal and piano

Location: ORTF Studio 14, Buttes-Chaumont, Paris, France. Tuesday 27 March 1973

Titles performed:

'Whisky And Blues'	Jazz Averty 665031
'Mr. Freddie's Blues'	Jazz Averty 665031
'Misery'	Jazz Averty 665031
'Darling, I Miss You So'	Jazz Averty 665008
'Arkansas Road House Blues'	Jazz Averty 665008
'El Capitain'	Jazz Averty 665008
'Angel Child'	Jazz Averty 665008
'Pinetop's Boogie Woogie'	Jazz Averty 665008
'Pigalle Love'	Jazz Averty 665008
'Boogien' And Bluesin'' [*sic*]	Jazz Averty 665008
'What's The Matter'	Jazz Averty 665008
'Memphis Slim, USA'	Jazz Averty 665008

'Cow Cow Blues' Jazz Averty 665008
'I Heard The Blues Everywhere' Jazz Averty 665008
'Didn't We, Babe' Jazz Averty 665008
'Rack 'em Back' Jazz Averty 665008
'Smiling To Keep From Crying' Jazz Averty 665008
'Three And One Boogie' Jazz Averty 665008
'All By Myself' Jazz Averty 665008

Source: *ORTF*

Vocal and piano accompaniment: Mickey Baker (electric guitar); Charlie Myers (bass); Benny Turner (drums)

Location: Montreux, Switzerland. July 1973

Titles performed:
'Everyday I Have The Blues'
'Baby Please Come Home'
'Wish Me Well'
'Watergate Blues'
'Last Night'
'All By Myself'
'My Little Angel Child'
untitled boogie instrumental
'Bye Bye'

Source: *Montreux Jazz*

Vocal and piano

Location: Paris, France. 1976

Titles performed:
'Last Night'
'All By Myself'

Source: *All You Need Is Love*

Vocal and piano

Location: France. 1982

Titles performed:
'Bluesin' And Boogien'' [*sic*]
'Misery'
'All By Myself'
'Lowdown Dirty Shame'
untitled boogie instrumental
untitled blues instrumental

Source: *French TV broadcast* [C]

Vocal and piano accompaniment: Michel St. Denis (drums)

Location: probably Nice, France. c. 1980–81

Titles performed:
'Rockin' The Blues' Magnum MMGV020
'Misery' Magnum MMGV020
'I'm Lost Without You' Magnum MMGV020
'It's Too Late' Magnum MMGV020
'Dimples' Magnum MMGV020
'Kansas City' Magnum MMGV020
'Baby Please Come Home' Magnum MMGV020
'Everyday I Have The Blues' Magnum MMGV020
'Nashville' Magnum MMGV020
'What Is The Blues' Magnum MMGV020
'Shake Rattle And Roll' Magnum MMGV020
'All By Myself' Magnum MMGV020
'She Brings Out The Animal In Me' Magnum MMGV020
'Mean Ole Frisco' Magnum MMGV020
'Pigalle Love' Magnum MMGV020
'Let The Good Times Roll' Magnum MMGV020
'That Train Has Gone' Magnum MMGV020
'This Is A Good Time To Write A Song' Magnum MMGV020
'You're Never Gonna Let Me Go' Magnum MMGV020
'I'm Goin' Back Home' Magnum MMGV020
'Low Down Dirty Shame' Magnum MMGV020
'I May Be Wrong' Magnum MMGV020
'Big Fat Mama' Magnum MMGV020
'Wish Me Well' Magnum MMGV020
'Next Time You See Me' Magnum MMGV020
'All By Myself' Magnum MMGV020

Source: *French TV broadcast* [C]

Piano solo–1
Vocal duet with George Melly accompaniment: own piano–2

Location: London, England. 1983

Titles performed:
'Rockin' The House'–1
'Sent For You Yesterday'–2

Source: *Good Time George*

Vocal and piano

Location: Cambridge, England. Summer 1984

Titles performed:
'Movin' On'
'Misery'
'We're Gonna Rock'
'Baby Please Come Home'
'All By Myself'

Source: *Festival* [2]

Vocal and piano accompaniment: Danny Adler (electric guitar); Bob Brunning (electric bass); George Collier (drums); add Paul Jones (harmonica)–1 and Slim Gaillard (vocal)–2

Location: Ronnie Scott's Jazz Club, London, England. 1986

Titles performed:
'Baby Please Come Home'
'Where Do I Go From Here'
'Didn't We'
'Lost Without You'
'Lonesome Traveller'
'Stepping Out'
'Christina'
'Beer Drinkin' Woman'
'You Bring Out The Animal In Me'
'Misery'
'Please Send Me Someone To Love'
'All By Myself'
'Four Hundred Years'–1
'Hip Shaking'–1
'Mother Earth'–1
'If You See Kay'–1
'Feel So Good'–1
'How Long'–1
'Tribute To Gaillard'–1, –2
'What Is The World Coming To'–1, –2
'Bye Bye Blues'–1, –2

Source: *Live At Ronnie Scott's*
Memphis Slim also appears in *Memphis Slim Live At Nice*, which may or may not be catalogued above. See Commercially Issued Videos, under Videoplus.

MEMPHIS WILLIE B

See [Memphis] Willie Borum.

MAE MERCER

Vocal accompaniment: Sonny Boy Williamson (harmonica); Hubert Sumlin (guitar); Sunnyland Slim (piano); Willie Dixon (bass); Clifton James (drums)

Location: Baden-Baden, Germany. October 1964

Title performed:
[introduction by Willie Dixon;]
'Careless Love'

Source: *American Folk Blues Festival 1964*

ELDER LIGHFOOT SOLOMON MICHAUX

Vocal accompaniment: unknown (harmonica); congregation (vocals)

Location: Church Of God In Christ, Washington DC. Monday 18 February 1935

Titles performed;
'Happy Am I' [part only] Yazoo 512
[monologue] Yazoo 512

Source: *Fox Movietone newsreel*

Probably similar to above

Location: Church of God In Christ, Washington DC. 1946 to 1949

Titles performed:
unknown

Source: *Elder Michaux*. Michaux also produced, and possibly featured in *We've Got The Devil On The Run* and *We've Come A Long Way*.

MICKEY AND SYLVIA (McHouston Baker and Sylvia Vanderpool)

Vocal duet accompaniment: probably Mickey (electric guitar) and others, unknown

Location: probably New York City. January–June 1957

Title performed:
[probably] 'Love Is Strange'

Source: *Circus Time*

Vocal duet accompaniment: probably Mickey (electric guitar) and the Alan Freed orchestra: Big Al Sears and Sam 'The Man' Taylor (tenor saxophones) and others, unknown

Location: New York City. July–August 1957

Title performed:
'Love Is Strange'

Source: *The Big Beat* [2]

MIGHTY CHARIOTS

Vocal quartet accompaniment: unknown

Location: New Orleans, Louisiana. 1985

Title performed:
'The Lord Will Make A Way'

Source: *New Orleans Now: In The Revival Tent*

MIGHTY CLOUDS OF HARMONY

Probably Julius La Rosa Hicks, Mose Ladson, Walter Alston Jr., James Madison Riley, Curtis Cleveland (vocals) accompaniment: possibly Masnon Williams (electric guitar); Quillie McMillian (electric bass)

Location: Chicago, Illinois. Wednesday 20th August 1969

Titles performed:
unknown

Source: *Jubilee Showcase* [prog # 4–1]

MIGHTY CLOUDS OF JOY

Joe Ligon (lead vocal) accompaniment: probably Ermant Franklin Jr, Leon Polk, Johnny Martin, Elmer Franklin (vocals); Richard Wallace (electric guitar); unknown (electric bass)–1
as above with Jessie Mae Renfro (vocal)–2
as –1 accompaniment: the Echoneers Young People's Choir–3

Location: Baltimore, Maryland. Sunday 5 September 1964

Titles performed:
'Steal Away'–1
'Golden Bells'–1
'He's So Wonderful'–2
'Just Look'–3

Source: *TV Gospel Time* #32

Probably as above accompaniment: unknown

Location: Chicago, Illinois

The following appearances are known:
1964
Sunday 5 April [prog #8–1]
1968
Saturday 19 October [prog #2–3]
1969
Saturday 20 September [prog #4–1]

Titles performed:
unknown

Source: *Jubilee Showcase*

Ligon (lead vocal) accompaniment: similar to above

Location: Chicago, Illinois. 1976

Titles performed:
unknown

Source: *Here Comes Gospel*

As last

Location: Montreux, Switzerland. July 1981

Titles performed:
unknown

Source: *Montreux Jazz*

As last

Location: unknown {USA}. 1984

Titles performed:
unknown

Source: *Gospel*

As last

Location: Chicago, Illinois. Sunday 25 November 1990

Title performed:
'I Been In The Storm Too Long'

Source: *Soundstage*
See also the Gospel Clouds Of Joy and Joe Ligon.

MIGHTY FLEA (Gene Connors)

Trombone accompaniment: the Johnny Otis band

Location: Monterey, California. Saturday 19 September 1970

Title performed:
'Preacher's Blues' [part only]

Source: *Play Misty For Me*

AMOS MILBURN

Vocal and piano accompaniment: Paul Williams (baritone saxophone); Jimmy Brown (trumpet); unknown (tenor saxophone, bass, drums); Willie Bryant, spoken comments–1

Location: New York City. 1955

Titles performed:

[spoken introduction by Willie Bryant, leading to;]	Fil A Film 2023, Storyville SV6016
'Rocky Mountain'	Fil A Film 2023, Storyville SV6016, Video Images 74
'Bad, Bad Whiskey'	Storyville SV6016, Video Images 73R
'Bewildered'	Storyville SV6016
[spoken introduction by Willie Bryant, leading to;]	Storyville SV6106, Video Images 73R
'Down The Road Apiece'–1	Storyville SV6016, Video Images 73R

Source: *Showtime At The Apollo*
'Rocky Mountain' is mistitled as 'I'm Gonna Tell My Mama' on both the Fil A Film and Video Images issues.

ALFRED MILLER

Vocal accompaniment: unknown, possibly own piano

Location: New York City. Sunday 4 November 1962

Title performed:
'Wade In The Water'

Source: *TV Gospel Time* #8
See also the Sanctuary Choir.

JAMES MILLER

Vocal and piano accompaniment: unknown (trumpet, clarinet, bass, drums)

Location: New Orleans, Louisiana. February 1985

Title performed:

'Hurry Sundown' [part only]	Vestapol 13076

Source: *Feet Don't Fail Me Now*

MILLER SISTERS

Vocal group accompaniment: unknown

Location: probably New York City. 1956

Title performed:
'Everybody's Having A Ball'

Source: *Rockin' The Blues*

LUCIUS [LUCKY] MILLINDER AND HIS BAND

Millinder appears in the 1933 production *Gig And Saddle* which may fall within the scope of this work, but it has not been possible to view it. For accompaniments by this band to a number of blues singers, see the accompanists index.

MILLS BROTHERS

Details of film performances by this group will be found in the third edition of *Jazz In The Movies* by David Meeker.

HAYWOOD MILLS
Vocal accompaniment: unknown

Location: Mississippi. 1984

Titles performed:
unknown

Source: *In The Delta Of Mississippi*

MAUDE MILLS
Vocal accompaniment: 'Club Alabama Stompers' [Billy Fowler and his orchestra]; Jack Butler and unknown (trumpets); Doc Crawford (trombone); three unknown reeds; unknown (piano); Eddie Gibbs (banjo); unknown (bass); Herbie Owens (drums)

Location: New York City. 1929

Title performed:
'I'm Gonna Lose Myself Down In Louisville'

Source: [probably] *Dark Town Scandals Review*

ROY MILTON
Vocal accompaniment probably Hosea Sapp (trumpet); Earl Sims (alto saxophone); Lorenzo 'Buddy' Floyd (tenor saxophone); Camille Howard (piano); David Robinson (bass); Roy Milton (drums); June Richmond (vocal) at least–1, and probably others

Location: Hollyowood, California. Early 1944

Titles performed:
[8308] 'We're Steppin' Out Tonight'–1
[16808] 'Hey Lawdy Mama' Charly 5, Rhino R3.2101, Storyville SV6003, Virgin VVD868
[17908] '47th Street Jive'–1 Charly 5
[17108] 'Ride On, Ride On'–1 Charly 5
[89108] 'Mr. Jackson From Jacksonville'–1 Storyville SV6003, Virgin VVD868
[13M2] 'Baby, Don't You Love Me Anymore'–1
[24M2] 'My Bottle Is Dry'–1
[25M2] 'Time Takes Care Of Everything'
[25M4] 'Who Dunnit To Who?'–1

Source: *Soundies*

The personnel quoted is that which appeared on Milton's first recording session in December 1945, by which time it may have altered. 16808 copyrighted 5 June 1944; 17108 27 June 1944; 17908 28 August 1944; 13M2 26 November 1945; 24M2 10 July 1946. One, at least, of the above titles appears in *Ebony Parade*, but it is not known which.

MITCHELL GOSPEL CHORAL ENSEMBLE
Mixed vocal choir accompaniment: unknown
Solists: Francis Heeden–1; Rose Miner–2

Location: Brooklyn, New York City. Saturday 15 December 1962

Titles performed:
'Jesus, I Love You'–1
'I Need Thee Every Hour'
'Good Enough'–2

Source: *TV Gospel Time* #18

FLORA MOLTON
Vocal and guitar accompaniment, if any: unknown

Location: Fairfax Station, Virginia. 1985

Titles performed:
unknown Blues Houseparty BH-01

Source: *Blues Houseparty*

Vocal, guitar and foot-operated tambourine

Location: WDBJ TV Studios, Roanoke, Virginia. Spring/Summer 1987

Title performed:
'Do Lord Remember Me' [part only]

Source: *Black Musical Traditions In Virginia: Sacred Music*

LITTLE BROTHER MONTGOMERY (Eurreal Wilford Montgomery)
Piano solo–1 : speech–2

Location: Chicago, Illinois. Thursday 14 July 1960

Titles performed:
blues piano solo–1 [ST] K-Jazz 014, Rhapsody 8022
monologue–2 [ST] K-Jazz 014, Rhapsody 8022

Source: *Blues Like Showers Of Rain*

Vocal and piano accompaniment: probably Fred Below (drums)

Location: Baden-Baden, Germany. c. December 1966

Titles performed:
unknown

Source: *American Folk Blues Festival 1966*

Vocal and piano

Location: Chicago, Illinois. Thursday 29 January 1976

Titles performed:
'Vicksburg Blues'
'No Special Rider' (unbroadcast)
untitled instrumental (unbroadcast)

Source: *The Devil's Music series 2*

Vocal and piano accompaniment, if any: unknown

Location: Chicago, Illinois. 1977

Titles performed:
unknown

Source: *Made In Chicago*
Montgomery appears on camera in *Nothing But The Blues*, accompanying Big Joe Turner, but he does not sing.
See also Edith Wilson.

MOONGLOWS
Vocal group accompaniment: Harvey Fuqua (see 'Harvey' entry). Founding line-up was (1951); Fuqua, Bobby Lester, Alexander Graves, Prentis Barnes (vocals); Billy Johnson (guitar)

Location: unknown {USA}. 1956

Titles performed:
'I Knew From The Start' Gold Star BSG203
'Over And Over Again' Gold Star BSG203

Source: *Rock, Rock, Rock*

Vocal group, accompaniment: unknown

Location: unknown {USA}. c. 1957

Title performed:
'Barcelona Rock'

Source: *Mister Rock And Roll*

[WHISTLING] ALEX MOORE (Alexander Herman Moore)
Piano solo with whistling

Location: Dallas, Texas. Spring 1963

Title performed:
untitled boogie instrumental Yazoo 520

Source: *Die Blues*

REVEREND A D [GATEMOUTH] MOORE
Preaching, speech, singing accompaniment: unknown (electric guitar, organ)

Location: E M Coleman church, Lexington, Mississippi. 1994

Titles performed:
[sermons] California Newsreel 01, Multicultural Media 1008
'This Little Light Of Mine' California Newsreel 01, Multicultural Media 1008

Source: *Saturday Night, Sunday Morning*

Speech

Locations: the Moore residence, Lexington, Mississippi; Beale Street, Memphis and elsewhere. 1994

[interviews] California Newsreel 01, Multicultural Media 1008

Source: *Saturday Night, Sunday Morning*

Vocal, in duet with Rufus Thomas, accompaniment: unknown (electric guitar, brass, piano, electric bass, drums)

Location: Memphis, Tennessee. 1994

Title performed:
'Did You Ever Love A Woman'
California Newsreel 01, Multicultural Media 1008

Source: *Saturday Night And Sunday Morning*

Preaching, accompaniment: congregation

Location: Lexington, Mississippi. August 1995

Titles performed:
untitled sermon

Source: *Too Close To Heaven*

[BIG] BILL MORGANFIELD

Vocal accompaniment: unknown, but probably including Bo Diddley, Buddy Guy, Keb' Mo', Mem Shannon, Koko Taylor, and others (vocals) accompaniment: G E Smith's band

Location: Washington DC. Saturday 11 October 1997

Title performed:
'Got My Mojo Working'

Source: *Tribute To Muddy Waters*
This artist is the son of Muddy Waters.

BARBARA MORRISON

Vocal accompaniment: the Johnny Otis band–1
Vocal accompaniment Delmar Evans, Linda Hopkins, Charles Williams (vocals) accompaniment: the Johnny Otis band–2

Location: Monterey, California. 1987

Titles performed:
'Shake'–1
Gospel medley–2

Source: *Monterey Jazz Festival*

BILL MOSS AND THE CELESTIALS

Vocal group accompaniment: unknown

Location: Chicago, Illinois

The following appearances are known:
1969
Saturday 15 March [prog #32–2]
Saturday 29 November [prog #25–2]
1972
Saturday 26 August [prog #13–3]

Titles performed:
unknown

Source: *Jubilee Showcase*

MOUNT CARMEL BAPTIST CHURCH CHOIR

Mixed vocal choir accompaniment: unknown
Soloists: Dallas Sullivan–1; Louise Walker–2

Location: Charlotte, North Carolina. Saturday 1 August 1964

Titles performed:
'Nothing Between'
'Oh, What A Time'–1
'When We All Get to Heaven'–2

Source: *TV Gospel Time* #30

MOUNT OLLIE BAPTIST CHURCH CHOIR

Mixed vocal choir accompaniment: unknown
Soloists: Anthony Glover–1; Joyce Williams–2; Geraldine Giles–3

Location: Brooklyn, New York City. Sunday 27 January 1963

Titles performed:
'Sit Down, Servant'–1
'Lord, I Want To Be A Christian'–2
'I'm Coming Home On The Morning Train'–3

Source: *TV Gospel Time* #16

MOUNT SINAI GOSPEL CHORUS
Mixed vocal choir accompaniment: unknown
Soloist: Marie McDougal–1

Location: Brooklyn, New York City. Sunday 2 December 1962

Titles performed:
'Come On Children, Let's Sing'–1
'I'm Getting Ready To Go'
'Jesus Is The King Of Kings'–1

Source: *TV Gospel Time* #4

MOVING STAR HALL SINGERS
Mixed vocal group, unaccompanied

Location: Newport, Rhode Island. 1963–4

Titles performed:
unknown

Source: *Festival* [1]
There is probably also footage of this group at Newport in 1966 in the Alan Lomax collection.

MUDDY WATERS (McKinley Morganfield)
Vocal accompaniment: Otis Spann (piano); James Cotton (harmonica); Pat Hare and Lafayette Thomas (electric guitars); Andrew Stephenson (electric bass); Francis Clay (drums)–1
as above, joined by Betty Jeanette, Sam Price, Jimmy Rushing (vocals); Butch Cage (violin); Willie Thomas (guitar)–2

Location: Newport, Rhode Island. Sunday 3 July 1960

Titles performed:
'Rollin' Stone'–1
'I Wanna Put A Tiger In Your Tank'–1
'I'm Your Hoochie Coochie Man'–1
'Soon Forgotten'–1
'Mean Mistreater'–1
'Got My Mojo Working'–1
'Goodbye Newport Blues'–2

Source: *Jazz-USA*
See also Otis Spann.

Vocal accompaniment, presumably, as above

Location: unknown {USA} (or Newport). 1960

Titles performed:
unknown

Source: *The Subterraneans*

Vocal accompaniment: unknown

Location: unknown {USA}. 1963

Titles performed:
unknown

Source: *International Hour* [unconfirmed]

Vocal accompaniment: unknown

Location: London, England. October 1963

Titles performed:
unknown
[interview]

Source: *Tonight*

Vocal accompaniment: Otis Spann (piano); Matt Murphy (electric guitar); Willie Dixon (bass); Billie Stepney (drums)

Location: Manchester, England. October 1963

Title performed:
'Got My Mojo Working'

Source: *I Hear the Blues*

Probably as above

Location: Baden-Baden, Germany. c. November 1963

Titles performed:
unknown

Source: *American Folk Blues Festival 1963*

Vocal and electric guitar accompaniment: Otis Spann (piano); Ramsom Knowling (bass); Willie Smith (drums)–1
Vocal only accompaniment: Rosetta Tharpe and Cousin Joe Pleasants (vocals); Brownie McGhee (vocal and guitar); Sonny Terry (vocal and harmonica); Otis Spann (piano); Ransom Knowling (bass); Willie Smith (drums)–2

Location: Alexandra Park railway station, Chorlton-cum-Hardy, Manchester, England. May 1964

Titles performed:
'Hoochie Coochie Man' (unbroadcast)–1
'Got My Mojo Working' (unbroadcast)–1
'When The Sun Rose This Morning'–1
'You Can't Lose What You Ain't Never Had'–1
'He's Got The Whole World In His Hands'–2

Source: *The Blues And Gospel Train*

Vocal accompaniment: unknown

Location: unknown {USA}. 1965

Titles performed:
unknown

Source: *Like Young* [unconfirmed]

Vocal accompaniment: unknown

Location: Boston, Massachusetts. 1965–6

Titles performed:
unknown

Source: *Dateline Boston*

Vocal and electric guitar accompaniment: James Cotton (harmonica); Sammy Lawhorn and James Madison (electric guitars); Otis Spann (piano); Jimmy Lee Morrison (electric bass); S.P. Leary (drums)–1
Vocal and electric guitar accompaniment: Sunnyland Slim (piano); Willie Dixon (bass); S.P. Leary (drums)–2
Vocal accompaniment as –1, with James Cotton, Willie Dixon, Jesse Fuller, Mable Hillery, Brownie McGhee, Otis Spann, Sunnyland Slim, Bukka White and Big Joe Williams (vocals)–3

Location: Toronto, Canada. Thursday 27 to Saturday 29 January 1966

Titles performed:
'You Can't Lose What You Ain't Never Had'–1 Rhino 3.2313
'Got My Mojo Working'–1 Rhino 3.2313
'Little Anna Mae'–2 Rhino 3.2313
jam session–2 Rhino 3.2313
[and conversation with Barry Callaghan, Willie Dixon, Brownie McGhee, Otis Spann and Sunnyland Slim]

Source: *Festival Presents The Blues*

Vocal accompaniment: Otis Spann (piano); Paul Oscher (harmonica); Luther Johnson and Sammy Lawhorn (electric guitars); Little Sonny Wimberley (electric bass); S.P. Leary (drums)

Location: London, England. c. late November 1967

Titles performed:
unknown

Source: BBC-TV programme, title unknown, broadcast Sunday 26 November. This may have been a live broadcast, in which case it is also the correct recording date. See also Otis Spann.

Vocal accompaniment: unknown

Location: unknown {USA}. 1968

Titles performed:
unknown

Source: *For Blacks Only* [unconfirmed]

Vocal and electric guitar accompaniment: Otis Spann (piano); Paul Oscher (harmonica); Luther Johnson and James 'PeeWee' Madison (electric guitars); Sonny Wimberley (electric bass); S.P. Leary (drums)

Location: Maltings Theatre, Snape, England. Monday 21 October 1968

Titles performed:
untitled instrumental [band only]
'You Can't Lose What You Ain't Never Had'
'Bloodstains On The Wall'
'Hoochie Coochie Man'
'Got My Mojo Working'
'Long Distance Call'
'Country Boy'
'Five Long Years' [part only]

Source: *Jazz At The Maltings*

As above

Location: London, England. Late October 1968

Titles performed;
'Blow Wind Blow'
'You Can't Lose What You Ain't Never Had'

Source: *Once More With Felix*

Vocal accompaniment: unknown

Location: unknown {USA}. 1969

Titles performed:
unknown

Source: *Blackbook*

Vocal accompaniment: Buddy Guy (electric guitar); Paul Oscher (harmonica); unknown (electric bass, drums)

Location: Chicago, Illinois. April–May 1970

Titles performed:
'Hoochie Coochie Man' [part only] K-Jazz 004, Rhapsody 9012
'She's Nineteen Years Old' [part only] K-Jazz 004, Rhapsody 9012
[interview] K-Jazz 004, Rhapsody 9012

Source: *Chicago Blues*
An audio recording from this session of *Got My Mojo Working* exists, but the accompanying film appears not to have survived.

Vocal and electric guitar accompaniment: Luther Johnson and Bob Margolin (electric guitars); Jerry Portnoy (harmonica); Pinetop Perkins (piano); probably Calvin Jones (electric bass); Willie Smith (drums)

Location: Bologna, Italy. Late 1970

Titles performed:
band instrumental
'I've Had My Fun'
'Hoochie Coochie Man'
'Baby Please Don't Go'
'I'm A Howlin' Wolf'
'Sun Rose This Morning'
'County Jail'

Source: *Italian TV broadcast* [C]

Vocal accompaniment: unknown, probably as above

Location: Chicago, Illinois. 1970

Titles performed:
unknown

Source: *The Blues Is Alive And Well In Chicago*

Vocal accompaniment: unknown

Location: unknown {USA}. 1971

Titles performed:
unknown

Source: *The Cromie Circle Show* [unconfirmed]

Vocal accompaniment: unknown

Location: New York City. 1971

Titles performed:
unknown

Source: *The David Frost Show*

Vocal accompaniment: unknown

Location: unknown {USA}. 1971

Titles performed:
unknown [probably ST only]

Source: *Dynamite Chicken*

Speech

Location: London, England. Probably December 1971

[interview with disc jockey Mike Raven]

Source: *BBC*

Vocal and electric guitar accompaniment: George 'Mojo' Buford (harmonica); Lafayette Leake (piano); Louis Myers (electric guitar); David Myers (electric bass); Fred Below (drums)
Duet with T-Bone Walker (vocal and electric guitar), accompaniment: as above–1; duet with Koko Taylor (vocal), accompaniment: as above–2

Location: Montreux, Switzerland. Saturday 17 June 1972

Titles performed:
'Sail On'
'Hoochie Coochie Man'
'County Jail'
'Long Distance Call'
'Rock Me Baby'
'Trouble No More'
'Rosalie'
'Rollin' And Tumblin''
'Feel Like Going Home'
'Got My Mojo Working'
'They Call It Stormy Monday'–1
'She Says She Loves Me'–1
'I Got What it Takes'–2

Source: *Montreux Jazz*

Vocal and guitar accompaniment: Buddy Guy (electric guitar); Junior Wells (harmonica); Terry Taylor (second electric guitar); Pinetop Perkins (piano); Bill Wyman (electric bass); Dallas Taylor (drums)–1;
accompaniment as above, vocal only–2

Location: Montreux, Switzerland. Friday 28 June 1974

Titles performed:

'Hoochie Coochie Man'–1	BMG 791051, Rhino R3.1991
'Manish Boy'–1	BMG 791051, Rhino R3.1991
'The Same Thing'–2	BMG 791051, Rhino R3.1991
'I've Got My Mojo Working'–2	BMG 791051, Rhino R3.1991

Source: *Montreux Jazz*
See also Buddy Guy and Junior Wells.

Vocal accompaniment: Junior Wells (harmonica); Dr. John (piano); Michael Bloomfield and Johnny Winter (electric guitars); Willie Dixon (bass); Buddy Miles (drums)

Location: Chicago, Illinois. Tuesday 18 July 1974

Titles performed:
'Blow Wind Blow'
'Hootchie Cootchie Man'
'Long Distance Call'
'Mannish Boy'
'Got My Mojo Working'

Source: *Soundstage; 'Muddy And Friends'*

Vocal accompaniment: unknown (banjo, washboard) and the Maurice Jarre orchestra

Location: Los Angeles, California. 1974

Titles performed:
'Born In This Time' [ST]

Source: *Mandingo*

Vocal and electric guitar accompaniment: Jerry Portnoy (harmonica); Luther Johnson and Bob Margolin (electric guitars); Pinetop Perkins (piano); Calvin Jones (electric bass); Willie Smith (drums) add Junior Wells, (harmonica)–1

Location: Dortmund, Germany. Friday 29 October 1976

Titles performed:
'Soon Forgotten'
'I'm A Howlin' Wolf'
'Hoochie Coochie Man'
'Blow Wind Blow'
'What's The Matter With The Mill'
'Long Distance Call'
'Got My Mojo Working'–1

Source: *German TV broadcast* [C]

Vocal and electric guitar accompaniment: Luther Johnson, Johnny Winter, Bob Margolin and Robbie Robertson (electric guitars); Pinetop Perkins (piano); Richard Manuel and Gareth Hudson (keyboards); Rick Danko (electric bass); Levon Helm (drums)

Location: Winterland ballroom, San Francisco, California. Thursday 25 November 1976

Title performed:
'Mannish Boy'

Source: *The Last Waltz*

Vocal and electric guitar accompaniment: Jerry Portnoy (harmonica); Pinetop Perkins (piano); Luther Johnson and Bob Margolin (electric guitars); Calvin Jones (electric bass); Willie Smith (drums): Clark Terry (trumpet)–1

Location: Nice, France. Sunday 10 July 1977

Titles performed:
'The Honeydripper' (band only)
'I'm Through'
'Baby Please Don't Go'
'What's The Matter With The Mill'–1
'Stormy Monday Blues'
'Everything's Gonna Be Alright'

Source: *French TV broadcast* [C]

As last; Muddy Waters and Pinetop Perkins, vocal duet–2

Location: Nice, France. Thursday 14 July 1977

Titles performed:
'Clouds In My Heart'
'Blow Wind Blow'
'She's So Pretty'
'Hoochie Coochie Man'
'Caldonia'–1
'Got My Mojo Working'

Source: *French TV broadcast* [C]

Vocal accompaniment: unknown

Location: Los Angeles, California. 1977

Titles performed:
unknown

Source: *The Mike Douglas Show*

Vocal and electric guitar accompaniment: unknown

Location: unknown {USA}. 1978

Titles performed:
unknown

Source: *Don Kirshner's Rock Concert*

Vocal and electric guitar accompaniment: probably Jerry Portnoy (harmonica); Pinetop Perkins (piano); Bob Margolin (electric guitar); Calvin Jones (electric bass); Willie Smith (drums);
Muddy Waters and Pinetop Perkins (vocal duet), accompaniment as above–1

Location: Germany. December 1978

Titles performed:
'They Call Me Muddy Waters'
'Country Boy'
'Caldonia'–1
'Mannish Boy'
'Got My Mojo Working'

Source: *Rockpalast*

Vocal accompaniment: unknown

Location: unknown {USA}. Early–mid-1979

Title performed:
unknown

Source: *US TV advert for Budweiser beer*

Vocal and electric guitar accompaniment: probably as last

Location: Nice, France. July 1979

Titles performed:
band instrumental
'Hoochie Coochie Man'
'Walking Through The Park'
'Soon Forgotten'
'Baby Please Don't Go'
'They Call Me Muddy Waters'
'Champagne And Reefers'
'Trouble No More'

Source: *La Grande Parade Du Jazz*

Vocal and electric guitar accompaniment: probably as last

Location: Northsea Jazz Festival, Den Haag, Netherlands. c.1979

Titles performed:
'Hoochie Coochie Man'
'Baby Please Don't Go'
'Mean Mistreater'

'Kansas City'
'I'm A Man'
'Got My Mojo Working'

Source: *Dutch TV broadcast* [C]

Vocal and electric guitar accompaniment: George 'Mojo' Buford (harmonica); Lovie Lee (piano); Rick Kreher (electric guitar); Ernest Johnson (electric bass); Ray Allison (drums)

Location: Antibes, France. Tuesday 22 July 1980

Titles performed:
'They Call Me Muddy Waters'
'Blow Wind Blow'
'My Home Is In The Delta'
'Hoochie Coochie Man'
'Baby Please Don't Go'
'Everything Gonna Be Alright'
'Kansas City'
'Got My Mojo Working'

Source: *French TV broadcast* [C]

Vocal and electric guitar accompaniment: George 'Mojo' Buford (harmonica); John Primer (electric guitar); Eddie Lee Watson (piano); Jesse Clay (electric bass); unknown (drums)

Location: Helsinki, Finland. 1980

Titles performed:
'Blues Before Sunrise'
'Nine Below Zero'
'I'm A Howlin Wolf'
'Everything's Gonna Be Alright'
'Baby Please Don't Go'
'Nineteen Years Old'
'Blow Wind Blow'
'Mannish Boy'

Source: *Finnish TV broadcast*

Vocal and electric guitar accompaniment: probably as above

Location: Montreux, Switzerland. Summer 1981

Titles performed:
band instrumental
'Hoochie Coochie Man'
'They Call Me Muddy Waters'
'I'm Gonna Get High'
'Ninety-Nine Years Blues'
'Blow Wind Blow'
'Country Boy'

Source: *Montreux Jazz*

Vocal and electric guitar accompaniment: George 'Mojo' Buford (harmonica); John Primer (electric guitar); Lovie Lee (piano) and others, unknown; with Johhny Winter (electric guitar) and Buddy Miles (drums) guesting.

Location: Chicago, Illinois. Tuesday 4 August 1981

Titles performed:
'Mannish Boy' BMG5013
'You Don't Have To Go' BMG5013
'Baby Please Don't Go' BMG5013
'I'm A King Bee' BMG5013
'Trouble No More' BMG5013
'They Call Me Muddy Waters' BMG5013
'Goin' Down Slow' BMG5013
'Nineteen Years Old' BMG5013
'Look What You've Done' BMG5013
'Mean Mistreatin' Mama' BMG5013
'Got My Mojo Working' BMG5013

Source: *Chicago Blues Festival 1981*

Vocal and electric guitar accompaniment: unknown, probably similar to above

Location: Germany. 1981

Titles performed:
'Hoochie Coochie Man'
'Got My Mojo Working'

Source: *Rockpalast* [C]

Vocal and electric guitar accompaniment: George 'Mojo' Buford (harmonica); Lovie Lee (piano); John Primer and Rick Kreher (electric guitars); Ernest Johnson (electric bass); Ray Allen (drums)

Location: Ames, Iowa. 1981

Titles performed:
'Hoochie Coochie Man' K-Jazz 143
'My Home Is On The Delta' K-Jazz 143
'You Don't Have To Go' K-Jazz 143

'I'm A King Bee' K-Jazz 143
'Baby, Please Don't Go' K-Jazz 143
'Long Distance Call' K-Jazz 143
'Trouble No More' K-Jazz 143
'Goin' Down Slow' K-Jazz 143
'Got My Mojo Working' K-Jazz 143
'Mannish Boy' K-Jazz 143

Source: *Maintenance Shop Blues*

Vocal accompaniment: unknown

Location: unknown {USA}. 1981–2

Titles performed:
unknown [probably ST only]

Source: *Street Music*

Vocal and electric guitar accompaniment: Keith Richards and John Primer (electric guitars); Ray Allison (drums)
As above, accompaniment: Mojo Buford (harmonica)–1; Buddy Guy (vocal and electric guitar)–2; Mick Jagger (vocal)–3; Ernest Johnson (electric bass)–4; Mick Jones (electric bass)–5; Rick Kreher (electric guitar)–6; Lefty Dizz (electric guitar)–7; Lovie Lee (piano)–8; Ian Stewart (piano)–9; Junior Wells (vocal and harmonica)–10; Ron Wood (electric guitar)–11

Location: Checkerboard Lounge, Chicago, Illinois. Sunday 22 November 1981

Titles performed:
[band only:]
band theme and introduction
'Sweet Little Angel' (vocal, Lovie Lee)
'Flip, Flop And Fly' (vocal, Lovie Lee)
[introduction of and monologue by Muddy Waters, leading to;]
'Down The Road I Go'–1, –4, –6, –8
'Country Boy'–1, –4, –6, –8
'County Jail'–1, –4, –6, –8
'I'm A King Bee'–1, –4, –6, –8
'Someday Baby'–1, –4, –6, –8
'Baby Please Don't Go'–1, –3, –4, –6, –8, –11
'Hoochie Coochie Man'–1, –3, –4, –6, –8, –11
'Long Distance Call'–1, –3, –4, –6, –8, –11
'Mannish Boy'–2, –4, –5, –6, –8, –10, –11
'Got My Mojo Working'–2, –4, –6, –8, –10, –11
'Next Time You See Me'–2, –4, –6, –9, –10, –11
'Ugly Woman Blues'–5, –6, –7, –9, –10, –11
'Baby Please Don't Go' (instrumental)–5, –6, –7 ,–8, –11
'Clouds In My Heart'–5, –6, –7, –8, –11
'Champagne And Reefers'–5, –6, –7, –8, –11
untitled instrumental #1 (1–11 inclusive)
untitled instrumental #2 (1–11 inclusive)

Source: unknown

Vocal accompaniment: George 'Mojo' Buford (harmonica); Lovie Lee (piano); John Primer (electric guitar); Ernest Johnson (electric bass); Ray Allen (drums)

Location: Chicago, Illinois. 1981

Titles performed:
'Got My Mojo Working'
'I'm A Man'

Source: *Melody Of A City; Chicago*
There are believed to be TV broadcasts by Muddy Waters made in Poland during 1974, Australia during 1975, and Mexico and Japan during 1979. There also remains the possibilty of his appearing on British TV during his October 1958 tour, and German TV during late 1962. A brief silent clip of amateur colour footage of this artist, dating from c. early 1960s, appears in 'Record Row'.

MATT [GUITAR] MURPHY
Electric guitar ccompaniment: Memphis Slim (piano); Willie Dixon (bass); Billie Stepney (drums)

Location: Manchester, England. October 1963

Title performed:
'Matt's Guitar Boogie'

Source: *I Hear The Blues*

Probably as above

Location: Baden-Baden, Germany. c. October 1963

Titles performed:
unknown

Source: *American Folk Blues Festival 1963*
Murphy also appeared, in an acting role and as a member of the band, in both *The Blues Brothers* and *Blues Brothers 2000*

DAVID MYERS
Vocal and electric bass accompaniment: Jimmy Johnson and Eddie Clearwater (electric guitars); Odie Payne (drums)

Location: Montreux, Switzerland. 1979

Title performed:
'Blue Shadows Falling'

Source: *Montreux Jazz*
See also the Aces.

LOUIS MYERS
Vocal accompaniment: unknown

Location: unknown {USA}. 1976

Titles performed:
unknown

Source: *Music In America* [unconfirmed]
See also the Aces.

SAMMY MYERS
Vocal and harmonica accompaniment: Anson Funderburgh and the Rockets [G]

Location: Chicago, Illinois. 1991

Title performed:
Look On Yonders Wall BMG 791.151

Source: *Blues Alive*

N

[REVEREND KING] LOUIS H NARCISSE
Vocal accompaniment: unknown (piano) and congregation–1
Vocal accompaniment: own piano–2

Location: Mount Zion Spiritual Temple, Oakland, California [A]
the Narcisse residence, Oakland, California [B]. Spring 1963

Titles performed:
[preaching] [A]
'This Little Light Of Mine–1 [A]
'Leaning On Jesus'–1 [A]
'Move On Up A Little Higher'–1 [A]
'Walk To Jerusalem'–1 [A]
[sermons] [A]
'On The Battlefield'–2 [B]
[and film of Narcisse administering to his church members, in San Francisco, of Narcisse at home, of his family and friends]

Source: *Dietrich Wawzyn film collection*

CHARLES NEAL
Vocal accompaniment: unknown

Location: New York City. Sunday 16 December 1962

Title performed:
'Peace in The Valley'

Source: *TV Gospel Time* #12

KENNY NEAL
Vocal accompaniment: unknown

Location: Nice, France. 1978

Title performed:
'There Ain't Nothin' You Can't Do'

Source: *La Grande Parade Du Jazz*

Vocal accompaniment: unknown

Location: Chicago, Illinois. 1991

Titles performed:
unknown

Source: *Blues And The Alligator*

RAFUL NEAL
Vocal accompaniment: unknown (two electric guitars, electric bass, drums)

Location: Baton Rouge, Louisiana. 1984

Title performed:
'I'm Downhearted Baby'

Source: *Baton Rouge Blues*

SONNY BOY NELSON
See Eugene Powell.

NEW DESIGN PENTECOSTAL CHURCH SINGERS
Female choir group accompaniment: unknown (electric guitar, electric bass, drums)

Location: WDBJ TV Studios, Roanoke, Virginia. Spring/Summer 1987

Title performed:
'Sit Down By The Banks' [part only]

Source: *Black Musical Traditions In Virginia: Sacred Music*

NEW HOPE CHOIR OF NEWARK, NEW JERSEY
Mixed vocal choir accompaniment: unknown

Location: probably New York City. 1966

Titles performed:
unknown

Source: *TV Gospel Time* #65

NEW METROPOLITAN GOSPEL CHOIR
Mixed vocal choir accompaniment: unknown
Soloist: Joseph Bailey

Location: Baltimore, Maryland. Sunday 20 December 1964

Titles performed:
'Great Day'
'Jesus Is Tenderly Calling'
'By And By'–1

Source: *TV Gospel Time* #24

NEW ORLEANS HARMONIZERS
Vocal quintet accompaniment: one of them (electric guitar)

Location: New Orleans, Louisiana. Spring 1963

Title performed:
'Oh Lord, Stand By Me'
'Farther Along'

Source: *Dietrich Wawzyn film collection*

NEW SALEM BAPTIST CHOIR
Mixed vocal choir accompaniment: unknown

Location: Memphis, Tennessee. Saturday 19 January 1963

Titles performed:
'Old Time Religion'
'Saved, Saved, Saved'
'Just Like Fire Shut Up In My Bones'

Source: *TV Gospel Time* #22

NEW YORK STATE CHOIR
Mixed vocal choir accompaniment: unknown

Location: probably New York City. 1965–66

Titles performed:
unknown

Source: *TV Gospel Time* #52

ROBERT NIGHTHAWK (Robert Lee McCollum aka Robert Lee McCoy)
Vocal and electric guitar accompaniment: Johnny Young (second electric guitar); Robert Whitehead (drums)

Location: Maxwell Street, Chicago, Illinois. September 1964

Titles performed:
'Dust My Broom' (instrumental) [ST] Shanachie 1403
'The Time Has Come' [ST] Shanachie 1403
'I'm Gonna Murder My Baby' [part only] Shanachie 1403

Source: *And This Is Free*

NIGHTINGALES

Probably Rudolph Leamon, Horace Thompson, Joseph Wallace, Charles Johnson, Arthur Crume, Bill Woodruff, Carl Coates (vocals) accompaniment: probably Joseph Wallace (electric guitar)–1;
as above, accompaniment: Emily Bram (vocal)–2

Location: Charlotte, North Carolina. Sunday 1 August 1964

Titles performed:
'Somewhere To Lay My Head'–1
'To The End'–1
'Bye And Bye'–2

Source: *TV Gospel Time* #29

The following appearances are known:
1963:
Sunday 10 November [prog #30–2]
Sunday 17 November [prog #27–3]
1964:
Sunday 12 January [prog #22–1–]
Sunday 26 January [prog #7–3]
Sunday 2 February [prog #20–1]
Sunday 9 February [prog #12–1]
Sunday 16 February [prog #10–3]
Sunday 23 February [prog #28–1]
Sunday 8 March [prog #17–3]
Sunday 15 March [prog #7–1]
Sunday 5 April [prog #8–1]
Sunday 12 April [prog #18–1]
Sunday 19 April [prog #22–3]
Sunday 26 April [prog #9–3]
Saturday 2 May [prog #8–1]
Saturday 9 May [prog #10–3]
Saturday 17 May [prog #21–2]
Sunday 31 May [prog #29–2]
Sunday 7 June [prog #16–2]
Sunday 14 June [prog #10–2]
Sunday 12 July [prog #15–1]
Sunday 19 July [prog #23–3]
Sunday 26 July [prog #26–1]
Sunday 2 August [prog #26–2]
Sunday 20 September [prog #9–2]
1965:
Sunday 19 December [prog #29–1]
1966:
Tuesday 8 March [prog #26–3]
Sunday 8 May [prog #23–1]
Friday 13 May [prog #34–2]
Sunday 2 October [prog #15–2]
Sunday 11 December [prog #15–3]
1967:
Sunday 5 March [prog #17–1]
Sunday 12 March [prog #17–2]
Thursday 6 April [prog #21–2]
Sunday 4 June [prog #21–2]
Sunday 16 July [prog #31–3]
1968:
Saturday 21 September [prog #28–2]
Saturday 5 October [prog #27–2]
Saturday 26 October [prog #24–2]
1969:
Saturday 1 February [prog #25–1];
Saturday 15 February [prog #1–2]
Saturday 8 March [prog #31–2]
Saturday 5 April [prog #13–1]
Wednesday 7 May [prog #12–2]
Monday 26 May [prog #33–1]
Saturday 21 June [prog #24–3]
Saturday 5 July [prog #12–2]

HAMMIE NIXON

Vocal and harmonica, kazoo, blown jug

Location: Freedom Village, Greenville, Mississippi. Saturday 8 September 1979

Titles performed:
'I'm A Tater Diggin' Man — K-Jazz 081
'Sent My Baby A Brand New Twenty Dollar Bill' — K-Jazz 081
'Rock Me Baby' — K-Jazz 081

Source: *Mississippi Blues*
See also John Henry Barbee and John Estes.

JOHN HENRY [BONES] NOBLES

Vocal and bones, accompaniment Taj Mahal (guitar)

Location: Beaumont, Texas. 1979

Titles performed:
unknown — K-Jazz 014

Source: *Bones*

NORFLEET BROTHERS

Arthur, Joseph, George, Peter, Junious and Nathaniel Norfleet, (vocals) accompaniment: one of them (guitar)

Location: Chicago, Illinois.

Saturday 16 August [prog #25–3]
Saturday 27 September [prog #11–3]
Saturday 1 November [prog #12–3]
Friday 11 December [prog #12–3]
1971:
Sunday 29 August [prog #4–2]
1974:
Sunday 25 August [prog #1–3]
1982:
Sunday 20 September [prog #33–3]

Titles performed:
unknown

Source: *Jubilee Showcase*

NORTH INDIANA STATE CHURCH OF GOD IN CHRIST CHOIR

Mixed vocal choir accompaniment: unknown

Location: Chicago, Illinois. Saturday 10 October 1964

Titles performed:
'Hallelujah!'
'There Is Not A Friend Like Jesus'
'Just A Little Talk'

Source: *TV Gospel Time* #39

DOROTHY NORWOOD SINGERS

Vocal group accompaniment: unknown

Location: Chicago, Illinois. Sunday 3 May 1964

Titles performed:
unknown

Source: *Jubilee Showcase* [prog #30–1]

Vocal group accompaniment: unknown

Location: Chicago, Illinois. Saturday 10 October 1964

Titles performed:
'Why Can't I?'
'Jesus Is A Rock'
'The Failure Is Not In God, It's In Me'

Source: *TV Gospel Time* #38

Dorothy Norwood, Melvic Jean Latham, Shirley Peppers (vocals)
accompaniment: Melton McLendon (piano)

Location: Fairfield Halls, Croydon, England. February 1966

Titles performed:
unknown

Source: *American Gospel And Spiritual Festival 1966*

Vocal group accompaniment: unknown

Location: Chicago, Illinois. Saturday 20 September 1969

Titles performed:
unknown

Source: *Jubilee Showcase* [prog #4–1]

As above

Location: Chicago, Illinois. Saturday 19 August 1972

Titles performed: unknown

Source: *Jubilee Showcase* [prog #13–2]

O

O'NEAL TWINS

Edgar and Edward O'Neal (vocal duet)
accompaniment: Alfred Miller (piano)

Location: New York City. c. 1965

Titles performed:
'Power In The Blood'
'Prayer Is The Key'
'Keep In Touch With Jesus'

Source: *TV Gospel Time* #48

As above accompaniment: unknown

Location: Chicago, Illinois. Saturday 12 October 1968

Titles performed:
unknown

Source: *Jubilee Showcase* [prog # unknown]

As above accompaniment: unknown

Location: Chicago, Illinois. 1976

Titles performed:
unknown

Source: *Here Comes Gospel*

Edgar and Edward (vocals) accompaniment: one of them (piano)–1;
as above accompaniment unknown (organ) and congregational vocal–2

Location: Antioch Baptist church, St. Louis, Missouri. 1982

Titles performed:
'I Gave Him My Heart'–1 FRF un-numbered
'Jesus Dropped The Charges'–2 FRF un-numbered
[interviews and conversation] FRF un-numbered

Source: *Say Amen Somebody!*

LORETTA OLIVER

Vocal accompaniment: unknown

Location: Chicago, Illinois

The following appearances are known:
1964
Sunday 12 April [prog #18–1]
Sunday 26 July [prog # 26–1]
1965
Sunday 11 July [prog #29–3]
1966
Friday 13 May [prog #34–2]
1974
Saturday 7 September [prog #5–1]

Titles performed:
unknown

Source: *Jubilee Showcase*

OLIVET INSTITUTIONAL BAPTIST CHURCH CHOIR

Mixed vocal choir
accompaniment: unknown

Location: probably New York City. 1965

Titles performed:
'Guide Me, Oh Jehovah'
'Great Day'

Source: *TV Gospel Time* #44

OMEGA BAPTIST CHURCH RADIO CHOIR

Mixed vocal choir accompaniment: unknown
Soloists: Jessy Dixon–1; Gwendolyn Gooley–2

Location: Chicago, Illinois. Saturday 10 October 1964

Titles performed:
'My Soul's Been Anchored In The Lord'–1
'A Child Of The King'–1
'I Thank You Lord'–2

Source: *TV Gospel Time* #36

Probaby similar to above. Dixon may not be present.

Location: Chicago, Illinois

The following appearances are known:
1965
Sunday 21 November [prog #10–1]
1966
Friday 13 May [prog #34–2]
1969
Saturday 15 February [prog #18–2]

Titles performed:
unknown

Source: *Jubilee Showcase*

ORIGINAL GOSPEL HARMONETTES

See Gospel Harmonettes.

JOHN OSCAR
Vocal accompaniment: unknown

Location: probably Los Angeles, California. c. 1948

Titles performed:
unknown

Source: *The Joint Is Jumping*

JOHNNY OTIS (John Veliotes)
Otis, vocal accompaniment: unknown

Location: New York City. 1956

Title performed:
'Willie And The Hand Jive' MMGV010

Source: *Scope-A-Tone* [FS] [M]

Otis, vocal and piano accompaniment: unknown (guitar, bass, drums)

Location: probably Hollywood, California. 1958

Title performed:
'Willie And The Hand Jive' [part only]

Source: *Juke Box Rhythm*

Johnny Otis, vocal accompaniment: the Johnny Otis band–1;
featured artists accompanied by the Johnny Otis band; Marie Adams and the Three Tons of Joy–2; The Eligibles–3; Marti Barris–4; Lionel Hampton–5; Mel Williams–6

Location: Los Angeles, California. 1959

Titles performed:
untitled boogie instrumental–1
'Goody Goody'–2
'Tom Dooley'–3
'The Nearness of You'–4
'It Don't Mean A Thing'–5
'Stay With Me'–6
'Hand Jive'–1
'Flying Home'–5

Source: *The Johnny Otis Show*

Otis, vocal, accompaniment: the Johnny Otis band

Location: Monterey, California. Saturday 19 September 1970

Title performed:
'Willie And The Hand Jive' [part only]

Source: *Play Misty For Me*
See also Mighty Flea.

Speech

Location: Los Angeles, California. 1986

[interview]

Source: *Remembering Black Music*

Otis, vocal accompaniment: Ernestine Anderson, Etta James, Delmar Evans, Linda Hopkins, Barbara Morrison, Eddie Vincent, Charles Williams (vocals); Big Jay McNeely (tenor saxophone); the Johnny Otis band

Location: Monterey, California. 1987

Titles performed:
'Hand Jive'

Source: *Monterey Jazz Festival*

JOHNNY [SHUGGIE] OTIS Jr.
Guitar accompaniment: the Johnny Otis band

Location: Monterey, California. 1987

Titles performed:
untitled instrumental

Source: *Monterey Jazz Festival*
This artist is the son of Johnny Otis.

[REVEREND] LOUIS OVERSTREET, HIS FOUR SONS, AND THE CONGREGATION OF THE ST. LUKE POWERHOUSE CHURCH OF GOD IN CHRIST OF PHOENIX, ARIZONA
Overstreet, vocal and electric guitar accompaniment: Alvin Sydney, Louis Jr, Robert Lee Overstreet (vocals)–1;
Overstreet, vocal and electric guitar accompaniment: congregation–2;
Overstreet, electric guitar solo to accompany congregational dancing–3;
Alvin Sydney, Louis Jr, Albert Lee, Robert Lee Overstreet (vocals) accompaniment: Louis Overstreet (electric guitar); and congregation (vocals)–4

Location: Phoenix, Arizona. Spring 1963
[A] on the street
[B] St. Luke Powerhouse Church Of God In Christ.

Titles performed:
'I'm Gonna Walk Through The City'–1 [A] [part only] Yazoo 520
'We're Gonna Walk'–2 [B] Yazoo 520
'Working On The Building'–3 [B] Yazoo 520
'I'm Pressing On'–4 [B] Yazoo 520
'Working On The Building'–4 [B] Yazoo 520

Source: *Dietrich Wawzyn film collection*

JACK OWENS (L F Nelson)
Vocal and guitar accompaniment: Bud Spires (harmonica)
Vocal and guitar accompanying Bud Spires (dancing)–1

Location: Bentonia, Mississippi. Between 11 August and 9 September 1978

Titles performed:
'Hard Time Killing Floor Blues' [A] Vestapol 13078
'Catfish Blues' [A] Vestapol 13078
[interview] [A] Vestapol 13078
'That's All Right' [fragment] [B] Vestapol 13080
'I'd Rather Be The Devil' [fragment] [B] Vestapol 13080
'Mama Don't Allow'–1 [part only] [B] Vestapol 13080
'Catfish Blues' [part only] [B] Vestapol 13080
[interview] [B]

Source: *Land Where The Blues Began* [A]; *Dreams And Songs of The Noble Old* [B]

Vocal and guitar accompaniment: Bud Spires (harmonica)

Location: Bentonia, Mississippi. Autumn 1990

Titles performed:
'The Devil Blues' Anxious 45099-29643, BMG un-numbered
'Hard Time Killin' Floor Blues' Anxious 45099-29643, BMG un-numbered

Source: *Deep Blues*
The version of 'The Devil Blues' that appears on the soundtrack CD on Atlantic is longer than the version in the film, and was recorded some days earlier. This is not, in any real sense, the same song as Skip James' 'I'd Rather Be The Devil'.
See also Bud Spires.

P

ORAN THADDEUS [HOT LIPS] PAGE
Probably vocal and trumpet accompaniment: unknown

Location: New York City. January–June 1949

Titles performed:
unknown

Source: *Adventures In Jazz*

Probably vocal and trumpet accompaniment: The Three Flames: Tiger Haynes (guitar); Roy Testemark (piano); Bill Pollard (bass)

Location: New York City. June–August 1949

Titles performed:
unknown

Source: *The Three Flames Show*

Probably vocal and trumpet accompaniment: the Eddie Condon orchestra

Location: New York City. Late 1949–early 1950

Titles performed:
unknown

Source: *Eddie Condon's Floor Show*

Probably vocal and trumpet accompaniment: unknown

Location: New York City. 1951

Titles performed:
unknown

Source: *Toast of The Town*

KITTY PARHAM

Vocal accompaniment: unknown

Location: Chicago, Illinois. Sunday 15 December 1963

Titles performed:
unknown

Source: *Jubilee Showcase* [prog #11–1]
See also the Stars of Faith.

ROBERT PARKER

Vocal accompaniment: The Blue Beats; Clarence 'Gatemouth' Brown and Johnnie Johnson (electric guitars); Dave 'Fathead' Newman and one unknown (trumpets); Harrison Calloway and one unknown (tenor saxophones); 'Skip' [possibly Skippy Brooks] (piano); Finis Tasby (electric bass); Freeman Brown (drums)

Location: WFAA-TV studios, Dallas, Texas. c. summer 1966

Titles performed:
Barefootin'
'Just A Little Bit'
[interview with Hoss Allen]
'Where The Action Is'

Source: *The Beat*

PATTERSON SINGERS

Probably Lee Patterson (vocal) and others, unknown (vocal)
accompaniment: unknown

Location: New York City. c. 1966

Title performed:
unknown

Source: *TV Gospel Time* #63

PATTERSONAIRES

Vocal group accompaniment: unknown (piano)

Location: Friendship Baptist Church, Brighton, Alabama. Early 1984

Titles performed:
'The Old Landmark'

Source: *On The Battlefield*

ODIE PAYNE

Vocal and drums accompaniment: Jimmy Johnson, Willie James Lyons (electric guitars); Big Mojo Elem (electric bass); John 'Big Moose' Walker (piano)

Location: unknown {Europe}. c.1978–79

Title performed:
'The Woman I Got'

Source: *European TV broadcast* [C]. Origin unknown.

Vocal and drums accompaniment: Robert Lockwood (electric guitar); Sumito Amiyoshi (piano); Eugene Schwartz (drums)

Location: Tokyo, Japan. Wednesday 10 July 1985

Title performed:
'I Don't Know'

Source: *Japanese TV broadcast* [C]
See also Robert Lockwood.

PEEDEE CHORAL ENSEMBLE
Mixed vocal choir accompaniment: unknown
Soloists: Robert Lewis McCall–1; Geneva Thomas–2

Location: Charlotte, North Carolina. Sunday 27 September 1964

Titles performed:
'I'm Ready'–1
'Windstorm'
'I'm Gonna Pray Every Step Of The Way'–2

Source: *TV Gospel Time* #29

PEG LEG SAM (Arthur Jackson)
Vocal and harmonica

Location: Chapel Hill, North Carolina. 1976

Titles performed:
unknown

Source: *Born For Hard Luck*

PENTECOSTAL TEMPLE CHURCH OF GOD IN CHRIST CHOIR
Mixed vocal choir accompaniment: unknown
Soloists: Mattie Wigley–1; Anne Fletcher–2; Madye Porter–3

Location: Memphis, Tennessee. Saturday 19 January 1963

Titles performed:
'Jesus Lifted Me' [A]–1
'Power In The Blood Of The Lamb' [B]–1
'Lord, I Want To Be A Christian' [A]–2
'Somebody Touched Me' [A]–3
'Hark, The Voice Of Jesus Calling' [B]
'He's A Rock In A Weary Land' [B]

Source: *TV Gospel Time* #19 [A], 23 [B]

As above
Soloists: Madye Porter and Bernice McClellan–1; Anne Fletcher–2; Mattie Wigley–3

Location: probably New York City. 1965

Titles performed:
'Oh Heaven!'–1
'Peace Be Still'–2
'I Thank You Lord'–3
'Get Away, Jordan'
'Write My Name Above'–3

Source: *TV Gospel Time* #45

ALBERTA PERKINS
Vocal accompaniment: unknown

Location: probably New York City. 1934

Titles performed:
unknown

Source: *Voodoo Drums*

Vocal accompaniment: Donald Heywood and his orchestra

Location: New York City. c.1940

Title performed:
'Who'll Buy My Fresh Tarts'
Timeless Video 5058

Source: *Murder On Lenox Ave*

JOE WILLIE [PINETOP] PERKINS
Vocal and piano accompaniment: unknown

Location: Chicago, Illinois. 1978

Titles performed:
unknown

Source: *Soundstage*

Vocal and piano accompaniment: Jerry Portnoy (harmonica); Peter Ward (electric guitar); Calvin Jones (electric bass); Willie Smith (drums)

Location: Chicago, Illinois. c. 1979

Title performed:
'Pinetop's Boogie Woogie'

Source: *Chicago On The Good Foot*
The above group are also known as the Legendary Blues Band.

Vocal and Yamaha electric piano

Location: Topanga Canyon, California
Saturday 25 June 1988

Titles performed:
monologue on his life in the blues
'Blues After Hours'
[interview]

Source: *Topanga Blues Festival*

Vocal and piano accompaniment, if any: unknown

Location: Washington, DC. Saturday 11 October 1997

Titles performed:
unknown

Source: *Tribute To Muddy Waters*
See also Muddy Waters.

JAMES [LUCKY] PETERSON
Vocal and piano accompaniment: unknown

Location: Chicago, Illinois. 1991

Titles performed:
unknown

Source: *Blues And The Alligator*

CORA PHILLIPS
Guitar accompaniment: Etta Baker (banjo)

Location: North Carolina. 1988

Titles performed:
untitled instrumental #1 [part only]
untitled instrumental #2 [part only]
[interview]

Source: *Step It Up And Go*
See also Etta Baker.

[LITTLE] ESTHER PHILLIPS (Esther Mae Jones)
Vocal accompaniment: unknown

Location: ATV Studios, London, England.
1965

Titles performed:
unknown

Source: *Ready Steady Go*

Vocal accompaniment: Clarence 'Gatemouth' Brown and Johnnie Johnson (electric guitars); David 'Fathead' Newman and one other (trumpets); Harrison Calloway and one unknown (tenor saxophones); 'Skip' [possibly Skippy Brooks] (piano); Finis Tasby (electric bass); Freeman Brown (drums)

Location: WFAA TV Studios, Dallas, Texas.
May–August 1966

Title performed:
'I Could Have Told You'
[interview with Hoss Allen]

Source: *The Beat*

Vocal accompaniment: unknown

Location: New York City. 1969

Titles performed:
unknown

Source: *The Tonight Show Starring Johnny Carson*

Vocal accompaniment: unknown

Location: unknown {USA}. 1971

Titles performed:
unknown

Source: *Soul*

Vocal accompaniment: unknown

Location: New York City. 1972

Titles performed:
unknown

Source: *The Tonight Show Starring Johnny Carson*

Vocal accompaniment; the Johnny Otis band

Location: Monterey, California. 1973

Titles performed:
unknown

Source: *Monterey Jazz*

Vocal accompaniment: the Duke Ellington orchestra

Location: Monterey, California. 1973

Title performed:
'Release Me'

Source: *The Duke At Monterey*

Vocal accompaniment: unknown

Location: unknown {USA}. 1974

Titles performed:
unknown

Source: *Boarding House*

Vocal accompaniment: unknown

Location: unknown {USA}. 1975

Titles performed:
unknown

Source: *AM America*

Vocal accompaniment: unknown

Location: New York City. 1975

Titles performed:
unknown

Source: *Saturday Night Live*

Vocal accompaniment: unknown

Location: unknown {USA}. 1976

Titles performed:
unknown

Source: *Dinah And Her New Best Friends*

Vocal accompaniment: unknown

Location: unknown {USA}. 1976

Titles performed:
unknown

Source: *Don Kirschner's Rock Concert*

Vocal accompaniment: unknown

Location: Montreux, Switzerland. Summer 1979

Titles performed:
'Love Addict'
and other, unknown, titles

Source: *Montreux Jazz*

Vocal accompaniment: the Tim Hinckley band

Location: the Millionaire Club, Manchester, England. 1982

Titles performed:
'What A Difference A Day Makes'
'Too Many'
'Long Gone'
'Jelly Jelly'
'In The Evening'

Source: *Live At The Millionaire*

Vocal accompaniment: the Gerald Wiggins orchestra.

Location: unknown {USA}. 1982

Titles performed:

'Early In The Morning'	Magnum MMGV–037
'In The Evening'	Magnum MMGV–037

Source: *America's Music Blues – Volume 2*

PIANO RED (William Lee Perryman)
Unknown contribution

Location: unknown {USA}. 1972

Titles performed:
unknown

Source: *The Catcher* [unconfirmed]

Vocal and piano accompaniment, if any:
unknown

Location: Berlin, Germany. 1980

Titles performed:
'Shake Rattle And Roll'
'Corrine, Corrina'
'Right String But The Wrong Yo Yo'
'Ain't Gonna Be Your Low Down Dog'
'Do She Love Me'
'You Got The Thing On Me'
'Dr Feelgood'

Source: *German TV broadcast* [C]

EDWIN [BUSTER] PICKENS
Speech

Location: Houston Texas. Tuesday 9 August 1960

monologue [ST] K-Jazz 014, Rhapsody 8022

Source: *Blues Like Showers Of Rain*

Piano solo

Location: Houston, Texas. Spring 1963

Title performed:
short untitled instrumental Yazoo 520
[and film of Pickens in his local environment]

Source: *Die Blues*

JOSEPH LA CROIX [DEDE] PIERCE
Vocal and trumpet accompaniment: probably George Guesnon (guitar or banjo)

Location: New Orleans, Louisiana. 1961

Titles performed:
unknown

Source: *David Brinkley's Journal*

Probably as above

Location: New Orleans, Louisiana. 1964

Titles performed:
unknown

Source: *New Orleans Jazz*

Vocal accompaniment: unknown

Location: probably New Orleans, Louisiana. 1966

Titles performed:
unknown

Source: *Anatomy Of Pop*

Vocal accompaniment: unknown

Location: probably New Orleans, Louisiana. 1968

Titles performed:
unknown

Source: *Beat Of The Brass*

PILGRIM JUBILEES
Probably Clay Graham, Major Roberson and others (vocals) accompaniment: unknown

Location: Chicago, Illinois.

The following appearances are known:
1964
Sunday 20 September [prog #9–2]
1966
Sunday 23 January [prog #6–2]
1968
Saturday 12 October [prog #16–3]
1972
Saturday 12 Aug [prog #4–3]
Saturday 19 Aug [prog #13–2]

Titles performed:
unknown

Source: *Jubilee Showcase*

Also, the following;

probably as above

Location: New York City. c.1965

Title performed:
unknown

Source: *TV Gospel Time* #47

LONNIE PITCHFORD
Vocal and 1-string guitar–1
Vocal and 1-string electric guitar–2
Vocal and 'Diddley-bow' [a wall-mounted 1-string instrument played with a pick and a slide]–3

Location: probably Lexington, Mississippi. Between 11 August and 9 September 1978

Titles performed:

untitled instrumental–1	Vestapol 13078
untitled instrumental–2	Vestapol 13078
[interview]	
untitled instrumental–3	Vestapol 13078

Source: *Land Where The Blues Began*

Vocal and one string guitar

Location: unknown {Europe}. 1983

Titles performed:
'Why I Sing The Blues'
'One String Boogie'

Source: *European TV broadcast* [C]. Origin unknown.

As above

Location: Atlanta, Georgia. October 1984

Title performed:
'That Train'

Source: *National Down Home Blues Festival*

Vocal and 'Diddley-bow'–1
Vocal and guitar–2

Location: Lexington, Mississippi. Autumn 1990

Titles performed:
'Johnny Stole An Apple'–1
Anxious 45099-26941, BMG un-numbered
'If I Had Possession Over Judgement Day'–2
Anxious 45099-26941, BMG un-numbered
'Come On In My Kitchen'–2
Anxious 45099-26941, BMG un-numbered

Source: *Deep Blues*

PLATTERS
Tony Williams, David Lynch, Paul Robi, Herbert Reed, Zola Taylor (vocals) accompaniment: the Ernie Freeman orchestra

Location: unknown {USA}. 1956

Titles performed:
'Only You'
'The Great Pretender'

Source: *Rock Around The Clock*

As above

Location: Hollywood, California. 1957

Title performed:
'You'll Never Know'

Source: *The Girl Can't Help It*

As above

Location: probably Hollywood, California. 1957

Title performed:
'Remember When'

Source: *Carnival Rock*
Later material by this group, with significantly altered personnel, has been excluded from this work.

PLEASANT GREEN BAPTIST CHURCH CHOIR
Mixed vocal choir accompaniment: unknown
Soloists: Leroy Bogart–1; Charles Parker and Spencer Wiggins–2

Location: probably New York City. 1965

Titles performed:
'Yes, I Love Him'–1
'I'm On My Way To Heaven'–2

Source: *TV Gospel Time* #48

[COUSIN] JOE PLEASANTS (Pleasant Joseph)
Vocal and piano accompaniment: Ransom Knowling (bass); Willie Smith (drums)–1
Vocal accompaniment: Muddy Waters, Rosetta Tharpe (vocals); Brownie McGhee (vocal and guitar); Sonny Terry (vocal and harmonica); Otis Spann (piano); Ransom Knowling (bass); Willie Smith (drums)–2

Location: Alexandra Park Railway Station, Chorlton-cum-Hardy, Manchester, England. May 1964

Titles performed:
'No More Hot Dogs'–1
'Railroad Porter Blues'–1
'He's Got The Whole World In His Hands'–2

Source: *The Blues And Gospel Train*
Most of 'Railroad Porter Blues' is performed in the open air during a sudden and unexpected rainstorm.

Vocal and piano

Location: New Orleans, Louisiana. 1985

Titles performed:
'Life Is A One Way Ticket'
'I Wouldn't Give A Blind Sow An Acorn'
'Me And Hard Work Fell Out'

Source: *In Concert* [3]

LORENZA BROWN PORTER
Vocal accompaniment: unknown

Location: Chicago, Illinois

The following appearances are known:
1963
Sunday 17 November [prog #27–3]
1964
Sunday 2 August [prog #26–2]
1967
Sunday 4 June [prog #21–2]
1968
Saturday 5 October [prog #27–2]

Titles performed:
unknown

Source: *Jubilee Showcase*

ANTHONY POUGH
Percussive spoons solo

Location: Philadelphia, Pennsylvania. 1988

Titles performed:
untitled
[interview]
[demonstration of how the spoons are played]

Source: *Step It up And Go*

EUGENE POWELL (Sonny Boy Nelson)
Vocal and guitar

Location: probably Anguilla, Mississippi. Between 11 August and 9 September 1978

Title performed:
'How You Want Your Rolling Done' Vestapol 13078
[interview]

Source: *Land Where The Blues Began*

Vocal and guitar accompaniment: Sam Chatman (vocal and guitar)

Location: Freedom Village, Greenville, Mississippi. Saturday 8 September 1979

Titles performed:
'We Going Round The Mountain' K-Jazz 081
'How Long Has That Evening Train Been Gone?' K-Jazz 081

Source: *Mississipi Blues*

SARAH JORDAN POWELL
Vocal accompaniment: unknown

Location: Chicago, Illinois

The following appearances are known:
1964
Sunday 17 May [prog #21–3]
1968
Saturday 28 September [prog #28–3]

Titles performed:
unknown

Source: *Jubilee Showcase*

Vocal duets with Carl Preacher accompaniment: unknown

Location: unknown {USA}. c. 1969

Titles performed:
'I Find No Fault In Him'
'Gospel Medley'
'I Must Tell Jesus'
'When Jesus Comes'

Source: *Soul Set Free*

BILLY PRESTON

Vocal and probably electric organ, accompaniment: unknown

Location: Chicago, Illinois. Monday 4 May 1964

Titles performed:
unknown

Source: *Jubilee Showcase* [prog #8–1]
This is the Billy Preston who later became associated with the Beatles.

LLOYD PRICE

Vocal accompaniment: unknown

Location: probably New York City. c.1974

Titles performed:
'Personality'
'Stagger Lee'

Source: *The Midnight Special*

Vocal accompaniment: unknown

Location: probabably New York City. c. 1977–79

Title performed:
'Personality'

Source: *Sha Na Na*

Speech

Location: unknown {USA}. 1995

[interview]

Source: *Rock And Roll Part 1*
Lloyd Price went into concert promotion – he appears in this role (as a non-performer) in *When We Were Kings*.

SAM PRICE

Speech

Location: New York City. Late June–early July 1960

monologue[ST] K-Jazz 014, Rhapsody 8022

Source: *Blues Like Showers Of Rain*

Piano solo accompanpment: Pat Hare (electric guitar); Andrew Stephens (electric bass); Francis Clay (drums)

Location: Newport, Rhode Island. Sunday 3 July 1960

Titles performed:
untitled boogie instrumental #1
untitled boogie instrumental #2

Source: *Jazz-USA*
See also Muddy Waters.

Piano accompaniment: Adolphus 'Doc' Cheatham (trumpet, vocal–1); Gene 'Mighty Flea' Connors (trombone); Ted Buckner (alto saxophone); Carl Pruitt (bass); J C Heard (drums); Marie Buggs (vocal–2)
Price, Pruitt and Heard only–3

Location: Sysmo studio, Paris, France. Monday 12 May 1975

Titles performed:
untitled boogie–3 Fil A Film 2022
'Squeeze Me' Fil A Film 2022
'Willow Weep For Me' Fil A Film 2022
'What Can I Say After I Say I'm Sorry'–1 Fil A Film 2022
untitled instrumental–3 Fil A Film 2022
'Backwater Blues'–2 Fil A Film 2022

'Boogie With Riffs'–3
'Rockin' Boogie'–3
'Last Boogie'–3

Source: *Black & Blue Records*
All titles appear on Black & Blue LP 233.111 and CD 59–111–2.

Vocal and piano accompaniment, if any: unknown

Location: Birmingham, England. Tuesday 6 February 1979

Titles performed:
unknown

Source: *Pebble Mill At One*

Vocal and piano accompaniment: the K&K Dixieland Band, personel unknown

Location: Switzerland. 1980

Titles performed:
'Boogie Woogie'
'Please Don't Talk About Me'
'I Can't Give You Anything But Love'
'When You're Smiling'
'How Long Blues'
'Boogie'
'Jonah Wails Again'
'Pee Wee Blues'
untitled instrumental
'Sleepy Time Down South'

Source: *Swiss TV broadcast* [C]

Piano solo

Location: Zurich, Switzerland. 1987

Title performed:
'Honky Tonk Train Blues'

Source: *Karussel*

Vocal and piano accompaniment: George Kelly and Percy France (tenor saxophones); Leonard Gaskin (bass); Ronnie Cole (drums)

Location: Bern, Switzerland. Saturday 2 May 1987

Titles performed:
'I Want A Little Girl'
'Kansas City'
'Body And Soul'
'Shake That Thing'

Source: *Swiss TV broadcast* [C]

Speech

Location: probably Chicago, Illinois. 1989

[interview]

Source: *Wild Women Don't Have The Blues*

ZELLA JACKSON PRICE
Vocal accompaniment: unknown (organ) and congregational vocal

Location: Antioch Baptist church, St. Louis, Missouri. 1982

Title performed:
'His Name Is Jesus' FRF un-numbered

Source: *Say Amen Somebody!*

LYNN PROCTOR TRIO
Proctor, vocal and piano accompaniment: unknown (bass and drums)

Location: New York City. 1948

Title performed:
'Watch Out Hollywood' Select 97803

Source: *Miracle In Harlem*

PROFESSOR LONGHAIR (Henry Roeland 'Roy' Byrd)
Vocal and piano accompaniment, if any, unknown

Location: probably New Orleans, Louisiana. 1971

Titles performed:
unknown

Source: *Dr. John*

Vocal and piano accompaniment, if any, unknown

Location: Montreux, Switzerland. Summer 1973

Titles performed:
'Go To The Mardi Gras'
'Cry To Me'

Source: *Montreux Jazz*

Vocal and piano accompaniment, if any, unknown

Location: Chicago, Illinois. 1974

Titles performed:
unknown Rhino R3.2076

Source: *Dr. John's New Orleans Swamp*

Vocal and piano

Location: New Orleans, Louisiana. c. 1977–78

Title performed:
'Big Chief' Flower 6, K-Jazz 054

Source: *Always For Pleasure*

Vocal and piano

Location: London, England. Wednesday 22 March 1978

Titles performed:
[interview]
untitled instrumental

Source: *Thames At Six*

Vocal and piano accompaniment: unknown

Location: Nice, France. 1978

Titles performed:
'Every Day I Have The Blues'
'How Long Has The Train Been Gone'

Source: *French TV broadcast* [C]

Vocal and piano; solo, and in the company of Allen Toussaint and Tuts Washington (pianos)

Location: New Orleans, Louisiana. Late 1979

Titles performed:
unknown K-Jazz 084

Source: *Piano Players Rarely Ever Play Together*

ALBERTA PRYNE

Vocal accompaniment: unknown

Location: probably New York City. 1946

Title performed:
[probably] 'Mama's Got To Get That Rent'

Source: *House Rent Party*

JAMES EDWARD [SNOOKY] PRYOR

Vocal and harmonica accompaniment: Homesick James (electric guitar); Boogie Woogie Red (piano); Roger Hill (electric bass); Tom Parnell (drums)

Location: Brighton Polytechnic, Sussex, England. Friday 16 February 1973

Title performed:
'Boogie Twist'

Source: *Blues Legends 73*

Vocal and harmonica accompaniment: Homesick James (electric guitar)

Location: Atlanta, Georgia. October 1984

Titles performed:
'Why You Want To Treat Me Like That'
[interview]

Source: *National Down Home Blues Festival*

Vocal and harmonica–1;
as above accompaniment: the Cash McCall band. McCall (electric guitar); unknown (tenor saxophone, piano, electric bass, drums)

Location: Topanga Canyon, California. Saturday 25 June 1988

Titles performed:
'That's The Way To Do It' ['That Ain't The Way To Do It']–1
untitled instrumental–2
[interview]

Source: *Topanga Blues Festival*

PULLMAN PORTERS QUARTETTE

Vocal quartet, unaccompanied–1; accompanied by studio orchestra–2; unknown (incidental harp)–3

Location: unknown {USA}. Late 1928

Titles performed:
'Calliope Song'–1
'Shine'–2
'Little David Play On Your Harp'–3
'Ain't It A Shame'–1
'Goodnight Ladies'–2

Source: *Vitaphone*. These titles comprise the soundtrack for and unidentified Vitaphone short.

EVA JEAN PURNELL

Vocal accompaniment: unknown

Location: Chicago, Illinois.

The following appearances are known:
1964
Sunday 16 February [prog # 30–3]
1968
Saturday 26 October [prog #31–1]

Titles performed:
unknown

Source: *Jubilee Showcase*

Q

QUEEN IDA (Lewis) AND THE BON TON ZYDECO BAND

Queen Ida, vocal and accordeon accompaniment: Lisa Haley (violin); Kid James Dyson (electric guitar); François Calloway (electric bass); Wilbert Lewis (rub-board); 'Pepe Depew' [*sic*] (drums)

Location: Stockholm, Sweden. 1982

Titles performed:
'Capitaine'
'Rosa Majeur'
'Mazurka'
'Lady Fingers'
'Bayou Polka'
'Jambalaya'
'Capitaine' (take 2)

Source: *Swedish TV broadcast* [C]

Probably as above

Location: unknown {USA}. 1984

Titles performed:
unknown

Source: *Rumble Fish*

Probably as above

Location: Ames, Iowa. 1985

Titles performed:
unknown

Source: *Maintenance Shop Blues*

Probably as above

Location: Austin, Texas. 1987

Titles performed:
'Every Now And Then'
'Where Did You Go Last Night'
'Alligator Song'
'Tell Me What You're Looking For'
'Jambalaya'
and other, unknown, titles

Source: *Austin City Limits*

Probably as above

Location: San Francisco Jazz Festival, San Francisco, California. 1987 or 1988

Title performed:
Ful Il Sa Flower 7
[interview] Flower 7

Source: *J'ai Eté Au Bal*

Probably as above

Location: Louisiana. 1988

Titles performed:
'Stay Out All Nght'
'Good Morning Heartache'
'Every Now And Then'

Source: *Aly Bain And Friends*

Probably as above

Location: Louisiana. 1988

Titles performed:
'Rosa Majeur'
'Raywood'

Source: *Aly Meets The Cajuns*
The last two entries are probably drawn from the same session[s]. See also *Cajun Country*, which presents re-edited material from the above two broadcasts.

R

JAMES [YANK] RACHELL

Vocal and mandolin accompaniment: probably John Estes (guitar)

Location: Baden-Baden, Germany. c. December 1966

Titles performed:
unknown

Source: *American Folk Blues Festival 1966*

Vocal and mandolin accompaniment: Howard Armstrong (violin); Banjo Ikey Robinson (banjo); Tom Armstrong (bowed bass)

Location: Chicago, Illinois. 1985

Title performed:
'Diving Duck Blues'
[conversation with Armstrong and Bogan]

Source: *Louie Bluie*

Vocal and mandolin, accompaniment, if any: unknown

Location: unknown {USA}. 1989

Titles performed:
unknown

Source: *Tennessee Tornado*

Vocal and electric mandolin accompaniment: unknown (electric guitar, electric bass, drums)–1;
electric mandolin accompaniment: as above–2

Location: Rosa's Lounge. Chicago, Illinois. c.1989

Titles performed:
'Early In The Morning'–1
'Late In The Evening'–1
'Bugle Call Rag'–2

Source: *Live At Rosa's*
See also Howard Armstrong and John Estes.

BIG MEMPHIS MA RAINEY

See Under 'B'

CLEO RANDALL

Vocal accompaniment: The Blue Beats; Clarence 'Gatemouth' Brown (electric guitar); Johnnie Johnson (electric guitar); Dave 'Fathead' Newman and one unknown (trumpets); Harrison Calloway and one unknown (tenor saxophones); 'Skip' [possibly Skippy Brooks] (piano); Finis Tasby (electric bass); Freeman Brown (drums)

Location: WFAA-TV studios, Dallas, Texas. Tuesday 15 February 1966

Titles performed:
'Big City Lights'
'I Need Your Love So Bad'

Source: *The Beat*
Cleo Randall was a Chicago-based artist

FORBES RANDOLPH'S KENTUCKY SINGERS
Vocal group accompaniment, if any, unknown

Location: unknown {USA}. c. 1929

Titles performed:
unknown

Source: *Several short monochrome films, titles unknown*. Reportedly directed by William DeForest.

R S RANKIN
Unknown contribution

Location: Hollywood, California. 1960

Titles performed [if any]
unknown

Source: *Soupy Sales*
This artist recorded under the pseudonym T-Bone Walker Jr., for Midnite records of Los Angeles, California. He is Walker's nephew.

MOSES RASCOE
Vocal and guitar–1
as above in duet with Thomas Burt–2

Location: North Carolina. 1988

Titles performed:
'Mama, Let Me Scoop For You'–1
'Step It Up And Go'–2
[interview]

Source: *Step It Up And Go*

RAYMOND RASPBERRY SINGERS
Raymond Raspberry (vocal) accompaniment: unknown (vocals)

Location: Chicago, Illinois. Saturday 10 October 1964

Titles performed:
'Only What You Do For Christ'
'Deliverance Will Come'
'Way Over Yonder'

Source: *TV Gospel Time* #36

As above

Location: New York City. c. April 1965

Titles performed:
'No Tears In Heaven'
'You'll Never Be Left To Walk Alone'

Source: *TV Gospel Time* #41

RAVENS
Vocal group accompaniment: unknown

Location: New York City. c.1949–50

Titles performed:
unknown

Source: *The Perry Como Show*

A C REED (Aaron Cortier)
Vocal accompaniment: Larry Davis (electric guitar–1; electric guitar and vocal–2); Maurice John Vaughn (vocal–2); Byther Smith (vocal and electric guitar–2) and others, unknown

Location: unknown {Europe}. 1985

Titles performed:
'I Wanna Boogie'–1
'Blues Medley'–2

Source: *Chicago Blues Festival* [2]
See also Albert Collins.

JIMMY REED (Mathis James Reed)
Vocal and guitar, miming to VJ 509

Location: ATV studios, London, England. Friday 30 October 1964

Title performed:
'Shame, Shame, Shame'

Source: *Ready Steady Go*

Vocal and electric guitar accompaniment: Eddie Taylor (electric guitar); T-Bone Walker (piano); Jerome Arnold (electric bass); J.C. Lewis (drums); Reed (harmonica)

Location: BBC-TV studios, White City, London, England. Tuesday 22 October 1968

Titles performed:
'Ain't That Lovin' You Baby'
'You Know It's A Sin'

Source: *American Folk Blues Festival 1968* [1]

Probably as above

Location: Germany. November 1968

Titles performed:
unknown

Source: *American Folk Blues Festival 1968* [2]

REFRESHING SPRING CHURCH CHOIR OF WASHINGTON DC

Mixed vocal choir accompaniment: unknown

Location: probably Washington DC. 1966

Titles performed:
unknown

Source: *TV Gospel Time* #55

REFUGE TEMPLE CHOIR

Mixed vocal choir accompaniment: unknown
Soloists: Robert White–1; Thelma Jones–2

Location: New York City. Saturday 15 December 1962

Titles performed:
'God Is Great'
'Lift Up Your Heads, Oh Ye Gates'–1
'Do You Love Him?'–2

Source: *TV Gospel Time* #15

JESSIE MAE RENFRO

Vocal accompaniment: unknown (piano)–1
Vocal accompaniment: the Mighty Clouds Of Joy–2
Vocal accompaniment: Julius Cheeks and the Four Knights–3

Location: Baltimore, Maryland. Saturday 5 September 1964

Titles performed:
'There Is A Fountain'–1 [A]
'Can't No Grave Hold My Body Down'–1 [A]
'Near The Cross'–1 [B]
'Mountain Railroad'–1 [B]
'He's So Wonderful'–2 [A]
'That's Worrying Me'–3 [B]

Source: *TV Gospel Time* #32, 33 [B]

TEDDY [CRY CRY] REYNOLDS

Vocal accompaniment: The Texas Houserockers [G]

Location: Houston, Texas. Friday [*sic*] 8 October 1993

Title performed:
'I Don't Want To Love Her'

Source: *Saturday Night At Rockefellers*

R & H GOSPEL SINGERS

Mixed a cappella vocal group

Location: unknown church, Atlanta, Georgia. 1977

Title performed:
'Jesus, Be By My Side' Shanachie 1401

Source: *It's A Mean Old World*

SONNY RHODES (Clarence Smith)

Vocal and pedal steel guitar accompaniment: unknown (electric guitar, electric bass, drums)

Location: Oakland, California. 1981

Title performed:
'Cigarette Blues' [part only]
[interview]

Source: *Long Train Running*

Vocal and pedal steel guitar accompaniment: The Texas Twisters [G]

Location: Oakland, California. 1984

Title performed:
'Cigarette Blues'

Source: *Cigarette Blues*

ZACHARY RICHARD
Vocal accompaniment: unknown

Location: New Orleans, Louisiana. 1990

Titles performed:
'Ton Ton Girls'
'No French No More'
'Take Me Away'

Source: *New Orleans Jazz And Heritage Festival 1990*

Vocal accompaniment: unknown

Location: Austin, Texas. 1994

Titles performed:
'Somebody Stole My Monkey'
'Come On Sheila'
'Let's Run'
'Zydeco Jump'
'Since The Industry Came To Town'
'Down At The Double L'

Source: *Austin City Limits*

BENNY RICHARDSON
Vocal accompaniment: male convicts (vocals and felling trees)

Location: Ellis Unit, Huntsville State Farm, Texas. 22–24 March 1966

Titles performed:
'Grizzly Bear' Vestapol 13042
'Jody'

Source: *Afro-American Songs In A Texas Prison*
See also Unidentified Artists [B] (26)

RICHBURG SINGERS
Probably Wilhemina, John and Julius Richburg accompaniment: unknown

Location: Jacksonville, Florida. c. 1966

Title performed:
unknown

Source: *TV Gospel Time* #60

JUNE RICHMOND
Vocal accompaniment: Roy Milton And Orchestra: probably Hosea Sapp (trumpet); Earl Sims (alto saxophone); Lorenzo 'Buddy' Floyd (tenor saxophone); Camille Howard (piano); David Robinson (bass); Roy Milton (drums)

Location: Hollywood, California. Early 1944

Titles performed:
[8308] 'We're Steppin' Out Tonight '
[17908] '47th Street Jive' Charly #5
[17108] 'Ride On, Ride On' Charly #5
[89108] 'Mr Jackson From Jacksonville' Storyville SV6003, Virgin VVD868
[13M2] 'Baby, Don't You Love Me No More'
[24M2] 'My Bottle Is Dry'
[25M4] 'Who Dunnit To Who?'

Source: *Soundies*
The personnel quoted is that which appeared on Milton's first recording session in December 1945, by which time it may have altered. 17108 copyrighted 27 June 1944; 17908 28 August 1944; 123M2 26 November 1945; 24M2 10 July 1946. One, at least, of the above titles appears in *Ebony Parade*, but it is not known which.

Vocal accompaniment: Tiny Grimes and his band, details unknown

Location: unknown {USA}. 1944

Titles performed:
'Joseph 'N His Brudders' [*sic*]

Source: *Soundie*
'Romance Without Finance', from the same session, may also be a vocal by Richmond. See Tiny Grimes.

Vocal accompaniment: Louis Jordan And The Tympany Five

Location: probably New York City. 1947

Title performed:
'You Got Me Where You Want Me'

Source: *Reet-Petite And Gone*

Vocal accompaniment: unknown

Location: probably New York City. 1948

Titles performed:
'All You Want To Do Is Eat'
'My Man Is Working Again'

Source: *The Dreamer*

RISING ECHOES

Vocal quartet accompaniment: unknown

Location: New York City. Wednesday 5 December 1962

Titles performed:
'Jesus Is Calling Me'
'Jesus, Keep Me Near The Cross'

Source: *TV Gospel Time* #17

BOYD RIVERS

Vocal and electric guitar

Location: Freedom Village, Greenville, Mississippi. Saturday 8 September 1979

Titles performed:
'You Got To Take Sick And Die One Of These Days' K-Jazz 081
'When I Cross Over' K-Jazz 081

Source: *Mississippi Blues*

ROBERT-ETTES

Female vocal group accompaniment: unknown–1;
North Indiana State Church Of God In Christ Choir–2

Location: Chicago, Illinois. Monday 10 October 1964

Titles performed:
'Whiter Than Snow'–1
'Hallelujah!'–2

Source: *TV Gospel Time*

ROBERTS SINGERS

Vocal group accompaniment: unknown

Location: New York City. Sunday 16 December 1962

Titles performed:
'Rock My Soul'
'Joy'

Source: *TV Gospel Time* #12

CARRIE ROBERTSON

Vocal and dancing accompaniment: Blind James Brewer (electric guitar); unknown (second electric guitar); two unknown females and one male (tambourines)

Location: Maxwell Street. Chicago, Illinois. 1964

Titles performed:
'Just A Closer Walk With Thee' [part only] Shanachie 1403
'Power' [part only] Shanachie 1403

Source: *And This Is Free*

Vocal and dancing accompaniment: Blind James Brewer (electric guitar); Albert Holland (electric bass)

Location: Maxwell Street, Chicago, Illinois. 1980

Titles performed:
'Life Is A Ball Game' K-Jazz 031, Rhapsody 8045
'Thank You Lord' K-Jazz 031, Rhapsody 8045
[interview] K-Jazz 031, Rhapsody 8045

Source: *Maxwell Street Blues*
See also Blind James Brewer.

[REVEREND] CLEOPHUS ROBINSON

Vocal accompaniment: unknown

Location: New York City. c. 1965

Titles performed:
'We Shall Gain The Victory'
'Jesus, Keep Me Near The Cross'

Source: *TV Gospel Time* #45

Vocal accompaniment: unknown

Location: Chicago, Illinois. Saturday 5 April 1969

Titles performed:
unknown

Source: *Jubilee Showcase* [prog # unknown]

Vocal accompaniment: the Greater Bethlehem Church Choir

Location: unknown {USA}. c.1969

Title performed:
'Meditation'

Source: *Soul Set Free*

Vocal accompaniment: unknown

Location: unknown {USA}. 1970

Titles performed:
unknown

Source: *Look Up And Sing Out*

Vocal accompaniment: unknown

Location: Montreux, Switzerland. July 1975

Titles performed:
unknown

Source: *Montreux Jazz*

FENTON ROBINSON

Vocal and electric guitar accompaniment: Bill Heid (electric piano); Bob Stroger (electric bass); Jesse Green (drums)

Location: Chicago, Illinois. Saturday 28 January 1976

Titles performed:
'You Don't Know What Love Is'
'Somebody Loan Me A Dime'

Source: *The Devil's Music series 2*

Vocal and electric guitar accompaniment: Pat Hall (piano); Ike Anderson (electric bass); Michael Linn (drums)

Location: Groningen, Netherlands. Wednesday 7 November 1984

Titles performed:
'Blue Monday'
'You Don't Know What Love Is'
'Checkin' On My Woman'
'Schoolboy'
'Country Girl'
'Goin' To Chicago'
'Somebody Loan Me A Dime'
'Stormy Monday'
'Everything's Gonna Be Alright'
'As The Years Go Passing By'
'I Lost My True Love'

Source: *Swingmaster Presents*
There are believed to be Japanese TV broadcasts by this artist from the 1980s

FRANK [SUGAR CHILE] ROBINSON

Vocal and piano; introductions by, and dialogue with, Count Basie

Location: Universal City, Hollywood, California. August 1950

Titles performed:
'After School Boogie'
'Numbers Boogie'

Source: *Sugar Chile Robinson, Billie Holiday, Count Basie And His Sextet*

Vocal and piano accompaniment, if any: unknown

Location: New York City. c. early 1950s

Titles performed:
unknown

Source: *The Milton Berle Show*

Vocal and piano accompaniment, if any: unknown

Location: New York City. c. early 1950s

Titles performed:
unknown

Source: *This Is Show Business*

HELEN ROBINSON YOUTH CHORUS

Mixed juvenile vocal choir accompaniment: unknown
Soloists: Jeanette Robinson–1; Aubrey Pettis–2

Location: Chicago, Illinois. Sunday 28 March 1965

Titles performed:
'Lord, Don't Let Me Fall'–1
'Tramping'–1
'Worthy Of Thee'–2

Source: *TV Gospel Time* #38

[BANJO] IKEY ROBINSON

Vocal and banjo accompaniment: Howard Armstrong (mandolin)

Location: Chicago, Illinois. 1985

Titles performed:
'My Four Reasons'
[conversation with Armstrong]

Source: *Louie Bluie*
See also Howard Armstrong, Ted Bogan and Yank Rachell.

[LONESOME] JIMMY LEE ROBINSON

Vocal and guitar accompaniment: Fred Below (drums)

Location: Baden-Baden, Germany. October 1965

Title performed:
[introduction by Eddie Boyd;]
'I'm Coming Home'

Source: *American Folk Blues Festival 1965*

LILLIAN ROBINSON

Guitar solo–1
Vocal and guitar–2

Location: WDBJ TV Studios, Roanake, Virginia. Spring/Summer 1987

Titles performed:
'Sitting On Top Of The World'–1 [A][part only]
'John Henry'–2 [B] [part only]

Source: *Black Musical Traditions In Virginia: Blues* [A]; *Black Musical Traditions In Virginia: Non-blues Secular Music* [B]

REVEREND R L ROBINSON

Vocal accompaniment: The Heavenly Choir [*sic*]

Location: Dallas, Texas. c. 1941

Titles performed:

'Good News'	Hollywood Select 50543
'Go Down Moses'	Hollywood Select 50543
'All God's Children Got Shoes'	Hollywood Select 50543
'On Jordan's Stormy Banks	Hollywood Select 50543
'I Heard A Child Of Heaven Call'	Hollywood Select 50543
'Amazing Grace	Hollywood Select 50543
'Swing Low, Sweet Chariot	Hollywood Select 50543
'Run Children'	Hollywood Select 50543
'Good News' (reprise)	Hollywood Select 50543

Source: *The Blood Of Jesus*

Probably similar to above

Location: probably Dallas, Texas. 1944

Titles performed:
unknown — Timeless Video 5055

Source: *Go Down Death*

MAURICE ROCCO
Vocal and piano accompaniment: off-screen studio orchestra; Mabel Scott, vocal–1

Location: probably New York City. Late 1943

Titles performed:
[14708] 'Rock It For Me'
[15008] 'Beat Me Daddy, Eight To The Bar'–1 — Charly #2, Storyville SV6013, Virgin VVD762
[15308] 'Rhumboogie' — Charly #2, Storyville SV6013, Virgin VVD762
[15608] 'Rocco Blues' — Charly #2, Storyville SV6013, Virgin VVD762

Source: *Soundies*
14708 copyrighted 27 December 1943; 15008 29 December 1943; 15308 and 15608 31 December 1943

ROCKIN' DOPSIE (Alton Ray Rubin) AND HIS CAJUN TWISTERS
Vocal and accordion accompaniment: unknown (electric guitar, rub-board, electric bass, drums)

Location: Germany. 1981

Titles performed:
'Colinda'
'Hold On To That Tiger'
'Cajun Two Step'
'Baby Please Don't Leave Me'
'You Used To Call Me Every Morning'
'My Baby, She's Gone'
'Hot Tamali Baby'
'Dopsie's Boogie'

Source: *Rockpalast* [C]

Vocal and accordion accompaniment: Dewey Balfa (violin); Nathan Abshire (accordion); unknown (guitar)

Location: High School, Mamou, Louisiana. 1983

Title performed:
'Oh Papa' — Vestapol 13001

Source: *Les Blues De Balfa*

Vocal accompaniment: probably as above

Location: New Orleans, Louisiana. 1990

Title performed:
'It's Alright'

Source: *New Orleans Jazz And Heritage Festival 1990*

Vocal and accordion accompaniment: The Zydeco Twisters: John Hart (tenor saxophone); unknown (electric guitar, electric bass, rub-board, drums)

Location: Louisiana. 1990

Titles performed:
'Harlem Shuffle' — Channel 5 083 258-3, Island 083 258-3
'Who's Loving You Tonight?' — Channel 5 083 258-3, Island 083 258-3
'I'm A Hog For You, Baby' — Channel 5 083 258-3, Island 083 258-3

Source: *Zydeco Nite'N'Day*

ROCKIN' SYDNEY (Semien)
Vocal accompaniment: unknown

Location: Austin, Texas. 1986

Titles performed:
'Let Me Take You To The Zydeco'
'Joe Pete's In The Bed'
'Zydeco Shoes'
'Jalepeno Lena'
'Dance And Show Off'
'My Toot Toot'

Source: *Austin City Limits*

Vocal and accordion accompaniment: unknown

Location: Louisiana. 1987–88

Titles performed;
'My Toot Toot' Flower 7
[interview] Flower 7

Source: *J'ai Eté Au Bal*

Speech

Location: Plaisance, Louisiana. 1988

[interview] K-Jazz 098, Rhapsody 8062

Source: *Zydeco Gumbo*

[DOCTOR] ISAIAH ROSS

Vocal, guitar, harmonica, bass drum, hi-hat cymbal

Location: Baden-Baden, Germany. October 1965

Titles performed:
[introduction by Jimmy Lee Robinson;]
'Boogie Disease'

Source: *American Folk Blues Festival 1965*
The above title includes some verses from Ross's original recording of 'Boogie Disease', but it is largely a version of the Junior Parker recording of 'Feeling Good'.

Vocal, guitar, harmonica

Location: London, England. c. 1974

Titles performed:
unknown
[interview]

Source: *The Old Grey Whistle Test*

Vocal, guitar, harmonica, bass-drum, hi-hat cymbal–1
Guitar and harmonica only–2

Location: Berlin, Germany. 1980

Titles performed:
'Trouble Blues'–1
'That's Alright Mama'–1
'General Motors Blues'–1
'Chicago Breakdown'–2

Source: German TV broadcast [C]

Vocal and harmonica

Location: Atlanta, Georgia. October 1984

Title performed:
'Biscuit Bakin' Woman'

Source: *National Down Home Blues Festival*

ROYAL TRAVELLERS

Vocal group accompaniment: unknown

Location: New York City. Sunday 18 November 1962

Titles performed:
'He's Mine'
'So Sad'
'Prayer Is The Key To The Kingdom'

Source: *TV Gospel Time* #10

SPARKY RUCKER

Vocal and guitar

Location: unknown {Europe}. 1983

Title performed:
'Kind Hearted Woman'

Source: *European TV broadcast* [C]. Origin unknown.

ERNESTINE AND LAURA RUNDLESS

Vocal duet accompaniment: unknown

Location: Chicago, Illinois. Sunday 19 July 1964

Titles performed:
unknown

Source: *Jubilee Showcase* [prog #23–3]
See also Meditation Singers.

OTIS RUSH

Vocal and electric guitar accompaniment: Junior Wells (harmonica); Roosevelt Sykes (piano); Jack Meyers (electric bass); Fred Below (drums)

Location: Baden-Baden, Germany. c. December 1966

Titles performed:
unknown

Source: *American Folk Blues Festival 1966*

Vocal and electric guitar accompaniment: Danny Draker (electric guitar); Tyrn Green (electric bass); Jonni Inserno (drums)

Location: Camden Town, London, England. 1981

Titles performed:
'All Your Love'
'Let's Have A Natural Ball'
'Love's Proposition'
'Cross Cut Saw'
and other, unknown, titles

Source: *Individual Voices*

Electric guitar–1, vocal and electric guitar–2, accompaniment: The Cash McCall band. McCall (electric guitar); unknown (tenor saxophone, piano, electric bass, drums)

Location: probably Topanga Canyon, California. Saturday 25 June 1988

Titles performed:
untitled instrumental boogie
untitled instrumental blues
'Cross Cut Saw'
[interview]

Source: *Topanga Blues Festival*

Vocal and electric guitar accompaniment: unknown

Location: Checkerboard Lounge, Chicago, Illinois. 1991

Titles performed:
'It's My Own Fault' BMG 791.151, Rhino R91226
'Cross Cut Saw' BMG 791.151, Rhino R91226

Source: *Blues Alive*

Vocal and electric guitar accompaniment: unknown

Location: London. c.1993–94

Title performed:
'Homework'

Source: *Later...With Jools Holland*
Rush appears on camera in the 1966 production *Nothing But The Blues* but he does not sing. He also appears in a tutorial video issued on Hot Licks 3032A and in *Blues Brothers 2000.*

JAMES ANDREW [JIMMY] RUSHING

Vocal accompaniment: the Count Basie orchestra

Location: probably Hollywood, California. 1941

Title performed:
[4406] 'Air Mail Special' Storyville SV6000, Virgin VVD865

Source: *Soundie*. Probably also in *Big Name Bands No. 1.* Copyrighted 8 December 1941

Vocal accompaniment: the Count Basie orchestra

Location: probably Hollywood, California. c.1943

Titles performed:
[4501] 'Take Me Back Baby'
Jazz Classics JCVC 111, Parkfield MJK0007, Proserpine 611, Rhino R3.2101, Verve CFV1022

Source: *Soundie.* Copyrighted c.1941 [*sic*]

Vocal accompaniment: the Count Basie orchestra

Location: probably Hollywood, California. 1943

Titles performed:
unknown

Source: *Crazy House*

Vocal accompaniment: the Count Basie orchestra

Location: probably Hollywood, California. 1943

Titles performed:
unknown

Source: *Top Man*

Vocal accompaniment: unknown

Location: New York City. 1954

Titles performed:
unknown

Source: *The Tonight Show*

Vocal accompaniment: unknown

Location: New York City. 1956

Titles performed:
unknown

Source: *The Tonight Show*

Vocal and piano

Location: New York City. 1957

Titles performed:
'Am I To Blame'
'Please Don't Tell On Me'
'Tricks Ain't Working No More' [*sic*]
'How Long Blues'
untitled boogie instrumental

Source: *Jazz Casual*

Vocal accompaniment: Count Basie's All-Stars

Location: New York City. Sunday 8 December 1957

Title performed:
'I Left My Baby' Vintage Jazz Classics 2001, Warner 9031-74506-3

Source: *The Sound Of Jazz*

Vocal accompaniment: Buck Clayton (trumpet) and others, unknown

Location: New York City. 1957–58

Titles performed:
'Sent For You Yesterday'
'Goin' To Chicago'
'St. Louis Blues'
'I Want A Little Girl'
'Billie's Bounce'
'Boogie Woogie'

Source: *Seven Lively Arts – The Subject is Jazz*

Vocal accompaniment: probably the Jack Kane orchestra

Location: unknown {USA}. 1959

Titles performed:
unknown

Source: *The Jack Kane Show*

Vocal accompaniment: unknown

Location: unknown {USA}. 1959

Titles performed:
unknown

Source: *John Gunther's High Road*

Vocal accompaniment: Otis Spann (piano); Pat Hare (electric guitar); Andrew Stephens (electric bass); Francis Clay (drums)

Location: Newport, Rhode Island. Sunday 3 July 1960

Title performed:
'Mean Mistreater'

Source: *Jazz-USA*
See also Muddy Waters.

Vocal accompaniment: the Count Basie orchestra. Vocal duet with Joe Williams accompaniment as above–1

Location: Newport, Rhode Island. Summer 1962

Titles performed:
'I'm Coming, Virginia'
'Going To Chicago'–1

Source: *Newport Jazz Festival 1962*

Vocal accompaniment: unknown

Location: unknown {USA}. 1965

Titles performed:
unknown

Source: *Kaleidoscope*

Vocal accompaniment: unknown

Location: unknown {USA}. 1967

Titles performed:
unknown

Source: *The Mike Douglas Show*

Vocal accompaniment: unknown

Location: unknown {USA}. 1969

Title performed:
'My Baby's Gone' [ST only]

Source: *The Learning Tree*
Rushing also has a dramatic role in this film.

Vocal accompaniment: unknown

Location: unknown {USA}. 1971

Titles performed:
unknown

Source: *Our Musical Heritage*

Vocal accompaniment: probably the Johnny Otis band

Location: Monterey, California. 1973

Titles performed:
unknown

Source: *Monterey Jazz*

Vocal accompaniment: Duke Ellington Orchestra

Location: Monterey, California. 1973

Title performed:
'Sent For You Yesterday'

Source: *The Duke At Monterey*

S

OLIVER SAIN
Tenor saxophone accompaniment: unknown

Location: St. Louis, Missouri. 1989

Titles performed:
'Honky Tonk'
'Soul Serenade'
untitled instrumental

Source: *St. Soul – Soul Of St. Louis R&B*
See also Ike Turner.

ST. LOUIS JIMMY (James Burke Odum)
Speech

Location: Chicago, Illinois. Summer 1960

[monologue] K-Jazz 014, Rhapsody 8022

Source: *Blues Like Showers Of Rain*

ST. MARY'S CHURCH CHOIR
Mixed vocal choir accompaniment: unknown
Soloist: John Washington–1

Location: New York City. Sunday 4 November 1962

Titles performed:
'Great Change In Me'–1
'Behold, I Stand At The Door'
'Send Me'

Source: *TV Gospel Time #8*

As above
Soloist: Elsie Bush–1

Location: New York City. Sunday 23 December 1962

Titles performed:
'Jesus Is The Light Of The World'–1
'Yield Not To Temptation'

Source: *TV Gospel Time* #9

ST. PAUL'S DISCIPLE CHOIR

Mixed vocal choir accompaniment: unknown
Soloists: Daniel White–1; Robert Moore–2; Troy Keyes–3

Location: New York City. Sunday 15 December 1962

Titles performed:
'When The Saints Go Marching In'–1
'Zion's Walls'–2
'Jesus Paid It All'–3

Source: *TV Gospel Time* #14

ST. TIMOTHY MALE CHORUS

Male vocal choir accompaniment: unknown
Soloist: Ernest McGhee–1

Location: probably New York City. 1965

Titles performed:
'Dry Bones'
'Chariot's Coming'–1

Source: *TV Gospel Time* #43

SALEM TRAVELLERS

Probably Chester Feemster, Arthur Davis, Samuel Hanchett, Timothy Bailey, Talmon Thomas, Bill Ford (vocals)
accompaniment: unknown

Location: Chicago, Illinois

The following performances are known:
1964
Sunday 12 July [prog #15–1]
1965
Sunday 21 November [prog #10–1]
1969
Saturday 8 February [prog #34–3]
Saturday 28 June [prog #7–2]
1976
Sunday 21 November [prog #8–2]

Titles performed:
unknown

Source: *Jubilee Showcase*

AMBROSE SAM

Vocal and accordion

Location: Louisiana. 1990

Title performed:
'She's Calling Me' Channel 5 083 258–3, Island 083 258–3
[interview] Channel 5 083 258–3, Island 083 258–3

Source: *Zydeco Nite'N'Day*

SAM BROTHERS FIVE

Probably Herbert Sam, vocal and accordion accompaniment: his sons. In 1979 the band was Leon Sam (vocal accompaniment); Carl Sam (guitar); Rodney Sam (drums); Glen Sam (bass); Calvin Sam (rub-board)

Location: Louisiana. 1990

Title performed:
'I'm Comin' Home' Channel 5 083 258-3, Island 083 258-3

Source: *Zydeco Nite'N'Day*

DERYCK SAMPSON

Piano solos with Mabel Lee, dancing–1
as above accompaniment: unknown (guitar, bass, drums)–2

Location: probably New York City. Late 1945

Titles performed:
[22408] 'Half Past Jump Time'–1 Charly #2
[87608] 'Cats Can't Dance'–2 Charly #2, Storyville SV6003
[16M1] 'Baby, Don't Go Away From Me'–1 Charly #2

Source: *Soundies*
22408 copyrighted 30 December 1945; 16M1 4 February 1946

SANCTUARY CHOIR

Mixed vocal choir accompaniment: unknown
Soloists: Alfred Miller–1; Rosalie Williams–2

Location: Washington DC. Saturday 15 December 1962

Titles performed:
'I'm Leaning On The Lord'–1
'I Heard The Voice Of Jesus Say'
'Come And Go With Me'–2

Source: *TV Gospel Time* #17
See also Alfred Miller.

[REVERENCE] W J SANKEY

Speech with sung responses by congregation

Location: Friendship Baptist Church, Brighton, Alabama. Early 1985

Title performed:
[prayer]

Source: *On The Battlefield*
Reverend Sankey was pastor of Friendship Baptist Church.

SATAN AND ADAM

Sterling Magee [Satan] (vocal and guitar), Adam Gussow [Adam] (vocal and harmonica)

Location: 125th Street, New York City. 1988

Titles performed:
'Freedom For My People'

Source: *U2: Rattle And Hum*

JOE SAVAGE AND GROUP

Savage, vocal–1, comments and monologues : William S. Hart [*sic*], vocal–2, comments and monologues; Walter Brown and Bill Gordon (comments and monologues)–3

Location: Greenville, Mississippi. Between 11 August and 9 September 1978

Titles performed:
untitled mule song #1–1 Vestapol 13078
untitled mule song #2–2 Vestapol 13078
discussion on the mule trade–1, –2, –3

Source: *Land Where The Blues Began*
See also Walter Brown.

CHARLIE SAYLES

Vocal and harmonica

Location: Times Square, New York City. April 1976

Titles performed:
'Vietnam Blues'
'Banjo' (instrumental)

Source: *Omnibus*

MABEL SCOTT

Vocal accompaniment: Maurice Rocco (piano) and off-screen studio orchestra–1
Vocal accompaniment: The Flennoy Trio, Lorenzo Flennoy (piano); unknown (guitar, bass)–2

Location: probably Los Angeles, California. 1944

Titles performed:
[15008] 'Beat Me Daddy, Eight To The Bar'–1
[19008] 'Steak And Potatoes'–2
[19308] 'Gee'–2
[89808] 'Yankee Doodle Never Went To Town' –2

Source: *Soundies*
19008 copyrighted 27 November 1944; 89808 31 December 1944

UNCLE JOHN SCRUGGS
Vocal and 4-string banjo

Location: Powhatan County, Virginia. Thursday 8 November 1928

Title performed:
'Little Old Log Cabin In The Lane' Yazoo 512

Source: *Fox Movietone newsreel*

FRANK [SON] SEALS
Vocal and electric guitar accompaniment: unknown (second electric guitar, keyboards, electric bass, drums)

Location: Chicago, Illinois. 1980

Titles performed:
'Sweet Home Chicago' K-Jazz 075, Rhapsody 8020
untitled instrumental [part only] K-Jazz 075, Rhapsody 8020
[interview] K-Jazz 075, Rhapsody 8020

Source: *Big City Blues*

Vocal and electric guitar accompaniment: Lacey Gibson (electric guitar); and others, unknown

Location: Paris, France. 1978

Titles performed:
'Hot Sauce'
'The Woman I Love'
'Go Johnny Go'

Source: *French TV broadcast* [C]

Vocal and electric guitar accompaniment: probably Mighty Joe Young (electric guitar) and others, unknown

Location: Chicago, Illinois. Thursday 1 November 1979

Title performed:
'Cotton Pickin' Blues'

Source: *Soundstage*

SELAH JUBILEE SINGERS
Vocal group accompaniment: unknown (guitar)–1;
as above accompaniment: the Mount Carmel Baptist Church Choir–2

Location: Charlotte, North Carolina. Sunday 4 October 1964

Titles performed:
'Gospel Train'–1
'Don't Blame The Children'–1
'God Almighty's Gonna Cut You Down'–2

Source: *TV Gospel Time* #30
The personel of this group changed frequently during the above period, and the presence of either Thermon Ruth or Alden Bunn (Tarheel Slim) cannot therefore be confirmed.

[BROTHER] JOHN SELLERS
Vocal accompaniment: unknown

Location: unknown {USA}. 1957

Titles performed:
unknown

Source: *Ethnic Folk Songs Of The Southland*

Vocal accompaniment: unknown

Location: New York City. 1962

Titles performed:
unknown

Source: *Camera Three: One Hundred Years From Today*

Vocal accompaniment: unknown

Location: Chicago, Illinois

The following appearances are known:
1964
Sunday 9 February [prog #12–1]
1967
Sunday 5 March [prog #17–1]
Sunday 12 March [prog #17–2]

Titles performed:
unknown

Source: *Jubilee Showcase*

SENSATIONAL NIGHTINGALES
See the Nightingales.

SHADRACK BOYS
Vocal group accompaniment unknown orchestra

Location: probably New York City. 1941

Titles performed:
[W110] 'Samoa (I'd Like To See More Of)'
[W140] 'Shadrack'

Source: *Associated Featurettes*
Reviewed in *Billboard* 2 August 1941.

Vocal group accompaniment, if any, unknown

Location: probably New York City. c. late 1943–early 1944

Titles performed:
[15508] 'Lazy River'
[16108] 'Jonah And The Whale'

Source: *Soundies*
15508 copyrighted 28 February 1944; 16108 10 April 1944

SHADY GROVE CHURCH CHOIR
Mixed vocal choir accompaniment: unknown
Soloists: Lester Baskin–1; Clemmie Lee Backus–2

Location: Memphis, Tennessee. Saturday 19 January 1963

Titles performed:
'Old Camp Ground'–1
'I've Been Born Again'
'Meet Me At The River'–2

Source: *TV Gospel Time* #21

MEM SHANNON
Vocal and guitar accompaniment: probably G E Smith's band

Location: Washington, DC. Saturday 11 October 1997

Titles performed:
unknown

Source: *Tribute To Muddy Waters*

WILL SHADE
Vocal and bass accompaniment: Charlie Burse (vocal and tenor guitar)

Location: Memphis, Tennessee. 1962

Title performed:
'Bottle Up And Go'

Source: *Local TV broadcast* [M]

SHAKEY JAKE (James D Harris)
Vocal and harmonica accompaniment: probably Memphis Slim (piano); Willie Dixon (bass); Clifton James (drums)

Location: Baden-Baden, Germany. c. October 1962

Titles performed:
unknown

Source: *American Folk Blues Festival 1962*

Presumably speech, vocal and harmonica accompaniment, if any: unknown

Location: probably Chicago, Illinois. 1972

Titles performed:
unknown

Source: *Conversations With Shakey Jake*

SHARPEES
Vernon Guy and Stacey Johnson, vocals accompaniment: unknown

Location: St. Louis, Missouri. 1989

Title performed:
'When Something Is Wrong With My Baby'

Source: *St. Soul – Soul Of St. Louis R&B*

OMAR SHARRIFF
See Dave Alexander.

ROBERT SHAW
Vocal and piano

Location: unknown {USA}. 1978

Titles performed:
unknown

Source: *Visions* (unconfirmed)

Vocal and piano

Location: Austin, Texas. 1979

Titles performed:
'Piggly Wiggly'
'It's A Lowdown Dirty Shame'
'Hattie Green'

Source: *Austin City Limits*

SHILOH CHRISTIAN COMMUNITY CHURCH CHOIR
Mixed vocal choir accompaniment: unknown
Soloists: Thelma Jackson–1; Clifton Bennett–2

Location: Baltimore, Maryland. Saturday 5 September 1964

Titles performed:
'When He Calls Me'
'I Feel Like Travelling On'–1
'I Shall Wear A Crown'–2

Source: *TV Gospel Time* #34

Probably as above

Location: New York City. 1966

Titles performed:
unknown

Source: *TV Gospel Time* #61

JOHNNY SHINES
Vocal and guitar, accompaniment: David 'Honeyboy' Edwards (guitar); Walter Horton (harmonica)

Location: Thunderbird Motel, Chicago, Illinois. 1969

Titles performed:
'This Love Of Mine' K-Jazz 030, Vestapol 13038, Yazoo 505
'Going To Algiers' Vestapol 13038
'Ramblin'' Vestapol 13038
'Tell Me How You Want Your Rolling Done' Vestapol 13038

Source: *Adelphi Productions* [C]

Vocal and guitar

Location: KCTS TV studios, Seattle, Washington. November 1970

Titles performed:
'Ramblin'' Vestapol 13002
'Tell Me Mama' Vestapol 13002
'Mister Tom Green's Farm' Vestapol 13002
'Sweet Home Chicago' Vestapol 13038
'Kindhearted Woman' Vestapol 13038
'I Don't Know' Vestapol 13038

Source: *University of Washington/Seattle Folklore Society*
One or more of the above titles are probably included in *Roots Of American Music*.

Vocal and guitar

Location: unknown {USA}. 1971

Titles performed;
unknown

Source: *Velvet Vampire*. May be [ST] only

Vocal and guitar

Location: unknown {USA}. 1973

Titles performed:
unknown

Source: *Johnny Shines: Black And Blue* [unconfirmed]

Vocal and guitar

Location: Vienna, Austria. 1975

Titles performed:
'The Blues Walked In This Morning'
'Good Morning Blues'
'Milkcow Blues'
'Good Morning Little Schoolgirl'
and 2 other, unknown, titles

Source: *Austrian TV broadcast*

Vocal and guitar accompaniment, if any: unknown

Location: unknown {USA}. February 1977

Titles performed:
unknown

Source: *US TV broadcast* [C]. Origin unknown

Vocal and guitar

Location: Freedom Village, Greenville, Mississippi. Saturday 8 September 1979

Titles performed:
'You Got To Pay The Cost' K-Jazz 081
'I Walked All The Way From East St. Louis' K-Jazz 081

Source: *Mississippi Blues*

Vocal and electric guitar in duet with Robert Lockwood (vocal and electric guitar) accompaniment: unknown (drums)

Location: Sacramento, California. September 1987

Titles performed:
'Hey Ba-ba Re Bop'

Source: *Sacramento Blues Festival 1987*

Vocal and guitar

Location: unknown {USA}. 1991

Title performed:
'Dust My Broom' CMV491132
[interview] CMV491132

Source: *The Search For Robert Johnson*

J D SHORT

Vocal, guitar, harmonica and bass drum

Location: St. Louis, Missouri. Summer 1962

Titles performed:
[untitled introduction]
'Slidin' Delta'

Source: *The Blues* [1]

TERRENCE SIMIEN AND THE MALLET PLAYBOYS

Vocal and accordion accompaniment: unknown (rub-board, electric guitar, electric bass, drums)

Location: Plaisance, Louisiana. 1988

Title performed:
unknown [fragment] K-Jazz 098, Rhapsody 8062

Source: *Zydeco Gumbo*

Vocal and accordion accompaniment: unknown (2 electric guitars, electric bass, rub-board, drums)

Location: Louisiana. 1990

Titles performed:
'Mon Chatife' Channel 5 083 258-3, Island 083 258-3
'Will The Circle Be Unbroken' Channel 5 083 258-3, Island 083 258-3

Source: *Zydeco Nite'N'Day*

SARAH SIMMONS

Vocal accompaniment: unknown

Location: Chicago, Illinois

The following appearances are known:
1965
Sunday 11 July [prog #29–3]
1972
Friday 25 August [prog #2–2]

Titles performed:
unknown

Source: *Jubilee Showcase*

SINGERS OF JOY
Vocal group accompaniment: unknown

Location: Chicago, Illinois. Sunday 26 April 1964

Titles performed:
unknown

Source: *Jubilee Showcase* [prog #9–3]

SINGING ANGELS
Vocal group accompaniment: unknown

Location: New York City. Sunday 30 September 1962

Titles performed:
'Meet My Saviour'
'They Called Me Crazy'

Source: *TV Gospel Time* #6

As above

Location: New York City. Saturday 15 December 1962

Title performed:
'So Many Years I Lived In Sin'

Source: *TV Gospel Time* #1

DRINK SMALL
Vocal and guitar

Location: Columbia, South Carolina. 1992

Title performed:
'I'm Getting Tired Now' JVC 225

Source: *University of Carolina, Concert of Heritage*

BESSIE SMITH
Vocal, unaccompanied–1
Vocal accompaniment: Joe Smith (cornet); Russell Smith (trumpet); Charlie Green (trombone); unknown (clarinet and tenor saxophone); James P. Johnson (piano); Charles Dixon (banjo); Harry Hull (bass); Kaiser Marshall (drums); Rosamund Johnson and the Hall Johnson Choir (vocal chorus)–2

Location: Astoria, Queens, New York City. Late June 1929

Titles performed:
[dialogue leading to:]
'My Man'–1 Blacast VY328, Jazz & Jazz Vidjazz 13, Jazz Classics JCVC108, Storyville SV6032, Video Images 328, Yazoo 514
[unaccompanied fragment of 'St. Louis Blues']
[dialogue leading to:]
'St. Louis Blues'–2 Blacast VY328, Jazz & Jazz Vidjazz 13, Jazz Classics JCVC108, Rhino R3.2101, Storyville SV6032, View Video 1313, Video Images 328, Vintage Jazz Classics VJC2002, Yazoo 514

Source: *St. Louis Blues* [1]
The complete film is included on Blacast, Jazz & Jazz, Jazz Classics, Storyville and Video Images. The Storyville print is taken from the original negative. The Rhino, View Video, Vintage Jazz Classics and Yazoo issues offer excerpts.

BYTHER SMITH
See A.C. Reed.

REVEREND CAESAR SMITH
Speech–1
Vocal accompaniment church congregation (vocals and foot-stomping)–2

Location: Mississippi. Between 11 August and 9 September 1978

Titles performed:
Sermon–1 Vestapol 13078
Lining out hymn–2
'Do What Your Spirit Say'–2

Source: *Land Where The Blues Began*

CARRIE SMITH
Vocal accompaniment: piano

Location: New York City. Sunday 9 December 1962

Titles performed:
'He's A Rock All The Way'
'Down By The Riverside'

Source: *TV Gospel Time* #7

COLUMBUS SMITH
Vocal accompaniment: unknown

Location: New York City. c.1966

Title performed:
unknown

Source: *TV Gospel Time* #61

GOSSIE SMITH
Vocal accompaninment: unknown (orchestra)

Location: Dallas, Texas. 1941

Title performed:
'Weary Blues' Hollywood Select 50543

Source: *The Blood Of Jesus*

LAURA SMITH
Vocal accompaniment: unknown

Location: unknown {USA}. 1929

Titles performed:
unknown

Source: *Lady Liz*

MAMIE SMITH
Vocal accompaniment: Porter Grainger (piano); unknown (1-string fiddle)

Location: Camden, New Jersey. Tuesday 9 April 1929

Titles performed:
[50603–1] 'The Jail House Blues/You Can't Do It'

Source: *The Jail House Blues*
[This was a Victor custom recording. The matrix number shown in parenthesis was allocated by Victor.]

Vocal accompaniment: unknown

Location: probably New York City. 1938

Titles performed:
unknown

Source: *Mystery In Swing*

Vocal accompaniment: Donald Heywood and his orchestra

Location: New York City. c. 1940

Titles performed:
'I'll Do Anything For Love' Timeless Video 5060
'Good Times Are Here Again' Timeless Video 5060

Source: *Sunday Sinners*

Vocal accompaniment: Donald Heywood and his orchestra

Location: New York City. c.1940

Title performed:
'I'll Get Even With You' Blacast BC8035, Timeless Video 5058

Source: *Murder On Lenox Avenue*

Vocal accompaniment: Lucky Millinder and his Cotton Pickers; unknown (three trombones, two tenor saxophones, bass saxophone, piano, guitar, bass, drums)–1
As above, accompaniment: The Alphabetical Four (vocal group); Johnny Smith, (lead); Curtis Brown (tenor); Asher Short or Johnny Pierce, (baritone); — Lockwood (bass)–2

Location: New York City. c. March–April 1940

Titles performed:
'Lord Lord (Because I Love You)'–1 Rhino R3.2101, Storyville SV6032, Timeless Video 5048, Video Images 517
'Harlem Blues'–2 Rhino R3.2101, Timeless Video 5048, Video Images 517

Source: *Paradise In Harlem*
'Lord Lord (Because I Love You)' was also issued as Soundie 2M1. Rhino R3.2101 features the two songs only. Video Images 517 and Hollywood Select 5048 contain the full film.

MOSES [WHISPERING] SMITH
Vocal and harmonica accompaniment: probably Boogie Woogie Red (piano); Homesick James (electric guitar); Roger Hill (electric bass); Tom Parnell (drums)

Location: Brighton Polytechnic, Sussex, England. February 1973

Titles performed:
unknown

Source: *Blues Legends 73*

Vocal and harmonica accompaniment: unknown (electric guitar, electric bass, drums)

Location: Baton Rouge, Louisiana. 1984

Titles performed:
'Got My Mojo Working'
'Texas Flood'
'Raining In My Heart'
[interview]

Source: *Baton Rouge Blues*

PREACHER SMITH AND THE DEACONS
Tenor saxophone accompaniment: unknown orchestra

Location: probably Houston, Texas. 1956

Titles performed:
'Eat Your Heart Out' Rhino R3.2410
'Roogie Doogie' Rhino R3.2410

Source: *Rock Baby, Rock It!*

TRIXIE SMITH
Vocal accompaniment: unknown

Location: probably New York City. c. 1932

Titles performed:
unknown

Source: *The Black King*
Smith is reported to also have a dramatic role in this film.

Vocal accompaniment: unknown (two trumpets, tenor saxophone, piano, bass, drums)

Location: probably New York City. 1938

Title performed:
'That's How Rhythm Was Born'

Source: *Birthright*

Vocal accompaniment: unknown

Location: probably New York City. 1938

Titles performed:
unknown

Source: *God's Stepchildren*
This artist also had a dramatic cameo in the 1931 Mae West film *The Constant Sinner.*

WILLIE MAE FORD SMITH
Vocal accompaniment: Bertha Smith (piano)–1
Vocal accompanment: unknown (piano)–2
Vocal accompaniment: unknown (electric organ), congregational vocals–3

Locations: [A] Senior citizens home, Chicago, Illinois
[B] the Smith residence, Chicago, Illinois
[C] Antioch Baptist church, St. Louis, Missouri

Titles performed:
'Singing In My Soul'–2 [B] FRF un-numbered
'Go Preach My Gospel'–3 [C] FRF un-numbered
'I'll Never Turn Back'–3 [C] FRF un-numbered
'Highway To Heaven'–3 [C] FRF un-numbered

'That's Allright' 3 [C] FRF un-numbered
'I Long To See My Saviour'–3 [C] FRF un-numbered
[interviews and conversation] FRF un-numbered

Source: *Say Amen Somebody!*

[REVEREND] MELVIN SMOTHERSON
Preaching and singing

Location: St. Louis, Missouri. 1982

[sermon] FRF un-numbered

Source: *Say Amen, Somebody!*

VANITA SMYTHE
Vocal accompaniment: Dan Burley (piano); unknown (bass)

Location: New York City. Early 1946

Titles performed:
[19M4] 'Back Door Man' Charly #5
[21M3] 'They Raided The Joint' Storyville SV6003, Virgin VVD868
[22M1] 'Does You Do, Or Does You Don't?'
[24M3] 'I Need A Playmate'
[25M3] 'Sho' Had A Wonderful Time'
[26M1] 'Low, Short And Squatty' Charly #5

Source: *Soundies*. One, at least, of the above titles also appears in *Ebony Parade*. 19M4 registered 1 June 1946; 21M3 15 July 1946; 22M1 5 August 1946; 24M3 14 October 1946; 25M3 18 November 1946; 26M1, 2 December 1946.

SOUL STIRRERS
Vocal group; Paul Foster (lead vocal)–1; Jimmy Outler (lead vocal)–2 Jesse James Farley (lead vocal)–3; accompaniment: unknown (bass vocal); Outler (electric guitar); Paul Foster accompaniment: the Shady Grove Choir–4

Location: Memphis, Tennessee. Saturday 19 January 1963

Titles performed:
'Must Jesus Bear The Cross Alone'–1 [A]
'I Love The Lord'–1 [B]
'Wade In The Water'–1 [B]
'I'm A Pilgrim'–1 [C]
'Shelter For Me'–1 [C]
'I'm Thankful'–2 [B]
'I'm A Soldier In The Army Of The Lord'–2 [C]
'Listen To The Angels Sing'–2 [C]
'Ride On, King Jesus'–3 [C]
'The End Of My Journey'–3 [C]
'Toiling On'–4 [A]

Source: *TV Gospel Time* #21 [A], #22 [B], #23 [C]

Probably Willie Rogers, Martin Jacox, Sonny Mitchell, Jesse James Farley (vocals) accompaniment, if any: Arthur Crume (electric guitar) and Sonny Mitchell (electric bass)

Location: Chicago, Illinois

The following performances are known:
1964
Sunday 12 January [prog #22–1]
Saturday 9 May [prog #10–3]
1969
Saturday 11 January [prog #8–3]
1971
Saturday 14 August [prog #1–2]
1972
Sunday 24 September [prog #2–2]
1973
Tuesday 22 May [prog #5–3]
1976
Saturday 9 October [prog #9–1]

Titles performed:
unknown

Source: *Jubilee Showcase*

J J Farley And the Original Soul Stirrers: Farley, Martin Jacox, Ben Odom, Will Rogers (vocals) accompaniment: The Colonus Messengers

Location: Annenberg Center, Philadelphia, Pennsylvania. 1985

Titles performed:
[see note in Programme Index.]

Source: *The Gospel At Colonus*
Martin Jacox played the dramatic role of Choragos.There is no evidence to suggest that any film, video or kinescope of the Soul Stirrers featuring Sam Cooke exists; there is, however, considerable footage of Cooke as a secular artist, available from Historic. See also Jesse James Farley and Robert Harris.

SOUTHERNAIRES

Vocal quartet; Roy Yeates, Lowell Peters, Jay Stone Toney and William Anderson accompaniment: Clarence Jones (piano).

Location: New York City. September 19 to November 21 1948

Titles performed:
unknown

Source: *Southernaires Quartet*

OTIS SPANN

Vocal and piano–1 ; piano solo–2

Location: Newport, Rhode Island. Sunday 3 July 1960

Titles performed;
'St. Louis Blues'–1
'Boogie Woogie'–2
'Sweet Slow Blues' [*sic*]–2
untitled boogie instrumental–2

Source: *Jazz-USA*

Vocal and piano

Location: Chicago, Illinois. Thursday 14 July 1960

Titles performed:
'Some People Call Me Lucky' K-Jazz 014, Rhapsody 8022
[monologue] K-Jazz 014, Rhapsody 8022

Source: *Blues Like Showers Of Rain*

Vocal and piano accompaniment: Willie Dixon (bass); S.P. Leary (drums)–1
Vocal accompaniment: Muddy Waters Blues Band and James Cotton, Willie Dixon, Jesse Fuller, Mable Hillery, Brownie McGhee, Muddy Waters, Sunnyland Slim, Sonny Terry, Bukka White, Big Joe Williams, (vocals)–2

Location: Toronto, Canada. Thursday 27 to Saturday 29 January 1966

Titles performed:
'Ain't Nobody's Business'–1 Rhino R3.2313
'The Blues Don't Like Nobody'–1 Rhino R3.2313
jam session–2 Rhino R3.2313

Source: *Festival Presents The Blues*

Vocal and piano accompaniment: Muddy Waters (electric guitar); probably Paul Oscher (harmonica); Luther Johnson and Sammy Lawhorn (electric guitars); Sonny Wimberly (electric bass); S.P. Leary (drums)

Location: London, England. c. November 1967

Title performed:
Bloody Murder
and possibly other, unknown, titles

Source: *UK BBC-TV broadcast* [M], title unknown. Broadcast Sunday 26 November 1967. This may have been live, in which case the broadcast date is the correct recording date.

Vocal and piano accompaniment, if any, unknown

Location: Ronnie Scott's Jazz Club, London, England. Thursday 11 June 1970

Titles performed:
'Going Down Slow'
'T–99'

Source: *Jazz Scene At Ronnie Scott's*

As above

Location: Ronnie Scott's Jazz Club, London, England. Saturday 10 September 1970

Titles performed:
untitled boogie instrumental
'Ain't Nobody's Business'

Source: *Jazz Scene at Ronnie Scott's*
Otis Spann may also have appeared on British TV during October 1958, when he toured with Muddy Waters. A brief silent clip of amateur colour footage of this artist, dating from c. early 1960s, appears in *Record Row*.

SPECKLED RED (Rufus Perryman)
Speech

Location: Newberry Terrace, St. Louis, Missouri. 1960

monologue [ST] K-Jazz 014, Rhapsody 8022

Source: *Blues Like Showers Of Rain*

BUD SPIRES
Vocal and harmonica

Location: probably Bentonia, Mississippi. Between 11 August and 9 September 1978

Title performed:
'Easy Ridin' Buggy' [fragment only] Vestapol 13078

Source: *Land Where The Blues Began*

Speech and guitar accompaniment: Jack Owens (guitar)

Location: Bentonia, Mississippi. Autumn 1990

Title performed:
[monologue regarding the preacher and devil at the crossroads] Anxious 45099-29643, BMG un-numbered

Source: *Deep Blues*
See also Jack Owens.

SPIRIT OF MEMPHIS QUARTET
Vocal group, unaccompanied

Location: Handy Park, Memphis, Tennessee. c. early–mid-1950s

Title performed:
'He's A Way Maker' [part only] California Newsreel 01, Multicultural Media 1008

Source: *Origin unknown, probably newsreel* [M]. The personnel of this group changed frequently enough that it has not been possible accurately to establish who appears in this brief clip.

SPIRITS OF RHYTHM
Vocal group accompaniment: probably Leo Watson, Wilbur Daniels, Douglas Daniels (vocals, tiples); Teddy Bunn (guitar); Virgil Scoggins (vocals, drums); and sometimes a bass player
Vocal interjections by Dorothy Dandridge

Location: probably New York City. Mid 1942

Title performed:
'Yes, Indeed!'

Source: *Soundie*

SPIRITUAL FIVE
Vocal group accompaniment: unknown

Location: Chicago, Illinois. Sunday 23 February 1964

Titles performed:
unknown

Source: *Jubilee Showcase* [prog #28–1]
This group may possibly include Wilson Pickett.

VICTORIA SPIVEY (Victoria Regina Spivey)
Vocal and harmonium, leading choir

Location: unknown {USA}. 1929

Title performed:
'I Belong To That Band' [part only]

Source: *Hallelujah*
Spivey has a dramatic role, as Missy Rose, in this production. Despite some claims to the contrary, there is no evidence of her singing secular songs in any inspected print of this film.

Vocal accompaniment: unknown

Location: unknown {USA}. 1963

Titles performed:
unknown

Source: *Lyrics And Legends: The Blues*

Vocal and piano, accompaniment: Matt Murphy (electric guitar); Willie Dixon (bass); Billie Stepney (drums)

Location: Manchester, England. October 1963

Title performed:
'T.B. Blues'

Source: *I Hear The Blues*

Vocal and piano accompaniment: probably similar to above

Location: Baden-Baden, Germany. October 1963

Title performed:
unknown

Source: *American Folk Blues Festival 1963*

Vocal accompaniment: unknown

Location: unknown {USA}. 1971

Titles performed:
unknown

Source: *Free Time* [unconfirmed]

Vocal accompaniment: unknown

Location: Philadelphia, Pennsylvania. 1974

Titles performed:
unknown

Source: *Philadelphia Folk Festival*

Vocal and piano

Location: Brooklyn, New York City. Monday 2 February 1976

Titles performed:
'T.B. Blues'
'Back Snake Blues'

Source: *The Devil's Music series 2*

HORACE SPROTT

Vocal, harmonica, possibly other instruments

Location: probably Alabama. 1956

Titles performed:
unknown

Source: *Odyssey: They Took A Blue Note*

HOUSTON STACKHOUSE

Vocal and electric guitar accompaniment: probably Joe Willie Wilkins (guitar) and others, unknown

Location: probably Memphis, Tennessee. 1975

Titles performed:
unknown

Source: *The Friendly Invasion*

Vocal and electric guitar accompaniment: unknown

Location: unknown {USA}. 1975

Titles performed:
unknown

Source: *Born in The Blues* [unconfirmed]

Vocal and electric guitar accompaniment: Joe Willie Wilkins (guitar); L.T. Lewis (drums)

Location: Memphis, Tennessee. Monday 19 January 1976

Titles performed:
'Cool Drink of Water' [unbroadcast] Vestapol 13016
'Mean Red Spider'
[interview]

Source: *The Devil's Music series 2*

Vocal and electric guitar

Location: Memphis, Tennessee. 1978

Titles performed:
[monologue regarding Tommy Johnson] K-Jazz 030, Yazoo 505
leading to;
'Canned Heat Blues' [part only] K-Jazz 030, Yazoo 505

Source: *Good Morning Blues*

STAPLE SINGERS
Probably Mavis, Yvonne, Cleotha, Purvis Staples (vocals) accompaniment: Roebuck 'Pop' Staples (electric guitar)

Location: Newport, Rhode Island. Sunday July 26 1964

Titles performed:
unknown [fragments]

Source: *Festival* [1]

Probably as above

Location: Chicago, Illinois

The following appearances are known:
1964
Saturday 9 May [prog #10–3]
1966
Saturday 11 June [prog #23–2]
1968
Saturday 28 September [prog #28–3]
1969
Saturday 8 March [prog #31–2]

Titles performed:
unknown

Source: *Jubilee Showcase*
Later recordings by the Staples Singers fall outside the scope of this work and are therefore excluded.

STARLIGHT GOSPEL SINGERS
Vocal quartet accompaniment: unknown (two electric guitars, electric bass, drums)

Location: WDBJ TV Studios, Roanoke, Virginia. Spring/summer 1987

Title performed:
'It's Gonna Rain' [part only]

Source: *Black Musical Traditions In Virginia: Sacred Music*

BOB [BLUES] STARR
Vocal and electric guitar accompaniment: the Milton DeLugg orchestra and Gene-Gene the Dancing Machine (resident *Gong Show* dancer)

Location: Burbank, California. 1978–79

Title performed:
'This Energy Crisis Is Killin' Me' [part only]

Source: *The Gong Show*

STARS OF FAITH
Marion Williams, Mattie Williams, Frances Steadman, Kitty Parham, Henrietta Waddy, Esther Ford (vocals) accompaniment: probably Alex Bradford (piano) and others, unknown

Location: London, England. c. November 1962

Titles performed:
[probably];
'My Way Is Cloudy'
''Most Done Travelling'
'Baby Born Today'
'Poor Little Jesus Boy'
'Mary, What You Gonna Name That Pretty Little Boy'

Source: *Black Nativity*

Probably Marion Williams, Frances Steadman, Mattie Williams, Henrietta Waddy, Rita Palmer (vocals) accompaniment: unknown

Location: London, England. Sunday 27 October 1963

Titles performed:
unknown

Source: *Tempo*

Probably as last

Location: Chicago, Illinois. Sunday 15 December 1963

Titles performed:
unknown

Source: *Jubilee Showcase* [prog #11–1]

Probably Frances Steadman, Henrietta Waddy, Matty Dozier Belk, Kitty Parham, Elaine Murphy (vocals) accompaniment: unknown

Location: New York City. c.1966

Titles performed:
unknown

Source: *TV Gospel Time* #66

Probably as above

Location: Chicago, Illinois. Sunday 13 March 1966

Titles performed:
unknown

Source: *Jubilee Showcase* [prog #34–2]

Probably Frances Steadman, Kitty Parham, Henrietta Waddy, Willie DeJohn, Sadie Keys (vocals) accompaniment: unknown

Location: Maltings theatre, Snape, England. Thursday 20 February 1969

Titles performed:
unknown

Source: *Jazz At The Maltings*

Probably as last

Location: Ronnie Scott's Jazz Club, London, England. Thursday 23 April 1970

Titles performed:
unknown

Source: *Jazz Scene At Ronnie Scott's*

Probably as last

Location: Ronnie Scott's Jazz Club, London, England. Thursday 28 May 1970

Titles performed:
unknown

Source: *Jazz Scene At Ronnie Scott's*

Probably as last

Location: Berlin, Germany. 1971

Title performed:
'We Shall Be Changed'

Source: *Just For Fun*

Probably as last

Location: Montreux, Switzerland. 1974

Titles performed:
unknown

Source: *Montreux Jazz*

Probably as last

Location: Pebble Mill TV studios, Birmingham, England. Thursday 30 October 1980

Titles performed:
unknown

Source: *Pebble Mill At One*

Probably as last

Location: Montreux, Switzerland. 1983

Titles performed:

Source: *Montreux Jazz*

Probably as last

Location: Montreux, Switzerland. 1987

Titles performed:
unknown

Source: *Montreux Jazz*
See also Kitty Parham, Francis Steadman and Marion Williams.

STARS OF ZION

Vocal group accompaniment: unknown

Location: Gary, Indiana. June 1976

Titles performed:
unknown

Source: *Gospel In Gary*

FRANCIS STEADMAN

Vocal accompaniment: unknown

Location: Chicago, Illinois. Sunday 15 December 1963

Titles performed:
unknown

Source: *Jubilee Showcase* [prog #11–1]
See also the Stars of Faith.

THE J D STEELE SINGERS

J D Steele, Frederick Steel, Jearlyn Steele Battle, Jevetta Steel (vocals) accompaniment: The Colonus Messengers

Location: Annenberg Center, Philadelphia, Pennsylvania. 1985

Titles performed:
[see note in Programme Index]

Source: *The Gospel at Colonus*
Jevetta Steel played the dramatic role of Ismene.

STERLING JUBILEE SINGERS

Vocal quartet, unaccompanied

Location: [A] probably Alabama. Early 1984
[B] Birmingham or Bessemer, Alabama. Early 1984
[C] Lily Grove Baptist Church, Bessemer, Alabama. Early 1984
[D] Friendship Baptist Church, Brighton, Alabama. Early 1984

Titles performed:
'The Lord's Prayer' [A]
[rehearsing 'When I Was A Sinner' and My Home Is Over In Canaan' with the Birmingham Sunlights] [B]
[sung prayer and business meeting leading to;]
'When They Ring the Golden Bells' leading to;]
[closing prayer] [C]
'My Jesus Knows' [D]

Source: *On The Battlefield*

STEVENS SINGERS

probably Herman Stevens, Helen Bryant, Evelyn Archer, Carnegie Burruso (vocals) accompaniment: unknown

Location: New York City. c. 1965–66

Title performed:
unknown

Source: *TV Gospel Time* #50

JAMES [GUITAR SLIM] STEVENS

Vocal and piano–1
Vocal and electric guitar–2

Location: North Carolina. 1988

Titles performed:
'Please Don't Go'–1
untitled slow blues instrumental–1
'I Know His Blood Can Make Me Whole'–2
[interview]

Source: *Step It Up And Go*
This is not the same artist as Eddie (Guitar Slim) Jones who recorded for Bullet, Specialty and Imperial records.

PRINCESS STEWART
Vocal accompaniment: unknown

Location: Chicago, Illinois

The following appearances are known:
1963
Sunday 15 December [prog #11–1]
1964
Sunday 16 February [prog #30–3]
1965
Tuesday 25 May [prog #21–1]

Titles performed:
unknown

Source: *Jubilee Showcase*

ARBEE STIDHAM
Vocal accompaniment and electric guitar

Location: probably Chicago. c. early 1950s

Titles performed:
unknown

Source: *I Come For To Sing*

Vocal accompaniment and electric guitar

Location: Chicago, Illinois. 1973

Titles performed:
unknown

Source: *The Bluesman*

CHARLES STORY
Vocal accompaniment: unknown

Location: New York City. c. 1965–66

Title performed:
unknown

Source: *TV Gospel Time* #51

JIMMY STREETER
See unidentified artist #36.

NAPOLEON STRICKLAND
Vocal and one string guitar–1
Vocal and steel guitar–2
Fife, accompaniment: unknown (2 snare drums and one bass drum)–3

Location: Mississippi. Between 11 August and 9 September 1978

Titles performed:
'Back Door Blues'–1 Vestapol 13078
'Shake 'em On Down'–2 Vestapol 13078
untitled instrumental ['Oree']–3 Vestapol 13078
[interview]

Source: *Land Where The Blues Began*
Aee also Jessie Mae Hemphill, Othar Turner and Ed Young.

NOLAN STRUCK
Vocal and electric bass accompaniment: Eddie C Campbell (electric guitar); Lester Davenport (harmonica); Chico Chism (drums)

Location: South Bank Arts Centre, London, England. Tuesday 27 November 1979

Title performed:
'Everyday I Have The Blues'

Source: *Mainstream*

SUGAR BLUE (James Whiting)
Vocal and harmonica accompaniment, if any: unknown

Location: Chicago, Illinois. c.1978

Title performed:
'Chicago Blues'

Source: *Chicago Melodie*

Vocal and harmonica accompaniment: Paul Cooper (electric guitar); Vic Pitts (drums)

Location: Antibes, France. Tuesday 22 July 1980

Titles performed:
'Rock Me Baby'
'Little Red Rooster'
'Another Man Done Gone'

Source: *French TV broadcast* [C]

Vocal and harmonica accompaniment: Fred Grady, Michael Robinson, Laverne Tayton, Lafayette Evans, (unknown instrumentation)

Location: Tessin, Switzerland. 1982

Titles performed:
'Who's Loving My Girl Tonight'
'Hoochie Coochie Man'
'Messin' With The Kid'
'I Just Want To Make Love To You'
untitled blues
[interview in French]

Source: *Swiss TV broadcast* [C]

Vocal and harmonica accompaniment: the BB King orchestra

Location: Montreux, Switzerland. Tuesday 27 July 1982

Title performed:
'Whiskey Drinkin' Woman'

Source: *Montreux Jazz*

HUBERT SUMLIN
Vocal and electric guitar accompaniment: Carey Bell (harmonica); Eddie Taylor (electric guitar); Bob Stroger (electric bass); Odie Payne (drums)

Location: Germany. 1980

Titles performed:
'Gamblin' Woman'
untitled blues

Source: *American Folk Blues Festival 1980*

Electric guitar accompaniment: unknown (electric guitar, electric bass, drums)

Location: Chicago, Illinois. 1994

Title performed:
untitled instrumental — MCA V10944
[interview]

Source: *Sweet Home Chicago* [2]
Sumlin is the subject of an undated documentary entitled *Living The Blues*, details unknown.
See also Howlin' Wolf and Sunnyland Slim.

SUNNYLAND SLIM (Albert Luandrew)
Vocal and piano accompaniment: Robert Lockwood (electric guitar)–1; speech–2

Location: Chicago, Illinois. Wednesday 13 July 1960

Titles performed:
'Prison Bound'–1 [ST] — K-Jazz 014, Rhapsody 8022
monologue–2 [ST] — K-Jazz 014, Rhapsody 8022

Source: *Blues Like Showers Of Rain*

Vocal and piano accompaniment: Hubert Sumlin (electric guitar); Willie Dixon (bass); Clifton James (drums)

Location: Baden-Baden, Germany. October 1964

Title performed:
[intoduction by Sonny Boy Williamson;]
'Come On Home'

Source: *American Folk Blues Festival 1964*
Hubert Sumlin contributes a long guitar solo to the above performance.

Probably as above

Location: Free Trade Hall, Manchester, England. Thursday 22 October 1964

Title performed:
unknown

Source: *The Blues Came Walking*

Vocal and piano accompaniment: Muddy Waters, Sammy Lawhorn (electric guitars); Jimmy Lee Morrison (electric bass); S.P. Leary (drums)–1
Vocal accompaniment: Willie Dixon (bass); S.P. Leary (drums)–2
Vocal accompaniment: Muddy Waters Blues Band and James Cotton, Willie Dixon, Jesse Fuller, Mable Hillery, Brownie McGhee, Muddy Waters, Otis Spann, Sonny Terry, Bukka White and Big Joe Williams, (vocals)–3

Location: Toronto, Canada. Thursday 27 to Saturday 29 January 1966

Titles performed:

'The Devil's Got Me'–1	Rhino 3.2313
'Tin Pan Alley'–2	Rhino 3.2313
short untitled blues–2	Rhino 3.2313
jam session–3	Rhino 3.2313

[and conversation with Barry Callaghan, Willie Dixon, Muddy Waters, Brownie McGhee, Otis Spann and Sonny Terry]

Source: *Festival Presents The Blues*

Vocal and piano accompaniment: unknown

Location: Chicago, Illinois. c. 1978

Title performed:
'Election Day'

Source: *Chicago Melodie*

Vocal and piano accompaniment: Hubert Sumlin and Eddie Taylor (electric guitars); Bob Stroger (electric bass); Odie Payne (drums)

Location: Germany. 1980

Title performed:
'She's Got A Thing Goin' On'

Source: *American Folk Blues Festival 1980*

Vocal and piano

Location: Belgium. 1981

Title performed:
'You Drove My Love Away'

Source: *American Folk Blues Festival 1981*

Vocal and piano

Location: Atlanta, Georgia. 1984

Title performed:
'Don't Put That Thing On Me'

Source: *National Downhome Blues Festival*

SUPREME ANGELS [male vocal group]

Vocal group, probably including Howard 'Slim' Hunt (lead vocal) accompaniment: unknown

Location: Chicago, Illinois. Saturday 22 February 1969

Titles performed:
unknown

Source: *Jubilee Showcase* [prog #19–3]

BELTON SUTHERLAND

Vocal and guitar

Location: Mississippi. Between 11 August and 9 September 1978

Title performed:

'Grey Mule Blues'	Vestapol 13078

Source: *Land Where The Blues Began*

SWANEE QUINTET

Probably Johnny Jones, Ruben Willingham, Charles Barnwell, James Anderson, Rufus Washington, William Crawford (vocals) accompaniment: unknown

Location: Apollo theatre, Harlem, New York City. 1959

Titles performed:
unknown

Source: *World By Night*

Probably as last

Location: Chicago, Illinois. Sunday 11 July 1965

Titles performed:
unknown

Source: *Jubilee Showcase* [prog #29–3]

probably as last accompaniment: unknown (electric guitar, organ), with Reverend Ruben Willingham (lead vocal and dancing)

Location: Jacksonville, Florida. c.1966

Title performed:
'I've Got A New Walk'

Source: *TV Gospel Time* #57

Probably as last

Location: Chicago, Illinois. Saturdy 14 June 1969

Titles performed:
unknown

Source: *Jubilee Showcase* [prog #19–1]

Probably as last

Location: unknown {USA}. 1970s

Titles performed:
unknown

Source: *Look Up And Sing Out*

SWAN SILVERTONE SINGERS

Claude Jeter (vocal); John Myles, Louis Johnson, probably William Connor (vocals) accompaniment: probably Linwood Hargrove (electric guitar)–1;
as above, in the company of the Dixie Hummingbirds and the Gospel Harmonettes (vocal groups)–2

Location: Newport, Rhode Island. July 1966

Titles performed:
'Feed Me Jesus'–1
'Only Believe'–1
'Jesus Is The Key'–2

Source: *Alan Lomax film collection*

DOLORES SYKES

Vocal accompaniment: unknown

Location: Chicago, Illinois. Sunday 26 July 1964

Titles performed:
unknown

Source: *Jubilee Showcase* [prog #26–1]

ROOSEVELT SYKES

Vocal and piano

Location: unknown {USA}. 1940s

Titles performed:
unknown

Source: *Toast of The Coast* [unconfirmed]

Vocal and piano

Location: Brussels, Belgium. Early 1961

Titles performed:

'The Honeydripper'	K-Jazz 096, Yazoo 518
'Poor Me'	K-Jazz 096, Yazoo 518
'Night Time Is The Right Time'	K-Jazz 096, Yazoo 518
'Sweet Old Chicago'	K-Jazz 096, Yazoo 518
'Sykes Boogie'	K-Jazz 096, Yazoo 518
'Speculatin' Daddy'	K-Jazz 096, Yazoo 518
'On The Sunny Side Of The Street'	K-Jazz 096, Yazoo 518

Source: *Roosevelt Sykes*

Vocal and piano

Location: Baden-Baden, Germany, c. October 1965

Title performed:
'North Gulfport Boogie'

Source: *American Folk Blues Festival 1965*

Vocal and piano accompaniment: Otis Rush (electric guitar); Jack Meyers (electric bass); Fred Below (drums)

Location: Studio 6, Granada TV Centre, Manchester, England. Friday 30 September 1966

Titles performed:
[band theme and introductions]
'No Better Time Than Now'

Source: *Nothing But The Blues*

Probably as above

Location: Baden-Baden, Germany. c. October 1966

Title performed:
unknown

Source: *American Folk Blues Festival 1966*

Vocal and piano

Location: New Orleans, Louisiana. 1971

Titles performed:

'Running The Boogie' [A]	K-Jazz 020, Yazoo 506
'Driving Wheel' [A]	K-Jazz 020, Yazoo 506
'Sweet Home Chicago' [A]	K-Jazz 020, Yazoo 506
'I'm Going Away' [B]	

Source: *Out Of The Blacks, Into The Blues Part 1* [A]; *Le Blues Entre Les Dents* [B]

Vocal and piano–1; Vocal and guitar–2

Location: New Orleans, Louisiana. 1973

Titles performed:

'Night Time Is The Right Time'–1	Yazoo 513
'Hoochie Coochie Yes Mam'–1	Yazoo 513
'I Ain't Mad At You'–1	Yazoo 513
'A Woman Is In The Man'–1	Yazoo 513
'Blue Moon'–1	Yazoo 513
'Driving Wheel'–1	Yazoo 513
'Going Down Slow'–1	Yazoo 513
'The Man Is Crazy'–2	Yazoo 513
[interviews]	Yazoo 513

Source: *Roosevelt Sykes In New Orleans*

Vocal and piano accompaniment: Henry Townsend (electric guitar)

Location: St. Louis, Missouri. 1982

Titles performed:
unknown

Source: *KSDK-TV, Channel 5, St. Louis, Missouri*
A fragment of one performance from the above appears in *That's The Way I Do It.*

T

TAJ MAHAL (Henry St. Clair Fredericks)
Vocal and guitar

Location: New York City. Wednesday 11 December 1968

Title performed:

'Ain't That A Lot Of Love'	Arista 1003-3

Source: *Rolling Stones Rock And Roll Circus*

Vocal and guitar accompaniment, if any: unknown

Location: unknown {USA}. 1969

Titles performed:
unknown

Source: *Upbeat* [unconfirmed]

Vocal and guitar

Location: Germany. c.1970

Titles performed:
'Baby Don't You Wait'
'If A Man Gets Worried'

Source: *Beat Club*

Vocal and guitar

Location: unknown {USA}. 1970

Titles performed:
unknown

Source: *NET Playhouse; Thoughts Of The Artist On Leaving The Sixties*

Vocal and guitar accompaniment, if any:
unknown

Location: unknown {USA}. 1970

Titles performed:
unknown

Source: *The Show* [unconfirmed]

Vocal and guitar accompaniment: unknown

Location: unknown {USA}. 1971

Titles performed:
unknown

Source: *Clay Pigeon*. May be [ST] only.

Vocal and guitar accompaniment: unknown

Location: unknown {USA}. 1971

Titles performed:
unknown

Source: *Free Time*

Vocal and guitar accompaniment: unknown

Location: unknown {USA}. 1971

Titles performed:
unknown

Source: *Mark Of Jazz*

Vocal and guitar accompaniment: unknown

Location: unknown {USA}. 1971

Titles performed:
unknown

Source: *Sound Of The Seventies*

Vocal and guitar accompaniment: Red Callender (tuba)

Location: Los Angeles, California. 1972

Titles performed:
'Cake Walking Babies From Home'

Source: *The Flip Wilson Show*

Vocal and guitar accompaniment: unknown

Location: unknown {USA}. 1972

Titles performed:
unknown

Source: *Soul*

Vocal and guitar accompaniment: unknown

Location: unknown {USA}. 1972

Titles performed:
unknown

Source: *The Tilmon Tempo Show*

Vocal and guitar–1; banjo solo–2; harmonica solo–3

Location: unknown {USA}. 1972

Titles performed:
'Jesus Come By Here'–1 [ST only]
incedental music–2, 3 [ST only]

Source: *Sounder*
Taj Mahal also has a cameo role in this production.

Vocal and guitar accompaniment: unknown

Location: unknown {USA}. 1973

Titles performed:
unknown

Source: *Boarding House*

Vocal and guitar accompaniment: unknown

Location: unknown {USA}. 1974

Titles performed:
unknown

Source: *Fighting For Our Lives*

Vocal and guitar accompaniment: unknown

Location: unknown {USA}. 1975

Titles performed:
unknown

Source: *Play It Again Sam*

Vocal and guitar accompaniment: unknown

Location: unknown {USA}. 1976

Titles performed:
unknown

Source: *Apollo*

Vocal and guitar accompaniment: unknown

Location: unknown {USA}. 1976

Titles performed:
unknown

Source: *At The Top*

Vocal and guitar

Location: unknown {USA}. 1976

Title performed:
'Hangover Blues'

Source: *Scott Joplin*

Vocal and guitar accompaniment: unknown

Location: unknown {USA}. June–July 1976

Titles performed:
unknown

Source: *Dinah And Her New Best Friends*

Vocal and guitar accompaniment: unknown

Location: unknown {USA}. 1977

Titles performed:
unknown

Source: *Brothers*. May be [ST] only.

Vocal and guitar accompaniment: unknown

Location: unknown {USA}. 1977

Titles performed:
unknown

Source: *Me And Stella*

Vocal and guitar accompaniment: unknown

Location: New York City. 1977

Titles performed:
unknown

Source: *Saturday Night Live*

Vocal and guitar

Location: Melbourne, Australia. 1978

Titles performed:
'Candy Man'
'Statesboro Blues'
'Built For Comfort'
'Caldonia'
'Sweet Home Chicago'

Source: *Australian TV broadcast* [C]

Vocal and guitar

Location: Montreux, Switzerland. Summer 1978

Titles performed:
'Gonna Get Me Religion'
'Queen Bee'

Source: *Montreux Jazz*

Vocal and guitar

Location: unknown {USA}. 1979

Titles performed:
'Dust My Broom' K-Jazz 014
'Stagger Lee' K-Jazz 014

Source: *Bones*

Vocal and guitar accompaniment: unknown

Location: Ames, Iowa. 1979

Titles performed:
unknown

Source: *Maintenance Shop Blues*

Vocal and piano

Location: Atlanta, Georgia. October 1984

Title performed:
'Statesboro Blues'

Source: *National Down Home Blues Festival*

Vocal and guitar accompaninment: unknown

Location: Germany. c.1985

Titles performed:
'Come On In My Kitchen'
'Baby, You're My Destiny'
'Kanui Kalypso'

Source: *Ohne Filter*

Vocal and guitar accompaniment: unknown

Location: Ronnie Scott's club, London, England. 1988

Titles performed:
'My Country Sugar Mama'
'Move Up To The Country'
'Stagger Lee'
'Come On In My Kitchen'
'Loco Motion'
'Soothin'
'Goin' Fishin''
'Statesboro' Blues'

Source: *Live at Ronnie Scott's*

Vocal and guitar

Location: unknown {USA}. September 1988.

Title performed:
'Bourgeois Blues'

Source: *All Star Tribute To Leadbelly And Woody Guthrie*

Speech

Location: probably New York City. 1990

monologues on the careers of:

Gary Davis	Yazoo 501
Lightnin' Hopkins	Yazoo 502
Son House	Yazoo 500
Mance Lipscomb	Yazoo 502
Sonny Terry	Yazoo 501
Bukka White	Yazoo 500

Source: *Shanachie Entertainment.* These monologues were recorded especially to introduce performances by the above artists. The material all originates from the archives of the Seattle Folklore Society and details will be found under the relevant artist entries.

Vocal and guitar

Location: Austin, Texas. 1993

Titles performed:
'Mailbox Blues'
'Queen Bee'
'Blues With A Feeling'
'Fishin' Blues'
'Freight Train'

Source: *Austin City Limits*
Taj Mahal also appears in *Blues Brothers 2000.*

TARHEEL SLIM (Alden Bunn)

Vocal accompaniment: unknown

Location: New York City. Early 1950s

Titles performed:
unknown

Source: *Arthur Godfrey Talent Scouts* [unconfirmed]

CHARLES HENRY [BABY] TATE

Vocal and guitar–1
Guitar solo–2

Location: Spartanburg, North Carolina. July 1962

Titles performed:
'If I Could Holler Like A Mountain Jack'–1
'When I First Started To Hoboing'–1
'Bad Blues'–2

Source: *The Blues* [1]

CHARLES TAYLOR

Vocal accompaniment: unknown (male vocal trio and piano)

Location: New York City. Saturday 15 December 1962

Titles performed:
'The Bells'
'He's My Rock, My Shield'
'Jesus, I'll Never Forget You'

Source: *TV Gospel Time* #18

Vocal accompaniment: unknown

Location: New York City. 1966

Title performed:
unknown

Source: *TV Gospel Time* #66

EDDIE TAYLOR

Vocal and electric guitar accompaniment: Walter Horton (harmonica); T-Bone Walker (piano); Jerome Arnold (electric bass); J C Lewis (drums)

Location: BBC TV studios, White City, London, England. Tuesday 22 October 1968

Titles performed:
'Big Town Playboy'

Source: *American Folk Blues Festival 1968* [1]

Probably as above

Location: Germany. c. November 1968

Titles performed:
unknown

Source: *American Folk Blues Festival 1968* [2]

Vocal and electric guitar accompaniment: Sunnyland Slim (piano); Hubert Sumlin (second electric guitar); Bob Stroger (electric bass); Odie Payne (drums)

Location: Germany. 1980

Titles performed:
unknown

Source: *American Folk Blues Festival 1980*

EVA TAYLOR

Vocal accompaniment: unknown

Location: unknown {USA}. 1967

Titles performed:
unknown

Source: *Joe Franklin Show*

HOUND DOG TAYLOR

See Theodore Roosevelt (Hound Dog) Taylor.

KOKO TAYLOR (Cora Taylor, née Walton)

Despite claims in some published sources that this artist appeared in the 1966 TV programme *The Beat*, no evidence can be found to support this.

Vocal accompaniment: unknown

Location: Chicago, Illinois. 1970

Titles performed:
unknown

Source: *The Blues Is Alive And Well In Chicago*

Vocal accompaniment: unknown, probably including Mighty Joe Young (electric guitar)

Location: Chicago, Ilinois. April–May 1970

Titles performed:
unknown

Source: *Chicago Blues*. Not used in the final edit.

Vocal accompaniment: unknown (electric guitar, piano, electric bass, drums)

Location: Sweden. 1970

Titles performed:
'Got My Mojo Working'
'Please Don't Dog Me Around'
'Kansas City'
'Sweet Home Chicago'
'I Got What It Takes'

Source: *Swedish TV broadcast* [C]

Vocal duet with Muddy Waters accompaniment: Lafayette Leake (piano); Louis Myers (electric guitar); David Myers (electric bass); Fred Below (drums)

Location: Montreux, Switzerland. Sunday 17 June 1972

Titles performed:
'I Got What It Takes'
and other, unknown, solo titles by Taylor

Source: *Montreux Jazz*

Vocal accompaniment: Willie Dixon (vocal and bass) and others, unknown

Location: Chicago, Illinois. Thursday 18 July 1974

Titles performed:
'Wang Dang Doodle'

Source: *Soundstage*

Vocal accompaniment: The Blues Machine [G]

Location: Montreux, Switzerland. July 1978 or July 1979

Titles performed:
'Please Don't Dog Me'
'Hey Bartender'

Source: *Montreux Jazz*

Vocal accompaniment: unknown

Location: Ames, Iowa. 1979

Titles performed:
unknown

Source: *Maintenance Shop Blues*

Vocal accompaniment: unknown

Location: Montreux, Switzerland. 1981

Titles performed:
'Let The Good Times Roll'
'I'm A Woman'
'Twenty Nine Ways'
'Baby Please Don't Go'

Source: *Montreux Jazz*

Vocal accompaniment: unknown

Location: Chicago, Illinois. 1983

Titles performed:
unknown

Source: *Sweet Home Chicago* [1]

Speech

Location: Chicago, Illinois. 1989

[interview]

Source: *Wild Women Don't Have The Blues*

Vocal accompaniment: Buddy Guy (electric guitar); Willie Dixon (bass) and others, unknown

Location: Chicago, Illinois. Monday 1 January 1990

Titles performed:
'Beer Bottle Boogie'
'Fishing Trip'
'Hey Baby'
'I'd Rather Go Blind'
'I'm A Woman'
'Let The Good Times Roll'
'Wang Dang Doodle'

Source: *Soundstage*

Vocal accompaniment: unknown (two electric guitars, keyboards, electric bass, drums)
As above, in duet with Willie Dixon, accompaniment: Buddy Guy (electric guitar)–1

Location: Legends nightclub, Chicago, Illinois. 1990

Titles performed:

'Let The Good Times Roll'	MPI 6243
'Fishin' Trip'	MPI 6243
'Beer Bottle Boogie'	MPI 6243
'I'm A Woman'	MPI 6243
'I'd Rather Go Blind'	MPI 6243
'Hey Baby'	MPI 6243
'Jump For Joy'	MPI 6243
'Wang Dang Doodle'–1	MPI 6243
[interviews]	MPI 6243

Source: *Queen Of The Blues*

Vocal accompaniment: unknown

Location: Chicago, Illinois. 1991

Titles performed:
unknown

Source: *Blues And The Alligator*

Vocal accompaniment: The Blues Machine: James Johnson (electric guitar); Eddie King (tenor saxophone); Jim Doren (keyboards); Jerry Murphy (electric bass); Frank Alexander (drums)–1;
as above, in duet with Lonnie Brooks (vocal and electric guitar)–2;
as above, in jam session with Li'l Ed (vocal and electric guitar); Elvin Bishop (vocal and electric guitar); Katie Webster (vocal)–3

Location: Chestnut Cabaret, Philadelphia, Pennsylvania. Thursday 12 March 1992

Titles performed:

'I'd Rather Go Blind'–1	BMG 80046-3
'It's A Dirty Job'–2	BMG 80046-3
'Sweet Home Chicago'–3	BMG 80046-3
[interview]	BMG 80046-3

Source: *Pride And Joy – The Story Of Alligator Records*

Speech

Location: Chicago, Illinois. 1993

[interview]	MCA V10944

Source: *Sweet Home Chicago* [2]

Vocal accompaniment: G E Smith's band

Location: Washington, DC. Saturday 11 October 1997

Title performed:
'Long Distance Call'

Source: *Tribute To Muddy Waters*
Taylor is also reported to have appeared on Brazilian television.

REVEREND L O TAYLOR

Reverend Taylor was a Memphis-based Baptist minister who, during the 1930s and 1940s, made many hundreds of hours of amateur film of his family, friends, congregation, church, neighbourhood, trips out of the city, baptismal scenes, etc.

He also made seperate sound recordings using a direct-disc machine. Some of this material has been edited together by director Lynn Sachs to make the film *Sermons And Sacred Pictures.* Much more is still unused. [Available from Historic.]

THEODORE ROOSEVELT [HOUND DOG] TAYLOR

Vocal and electric guitar accompaniment: probably Brewer Phillips (electric bass); Ted Harvey (drums)

Location: Ann Arbor Blues Festival, Ann Arbor, Michigan. Summer 1972

Titles performed:
unknown

Source: *unknown*. Used in *Blues And The Alligator*

Vocal and electric guitar accompaniment: probably Brewer Phillips (electric bass); Ted Harvey (drums)

Location: Australia. February/March 1975

Titles performed:
unknown

Source: *Australian TV broadcast* [C]
Taylor can also be seen briefly in the film *Chicago Blues* (1970, Harley Cokliss) but he does not perform.

TEARS OF MUSIC
Vocal group accompaniment unknown

Location: New York City. Sunday 25 November 1962

Titles performed:
'Brother Afar'
'Tramping'
'No Hiding Place'

Source: *TV Gospel Time* #3

As above

Location: New York City. Sunday 10 February 1963

Titles performed:
'In The Word Of God'
'Going To Need The Lord'

Source: *TV Gospel Time* #14

TEMPLE RADIO COMBINED CHOIRS
Large mixed vocal choir, accompaniment: unknown
Soloist: Reverend Eugene W Ward–1

Location: probably New York City. April 1965

Titles performed:
'Stand By Me'–1
'It Is Well'
'Wonderful Jesus'

Source: *TV Gospel Time* #41

SONNY TERRY (Saunders Terrell)
Vocal and harmonica accompaniment: J C Burris (bones)–1
Terry and Burris, step dancing and body slapping–2

Location: either New York City or the Pete Seeger residence, New York. 1958

Titles performed:
'Crazy 'bout You Baby–1' Vestapol 13042, 13057
'Buck Dance'–2 Vestapol 13042, 13057
'Hand Jive'–2 Vestapol 13042, 13057

Source: *Pete Seeger film collection*

Vocal and harmonica

Location: Oakland, California. 1969

Titles performed:
'Shoutin' The Blues' Vestapol 13057
[monologue leading to;]
'My Baby Done Changed The Lock' Vestapol 13057
[monologue on the perils of infidelity]
[monologue leading to;]
'Sweet Woman Blues' Vestapol 13057
'Talking Harmonica Blues'

Source: *Shoutin' The Blues*

Vocal and harmonica

Location: KCTS-TV studios, Seattle, Washington. 1971

Titles performed:
[monologue leading to;]
'Easy Rider' Yazoo 501
[monologue leading to;]
'Beautiful City' Yazoo 501
[monologue leading to;]
'I Got My Eye On You' Yazoo 501
[monologue leading to;]
'Somebody Changed The Lock On My Door' Yazoo 501
[monologue leading to;]
'Hooting The Blues' Yazoo 501

Source: *Masters Of American Traditional Music*

Vocal and harmonica

Location: unknown {USA}. 1971

Title performed:
'Somebody Changed The Lock On My Door' K-Jazz 020, Yazoo 506

Source: *Out Of The Blacks, Into The Blues part 2*

Vocal and harmonica

Location: unknown {USA}. 1972

Titles performed:
unknown

Source: *Playing That Thing* [unconfirmed]

Vocal and harmonica

Location: unknown {USA}. 1972

Title performed:
'Wailin' and Whoopin'' [ST only]

Source: *Cisco Pike*

Vocal and harmonica

Location: Chicago, Illinois. Tuesday 14 December 1976

Titles performed:
'My Woman Chained The Door' [*sic*] [probably; 'Somebody Changed The Lock On My Door']
'Whoopin' The Blues'

Source: *Soundstage*

Vocal and harmonica accompaniment: unknown (guitar)

Location: Atlanta, Georgia. October 1984

Title performed:
'Rock Me Baby'

Source: *National Down Home Blues Festival*

Harmonica solos

Location: unknown {USA}. 1986

Titles performed:
Main theme
incidental music

Source: *Crossroads*
Terry also supplied some soundtrack material to the film *Woody Guthrie – Hard Travelin'* and appeared in it. See also Brownie McGhee.

SONNY BOY TERRY AND KINNY ADAIR
Vocal accompaniment: unknown

Location: Houston, Texas. Friday [*sic*] 8 October 1993

Titles performed:
'Wigs And Pig's Feet'
'Green Hair On Her Legs'

Source: *Saturday Night At Rockefellers*

TEXAS GUITAR SLIM
Vocal and electric guitar accompaninent: Clarence Green and the Rhythmaires

Location: Houston, Texas. Friday [*sic*] 8 October 1993

Titles performed:
'The Blues Is Alright'
'Things I Used To Do'

Source: *Saturday Night At Rockefellers*

[SISTER] ROSETTA THARPE (née Rosetta Nubin)
Vocal accompaniment: Lucky Millinder and his orchestra: William 'Chiefy' Scott, Archie Johnson, Nelson Bryant (trumpets); George Stevenson, Floyd Brady, Edward Morant (trombones); Ted Barnett, George James (alto saxophones); Stafford 'Pazzuza' Simon (tenor saxohone); Ernest Purce (baritone saxophone); Bill Doggett (piano); Abe Bolard (bass); Trevor Bacon (guitar); Panama Francis (drums) Lucky Millinder (director, vocal–1); members of the band (vocal chorus–2, clapping–3)

Location: New York City. Week of 22 August 1941

Titles performed:
[3608] 'Four Or Five Times'–2, –3
Storyville SV6000,
Virgin VVD865,
[3701] 'Shout Sister Shout'–1, –2, –3
Storyville SV6000,
Virgin VVD865,

[4106] 'That Lonesome Road'–3
Jazz Classics JCVC110,
Storyville SV6003,
View Video 1313,
Virgin VVD868

Source: *Soundies*
The above date is for the studio soundtrack recordings. The film to which these titles were mimed was made on 3 and 4 September 1941, and there remains a possibilty that some of the personnel may have altered between the two sessions.

Vocal accompaniment: unknown

Location: New York City. 1952–1956

Titles performed:
unknown

Source: *The Jackie Gleason Show*

Vocal and electric guitar accompaniment: unknown

Location: London, England. Friday 15 November 1957

Title performed:
unknown

Source: *Six-Five Special*

Vocal and electric guitar accompaniment: Chris Barber's Jazz Band; Barber (trombone); probably Pat Halcox (trumpet); Monty Sunshine (clarinet); Eddie Smith (banjo); Dick Smith (bass); Graham Burbidge (drums)

Location: Manchester, England. Thursday 19 December 1957

Titles performed:
'Joshua Fit The Battle'
'Peace In The Valley'
'Up Above My Head'

Source: *Chelsea At Nine*

Vocal and electric guitar accompaniment: Otis Spann (piano); Ransom Knowling (bass); Willie Smith (drums)–1;
as above, with Muddy Waters, Cousin Joe Pleasants, Brownie McGhee and Sonny Terry, (vocals)–2

Location: Alexandra Park railway station, Chorlton-cum-Hardy, Manchester. May 1964

Titles performed:
'Didn't It Rain'–1
[monologue leading to;]
'Trouble In Mind'–1
'Whole World In His Hands'–2

Source: *The Blues And Gospel Train*

Vocal and electric guitar accompaniment: unknown

Location: Studio 6, Granada TV Centre, Manchester, England. Monday 16 November 1964

Titles performed:
unknown

Source: *unbroadcast and untitled show made for Granada TV by Philip Casson and John Hamp.*
See also Sonny Boy Williamson.

Vocal and electric guitar accompaniment: the St. Timothy male voice choir–1
Vocal and electric guitar accompaniment: Deloris Barrett Campbell (vocal); Alfred Miller (piano)–2
Speech only–3

Location: probably Chicago, Illinois. 1965

Titles performed:
'Down By The Riverside'–1 [A]
'God Has Done So Much For Me'–1 [B]
'In The Garden'–2 [A]
'Up Above My Head'–1 [B]
'Feenamint' laxative chewing gum advert–3 [A]
'Artria' Skin Tone Cream advert–3 [B]

Source: *TV Gospel Time* #43 [A], #44 [B]
Artria and Feenamint were the commercial sponsors for *TV Gospel Time*.

Vocal and electric guitar

Location: New York City. Spring 1969

Titles performed:
'That's All'
'Go Ahead'
'I Shall Not Be Moved'

Source: *L'Aventure Du Jazz*

Vocal and electric guitar accompaniment: probably Lee Jackson (second electric guitar); Lafayette Leake (piano); Willie Dixon (bass); Clifton James (drums)

Location: Baden-Baden, Germany. c. May 1970

Titles performed:
'That's All'
'Didn't It Rain'

Source: *American Folk Blues Festival 1970*

CHRIS THOMAS

Vocal and electric guitar accompaniment: unknown (electric bass and drums)

Location: Baton Rouge, Louisiana. 1984

Title performed:
'Stormy Monday Blues'
[interview]

Source: *Baton Rouge Blues*

EDDIE THOMAS AND CARL SCOTT

Thomas, vocal, washboard, kazoo and coffee-pot accompaniment: Scott (ukelele)

Location: Richmond, Virginia. Wednesday 21 November 1928

Titles performed:

'Tomorrow'	Yazoo 512
'My Ohio Home'	Yazoo 512

Source: *Fox Movietone newsreel*
Thomas employs the coffee-pot as amplification for his kazoo, inserting the instrument into the spout and then using the pot lid to alter the tone.

ERNEST [TABBY] THOMAS

Vocal and electric guitar accompaniment: unknown (second electric guitar, electric bass, drums)

Location: Baton Rouge, Louisiana. 1984

Titles performed:
'Next Time You See Me'
'Hoochie Coochie Man'
'Ain't That Loving You Baby'
'Crawling Kingsnake'
'Hoodoo Working'

Source: *Baton Rouge Blues*

IRMA THOMAS

Vocal accompaniment: unknown

Location: Germany. Mid-1980s

Titles performed:
'New Rules'
'I Needed Somebody'

Source: *Ohne Filter*

Vocal accompaniment: unknown

Location: Toulouse Theatre, New Orleans, Louisiana. 1988

Titles performed:
'Ruler Of My Heart'
'Breakaway'
'Time Is On My Side'
'Done Got Over It'

Source: *Big Easy Music*

Vocal accompaniment: unknown

Location: New Orleans, Louisiana. 1990

Title performed:
'Old Records'

Source: *New Orleans Jazz And Heritage Festival 1990*

Vocal accompaniment: unknown (two tenor saxophones, trumpet, keyboards, electric guitar, electric bass, drums)

Location: New Orleans, Louisiana. 1994

Title performed:
'Smoke Filled Room' BMG un-numbered

Source: *True Believers – The Musical Family Of Rounder Records*

[REVEREND] ISAAC THOMAS
Vocal accompaniment: unknown

Location: Mississippi. 1977

Titles performed:
unknown CFSC 1219

Source: T*wo Black Churches*

JAMES [JUNIOR] THOMAS
Glass bottle solo–1
Glass bottle accompaniment: unknown (second glass bottle, spoons)–2

Location: North Carolina. 1988

Titles performed:
untitled instrumental–1
untitled instrumental–2
[interview]

Source: *Step It Up And Go*
The glass bottle is played by blowing across the top of the bottle's open mouth with pursed lips. The tone is controlled by the level of water in the bottle. The spoons are played in the traditional percussive manner.

JAMES [SON] THOMAS (aka Sonny Ford)
Vocal and electric guitar–1
Vocal and guitar–2
Guitar solo accompanying unknown male (step-dancing)–3
Vocal and guitar accompanying unknown male (harmonica)–4
Vocal and electric guitar accompaniment: unknown (electric bass and drums)–5

Location: Leland, Mississippi. 1969

Titles performed:
'61 Highway'–1 CFSC 1219
'Rock Me Mama'–2 CFSC 1219
untitled instrumental–3 CFSC 1219
'Bluebird Blues'–4 CFSC 1219
'Dust My Broom'–5 CFSC 1219

Source: *Sonny Ford, Delta Artist*
See also unknown artists.

Vocal and guitar

Location: probably Mississippi. 1972

Titles performed:
unknown CFSC 1056

Source: *Mississippi Delta Blues* [2]

Vocal and guitar

Location: probably Mississippi. 1973

Titles performed:
unknown

Source: *CBS News*

Vocal and guitar

Location: Mississippi. 1974

Titles performed:
unknown CFSC 1136

Source: *Mississippi Delta Blues* [3]

Vocal and guitar–1
Vocal and electric guitar accompaniment: Shelby 'Papa Jazz' Brown (second electric guitar)–2
Vocal and electric guitar accompaniment: Shelby 'Papa Jazz' Brown (second electric guitar) and Cleveland 'Broom Man' Jones (broomhandle percussion)–3

Location: Juke joint, Leland, Mississippi. 1975

Titles performed:
'61 Highway' [ST]–1 CFSC 1077
'I Wanna Ramble'–2 CFSC 1077
'Rock Me Baby'–1 CFSC 1077
'61 Highway'–3 CFSC 1077

Source: *Give My Poor Heart Ease*

Vocal and guitar

Location: New York City. 1976

Titles performed:
unknown

Source: *The Today Show*

Vocal and guitar

Location: Sweden. 1981

Titles performed:
'Worried Man Blues'
'Hoochie Coochie Man'
'Catfish Blues'

Source: *Swedish TV broadcast* [C]

Vocal and guitar

Location: Leland, Mississippi. 1984

Titles performed:

'Bumble Bee Blues'	Arrow AV015
'Beefsteak Blues'	Arrow AV015
'Cairo Blues'	Arrow AV015
'Big Fat Mama'	Arrow AV015

Source: *Saturday Blues*

Vocal and guitar

Location: Atlanta, Georgia. October 1984

Title performed:
'Rollin' And Tumblin''

Source: *National Downhome Blues Festival*

JESSIE MAE THOMAS

Vocal accompaniment: unknown

Location: New York City. 1965–66

Titles performed:
unknown

Source: *TV Gospel Time* #64

JIMMY THOMAS

Vocal accompaniment: Ike Turner's Kings of Rhythm: Ike Turner (electric guitar); Carlson Oliver (tenor saxophone); Erskine Ogelsby (baritone saxophone); Jesse Knight (electric bass); John 'Booty-Lip' Wings (drums)

Location: St.Louis, Missouri. 1958

Title performed:
'Splish Splash'

Source: *George Edick's Showtime*

Vocal accompaniment: Ike Turner's Kings of Rhythm; Ike Turner (electric guitar); Ernest Lane (piano); Herb Sadler (second electric guitar); Sam Rhodes (electric bass); James 'Nose' Norwood (drums)

Location: Civic Auditorium, Santa Monica, California. 1964

Title performed:
[short vocal contribution followed by dancing]

Source: *The TAMI Show*
See also Tommy Hodge and Ike Turner.

RAYMOND THOMAS

Vocal accompaniment: unknown

Location: Mississippi. 1984

Titles performed:
unknown

Source: *In The Delta of Mississippi*

RUFUS THOMAS

Probably miming to Stax 130

Location: London, England. Friday 3 or 11 December 1964

Title performed:
'Walkin' The Dog'

Source: *Ready Steady Go*

Vocal accompaniment: unknown

Location: London, England. Monday 14 December 1964

Title performed;
'Walkin' The Dog'
'Jump Back'

Source: *Beat Room*

Vocal accompaniment: unknown

Location: Philadelphia, Pennsylvania. 1965

Titles performed:
unknown

Source: *Dick Clark's American Bandstand*

Vocal accompaniment: unknown

Location: unknown {USA}. 1968

Titles performed:
unknown

Source: *Shade of Soul*

Vocal accompaniment: unknown

Location: Memphis, Tennessee. 1969

Titles performed:
unknown

Source: *Sounds Of Summer: Memphis Blues Festival*

Vocal accompaniment: unknown

Location: unknown {USA}. 1971

Titles performed:
unknown

Source: *Soul*

Vocal accompaniment: unknown

Location: Coliseum Stadium, Los Angeles, California. Sunday 20 August 1972

Titles performed:
'Funky Chicken'

Source: *Wattstax*

Vocal accompaniment: unknown

Location: unknown {USA}. 1973

Titles performed:
unknown

Source: *Black Omnibus*

Vocal accompaniment: unknown

Location: London, England. 1974

Titles performed:
unknown

Source: *In Concert* [2]

Speech

Location: Memphis, Tennessee. 1978

[interview]

Source: *Beale Street*

Speech

Location: Memphis, Tennessee. 1989

[dramatic role]

Source: *Mystery Train*

Vocal accompaniment: unknown (tenor saxophone, electric guitar, piano, electric bass, drums)–1
As above, in duet with Gatemouth Moore–2
Vocal, unaccompanied–3

Location: Memphis, Tennessee. c. 1994
[A] On stage in an unnamed nightclub
[B] in radio station WDIA's broadcasting studio

Titles performed:
'Woman, You Gotta Go'–1 [A] California Newsreel 01, Multicultural Media 1008
'Did You Ever Love A Woman'–2 [A] California Newsreel 01, Multicultural Media 1008
'Happy Birthday To You'–3 [B] California Newsreel 01, Multicultural Media 1008
[interview] California Newsreel 01, Multicultural Media 1008

Source: *Saturday Night, Sunday Morning*

Speech
Location: Memphis, Tennessee. 1995

[iinterview]

Source: *Rock And Roll Part 1*

WILLIE THOMAS

Vocal and guitar accompaniment: James 'Butch' Cage (vocal and violin)

Location: Newport, Rhode Island. Sunday 3 July 1960

Titles performed:
'44 Blues'
untitled instrumental duet
'Take The Children Out Of Pharoh's Land'

Source: *Jazz-USA*
See also Muddy Waters.

Vocal and guitar accompaniment: James 'Butch' Cage (violin)–1;
guitar accompaniment to his grandson, (vocal), accompaniment: Cage (violin)–2;
speech–3

Location: Zachary, Louisiana. Sunday, 7 August 1960

Titles performed:

'Prisoner's Song'–1 [ST]	K-Jazz 014, Rhapsody 8022
'Kill That Nigger Dead'–1 [ST]	K-Jazz 014, Rhapsody 8022
'Rooster Blues'–2 [ST]	K-Jazz 014, Rhapsody 8022
monologue–3ST	K-Jazz 014, Rhapsody 8022

Source: *Blues Like Showers Of Rain*

Thomas, vocal and guitar;
as above, accompaniment: Martha Thomas (percussion)–1

Location: Zachary, Louisiana. Spring 1963

Titles performed:
'Love Like A River' [part only]
'Wreck Of The Old '97'–1 [part only]

Source: *Die Blues*

Thomas, vocal and guitar accompaniment: Cage (vocal and violin)

Location: unknown {USA}. 1963

Titles performed:
unknown

Source: *Lyrics And Legends: The Blues*

Thomas, vocal and guitar accompaniment: Cage (vocal and violin)

Location: unknown {USA}. 1976

Titles performed:
unknown

Source: *People's Music ... And All That Jazz*
See also James [Butch] Cage.

THOMPSON COMMUNITY SINGERS

Mixed vocal choir accompaniment: unknown
Soloist: Loretta Oliver–1

Location: Chicago, Illinois. Saturday 10 October 1964

Titles performed:
'I Don't Mind'
'In My Father's House'
'Joy Will Come On The Morning'–1

Source: *TV Gospel Time* #37

As above

Location: Chicago, Illinois

The following performances are known:
1966
Friday 13 May [prog #34–2]
1969
Saturday 5 July [prog #12–2]
1974
Sunday 14 July [prog #6–1]

Titles performed:
unknown

Source: *Jubilee Showcase*

THOMPSON FAMILY

Odell Thompson (banjo); Joe Thompson (violin)

Location: Orange County, North Carolina. 1983–85

Titles performed:

'Goin' Down Town' [part only]	Vestapol 13079
untitled instrumental [part only]	Vestapol 13079
[interview]	

Source: *Appalachian Journey*

Odell Thompson (banjo); Joe Thompson (violin); Nate Thompson (guitar)

Location:. Orange County, North Carolina. 1988

Titles performed:
untitled instrumental breakdown [part only]
untitled instrumental square dance [part only]

Source: *Step It Up And Go*

WILLIE MAE [BIG MAMA] THORNTON
Vocal accompaniment: Buddy Guy (electric guitar); Eddie Boyd (piano); Jimmy Lee Robinson (electric bass); Fred Below (drums)

Location: Baden-Baden, Germany. October 1965

Titles performed:
[introduction by Buddy Guy;]
'Hound Dog'

Source: *American Folk Blues Festival 1965*

Vocal accompaniment: unknown

Location: unknown {USA}. 1969

Titles performed:
unknown

Source: *Della*

Vocal accompaniment: unknown–1; Pete Seeger (vocal and banjo)–2; Brownie McGhee (vocal and guitar); Sonny Terry (vocal and harmonica)–3

Location: Newport, Rhode Island. July 1969

Titles performed:
'Lord, Lord, Lord'–1
'Walk Through The Valley'–2
'Rock Island Line'–3

Source: *Folklife Productions*

Vocal accompaniment: unknown

Location: unknown {USA}. 1969

Titles performed:
unknown

Source: *Black, White And Blues*

Vocal accompaniment: unknown

Location: unknown {USA}. 1970

Titles performed:
unknown

Source: *Rock 1* [unconfirmed]

Vocal accompaniment: unknown

Location: New York City. 1971

Titles performed:
unknown

Source: *The Dick Cavett Show*

Vocal accompaniment: unknown [G]

Location: probably Los Angeles, California. 1971

Title performed:
'Sing Out For Jesus' [ST only]

Source: *Vanishing Point*

Vocal accompaniment: unknown

Location: unknown {USA}. 1974

Titles performed:
unknown

Source: *The Midnight Special*

Vocal accompaniment: unknown

Location: Belly Up Tavern, San Diego, California 1983

Titles performed:
'It's Alright'
'Why Do Everything Happen To Me'
'Hound Dog'
'Walkin' The Dog'

Source: *Three Generations Of The Blues part 1*

Vocal accompaniment: probably Joe Liggins' Honeydrippers

Location: Los Angeles, California. 1984

Titles performed:
'Early One Morning'
'Ball And Chain'
'Hound Dog'

Source: *Legends Of Rhythm And Blues*

THREE FLAMES

Tiger Haynes (vocal and guitar); Roy Testemark (piano); Bill Pollard (bass)

Location: probably New York City. Monday 13 June to Saturday 20 August 1949

Titles performed:
[probably] 'Open The Door Richard'
and others, unknown

Source: *The Three Flames Show*

THREE GOSPEL PROFESSORS

Vocal trio accompaniment: unknown (piano)

Location: New York City. Sunday 23 December 1962

Titles performed:
'Go Tell It On The Mountain'
'If It Wasn't For The Lord'

Source: *TV Gospel Time* #9

As above–1;
as above with Ernestine Washington (vocal)–2

Location: Baltimore, Maryland. Saturday 16 February 1963

Titles performed:
'How Did You Feel?'–1
'I Know It Was The Hand Of The Lord'–1
'Breathe On Me'–2

Source: *TV Gospel Time* #27

THREE PEPPERS

Vocal trio accompaniment: the Lennox Trio (presumably piano, bass, drums)

Location: unknown {USA}. 1945

Titles performed:
[89408] 'Take Everything'
[20M2] 'Rhythm Sam'

Source: *Soundies*
89408 copyrighted 23 April 1945; 20M2 17 June 1946.

CAMPBELL [SKEETS] TOLBERT AND HIS ORCHESTRA

Probably Robert Hicks (trumpet); Skeets Tolbert (alto saxophone and vocal–1); probably Otis Hicks (tenor saxophone); unknown (piano, bass, drums); Lupe Castel (vocal)–2; ensemble vocal–3

Location: New York City. Late 1944

Titles performed:

[9M1] 'Blitzkrieg Bombadier'–1, –3	Charly #5
[9M2] 'Corn Pone'–2	Charly #5
[12M1] 'Tis You Baby'–1	Charly #5
[89608] 'No No Baby'–1	Charly #5

Source: *Soundies*
9M1 registered 31 December 1944; 9M2, 16 March 1945; 12M1, 10 September 1945 89608, 16 July 1945.

The two Hicks brothers noted here are in no way connected with either Barbecue Bob or Lightnin' Slim, whose real names were respectively Robert Hicks and Otis Hicks,

[REVEREND] MARSHALL TOMKIN

Vocal accompaniment: church congregation

Location: unnamed Baptist church, rural Alabama. 1964

Title performed:
Lining out hymn

Source: *Nothin' But A Man*

RUDOLPH [RUDY] TOOMBS

Vocal and piano or piano only accompaniment, if any: unknown.

Location: probably New York City. 1946

Titles performed:
unknown [possibly 'Rockaway' and/or 'The Rent Party']

Source: *House Rent Party*

ALLEN TOUSSAINT

Vocal and piano–1
Vocal and piano accompaniment Dr. John (piano)–2

Location: Chicago, Illinois. Sunday 7 November 1982

Titles performed:
'What You Want The Girl To Do'–1
'With You In Mind'–1
'Amazing Grace'–2

Source: *Soundstage*

Vocal and piano, in the company of Professor Longhair and Tuts Washington (pianos)

Location: New Orleans, Lousiana. Late 1979

Titles performed:
unknown K-Jazz 084

Source: *Piano Players Rarely Ever Play Together*

HENRY TOWNSEND

Speech

Location: St. Louis, Missouri. Summer 1960

monologue [ST] K-Jazz 014, Rhapsody 8022

Source: *Blues Like Showers Of Rain*

Vocal and guitar–1 : Vocal and piano–2

Location: St.Louis, Missouri. Friday 23 January 1976

Titles performed:
'Tears Came Rolling Down' [fragment only] [A]– 1
'Wave My Hands Bye Bye' [B]–2
[interview]

Source: *The Devil's Music series 1* [A]; *series 2* [B]

Vocal and guitar accompaniment: Robert Lockwood (electric guitar)

Location: New Orleans, Louisiana. 1984

Title performed:
'Biddle Street Blues' [part only]

Source: *That's The Way I Do It*

Vocal and steel guitar–1; vocal and piano–2; vocal and guitar–3; vocal duet with Vernell Townsend–4

Location: St. Louis, Missouri. 1986

Titles performed:
'All I Got Is Gone'–1
'All My Money Gone' [part only]–2
'That's All Right Baby'–2
'You Never Find Another Love'
'Like Me' [part only]–4
'Lonesome Road'–1
'Cairo Blues'–1 Vestapol 13003
'Tears Came Rolling Down' [part only]–1
'Tears Came Rolling Down' [part only]–4
'Blow My Blues Away'–2
[interviews]

Source: *That's The Way I Do It*
See also Roosevelt Sykes.

TRENIERS

Vocal group accompaniment: unknown

Location: probably Los Angeles, California. c.1953–55

Titles performed:
'Rag Mop' Parkfield MJK0007, Proserpine 611
'It's Rock And Roll, It's Swing' Parkfield MJK0007, Proserpine 666

Source: *unknown*

Vocal group accompaniment: unknown orchestra

Location: Hollywood, California. 1957

Title performed:
'Rockin' Is Our Business'

Source: *The Girl Can't Help It*

Vocal group accompaniment: unknown orchestra

Location: probably Hollywood, California. 1957

Titles performed:
'Calypso Joe'
'Day Old Bread And Canned Beans'

Source: *Calypso Heatwave*

Vocal group accompaniment: unknown

Location: New York City. c.1957–58

Titles performed:
unknown

Source: *The Steve Allen Show*

Vocal group accompaniment: unknown orchestra

Location: probably Hollywood, California. 1958

Title performed:
'Get Out Of The Car'

Source: *Juke Box Rhythm*

TRINITY BAPTIST CHURCH RADIO CHOIR

Mixed vocal choir accompaniment: unknown

Location: New York City. 1966

Titles performed:
unknown

Source: *TV Gospel Time* #58

TRUMPETEERS

Probably Raleigh Turnage, Carey Bradley, Joseph E Johnson, Calvin Stewart, Roland Allen (vocals) accompaniment: unknown

Location: probably Baltimore, Maryland. c. 1966

Title performed:
unknown

Source: *TV Gospel Time* #54

EMMA TUCKER

Vocal accompaniment: unknown

Location: New York City. c. 1966

Title performed:
unknown

Source: *TV Gospel Time* #59

IRA TUCKER

Vocal accompaniment: unknown

Location: Chicago, Illinois. Sunday 14 June 1964

Titles performed:
unknown

Source: *Jubilee Showcase* [prog #10–2]

Speech

Location: Chicago, Illinois. August 1995

[interview]

Source: *Too Close To Heaven*
See also The Dixie Hummingbirds.

J R TUCKER AND GROUP (track lining gang)

Tucker, lead vocal accompaniment: seven male singers including Wilbert Puckett and George Johnson

Location: Mississippi. Between 11 August and 9 September 1978

Titles performed:
three untitled track lining songs
[interview with Tucker, Johnson and Puckett]
Vestapol 13078

Source: *Land Where The Blues Began*
See also unidentified artists [B] #4.

TOMMY TUCKER (Robert Higginbotham)
Vocal accompaniment: unknown [G]

Location: London, England. Monday 17 August 1964

Title performed:
[probably] 'Hi Heel Sneakers'

Source: *Beat Room*

As above

Location: London, England. Monday 24 August 1964

Titles performed:
[probably] 'Hi Heel Sneakers'

Source: *Beat Room*

Vocal accompaniment: unknown

Location: Los Angeles, California. 1965

Titles performed:
unknown

Source: *Shindig*

BABE KYRO LEMON [BUCK] TURNER
See Black Ace.

IKE TURNER
Speech, occasional piano

Location: unknown {USA}. 1995

[interview]

Source: *Rock And Roll Part 1*

IKE TURNER AND THE KINGS OF RHYTHM
Ike Turner, vocal and electric guitar accompaninment; The Kings of Rhythm: Carlson Oliver (tenor saxophone); Erskine Ogelsby (baritone saxophone); Jesse Knight (electric bass); John 'Booty Lip' Wings (drums)

Location: St. Louis, Missouri. 1958

Titles performed:
untitled instrumental
'So Fine'
'Charlie Brown'
[interview with George Edick]
'Señor Blues' [instrumental]

Source: *George Edick's Showtime*
See also Tommy Hodge and Jimmy Thomas.

IKE AND TINA TURNER
Tina, vocal accompaniment: Ike Turner (electric guitar) and the Kings of Rhythm: Ernest Lane (piano); Herb Sadler (second electric guitar); Sam Rhodes (electric bass); James 'Nose' Norwood (drums); the Ikettes, (female vocal trio); Ike and Tina Turner, vocal duet, accompaniment as above–1

Location: Civic Auditorium, Santa Monica, California. 1964

Titles performed:
'Shake'
'Fool In Love'
'It's Gonna Work Out Fine'–1
'Please Please Please'
'Hurt By Love'
'Things Ain't What They Used To Be'–1

Source: *The TAMI Show*

Tina, vocal accompaniment: Ike, vocal and electric guitar and others, unknown

Location: London, England. Friday 30 September 1966

Titles performed:
unknown

Source: *Ready Steady Go*
Later material by Ike and Tina Turner, both together and separately, falls outside the scope of this work and is therefore excluded.

[BIG] JOE TURNER

Vocal accompaniment: Meade Lux Lewis (piano)

Location: Hollywood, California. Early 1944

Title performed:
[16507] 'Low Down Dog' Charly #2, Jazz & Jazz Vidjazz 20, Jazz Classics JCVC105, Storyville SV6013, Virgin VVD–762

Source: *Soundie*

Turner does not appear in this *Soundie*; his singing is mimed by Dudley Dickerson in a sketch featuring Meade Lux Lewis. The copyright date for this title is 15 May 1944. The title is frequently shown as 'Ain't Gonna Be Your Low Down Dog', but the above is correct according to copyright registration.

Vocal accompaniment: Paul Williams (baritone saxophone); Jimmy Brown (trumpet); unknown (tenor saxophone, piano, bass, drums)

Location: New York City. 1955

Titles performed:
[introduction by Willie Bryant, leading to;]
'Shake Rattle And Rock' Storyville SV6016
[introduction by Willie Bryant and Leonard Reed leading to;]
'Oke-She-Moke-She-Pop' Storyville SV6016

Source: *Showtime At The Apollo*

Miming to [A] Atlantic 1100: [B] Atlantic 1122

Location: unknown {USA}. 1956

Titles performed:
'Lipstick, Powder And Paint' [A]
'Feelin' Happy' [B]

Source: *Shake Rattle And Rock*

Vocal accompaniment: Buck Clayton (trumpet); Edmund Hall (clarinet); and the Humphrey Lyttelton band

Location: London, England. Sunday 16 May 1965

Titles performed:
'Feelin' Happy'
'I Want A Little Girl'
'Morning Glory'
'Cherry Red'
'Roll 'em Pete'
'Wee Baby Blues' PNE PNV1043
'Shake Rattle And Roll' PNE PNV1043
'Chains Of Love' PNE PNV1043
'Ain't Gonna Be Your Lowdown Dog' PNE PNV1043
'Bye Bye Baby'

Source: *Jazz 625*

Vocal accompaniment: Little Brother Montgomery (piano); Otis Rush (electric guitar); Jack Meyers (electric bass); Fred Below (drums)

Location: Studio 6, Granada TV Centre, Manchester, England. Friday 30 September 1966

Titles performed:
'Well, Oh Well'
'My Baby's A Jockey'

Source: *Nothing But The Blues*

Probably as above

Location: Baden-Baden, Germany. c. December 1966

Titles performed:
unknown

Source: *American Folk Blues Festival 1966*

Vocal accompaniment: Hampton Hawes (piano); Harry 'Sweets' Edison (trumpet); Teddy Edwards and Sonny Criss (saxophones); Leroy Vinnegar (bass); Bobby Thompson (drums)

Location: Los Angeles, California. c. 1970

Titles performed:
'Feelin' Happy' Rhapsody 8037
'Shake, Rattle and Roll' Rhapsody 8037

Source: *Jazz on Stage*

Vocal accompaniment: unknown

Location: unknown {USA}. 1970

Titles performed:
unknown

Source: *Della*

Vocal accompaniment: unknown

Location: unknown {USA}. 1970

Titles performed:
unknown

Source: *The Homewood Show* [unconfirmed]

Vocal accompaniment: unknown

Location: unknown {USA}. 1973

Titles performed:
unknown

Source: *All Together Now* [unconfirmed]

Vocal accompaniment: probably the Johnny Otis band

Location: Monterey, California. 1973

Titles performed:
unknown

Source: *Monterey Jazz*

Vocal accompaniment: the Duke Ellington orchestra

Location: Monterey, California. 1973

Title performed:
'Hide And Seek'

Source: *The Duke At Monterey*

Vocal accompaniment: Oscar Peterson (piano); Nils-Henning Ørsted-Pedersen (bass); unknown (drums)

Location: unknown {USA}. c.1973–4

Titles performed:
'Flip Flop And Fly'
'Wee Baby Blues'
'Honey Hush'

Source: *Oscar Peterson Presents*

Vocal accompaniment: Jay McShann (piano) and others, unknown

Location: Kansas City, Missouri. 1974–79

Titles performed:

'Piney Brown Blues'	K-Jazz 012, Rhapsody 8039
'Shake Rattle And Roll'	K-Jazz 012, Rhapsody 8039
'Roll 'em Pete'	K-Jazz 012, Rhapsody 8039
'Kansas City Blues'	K-Jazz 012, Rhapsody 8039

Source: *Last Of The Blue Devils*

Vocal accompanient: unknown

Location: unknown {USA}. 1977

Titles performed:
unknown

Source: *Roots*. [ST only]

Speech

Location: Los Angeles, California. 1981

[interview]

Source: *Remembering Black Music*

OTHAR TURNER AND THE GRAVEL SPRINGS FIFE AND DRUM BAND

Turner, cane fife accompaniment: unknown (snare drum and bass drum)

Location: Mississippi. Between 11 August and 9 September 1978

Title performed:
untitled instrumental — Vestapol 13078

Source: *Land Where The Blues Began*
See also Jesse Mae Hemphill, Napoleon Strickland and Ed Young.

TWILIGHT GOSPEL SINGERS

Vocal group, including Ann Walker and Carolyn Bush, accompaniment: unknown

Location: New York City. Sunday 21 October 1962

Titles performed:
'Oh Lord, Save Me'
'Help Us To Tell It'

Source: *TV Gospel Time* #13

As above

Location: New York City. Sunday 2 December 1962

Titles performed:
'Does Jesus Care'
'Who'
'I'm Willing To Go'

Source: *TV Gospel Time* #4

BRADY TWINE

Guitar solo

Location: WDBJ TV Studios, Roanoke, Virginia. Spring/Summer 1987

Title performed:
untitled instrumental [part only]

Source: *Black Music Traditions In Virginia: Non-blues Secular Music*

JOHNNY TWIST (John Lee Williams)

Vocal and electric guitar accompaniment; unknown

Location: Chicago, Illinois. c. 1978

Titles performed:
unknown

Source: *Chicago Melodie*

U

UNIDENTIFIED ARTISTS [A]

The following performances were filmed by Dr. Milton Metfessel, in an experimental speech analysis programme conducted by the University of North Carolina at Chapel Hill. The un-named performers were all recorded using what Metfessel describes as 'phonophotography', a term coined by him that is, in fact, the earliest known use of synchronised sound-film recording for folkloric purposes. The following recordings may not represent everything that Metfessel and his associates made, but they are those cited in his subsequently published book *Phonophotography In Folk Music* (University of North Carolina at Chapel Hill, 1928). Metfessel names no artists in his work, and the partial identification presented here is drawn from examining the photographic evidence Metfessel published. No two songs are performed by the same artist.

All titles are given exactly as Metfessel gives them, though the titles in parentheses represent the more likely alternatives. The chronology is as it appears in the book, and probably does not represent the order in which the songs were recorded.

Un-named artists, vocal, unaccompanied unless otherwise stated.

Location: Chapel Hill, North Carolina and its immediate environs. 1926

Titles performed:
Young male;
1. 'I Heard The Voice' [I Heard The Voice Of Jesus]

unknown;
2. 'Do Lawd' ['Do Lord Remember Me']

Young male;
3. 'Burden Down' ['Since I Laid My Burden Down']

unknown;
4. 'Roll, Jordan, Roll'

unknown;
5. 'All My Days'

unknown;
6. 'Let The Heaven Light Shine' ['Let The Heavenly Light Shine On Me']

unknown;
7. 'Go Down Moses'

Older male from Hampton Institute;
8. 'By And By'

Young female;
9. 'I'm So Glad Trouble Don't Last Always'
Young female;
10. 'Nobody Knows The Trouble I've Seen'
unknown;
11. 'God Is A God' ['My God Is A Real God']
unknown;
12. 'Little David' ['Little David, Play On Your Harp']
unknown;
13. 'Swing Low, Sweet Chariot'
Middle aged male employing axe as percussion;
14. 'You Ketch Dis Train'
Middle aged male;
15. 'John Henry'
unknown;
16. 'Shoot Dat Buffey'
Young male;
17. 'I Got A Muly' (first version)
unknown;
18. 'I Got A Muly' (second version)
Young male;
19. 'I Got A Muly' (third version, unwillingly performed)
unknown;
20. 'My Gal Ain't Actin' Right'
unknown;
21. 'West Indies Blues'
unknown;
22. 'You Doan Know My Mind'
Young male;
23. 'It Ain't Gonna Rain No Mo' '
Young female with ukelele;
24. 'My Lovie Come Back'
Middle aged male;
25. 'Shot Ma Pistol'
unknown;
26. 'Obscene Song'
Young male college quartet (probably Hampton Institute);
27. 'Look At De Biscuits' (lead)
as 27;
28. 'Look At De Biscuits' (bass)
unknown;
29. 'Cornfield Holler' (1)
unknown;
30. 'Cornfield Holler' (2)
unknown;
31. 'A Negro Laugh'
Group of male youths;
32. High School Boys' Voices
Group of female youths;
33. High School Girls' Voices

Source: *Milton Metfessel Phonophotographic Recordings*

UNIDENTIFIED ARTISTS [B] (in date order)

[1] Group of c. 25 mixed-sex juvenile cotton pickers, vocal, lead by older female

Location: unknown {USA}. c.1928–31

Title performed:
'Nobody Knows The Trouble I've Seen'

Source: *Fox Movietone newsreel*

[2] Group of c.20 chained male convicts, a cappella ensemble vocal; filmed three times, in long, medium and close up shots

Location: Richmond County, unknown US state. c.1928–31

Titles performed:
'Build Right On That Shore' (takes 1 to 3)
[dialogue]

Source: *Fox Movietone newsreel*
There are Richmond counties in Georgia, North Carolina and Virginia. It is not known which of these three is the correct location.

[3] Group of five male convicts drawn from above group.
Vocal accompaniment: striking of picks

Location: as above

Title performed:
'Water Boy'
[dialogue]

Source: *Fox Movietone newsreel*

[4] Group of 20 male track-liners, ensemble vocal accompaniment: track-lining rods used as percussion, led by caller; filmed from three different angles.

Location: unknown {USA}. c.1928–31

Title performed:
Track lining song (takes 1 to 4)

Source: *Fox Movietone newsreel*

[5] Male quartet, a cappella vocal

Location: Oyster shucking yard, unknown location, eastern US seaboard. c.1928–31

Titles performed:
'Do You Call That Religion' (takes 1 to 4)

Source: *Fox Movietone newsreel*
These artists were filmed sitting on a vast pile of emptied oyster shells. The likely locations are Maryland or Virginia.

[6] Different group of [mixed sex] oyster shuckers, vocal

Location: as above

Title performed:
untitled song

Source: *Fox Movietone newsreel*

[7] Washerwoman, a cappella vocal

Location: unknown {USA}. c.1928–31

Title performed:
'I Want To Live Like Jesus'
[dialogue]

Source: *Fox Movietone newsreel*

[8] 30 voice mixed sex choir, a cappella vocal

Location: unknown {USA}. c.1928–31

Title:
'Rise And Shine'

Source: *Fox Movietone newsreel*
This could possibly be the Hall Johnson Choir, and the location therefore likely to be New York City.

[9] Male vocal accompaniment: unknown male (guitar)

Location: prison yard, unknown state, USA. c. 1928–31

Title performed:
'He's In The Jailhouse Now'

Source: *Fox Movietone newsreel*
This is included in *Ain't Misbehavin'* and [in part] in *Brother Can You Spare a Dime.*

[10] Five males, vocal, accompaniment: one of them (banjo)

Location: Augusta, Georgia. Thursday 21 March 1929

Title performed:
'Mary, Don't You Weep' Yazoo 512

Source: *Fox Movietone newsreel*
[All Fox Movietone newsreels are available from Historic.]

[11] Male (vocal and banjo) accompaniment: two others (guitar, blown jug and alto saxophone) accompanying: young male (dancing)

Location: unknown {USA}. c.1929–30

Title performed:
'He's In The Jailhouse Now'

Source: *Fox Movietone or Hearst Metrotone News*
This performance appears in the documentary *Louie Bluie.*

[12] Female vocalist, a cappella

Location: unknown, possibly New York City. 1930

Titles performed:
'Will There Be Any Stars In My Crown'
'Dear Lord'

Source: *Georgia Rose*

[13] Two males, vocal, accompaniment: one of them (piano)

Location: unknown {USA}. c.1933

Titles performed:
fragment of untitled urban blues song
[first line; 'Have You Ever Been Lonely?']
'You Got To Do Better Than That' [two verses only]
[dialogue]

Source: *Knee Deep In Music*

[13a] Unidentified female blues singer
accompaniment: unknown

Location: New York City or Los Angeles, California. 1942

Title performed:
[2M2] 'I Won't Miss You'

Source: *Soundie*
Copyrighted 30 December 1942.

[14] Male, guitar and rack harmonica

Location: Ruleville, Mississippi. 1942

[unknown fragment]

This four second segment of an eight minute monochrome, silent film has been said to show Robert Johnson, but does not. The artist is pictured in front of a poster for the film *Blues In The Night*, released in December 1941, after Johnson's death. The film was shot by B F Jackson; the original is held by his stepson. Film and video copies are held by the Mississippi Department of Archives and History.

[15] Group of children, vocals and dancing, unaccompanied. Strong possibility these are Emma Jane Davis lead vocal with group: 'Little Sally Walker'/'Pullin' The Skiff', and Florence Mason lead vocal with Emma Jane Davis, Alice Austin, Dorothy May Ward, vocals/clapping: 'Mary Mack'.

Location: Anne William's house, Friar's Point, Mississippi. Sunday 26 July 1942

Titles performed:
'Little Sally Walker'
'Pullin' The Skiff'
'Mary Mack'

Source: *Library Of Congress*

[16] Group of children, vocals and dancing, unaccompanied

Location: Coahoma County Training School, Mississippi. August 1942

Titles performed:
'Lazy Motion' (two versions)
'Take Your Outside Partner'
'Down By The Green Apple Tree'
'How Many Miles To Bethlehem?'
'Who De Cat?' [*sic*]
'Hop Burr Rabbit In The Pea-Vine' [*sic*]
'Good Ole Man'
'Satisfy'
'Pulling The Skiff'
'Shoo Fly'
'Did You Ever See A Monkey Do The Motion?'

Source: *Library Of Congress*

[17] Old man, dancing, unaccompanied

Location: un-named plantation, Northwest Coahoma County, Mississippi. 1942

Title performed:
Buck dance

Source: *Library Of Congress*

[18] Male piano player

Location: probably Hollywood, California. 1945

Titles performed:
untitled instrumental blues
untitled mid-tempo boogie

Source: *Dillinger*

[19] Male vocal, accompaniment: own harmonica and foot-stomping

Location: Benoit, Mississippi. 1956

Title performed:
'Baby, Please Don't Go' [part only]

Source: *Baby Doll*

[20] Male vocal and harmonica

Location: unknown {USA}. 1958

Title performed:
'Long Gone' [ST]

Source: *The Defiant Ones*

[21] Female vocal accompaniment: own piano

Location: the King Louis Narcisse residence, Oakland, California. Spring 1963

Title performed:
'I Turn To Thee' [part only]

Source: *Dietrich Wawzyn film collection*

[22] Members of a Pentecostal church, ensemble vocals accompaniment: unknown (trumpet, drums and sundry percussion)

Location: Texas. Spring 1963

Title performed:
untitled instrumental accompanying religious dancing

Source: *Dietrich Wawzyn film collection*

[23] Group of three male children accompaniment: body-slapping and shoe-shine cloths used as percussion

Location: New Orleans, Louisiana. Spring 1963

Title performed:
'Hambone, Hambone'

Source: *Dietrich Wawzyn film collection*

[24] Male youth, vocal accompaniment: percussion on cardboard box

Location: Maxwell Street, Chicago, Illinois. 1964

Title performed:
'Bo Diddley' ['Hambone'] Shanachie 1403

Source: *And This Is Free*

[25] Old man, vocal and harmonica

Location: Maxwell Street, Chicago, Illinois. 1964

Title performed:
'John Came North' Shanachie 1403

Source: *And This Is Free*

[26] Two blind females, vocals and guitars

Location: Maxwell Street, Chicago, Illinois. 1964

Title performed:
'I'll Overcome Someday' [fragment only]

Source: *And This Is Free*

[27] Group of male convicts, vocal

Location: Ellis Unit, Huntsville State Farm, Texas. March 1966

Titles performed:
'Working All Day Long' Vestapol 13042
'Down The Line' Vestapol 13042
'I Believe I'll Call My Baby' Vestapol 13042

Source: *Afro-American Songs In A Texas Prison*
Vestapol claims a date of 1964, but this is not correct. Some of these songs may be led by Willie [Cowboy] Craig, Joseph [Chinaman] Johnson or Benny Richardson.

[27a] Male step-dancer accompanied by Clark Kessinger (violin); Gene Meade (guitar); Wayne Hauser (banjo)

Location: Newport, Rhode Island. Summer 1966

Titles performed:
'Billy In The Lowgrounds' Vestapol 13051
'Leather Britches' Vestapol 13051

[28] Congregation of church, vocals

Location: Centerville, Texas. 1967

Title performed:
'I Know His Blood Can Make Me Whole' Flower 1, K-Jazz 053

Source: *The Blues According To Lightnin' Hopkins*

[29] Male instrumentalist, one string guitar solos and commentary

Location: Mississippi. 1969

Titles performed:
two untitled blues CFSC 1135

Source: *Mississippi Delta Blues* [1]

[30] Male singer accompaniment own guitar

Location: Mississippi. 1969

Title performed:
untitled blues CFSC 1135

Source: *Mississippi Delta Blues* [1]

[31] Female vocalist accompaniment: male pianist

Location: Mississippi. 1969

Title performed:
untitled blues CFSC 1135

Source: *Mississippi Delta Blues* [1]

[32] Male trio, vocal, guitar, broom handle percusson

Location: juke-joint, Mississippi. 1969

Title performed:
untitled blues CFSC 1135

Source: *Mississippi Delta Blues* [1]

[33] Male harmonica player

Location: Leland, Mississippi. 1969

Title performed:
'Train Time' CFSC 1056

Source: *Sonny Ford – Delta Artist*

[34] Preacher and congregation

Location: Chicago, Illinois. April–May 1970

Title performed:
untitled song K-Jazz 004, Rhapsody 9012

Source: *Chicago Blues*

[35] Two females (electric guitars); one male (harmonica)

Location: Maxwell Street, Chicago, Illinois. April–May 1970

Title performed:
untitled instrumental [fragment only] K-Jazz 004, Rhapsody 9012

Source: *Chicago Blues*

[36] Male vocalist accompaniment: own washtub bass

Location: unknown {USA}. 1971

Titles performed:
'Sit Right Down And Right Myself A Letter' [A] K-Jazz 020, Yazoo 507
'Wrap Your Troubles In Dreams' [A] [B] K-Jazz 020, Yazoo 507

Source: *Out Of The Blacks, Into The Blues part 1*[A]; *Le Blues Entre Les Dents* [B]
The washtub bass is constructed from an inverted galvanized washtub, to which is attached a a length of string or wire, which in turn is attached to an approximately 3 foot length of wood. The bottom, free end, of the wood is then placed on the surface of the inverted tub and the string or wire is plucked, causing the tub to resonate. The tone is altered by pressing the string or wire to the wood at various positions along its length.
This artist's name may be Jimmy Streeter.

[36A] Male vocalist accompaniment: unknown (electric guitar, electric bass, drums)

Location: Prison, unknown location, New York. 1971

Title performed:
'It's A Low Down Dirty Shame'

Source: *Le Blues Entre Les Dents*

[36B] Group of male convicts, vocal accompaniment: axes used as percussion.

Location: probably State Farm, unknown location, Texas. 1971

Title performed:
'Hammer Ring (Let Your Hammer Ring)'

Source: *Le Blues Entre Les Dents*

[37] Church congregation, unaccompanied

Location: Eunice, Louisiana. 1973

Title performed:
'Kumbaya' Flower 4, K-Jazz 067

Source: *Dry Wood*

[38] Male harmonica player

Location: Festival of American Folklife, Washington DC. Summer 1974

Title performed:
untitled instrumental

Source: *Oh Happy Day*

[39] Male vocalist and guitar player

Location: Festival of American Folklife, Washington DC. Summer 1974

Title performed:
untitled blues

Source: *Oh Happy Day*

[40] Church congregation–1; church group accompaniment guitar–2

Location: Rose Hill, Mississippi. 1974

Titles performed:
unknown number of untitled songs–1 CFSC 1025
Lining out–1 CFSC 1025
'Half Ain't Never Been Told'–2 CFSC 1025

Source: *Black Delta Religion*

[41] Group of children, unaccompanied vocal

Location: John's Island, South Carolina, 1975

Title performed:
'Mama Lamma Cooma Lamma' JVC V-225

Source: *Musical Holdouts*

[42] Male prison inmates, vocal accompaniment: two electric guitars, electric bass and drums

Location: Cummins Prison Farm, Arkansas. 1984

Title performed:
'Downhome Blues' Arrow AV015

Source: *Saturday Blues*

[43] Group of males, vocal accompaniment: electric guitar, electric organ and drums

Location: juke-joint, Clarksdale, Mississippi. 1984

Title performed:
untitled blues [part only] Arrow AV015

Source: *Saturday Blues*

[44] Unknown number of singers

Location: Mississippi. 1985

Titles performed:
unknown

Source: *Delta Blues Festival*

UNITED SONS AND DAUGHTERS OF ZION NUMBER NINE FIFE AND DRUM BAND

Columbus Griffin, James Mitchell, John Mitchell, possibly others, unknown number of fifes and drums

Location: KCTS-TV studios. Seattle, Washington. c.1966–70

Titles performed:
unknown

Source: *Seattle Folklore Society*. Video only, currently unavailable

UTICA JUBILEE SINGERS

Vocal group accompaniment: unknown

Location: unknown {USA}. c.1930

Titles performed:
unknown

Source: [FS] [M]. Origin unknown.

V

MAURICE JOHN VAUGHN
See A C Reed.

TATA VEGA (Carmen Rosa Vega)
Sonny Terry (harmonica–1, jew's harp–2); Freg Phillinganes (piano–1); Bobby Scott (piano–2); Roy Graines (guitar, footstomping–1);Paul Jackson Jr. (guitar–1); Ry Cooder (mandolin–2)

Titles performed:
'Dirty Mistreater'–1
'Miss Celie's Blues'–2

Source: *The Color Purple*
These performances are mimed in the film by Margaret Avery. Vega does not appear on camera.

VENSON'S PLAYBOYS
Adair King, vocal and electric guitar accompaniment: Pat Rush (electric bass); Tenner 'Playboy' Venson (drums)

Location: Maxwell Street, Chicago, Illinois. 1980

Titles performed:

'Killin' Floor'	K-Jazz 031, Rhapsody 8045
untitled instrumental blues	K-Jazz 031, Rhapsody 8045

Source: *Maxwell Street Blues*
See also Floyd Jones.

JACKIE VERDELL
Vocal accompaniment: unknown

Location: Chicago, Illinois. Saturday 7 September 1974

Titles performed:
unknown

Source: *Jubilee Showcase* [prog #5–1]
See also The Davis Sisters and Brother Joe May.

VICTORY TRAVELLERS
Male vocal quartet accompaniment: unknown (electric guitar, electric bass, drums)

Location: Chicago, Illinois. c.1979

Title performed:
'Everything's Gonna Be Alright'

Source: *Chicago On The Good Foot*

EDDIE [CLEANHEAD] VINSON
Vocal accompaniment: the Cootie Williams orchestra

Location: New York City. c. mid -1944

Title performed:
'Things Ain't What They Used To Be'

Source: *Film Vodvil, series 2, No. 2*

Vocal accompaniment: the Cootie Williams orchestra

Location: unknown {USA}. c.1944

Titles performed:
unknown

Source: *Cootie Williams And His Orchestra*
This may be the same material as that listed in the previous entry.

Vocal accompaniment: unknown

Location: probably Los Angeles, California. 1970

Titles performed:
unknown

Source: *The Homewood Show* [unconfirmed]

Vocal accompaniment: unknown

Location: Montreux, Switzerland. 1971

Titles performed:
'They Call Me Mr Cleanhead'
'I'm Still In New York City'
'Just a Dream'
'Person to Person'

Source: *Montreux Jazz*

Vocal accompaniment: probably the Johnny Otis band

Location: Monterey, California. 1973

Titles performed:
unknown

Source: *Monterey Jazz*

Vocal accompaniment: the Duke Ellington orchestra

Location: Monterey, California. 1973

Title performed:
'They Call Me Mr. Cleanhead'

Source: *The Duke At Monterey*

Vocal accompaniment: probably the Johnny Otis band

Location: Montreux, Switzerland. July 1981

Titles performed:
'Is You Is Or Is You Ain't My Baby'
'Judge Oh Judge'
'Kidney Stew'
'Railroad Porter Blues'

Source: *Montreux Jazz*

Vocal accompaniment: the Gerald Wiggins orchestra

Location: unknown {USA}. 1982

Titles performed:
'Cleanhead Blues' Magnum MMGV-035

Source: *America's Music – Blues Volume 1*

Vocal accompaniment: the Johnny Otis band

Location: Monterey, California. 1987

Titles performed:
'Kidney Stew'
'They Call Me Mr. Cleanhead'

Source: *Monterey Jazz Festival*

MOSE VINSON

Vocal and piano accompaniment: Sonny Blake (harmonica); L T Lewis (drums)

Location: Memphis, Tennessee. Monday 19 January 1976

Titles performed:
'One Room Country Shack'
'When You Got Rid of My Mule'
'Bugle Call Blues'

Source: *Devil's Music series 2*

Vocal and piano accompaniment, if any, uknown

Location: Memphis, Tennessee. 1978

Titles performed:
unknown CFSC 1139

Source: *Mr. Boogie Woogie*

VIOLINAIRES

Probably Robert Blair, Isaiah Jones, James Byers, Charles Brown, Robert Wilson, James McCurdy (vocals) accompaniment: unknown

Location: Chicago, Illinois. Monday 5 May 1969

Titles performed:
unknown

Source: *Jubilee Showcase* [prog # unknown]

Vocal group accompaniment: unknown

Location: Chicago, Illinois. Saturday 24 November 1973

Titles performed:
unknown

Source: *Jubilee Showcase* [prog # unknown]

VIRGINIA CHOIR ENSEMBLE
Mixed vocal choir accompaniment: unknown

Location: New York City. 1966

Titles performed:
unknown

Source: *TV Gospel Time* #63

VOICES OF FAITH CHOIR
Mixed vocal choir accompaniment: unknown

Location: Jacksonville, Florida. 1966

Titles performed:
unknown

Source: *TV Gospel Time* #57

VOICES OF MELODY
Vocal group accompaniment: unknown

Location: Chicago, Illinois

The following appearances are known:
1964
Sunday 17 May [prog #21–3]
1968
Saturday 28 September [prog #28–3]
1975
Saturday 28 June [prog #20–2]

Titles performed:
unknown

Source: *Jubilee Showcase*

VOICES OF PRAISE
Vocal group accompaniment: unknown

Location: Chicago, Illinois. Saturday 22 November 1975

Titles performed:
unknown

Source: *Jubilee Showcase*

VOICES OF SHILOH
Mixed vocal choir accompaniment: unknown
Soloist: Esther Anthony–1

Location: New York City. Sunday 25 November 1962

Titles performed:
'I'm Going To Wait On The Lord'–1
'Joshua Fit The Battle Of Jericho'
'All Over God's Heaven (I Got Shoes)'

Source: *TV Gospel Time* #3

VOICES OF SOUTHERN [*sic*]
Mixed vocal choir accompaniment: unknown
Soloists: Cleo Jackson–1; Alvin Cannon–2

Location: Baltimore, Maryland. Saturday 5 September 1964

Titles performed:
'Travelling Home'–1
'Rock Of Ages'–2
'Camp Meeting Song'–2

Source: *TV Gospel Time* #33

VOICES OF TRIUMPH
Vocal group accompaniment: unknown

Location: Chicago, Illinois. Saturday 8 February 1969

Titles performed:
unknown

Source: *Jubilee Showcase*

W

AARON THIBEAUX [T-BONE] WALKER
Vocal and electric guitar accompaniment: unknown

Location: New York City. Early 1950s

Titles performed:
unknown

Source: *Toast Of The Town*

Vocal and electric guitar accompaniment: probably Memphis Slim (piano); Willie Dixon (bass); Clifton James (drums)

Location: Baden-Baden, Germany. c. October 1962

Titles performed:
unknown

Source: *American Folk Blues Festival 1962*

Vocal and electric guitar accompaniment: unknown

Location: Manchester, England. c. December 1963

Titles performed:
unknown

Source: *More Jazz Unlimited – A Rebirth Of The Blues*

Vocal and electric guitar accompaniment: John Mayall's Blues Breakers: Mayall (piano); Bernie Watson (second electric guitar); John McVie (electric bass); Peter Ward (drums)

Location: ATV Studios, London, England. Friday 5 March 1965

Title performed:
'I'm In Love'

Source: *Ready Steady Go*

Vocal and electric guitar accompaniment: as above

Location: London, England. Thursday 18 March 1965

Title performed:
'I'm In Love'

Source: *The Ollie And Fred Show*

Vocal and electric guitar accompaniment: the Kenny Salmon Quintet

Location: London. Saturday 20 March 1965

Title performed:
[introduction by Peter Cooke, leading to;]
'I'm In Love'
[followed by brief conversation between Cooke, Walker, Dudley Moore and Peter Sellers]

Source: *Not Only ... But Also ...*

Vocal and electric guitar accompaniment: Dizzy Gillespie (trumpet); Clark Terry (flugel horn); Zoot Sims and James Moody (tenor saxophones); Teddy Wilson (piano); Bob Cranshaw (bass); Louis Bellson (drums); Terry (flugel horn mouthpiece solo)–1
As above, without vocal and including Benny Carter and Coleman Hawkins (tenor saxophones)–2

Location: Poplar Town Hall, London, England. Saturday 25 November 1967

Titles performed:
'Woman, You Must Be Crazy'–1 Jazz & Jazz Vidjazz 13
'Sometimes I Wonder'–1 Jazz & Jazz Vidjazz 13
'Old Time Used To Be'–1
'Goin' To Chicago'–1
'The Real BBC Blues'–2

Source: *Jazz At The Philharmonic*

Vocal and electric guitar accompaniment: Lloyd Glenn (piano) and others, unknown–1;
as above, in duet with BB King–2

Location: Monterey, California. 1968

Titles performed:
'Mistreatin' Woman'–1
'Crazy 'bout My Baby'–1
'Stormy Monday'–1
untitled instrumental–2
'What In The World's Going To Happen'–2

Source: *Monterey Jazz*

Vocal and electric guitar accompaniment: Eddie Taylor (electric guitar); Jerome Arnold (electric bass); J C Lewis (drums)

Location: BBC TV studios, White City, London, England. Tuesday 22 October 1968

Titles performed:
'I Love My Baby'
and two other, unknown, titles

Source: *American Folk Blues Festival 1968* [1]

Probably as above

Location: Germany. November 1968

Titles performed:
unknown

Source: *American Folk Blues Festival 1968* [2]

Vocal and electric guitar accompaniment: unknown

Location: probably Los Angeles, California. 1970

Titles performed:
unknown

Source: *The Homewood Show* [unconfirmed]

Vocal and electric guitar in duet with Muddy Waters, vocal and electric guitar, accompaniment: Mojo Buford (harmonica); Lafayette Leake (piano); Louis Myers (electric guitar); David Myers (electric bass); Fred Below (drums)

Location: Montreux, Switzerland. Saturday 17 June 1972

Titles performed:
'They Call It Stormy Monday'
'She Says She Loves Me'
'Shake It Baby'
'Reconsider Baby'
'Everyday I Have The Blues'

Source: *Montreux Jazz*

Vocal accompaniment: unknown

Location: Los Angeles, California. 1972

Titles performed:
unknown

Source: *The Mike Douglas Show*

ALBERTINA WALKER

Vocal accompaniment: unknown

Location: Chicago, Illinois

The following appearances are known:
1964
Sunday 26 January [prog #7–3]
Sunday 15 March [prog #7–1]
1966
Sunday 23 January [prog #6–2]
1967
Sunday 5 March [prog #17–1]
1968
Saturday 19 October [prog #2–3]
1969
Saturday 24 May [prog #18–3]
1972
Saturday 2 September [prog #24–1]
1975
Sunday 13 April [prog #19–2]
1982
Monday 20 September [prog #14]

Titles performed:
unknown

Source: *Jubilee Showcase*

Also, the following;

Vocal accompaniment: unknown

Location: unknown {USA}. 1970s

Titles performed:
unknown Savoy 9500

Source: *Down Memory Lane*

Vocal accompaniment: unknown

Location: Chicago, Illinois. Sunday 25 November 1990

Title performed:
'I Can Go To God In Prayer'

Source: *Soundstage*

Speech

Location: Chicago, Illinois. August 1995

[interview]

Source: *Too Close To Heaven*
See also the Caravans.

JOHN [BIG MOOSE] WALKER

Vocal and piano accompaniment: Jimmy Johnson, Lefty Dizz and Willie James Lyons (electric guitars); Big Mojo Elem (electric bass); Odie Payne (drums)

Location: unknown {Europe}. c.1978–79

Titles performed:
'Would You Baby'
'The Sky Is Crying'

Source: *European TV broadcast* [C]. Origin unknown.

MARIE WALKER

Vocal accompaniment: unknown

Location: New York City. Sunday 16 December 1962

Title performed:
'Ask God'

Source: *TV Gospel Time* #12

PHILLIP WALKER

Vocal and electric guitar accompaniment: unknown Swedish musicians, (electric guitar, piano, electric bass, drums)

Location: Stockholm, Sweden. 1979

Titles performed:
unknown

Source: *Swedish TV broadcast* [C]

T-BONE WALKER

See Aaron Thibeaux [T-Bone] Walker.

T-BONE WALKER Jr.

See R S Rankin.

BEULAH [SIPPIE] WALLACE (née Thomas)

Vocal accompaniment: Little Brother Montgomery (piano); Fred Below (drums)

Location: Studio 6, Granada TV Centre, Manchester, England. Friday 30 September 1966

Title performed:
'Women Be Wise'

Source: *Nothing But The Blues*

Probably as above

Location: Baden-Baden, Germany. c. December 1966

Titles performed:
unknown

Source: *American Folk Blues Festival 1966*

Vocal accompaniment: The BB King orchestra

Location: Montreux, Switzerland Tuesday 27 July 1982

Title performed:
'Po' Gal Blues'

Source: *Montreux Jazz*

Vocal accompaniment: John Mayall's Bluesbreakers; Mayall (piano); Mick Taylor (electric guitar); John McVie (electric bass); Colin Allen (drums)

Location: New Jersey. 1982

Title performed:
'Short Joy Blues' Castle Hendring 6 086

Source: *Blues Survivors*

Vocal accompaniment: unknown

Location: Belly Up tavern, San Diego, California. 1983

Titles performed:
'Shake It To A Jelly'
'Women Be Wise'
'You Can Make Me Do What You Want, But You Gotta Know How'

Source: *Three Generations Of The Blues Part 1*

Vocal and piano

Location: Ann Arbor, Michigan. 1983

Titles performed:
'Up The Country Blues' K-Jazz 073, Rhapsody 8054
'Mighty Tight Woman' K-Jazz 073, Rhapsody 8054
spontaneous blues [fragments only] K-Jazz 073, Rhapsody 8054
[interview] K-Jazz 073, Rhapsody 8054

Source: *Sippie*

WADE WALTON
Guitar solo–1; speech–2

Location: Clarksdale, Mississippi. Sunday 24 July 1960

Titles performed:
instrumental blues–1 [ST] K-Jazz 014, Rhapsody 8022
monologue–2 [ST] K-Jazz 014, Rhapsody 8022

Source: *Blues Like Showers Of Rain*

Vocal, harmonica and razorstrop percussion accompaniment: unknown (guitar)

Location: Clarksdale, Mississippi. 1969

Titles performed:
unknown CFSC 1056

Source: *Sonny Ford – Delta Artist*

Guitar solo–1; vocal accompaniment: own guitar–2

Location: Clarksdale, Mississippi. 1974

Titles performed:
instrumental–1 CFSC 1136
'Rock Me Baby'–2 CFSC 1136

Source: *Mississippi Delta Blues* [3]

Guitar solo–1; vocal and guitar–2; razorstrop percussion solo–3

Location: Clarksdale, Mississippi. 1975

Titles performed:
untitled instrumental–1 CFSC 1077
'Rock Me Baby'–2 CFSC 1077
untitled instrumental–3 CFSC 1077

Source: *Give My Poor Heart Ease*

Vocal and harmonica–1; harmonica solo–2; razor strop percussion solo accompaniment: unknown (guitar)–3

Location: Clarksdale, Mississippi. 1984

Titles performed:
'Caldonia'–1 Arrow AV015
untitled instrumental–2 Arrow AV015
untitled instrumental ['Barbershop Rhythm']–3 Arrow AV015

Source: *Saturday Blues*

Vocal accompaniment: unknown

Location: Clarksdale, Mississippi. 1984

Titles performed:
unknown

Source: *In The Delta Of Mississippi*
This may comprise material from *Saturday Blues*.

Vocal and electric guitar

Location: Clarksdale, Mississippi. Autumn 1990

Title performed:
'Rock Me Baby' Anxious 45099-29643, BMG un-numbered
[interview] Anxious 45099-29643, BMG un-numbered

Source: *Deep Blues*
All Walton's performances take place in the front salon of his barber shop on 6th Street except for the 1960 performance, which was recorded in his original barber shop on 4th Street.

The leather razor strop is played by alternately dragging and then slapping an open cut-throat razor along the strop in short, quick strokes.

WANDERERS

Vocal group accompaniment: unknown–1
Vocal group featuring Pearl Woods (vocal) accompaniment: unknown–2

Location: probably New York City. 1956

Titles performed:
'Oozin' Down'–1
'I Can't Wait'–2
'He's So Lazy'–2

Source: *Rockin' The Blues*

CLARA WARD SINGERS

Clara Ward, vocal accompaniment: probably Bessie Tucker, Dorothy Robinson, Mildred Means (vocals)

Location: London, England. April 1959

Titles performed:
unknown

Source: *UK ITV TV broadcast* [M]. Title unknown

Probably as above

Location: New York City. c.1959

Titles performed:
'Nobody Knows The Trouble I've Seen'
'Swing Low, Sweet Chariot'

Source: *The Steve Allen Show*

Probably Clara Ward, Gertrude Ward, Thelma Bumpess, Vermettya Royster, and others, unidentified (vocals) unaccompanied

Location: Newport, Rhode Island. July 1962

Titles performed:
'This Little Light of Mine'
'When The Saints Go Marching In'

Source: *Newport Jazz Festival 1962*

Probably Clara Ward, Vermettya Royster, Geraldine Jones, Thelma Bumpess, Mildred Menas, Voyla Crowley, Malvilyn Simpson (vocals) accompaniment: unknown

Location: unknown {USA}. 1963–64

Titles performed:
unknown

Source: *Hootenanny*

Probably as above

Location: Los Angeles, California. 1964

Titles performed:
unknown

Source: *Shindig*

Probably as above

Location: Newport, Rhode Island. July 1966

Titles performed:
unknown

Source: *Alan Lomax collection*

Probably as above

Location: unknown {USA}. 1968

Titles performed:
unknown

Source: *A Time To Sing, A Time To Cry*

Probably as above

Location: Monterey, California. 1968

Titles performed:
'The Old Camp Ground'
'Down By The Riverside'
'He's Got The Whole World In His Hands'
'Dry Bones'
'Amen'

Source: *Monterey Jazz*

Probably as above

Location: probably Hollywood, California. 1969

Titles performed:
unknown Rhino R3.2284

Source: *Thirty Three And A Third Revolutions Per Monkee*

Probably as above

Location: Chicago, Illinois. c.1969–70

Titles performed:
unknown

Source: Dial M For Music

Probably as above, in support of Flip Wilson, in the comic persona of 'Brother Leroy of the Church Of What's Happenin''

Location: Los Angeles, California. Thursday 18 November 1971

Title performed:
dialogue, comic response and short untitled song

Source: *The Flip Wilson Show*

Probably as above

Location: Yankee Stadium, New York City. 1970

Titles performed:
unknown

Source: *It's Your Thing*

DIONNE WARWICK

See Calvin And The Majestics and the Washington Temple Angelic Choir.

WASHBOARD WILLIE

Vocal and washboard, accompaniment: probably Snooky Pryor (harmonica); Homesick James (electric guitar); Boogie Woogie Red (piano); Roger Hill (electric bass); Tom Parnell (drums)

Location: Brighton Polytechnic, Sussex, England. Friday 16 February 1973

Titles performed:
unknown

Source: *Blues Legends 73*

ALBERT WASHINGTON

Vocal and electric guitar accompaniment: unknown

Location: unknown {USA}. 1975

Titles performed:
unknown

Source: *Night Life* [unconfirmed]

DINAH WASHINGTON (Ruth Lee Jones)

Vocal accompaniment: the Three Flames: Tiger Haynes (guitar); Roy Testemark (piano); Bill Pollard (bass)

Location: New York City. June–August 1949

Titles performed:
unknown

Source: *The Three Flames Show*

Vocal accompaniment: Paul Williams (tenor saxophone); Jimmy Brown (trumpet); unknown (piano, guitar, bass, drums)

Location: New York City. 1955

Titles performed:

'My Lean Baby	View Video 1313
'I Don't Hurt Anymore'	Fil A Film 2023, Storyville SV6017
'Only A Moment Ago'	Bavaria 12177, Storyville SV6017, View Video 1313
'Such A Night'	Storyville SV6017, Video Images 73R

Source: *Showtime At The Apollo*

Vocal accompaniment: unknown

Location: New York City. 1957

Titles performed:
unknown

Source: *DuPont Show Of The Month*

Vocal accompaniment: unknown

Location: Newport, Rhode Island. Summer 1958

Title performed:
'All Of Me' Castle Hendring 2.239, New York Video 16590

Source: *Jazz On A Summer's Day*

Vocal accompaniment: orchestra led by Louis Jordan

Location: Apollo Theatre, Harlem, NYC. 1960

Title performed:
'What A Difference A Day Makes' Video Images 511, Vintage Jazz Classics VJC2003

Source: *Those Singing, Swinging Years*

ERNESTINE WASHINGTON
Vocal accompaniment: unknown–1
Vocal accompaniment: the Washington Temple Angelic Choir–2

Location: New York City. Sunday 30 September 1962

Titles performed:
'He's The One'–1
'Breathe On Me'–1
'I'll Fly Away'–2

Source: *TV Gospel Time* #6

Vocal accompaniment: unknown.

Location: New York City. Sunday 23 December 1962

Title performed:
'The Advent'

Source: *TV Gospel Time* #9

Vocal accompaniment: unknown–1
Vocal accompaniment: the Three Professors Of Gospel (vocal trio)–2

Location: Baltimore, Maryland. Sunday 23 May 1965

Titles performed:
'Walk Through The Valley'–1
'There's Not A Friend Like Jesus'–1
'Breathe On Me'–2

Source: *TV Gospel Time* #27

Vocal accompaniment: unknown

Location: Baltimore, Maryland. Sunday 20 December 1964

Titles performed:
'Father, I Stretch My Hand To Thee'
'Walk On By Faith'

Source: *TV Gospel Time* #24

Vocal accompaniment: unknown

Location: New York City. c.1966

Title performed:
unknown

Source: *TV Gospel Time* #52

WASHINGTON GOSPEL CHORUS
Mixed vocal choir accompaniment: unknown
Soloist: Ernest Alexander–1

Location: New York City. Sunday 16 December 1962

Titles performed:
'Ninety Nine And A Half Won't Do'–1
'Showers Of Blessings'
'There's Not A Friend Like Jesus'

Source: *TV Gospel Time* #12

ISIDORE [TUTS] WASHINGTON

Vocal and piano, in the company of Professor Longhair and Allen Toussaint

Location: New Orleans, Louisiana. Late 1979

Titles performed:
unknown K-Jazz 084

Source: *Piano Players Rarely Ever Play Together*

WASHINGTON TEMPLE ANGELIC CHOIR

Mixed vocal choir accompaniment: unknown
Soloists: Nanny McNeil–1; James Hayward–2

Location: New York City. Sunday 30 September 1962

Titles performed:
'Heaven's So High'–1
'What A Friend We Have In Jesus'
'All Right!'–2

Source: *TV Gospel Time* #6 [*sic*]

As above
Soloist: Ezerline Jenkins–1

Location: New York City. Sunday 28 October 1962

Titles performed:
'Just Like Fire Shut Up In My Bones'–1
'The Twenty–third Psalm'
'He's My Rock, My Shield'

Source: *TV Gospel Time* #5 [*sic*]

As above
Soloist: Dionne Warwick–1

Location: New York City. Sunday 9 December 1962

Titles performed:
'Swing Down Chariot, Let Me Ride'–1
'Tell The World About This'
'I'll Never Turn Back'

Source: *TV Gospel Time* #7
See also Ernestine Washington.

WASHINGTON TEMPLE CELESTIAL CHORUS

Mixed vocal choir accompaniment: unknown
Soloists: Laura Brown–1; Louise Bynoe, Laura Brown, Robert Madison and Robert Taylor–2; Henry Costen, Robert Madison and Robert Taylor–3

Location: New York City. Sunday 7 October 1962

Titles performed:
'Have You Been Down To The River'–1
'God Is Moving'–2
'Stand Still'–3

Source: *TV Gospel Time* #1

As above
Soloists: James Wyns–1; Ernest Alexander–2

Location: New York City. Sunday 11 November 1962

Titles performed:
'I'll Go With Him'
'Softly And Tenderly'–1
'Ninety Nine And A Half Won't Do'–2

Source: *TV Gospel Time* #2
There is probably some relationship between the Washington Gospel Chorus, the Washington Temple Angelic Choir and the Washington Temple Celestial Chorus. They may actually all be parts of one large group. See also Abner Jay and James Wyns. The following entry is definitely related to the Washington Temple Angelic Choir.

WASHINGTON TEMPLETTES

Female vocal group; probably Laura Brown, Louise Bynoe and others, unknown

Location: New York City. Sunday 7 October 1962

Titles performed:
'Tired'
'Holy City'

Source: *TV Gospel Time* #1

[MISSISSIPPI] JOHNNY WATERS (John Sandifer)
Vocal and electric guitar accompaninent: unknown (second electric guitar, harmonica, electric bass, drums)

Location: Oakland, California. 1981

Titles performed:
untitled instrumental
'So Much Trouble'
[interview]

Source: *Long Train Running*

JOHNNY [GUITAR] WATSON
All the known film and video by this artist is in the funk genre, and therefore falls outside the scope of this work.

LOUISE WEAVER
Vocal accompaniment: unknown

Location: Chicago, Illinois

The following performances are known:
1963
Sunday 10 November [prog # 30–2]
1964
Sunday 12 January [prog #22–1]
Sunday 26 January [prog #7–3]
Sunday 2 February [prog #20–1]
Sunday 9 February [prog #12–1]
Sunday 16 February [prog #30–3]
Sunday 23 February [prog #28–1]
Sunday 8 March [prog # 26–3]
Sunday 15 March [prog #7–1]
Sunday 5 April [prog # 8–1]
Sunday 19 April [prog # 22–3]
Sunday 26 April [prog #9–3]
Sunday 3 May [prog #30–1]
Saturday 9 May [prog #10–3]
Sunday 31 May [prog # 28–2]
Sunday 7 June [prog #16–2]
Sunday 14 June [prog #10–2]
Friday 19 July [prog #23–3
Friday 26 July [prog #26–1]
Sunday 2 August [prog #26–2]
1965
Sunday 25 April [prog #21–1]
1966
Sunday 11 December [prog #15–3]
1968
Saturday 21 September [prog #28–2]
1969
Saturday 4 October [prog #27–1]

Titles performed:
unknown

Source: *Jubilee Showcase*

[BOOGIE] BILL WEBB
Presumably vocal and guitar

Location: unknown {USA}. 1949

Titles performed:
unknown

Source: *Jackson Jive* [unconfirmed]

Vocal and guitar accompaniment: Harmonica Slim (harmonica)

Location: New Orleans, Louisiana. 1985

Titles performed:
'Ninth Ward Blues' [A] [B]
unknown titles [B]

Source: *New Orleans Now – All Alone With The Blues* [A]; *In Concert* [3] [B]

KATIE WEBSTER (Kathryn Thorne)
Vocal and piano accompaniment: unknown

Location: Hamburg, Germany. Saturday 16 April 1983

Titles performed:
'Let The Good Times Roll'
'The Katie Lee'
'Tomorrow Night'
'I Wish Those Days Would Come Back'
'Stormy Weather'
'Blue Suede Shoes'
'Since I Fell For You'
'Hallelujah I Love Him So'
'If You Should Lose Me'
'Good Golly Miss Molly'

Source: *German TV broadcast* [C]

The following may be part of the above, but was broadcast separately:

Vocal and piano accompaniment: unknown

Location: Hamburg, Germany. 1983

Titles performed:
'Everyday I Have The Blues'
'Jelly, Jelly'

Source: *German TV broadcast* [C]

Vocal and piano accompaniment Hot Links [G]

Location: unknown {USA}. c.1983–84

Titles performed:
unknown

Source: *The Afternoon Show* [C]. US TV broadcast. Origin unknown.

Vocal and piano accompaniment: Little Willie Littlefield and Axel Zwingenberger (pianos); Big Jay McNeeley (tenor saxophone), and others, unknown

Location: Germany. c.1984–5

Title performed:
'Mama Don't Allow'

Source: *German TV broadcast* [C]

Vocal and piano

Location: Lone Star Cafe, New York City. Wednesday 7 August 1985

Titles performed:
'I Know That's Right'
'Don't Accuse Me'
'Tutti Frutti'
'St. Louis Blues'
'If You Could See Me Now'
'How Much Longer Will I Have To Sing The Blues'
'Texas Stew Boogie'
'I Know You Don't Love Me No More'
'My Train Is Gonna Come'
'Sittin' On The Dock Of The Bay'
'Worried Life Blues'
'You're So Fine'
'Shake Rattle And Roll'
'Honey Hush'
'Ooh-whee Sweet Daddy'
'Real Gone Daddy'
'What A Difference'
'Let The Good Times Roll'
'It's A Sin To Tell A Lie'

Source: *unknown, probably US TV broadcast* [C]

Vocal and piano accompaniment: Hot Links: John Lumsdain and Danny Caron (electric guitars); Nancy Wright and Bruce Unswal (tenor saxophones); Steve Erhmann (electric bass); Steve Griffiths (drums)

Location: Veteran's Hall, Albany, California. November 1985

Titles performed:

'Misty Blue'	Arhoolie ARV402
'Snatch And Grab It'	Arhoolie ARV402
'Katie's Boogie'	Arhoolie ARV402

Source: *It's Got To Be Rough To Be Sweet*

Vocal and piano accompaniment: unknown

Location: Zurich, Switzerland. 1985

Titles performed:
'I Wish Those Days Would Come Back'

Source: *Swiss TV broadcast* [C]

Vocal and piano

Location: Oasis club, San Francisco, California. Monday 17 February 1986

Titles performed:
'That's Right'
'Texas Boogie Stew'
'Sea Of Love'
'Tutti Frutti'
'Who Will The Next Fool Be'
'My Train Is Gonna Come'
'Sittin' On The Dock Of The Bay'
'Ooh-whee Sweet Daddy'
'Blue Monday'
'Hallelujah I Just Love Him So'
'Since I Fell For You'
'How Much Longer Will I Have To Sing The Blues'

Source: *probably US PBS TV broadcast* [C]

Vocal and piano

Location: Cologne, Germany. Monday 29 June 1987

Titles performed:
'Real Gone Daddy'
'Take My Hand, Precious Lord'

Source: *German TV broadcast* [C]

Vocal and piano accompaniment: the Sunday Night band: unknown (alto saxophone, electric guitar, keyboards, electric bass, drums)–1; as above, vocal only, with Paul Shaffer (piano)–2

Location: New York City. 1989

Titles performed:
'Ooh-whee Sweet Daddy'–1
'Who's Making Love'–2

Source: *Sunday Night*

Vocal and piano

Location: New Orleans, Louisiana. 1990

Title performed:
'Two Fisted Woman'

Source: *New Orleans Jazz And Heritage Festival 1990*

Vocal and piano

Location: Chestnut Cabaret, Philadelphia, Pennsylvania. Thursday 12 March 1992

Titles performed:
'Pussycat Moan' BMG 80046-3
'Lord, I Wonder' BMG 80046-3
'How Much Longer Must I Sing The Blues' BMG 80046-3
[interview] BMG 80046-3

Source: *Pride And Joy; The Story Of Alligator Records*
See also Koko Taylor.

Vocal and piano–1

Vocal and piano accompaniment: Jools Holland (piano)–2

Location: London, England. 1992

Titles performed:
'Have A Little Meat On The Side'–1
'CQ Boogie'–2

Source: *Later ... with Jools Holland*

VALERIE WELLINGTON

Vocal accompaniment: Willie Murphy and the Bees: Willie Murphy (electric guitar); unknown (piano, electric bass); Donal Robinson and Howard Merriweather (drums)

Location: Wilibeski's Blues Saloon, St. Paul, Minnesota. Tuesday 13 March 1984

Title performed:
'Independent Blues'
'200 Pounds Of Joy' (not used in final edit)

Source: *Survivors: The Blues Today*

Vocal accompaniment: unknown band

Location: Chicago, Illinois. 1985

Title performed:
untitled blues

Source: *Chicago Tribune TV advert #1*

As above

Location: Chicago, Illinois. 1986

Title performed:
untitled blues

Source: *Chicago Tribune TV advert #2*

Vocal accompaniment: unknown (two electric guitars, piano, electric bass, drums

Location: Chicago, Illinois. 1986

Title performed:
'Old Man Blues' [part only]

Source: *local TV news broadcast*

Vocal accompaniment: the Cash McCall band: McCall (electric guitar); unknown (tenor saxophone, piano, electric bass, drums); Otis Rush (electric guitar); Snooky Pryor (harmonica)

Location: Topanga Canyon, California. Saturday 25 June 1988

Titles performed:
'Let The Good Times Roll'
'The Blues Is All Right'

Source: *Topanga Blues Festival*

Vocal accompaniment: Booker T. Laury and Jerry Lee Lewis (pianos); unknown (2 tenor saxophones, baritone saxophone, bass, drums)

Location: probably Memphis, Tennessee. 1989

Title performed:
'Whole Lotta Shakin' Goin' On'

Source: *Great Balls Of Fire*
Wellington appears in this production as Big Maybelle.

Speech

Location: Chicago, Illinois. 1989

[interview]

Source: *Wild Women Don't Have The Blues*

JUNIOR WELLS (Amos Blackmore)
Vocal and harmonica accompaniment: Roosevelt Sykes (piano); Otis Rush (electric guitar); Jack Meyers (electric bass); Fred Below (drums)

Location: Studio 6, Granada TV Centre, Manchester, England. Friday 30 September 1966

Title performed:
'What'd I Say'

Source: *Nothing But The Blues*

Probably as above

Location: Baden-Baden, Germany. c. December 1966

Titles performed:
unknown

Source: *American Folk Blues Festival 1966*

Vocal and harmonica accompaniment: Buddy Guy (electric guitar); David Myers (electric bass); unknown (drums)

Location: Chicago, Illinois. April–May 1970

Title performed:
'Cryin' Shame' K-Jazz 004, Rhapsody 9012

Source: *Chicago Blues*

Vocal and harmonica accompaniment: Buddy Guy (electric guitar); unknown (electric bass, drums)

Location: Chicago, Illinois. 1971

Title performed:
'Ship In The Ocean' [A] K-Jazz 019, Yazoo 507
'Tell Me What's Inside Of You' [B]

Source: *Out Of The Blacks, Into The Blues Part 2* [A]; *Le Blues Entre Les Dents* [B]

Vocal and harmonica accompaniment: Buddy Guy (electric guitar); Terry Taylor (second electric guitar); Pinetop Perkins (piano); Bill Wyman (electric bass); Dallas Taylor (drums)

Location: Montreux, Switzerland. Friday 28 June 1974

Titles performed:
'Lowdown Dirty Shame'
'Lord Have Mercy'
'Don't Do It No More'
'Don't Start Me To Talking'
'Messin' With The Kid' BMG791051, Rhino R3.1991
'Hoodoo Man' BMG791051, Rhino R3.1991
'Ain't No Need'

Source: *Montreux Jazz*
See also Buddy Guy and Muddy Waters.

Vocal and harmonica accompaniment: Nick Gravenites band, and Bonnie Raitt (vocal and guitar)

Location: Chicago, Illinois. Tuesday 18 July 1974

Titles performed:
'Messin' With The Kid'
'Stop Breaking Down'

Source: *Soundstage*

Vocal and harmonica accompaniment: Buddy Guy, Jimmy Johnson and Eddie Clearwater (electric guitars); David Myers (electric bass); Odie Payne (drums)

Location: Montreux, Switzerland. July 1979

Titles performed:
'Help Me'
'Messin' With The Kid'

Source: *Montreux Jazz*

Vocal accompaniment: Phil Guy and Sammy Lawhorn (electric guitars); Leo Davis (keyboards); Ike Addison (electric bass); Jerry Porter (drums)

Location: Chicago, Illinois. c.1979

Title performed:
'Junior, Do You Love Me?'

Source: *Chicago On The Good Foot*

Vocal and harmonica accompaniment: Southside Johnny And The Asbury Dukes [G]

Location: Chicago, Illinois. Saturday 12 January 1980

Titles performed:
'Messin' With The Kid'
'Hearts Of Stone'
'Hoodoo Man'

Source: *Soundstage*

Vocal and harmonica accompaniment: Buddy Guy (vocal and electric guitar) and others, unknown

Location: Chicago. 1981

Titles performed:
unknown

Source: *Chicago Blues Festival 1981*

Vocal and harmonica accompaniment: unknown (electric guitar, electric bass, drums)

Location: Theresa's Lounge, Chicago, Illinois. 1981

Titles performed:
'Mystery Train'
'Help Me'

Source: *Melody Of A City; Chicago*

Vocal and harmonica accompaniment: Buddy Guy (electric guitar) and others, unknown

Location: Chicago, Illinois Tuesday 20 July 1982

Title performed:
'What My Mama Told Me' [*sic*] (probably 'Stop Breaking Down')

Source: *Soundstage*

Vocal and harmonica accompaniment: Buddy Guy (electric guitar) and John Mayall's Blues Breakers; Mayall (keyboards); Mick Taylor (electric guitar); John McVie (electric bass); Colin Allen (drums)

Location: New Jersey. 1982

Titles performed:
'Messin' With The Kid' Castle Hendring 6 086
'Don't Start Me Talkin'' Castle Hendring 6 086

Source: *Blues Survivors*

Vocal and harmonica in duet with Buddy Guy (vocal and electric guitar) accompaniment: the Gerald Wiggins orchestra

Location: unknown {USA}. 1982

Title performed:
'Who's Loving You Tonight' ['That's Alright']

Source: *America's Music – Blues Volume 2*

Vocal and harmonica accompaniment: Buddy Guy (electric guitar) and others, unknown

Location: Checkerboard Lounge, Chicago, Illinois. 1990

Title performed:
'Everything's Gonna Be Alright' BMG 791.151, Rhino R91226

Source: *Blues Alive*

Speech

Location: Chicago, Illinois. 1993

[interview] MCA V10944

Source: *Sweet Home Chicago* [2] [D] [C]
Wells also appears in a tutorial video on Hot Licks 22234, and in *Blues Brothers 2000.*

CLIFTON WEST

Vocal accompaniment: unknown

Location: New York City. Sunday 21 October 1962

Titles performed:
'Belonging To God'

Source: *TV Gospel Time* #13

Vocal accompaniment: unknown

Location: New York City. Sunday 25 November 1962

Title performed:
'Wake Up In Glory'

Source: *TV Gospel Time* #3 [*sic*]

[REVEREND] E S WHEELER

Preaching and singing accompaniment: members of the St. John's Mission Baptist Church of Navasota, Texas

Location: Navasota, Texas. 1967

Titles performed:
'I Shall Not Be Moved' Flower 2, K-Jazz 055
'Old Ship Of Zion' Flower 2, K-Jazz 055
'Get On Board, Little Children' Flower 2, K-Jazz 055

Source: *A Well Spent Life*

WHISTLER AND HIS JUG BAND

Buford Threlkeld, vocal and guitar accompaniment: unknown (banjo, three blown jugs)

Location: Louisville, Kentucky. Sunday 25 May 1930

Title performed:
'Foldin' Bed (Tear It Down, Bed Slats And All)' Yazoo 512

This film was not originally used, and remained in storage until the mid-1980s. The version that appears on the Yazoo video is edited together by Sherwin Dunner from the fifteen takes that the Hearst crew originally made, placing both the camera and the microphone in different positions. Some of these takes suffered from speed fluctuations. They are as follows:

Tk. 1 incomplete; group shot
Tk. 2 complete; ST only, accompanying shots of mules in field
Tk. 3 complete; ST only, accompanying shots of cows in field
Tk. 4 incomplete; ST only, accompanying shots of cows in field
Tk. 5 incomplete; group shot
Tk. 6 complete; one jug only in close up shot
Tk. 7 incomplete; Threlkeld and banjo player only in shot
Tk. 8 incomplete; group shot
Tk. 9 incomplete; three jugs in shot
Tk. 10 incomplete; Threlkeld and banjo player only in shot

Tk. 11 incomplete; three jugs only in shot
Tk. 12 as tk. 11
Tk. 13 incomplete (end of song); Threlkeld and banjo player only in shot
Tk. 14 incomplete (end of song); three jugs only in shot
Tk. 15 incomplete (end of song); three jugs only in shot

Source: *Hearst Metrotone Newsreel*. Available from Historic.
A different and shorter edit of this performance appears in the film *Louie Bluie*.

BOOKER T WASHINGTON [BUKKA] WHITE

Vocal and steel guitar accompaniment: Willie Dixon (bass)–1
Vocal accompaniment: Muddy Waters Blues Band with James Cotton, Willie Dixon, Jesse Fuller, Mable Hillery, Brownie McGhee, Muddy Waters, Otis Spann, Sunnyland Slim, Sonny Terry, and Big Joe Williams, (vocals)–2

Location: Toronto, Canada. Thursday 27 to Saturday 29 January 1966

Titles performed:
[spoken introduction leading to];
'Aberdeen, Mississippi'–1
jam session–2

Source: *Festival Presents The Blues*

Vocal and steel guitar–1
Vocal and steel guitar accompaniment: Howlin Wolf (guitar); Reverend Pearly Brown (comments); Kilby Snow (percussion [tapping the back of his autoharp])–2
Vocal and steel guitar in the company of Son House (vocal and steel guitar); Skip James (vocal and guitar)–3
Vocal and steel guitar accompaniment: Skip James (guitar)–4

Location: Newport, Rhode Island. July 1966

Titles performed:
'Baby, You're Killing Me'–1 Vestapol 13049
'Old Lady Blues'–2 Vestapol 13049
'Please Don't Put Your Daddy Outdoors'–2 Vestapol 13049
'One Hundredth Man'–2 Vestapol 13049
participation in 'Blues Contest';
'Aberdeen, Mississippi'–3 Vestapol 13050
'Tombstone Blues'–4 Vestapol 13050

Source: *Alan Lomax film collection*
White can also be seen in the background during performances by Kilby Snow and Jimmy Driftwood, recorded on the same day as most of the above. See Vestapol 13051.

Vocal and steel guitar–1
Vocal and piano–2

Location: KCTS-TV studios, Seattle, Washington. 1967

Titles performed:
'Mama Don't Allow'–1 Yazoo 500
'Aberdeen, Mississippi Blues'–1 Yazoo 500
untitled blues
['I Wonder Why We Can't Get Along']–2 Yazoo 500
'Miss Rosa Lee'–1 Yazoo 500
'Poor Boy'–1 Yazoo 500
'World Boogie'–1 Yazoo 500

Source: *Masters Of American Traditional Music*

Vocal and steel guitar or guitar

Location: Memphis, Tennessee. 1969

Titles performed:
unknown

Source: *Sounds Of Summer – Memphis Blues Festival*

Vocal and guitar

Location: probably Memphis, Tennessee. 1969

Title performed:
'Mama Don't Allow' K-Jazz 030, Yazoo 505

Source: *Adelphi Productions*

Vocal and steel guitar

Location: Memphis, Tennessee. c.1970

Titles performed:
'Old Lady' Vestapol 13038
'Freight Train Blues' Vestapol 13038
'I'm Going To Settle Down' Vestapol 13038

Source: *uncredited* [C]

Vocal and guitar or steel guitar

Location: Baden-Baden, Germany. c. May 1970

Titles performed:
unknown

Source: *American Folk Blues Festival 1970*

Vocal and steel guitar

Location: probably Memphis, Tennessee. 1971

Titles performed:
'Poor Boy' [A] K-Jazz 020, Yazoo 506
'Jelly Roll Blues' [A] K-Jazz 020, Yazoo 506
'I'm Gonna Lay My Burden Down' [B]

Source: *Out Of The Blacks, Into The Blues Part 1* [A]; *Le Blues Entre Les Dents* [B]

Vocal and steel guitar

Location: probably Memphis, Tennessee. 1972

Titles performed:
unknown

Source: *Mr. Crump's Blues*
This may contain previously documented material.

Vocal and steel guitar

Location: Memphis, Tennessee. Sunday January 18 1976

Titles performed:
'Aberdeen, Mississippi Blues' Vestapol 13016
'Poor Boy' Vestapol 13016
'Slavery Time Blues'

Source: *The Devil's Music series 2*

Vocal and steel guitar

Location: unknown {USA}. 1976

Titles performed:
unknown

Source: *Cocksucker Blues*

JOSHUA DANIEL [JOSH] WHITE
Vocal and guitar accompaniment: Burl Ives and two unidentified singers (chorus)

Location: unknown {USA}. 1941

Title performed:
'John Henry'

Source: *Tall Tales*

Vocal and guitar

Location: unknown {USA}. 1945

Titles performed:
'Walls Of Jericho'
'One Meat Ball'

Source: *The Crimson Canary*

Vocal and guitar

Location: unknown {USA}. 1948

Titles performed:
unknown

Source: *Dreams That Money Can't Buy*

Vocal and guitar

Location: New York City. January–June 1949

Titles performed:
unknown

Source: *Adventures In Jazz*

Vocal and guitar

Location: unknown {USA}. 1949

Titles performed:
unknown

Source: *The Walking Hills*

Vocal and guitar

Location: New York City. 1950

Titles performed:
unknown

Source: *Arthur Godfrey And Friends* [unconfirmed]

Vocal and guitar

Location: New York City. 1957

Titles performed:
unknown

Source: *Art Ford's Greenwich Village Party*

Vocal and guitar

Location: New York City. 1958

Titles performed:
unknown

Source: *Art Ford's Jazz Party*

Vocal and guitar

Location: probably New York City. 1961

Titles performed:
unknown

Source: *Look Up And Live* [unconfirmed]

Vocal and guitar accompaniment, if any:
unknown

Location: probably Manchester, England. 1961

Titles performed: the following songs were performed in the series of 13 weekly programmes, transmitted between 21 September and 14 December 1961, but the order of performance is not known.
'Baby, Baby, Baby'
'Betty and Dupree'
'Black Girl'
'Blind Man Stood on the Road and Cried'
'Cindy'
'Delia's Gone'
'Don't Lie, Buddy'
'Every Time I Feel the Spirit'
'Foggy, Foggy Dew'
'Frankie and Johnnie'
'Good Morning Blues'
'Hard Time Blues'
'He Never Said a Mumbling Word'
'He's Got the Whole Wide World in His Hand'
'I Don't Intend to Die in Egypt's Land'
'I Had a Woman'
'I Know King Jesus is My Friend'
'If That Ain't the Holy Ghost'
'I'm Going to Live the Life I Sing About'
'I'm Marching Down Freedom's Road'
'In the Evening'
'I've Been 'Buked and I've Been Scorned'
'I've Got a Head Like a Rock'
'Joshua'
'Just a Closer Walk with Thee'
'Lonesome Town'
'My Captain'
'My Guitar is as Old as Father Time'
'Nobody Knows You When You're Down and Out'
'Number 12 Train'
'Old Ark's A-Movering'
'One Meat Ball'
'One Mint Julep'
'Outskirts of Town'
'Peter on the Sea'
'Raise a Rukus Tonight'
'Riddle Song'
'Run, Mona, Run'
'St. James Infirmary Blues'
'Scandalise My Name'
'Scotch and Soda for the Lady'
'Sometimes I Feel Like a Motherless Child'
'So Soon in the Morning'
'Strange Fruit'
'Take a Girl Like You'
'There's a Man Going Round Taking Names'
'The Story of the Grey Goose'
'They Call the Wind Maria'
'Timber'
'Two Little Fishes and Five Loaves of Bread'
'Waltzing Matilda'
'Wanderings'
'You Don't Know My Mind'
'You're a Mean Mistreating Woman'

Source: *Josh White Sings Music of the New World*
Studio photographs indicate that Josh White Jr. (presumably vocal and possibly guitar) took part in one broadcast at least.

Vocal and guitar accompaniment: unknown (bass)

Location: Sweden. 1962

Titles performed:
'You Know Baby What I Want' Vestapol 13037
'Number Twelve Train' Vestapol 13037

Source: *Swedish TV broadcast*

Vocal and guitar

Location: unknown {USA}. 1963

Titles performed:
unknown

Source: *Dinner With The President*

Vocal and guitar accompaniment, if any, unknown

Location: probably New York City. 1963

Titles performed:
unknown

Source: *Hootenanny*

Vocal and guitar

Location: probably New York City. 1964

Titles performed:
unknown

Source: *Hootenanny*

Vocal and guitar accompaniment: unknown (bass and drums).
Possibly Julie Felix (second vocal)–1

Location: London, England. 1965

Titles performed:
'John Henry' Vestapol 13004
'Timbers Gotta Roll'
'Ride Back Home'
'Battle of Jericho'
'Give Me Back My Sign'
'Strange Fruit'
'Jelly, Jelly'–1 Vestapol 13003
'Jim Crow'
'Free And Equal Blues'
'My Guitar Is As Old As Father Time'

Source: *BBC TV broadcast* [M]. Title unknown

Vocal and guitar

Location: unknown {USA}. 1966

Titles performed:
unknown

Source: *World Of Music*

Vocal and guitar

Location: unknown {USA}. 1967

Titles performed:
unknown

Source: *Live From The Bitter End*

Vocal and guitar

Location: unknown {USA}. 1967

Titles performed:
unknown

Source: *The Woody Woodbury Show*

Vocal and guitar accompaniment: Carolyn White (vocal)

Location: Sweden. 1967

Title performed:
'Nobody Knows You When You're Down And Out' Vestapol 13037

Source: *Swedish TV broadcast* [M]

PHIL WIGGINS
See John Cephas.

SPENCER WIGGINS
See Pleasant Green Choir.

JOE WILLIE WILKINS

Vocal and guitar accompaniment: Mose Vinson (piano); Houston Stackhouse (electric guitar); L T Lewis (drums)

Location: Memphis, Tennessee. Monday 19 January 1976

Title performed:
'Mr Downchild' [part only]

Source: *The Devil's Music series 1*
See also Houston Stackhouse.

[REVEREND] ROBERT WILKINS

Wilkins was filmed at the Newport Folk Festival in July 1964, and a fragment of one song was used on the soundtrack of the documentary *Festival* [1]. The possibility of the original footage surviving certainly must exist but currently remains unproved.

BILL WILLIAMS

Vocal and guitar

Location: probably Louisville, Kentucky. Summer 1970

Titles performed:
unknown

Source: *Kentucky Educational Television*

Location: unknown {USA}. 1971

Titles performed:
unknown

Source: *CBS News*

Vocal and guitar

Location: unknown {USA}. 1972

Titles performed:
unknown

Source: *Thinking Out Loud* [unconfirmed]

CHARLES WILLIAMS

Vocal accompaniment: the Johnny Otis band–1
Vocal accompaniment: Delmar Evans, Linda Hopkins, Barbara Morrison (vocals) and the Johnny Otis band–2

Location: Monterey, California. 1987

Titles performed:
'Every Beat Of My Heart'–1
Gospel medley–2

Source: *Monterey Jazz Festival*
See also Johnny Otis.

[BIG] JOE WILLIAMS (Joe Lee Williams)

Vocal accompaniment: presumably own 9-string guitar

Location: probably Chicago, Illinois. c. early 1950s

Titles performed:
unknown

Source: *I Come For To Sing* [unconfirmed]

Vocal and 9-string electric guitar

Location: London, England. October 1963

Titles performed:
unknown
[interview]

Source: *Tonight*

Vocal and 9-string electric guitar–1
Vocal accompaniment Lonnie Johnson (vocal); Memphis Slim (vocal and piano); Muddy Waters (vocal); Matt Murphy (electric guitar); Victoria Spivey (vocal); Billie Stepney (drums); Sonny Boy Williamson (vocal)–2

Location: Manchester, England. October 1963

Titles performed:
'Baby Please Don't Go'–1
'Bye Bye Baby'–2

Source: *I Hear the Blues*

Probably as above

Location: Baden-Baden, Germany. October 1963

Titles performed:
unknown

Source: *American Folk Blues Festival 1963*

Vocal accompaniment: the Muddy Waters Blues Band, with James Cotton, Willie Dixon, Jesse Fuller, Mable Hillery, Brownie McGhee, Muddy Waters, Otis Spann, Sunnyland Slim, and Bukka White (vocals)

Location: Toronto, Canada. Thursday 27 to Saturday 29 January 1966

Title performed:
jam session

Source: *Festival Presents The Blues*
Although Williams appears in the finale, he does not appear either on camera or soundtrack anywhere else in this programme. His presumed solo contribution[s] must therefore be regarded as unbroadcast, but potentially still extant.

Vocal and 9-string electric guitar

Location: KCTS-TV studios, Seattle, Washington. 1967

Titles performed:

'Little Annie Mae'	Yazoo 504
'Baby Please Don't Go'	Yazoo 504
'Low Down Dirty Shame'	Yazoo 504
'Doctor Martin Luther King'	Yazoo 504
'Shake Your Boogie'	Yazoo 504
'Shake Your Boogie' take 2	Yazoo 504
'My Baby Left Me'	Yazoo 504
'Don't You Leave Me Here'	Yazoo 504
'Something Wrong With My Little Machine'	Yazoo 504
'Juanita'	Yazoo 504
'Tailor Made Baby'	Yazoo 504
'Mean Mistreater'	Yazoo 504
'Peach Orchard Mama'	Yazoo 504
'Tijuana'	Yazoo 504
'Peach Orchard Mama' take 2	Yazoo 504

Source: *Masters Of American Traditional Music*
The bulk of these performances are relatively short, and the total running time of the session is 29 minutes.

Vocal and 9-string electric guitar

Location: BBC TV studios, White City, London, England. Tuesday 22 October 1968

Titles performed:
'Four Corners Of The World'
'Baby Please Don't Go'
and two other, unknown, titles

Source: *American Folk Blues Festival 1968* [1]

Probably as above

Location: Germany. November 1968

Titles performed:
unknown

Source: *American Folk Blues Festival 1968* [2]

Vocal and 9-string guitar

Location: Crawford, Mississippi. Wednesday 21 January 1976

Titles performed:

'Sloppy Drunk Blues'	Vestapol 13016
'Highway 49'	Vestapol 13016
'Providence Help The Poor People'	Vestapol 13016
'Meet Me in The Bottom'	
'Watergate Blues'	

Source: *The Devil's Music series 2*

Presumably vocal and 9-string electric guitar

Location: unknown {USA}. 1976

Titles performed:
unknown

Source: *The Glorious Fourth* [unconfirmed]

Vocal and 9-string electric guitar

Location: juke-joint, Crawford, Mississippi. 1978

Titles performed:
'Low Down Dirty Shame' K-Jazz 030, Yazoo 505
'Baby Please Don't Go' K-Jazz 030, Yazoo 505

Source: *Good Morning Blues*

Vocal and 9-string electric guitar

Location: Freedom Village, Greenville, Mississippi. Saturday 8 September 1979

Titles performed:
'Baby Please Don't Go' K-Jazz 081
'Tailor Made Baby' K-Jazz 081
'Came Home This Morning' K-Jazz 081

Source: *Mississippi Blues*
The 9-string electric guitar, with the bottom three strings double strung, was unique to Williams, who built it by adapting a standard 6-string model.

JOE WILLIAMS (Joseph Goreed)
Vocal accompaniment: the Count Basie orchestra

Location: unknown {USA}. 1957

Title performed:
'I Don't Like You Anymore'

Source: *Disk Jockey Jamboree*

Vocal accompaniment: probably the Mitchell Ayres orchestra

Location: New York City. 1958

Titles performed:
unknown

Source: *The Perry Como Show*

Vocal accompaniment: unknown

Location: New York City. 1959

Titles performed:
unknown

Source: *The Ed Sullivan Show*

Vocal accompaniment: unknown

Location: unknown {USA}. 1959

Titles performed:
unknown

Source: *The George Hamilton IV Show*

Vocal accompaniment: the Count Basie orchestra

Location: Zurich, Switzerland. 1959

Title performed:
'Roll 'em Pete'

Source: *Swiss TV broadcast* [M]

Vocal accompaniment: unknown

Location: unknown {USA}. 1960

Titles performed:
unknown

Source: *Cinderfella* [unconfirmed]

Vocal accompaniment: the Count Basie orchestra

Location: unknown {USA}. 1960

Titles performed:
unknown

Source: *The Fred Astaire Show*

Vocal accompaniment: the Count Basie orchestra

Location: unknown {USA}. 1961

Titles performed:
unknown

Source: *Moods In Melody* [unconfirmed]

Vocal accompaniment: the Count Basie orchestra

Location: Liège, Belgium. 1961

Titles performed:
'Gee Baby, Ain't I Good To You'
'Hallelujah I Love Her So'

Source: *Belgian TV broadcast* [M]

Vocal duet with Jimmy Rushing
accompaniment: the Count Basie orchestra

Location: Newport, Rhode Island. Summer 1962

Title performed:
'Goin' To Chicago'

Source: *Newport Jazz Festival 1962*

Vocal accompaniment: unknown

Location: New York City. 1963

Titles performed:
unknown
[probably interview]

Source: *The Steve Allen Show*

Vocal accompaniment: probably the Skitch Henderson orchestra

Location: New York City. 1963

Titles performed:
unknown
[probably interview]

Source: *The Tonight Show Starring Johnny Carson*

Vocal accompaniment: unknown

Location: New York City. 1964

Titles performed:
unknown

Source: *On Parade*

Vocal accompaniment: probably the Paul Weston orchestra

Location: unknown {USA}. 1966

Titles performed:
unknown

Source: *The Danny Kaye Show*

Vocal accompaniment: unknown

Location: unknown {USA}. 1966

Titles performed:
unknown

Source: *The Strollin' 20's*

Vocal accompaniment: unknown

Location: unknown {USA}. 1966–67

Titles performed:
unknown

Source: *Dial M For Music* [unconfirmed]

Vocal accompaniment: unknown

Location: unknown {USA}. 1967

Titles performed:
unknown

Source: *The Bruce Morrow Show*

Vocal accompaniment: unknown

Location: Los Angeles, California. 1967–68

Titles performed:
unknown

Source: *The Joey Bishop Show*

Vocal accompaniment: unknown

Location: Los Angeles, California. 1968

Titles performed:
unknown

Source: *The Donald O'Connor Show*

Vocal accompaniment: unknown

Location: unknown {USA}. 1968

Titles performed:
unknown

Source: *Here Come The Stars*

Vocal accompaniment: unknown

Location: New York City. 1968

Titles performed:
unknown
[probably interview]

Source: *The Steve Allen Show*

Vocal accompaniment: the Duke Ellington orchestra

Location: the White House, Washington DC. 1969

Titles performed:
unknown

Source: *Duke Ellington At The White House*

Vocal accompaniment: probably the Mort Lindsay orchestra

Location: unknown {USA}. 1969

Titles performed:
unknown

Source: *The Merv Griffin Show*

Vocal accompaniment: unknown

Location: unknown {USA}. 1969

Titles performed:
unknown [probably ST only]

Source: *The Moonshine War*

Vocal accompaniment: unknown

Location: unknown {USA}. 1969

Titles performed:
unknown

Source: *Peter Wolf*

Vocal accompaniment: unknown

Location: unknown {USA}. 1969

Titles performed:
unknown

Source: *Playboy After Dark*

Vocal accompaniment: probably the Doc Severinsen orchestra

Location: New York City. 1970

Titles performed:
unknown

Source: *The Tonight Show Starring Johnny Carson*

Location: New York City. 1970

Titles performed:
unknown

Source: *The Steve Allen Show*

Vocal accompaniment: probably the Mort Lindsay orchestra

Location: unknown {USA}. 1971

Titles performed:
unknown

Source: *The Merv Griffin Show*

Vocal accompaniment: unknown

Location: unknown {USA}. 1972

Titles performed:
unknown

Source: *Timex All Star Swing Festival*

Vocal accompaniment: the Duke Ellington orchestra

Location: Monterey, California. 1973

Title performed:
'Don't Get Around Much Anymore'
'Everyday I Have The Blues'

Source: *The Duke At Monterey*

Vocal accompaniment: the Duke Ellington orchestra

Location: unknown {USA}. 1973

Titles performed:
unknown

Source: *The Duke Ellington Special*

Vocal accompaniment: unknown

Location: unknown {USA}. 1974

Titles performed:
unknown

Source: *Feeling Good*

Vocal accompaniment: the Johnny Otis orchestra

Location: Monterey, California. 1973

Titles performed:
unknown

Source: *Monterey Jazz*

Vocal accompaniment: probably the Mort Lindsay orchestra

Location: unknown {USA}. 1974

Titles performed:
unknown

Source: *The Merv Griffin Show*

Vocal accompaniment: unknown

Location: unknown {USA}. 1974

Titles performed:
unknown

Source: *The Midnight Special*

Vocal accompaniment: Oscar Peterson (piano); Nils-Henning Ørsted-Pedersen (bass); unknown drums)

Location: unknown {USA}. 1974

Titles performed:
unknown

Source: *Oscar Peterson Presents*

Vocal accompaniment: unknown

Location: unknown {USA}. 1975

Titles performed:
unknown

Source: *AM America*

Vocal accompaniment: probably the George Rhodes orchestra

Location: Las Vegas, Nevada. 1975

Titles performed:
unknown

Source: *Sammy And Company*

Vocal accompaniment: unknown

Location: unknown {USA}. 1976

Titles performed:
unknown

Source: *At The Top*

Vocal accompaniment: unknown

Location: unknown {USA}. 1976

Titles performed:
unknown

Source: *Festival Of Lively Arts For Young People*

Vocal accompaniment: unknown

Location: unknown {USA}. 1976

Titles performed:
unknown

Source: *The Joe Franklin Show*

Vocal accompaniment: unknown

Location: unknown {USA}. 1976

Titles performed:
unknown

Source: *The Midnight Special*

Vocal accompaniment: probably the Mort Lindsay orchestra

Location: unknown {USA}. 1977

Titles performed:
unknown

Source: *The Merv Griffin Show*

Vocal accompaniment: unknown

Location: unknown {USA}. 1978

Titles performed:
unknown

Source: *Big Band Bash*

Vocal accompaniment: probably the Milton DeLugg orchestra

Location: Burbank, California. 1978

Titles performed:
unknown

Source: *The Chuck Barris Rah Rah Show*

Vocal accompaniment: probably the Doc Severinson orchestra

Location: Los Angeles, California. 1978

Titles performed:
unknown
[probably interview]

Source: *The Tonight Show Starring Johnny Carson*

Vocal accompaniment: the Count Basie orchestra

Location: Carnegie Hall, New York. 30 March 1981

Titles performed:
'Everyday I Have The Blues'
'Goin' To Chicago'
'Well Alright'
'Roll 'em Pete'

Source: *Count Basie At Carnegie Hall*

Vocal accompaniment: the Gerald Wiggins orchestra

Location: unknown {USA}. 1982

Title performed:
'She's Mine, She's Yours'
Magnum MMGV-037

Source: *America's Music – The Blues Vol. 2*

Dramatic performances and occasional vocals

Location: New York City. 1984–92

Williams appeared in several episodes of this programme as the father-in-law of Cosby's character Cliff Huxtable.

Source: *The Cosby Show*

MARION WILLIAMS

Vocal accompaniment: unknown

Location: London, England. Sunday 27 October 1963

Titles performed:
unknown

Source: *UK TV broadcast* [M]. Origin unknown.

Vocal accompaniment: unknown

Location: Chicago, Illinois. Sunday 15 December 1963

Titles performed:
unknown

Source: *Jubilee Showcase* [prog #11–1]

Vocal accompaniment: unknown

Location: New York City. c.1965–66

Titles performed:
unknown

Source: *TV Gospel Time* #60

Vocal accompaniment: unknown

Location: Chicago, Illinois. Friday 13 May 1966

Titles performed:
unknown

Source: *Jubilee Showcase* [prog #34–2]

Vocal accompaniment: unknown

Location: probably Paris, France. 1971

Titles performed:
'When The Saints Go Marching In'
and other, unknown, title[s]

Source: *Pan-African Festival*

Vocal accompaniment: unknown

Location: Chicago, Illinois. Monday 13 December 1976

Title performed:
'How I Got Over'

Source: *Soundstage*

Vocal accompaniment: unknown

Location: Paris, France. 1978

Titles performed:
unknown

Source: *Gospel Caravan*

Vocal accompaniment: unknown

Location: All Saints Church, Northampton, England. 1980

Titles performed:
unknown

Source: *In The Spirit*
See also the Stars Of Faith.

MEL WILLIAMS
See Johnny Otis.

NATHAN WILLIAMS AND THE ZYDECO CHA-CHAS
Vocal and accordion accompaniment: unknown (tenor saxophone, electric guitar, electric bass, rub-board, drums)
Nathan Williams, vocal and accordion accompaniment: Walter Williams Jr. (rub-board–1

Location: Louisiana. 1990

Titles performed:

'Hey Bébé'	Channel 5 083 258-3, Island 083 258-3
'Steady Rock'	Channel 5 083 258-3, Island 083 258-3
'Jolie Catin'–1	Channel 5 083 258-3, Island 083 258-3

Source: *Zydeco Nite'N'Day*

Vocal and accordion accompaniment: Mark Anthony Williams (rub-board)

Location: Louisiana. 1994

Title performed:

'Ma Pauvre Maman'	BMG un-numbered
[interview]	BMG un-numbered

Source: *The Kingdom Of Zydeco*

ROBERT PETE WILLIAMS
Vocal and guitar

Location: Studio 6, Granada TV centre, Manchester, England. Friday 30 September 1966

Title performed:
untitled blues

Source: *Nothing But The Blues*

Vocal and guitar

Location: Baden-Baden, Germany. c. December 1966

Titles performed:
unknown

Source: *American Folk Blues Festival 1966*

Vocal and guitar

Location: KCTS-TV studios, Seattle, Washington. Thursday 16 April 1970

Titles performed:
'Mamie' Vestapol 13003
'I Want To Know'
'I've Been Mistreated'
'We're Gonna Boogie'
'Dear Old Mother Of Mine' Vestapol 13037

Source: *Masters Of American Traditional Music*

Vocal and guitar

Location: KCTS-TV studios, Seattle, Washington. Probably Thursday 16 April 1970

Title performed:
'Baby, You Don't Treat Me Right'

Source: *Roots Of American Music*

Vocal and guitar

Location: Louisiana. 1971

Titles performed:
'Old Girl At My Door' [A] K-Jazz 020, Yazoo 506
'Scrap Iron Blues' [A] K-Jazz 020, Yazoo 506
[interview] [A] K-Jazz 020, Yazoo 506
'Woman Why You Treat Me So Mean?' [B]

Source: *Out Of The Blacks – Into The Blues part 1* [A]; *Le Blues Entre Les Dents* [B]

Vocal and guitar

Location: unknown {USA}. c.1972

Titles performed:
unknown

Source: *Thinking Out Loud*

SISTER WILLIAMS
Vocal with congregation, vocals

Location: Lily Grove Baptist Church, Bessemer, Alabama. Early 1984

Title performed:
'I Love The Lord' (part only)

Source: *On The Battlefield*

SONNY BOY WILLIAMSON (Aleck Ford aka 'Rice' Miller)
Vocal and harmonica accompaniment: Memphis Slim (piano); Matt Murphy (electric guitar); Willie Dixon (bass); Billie Stepney (drums)

Location: Studio 6, Granada TV studios, Manchester, England. October 1963

Title performed:
'Keep It To Yourself'

Source: *I Hear The Blues*

Probably as above

Location: Baden-Baden, Germany. October 1963

Titles performed:
unknown

Source: *American Folk Blues Festival 1963*

Vocal and harmonica accompaniment: unknown

Location: London, England. Late 1963

Titles performed:
unknown
[interview]

Source: *Tonight*
There was almost cerainly another appearance on the *Tonight* show within two weeks either side of the above.

Vocal and harmonica accompaniment: unknown Danish musicians (guitar, bass)

Location: Copenhagen, Denmark. Late 1963

Titles performed:
'When I'm Gone' ['Tell Me Baby'] Storyville SV6032, Jazz & Jazz Vidjazz 13
'Come On In This House' ['You're My Baby'] Storyville SV6032, Jazz & Jazz Vidjazz 13
'Goin' Back Home' Storyville SV6032, Jazz & Jazz Vidjazz 13

Source: Danish TV broadcast, subsequently released as *Sonny Boy Williamson* [FS]. Titles in parenthesis are those assigned by Storyville.

Vocal and harmonica–1;
as above accompaniment: Sunnyland Slim (piano); Hubert Sumlin (electric guitar); Willie Dixon (bass); Clifton James (drums)–2

Location: Baden-Baden, Germany. October 1964

Titles performed:
'Bye Bye Baby'–1
[short interview in English with Joachim Berendt]
'In My Younger Days'–2

Source: *American Folk Blues Festival 1964*
Sonny Boy Williamson can be seen – and heard – playing a fruit machine during a long introduction to the programme in German by the presenter, Joachim Berendt.

Probably as above

Location: Free Trade Hall, Manchester, England. Thursday 22 October 1964

Titles performed:
unknown

Source: *The Blues Came Walking*

Vocal and harmonica accompaniment: unknown

Location: London, England. Monday 9 November 1964

Titles performed:
'Lonesome Cabin'
and one other, unknown, title

Source: *Beat Room*

Vocal and harmonica accompaniment: probably the Five Dimensions[G]

Location: Studio 6, Granada TV Centre, Manchester, England. Monday 16 November 1964

Titles performed:
unknown

Source: *unbroadcast show* [M] made for UK Granada TV by Philip Casson and John Hamp

Vocal and harmonica accompaniment: unknown

Location: Southampton, England. Tuesday 22 December 1964

Title performed:
unknown

Source: *Day By Day*

Vocal and harmonica accompaniment: unknown

Location: ATV studios, London, England. Friday 8 Januuary 1965

Title performed:
unknown

Source: *Ready Steady Go*

Vocal and harmonica accompaniment: unknown British group, (piano, guitar, bass, drums)

Location: ATV Studios, London England. c. early 1965

Titles performed:
unknown

Source: *Hullabaloo* [2]

[REVEREND] RUBEN WILLINGHAM
Vocal accompaniment: unknown

Location: Chicago, Illinois.

The following appearances are known:
1965 Sunday 11 July [prog #29–3]
1969 Saturday 14 June [prog #19–1]

Titles performed:
unknown

Source: Jubilee Showcase
See also The Swanee Quintet.

AARON [LITTLE SONNY] WILLIS
Vocal and probably harmonica accompaniment: unknown

Location: Coliseum Stadium, Los Angeles, California. Sunday 20 August 1972

Titles performed:
unknown

Source: *Wattstax*

CHUCK WILLIS
Vocal accompaniment: unknown

Location: Philadelphia, Pennsylvania. c.1956

Title performed:
[probably] 'The Stroll'

Source *Dick Clark's American Bandstand*

EDITH WILSON
Vocal accompaniment: unknown

Location: unknown {USA}. 1940

Titles performed:
unknown

Source: *I'm Still Alive*

Vocal accompaniment: unknown

Location: probably New York City. 1950s

Titles performed:
unknown

Source: *The Garry Moore Show*

Vocal accompaniment: unknown

Location: New York City. 1950s

Titles performed:
unknown

Source: *The Jackie Gleason Show*

Vocal accompaniment: Little Brother Montgomery (piano)

Location: Chicago, Illinois. Thursday 29 January 1976

Title performed:
'He May Be Your Man'
'Yankee Doodle Blues' [unbroadcast]

Source: *The Devil's Music series 1*

Vocal accompaniment unknown, possibly Little Brother Montgomery (piano)

Location: Chicago, Illinois. 1977

Titles performed:
unknown

Source: *Made In Chicago*

HARDING [HOP] WILSON
Vocal and pedal steel guitar, accompaniment: unknown (electric bass); probably Ivory Lee Simien (drums)

Location: Houston, Texas. Spring 1963

Titles performed:
untitled blues [fragment only] Yazoo 520

Source: *Dietrich Wawzyn film collection*

SMOKEY WILSON

Vocal accompaniment: unknown

Location: San Diego, California. 1987

Titles performed:
unknown

Source: *Three Generations Of The Blues part 2*

U P WILSON

Vocal and electric guitar accompaniment: unknown

Location: unknown {USA}. c. early 1990s

Titles performed:
unknown Red Lightnin' 0083

Source: *U P Wilson – Texas Guitar Tornado*

JIMMY WITHERSPOON

Vocal accompaniment: Ben Webster (tenor saxophone) and the Vince Guaraldi trio (piano, bass, drums)

Location: unknown {USA}. Mid–late 1950s

Titles performed:
'Times Are Getting Tougher'
'Ain't Nobody's Business'
'Outskirts Of Town'
'Roll 'Em'

Source: *US TV broadcast* [M]. Origin unknown.

Vocal accompaniment: unknown

Location: New York City. 1961

Titles performed:
unknown

Source: *The Steve Allen Show*

Vocal accompaniment: unknown

Location: unknown {USA}. 1962

Titles performed:
unknown

Source: *The Paul Crump Story*. May be [ST] only.

Vocal accompaniment: unknown

Location: unknown {USA}. 1964

Titles performed:
unknown

Source: *Quest*

Vocal accompaniment: unknown

Location: Reading, Berkshire, England. 1964

Titles performed:
'No Rollin' Blues'

Source: *UK TV broadcast* [M]. Origin unknown.

Vocal accompaniment: unknown, but including tenor saxophone

Location: London, England. 1964

Title performed:
'Money's Getting Cheaper'

Source: *Tonight*

Vocal accompaniment: unknown

Location: unknown {USA}. 1965

Titles performed:
unknown

Source: *Hollywood A Go-Go*

Vocal accompaniment: unknown

Location: Los Angeles, California. 1965

Titles performed:
unknown

Source: *Shindig*

Vocal accompaniment: unknown

Location: unknown {USA}. 1965

Titles performed:
unknown

Source: *Shivaree*

Vocal accompaniment: unknown

Location: probably New York City. 1967

Titles performed:
unknown

Source: *Jazz-USA*

Vocal accompaniment: unknown

Location: unknown {USA}. 1971

Titles performed:
unknown

Source: *Soul*

Vocal accompaniment: unknown

Location: unknown {USA}. 1974

Titles performed:
unknown

Source: *The Black Godfather*. May be [ST] only

Vocal accompaniment: probably the Doc Severinsen orchestra

Location: Burbank, California. 1974

Titles performed:
unknown

Source: *The Tonight Show Starring Johnny Carson*

Vocal accompaniment: unknown

Location: unknown {USA}. 1974

Titles performed:
unknown

Source: *The Midnight Special*

Vocal accompaniment: Hal Singer (tenor saxophone); Richard Tee (piano); Cornell Dupree (electric guitar); Gordon Edwards (bass); Hersil Lovelle (drums)

Location: Montreux, Switzerland. Sunday 4 July 1976

Titles performed:
'Kansas City'
'Got My Mojo Working'
'Ain't Nobody's Business'
'Going To Chicago'
'Goin' Down Slow'
'Mean Ole Frisco'
'Hands Off'
'Pearly Whites'

Source: *Montreux Jazz*

Vocal accompaniment: Ray Alexander (piano); Eugene Edwards (electric guitar); and others, unknown

Location: Nice, France. Thursday 5–Sunday 15 July 1979

Titles performed:
'Everyday I Have The Blues'
'I'd Rather Drink Muddy Water'
'C C Rider'
'Big Boss Man'
'Outskirts Of Town'
'Stormy Monday'
'Everyday I Have The Blues'
'Gee Baby Ain't I Good To You'
'Kansas City'
'Hands Off'
'Got My Mojo Working'
'I'd Rather Drink Muddy Water'

Source: *La Grande Parade Du Jazz*

Vocal accompaniment: unknown, but including Art Pepper (tenor saxophone)

Location: Lighthouse Cafe, Los Angeles, California. 1981

Titles performed:
'Big Boss Man'
'You Got Me Runnin''
'Past Forty Blues'
'Jumpin' The Blues'
'Pearly Whites'
'Ain't Nobody's Business'

Source: *US PBS TV broadcast*[C]

Vocal accompaniment: unknown

Location: Covent Garden, London, England. 1983

Titles performed:
'Outskirts Of Town'
'Story Of My Life'
'Money's Getting Cheaper'
'Pearly Whites'
'Big Leg Woman'
'Kansas City'

Source: *Jazz On 4*

Vocal accompaniment: Danny Moss, Brian Dee, Roy Hawksford, Quinnie Lawrence, Len Skeat (individual instrumentation unknown)

Location: Leadmill nightclub, Sheffield, England. 1984

Titles performed:
'Gee Baby Ain't I Good To You'
'Pearly Whites'
'Big Leg Woman'
'I Want A Little Girl'
'Going To Chicago'
'Going Down Slow'
'Big Boss Man'

Source: *Jazz At The Leadmill*

Vocal accompaniment: unknown

Location: City Hall, Sheffield, England. 1984

Titles performed:
'Stormy Monday Blues'
'Goin' To Chicago'

Source: *Live At City Hall*

Vocal accompaniment: unknown quartet

Location: Lugano, Switzerland. 1985

Titles performed:
'The Shadow Of Your Smile'
'Come On And Love Me'
'It Don't Mean A Thing'
'Gee Baby Ain't I Good To You'
'Careless Love'
'Nobody Knows You When You're Down And Out'
'Anyway You Want Me'
'Ain't Nobody's Business'
'Big Boss Man'
'Pearly Whites'
'No Rollin' Blues'

Source: *Swiss TV broadcast* [C]

DANIEL WOMACK

Mouth-bow solo–1; vocal and guitar–2; body slapping–3

Location: WDBJ-TV Studios, Roanoke, Virgina. Spring/Summer 1987

Titles performed:
'I Heard A Mighty Rumblin''–1 [A]
'Let Us March'–2 [A]
'Hambone'–3 [A]
'Let Jesus Lead You'–2 [B]

Source: *Black Music Traditions In Virginia: Non–blues Secular Music* [A]; *Black Music Traditions In Virginia: Sacred Music* [B]
All the above performances are used in extract only.

A mouth bow is a 1-string instrument, shaped like a rudimentary archery bow and played by placing one end in the mouth, plucking the string with one hand and using the lips and mouth cavity to alter the tone.

JOHNNY AND VERLINA WOODS

Vocal and harmonica–1
Johnny and Verlina Woods, vocal duet, accompaniment: Johnny Woods (harmonica)–2

Location: Mississippi. 1976

Titles performed:
untitled blues–1
'My Home Is In The Rocky Mountains'–2
'Long Tall Baby'–1
unknown title–1

Source: *All You Need Is Love*

[REVEREND] MACEO WOODS
Vocal accompaniment: unknown

Location: Chicago, Illinois

The following appearances are known:
1968
Saturday 21 September [prog #28–2]
1973
Saturday 26 May [prog #32–3]
1975
Saturday 13 September [prog #20–3]
1982
Monday 20 September [prog #14]

Titles performed:
unknown

Source: *Jubilee Showcase*

ROBERT E WOOTEN
Vocal accompaniment : unknown

Location: Chicago, Illinois. Sunday 8 March 1964

Titles performed:
unknown

Source: *Jubilee Showcase* [prog #26–3]

JAMES WYNS
Vocal accompaniment: unknown

Location: New York City. Sunday 11 November 1962

Title performed:
'His Eye Is On The Sparrow'

Source: *TV Gospel Time* #2
See also the Washington Temple Celestial Chorus.

Y

ESTELLA [MAMA] YANCEY
Vocal accompaniment: unknown

Location: unknown {USA}. 1969

Titles performed:
unknown

Source: *Jazz Alley*

Vocal accompaniment: Erwin Helfer (piano)

Location: Chicago, Illinois. c.1978

Title performed:
'Make Me A Pallet On The Floor'

Source: *Chicago Melodie*
This artist is the widow of pianist Jimmy Yancey.

[REVEREND] MARVIN YANCEY
Vocal accompaniment: unknown

Location: Chicago, Illinois

The following appearances are known:
1968
Saturday 12 October [prog #16–3]
1969
Saturday 8 February [prog #34–3]
Saturday 28 June [prog #7–2]
Saturday 1 November [prog #12–3]
1972
Saturday 2 September [prog #24–1]
1973
Saturday 24 November [prog #32–1]
1974
Saturday 7 September [prog #5–1]
1975
Wednesday 13 April [prog #19–2]

Titles performed:
unknown

Source: *Jubilee Showcase*

ED AND LONNIE YOUNG

Ed Young (vocals and cane fife); Lonnie Young (bass drum); G.D. Young (snare drum)

Location: Newport, Rhode Island. July 1966
[A] Interior (bar area) (probably Thursday 21 July)
[B] In open air (probably as A)

Titles performed:

'Oree' (take 1) [A]	Vestapol 13050
[interview with Ed Young] [A]	Vestapol 13050
untitled instrumental [A]	Vestapol 13050
'Oree' (take 2) [B]	Vestapol 13050

Source: *Alan Lomax film collection*
The date for [A] is derived from a calendar on the wall of the liquor bar seen behind Ed Young during his interview.

Probably as above

Location: probably Como, Mississippi. c.1976

Titles performed:
'Sitting On Top Of The World' [part only]
'Jim And John' [part only]

Source: *All You Need Is Love*
See also Jesse Mae Hemphill, Napoleon Strickland and Othar Turner.

JOHNNY YOUNG

Vocal and guitar accompaniment: Robert Nighthawk (second guitar); Robert Whitehead (drums)

Location: Maxwell Street, Chicago, Illinois. 1964

Title performed:

'Liar Man Blues' [fragment]	Shanachie 1403

Source: *And This Is Free*

JOSEPH [MIGHTY JOE] YOUNG

Vocal accompaniment: The Blue Beats; Clarence 'Gatemouth' Brown and Johnnie Johnnson (electric guitars); Dave 'Fathead' Newman and one unknown (trumpets); Harrison Calloway and one unknown (tenor saxophones); 'Skip' [possibly Skippy Brooks] (piano); Finis Tasby electric bass); Freeman Brown (drums)–1
Vocal and electric guitar accompaniment: as above–2

Location: WFAA-TV studios, Dallas, Texas. Tuesday 14 February 1966

Titles performed:
'Suffering Soul'–1
'Tell Me Why You Want To Hurt Me'–2

Source: *The Beat*

Vocal and electric guitar accompaniment: unknown

Location: Chicago, Illinois. April–May 1970

Titles performed:
unknown

Source: *Chicago Blues*. Not used in the final edit.

Vocal and electric guitar accompaniment: unknown

Location: probably Chicago, Illinois. 1976

Title performed:
'One Thing You Can't Deny'

Source: *All You Need Is Love*

Vocal and electric guitar accompaniment: unknown

Location: Chicago, Illinois. 1977

Titles performed:
unknown

Source: *Made In Chicago*

Vocal and electric guitar accompaniment: probably Son Seals (electric guitar) and others, unknown

Location: Chicago, Illinois. Thursday 1 November 1979

Titles performed:
'Need A Friend'
'Why Baby'

Source: *Soundstage*

Z

ZION BAPTIST CHURCH FEMALE CHORUS OF JACKSONVILLE

Female choir, vocal accompaniment: unknown

Location: Jacksonville, Florida. 1966

Titles performed:
unknown

Source: *TV Gospel Time* #60

ZION HARMONIZERS

Vocal group accompaniment: unknown

Location: New Orleans, Louisiana. 1985

Title performed:
'I'll Fly Away'

Source: *New Orleans Now: In The Revival Tent*

ZION TRAVELLERS

Probably Bartha L Watkins, L C Cohen, L W Van, Garland Fate Mason, Wesley J Sherman, Felton Vernon (vocals) accompaniment: unknown

Location: probably Los Angeles, California. Early 1950s

Titles performed:
unknown

Source: [A] *A Miracle Through Song* [FS] [M]; [B] *God Of The Mountains* [FS] [M]

Origin unknown.

ZYDECO EXPRESS

Willis Prudhomme (vocal and accordion) accompaniment: unknown (electric guitar, electric bass, rub-board, drums)

Location: Plaisance, Louisiana. 1988

Title performed:
unknown [fragment] K-Jazz 098, Rhapsody 8062
[interview] K-Jazz 098, Rhapsody 8062

Source: *Zydeco Gumbo*

ZYDECO FORCE

Probably Jeffrey Broussard (vocal, accordion); Shelton Broussard (electric guitar); Robby Mann Robinson (electric bass); Herbert Broussard (rub-board); Raymond Thomas (drums)

Location: Louisiana. 1990

Titles performed:
'Dancing Shoes' Channel 5 083 258–3, Island 083 258–3

Source: *Zydeco Nite'N'Day*

ZYDECO STRAITS

Andrus Espre (vocal and accordion) accompaniment: unknown (rub-board, electric guitar, electric bass, drums)

Location: Plaisence, Louisiana. 1988

Title performed:
'Ai Ya Ya' [part only] K-Jazz 098, Rhapsody 8062

Source: *Zydeco Gumbo*
Andrus Espre is also known as Beau Jocque.

1 Programme, Film Title and Production Company Index

In order more easily to identify artists, this list employs an artist's most commonly-used name, thus Jalacy Hawkins is listed as Screamin' Jay Hawkins, Walter Lewis appears as Furry Lewis, etc. Where a film is untitled, or the title is unknown, the information will be found under the production company name or the original broadcasting organisation. Date parameters for TV broadcasts reflect the period during which the artists mentioned appeared, not the life of the programme itself. Specific dates mentioned in this appendix are those upon which the programme in question was first broadcast. Generally speaking, re-broadcast dates have been omitted. Feature films marked (#) are available on pre-recorded NTSC videotape and details may be found in *Video Hound's Golden Movie Retriever* (Visible Ink Press). Feature films marked with an asterisk are available on pre-recorded PAL videotape and details may be found in the Videoplus Catalogue.

A La Carte [M].
US TV broadcast. Origin unknown. 1964
Brownie McGhee/Sonny Terry

A Nous Deux, la France! [F] [C].
Origin unknown. 1970
Memphis Slim

ABC's Nightlife
US TV show. 1965
Jesse Fuller

Acoustic Routes [D] [C].
Directed by Jan Leman. UK BBC TV broadcast. 1992
Brownie McGhee

Adelphi Productions [C].
Produced and directed by Mike Stewart. 1969–72
George & Ethel McCoy/Johnny Shines/Bukka White

Adventures in Babysitting [F] [C]#.
Directed by Chris Columbus. 1987
Albert Collins

Adventures in Jazz [M].
US CBS TV broadcasts. 1949
Hot Lips Page/Josh White

Afro-American Worksongs in a Texas Prison [FS] [M].
Directed by Pete Seeger 1964 or 1966.
Willie 'Cowboy' Craig/Joseph 'Chinaman' Johnson/Benny Richardson/unidentified artists # 27
[Available from TCB Releasing]

The Afternoon Show
US TV broadcast. Origin unknown. c.1983–4
Katie Webster

Ain't Misbehavin' [D] [M].
Origin unknown. c.1974
Meade Lux Lewis/unidentified artist #9
[This is a compilation of vintage pornography, music shorts and newsreel footage made between 1920 and 1940]

Ain't Nothin' But the Blues [D] [C].
Origin unknown. 1987
Bo Diddley/Albert Collins/Robert Cray/BB King

Air Mail Special [FS] [M].
Origin unknown. 1941
Jimmy Rushing

Alan Lomax Film Collection [M].
Filmed at the Newport Folk Festival. 1966
Bois-Sec Ardoin/Reverend Pearly Brown/Dixie Hummingbirds/Canray Fontenot/Gospel Harmonettes/Son House/Howlin' Wolf/Skip James/Swan Silverton Singers/Ward Singers/ Bukka White/Ed & Lonnie Young
[Available from Historic. See also *American Patchwork* for more Lomax material.]

Alan Lomax Folk Special [M].
US TV broadcast, probably PBS. 1961
Mable Hillery

All Alone with the Blues [C].
Directed by Jim Gabbour. US Cox Cable TV New Orleans, Louisiana. 1985
James Booker/Henry Gray/Robert Lockwood/ Cousin Joe Pleasants/Boogie Bill Webb
[Available from Jim Gabbour Productions. See also *In Concert*]

All's Fair [FS] [M].
Educational Films Corporation. 1938
The Cabin Kids

All Star Tribute to Woody Guthrie and Leadbelly [C].
SHOWTIME, US syndicated TV broadcast. 1988
Little Richard/Taj Mahal

All Together Now [C].
US TV broadcast. Origin unknown. 1973
Lowell Fulson/BB King/Jimmy McCracklin/Joe Turner

All You Need is Love [D] [C].
Directed by Tony Palmer. UK LWT TV. 1977
Jimmy Dawkins/Memphis Slim/Johnny Woods/ Ed & Lonnie Young/Mighty Joe Young

Along the Old Man River
See *Out Of The Blacks, Into The Blues.*

Always for Pleasure [D] [C].
Directed by Les Blank. FLOWER FILMS. 1978
Professor Longhair
[Available from Flower Films]

Aly Bain and Friends [D] [C].
UK Channel 4 TV broadcast. 1988
Boozoo Chavis/Queen Ida

Aly Meets the Cajuns [D] [C].
UK Channel 4 TV broadcast. 1988
Queen Ida

AM America [C].
US TV broadcast. Origin unknown. 1975
Esther Phillips/Joe Williams

AM San Francisco [C].
US local TV broadcast. Origin unknown. 1975
J C Burris/Brownie McGhee/Sonny Terry

America's Music Blues, The, Volume 1 [C].
MERCURY FILMS. 1982
Pee Wee Crayton/Linda Hopkins/BB King/ Eddie Vinson

America's Music Blues, The, Volume 2 [C].
MERCURY FILMS. 1982
Buddy Guy/Brownie McGhee/Esther Phillips/ Junior Wells/Joe Williams

American Bandstand
See *Dick Clark's American Bandstand.*

American Folk Blues Festival 1962 [M].
German Sudwestfunk TV broadcast. Friday 26 October 1962
Willie Dixon/John Lee Hooker/Helen Humes/ Brownie McGhee/Memphis Slim/Shakey Jake/ Sonny Terry/T-Bone Walker
[Available from Sudwestfunk]

American Folk Blues Festival 1963 [M].
German Sudwestfunk TV broadcast. Thursday 10 October 1963
Willie Dixon/Lonnie Johnson/Memphis Slim/ Muddy Waters/Matt Murphy/Victoria Spivey/ Big Joe Williams/Sonny Boy Williamson
[Available from Sudwestfunk]

American Folk Blues Festival 1964 [M].
German Sudwestfunk TV broadcast. Tuesday 17 November 1964
John Henry Barbee/Willie Dixon/John Estes/ Lightnin' Hopkins/Howlin' Wolf/Mae Mercer/ Hammie Nixon/Hubert Sumlin/ Sunnyland Slim/Sonny Boy Williamson
[Available from Sudwestfunk]

American Folk Blues Festival 1965 [M].
German Sudwestfunk TV broadcast. Sunday 26 December 1965
Eddie Boyd/Buddy Guy/John Lee Hooker/ Walter Horton/J B Lenoir/ Fred McDowell/ Jimmy Lee Robinson/Doctor Ross/Roosevelt Sykes/Big Mama Thornton
[Available from Sudwestfunk]

American Folk Blues Festival 1966 [M].
German Sudwestfunk TV broadcast. Tuesday 6 December 1966
John Estes/Little Brother Montgomery/Otis Rush/Roosevelt Sykes/Joe Turner/Sippie Wallace/Junior Wells/Robert Pete Williams/Yank Rachell
[Available from Sudwestfunk]

American Folk Blues Festival 1968 [1] [C].
UK BBC TV unbroadcast programme. 1968
John Lee Hooker/Walter Horton/Curtis Jones/ Jimmy Reed/Eddie Taylor/T-Bone Walker/Big Joe Williams

American Folk Blues Festival 1968 [2] [C].
German TV broadcast. 1968
John Lee Hooker/Walter Horton/Curtis Jones/ Jimmy Reed/Eddie Taylor/T-Bone Walker/Big Joe Williams
[This does not appear to be a Sudwestfunk broadcast]

American Folk Blues Festival 1970 [C].
German Sudwestfunk TV broadcast. Monday 25 May 1970
Willie Dixon/Jack Dupree/Walter Horton/Lee Jackson/Lafayette Leake/Brownie McGhee/ Sonny Terry/Rosetta Tharpe/Bukka White
[Available from Sudwestfunk]

American Folk Blues Festival 1980 [C].
German TV broadcast. 1980
Carey Bell/Willie Mabon/Odie Payne/Bob Stroger/Hubert Sumlin/Sunnyland Slim/Eddie Taylor
[This does not appear to be a Sudwestfunk broadcast]

American Folk Blues Festival 1981 [C].
Belgian TV broadcast. 1981
Carey Bell/John Cephas/Sylvia Embry/Margie Evans/Louisiana Red/Sunnyland Slim/Phil Wiggins

All the *American Folk Blues Festival* programmes were drawn from the annual European autumn tours presented by the German promoters Horst Lipmann and Fritz Rau. See also *Blues Came Walking*, *I Hear The Blues* and *Nothing But The Blues*, for *American Folk Blues Festivals* broadcast in the UK. The following television broadcasts may also possibly exist:

1963: Denmark, France
1964: Denmark, France, USSR[Moscow]
1965: France
1966: France, USSR[East Berlin or Moscow]
1967: France, Germany
1968: France
1969: France, Germany, USSR [East Berlin and/ or Moscow]

American Gospel and Spiritual Festival 1966
See *Hallelujah* and *They Sing Like Someone's Happy*.

American Gospel and Spiritual Festival 966
UK BBC TV broadcast, 1966
Gospelaires/Harmonizing Four/Bishop Samuel Kelsey/Dorothy Norwood Singers

American Hot Wax [F] [C].
Directed by Floyd Mutrux. PARAMOUNT. 1978
Chuck Berry/Screaming Jay Hawkins

American Music Awards
US TV broadcast. Origin unknown. 1978
Chuck Berry

American Patchwork [D] [C].
Directed by Alan Lomax.
COLUMBIA UNIVERSITY/MAETV/PBS co-productions. 1990
See *Appalachian Journey*, *Cajun Country*, *Dreams And Songs Of The Noble Old*, *Feet Don't Fail Me Now* and *Land Where The Blues Began*.
[Compiled from videos made in 1979 and between 1983 and 1985. *Land Where The Blues Began* was originally produced in 1979 by the Mississippi Authority For Educational Television and subsequently included, complete, in the above series.]

Anatomy of Pop
See *From Folk To Jazz*.

And This is Free [D] [M].
Directed by Mike Shea. 1964
Blind James Brewer/Blind Arvella Gray/Robert Nighthawk/Carrie Robertson/unidentified artists #s 24–26/Johnny Young
[Available from Historic]

Andy Williams Show, The [C].
US NBC TV broadcast. 1967
Ray Charles

Angel Heart [F] [C]#*.
Directed by Alan Parker. CAROLCO INTERNATIONAL. 1987
Brownie McGhee

Animal House
See *National Lampoon's Animal House*.

Any Which Way You Can
Directed by Buddy Van Horn. 1980
Fats Domino

Appalachian Journey [D] [C].
COLUMBIA UNIVERSITY/PBS co-production. 1990
John Dee Holeman/Joe and Odell Thompson
[Also including white country artists]

Apollo [C].
US TV broadcast. Origin unknown. 1976
Taj Mahal

Arena – Blues Night [C].
UK BBC TV broadcast. 1984. A four hour special presentation of blues films, co-hosted by BB King and John Walters, presenting material documented in this volume.

Aretha [D] [C].
AMERICAN MASTERS. c. 1970
Reverend C L Franklin

Arhoolie's 25th Birthday Party
See *It's Got To Be Rough To Sweet*.

Art Ford's Greenwich Village Party [M].
US TV broadcast.
Origin unknown. 1957–58
Josh White

Art Ford's Jazz Party [M].
US TV broadcast. Origin unknown. 1958
Josh White

Arthur Crudup – Born with the Blues [D] [C].
Directed by David Deutsch. WETA-TV Washington DC. 1973
Arthur Crudup

Arthur Godfrey and Friends [M].
US CBS TV broadcast. 1950
Josh White

Arthur Godfrey Talent Scouts [M].
US CBS TV broadcast. 1952
Tarheel Slim

Artists in America
See *Sam Lightnin' Hopkins*.

Associated Featurettes [M].
Directed by Will Jason. 1941
The Shadrack Boys
[Available from ICE]

Aspel and Company [C].
UK ITV broadcast. 1988
Chuck Berry

At the Top [C].
US TV broadcast. Origin unknown. 1976
Taj Mahal/Joe Williams

At Travis County Jail [D] [C].
US TV broadcast, probably PBS. 1976
Freddy King

Austin City Limits [C].
US syndicated TV broadcasts. 1976–91
'Gatemouth' Brown/Ray Charles/C J Chenier/Clifton Chenier/Albert Collins/Robert Cray/Fats Domino/Buddy Guy/Lightnin' Hopkins/BB King/Queen Ida/Zachary Richard/Rockin' Sydney/Robert Shaw/Taj Mahal

Aventure du Jazz, L' aka Jazz Odyssey [D] [C]
Directed by L & C Panassié. Origin unknown. 1972
John Lee Hooker/Memphis Slim/Rosetta Tharpe/T-Bone Walker

B A in Music [C].
UK BBC TV broadcast. 1982. Director: Philip Chilvers
Ray Charles/Buddy Guy

BB King Revisits Cook County Jail [D] [C].
Origin unknown. 1973
BB King

Baby Doll [F] [M]#*.
Directed by Elia Kazan. WARNER BROTHERS. 1956
Smiley Lewis/unidentified artist # 19

Ballad in Blue aka Blues for Lovers [F] [M]#.
Directed by Paul Henried. 1964
Ray Charles

Barbara McNair Show, The [C].
US syndicated TV broadcast. 1969
BB King

Barbra Streisand Show, The [C].
US syndicated TV broadcast. 1973
Ray Charles

Bargain with Bullets aka Gangsters on the Loose [F] [M].
Directed by Ralph Cooper. MILLION DOLLAR PRODUCTIONS. 1937
Teresa Harris

Basin Street Revue
See *Showtime at The Apollo.*

Baton Rouge Blues [D] [C].
Directed by Beth Courtney. US PBS TV broadcast. 1984.
Henry Gray/Buddy Guy/Silas Hogan/Arthur 'Guitar' Kelly/Worth Long**/J D Miller**/ Raful Neal/Whispering Smith/Nick Spitzer**/Chris Thomas/Tabby Thomas
[Individuals marked with a double asterisk will be found in the index of non-performing interviewees.]

Beale Street [D] [C].
Directed by Alexis Krasilovsky. CENTRE FOR SOUTHERN CULTURE. 1978
Bobby Bland/BB King/Rufus Thomas
[Available from Centre For Southern Culture]

Beat, The [C].
US WFAA syndicated TV broadcast. Hosted by Bill 'Hoss' Allen; directed by Tommy Johnson. February–August 1966
Hoss Allen [resident host]/Big Amos/ 'Gatemouth' Brown/Clarence 'Frogman' Henry/ Etta James/Louis Jordan/Freddy King/Little Milton/Robert Parker/Esther Phillips/Cleo Randall/Mighty Joe Young
[This series also featured much contemporary soul music, including live performances by the following artists: Jimmy Church/Mitty Collier/Z Z Hill/Mighty Hannibal/Barbara Lynn/Lou Rawls/Otis Redding/Joe Simon/Percy Sledge/ Johnny Taylor/Jamo Thomas and others. Available from Historic.]

Beat Club [M].
German TV broadcast. 1960s
Taj Mahal
[Available from Historic]

Beat of the Brass [M] or [C].
US TV broadcast. Origin unknown. 1968
Joseph 'Dede' Pierce

Beat Room [M].
UK BBC TV broadcasts. 1964–66
Sugar Pie Desanto/John Lee Hooker/Howlin' Wolf/Little Walter/Memphis Slim/Rufus Thomas/Tommy Tucker/Sonny Boy Williamson
[Available from BBC. This programme also featured much contemporary soul, including performances by Inez and Charlie Foxx, Marvin Gaye, the Soul Sisters and others.]

Beatles Forever [C].
US TV broadcast. Origin unknown. 1977
Ray Charles

Beechnut Show
See *Dick Clark's Saturday Night Beechnut Show.*

Best Man, The [F] [C]#.
Directed by Franklin Schafner. UNITED ARTISTS. 1964
Mahalia Jackson

Beware [F] [M].
Directed by Bud Pollard. ASTOR FILMS. 1946
Louis Jordan

Big Band Bash [C].
US TV broadcast. Origin unknown. 1978
Helen Humes/Joe Williams

Big Beat, The [1] [F] [M].
Directed by Will Cowan. UNIVERSAL. 1957
Fats Domino

Big Beat, The [2] [M].
US ABC TV broadcasts. 12 July–2 August 1957.
Hosted by Alan Freed
Chuck Berry/Fats Domino/Alan Freed orchestra/Ivory Joe Hunter/ Johnnie & Joe/ Frankie Lymon & the Teenagers/Clyde McPhatter/Mickey & Sylvia

Big Bill Blues – Low Lights and Blue Smoke [FS] [M].
Directed by Jean Delire. 1956
Big Bill Broonzy
[Available from TCB Releasing. Every inspected print of this film is out of synchronisation.]

Big Bill Broonzy [M].
Filmed by Pete Seeger. 1957
Big Bill Broonzy
[Pete Seeger film collection. The BBC holds a copy of this film.]

Big City Blues [D] [C].
Directed by St.Clair Bourne. 1980.
Billy Branch/Blind James Brewer/Sylvia Embry/Bruce Iglauer**/Son Seals
[Bruce Iglauer will be found in the index to non-performing interviewees. See also *Blues And The Alligator* and *Pride And Joy* for more Alligator-related material.]

Big Easy Music [D] [C].
UK Channel 4 TV broadcast. 1988
Clarence 'Frogman' Henry/Ernie K-Doe/Irma Thomas/Allen Toussaint

Big Name Bands No. 1 [FS] [M].
Origin unknown. 1941
Jimmy Rushing

Big TNT Show
See *The TAMI Show*.

Big World [C].
UK Channel 4 TV broadcast. 1990
Antioch Gospel Choir/Chubby Carrier/Snooks Eaglin/Reverend Charlie Jackson/Ernie K-Doe

Bill Cosby Show [C].
US NBC TV broadcast. 1971.
Ray Charles
See also *The Cosby Show*.

Bip Bam Boogie
Origin unknown. c. mid-1940s
Ebony Trio

Birthright [F] [M].
Directed by Oscar Micheaux. MICHEAUX PICTURES CORPORATION. 1938
Trixie Smith

Black Delta Religion [D] [M].
Directed by William Ferris. CENTRE FOR SOUTHERN CULTURE. 1974
unidentified artists # 40
[Available from Centre For Southern Culture.]

Black Godfather [F] [C]#.
Directed by John Evans. Origin unknown. 1974
Jimmy Witherspoon

Black King, The
1932
Southland Pictures.
Trixie Smith

Black Musical Traditions in Virginia Parts 1–3: Blues; Non-blues secular music; Religious music [C]
Ferrum College, Roanake, Virgina. 1987
Leonard Bowles/Bobby Buford/Irvin Cook/Archie Edwards/First Baptist Church of Finscastle/Foddrell Family/Hiawatha Giles/Earl Gilmore/Harmonizing Five/John Jackson/Rufus Kasey/Flora Molton/New Design Pentecostal Church Singers/Lillian Robinson/Starlight Gospel Singers/Brady Twine/Daniel Womack
[Available from Ferrum College]

Black Nativity [M].
UK Associated Rediffusion TV broadcast. 1962
Alex Bradford/Bessie Griffin/Stars Of Faith

Black Omnibus [C].
US TV broadcast. Origin unknown. 1973
Rufus Thomas

Black on Black [C].
UK Channel 4. 1985
Little Willie Littlefield

Black Rodeo [F] [C].
Directed by Jeff Kanau. UTOPIA. 1972
Ray Charles/BB King/Little Richard

Black Roots [D] [C].
Directed by Lionel Rogosin. Impact Films. 1970
Joe Collier/Reverend Gary Davis/Larry Johnson

Black, White And Blues [M].
US TV broadcast. Origin unknown. 1969
Big Mama Thornton

Blackbook [F].
Origin unknown. 1969
Muddy Waters

Blind Gary Davis [FS] [M].
Directed by Harold Becker. Origin unknown. 1964
Reverend Gary Davis

Blood of Jesus, The [F] [M].
Directed and produced by Spencer Williams. AMEGRO FILMS. Distributed by SACK AMUSEMENT ENTERPRISES. 1941
Black Ace/Heavenly Choir/Reverend RL Robinson/Gossie Smith
[Available from Archive]

Blue Monday Party [C].
Directed by Elizabeth Radazzo
US PBS TV broadcasts. VIDEOTUNES. 1981
Lowell Fulson/John Lee Hooker/Percy Mayfield
[Available from TCB Releasing]

Blues, Die [D] [M].
German TV broadcast. Directed by Dietrich Wawzyn. 1963
Black Ace/Jesse Fuller/Lowell Fulson/Lightnin' Hopkins/Mance Lipscomb/Whistling Alex Moore/Buster Pickens/Willie Thomas
[Available from Tele-7-Film/Historic. See also *Dietrich Wawzyn collection.*]

Blues, The [1] [D] [C].
Directed by Samuel L Charters. Origin unknown. 1962
Pink Anderson/Memphis Willie Borum/Gus Cannon/John Estes/Furry Lewis/JD Short/Baby Tate
[This film is reported to be out of synchronisation.]

Blues, The [2].
1963 – see *Blues, Die.*

Blues, The [3].
1966 – see *Festival Presents The Blues.*

Blues, The [4].
1980 – see *Devil's Music, The, series 2.*

Blues According to Lightnin' Hopkins, The [D] [C].
Directed by Les Blank. FLOWER FILMS. 1967
Ruth Ames/Billy Bizor/Lightnin' Hopkins/Mance Lipscomb/unidentified artist # 28/Reverend ES Wheeler
[Available from Flower Films]

Blues Alive [C].
Origin unknown. 1982
Charles Brown/Ruth Brown/Albert Collins/Buddy Guy/Booker T Laury/Sammy Myers/Otis Rush/Junior Wells
[Available from Rhino Records]

Blues and Beyond, The [D] [C].
UK Channel 4 TV broadcast. 1984
Eddie C Campbell

Blues and Gospel Train, The [M].
Directed by Phillip Casson, produced by Johnny Hamp.
UK Granada TV broadcast. Wednesday 19 August 1964
Brownie McGhee/Muddy Waters/Cousin Joe Pleasants/Otis Spann/Sonny Terry/Rosetta Tharpe
[Available from Granada TV.]

Blues and the Alligator [D] [C].
Directed by Jim Downing. Origin unknown. 1991
Billy Branch/Lonnie Brooks/Kenny Neal/Lucky Peterson/Koko Taylor/'Hound Dog' Taylor
[See also *Big City Blues* and *Pride And Joy – The Story Of Alligator Records*, for more Alligator-related material.]

Blues Between the Teeth
See *Blues Entre Les Dents, Le.*

Blues Brothers, The [F] [C]#*.
Directed by John Landis. UNIVERSAL. 1980
Ray Charles/John Lee Hooker/Walter Horton/Matt Murphy

Blues Brothers 2000 [F] [C].
Directed by John Landis. UNIVERSAL. 1997
BB King/Matt Murphy/Otis Rush/Taj Mahal/Junior Wells

Blues Came Walking, The [M].
Directed by Helen Standage. UK ATV TV broadcast. 1964
Sugar Pie Desanto/Willie Dixon/John Estes/Lightnin' Hopkins/Howlin' Wolf/Sunnyland Slim/Sonny Boy Williamson
[This is the 1964 *American Folk Blues Festival.* The British Film Institute holds a copy of this programme]

Blues de Balfa, Les [D] [C].
Directed by Yasha Aginsky. SEARCHLIGHT PRODUCTIONS. 1983
Rockin' Dopsie [and other, white Cajun artists]

Blues Entre les Dents, Le [F] [C].
Directed by Robert Manthoulis. NEYRAE FILMS. 1971
Buddy Guy/BB King/Furry Lewis/Mance Lipscomb/Brownie McGhee/Roosevelt Sykes/Sonny Terry/Junior Wells/Robert Pete Williams/unidentified artists #s 36, 36A and 36B

Blues for a Black Film [F].
Origin unknown. 1973
Brownie McGhee/Sonny Terry

Blues for Lovers
See *Ballad In Blue.*

Blues Houseparty
Houseparty Productions
John Cephas/Flora Morton/Phil Wiggins

Blues is Alive and Well in Chicago [D] [C].
US TV broadcast. Origin unknown. 1970
Buddy Guy/Muddy Waters/Koko Taylor

Blues Legends 73 [C].
UK BBC TV broadcast. 1973
Boogie Woogie Red/Homesick James/Lightnin' Slim/Snooky Pryor/Whispering Smith/Washboard Willie

Blues Like Showers of Rain [D] [M].
Directed by John Jeremy. 1970
Blind James Brewer/Butch Cage/Gus Cannon/Walter Davis/BlindArvella Gray/Lonnie Johnson/James Stump Johnson/JB Lenoir/Robert Lockwood/Little Brother Montgomery/Buster Pickens/Sam Price/St. Louis Jimmy/Otis Spann/Speckled Red/Sunnyland Slim/Willie Thomas/Henry Townsend/Wade Walton
[Available from TCB Releasing. This is a rostrum camera montage of still photographs, accompanied by a soundtrack of field recordings made by Paul Oliver and Chris Strachwitz in the summer of 1960.]

Blues Night
See *Arena.*

Blues Survivors [C].
Monarch Entertainment. 1982
Buddy Guy/Etta James/Albert King/Sippie Wallace/Junior Wells

Bluesmaker, The [FS] [M].
Origin unknown. 1968
Fred McDowell
[Available from TCB Releasing]

Bluesman, The [D] [C].
Origin unknown. 1973
Arbee Stidham

Bo Diddley's Thirtieth Anniversary of Rock and Roll [C].
Origin unknown. 1985
Bo Diddley

Boarding House [C].
US TV broadcast. Origin unknown. 1973
Esther Phillips/Taj Mahal

Boarding House Blues [F] [M].
Directed by Jospeh Binney. ALL-AMERICAN NEWS CORPORATION. 1946
Anisteen Allen/Una Mae Carlisle/Bullmoose Jackson/Lucky Millinder orchestra

Bob Hope Show [C].
US syndicated TV broadcast. 1969
Ray Charles

Boboquivari [C].
US TV broadcast. Origin unknown. 1971
Lightnin' Hopkins/Freddy King/Robert Shaw

Bones [D] [C].
Directed by Carol Munday Lewis. 1979
John Henry Nobles/Taj Mahal
[Available from TCB Releasing]

Boogie Woogie [D] [C].
UK LWT TV broadcast. *South Bank Show* series. 1986
Big Joe Duskin/Paul Oliver**/Francis Wilford-Smith**
[Individuals marked with a double asterisk will be found in the index of non-performing interviewees.]

Boogie Woogie Blues [FS] [M].
ALL AMERICAN NEWS. 1948
Hadda Brooks
[Available from Archive/Phoenix]

Boogie Woogie Dream [FS] [M].
Directed by Hans Burger. FILMUSICAL/HOLLYWOOD PRODUCTIONS. 1941
Albert Ammons/Lena Horne/Pete Johnson
[Available from Archive/TCB Releasing]

Book of Numbers [F] [C].
Directed by Raymond St. Jacques. 1972
Brownie McGhee/Sonny Terry

Born for Hard Luck
1976
Peg Leg Sam

Born in the Blues [D] [C].
US PBS TV broadcast. Origin unknown. 1975
Jimmy Dawkins/John Estes/Hammie Nixon/Houston Stackhouse

Broadway Jamboree [M].
US NBC TV broadcast. 1948
Deep River Boys

Bronze Buckaroo [F] [M]#.
Produced by Richard C Kahn. HOLLYWOOD PRODUCTIONS.
Distributed by SACK AMUSEMENT ENTERPRISES. 1938
Four Tones

Bronze Venus
See *The Duke Is Tops*.

Brother Can You Spare A Dime [O]
UK film, origin unknown. 1975
unidentified artist #9

Brothers [F] [C].
Directed by Arthur Barron. WARNER BROTHERS. 1977
Taj Mahal

Bruce Morrow Show, The [M].
US TV broadcast. Origin unknown. 1967
Screaming Jay Hawkins/Joe Williams

Buck and the Preacher [F] [C]#.
Directed by Sidney Poitier. 1972
Brownie McGhee/Sonny Terry

Budweiser Beer advert [1] [C].
US TV broadcast. 1978
Muddy Waters

Budweiser Beer advert [2] [C].
UK ITV & Channel 4 broadcasts. 1992
unidentified artist

Budweiser Newport Jazz Festival [C].
Japanese TV broadcast. 1986
BB King

Cabin in the Sky [F] [M]#*.
Directed by Vincent Minelli. MGM. 1943
Hall Johnson Choir

Cable News Network [C].
24 hour networked news channel.
Turner Communications, Atlanta, Georgia. 1995
Johnny Copeland

Cajun Country [1] aka *Don't Drop the Potato*
COLUMBIA UNVERSITY/PBS co-production. 1990
Bois-Sec Ardoin/Canray Fontenot/Dorsinne Fontenot/Clinulm Jones
[also features white Cajun artists]

Cajun Country [2] [D] [C].
Channel 4 TV broadcast, 1996, from material filmed in 1988.
Boozoo Chavis/Queen Ida

Cajun Visits [D] [C].
Directed by Yasha Aginsky. SEARCHLIGHT PRODUCTIONS. 1983
Canray Fontenot (and other, white Cajun, artists)
[see also *Aly Meets The Cajuns*, *Dry Wood*, *Blues de Balfa* and *J'ai Eté Au Bal* for further Cajun material. See also *Zydeco*.]

Caldonia [FS] [M].
Directed by William Forest. ASTOR FILMS. An Adams Production. 1945
Louis Jordan
[Available from TCB Releasing.]

California Community Television [C].
1972
Freddy King

Calypso Heatwave [F] [M].
Directed by Fred F Sears. COLUMBIA. 1957
Treniers

Camera Three [M].
US CBS TV broadcasts. 1965–68
Buddy Guy/Son House/Alberta Hunter/John Sellers

Cannon and Ball Show [C].
US ITV TV broadcast. 1986
Little Richard

Can't You Hear the Wind Howl? [D] [C].
Directed by Peter W Meyer. SWEET HOME PICTURES. 1997
Keb' Mo'

Captain and Tennille [C].
US ABC TV broadcast. 1977–78
Bobby Bland/BB King

Captain and Tennille in New Orleans [C].
US ABC TV broadcast. 1978
Fats Domino

Captain Billy's Mississippi Music Hall [M]
US CBS TV broadcast. Friday 1 October–Friday 26 November 1948
Juanita Hall

Captain Billy's Showboat [M]
US local TV broadcast. Monday 1 August–Monday 13 September 1948
Juanita Hall
[This originally local TV show was picked up by CBS, renamed *Captain Billy's Mississippi Music Hall* and subsequently networked for two months before being cancelled.]

Carnival Rock [F] [M]#.
Directed by Roger Corman. 1957
Platters

Carol Burnett Show, The [C].
US CBS TV broadcast. 1972
Ray Charles

Carrefour [F] [M].
Directed by Kurt Bernhardt. British Unity Pictures. 1938
Una Mae Carlisle

Carry it On [F].
Origin unknown. 1970
Memphis Slim

Catalina Caper [F] [C]
Origin unknown. 1967
Little Richard

Catcher, The [F] [C].
Origin unknown. 1972
Piano Red

CBS News [C].
US CBS TV broadcasts. 1971–73
James Son Thomas/Bill Williams

Celebration: The American Spirit [C].
US TV broadcast. Origin unkown. 1976
Ray Charles

Change of Heart
See *Hit Parade of 1943*.

Charlie Smith and the Fritter Tree
See *Visions*.

Chelsea at Nine [M].
UK BBC TV broadcast. 1957
Rosetta Tharpe

Chicago Blues [D] [C].
Directed by Harley Cokliss. 1970
Willie Dixon/Buddy Guy/JB Hutto/Floyd Jones/Robert Koester**/Johnny Lewis/Muddy Waters/Koko Taylor/Junior Wells/unidentified artists #s 34 & 35/Mighty Joe Young
[Koester will be found in the index to non-performing interviewees. Available from TCB Releasing.]

Chicago Blues Festival [1] [C].
US TV broadcast. Origin unknown. 1981
Bobby Bland/Buddy Guy/Walter Horton/Junior Wells

Chicago Blues Festival [2] [C].
European TV broadcast. Origin unknown. 1985
Larry Davis/AC Reed/Byther Smith/Maurice John Vaughn

Chicago Blues Festival 1981 [C].
Origin unknown. 1981
Buddy Guy/Walter Horton/Muddy Waters/Junior Wells
[This may be related material to that found in *Chicago Blues Festival* [1].]

Chicago Melodie [D] [C].
German TV broadcast. 1978
Johnny Christian/Albert Collins/Homesick James/Lafayette Leake/Sugar Blue/Sunnyland Slim/Johnny Twist/Mama Yancey

Chicago on the Good Foot [D] [C].
US TV broadcast. MAINFRAME PRODUCTIONS. c.1979
Big Twist/James Cotton/Willie Dixon/Thomas A Dorsey/Rebert Harris/Pinetop Perkins/Victory Travellers/Junior Wells

'Chicago Tribune' TV adverts
US TV broadcasts. 1985–86
Valeriea Wellington

Chuck Barris Rah Rah Show, The [C].
US NBC TV broadcast. 1978
Chuck Berry/Ray Charles/Joe Williams

Cigarette Blues [FS] [C].
Directed by Les Blank. FLOWER FILMS. 1984
Sonny Rhodes
[Available from Flower Films]

Cincinatti Kid, The [F] [C]#*.
Directed by Norman Jewison. 1965
Ray Charles

Cinderfella [M].
US TV broadcast. Origin unknown. 1960
Joe Williams

Circus Time [M].
US ABC TV broadcast. 1957
Mickey & Sylvia

Cisco Pike [F] [C].
Directed by Bill L Norton. COLUMBIA. 1971
Sonny Terry

Citizen South – Citizen North [D] [M].
US PBS TV broadcast. Origin unknown. 1962
John Estes

City Limits
See *Austin City Limits*.

Clapton Sessions, The [C].
UK TV broadcast. Origin unknown. 1987
Buddy Guy

Clay Cole Show, The
US TV broadcast. Origin unkown. 1965
Bo Diddley

Clay Pigeon [F] [C].
Directed by Tom Stern. MGM. 1971
Taj Mahal

Clifton Chenier – The King of the Zydeco [D] [C].
Directed by Chris Strachwitz. 1987
Available from ARHOOLIE RECORDS
Clifton Chenier

Club, The
1980s
J B Hutto

CNN
See *Cable News Network*.

Cocksucker Blues [D] [C].
Origin unknown. 1976
Bukka White
[Cinéma-vérité documentary on the Rolling Stones.]

Color Purple, The [F] [C]#.
Directed by Stephen Spielberg. 1985
John Lee Hooker/Sonny Terry/Tata Vega

Comedy in America [C].
US TV broadcast. Origin unknown. 1976
Ray Charles

Conversations with Shakey Jake [D].
Origin unknown. 1972
Shakey Jake

Cooley High [F] [C]#.
Directed by Michael Schultz. AIP. 1976
Luther Allison

Cootie Williams and his Orchestra [FS] [M].
Origin unknown. 1944
Eddie Vinson

Cosby Show, The [C].
US NBC TV broadcasts. 1984–92
Ray Charles/BB King/Joe Williams
[See also *The Bill Cosby Show*.]

Cotton Club [C].
US TV broadcasts. Origin unknown. 1974–75
Ray Charles

Count Basie and his Orchestra [FS] [M].
Origin unknown. c. 1951
Helen Humes

Count Basie at Carnegie Hall [C].
Origin unknown. 1981
Joe Williams

Cow Cow Boogie [FS] [M].
Origin unknown. 1945
Dorothy Dandridge/Tiny Grimes orchestra

Crazy House
See *Funzapoppin'*.

Crimson Canary, The [F] [M].
Directed by John Hoffman. UNIVERSAL. 1943
Josh White

Cromie Circle Show, The [C].
US TV broadcast. Origin unknown. 1971
Muddy Waters

Crossroads [F] [C]#*.
Directed by Walter Hill. 1986
Terry Evans/Frank Frost/Bobby King/Sonny Terry

Crystal Gayle Show, The [C].
US TV broadcast. Origin unknown. 1978
BB King

Danny Kaye Show, The [M].
US CBS TV broadcast. 1966
Joe Williams

Dark Town Scandals Review aka *Le Jazz Noir* [in France] [M].
RED STAR FILMS. 1929
Sara Martin/Maude Mills

Dateline Boston [M].
US local TV broadcast. Origin unknown. 1966
Muddy Waters

David Brinkley's Journal [M].
US NBC TV broadcast. 1961
Creole George Guesnon/Joseph 'Dede' Pierce

David Frost Show, The [C].
US syndicated TV broadcasts. 1970–71
BB King/Muddy Waters

David Letterman Show
See *Late Night With David Letterman*.

Day by Day [M].
UK Southern ATV local news magazine. 1964
Sonny Boy Williamson

Dedans le Sud de Louisiane
See *Within Southern Louisiana*.

Deep Blues [D] [C].
Directed by Robert Mugge. MUG-SHOT PRODUCTIONS. 1991
Roosevelt 'Booba' Barnes/R L Burnside/Jesse Mae Hemphill/Jelly Roll Kings/Big Jack Johnson/Junior Kimbrough/Booker T Laury/Jack Owens/Robert Palmer**/Lonnie Pitchford/Abe Schwab**/Bud Spires/Napoleon Strickland/Wade Walton
[Individuals marked with a double asterisk will be found in the index of non-performing interviewees. Available from Mug-Shot Productions.]

Deep South [F] [M].
Distributed by SACK AMUSEMENT ENTERPRISES. 1930
Hall Johnson Choir

Defiant Ones, The [F] [M]*.
Directed by Stanley Kramer. UNITED ARTISTS. 1958
unidentified artist # 20

Delinquents [F] [M].
Origin unknown. 1957
Julia Lee

Della [C].
US TV broadcasts. Origin unknown. 1969–70
Ray Charles/Big Mama Thornton/Joe Turner/Joe Williams

Delta Blues Festival [D].
CENTRE FOR SOUTHERN CULTURE. 1985
unidentified artists # 44
[Available from Centre For Southern Culture.]

Delta Blues Singer
See *Sonny Ford, Delta Artist*.

Devil's Music, The, series 1 [D] [C].
BBC TV. 1978 – see series 2 for original material

Devil's Music, The, series 2 [D] [C].
UK BBC TV broadcasts.
Directed by Maddalena Fagandini and Giles Oakley. 1979
[Original broadcast dates: Mondays 9, 16, 23, 30 July 1979]
Aces/Billy Boy Arnold/Sonny Blake/Henry Brown/Gus Cannon/Joe Carter/Sam Chatmon/James DeShay/Thomas A Dorsey/Laura Dukes/Good Rockin' Charles/Little Brother Montgomery/Fenton Robinson/Purvis Spann**/Victoria Spivey/Houston Stackhouse/Henry Townsend/Mose Vinson/Bukka White/Joe Willie Wilkins/Big Joe Williams/Edith Wilson
[Available from BBC. Series 1 was a history of the blues, employing both original footage made in 1976 and archive material in excerpt. Series 2, also known as The Blues, and hosted by Alexis Korner, contained complete performances of entirely original 1976 BBC footage. Purvis Spann will be found in the index of non-performing interviewees.]

Dial M for Music [C].
US TV broadcast. Origin unknown. 1969–70
James Cotton/BB King/Ward Singers/Joe Williams

Dick Cavett Show, The [C].
US ABC TV broadcasts. 1969–72
Chuck Berry/Ray Charles/John Lee Hooker/BB King/Big Mama Thornton

Dick Clark Presents the Rock and Roll Years [C].
US syndicated TV broadcasts. 1973
Chuck Berry/Bo Diddley/BB King/Little Richard

Dick Clark's American Bandstand [M] & [C].
US ABC TV broadcasts. 1956–1970s; subsequently syndicated
Chuck Berry/Cadillacs/Eddy Clearwater/Fats Domino/Flamingos/Albert King/Little Richard/Frankie Lymon/Jimmy McCracklin/Clyde McPhatter/Rufus Thomas/Chuck Willis

Dick Clark's American Bandstand 23rd Birthday
US syndicated TV broadcast. 1975
Fats Domino

Dick Clark's American Bandstand 25th Anniversary
US syndicated TV broadcast. 1977
Chuck Berry

Dick Clark's Good Old Days [C].
US syndicated TV broadcasts. 1977
Bo Diddley

Dick Clark's Live Wednesday [C].
US syndicated TV broadcasts. 1978
Chuck Berry/Bo Diddley/Fats Domino

Dick Clark's Saturday Night Beechnut Show [M].
US ABC TV broadcasts 1958–59
Chuck Berry/Fats Domino

Dick Tracey [F] [C].
Directed by Warren Beatty. 1990
LaVern Baker

Dietrich Wawzyn Film Collection [M].
Directed by Dietrich Wawzyn. Sound by Chris Strachwitz. 1963
Sweet Emma Barrett/Black Ace/Blind James Campbell/Cortelia Clark/Ebenezer Baptist Church choir and soloists/Lowell Fulson/Jesse Fuller/Clarence 'Frogman' Henry/Lightning Hopkins/Mance Lipscomb/Alex Moore/King Louis Narcisse/New Orleans Harmonizers/Reverend Louis Overstreet/Buster Pickens/Willie Thomas/unidentified artists #s 21–23/Hop Wilson
[There is also footage of Jazz, Hillbilly, White evangelistic, Hawaiian, Native American, Mexican and African artists in this collection. Available from Dietrich Wawzyn/Historic]

Dillinger [F] [M]#.
Directed by Max Nosseck. KING BROTHERS. 1945
unidentified artist # 18

Dinah and her New Best Friends [C].
US CBS TV broadcasts. 1975–76
Chuck Berry/Ray Charles/Bessie Griffin/Little Richard/Esther Phillips/Taj Mahal

Dinah Shore Chevy Show, The [M].
US NBC TV broadcast. 1962
Ray Charles/Bessie Griffin

Dinner with the President [M].
US TV broadcast. Origin unknown. 1963
Josh White

Disk Jockey Jamboree [F] [M].
Directed by Roy Lockwood. WARNER BROTHERS. 1957
Fats Domino/Lewis Lymon/Joe Williams

Die Blues
See *Blues, Die.*

Do Re Mi
See *Girl Can't Help It, The.*

Dr. John [C].
US TV broadcast. Origin unknown. 1971
Professor Longhair

Dr. John's New Orleans Swamp [C].
US WTTW TV broadcast. 1974
Professor Longhair
[Available from Historic/WTTW]

Don Kirshner's Rock Concert [C].
US syndicated TV broadcasts. 1975–78
Chuck Berry/Honeyboy Edwards/John Lee Hooker/Muddy Waters/Esther Phillips

Don Sherwood Show, The [M].
US local TV broadcast. Probably San Francisco. Origin unknown. 1950s
Jesse Fuller

Don't Drop the Potato
See *Cajun Visits* [1].

Don't Knock the Rock [F] [M].
Directed by Fred F Sears. COLUMBIA. 1956
Little Richard

***Don't Knock the Rock* (1964)**
See *It's Little Richard!*

Donald O'Connor Show, The [C].
US syndicated TV broadcast. 1968
Joe Williams

Donny and Marie [C].
US ABC TV broadcasts. 1977
Chuck Berry/Bo Diddley/Little Richard

Down Memory Lane [C].
Origin unknown. 1980s
Inez Andrews/Barrett Sisters/Albertina Walker

Dreamer, The [F] [M].
ASTOR PICTURES. 1948
Mabel Lee/June Richmond

Dreamland [D] [C].
Directed by Oz Scott. 1980. Inter-American Productions.
Henry Butler/Joanne Crayton

Dreams and Songs of the Noble Old [D] [C].
COLUMBIA UNIVERSITY/PBS co-production. 1990
Sam Chatmon/Janie Hunter & group/Jack Owens/Bud Spires
[also features old-time and hillbilly artists]

Dreams That Money Can't Buy [F] [M].
Directed by Hans Richter. 1948
Josh White

Dry Wood [D] [C].
Directed by Les Blank. FLOWER FILMS. 1973
Bois-Sec Ardoin/Canray Fontenot/unidentified artists #37
[Available from Flower Films.]

Duchess of Idaho, The [F] [C]#.
Directed by Robert Z Leonard. 1949
Jubalaires

Duke at Monterey, The [D] [C].
Origin unknown. 1973
Esther Phillips/Jimmy Rushing/Big Joe Turner/Eddie Vinson/Joe Williams

Duke Ellington at the White House [C].
US TV broadcast. Origin unknown. 1969
Joe Williams

Duke Ellington Special [C].
US TV broadcast. Origin unknown. 1973
Ray Charles/Joe Williams

Duke is Tops, The [F] [M]#.
Directed by Leo Popkin, produced by Harry M Popkin.
TODDY PICTURES COMPANY. 1938
Cats And The Fiddle

DuPont Show of the Month [M].
US NBC TV broadcast. 1957
Dinah Washington

Dynamite Chicken [F] [C]#.
Directed by Ernest Pintoff. 1971
BB King/Muddy Waters

Ebb [F] [M].
Directed By Jim Potts. WADHAM FILM GROUP, Oxford. 1965
John Lee Hooker
[Hooker appears on the soundtrack only. Director Potts read lines from Shakespeare and T.S. Elliot to Hooker who then extemporised songs, mixing the quotations supplied by Potts with his own and traditional blues verses. The finished product was used as the soundtrack to this reportedly experimental film.]

Ebony [C].
UK Channel 4 TV broadcast. 1985
Little Richard

Ebony Parade [F] [M].
ASTOR PICTURES. 1947
Dorothy Dandridge/Jubalaires/Mabel Lee/Roy Milton/June Richmond/Vanita Smythe
[This film is a compilation of previously made *Soundies*.]

Ebony Readers' Music Poll Award Show [C].
US TV brodcast. Origin unknown. 1975
Ray Charles

Ed Sullivan Show, The [M]& [C].
US CBS TV broadcasts. 1955–72
LaVern Baker/Bo Diddley/Ray Charles/Fats Domino/Mahalia Jackson/Willis Jackson/Five Keys/BB King/Frankie Lymon/Joe Williams
[LaVern Baker, Bo Diddley, the Five Keys and Willis Jackson all appeared in a special 'Rhythm & Blues Review' segment of this show during November 1955. See also *Toast Of The Town*.]

Eddie Condon's Floor Show [M]
US NBC TV broadcast. 1949
Hot Lips Page

Elder Michaux [M] .
US DuMont TV broadcasts.
Sunday 31 October 1948 to Sunday 9 January 1949
Elder Solomon Lightfoot Michaux, his Happy-Am-I choir and congregation.
[This series stemmed from an earlier local Washington TV show of the same name, which was known to have been broadcasting in 1947, and may have started as early as 1946.]

Engelbert Humperdinck Show, The [C].
US ABC TV broadcast. 1970
Ray Charles

En Remontant la Mississippi.
See *Out Of The Blacks, Into The Blues*.

Ethnic Folksongs of the Southland.
Origin unknown. 1957
John Sellers

Eubie Blake 1883–1983 [D] [C].
UK BBC TV broadcast. 1983
Alberta Hunter

Evening Show [C].
US local TV broadcast. Probably San Francisco. Origin unknown. 1977
J C Burris

Fabrik, Der [C].
German TV broadcast. 1986
BB King

Face au Public [M].
Belgian TV broadcast. 1965
Chuck Berry

Face in the Crowd, A [F] [M]#.
Directed by Elia Kazan. WARNER BROTHERS. 1957
Brownie McGhee

Faces in Jazz [C].
US TV broadcasts, probably PBS. 1971–72
Alberta Hunter

Family Ties [C]
US NBC TV broadcast. 1988–89
Brownie McGhee

Fanfare [C].
US TV broadcast. Origin unknown. 1971
BB King

Fannie Bell Chapman – Gospel Singer [D] [C].
Directed by William Ferris. CENTRE FOR SOUTHERN CULTURE. 1975
Fannie Bell Chapman
[Available from Centre For Southern Culture.]

Farewell to Fillmore East [D] [C].
Origin unknown. 1971
Albert King

Fats Domino and Friends [C].
US TV broadcast. Origin unknown. 1986
Fats Domino

Feelin' Called the Blues, A [D] [C].
Directed by Ed Clement. Origin unknown. 1975
John Estes

Feeling Good [C].
US TV broadcast. Origin unknown. 1974
BB King/Joe Williams

Feet Don't Fail Me Now [D] [C].
COLUMBIA UNIVERSITY/PBS co-production. 1990
James Miller
[also features traditional New Orleans jazz and marching bands]

Festival [1] [USA] [D] [M].
Directed by Murray Lerner. PEPPERCORN WORMSER FILMS. 1967
Son House/Howlin' Wolf/John Hurt/Fred McDowell/Brownie McGhee/Moving Star Hall Singers/Staple Singers/Sonny Terry/Robert Wilkins

Festival [2] [UK] [C].
BBC TV broadcast. 1980
Brownie McGhee/Memphis Slim/Sonny Terry
[Available from BBC.]

Festival Culturel Panafricain, Le.
See *Pan-African Festival.*

Festival Express [C].
Origin unknown. 1970
Buddy Guy
[Available from Historic.]

Festival of Lively Arts for Young People [C].
US TV broadcast. Origin unknown. 1976
Joe Williams

Festival Presents the Blues [M].
Directed by Paddy Simpson. Canadian CBC TV broadcast.
Broadcast Sunday 23 February 1966
Willie Dixon/Jesse Fuller/Mable Hillery/Muddy Waters Band/Brownie McGhee/Otis Spann/Sonny Terry/Sunnyland Slim/Bukka White/Big Joe Williams
[Available from CBC/Showtime Archives. Note that the Rhino videotape R3 2313 includes material not shown in the original broadcast, and also omits some material orginally shown.]

Fifty Years of Country Music [C].
US syndicated TV broadcast. 1978
Ray Charles

Fighting for Our Lives [F] [C].
Origin unknown. 1974
Taj Mahal

Film Vodvil No. 2 [FS] [M].
COLUMBIA. 1943
Eddie Vinson

Film 79 [C].
UK BBC TV broadcast. 1979
Alberta Hunter

Five All Night Live [C].
Local US TV broadcast. 1980s
J B Hutto

Flip Wilson Show, The [C].
US NBC TV broadcasts. 1970–72
Ray Charles/BB King/Taj Mahal/Ward Singers

Floorshow.
See *Eddie Condon's Floor Show.*

Folklife Productions [M].
Directed by George Pickow. 1961 & 1969
Willie Dixon/Reverend Frederick Douglass Kirkpatrick/Brownie McGhee/Memphis Slim/Sonny Terry/Big Mama Thornton
[Available from Historic. See also *Lyrics and Legends*.]

Follow the Boys aka *Three Cheers For The Boys* [F] [M]#.
Directed by Edward Sutherland. UNIVERSAL PICTURES. 1944
Delta Rhythm Boys/Louis Jordan
Copyrighted 31 March 1944

For Blacks Only [M].
US TV broadcast. Origin unknown. 1968
Howlin' Wolf/Muddy Waters

For Love of Ivy [F] [C].
Directed by Daniel Mann. PALOMAR. 1968
BB King

Four Shall Die [M].
Directed by Leo Popkin. 1940
Dorothy Dandridge
Million Dollar Productions

Fox Movietone News [M].
1928–31
Elder Solomon Lightfoot Michaux/Uncle John Scruggs/Eddie Thomas and Carl Scott/unidentified artists #s 1–10 and possibly 11
[Available from Historic.]

Fred Astaire Show, The [M].
US TV broadcast. Origin unknown. 1960
Joe Williams

Free Time [C].
US TV broadcast. Origin unknown. 1971
Victoria Spivey/Taj Mahal

Friendly Invasion, The [D] [C].
UK BBC TV broadcast. Omnibus series. 1972
Houston Stackhouse

Fritz the Cat [AF] [C]#.
Directed by Ralph Bakshi. 1971
Bo Diddley/BB King

From Folk to Jazz [M].
US TV broadcast. Origin unknown. 1966
Scott Dunbar/Joseph 'Dede' Pierce
[This TV programme, also known as *Anatomy Of Pop*, was subsequently released as an educational film]

From Jumpstreet [C].
US TV broadcast. Origin unknown. 1980
Willie Dixon/Brownie McGhee/Sonny Terry

Funzapoppin' aka *Crazy House* [F] [M].
Directed by Edward F Cline. UNIVERSAL. 1943
Delta Rhythm Boys/Jimmy Rushing

Further Down the Road [D] [C].
Origin unknown. 1985
Albert Collins

Gadzooks! It's All Happening [M].
UK BBC TV broadcast. 1965
Screaming Jay Hawkins

Gangsters on the Loose
See *Bargain With Bullets.*

Garry Moore Show, The [M].
US CBS TV broadcast. 1950s
Martha Davis and Spouse/Edith Wilson

Gather No Moss
See *TAMI Show, The.*

George Carlin Monsanto Chemical Special [C].
US TV broadcast. Origin unknown. 1973
BB King

George Edick's Showtime [M].
Local US TV broadcast. 1958
George Edick [host]/Tommy Hodge/Kings Of Rhythm/Jimmy Thomas/Ike Turner
[This show ran for some time in the St Louis area. The episode detailed in this work is the only one known to have survived.]

George Hamilton IV Show, The [M].
US TV broadcast. Origin unknown. 1959
Joe Williams

Georgia Rose [F] [M].
ARISTO FILMS. 1930
unidentified artist # 12

Get Down [C].
US TV broadcast. Origin unknown. 1976
BB King

Gettin' Back [D] [M].
Origin unknown. 1974
Clifton Chenier/John Lee Hooker

Giants of Rock and Roll, The [C].
Italian TV broadcast. 1988
Bo Diddley/Little Richard

Gifts of Rhythm [FS] [M].
Origin unknown. 1936
The Cabin Kids

Gig and Saddle aka *Scandals of 1933* [F] [M].
GOLDBERG PRODUCTIONS. 1933
Lucky Millinder orchestra

Girl Can't Help It, The [F] [C]*.
Directed by Frank Tashlin. 20th CENTURY FOX. 1957
Fats Domino/Little Richard/Platters/Treniers

Give My Poor Heart Ease [D] [C].
Directed by William Ferris. CENTRE FOR SOUTHERN CULTURE. 1975
BB King/James Son Thomas/Wade Walton
[Available from Centre For Southern Culture.]

Glen Campbell Goodtime Hour, The [C].
US CBS TV broadcasts. 1971
Ray Charles/Little Richard/Brownie McGhee/Sonny Terry

Glorious Fourth, The [C].
US TV broadcast. Origin unknown. 1976
Big Joe Williams

Go Down Death [F] [M]#.
'Spencer Williams All-Negro Production'. Distributed by Sack Amusement Enterprises. 1944
Reverend Robinson and the Heavenly Choir

God's Stepchildren
Directed by Oscar Micheaux.
MICHEAUX PICTURES CORP. 1938
Trixie Smith

Go Johnny Go! [F] [M]#.
Directed by Paul Landres. HAL ROACH PRODUCTIONS. 1958
Chuck Berry/Cadillacs/Flamingos/Harvey

Going Places – New Orleans [D] [C].
US CPB PBS TV broadcast. 1997
Ebenezer Baptist Church congregation/Lois DeJean**
[Lois DeJean will be found in the index to non-performing interviewees. This film also contains some Cajun music.]

Gong Show, The [C].
US syndicated TV broadcast. 1978–79
Guitar Shorty/Bob [Blues] Starr

Good Morning [C].
US local TV newsbroadcasts. Origin unknown. 1970s
Eddie Clearwater/J B Hutto

Good Morning America [C].
US ABC TV broadcast. 1995
Johnny Copeland

Good Morning Blues [D] [C].
Directed by Walter Lowe.
MISSISSIPPI ASSOCIATION FOR EDUCATIONAL TELEVISION. 1978
Nathan Beauregard/Big Memphis Ma Rainey/Gus Cannon/Sam Chatmon/Honeyboy Edwards/Richard 'Hacksaw' Harney/Walter Horton/Mrs Van Hunt/BB King/Furry Lewis/Hayes McMullen/Johnny Shines/Houston Stackhouse/Bukka White/Big Joe Williams
[Available from TCB Releasing.]

Good Time George [C].
UK BBC TV broadcast. 1983
Memphis Slim

Gospel [D] [C].
GOLDEN DOOR PRODUCTIONS. 1984
Reverend James Cleveland/Mighty Clouds of Joy

Gospel According to Al Green [D] [C].
Directed by Robert Mugge. MUG-SHOT PRODUCTIONS. 1984
Al Green

Gospel at Colonus, The [D] [C].
US WNET-TV broadcast. Directed by Kirk Browning. 1985
Five Blind Boys of Alabama/Institutional Radio Choir/J D Steele Singers/Soul Stirrers
[This is a gospel-style adaptation of Sophocles' *Oedipus at Colonus*.]

Gospel Caravan [C].
French TV broadcast. 1978
Marion Williams

Gospel in Gary [D] [C].
Directed by John Husse. CENTRE FOR SOUTHERN CULTURE. 1976
Gospel Choice/Joiner's Five Trumpets/Little Dots/Stars of Zion
[Available from the Centre For Southern Culture, whose catalogue describes this film as being 'below broadcast standard'.]

Gospel in the Holy Land [D] [C].
MERCURY FILMS. 1985
Reverend James Cleveland

Gospel TV Time
See *TV Gospel Time*.

Got to Tell It [D] [C].
Directed by Jules Schwerin. 1974
Mahalia Jackson
[Available from Phoenix/TCB Releasing.]

Graeme Bell [D] [C].
UK TV broadcast. Origin unknown. Early 1980s
Amateur silent film of Big Bill Broonzy

Grande Parade du Jazz, La [C].
French TV broadcast. 1979
Phillip Guy/Helen Humes/BB King/Muddy Waters/Kenny Neal/Jimmy Witherspoon

Grass Roots Series #1 – Old Time Music [D].
Origin unknown. 1974
Elizabeth Cotten

Great Balls of Fire [F] [C]#.
Directed by Jim McBride. 1989. ORION
Booker T Laury/Valerie Wellington

Great White Hope, The [F] [C]#.
Directed by Martin Ritt. 20th CENTURY FOX. 1970
Jesse Fuller

Green Pastures [F] [M]#*
Directed by William Keighley and Marc Connelley. WARNER BROTHERS. 1936
Edna Harris/Hall Johnson Choir

Guitar, Guitar
See *Laura Weber's Guitar, Guitar.*

Guitar Legends [D] [C].
Spanish TV broadcast. 1992
Bo Diddley/Robert Cray/BB King

Hail, Hail Rock and Roll [D] [C].
Origin unknown. 1987
Chuck Berry

Hallelujah [F] [M].
Directed by King Vidor. 1929
Dixie Jubilee Singers/Victoria Spivey

Hallelujah! [M].
German TV broadcast. Sudwestfunk. 1965
Inez Andrews/Five Blind Boys of Mississippi/ Bishop Samuel Kelsey

Harlem Cultural Festival [M].
US TV broadcast. Origin unknown. 1967
Bobby Bland

Harlem Jam Session [F] [M].
Directed by Ray Sandford. Origin unknown. 1946
International Sweethearts Of Rhythm

Harlem Jazz Festival
See *Showtime At The Apollo.*

Harlem Jubilee
See *Sugar Hill Times.*

Harlem on the Prairie [F] [M]#.
Directed by Sam Newfield.
TODDY PRODUCTIONS/ASSOCIATED FEATURES. 1938
Four Tones

Harlem Rhythm and Blues
See *Showtime At The Apollo.*

Harlem Rides the Range [F] [M]#.
Produced by Richard C Kahn. HOLLYWOOD PRODUCTIONS.
Distributed by Sack Amusement Enterprises. 1939
Four Tones
[Available from Archive/Phoenix.]

Harlem Rock and Roll
See *Showtime At The Apollo.*

Harlem Roots
See *Showtime At The Apollo.*

Harlem Variety Review
See *Showtime At The Apollo.*

Hart and Lorne Terrific Hour, The [C].
US TV broadcast. Origin unknown. 1970
Brownie McGhee/Sonny Terry

Hearst Metrotone Newsreel [M].
1931
Whistler And His Jug Band/[possibly] unidentified artist #11
[Available from Historic.]

Hee Haw [C].
US CBS TV broadcasts. 1970–71
'Gatemouth' Brown/Ray Charles

Heineken beer adverts [C].
UK ITV/Channel 4 broadcasts. Origin unknown. 1992–3
Whitbread Beer Company/Lowe Howard-Spink.
Lonnie Brooks/Harmonica Fats

Heist, The
See *Million Dollars.*

Helen Reddy Show, The [C].
US NBC TV broadcast. 1973
BB King

Hep Cat Serenade [M].
Directed by William Forest Crouch. Sack Amusement Enterprises.
date unknown {c. late 1940s}
Una Mae Carlisle/Chanticleers/Louis Jordan/ Meade Lux Lewis
This is probably a compilation of *Soundies.*

Here Come the Stars [C].
US TV broadcast. Origin unknown. 1968
Joe Williams

Here Comes Gospel [D] [C].
UK BBC TV broadcast. Everyman series. 1976
Hoss Allen**/Inez Andrews/Reverend James Cleveland/Thomas A Dorsey/Gospel Stirrers/ Reverend Johnny Jones/Sallie Martin/Mighty Clouds Of Joy/O'Neal Twins/Shannon Williams**
[Individuals marked with a double asteriskwill be found in the index of non-performing interviewees.]

Hit Parade of 1943 [F] [M].
Directed by Albert S Rogell. REPUBLIC FILMS. 1943
Golden Gate Quartet/Wynonie Harris

Hold My Mule [D] [C].
MERCURY FILMS. 1993
Shirley Caesar

Hollywood A Go-Go [M].
US TV broadcast. Origin unknown. 1965
Chuck Berry/Jimmy Witherspoon

Hollywood Canteen [F] [M]#.
Directed by Delmar Davies. WARNER BROTHERS. 1943
Golden Gate Quartet

Hollywood Squares [C].
US NBC TV broadcast. 1970
Ray Charles

Homemade American Music [D].
Directed by Yasha Aginsky. 1979
Elizabeth Cotten

Homewood Show, The [C].
US TV broadcasts. Origin unknown, probably PBS. 1970
Charles Brown/Margie Evans/Lowell Fulson/ Furry Lewis/Joe Turner/Eddie Vinson/T-Bone Walker

Honky Tonk Man [F] [C]#*.
Directed by Clint Eastwood. 1982
Linda Hopkins

Hootenanny [M].
US ABC TV broadcasts. 1963–64
Ward Singers/Josh White

Hot Pepper [D] [C].
Directed by Les Blank. FLOWER FILMS. 1973
Clifton Chenier
[Available from Flower Films.]

House Rent Party [F] [M].
Directed by Sam Newfield. TODDY PICTURES. 1946
Alberta Pryne/Rudy Toombs

How About That Jive [F] [M].
Directed by Ray Sandford. Origin unknown. 1946
International Sweethearts Of Rhythm

Hugh Hefner Show, The
See *Playboy After Dark.*

Hullabaloo! [1] [M].
US NBC TV broadcast. 1965–66
Chuck Berry/Bessie Griffin

Hullabaloo! [2] [M].
UK ATV TV broadcast. 1965
Sonny Boy Williamson

I Am the Blues [C] [D].
Origin unknown. 1978
Baby Doo Caston/Chicago Blues All Stars/ Willie Dixon

I Call it Murder [D] [C].
UK BBC TV broadcast. Tuesday 27th November 1979
Eddie Clearwater

I Come For to Sing [M].
US TV broadcast. Probably local. Late 1940s–early 50s
Big Maceo/Big Bill Broonzy/Rosetta Howard/Arbee Stidham/Big Joe Williams
[This may have been hosted by Studs Terkel.]

I Hear the Blues [M].
Directed by Phillip Casson, produced by John Hamp.
UK Granada TV broadcast. Broadcast Wednesday 18 December 1963
Willie Dixon/Lonnie Johnson/Memphis Slim/Muddy Waters/Matt Murphy/Otis Spann/Victoria Spivey/Billie Stepney/Big Joe Williams/Sonny Boy Williamson
[Available from Granada TV. This is the 1963 American Folk Blues Festival.]

If You Feel the Feelin' You Was Feelin' [D] [C].
UK ITV TV broadcast. 1973
Jack Dupree
[This may be a retitling of *A Kind Of Freedom*.]

Il Mondo di Notte
See *World By Night*.

I'm Still Alive [F].
Origin unknown. 1940
Edith Wilson

Imitation of Life [F].
Directed by Douglas Sirk. UNIVERSAL. 1959
Mahalia Jackson

In a Lonely Place [F] [M].
Directed by Nicholas Ray. 1950
Hadda Brooks

In Concert [1] [C].
US ABC TV broadcast. 1973
BB King

In Concert [2] [C].
UK BBC TV broadcasts. Produced by Stanley Dorfmann. 1974
Brownie McGhee/Sonny Terry/Rufus Thomas
[Available from BBC.]

In Concert [3] [C].
Directed by Jim Gabbour. US Cox Cable Telecommunications
TV broadcast, New Orleans. 1985
James Booker/Henry Gray/Cousin Joe Pleasants/Robert Lockwood/Boogie Bill Webb
[Available from Jim Gabbour Productions.]

In the Delta of Mississippi [D] [C].
French TV broadcast. 1984
Roosevelt 'Booba' Barnes/Joe Cooper/Haywood Mills/Raymond Thomas/Wade Walton

In the Heat of the Night [F] [C]#*.
Directed by Norman Jewison. 1967
Ray Charles

In the Revival Tent [C].
Directed by Jim Gabbour. US Cox Cable Telecommunications TV broadcast, New Orleans. 1985
Heavenly Stars/Heralds of Christ/Mighty Chariots/Zion Harmonisers
[Available from Jim Gabbour Productions.]

In the Spirit [C].
UK Granada TV broadcast. 1980
Reverend James Cleveland/Marion Williams
[Available from Granada TV.]

In the Spotlight [C].
US TV broadcast. Origin unknown. 1982
Ray Charles

Individual Voices [C].
UK Channel 4 TV broadcast. 1984
Otis Rush

International Festival of Jazz [C].
UK TV broadcast. Origin unknown. 1979
Ray Charles

International Hour [M].
US TV broadcast. Origin unknown. 1968
Muddy Waters

International Sweethearts of Rhythm [D] [C].
Directed by Greta Schiller and Andrea Weiss. JEZEBEL PRODUCTIONS. 1986.
International Sweethearts Of Rhythm

Into the Night [F] [C]#.
Directed by John Landis. UNIVERSAL. 1985
BB King

It's a Mean Old World [D] [C].
Directed by John W English. 1978
Reverend Pearly Brown/R and H Gospel Singers
[Available from TCB Releasing.]

It's Got to be Rough to be Sweet [C].
Directed by John Lumsdain. ARHOOLIE PRODUCTIONS. 1987
J C Burris/Chris Strachwitz**/Katie Webster
[Arhoolie Records 25th Anniversary Party. This production also contains Cajun, jazz, country and Mexican music. Chris Strachwitz will be found in the index to non-performing interviewees. Available from Arhoolie Records.]

It's Little Richard! [M].
Directed by Phil Casson, produced by John Hamp.
UK Granada TV broadcast. 1964
Little Richard
[Available from Granada TV.]

J'ai Eté au Bal [D] [C].
Directed by Les Blank and Chris Strachwitz. FLOWER FILMS. 1989
Bois-Sec Ardoin/Boozoo Chavis/Cleveland Chenier/Clifton Chenier/John Delafose/Canray Fontenot/Queen Ida/Rockin' Sydney
[Available from Flower Films.]

Jack Kane Show, The [M].
US TV broadcast. Origin unknown. 1959
Jimmy Rushing

Jackie Gleason Show, The [M].
US CBS TV broadcast. 1950s
Rosetta Tharpe/Edith Wilson

Jackson Jive [F] [M].
Origin unknown. 1948
Boogie Bill Webb

Jail House Blues, The [F] [M].
COLUMBIA. 1929
Mamie Smith
[The only known surviving source for this film is its inclusion in the US NBC TV broadcast *Chicago And All That Jazz* (28th November 1961) and it is possible that edited versions of the songs were used for that programme. The original film remains unfound. The original sound recordings were custom-made by the Victor company.]

Jamboree
See *Disk Jockey Jamboree*.

Jazz 625 [M].
UK BBC TV broadcasts. 1964–65
Jack Dupree/Joe Turner/Jimmy Witherspoon
[Available from BBC.]

Jazz Alley [M].
US TV broadcast. Origin unknown. 1969
Mama Yancey

Jazz at the Leadmill [C].
UK Channel 4 TV broadcast. 1984
Jimmy Witherspoon

Jazz at the Maltings [M].
UK BBC TV broadcasts. 1968
Muddy Waters/Stars of Faith

Jazz at the Philharmonic [M].
UK BBC TV broadcast. 1967
T-Bone Walker

Jazz at the Smithsonian [C].
Produced by Larry Adler. ADLER ENTERPRISES. 1982
Alberta Hunter

Jazz Burghausen [C].
German TV broadcast. 1984
Lowell Fulson

Jazz Casual [M].
US TV broadcast. Origin unknown. 1950s
Jimmy Rushing

Jazz-In [C].
Swiss TV broadcasts. 1984 & 1987
Fats Domino/Linda Hopkins

Jazz Night [C].
Australian TV broadcast. 1986
Margie Evans

Jazz Noir, Le
See *Darktown Scandals Review*.

Jazz Odyssey
See *L'Aventure du Jazz*.

Jazz on a Summer's Day [D] [C].
Directed by Bert Stern. 1958
Chuck Berry/Big Maybelle/Mahalia Jackson/Dinah Washington
[Available from Historic. Commercially available on video]

Jazz on 4 [C].
UK Channel 4 TV broadcast. 1983
Jimmy Witherspoon

Jazz on Stage [C].
Directed by Jack Lewerkes. EURO-FILMS. 1970
Joe Turner

Jazz Scene [M].
UK BBC TV broadcast. 1958
Brownie McGhee/Sonny Terry

Jazz Scene at Ronnie Scott's [M].
UK BBC TV broadcasts. 1970
Jack Dupree/Albert King/Otis Spann/Stars Of Faith

Jazz Scrapbook [D] [C].
UK TV broadcast. Origin unknown. Early 1980s
Amateur silent film of Big Bill Broonzy

Jazz-USA [M].
US PBS TV broadcasts. Origin unknown. 1960
Butch Cage/Ray Charles/John Lee Hooker/Betty Jeanette/Muddy Waters/Sam Price/Jimmy Rushing/Otis Spann/Willie Thomas
[Available from Historic]

Jazz-USA [M].
US TV broadcast. Origin unknown. 1967
Jimmy Witherspoon
[This is presumed to be a different broadcast series from the above]

Jerk, The [F] [C].#
Directed by Carl Reiner. UNIVERSAL. 1979
Brownie McGhee/Sonny Terry

Jerry Blavatt Show, The [C].
US TV broadcast. Origin unknown. 1967
Little Richard

Jerry Lewis Show, The [C].
US NBC TV broadcast. 1968
Ray Charles

Jivin' in Be-Bop [F] [M].
Directed by Spencer Williams. ALEXANDER PRODUCTIONS. 1947
Dan Burley/Helen Humes

Joe Franklin Show, The [C].
US TV broadcast. Origin unknown. 1974
Screaming Jay Hawkins/Helen Humes/Eva Taylor/Joe Williams

Joey Bishop Show, The [M] or [C].
US ABC TV broadcast. 1967–69
Ray Charles/Joe Williams

John Gunther's High Road [M].
US ABC TV broadcast. 1959
Jimmy Rushing

John Hammond Presents [FS] [C].
JOHN HAMMOND JR FILM COLLECTION. 1971
Larry Johnson
[Available from TCB Releasing.]

John Henry Bones
See *Bones.*

John Jackson – An American Songster [D] [C].
Directed by Renato Tunelli. 1986
John Cephas/John Dee Holeman/John Jackson/Larry Johnson/Phil Wiggins

John Lee Hooker [D] [C].
South Bank Show. UK LWT TV broadcast. Directed and produced by Tony Knox. 1993
Bernie Besman**/Robert Cray/Famous Coachman**/John Lee Hooker/Zakiya Hooker**/BB King/Eddie Kirkland/Robert Koester**/Jim O'Neal**
[Individuals marked with a double asterisk will be found in the index of non-performing interviewees.]

Johnny B Goode [D] [C].
UK BBC TV broadcast. 1980
Chuck Berry/Johnny Johnson

Johnny Carson's Tonight Show
See *Tonight Show starring Johnny Carson.*

Johnny Cash Show, The [C].
US ABC TV broadcast. 1970
Ray Charles

Johnny Cash – Spring Fever **[C].**
US syndicated TV broadcast. 1978
Ray Charles

Johnny Otis Show **[M].**
US local TV broadcast. Origin unknown. 1959
Johnny Otis orchestra

Johnny Shines: Black and Blue **[C].**
Origin unknown. 1973
Johnny Shines

Joint Is Jumpin', The **[M] [FS].**
US. 1948
Hadda Brooks/John Oscar

Josh White Sings Music of the New World [M]
UK Granada TV series. 1961
Josh White/Josh White Jr.

Jubilaires **[*Soundie*] [M].**
Directed by William Forest Crouch.
FILMCRAFT PRODUCTIONS. 1948
Jubilaires

Jubilee Showcase **[M] from 1963 to 1970, [C] thereafter.**
Local TV broadcasts. SIDNEY ORDOWER PRODUCTIONS. 1963–82
Robert Anderson/Inez Andrews/Argo Singers/Harold Bailey Singers/Barrett Sisters/Bivens Specials/Maggie Bracey/Alex Bradford/Bradford Singers/Ethel Brooks/Willie Brown Jr/Milton Brunson/Shirley Caesar/Deloris Barrett Campbell/Caravans/Elaine Caston/Chansonettes/Chicago Community Choir/Clefs Of Faith/Reverend James Cleveland/Dorothy Love Coates/Davis Sisters/Ida Mae Davis/Dixie Hummingbirds/Jessy Dixon/Willie Dixon/Thomas A Dorsey/Reverend John Dowdy/Mattie Dozier/Roosevelt English/Lou Della Evans/Faith Community Choir/Jesse James Farley/Fellowship Missionary Baptist Church Choir/Clarence Fountain/Gertrude Fuller/Cassietta George/Gloryette Gospel Singers/Golden Tones/Gospel Chimes/Gospel Harmonettes/Gospel Songbirds/Bessie Griffin/Doris Grimes/Rebert Harris/James Herndon Singers/Highway Q C's/Robert Hodge/Joseph Hutchinson And The Hutchinson Sunbeams/Inspirational Gospel Singers/Reverend Jesse Jackson/Sister Josephine James/Reverend Johnny Jones/Reverend George Jordan/Reverend Stanley Keeble/Minnie Kennedy/Ladies Of Harmony/Joe Ligon/Dorothy Lipscomb/Little Criss/Loving Sisters/Reverend T E Lutcher/Gladys McPhatter/Roberta Martin/Sallie Martin/Meditation Singers/Mighty Clouds of Harmony/Mighty Clouds Of Joy/Bill Moss/Norfleet Brothers/Dorothy Norwood/O'Neal Twins/Loretta Oliver/Omega Baptist Church Radio Choir/Original Gospel Harmonettes/Kitty Parham/Pilgrim Jubilees/Lorenza Brown Porter/Sarah Jordan Powell/Billy Preston/Eva Jean Purnell/Reverend Cleophus Robinson/Ernestine and Laura Rundless/Salem Travelers/John Sellers/Sarah Simmons/Singers Of Joy/Soul Stirrers/Spiritual Five/Staple Singers/Stars Of Faith/Francis Steadman/Princess Stewart/Supreme Angels/Swanee Quintet/Doris Sykes/Thompson Community Singers/Ira Tucker/Jackie Verdell/Violinaires/Voices of Melody/Voices Of Praise/Voices Of Triumph/Albertina Walker/Ward Singers/Louise Weaver/Marion Williams/Reverend Ruben Willingham/Reverend Maceo Woods/Robert E Wooten/Reverend Marvin Yancey
[Available from Sidney Ordower.]

Juke Box Jury **[M].**
UK BBC TV broadcast. 1964
Howlin' Wolf

Juke Box Rhythm **[F] [M].**
Directed by Arthur Dreifuss. COLUMBIA. 1958
Johnny Otis/Treniers

Juke Joint Saturday Night **[D] [C].**
Origin unknown. 1991
Big Jack Johnson/Arthneice 'Gas Man' Jones

Jump the Blues Away **[C].**
Origin unknown. 1988
Albert Collins/Etta James
See Laserdisc file.

Jumpin' at the Jubilee **[FS] [M].**
A compilation of Louis Jordan soundies.
[Available from TCB Releasing]

Junior Prom **[F] [M].**
Directed by Arthur Dreifuss. MONOGRAM PICTURES. 1946
Louis Jordan
Copyrighted 17 February 1946

Just for Fun **[C].**
See *American Folk Blues Festival 1970.*

Kaleidoscope 4 [M].
US TV broadcast. Origin unknown. 1965
John Lee Hooker/Jimmy Rushing

Kansas City Jazz Story
See *Last of The Blue Devils.*

Karussel [C].
Swiss TV broadcast. 1987
Sam Price

Keep on Rockin' [D] [C].
Directed by D A Pennebaker. 1972
Chuck Berry/Bo Diddley/Little Richard
[Available from Historic. An edited version of this film, entitled *Sweet Toronto*, also exists.]

Kennedy Centre Awards Ceremony [C].
US PBS TV broadcast. Sunday 26 December 1997
Shirley Caesar

Kentucky Educational Television [C].
US PBS TV broadcast. 1970 & 1979
Lonnie Brooks/Bill Williams

Kentucky Fried Movie [F] [C]#.
Directed by John Landis. UNIVERSAL. 1977
BB King

KERA-TV, Dallas, Texas [C].
Untitled TV broadcast. Directed by Jim Rowley. 1973
Freddy King

Kind of Freedom, A [D] [C].
UK LWT TV broadcast Tuesday 10 July 1973
Jack Dupree

Kingdom of Zydeco, The [D] [C].
Directed by Robert Mugge. MUG-SHOT PRODUCTIONS. 1994
Beau Jocque/Boozoo Chavis/John Delafose/ Nathan Williams
[Available from Mug-Shot Productions.]

King of the Blues [D] [C].
UK BBC TV broadcast. Omnibus series. 1991
BB King

KLRU-TV [C].
Untitled TV broadcasts. Texas. 1969–72
Mance Lipscomb

Knee Deep in Music [FS] [M].
Directed by Alf Goulding. RADIO PICTURES. 1933
unidentified artist # 13

Kraft Music Hall, The [C].
USA NBC TV broadcast. 1967
Ray Charles

Kup's Show [C].
US TV broadcast. Origin unknown. 1972
BB King

LA All Stars
See *Jazz on Stage.*

Lady Liz [F] [M].
PARAMOUNT. 1929
Laura Smith
[*The Chicago Defender* of 22 November 1930 reported that Smith had just completed this film for Paramount but no copy has ever been found.]

Land Where the Blues Began [D] [C].
Directed by Alan Lomax.
COLUMBIA UNIVERSITY/MISSISSIPPI AUTHORITY FOR EDUCATIONAL TELEVISION/PBS co-production. 1979
Johnny Brooks/Walter Brown/R L Burnside/ Sam Chatmon/James Hall/George Johnson/ Beatrice Maxwell/Clyde Maxwell/Lonnie Pitchford/Jack Owens/Eugene Powell/Joe Savage/Reverend Caesar Smith/Bud Spires/Napoleon Strickland/Belton Sutherland/J R Tucker & group/Othar Turner & the Gravel Springs Fife & Drum Band
[Two versions of this film exist. The first, produced by the Mississippi Authority, and the second, with some subtitles added, broadcast as a part of the *American Patchwork* series in 1990. The only significant difference is the addition of on-screen commentary by Lomax to the *American Patchwork* edition.]

Larry Johnson
See *John Hammond Presents.*

Last of the Blue Devils [D] [C].
Directed by Bruce Ricker. MUTUAL MUSICIANS FOUNDATION. 1974–79
Joe Turner
[Available from TCB Releasing. This film was made over a five year period.]

Last Waltz, The [D] [C]#.
Directed by Martin Scorsese. 1978
Muddy Waters

Late Night Line Up [C].
UK BBC TV broadcasts. 1970
Juke Boy Bonner/Arthur Crudup/Son House/ Memphis Slim
[Available from BBC.]

Late Night with David Letterman [C].
US NBC TV broadcasts. 1989
Ruth Brown/Albert Collins/John Lee Hooker/ Memphis Slim

Late Night with Joan Rivers
US NBC TV broadcast. 1987
Bo Diddley

Later ... With Jools Holland [C].
UK Channel 4 TV broadcasts. 1992
Otis Rush/Katie Webster

Laura Weber's Guitar Guitar [M].
US PBS TV broadcast. 1969
Elizabeth Cotten
[Available from Historic.]

Le Jazz Noir
See *Dark Town Scandals*.

Leadbelly [F] [C].
Directed by Gordon Parks. PARAMOUNT. 1975
J C Burris/Hi-Tide Harris/Brownie McGhee/ Sonny Terry

Learning Tree, The [F] [C]#.
Directed by Gordon Parks. WARNER BROTHERS. 1969
Jimmy Rushing

Legend of Bo Diddley, The [FS] [M].
Origin unknown. 1966–67
Bo Diddley
[This film also includes scenes shot inside the Chess recording studios in Chicago.]

Legends of Rhythm and Blues [D] [C].
UK Channel 4 TV broadcast. *Repercussions* series. 1984
Charles Brown/Margie Evans/Lowell Fulson/ Lloyd Glenn/Joe Liggins/Big Jay McNeely/Big Mama Thornton

Les Crane Show, The [M].
US ABC TV broadcast. 1965
Jesse Fuller

Let the Church Say Amen [F] [C].
Origin unknown. 1973
BB King

Let the Good Times Roll [1] [F] [C].
Directed by Robert Abel and Sid Levin. COLUMBIA. 1973
Chuck Berry/Bo Diddley/Fats Domino/Little Richard

Let the Good Times Roll [2] [C].
Origin unknown. 1991
Buckwheat Zydeco/Five Blind Boys Of Alabama/BB King/Queen Ida
[New Orleans Jazz and Heritage Festival]

Levi Jeans advert [C].
Origin unknown. Broadcast in UK ITV regions and Channel 4. 1984
John Lee Hooker

Library of Congress, Washington DC [M].
1940, 1942 & 1976
Rich Amerson/Charles Edwards/Louisiana Red/ unidentified artists #s15–17

Like It Is [C].
US TV broadcast. Origin unknown. 1970
Reverend Gary Davis

Like Young [M].
US TV broadcast. Origin unknown. 1967
Muddy Waters

Limit Up [F] [C].
Directed by Richard Martini. 1989
Ray Charles

Little Richard – A Profile [D] [C].
UK LWT TV broadcast. *South Bank Show* series. 1985
Little Richard

Little Richard Story, The [D] [C].
Origin unknown. 1980
Little Richard/Billy Wright

Live Aid [C].
Worldwide charity TV broadcast in aid of famine relief. 1985
Albert Collins/BB King

Live at City Hall [C].
UK TV broadcast. Origin unknown. 1984
Jimmy Witherspoon

Live at Nick's [C].
Directed by Miles Kidder. 1983
BB King

Live at Ronnie Scott's [C].
WADHAM FILM GROUP. 1988
Memphis Slim/Taj Mahal

Live at Rosa's [FS] [C]
Directed by Jonathon Letchinger. c. 1989
Yank Rachell

Live at the Checkerboard [C].
Origin unknown. 1978
Buddy Guy/Muddy Waters

Live at the Millionaire
1982.
Esther Phillips

Live at the Roxy [C].
Origin unknown. 1982
Chuck Berry

Live at the Universal Amphitheatre [C].
US TV broadcast. Origin unknown. 1986
Fats Domino

Live from Her Majesty's [C].
UK BBC TV broadcast. 1984
BB King

Live from the Bitter End [C].
US TV broadcasts. Origin unknown. 1967–68
Chuck Berry/Little Richard
[Available from Historic.]

Live in Africa [C].
Origin unknown. 1974
BB King
[Some of this footage has also been used in *When We Were Kings* [D] [C].

Living Legends of the Blues [C].
Syndicated TV broadcasts. 1981
James Cotton/Blind John Davis
[Material compiled from Montreux festivals. See *Montreux Jazz*.]

Living with the Blues [D] [C].
Directed by Jim Kent. 1980s
Hubert Sumlin

London Rock and Roll Show, The [D] [C].
Directed by Peter Clifton. NOTTING HILL FILMS. 1972
Chuck Berry/Bo Diddley/Little Richard

Long Train Running [D] [C].
Directed by Marlon Riggs and Peter Webster. US PBS TV. 1981
Sugar Pie Desanto/Lowell Fulson/Bob Geddins**/Troyce Key & J J Malone/Frankie Lee/James Moore**/Paul Oliver**/Sonny Rhodes/Mississippi Johnny Waters
[Individuals marked with a double asterisk will be found in the index of non-performing interviewees.]

Look-Out Sister [F] [M].
Directed by Louis Jordan. ASTOR PICTURES. 1948
Louis Jordan

Look Up and Live [M].
US TV broadcast. Origin unknown. 1961
Josh White

Look Up and Sing Out [C].
Origin unknown. 1970s
Consolers/Gospel Harmonettes/Johnny Jones/Brother Joe May/Reverend Cleophus Robinson/Supreme Angels/Swanee Quintet/Reverend Ruben Willingham

Louie Bluie [D] [C].
Directed by Terry Zwigoff. SUPERIOR PICTURES. 1985
Howard Armstrong/Ted Bogan/Yank Rachell/Ikey Robinson/unidentified artist #11/Whistler And His Jug Band

Low Lights and Blue Smoke
See *Big Bill Blues*.

Lyrics and Legends [M].
US TV broadcast. Origin unknown. 1963
Butch Cage/John Lee Hooker/Victoria Spivey/Willie Thomas
[This may be part of the *Folklife Archive* series directed by George Pickow]

Mac Davis Show, The [C].
US NBC TV broadcast. 1976
Furry Lewis

Made in Chicago [D] [C].
US local TV broadcasts. Origin unknown. 1970–77
Carey Bell/Blind James Brewer/Blind John Davis/J B Hutto/Johnny Littlejohn/Little Brother Montgomery/Edith Wilson/Mighty Joe Young

Mahalia 1911–1972 [D] [C].
Origin unknown. 1985
Mahalia Jackson

Mahalia Jackson Sings [M].
UK BBC TV broadcast. Produced by Ernest Maxin. 1964
Mahalia Jackson

Mainstream [C].
UK BBC TV live outside broadcast. 1979
Eddie Campbell/Lester Davenport/Nolan Struck

Maintenance Shop Blues [C].
Directed by Doug Brooker.
Iowa Public Broadcasting System. 1979–81
Lonnie Brooks/'Gatemouth' Brown/James Cotton/Willie Dixon/Albert King/John Lee Hooker/Muddy Waters/Queen Ida/Taj Mahal/Koko Taylor

Man They Call the Genius, The [M]
UK ATV TV broadcast. Wednesday 26 August 1964.
Directed by Robert Fleming
Ray Charles

Mandingo [F] [C]#.
Directed by Richard Fleischer. 1973
Hi-Tide Harris/Muddy Waters

Mantan Messes Up [F] [M].
STAR PRODUCTIONS. 1946
Five Red Caps/Four Tones

March of Time [D] [M].
No. 2 April 1935
Leadbelly
[Available from Archive. For a full account of the making of this film, see the book *The Life And Legend Of Leadbelly* by Dr Kip Lornell and Charles Wolfe.]

March of Time [D] [M]
[unknown #] c.1945
Brownie McGhee/Sonny Terry
[This episode also includes film of the folk singer Woody Guthrie.]

Mardi Gras Funk [C].
UK TV broadcast. Origin unknown. 1984
Ernie K-Doe

Mark Naftalin's Blue Monday Party
See *Blue Monday Party*.

Mark of Jazz, The [C].
US TV broadcast. Origin unknown. 1971
Taj Mahal

Marty Faye Show [C].
US local TV broadcast. 1969
Magic Sam

Masters of American Traditional Music [M].
UNIVERSITY OF SEATTLE, WASHINGTON/SEATTLE FOLKLORE SOCIETY
1967-70
Reverend Pearly Brown/Elizabeth Cotten/Reverend Gary Davis/Jesse Fuller/John Lee Hooker/Lightnin' Hopkins/Son House/John Jackson/Furry Lewis/Mance Lipscomb/Fred McDowell Brownie McGhee/Martin, Bogan and Armstrong/Johnny Shines/Sonny Terry/United Sons And Daughters Of Zion Number Nine Fife And Drum Band/Bukka White/Big Joe Williams/Robert Pete Williams
[Available from Historic. See also *Roots Of American Music* for colour footage by many of the above artists.]

Maxwell Street Blues [D] [C].
Directed by Linda Williams and Raul Ziretsky. 1980
Blind James Brewer/John Henry Davis/Blind Arvella Grey/Floyd Jones/Carrie Robertson/Venson's Playboys
[Available from TCB Releasing. This also contains examples of amateur film shot by Blind Arvella Grey [*sic*] during the 1970s. See also *And This Is Free*, *Chicago Blues* and *Louie Bluie* for further footage of Maxwell Street.]

Me and Stella [C].
US TV broadcast. Origin unknown. 1977
Elizabeth Cotten/Taj Mahal
[Available from Phoenix.]

Medicine Ball Caravan aka *We Have Come for Your Daughters* [F] [C].
Directed by Francois Reichenbach. WARNER BROTHERS. 1971
BB King

Meet Miss Bobbysocks [F] [M].
Directed by Glenn Tryon. COLUMBIA. 1944
Louis Jordan
Copyrighted 12 October 1944

Melody of a City – Chicago [D] [C].
Directed by Linda Baldwin. WHA TV 1981
Muddy Waters/Junior Wells

Memphis Blues Festival
See *Sounds Of Summer*.

Memphis Slim [FS] [M].
Origin unknown. 1960
Memphis Slim

Merv Griffin Show, The [C].
US CBS TV broadcasts. 1968–77
Chuck Berry/Ray Charles/Fats Domino/Albert King/BB King/Little Richard/Joe Williams

Messin' With the Blues [C].
Montreux Jazz. 1974
Buddy Guy/Muddy Waters/Junior Wells
See also Commercially Available Laser Discs section, on p. 411.

Midday Show, The [C].
Australian TV broadcast. 1986
Margie Evans

Midnight Special, The [C].
US NBC TV broadcasts. 1970–76
Chuck Berry/Bobby Bland/Ray Charles/Bo Diddley/John Lee Hooker/BB King/Little Richard/Big Mama Thornton/Joe Williams/Jimmy Witherspoon

Mike Douglas Show, The [M] & [C].
US syndicated TV broadcasts. 1963–77
Chuck Berry/Bo Diddley/Ray Charles/Fats Domino/Alberta Hunter/BB King/Little Richard/Muddy Waters/Jimmy Rushing/Taj Mahal/T-Bone Walker/Jimmy Witherspoon
[Available from Historic.]

Million Dollars aka *The Heist* [F] [C].
Directed by Sergio Goff. FIRST AMERICAN FILMS. 1971
Little Richard

Milton Berle Show, The [M].
US NBC TV broadcast. 1950s
Mahalia Jackson/Sugar Chile Robinson

Milton Metfessel Phonophotographic Recordings [M].
Made by Dr Milton Metfessel.
University of North Carolina at Chapel Hill. 1926.
unidentified artists [A]
[reportedly still archived in the University of North Carolina at Chapel Hill.]

Miracle in Harlem [F] [M].
Directed by Jack Kemp. HERALD PICTURES. 1948
Lavada Carter/Savannah Churchill/Sheila Guyse/Juanita Hall/Lynn Proctor Trio
[Available from Archive.]

Mississippi Blues [1] [C].
Probably directed by Worth Long. MISSISSIPPI ACTION FOR COMMUNITY EDUCATION/ MISSISSIPPI AUTHORITY FOR EDUCATIONAL TELEVISION co-production. 1979
Sam Chatmon/Sylvia Embry/Betty Fikes/Lefty Dizz/Robert Lockwood/Clyde Maxwell/Eugene Powell/Boyd Rivers/Johnny Shines/Big Joe Williams
[Available from TCB Releasing]

Mississippi Blues [2]
See *Saturday Blues*.

Mississippi Days and Southern Nights [C].
US TV broadcast. Origin unknown. 1980
Brownie McGhee/Sonny Terry

Mississippi Delta Blues [1] [D] [M].
CENTRE FOR SOUTHERN CULTURE. 1969
unidentified artists #s 29–32
[Available from Centre For Southern Culture.]

Mississippi Delta Blues [2] [D].
Directed by Anthony Herrera. CENTRE FOR SOUTHERN CULTURE. 1972
James Son Thomas
[Available from Centre For Southern Culture.]

Mississippi Delta Blues [3] [D].
CENTRE FOR SOUTHERN CULTURE. 1974
James Son Thomas/Wade Walton
[Available from Centre For Southern Culture.]

Mississippi Department of Archives and History
B F Tucker silent movies
Unidentified artist #14

Mississippi Masala [F] [C]#.
Directed by Mira Nair. COLUMBIA. 1991
Willie Cobbs

Mister Boogie Woogie [D] [C].
Directed by Alexis Krasilovsky. CENTRE FOR SOUTHERN CULTURE. 1978
Mose Vinson
[Available from Centre For Southern Culture.]

Mister Brown [F] [C].
Directed by Roger Andrieux. ANDRIEUX PRODUCTIONS. 1972
John Lee Hooker

Mister Crump's Blues [D] [C].
US TV broadcast. Origin unknown. 1972
Bukka White

Mister Rock and Roll [F] [M].
Directed by Charles Dubin. PARAMOUNT. 1957
Lavern Baker/Chuck Berry/Wynonie Harris/Little Richard/Frankie Lymon/Clyde McPhatter

Mondo di Notte, Il
See *World by Night*

Monterey Jazz [D] [C].
Origin unknown. 1968
BB King/T-Bone Walker/Ward Singers

Monterey Jazz Festival [C].
US TV broadcast. Origin unknown. 1973
Ernestine Anderson/Margie Evans/Linda Hopkins/Etta James/Preston Love/Big Jay McNeely/Barbara Morrison/Johnny Otis/Shuggie Otis/Esther Phillips/Jimmy Rushing/Joe Turner/Eddie Vinson/Charles Williams/Joe Williams
[See also *The Duke At Monterey*.]

Montreux Jazz [C].
MONTREUX JAZZ. Produced by Claude Nobs. 1972-96
Luther Allison/Chuck Berry/Bo Diddley/Juke Boy Bonner/James Booker/'Gatemouth' Brown/Clifton Chenier/Eddie Clearwater/Albert Collins/Johnny Copeland/James Cotton/Robert Cray/Blind John Davis/Willie Dixon/Fats Domino/Jack Dupree/Bessie Griffin/John Lee Hooker/Helen Humes/J B Hutto/Etta James/Albert King/BB King/Freddy King/Little Willie Littlefield/Willie Mabon/Brownie McGhee/Magic Slim/Memphis Slim/Mighty Clouds Of Joy/Muddy Waters/David Myers/Esther Phillips/Sam Price/Professor Longhair/Reverend Cleophus Robinson/Stars of Faith/Sugar Blue/Taj Mahal/Koko Taylor/Sonny Terry/Eddie Vinson/T-Bone Walker/Sippie Wallace/Junior Wells/Jimmy Witherspoon
[Material from the annual Montreux Jazz Festivals. Originally broadcast on Swiss national TV. Available from Montreux Jazz.]

Moods in Melody [M].
US TV broadcast. Origin unknown. 1961
Joe Williams

Moonshine Wars, The [F] [C].
Directed by Richard Quine. 1970
Joe Williams

More Jazz Unlimited – A Rebirth of the Blues [M].
UK ATV TV broadcast. Directed by Joe McGrath. 1963
Memphis Slim/T-Bone Walker

MTV [Music Television] [C].
1980s & 1997
BB King

Muddy and Friends
See *Soundstage*.

Murder on Lenox Avenue [F] [M].
Directed by Arthur Dreifuss. COLONNADE PICTURES. 1940
Alberta Perkins/Mamie Smith

Music Hall America [C].
US syndicated TV broadcast. 1976
Ray Charles

Music in America [C].
US TV broadcast. Origin unknown. 1976
Louis Myers

Music Masters and Rhythm Kings [C].
Georgia Public Broadcasting System. 1992
Eddie Kirkland

Music Scene [C].
US ABC TV broadcast. 1969
Bo Diddley/BB King

Musical Holdouts [D] [C].
UNIVERSITY OF CALIFORNIA AT BERKELEY. 1975
unidentified artists #41

My Blue Heaven [F] [M]
Origin unknown. 1950
Helen Humes

My Castle's Rockin' [D] [C].
Origin unknown. 1982–83
Alberta Hunter

Mystery in Swing [F] [M]#.
Directed by Arthur Dreifuss. INTERNATIONAL ROAD SHOWS. 1940
Mamie Smith

Mystery Train [F] [C]#*.
Directed by Jim Jarmusch. 1989
Screaming Jay Hawkins/Rufus Thomas

Nat King Cole Show, The [M].
US NBC TV broadcasts. 1956–58
Mahalia Jackson

National Downhome Blues Festival [C].
Georgia Public Telecommunications Systems. 1984
Thomas Bird/Precious Bryant/John Cephas/Jessie Mae Hemphill/Homesick James/Thomas Hurt/John Jackson/Eddie Kirkland/Robert Lockwood/Albert Macon/Lonnie Pitchford/Snooky Pryor/Doctor Ross/Sunnyland Slim/Taj Mahal/Sonny Terry/James Son Thomas/Phil Wiggins

National Lampoon's Animal House [F] [C]#*.
Directed by John Landis. UNIVERSAL. 1978
Robert Cray

NBC Follies [C].
US NBC TV broadcast. 1973
Ray Charles

Nellie '82 [D] [C].
US KCET PBS TV broadcast. 1982
Nellie Lutcher

NET Jazz [M].
US National Educational Television PBS TV broadcast. 1968
BB King

NET Playhouse – Thoughts of the Artist on Leaving the Sixties [C].
US National Educational Television PBS TV broadcast. 1970
Taj Mahal

New Blues
See *Big City Blues*.

New Orleans [F] [M].
Directed by Arthur Lubin. UNITED ARTISTS. 1947
Meade Lux Lewis

New Orleans Jazz [M].
US TV broadcast. Origin unknown. 1964
Creole George Guesnon/Joseph 'Dede' Pierce

New Orleans Jazz and Heritage Festival 1990 [D] [C].
US TV broadcast. Origin unknown. 1990
C J Chenier/Followers Of Christ/Friendly Travellers/Clarence 'Frogman' Henry/Zachary Richard/Rockin' Dopsie/Irma Thomas/Katie Webster

New Orleans Now
See *All Alone With The Blues* and *In The Revival Tent*.

Newport Jazz Festival 1960
See *Jazz USA*.

Newport Jazz Festival 1962 [D] [M].
Origin unknown. 1962
Jimmy Rushing/Ward Singers/Joe Williams
[Available from TCB Releasing. See also the Alan Lomax film collection, *Festival, Folklife Productions*, *Jazz On A Summer's Day* and *Jazz USA* for other Newport footage.]

Night Life [1] [C].
US TV broadcast. Origin unknown. 1975
Albert Washington

Night Life [2] [C].
US TV broadcast. Origin unknown. 1981
J B Hutto
[The above are presumed to be different series. The Hutto performance is in Massachusetts, the origin of the Washington is unknown but was probably broadcast in Cincinatti.]

Night Scene [C].
US TV broadcast. Origin unknown. 1980s
J B Hutto

Nightmare [F] [M].
Directed by Maxwell Shane. 1955
Meade Lux Lewis

NIKE sports shoes adverts [C]
US & UK TV broadcasts. 1989
Bo Diddley

Noel avec Ray Charles
European TV broadcast. Origin unknown. 1979
Ray Charles

Not Only … But Also [M].
UK BBC TV broadcast. 1965
T-Bone Walker

Nothin' But a Man [F] [M]#.
Directed by Michael Roemer. DUARTE CINEMA. 1964
Gospel Stars/Reverend Marshall Tomkin

Nothing But the Blues [M].
Directed by Phillip Casson, produced by John Hamp. UK Granada TV.
Tuesday 27 December 1966
John Estes/Yank Rachell/Otis Rush/Roosevelt Sykes/Joe Turner/Sippie Wallace/Junior Wells/Robert Pete Williams
[This is the 1966 American Folk Blues Festival. Available from Granada.]

O'Voutie O'Rooney [F] [M].
Directed by Jack Reiger. ASTOR PICTURES. 1947
Mabel Lee
[Also featuring Slim Gaillard.]

Observer, The [M].
US TV broadcast, probably PBS. 1964
John Estes/Hammie Nixon/Yank Rachell

Odyssey: They Took a Blue Note [M].
US CBS TV broadcast. 1956
Horace Sprott

Oh Happy Day [D] [C].
UK BBC TV. Broadcast Tuesday 24 December 1974
Sam Chatmon/unidentified artists #s 38 & 39

Ohio University Telecommunications Centre [C].
1979-80
Elizabeth Cotten

Ohne Filter/Ohne Filter Blues/Ohne Filter Extra [C].
German TV broadcasts. SUDFUNKWEST. 1984
Johnny Adams/Johnny Copeland/Robert Cray/Little Willie Littlefield/Taj Mahal/Irma Thomas
[Available from Sudwestfunk]

Old Grey Whistle Test, The [C].
UK BBC TV broadcasts. 1974–85
Albert Collins/Robert Cray/BB King/Freddy King/Louisiana Red/Brownie McGhee/Cousin Joe Pleasants/Doctor Ross/Sonny Terry
[Available from BBC.]

Ollie and Fred Show, The [M].
UK ATV TV broadcast. 1965
T-Bone Walker
[This was a children's show, broadcast at 5pm; Walker was introduced by Ollie Beak and Fred Barker, the two glove puppets who hosted the programme.]

Omnibus [C].
UK BBC TV broadcast. 1978
Charlie Sayles

On the Battlefield [D] [C].
UK Channel 4 TV broadcast. *Repercussions* series. 1984
Birmingham Sunlights/Four Eagle Gospel Singers/Harps of Melody/Auguster Maul/Pattersonaires/Reverend W J Sankey/Sterling Jubilee Singers/Sister Williams

Once More with Felix [M].
UK BBC TV broadcast. 1968
Muddy Waters
[The other guest on this broadcast was Spike Milligan.]

One Dark Night [F] [M].
MILLION DOLLAR PRODUCTIONS. 1939
Four Tones

One Hundred Years From Today
See *Camera Three.*

One Night Stand [C].
US TV broadcast. Origin unknown. 1971
BB King

One of a Kind [C].
US TV broadcast. SIERRA SOUND AND VISION. 1970
Brownie McGhee/Sonny Terry

Open Studio [C].
US local TV broadcast. Origin unknown. 1975
J C Burris

Operation Entertainment [C].
US ABC TV broadcast. 1968
Ray Charles

ORTF
French TV broadcasts. 1962, 1970, 1973
Memphis Slim

Oscar Peterson Presents [C].
US syndicated TV broadcast. 1974
Big Joe Turner/Joe Williams

Oscar Peterson: Very Special [C].
US syndicated TV broadcast. 1976
Ray Charles

Our American Musical Heritage [C].
US TV broadcast. Origin unknown. 1971
Jimmy Rushing

Our Time [C].
US NBC TV broadcast. 1985
Coasters

Out of the Blacks, Into the Blues [D] [C].
Directed by Robert Manthoulis. 1971
Arthur Crudup/Willie Dixon/Buddy Guy/BB King/Furry Lewis/Mance Lipscomb/Brownie McGhee/Roosevelt Sykes/Sonny Terry/unidentified artist # 36/Junior Wells/Bukka White/Robert Pete Williams
[Available from TCB Releasing. In two parts; *Along The Old Man River* (part 1), *A Way To Escape The Ghetto* (part 2).]

Pan-African Festival aka *Le Festival Culturel Panafricain* [D] [C].
Directed by William Klein. ONCIC. 1971
Marion Williams

Panic in the Streets [F] [M].
Directed by Elia Kazan. 20TH CENTURY FOX. 1950
Helen Humes

Paradise in Harlem [F] [M].
Directed by Joseph Seiden. JUBILEE PICTURES CORPORATION. 1940
Sidney Easton/Babe Matthews/Mamie Smith

Pardon Us [F] [M].
Directed by James Parrott. MGM. 1931
Birmingham Jubilees
[The identification of the Birmingham Jubilees in this Laurel And Hardy feature is based upon aural and visual evidence, and therefore should not be regarded as conclusive.]

Passion Fish [F] [C].
Directed by John Sayles. ATCHAFALAYA. 1993
John Delafose

Patterns of Words and Music [M].
US TV broadcast. Origin unknown. 1960
Lightnin' Hopkins

Paul Crump Story, The [M].
US TV broadcast. Origin unknown. 1962
Jimmy Witherspoon

Pearl Bailey Show, The [C].
US ABC TV broadcast. 1971
BB King

Pebble Mill at One [C].
UK BBC TV news magazine. 1977 and 1980
Sam Price/Stars of Faith

People's Music – And All That Jazz [C].
US TV broadcast, probably PBS. 1976
Butch Cage/Willie Thomas

Perry Como Show, The [M].
US NBC TV broadcasts. 1952–58
Fats Domino/Larks/Ravens/Joe Williams

Perspective [C].
US TV broadcasts. Origin unknown. 1975
Dave Alexander/Floyd Dixon

Pete Seeger Film Collection
See Directors' index.
[See also *Three Songs By Leadbelly*, which Seeger edited]

Pete Seeger's Rainbow Quest [M].
US PBS TV brodcasts. 1966-68
Elizabeth Cotten/Reverend Gary Davis/John Hurt/Brownie McGhee/Sonny Terry
[Available from Historic.]

Peter Wolf [C] or [M].
US TV broadcast. Origin unknown. 1969
Joe Williams

Philadelphia Folk Festival [C].
US TV broadcasts, probably PBS. 1973–75
Larry Johnson/Fred McDowell/Victoria Spivey

Piano Players Rarely Play Together [D] [C].
Directed by Stephenson Palfi. 1980
Professor Longhair/Allen Toussaint/Tuts Washington

Playback [FS] [M].
Origin unknown. 1963
Mahalia Jackson

Play It Again Sam [C].
US TV broadcast. Origin unknown. 1975
Taj Mahal

Play Misty for Me [F] [C]*.
Directed by Clint Eastwood. 1971
Johnny Otis band/Mighty Flea

Playboy After Dark [C].
US TV broadcasts. Origin unknown. 1969
James Cotton/Joe Williams

Playing That Thing [C].
US TV broadcast. Origin unknown. 1972
James Cotton/Sonny Terry

Positively Black [C].
US TV broadcast. Origin unknown. 1973
BB King

Prairie Home Companion, The [C]
US KTCA PBS TV broadcast. 1987
Brownie McGhee

Pride and Joy – The Story of Alligator Records [D] [C].
Directed by Robert Mugge. MUG-SHOT PRODUCTIONS. 1992
Lonnie Brooks/Bruce Iglauer**/Robert Koester**/Li'l Ed and the Blues Imperials/Dick Shurman**/Koko Taylor/Katie Webster
[Individuals marked with a double asterisk will be found in the index of non-performing interviewees. Available from Mug-Shot Productions. See also *Big City Blues* and *Blues And The Alligator* for further Alligator-related material.]

Programme of Songs by Lightnin' Hopkins, A [FS] [M].
Origin unknown. 1971
Lightnin' Hopkins

Queen of the Blues [D] [C].
WTTW/WORMSER PRODUCTIONS. 1990
Willie Dixon/Buddy Guy/Pops Taylor**/Koko Taylor
[Pops Taylor will be found in the index of non-performing interviewees].

Quest [M].
US TV broadcast. Origin unknown. 1964
Jimmy Witherspoon

QVC (Quality, Value, Convenience).
US home shopping TV station. 1997
Shirley Caesar

Radio Parade of 1935 aka *Radio Follies* [F] [M].
Directed by Arthur Woods. ALLIANCE [England]. 1935
Alberta Hunter

Rage in Harlem, A [F] [C]#*.
Directed by Bill Duke. 1991
Screaming Jay Hawkins

Rattle and Hum
See *U2: Rattle And Hum.*

Ready Steady Go [M].
UK ATV TV broadcasts. Directed by Elkan Allen. 1963–66
Fontella Bass/Sugar Pie Desanto/Jesse Fuller/Buddy Guy/John Lee Hooker/Little Richard/Little Walter/Esther Phillips/Jimmy Reed/Rufus Thomas/Tommy Tucker/Ike & Tina Turner/T-Bone Walker/Sonny Boy Williamson
[This programme also featured live and mimed performances by contemporary soul artists including Arthur Alexander/James Brown/Roy C/Don Covay/Dixie Cups/Lee Dorsey/Inez & Charlie Foxx/Marvin Gaye/Ben E King/Wilson Pickett/ Otis Redding/Soul Sisters/Edwin Starr/Joe Tex]

Really the Country Blues
See *Camera Three.*

Record Row – Cradle of Rhythm and Blues
Produced by WTTW Chicago. 1997
Ewart Abner*/Jerry Butler*/Marshall Chess*/Phil Chess*/Bo Diddley/Buddy Guy/Bill Leaner*/ Keith Richards*

Reet-Petite and Gone [F] [M].
Directed by William Forest Crouch. ASTOR PICTURES. 1947
Louis Jordan/June Richmond

Remembering Black Music [D] [C].
Directed by Tom Reed. US KTLA-TV Los Angeles. 1986
Joe Adams**/Bumps Blackwell**/Bo Diddley/Hadda Brooks/Dave Clark**/Esther Crayton**/Clarence Fountain/Jack Gibson**/René Hall**/Harmonica Fats/Joe Liggins/Big Jay McNeely/Johnny Otis/Joe Turner/Dootsie Williams**
[Individuals marked with a double asterisk will be found in the non-performing intervewees appendix.]

Repercussions
See *Legends of Rhythm And Blues* and *On The Battlefield.*

Return to Macon County [F] [C]#.
Directed by Richard Compton. AIP. 1975
Fats Domino

Rhythm and Blues [C].
US TV broadcast. Origin unknown. 1974
BB King

Rhythm and Blues Revue
See *Showtime At The Apollo.*

Rhythms of the World [D] [C].
UK BBC TV broadcast. 1988 & 1993
Chris Barber**/Big Bill Broonzy/Robert Cray/John Lee Hooker/Bobbie & Sappho Korner**/Peggy Seeger**/Bert Wilcox**
[The 1993 programme on Big Bill Broonzy features extracts from the 1957 Pete Seeger film and interviews with people who knew him in Britain. Individuals marked with a double asterisk may be found in the appendix of non-performing interviewees.]

Rhythm Rodeo [F] [M].
Directed and produced by George Randol. GEORGE RANDOL PRODUCTIONS. 1938
Four Tones

Riverboat [F] [C].
Origin unknown. 1976
J C Burris

Rock 1 [C].
US TV broadcast. Origin unknown. 1970
Big Mama Thornton

Rock And Roll – Part 1: Renegades
Produced and directed by David Espar. 1995
WGBH-Boston/BBC TV co-production.
Bill 'Hoss' Allen*/Dave Bartholemew*/Marshall Chess*/Phil Chess*/Chuck Berry/Bo Diddley/Johnie Johnson*/Little Richard/Cosimo Matassa*/Earl Palmer*/Sam Phillips*/Lloyd Price/Rufus Thomas/Ike Turner/Alvin 'Red' Turner

Rock And Roll – Part 2: In The Groove
Produced and directed by Vicky Bippart and Daniel McCabe. 1995
WGBH-Boston/BBC TV co-production.
Carl Gardner*/Jerry Leiber*/Mike Stoller*

Rock and Roll Revival [C].
US TV broadcast. Origin unknown. 1974
Little Richard

Rock and Roll Revue
See *Showtime At The Apollo.*

Rock Around the Clock [F] [M].
1956
Platters

Rock Baby, Rock It! [F] [M].
Directed by Murray Douglas Sporup.
FREEBAR ENTERPRISES. 1957
Roscoe Gordon/Preacher Smith & The Deacons

Rock Gospel [C].
UK BBC TV broadcast. 1984
Shirley Caesar

Rock, Rock, Rock [F] [M]#.
Directed by Will Price. VANGUARD. 1956
Lavern Baker/Chuck Berry/Flamingos/Alan Freed orchestra/Frankie Lymon/Moonglows
[Available from Archive.]

Rockin' the Blues [F] [M].
Directed by Fritz Pollard. POLLARD ASSOCIATES. 1956
Connie Carroll/Harptones/Linda Hopkins/Hurricanes/Reese LaRue/Miller Sisters/Wanderers/Pearl Woods

Rockpalast [C].
German TV broadcasts. 1978–81
Muddy Waters/Rocking Dopsie

Rock Steady [C].
UK TV broadcast. Origin unknown. 1990
Robert Cray/Buddy Guy

Rockumentary [D] [C].
US MTV. 1997
BB King

Rolling Stones Rock and Roll Circus [C].
ARISTA. 1969
Taj Mahal

Roomful of Music [M].
US TV broadcast. Origin unknown. 1965
Brownie McGhee/Sonny Terry

Roosevelt Story, The [D] [M].
Origin unknown. 1947
Brownie McGhee

Roosevelt Sykes [FS] [M].
Directed by Yannick Bruynoghe. 1961
Roosevelt Sykes
[Available from TCB Releasing.]

Roosevelt Sykes in New Orleans [D] [C].
Directed by Dale and Dusty Nelson. 1972
Roosevelt Sykes
[Available from TCB Releasing.]

Roots [C].
US ABC TV mini-series. 1977
Joe Turner

Roots of American Music – Country and Urban Blues [C].
UNIVERSITY OF WASHINGTON, SEATTLE/SEATTLE FOLKLORE SOCIETY.
1969-70
Jesse Fuller/John Lee Hooker/Lightnin' Hopkins/Son House/Furry Lewis/Mance Lipscomb/Fred McDowell/Brownie McGhee/Johnny Shines/Sonny Terry/Robert Pete Williams
[Available from Historic. See also *Masters of Traditional American Music* for monochrome performances from the same source.]

Rumble Fish [F] [C]#*.
Directed by Francis Ford Coppola. 1983
Queen Ida

Sacramento Blues Festival 1987 [C].
Directed by Jerry Casey. US KKTV PBS TV. 1987
'Gatemouth' Brown/Robert Cray/Lowell Fulson/Rosco Gordon/Little Joe Blue/Robert Lockwood/Jimmy McCracklin/Johnny Shines

St. Louis Blues [1] [FS] [M].
Directed by Dudley Murphy. SACK AMUSEMENT ENTERPRISES. 1929
Hall Johnson Choir/Bessie Smith
[Available from Archive/Historic/TCB Releasing.]

St. Louis Blues [2] [F] [M].
Directed by Alan Reisner. PARAMOUNT. 1958
Mahalia Jackson

St. Soul-Soul of St. Louis R&B [D] [C].
US KETC PBS TV broadcast. Directed by Kinney Littlefield. 1989
Fontella Bass/George Edick(**)/Ikettes/Oliver Sain/Sharpees
[Edick will be found in the index to non-performing interviewees.]

Salute to the American Imagination [C].
US TV broadcast. Origin unknown. 1975
Ray Charles

Sammy and Company [C].
US syndicated TV broadcasts. 1975–76
Chuck Berry/Ray Charles/BB King/Joe Williams

Sammy Davis Jr. Show, The [C].
US syndicated TV broadcast. 1980
BB King

San Francisco Blues [C].
US local TV broadcast. Origin unknown. 1976
J C Burris

San Francisco Blues Festival [C].
Directed by Vincent Casalaima. IMAGE INTEGRATION. 1983
'Gatemouth' Brown/Clifton Chenier/Albert Collins/Robert Cray/Johnny Littlejohn

Sanford and Son [C].
US NBC TV broadcast. 1977
BB King

Sarge Goes to College [F] [M]
Origin unknown. 1947
Jack McVea

Saturday Blues aka *Mississippi Blues* [D] [C].
French TV broadcast. Directed by Bertrand Tavernier. 1984
Reverend Herbert Brewster/CeDell Davis/Obie Eatman/Nathan Hayes Septet/Jesse Mae Hemphill/Booker T. Laury/James Son Thomas/unidentified artists #s 42 & 43/Wade Walton

Saturday Night at Rockefellers [C].
Origin unknown. 1993
Clarence Green/Henry Hayes/Pete Mayes/Teddy Reynolds/Sonny Boy Terry & Kinny Adair/Texas Guitar Slim

Saturday Night Beechnut Show
See *Dick Clark's Saturday Night Beechnut Show*.

Saturday Night Live [C].
US NBC TV broadcasts. 1975–78
Chuck Berry/Ray Charles/Esther Phillips/Taj Mahal

Saturday Night, Sunday Morning [D] [C].
Directed by Louis Gilda. CALIFORNIA NEWSREEL. 1991
BB King/'Gatemouth' Moore/Spirit of Memphis Quartet/Rufus Thomas
[Available from Multicultural Media.]

Save the Children [D].
Origin unknown. 1973
Blind Arvella Gray

Say Amen, Somebody! [D] [C].
Directed by George Nierenberg. TAP PRODUCTIONS. 1982
Barrett Sisters/Thomas A Dorsey/Sallie Martin/O'Neal Twins/Zella Jackson Price/Willie Mae Ford Smith/Reverend Melvin Smotherson
[Available from TAP Productions.]

Say Brother [C].
US TV broadcast. Origin unknown. 1970
Larry Johnson

Scandals of 1933
See *Gig And Saddle*.

Scope-a-Tone [FS] [M]
1956
Johnny Otis

Scott Joplin [F] [C].
Origin unknown. 1976
Taj Mahal

Scorpio Rising [F].
Origin unknown. 1963
Ray Charles

Search for Robert Johnson, The [D] [C].
Produced and directed by Chris Hunt. IAMBIC PRODUCTIONS. 1991
Eric Clapton**/Wink Clark**/Honeyboy Edwards/John Hammond Jr**/Willie Mae Powell**/'Queen' Elizabeth**/Keith Richards**/Nat Richardson**/Johnny Shines
[Individuals marked with a double asterisk will be found in the index of non-performing interviewees.]

Second Barry Manilow Special [C].
US syndicated TV broadcast. 1978.
Ray Charles

Sergeant, The [F] [C].
Directed by John Flynn. WARNER BROTHERS. 1968
Memphis Slim

Sermons and Sacred Pictures [D] [M].
Directed by Lynne Sachs. 1989
Reverend L O Taylor
[Available from Canyon Cinema; raw footage available from Historic.]

Sesame Street [C].
US Children's Television Workshop TV broadcasts. 1970
Ray Charles/BB King

Seven Lively Arts – The Subject is Jazz [M].
US CBS TV broadcasts. 1957–58
Cat-Iron/Jimmy Rushing

Seven Minutes [F] [C]*.
Directed by Russ Meyer. 20th CENTURY FOX. 1971
BB King

Sha Na Na [C].
US syndicated TV broadcasts. 1978–79
Chuck Berry/Bo Diddley/Lloyd Price

Shade of Soul [C].
US TV broadcast. Origin unknown. 1968
Rufus Thomas

Shake Rattle and Rock [F] [M].
Directed by Edward L Kahn. AMERICAN INTERNATIONAL PICTURES. 1956
Fats Domino/Joe Turner

She's Crazy with the Heat [F] [M].
Alexander Productions. 1946–47
International Sweethearts Of Rhythm

She's Got It
See *Girl Can't Help It, The.*

Shindig [M].
US ABC TV broadcasts. 1964-66
Chuck Berry/Bo Diddley/Ray Charles/Coasters/Howlin' Wolf/Frankie Lymon/Tommy Tucker/Ward Singers/Jimmy Witherspoon
[This show also featured much contemporary soul music including performances by Booker T & the MGs/James Brown/Aretha Franklin/Jackie Wilson and many others. See Rhino Video R3 1456 for examples]

Shivaree [M].
US TV broadcast. Origin unknown. 1965
Jimmy Witherspoon

Shoutin' the Blues [FS] [C].
Directed by Yasha Aginsky. SEARCHLIGHT PRODUCTIONS. 1969
Sonny Terry
[Available from Searchlight Productions]

Show, The [C].
US TV broadcast. 1970
Taj Mahal

Showers of Stars [M].
US CBS TV broadcast. 1956
Frankie Lymon

Showtime at the Apollo [M].
Directed by Joseph Kohn. STUDIO FILMS INC./PATHE PICTURES. 1955
Faye Adams/Jimmy Brown/Ruth Brown/Willie Bryant/Clovers/Larry Darnell/Martha Davis/Delta Rhythm Boys/Helen Humes/Larks/Amos Milburn/Leonard Reed/Joe Turner/Dinah Washington/Paul Williams orchestra
[Available from Historic. This material was originally produced for a series of thirteen syndicated TV shows entitled *Harlem Variety Review.* It was subsequently repackaged for cinematic distribution under a variety of titles, all of which are cross-referenced. The balance of material in these programmes is jazz, dance and humour.]

Silver Shadow Production
Title unknown. 1987
Fats Domino

Sincerely the Blues [C].
US local TV broadcast. 1973
Carey Bell/Jimmy Dawkins/Brownie McGhee/Sonny Terry

Sing Sing Thanksgiving [D] [C].
Directed by David Hoffman. VARIED DIRECTIONS PICTURES. 1974
BB King
[Available from TCB Releasing.]

Singing Stream, A [D] [C].
Directed by Tom Davenport. 1986
Echoes Of Heaven of Akron, Ohio/Golden Echoes/Landis family

Sippie [D] [C].
Origin unknown. c. mid-1980s
Sippie Wallace
[Available from TCB Releasing.]

Six-Five Special [M].
UK BBC TV broadcasts. 1957
Big Bill Broonzy/Rosetta Tharpe
[Reports of an appearance by Frankie Lymon and the Teenagers on this programme are in error. What in fact appeared was an extract from the film *Rock, Rock, Rock*.]

Sixty Minutes [C].
US CBS TV news magazine. 1978
Alberta Hunter

Smothers Brothers Comedy Hour, The [C].
US ABC TV broadcasts. 1969–75
Ray Charles/Little Richard

Snader Telescriptions [M].
1951
Deep River Boys/Delta Rhythm Boys

Son of Ingagni [F] [M]#.
RICHARD C KAHN PRODUCTIONS.
Distributed by Sack Amusement Enterprises.
1940
Four Tones

Song is Born, A [F] [C]#.
Directed by Howard Hawks. RKO PICTURES. 1948
Golden Gate Quartet

Songmakers, The [D].
Directed by Frederick Ramsey Jr. Origin unknown. c.1965
Blind James Brewer/Blind Arvella Gray/Buddy Guy

Sonny and Cher Comedy Hour, The [C].
US CBS TV broadcast. 1973
Chuck Berry

Sonny Boy Williamson [FS] [M].
Danish TV broadcast. 1963
Sonny Boy Williamson
[Available from TCB Releasing.]

Sonny Ford – Delta Artist [D] [M].
CENTRE FOR SOUTHERN CULTURE. 1969
James Son Thomas/unidentified artist # 33/ Wade Walton
[Available from Centre For Southern Culture.]

Soul [C].
US syndicated TV broadcasts. 1969–71
BB King/Little Milton/Esther Phillips/Taj Mahal/Rufus Thomas/Jimmy Witherspoon

Soul Man [M].
UK BBC TV broadcast. Friday 7 February 1969.
Directed by Terry Henneberry
Ray Charles

Soul Set Free [C].
US TV broadcast. Origin unknown. c.1969
Shirley Caesar/Willa Dorsey/Sister Josephine James/Sarah Jordan Powell/Reverend Cleophus Robinson

Soul Train [C].
US syndicated TV broadcasts. 1972–75
Bobby Bland/BB King

Souls of Sin [F] [M].
Directed by Powell Lindsay. ALEXANDER PRODUCTIONS. 1949
Savannah Churchill/William Greaves
[Available from Archive/Phoenix.]

Sound of Jazz, The [M].
US CBS TV broadcast. 1957
Jimmy Rushing

Sound of the Seventies [C].
US TV broadcast. 1971
Taj Mahal

Sounder [F] [C]#.
Directed by Martin Ritt. 1972
Lightnin' Hopkins/Taj Mahal

Soundies [M].
The Soundies Corporation. 1941–46
Lynn Albritton/Anisteen Allen/Trevor Bacon/ Dallas Bartley/George Washington Brown/Una Mae Carlisle/Chanticleers/Savannah Churchill/ Dorothy Dandridge/Nat [King] Cole/Deep River Boys/Delta Rhythm Boys/Pat Flowers/Four Tones/Tiny Grimes/Teresa Harris/John 'Shadrack' Horace/Bob Howard/International Sweethearts Of Rhythm/Bull Moose Jackson/ Johnny and George/Louis Jordan/Jubilaires/

Mabel Lee/Meade Lux Lewis/Little Four/Roy Milton/June Richmond/Maurice Rocco/Jimmy Rushing/Deryck Sampson/Mabel Scott/ Shadrack Boys/Vanita Smythe/Spirits of Rhythm/Swinging Four/Rosetta Tharpe/Three Peppers/Skeets Tolbert/Joe Turner/unidentified artist #13a
[Available from International Creative Entertainment; Louis Jordan/Meade Lux Lewis/ Jimmy Rushing/Rosetta Tharpe/Joe Turner also available from TCB Releasing. *Soundies* were 2–3 minute film shorts created for visual juke-boxes, a short-lived phenomenon of the mid-1940s. Much jazz appeared in this series. TCB also carry two compilation programmes entitled *Jazz Juke Box*, tracing the history of *Soundies* and providing examples.]

***Sounds for Saturday* [C].**
UK BBC TV broadcast. 1972
Chuck Berry

***Sounds of Summer* [M].**
US TV broadcast. Origin unknown. 1969
Rufus Thomas/Bukka White

***Soundstage* [C].**
US WTTW (Windows To The World) TV broadcasts. 1974–90
Luther Allison/Barrett Sisters/Bobby Bland/ Willie Dixon/Buddy Guy/Etta James/Albert King/BB King/Earl King/Mighty Clouds Of Joy/Muddy Waters/Pinetop Perkins/Son Seals/ Koko Taylor/Sonny Terry/Allen Toussaint/ Albertina Walker/Junior Wells/Marion Williams/ Mighty Joe Young
[Available from Historic/WTTW.]

***Soupy Sales* [M].**
US ABC TV broadcast. 1960
R S Rankin [T-Bone Walker Jr.]

***South Bank Show* [C].**
UK LWT TV broadcast. 1991
Five Blind Boys of Alabama
See also *Boogie Woogie*, *John Lee Hooker* and *Little Richard – A Profile.*

***Spooky Loot* [F].**
Origin unknown. 1956. Unconfirmed.
George 'Papa' Lightfoot

***Spotlight* [C].**
Austrian TV broadcast. 1978
Fats Domino

***Star Spangled Rhythm* [F] [M]#.**
Directed by George Marshall. PARAMOUNT. 1941
Golden Gate Quartet

***Stars of Jazz* [M].**
US ABC TV broadcast. 1958
Jesse Fuller

***Step It Up and Go* [D] [C].**
North Carolina UNCI PBS TV broadcast. 1988
Directed by Susan Massengale
Etta Baker/Thomas Burt/John Dee Holeman/ Cora Phillips/Anthony Pough/Moses Rascoe/ James 'Guitar Slim' Stephens/James 'Junior' Thomas/Joe, Odell and Nate Thompson

***Steve Allen Show, The* [C].**
US syndicated TV broadcasts. 1963–70
BB King/Fats Domino/Mahalia Jackson/ Treniers/Ward Singers/Joe Williams/Jimmy Witherspoon
[Available from Historic. See also *Tonight.*]

***Stormy Weather* [F] [M]#*.**
Directed by Andrew Stone. 20th CENTURY FOX. 1943
Ada Brown

***Street Music* [F] [C]#.**
Directed by Jenny Bowen. PACIFICOM. 1982
Muddy Waters

***Strollin' 20's, The*[M].**
US TV broadcast. Origin unknown. 1966
Brownie McGhee/Joe Williams

***Studs Terkel Talks to Blind John Davis* [D] [C]**
Directed by Mike Ford. Origin unknown. c.1984–5

***Subterraneans, The* [F] [M].**
Directed by Ranald McDougal. MGM. 1960
James Cotton/Muddy Waters/Jimmy Rushing/ Otis Spann
[This is a dramatised biography of the poet Jack Kerouac, and employs music by jazz musicians Art Farmer and Art Pepper as well as the artists listed above. It is not known if the Muddy Waters band appears on screen or soundtrack only, but it does seem possible that the footage and/or soundtrack used may have been filmed at the 1960 Newport Jazz Festival, and it may possibly be the same as that found in *Jazz-USA*.]

Subject is Jazz, The
See *Seven Lively Arts*.

Sugar Chile Robinson, Billie Holiday, Count Basie and His Sextet [*sic*] **[FS] [M].**
Directed by Will Cowan. UNIVERSAL-INTERNATIONAL FEATURETTE. 1950
Sugar Chile Robinson
[The frequently quoted date of 1947 for this film is wrong.]

Sugar Hill Times **[M].**
US CBS TV broadcasts.
Six episodes, Tuesday 13 September–Tuesday 20 October 1949
The Jubilaires
[The first episode was called *Uptown Jubilee*, the second *Harlem Jubilee*, the remaining four *Sugar Hill Times*]

Sun's Gonna Shine, The **[FS] [C].**
Directed by Les Blank. FLOWER FILMS. 1967
Lightnin' Hopkins
[Available from Flower Films.]

Sunday Night **[C].**
US syndicated TV broadcasts. BROADWAY VIDEO INC. 1988–89
Robert Cray/Willie Dixon/Katie Webster

Sunday Night at the London Palladium **[M].**
UK ATV-TV broadcast. 1957
Frankie Lymon and the Teenagers

Sunday Sinners **[F] [M].**
Directed by Arthur Dreifuss. GOLDBERG PRODUCTIONS. 1941
Mamie Smith

Supershow **[C].**
Origin unknown. 1970
Buddy Guy

Survivors – The Blues Today **[D] [C].**
Directed by Robert Schwartz. Origin unknown. 1984
Baby Doo Caston/John Lee Hooker/Valerie Wellington

Sweethearts of Rhythm **[F] [M].**
Associated Pictures. 1947.
International Swethearts Of Rhythm

Sweet Home Chicago **[1] [D] [C].**
US local TV broadcast. Origin unknown. 1983
Billy Branch/James Cotton/Blind John Davis/Willie Dixon/Buddy Guy/Koko Taylor

Sweet Home Chicago **[2] [D] [C].**
Vanguard Productions. 1993
Marshall Chess**/Phillip Chess**/James Cotton/Buddy Guy/Mick Jagger**/Johnny Johnson/Hubert Sumlin/Koko Taylor/Junior Wells
[Individuals marked with a double asterisk will be found in the index of non-performing interviewees.]

Sweet Toronto
See *Keep On Rockin'*.

Swing Parade of 1946 **[F] [M]#.**
Directed by Phil Karlson. MGM. 1946
Louis Jordan
Copyrighted 2 March 1946

Swingin' the Dream **[F] [M].**
Origin unknown. 1939
Big Bill Broonzy/Louis Jordan

Swingmaster Presents **[C].**
Dutch TV broadcast. 1984
Fenton Robinson

Taking it Home Live in Concert **[C].**
BBC/Island Visual Arts
Buckwheat Zydeco

Tall Tales **[FS] [C].**
Origin unknown. 1941
Josh White

Tall, Tan and Terrific
See *Tan And Terrific*.

TAMI Show, The **[M].**
Produced and directed by Phil Spector.
American International Pictures. 1964
Chuck Berry/Bo Diddley/Ray Charles/Jimmy Thomas/Ike & Tina Turner
[Various edits of the above footage have been included in *The Big Beat, The Big TNT Show, Gather No Moss* and *Teenage Command Performance*. The balance of material in these shows is soul and rock, including James Brown, Marvin Gaye, Miracles, Ronettes, Supremes, Animals, Beach Boys and Rolling Stones.]

Tan and Terrific [F] [M].
Directed by Bud Pollard. 1947
Helen Humes

Teenage Command Performance
See *The TAMI Show*.

Tempo [M].
UK BBC TV broadcasts. Directed by Lloyd Shirley. 1962
Brownie McGhee/Stars of Faith/Sonny Terry

Texas Music Museum [C].
1987
Bells of Joy

Thames at Six [C].
UK Thames TV local news magazine. 1978
Professor Longhair

Thank You Rock and Roll [C].
US syndicated TV broadcast. 1978
Ray Charles

Thank Your Lucky Stars [M].
UK ATV TV broadcasts. 1963–66
Bo Diddley/Screaming Jay Hawkins/John Lee Hooker

That Rhythm – Those Blues [D] [C].
Directed by George T. Nierenberg. TAP productions. 1988
Charles Brown/Ruth Brown

That's Life [C].
US ABC TV broadcast. 1968
Mahalia Jackson

That's the Way I Do It [C].
US PBS TV broadcast. LEGACY PRODUCTIONS. 1986
Bill Greensmith**/Leroy Pierson**/Roosevelt Sykes/Henry Townsend/Vernell Townsend
[Bill Greensmith and Leroy Pierson will be found in the index to non-performing interviewees]

They Sing Like Someone's Happy [M].
UK ATV TV broadcasts. Sunday 14 March and Sunday 11 April 1965.
Directed by Helen Standage. 1965
Inez Andrews/Five Blind Boys of Mississippi/Bishop Samuel Kelsey
[The British Film Institute holds copies of these programmes. See also *Hallelujah*.]

They Took a Blue Note
See *Odyssey*.

Thinking Out Loud [D] [C].
Origin unknown. 1972
Scott Dunbar/John Estes/Furry Lewis/Bill Williams/Robert Pete Williams

Thirty Three and a Third Revolutions Per Monkee [C].
US NBC TV broadcast. 1969
Fats Domino/Little Richard/Ward Singers

This Country's Rockin' [C].
US syndicated TV broadcast. 1989
Etta James

This Hour Has Seven Days [M].
US TV broadcast. Origin unknown. 1965
John Hurt

This is Show Business [M].
US CBS TV broadcast. Early 1950s
Sugar Chile Robinson

This is Tom Jones [C].
US ABC TV broadcast. 1970 & 1972
Ray Charles/Little Richard

Those Singing, Swinging Years [M].
Directed by Barry Shear. NBC TV 'Ford Star Time' series.
Broadcast Tuesday 8 March 1960
Louis Jordan/Dinah Washington

Three Cheers for the Boys
See *Follow The Boys*.

Three Flames Show, The [M].
US NBC TV broadcast. Six episodes, 13 June-20 August 1949
Hot Lips Page/Three Flames/Dinah Washington
[There was also another *Three Flames Show* broadcast locally in New York just prior to this NBC network version. The probable dates for the New York broadcasts are mid-/late 1948].

Three Generations of the Blues Part 1 [C].
US PBS TV broadcast. 1983
Big Mama Thornton/Sippie Wallace
[The third artist on this broadcast is Jeannie Cheatham, whose work falls outside the scope of this volume.]

Three Generations of the Blues Part 2 [C].
US PBS TV broadcast. 1983
Robert Cray/John Lee Hooker/Smokey Wilson

Three Sides of Johnny Copeland, The [D] [C].
Origin unknown. 1988
Johnny Copeland

Three Songs by Leadbelly [FS] [C].
Produced by Blanding Sloan and Wah Monh Chong. 1944
Leadbelly
[Available from TCB Releasing. This film was originally shot silently, with Leadbelly miming to audio recordings made the day previously. Up to six songs were reportedly recorded and filmed in this way. The film was then stored unused for over twenty years, until Pete Seeger edited the current version from the raw footage. For a fuller description of these events, see both the book *The Life And Legend Of Leadbelly* by Dr Kip Lornell and Charles Wolfe, and the notes to Vestapol videotape 13042.]

Thunderbolt [F] [M].
Directed by Joseph Von Sternberg.
PARAMOUNT. 1929
Teresa Harris

Tilmon Tempo Show, The [C].
US TV broadcasts. Origin unknown. 1972–75
Magic Slim/Taj Mahal

Time to Sing, A Time to Cry, A [F].
MGM. 1968
Ward Singers

Timex All Star Swing Festival [C].
US TV broadcast. Origin unknown. 1972
Joe Williams

Tiny And Ruby: Hell Divin' Women
Directed by Greta Schiller and Andrea Weiss.
JEZEBEL PRODUCTIONS. 1986
Ernestine 'Tiny' Davis/International Sweethearts of Rhythm/Ruby Lucas

To Hear Your Banjo Play [FS] [C].
Directed Charles Korvin. Script by Alan Lomax. 1947
Brownie McGhee/Sonny Terry
[This film also features Woody Guthrie and Pete Seeger.]

To Tell the Truth [C].
US TV broadcast. Origin unknown. 1978
Alberta Hunter

Toast of the Coast [M].
US TV broadcast. Origin unknown. 1940s
Roosevelt Sykes

Toast of the Town aka *The Ed Sullivan Show* [M].
US CBS TV broadcasts. 1949–55
Ivory Joe Hunter/Louis Jordan/Hot Lips Page/T-Bone Walker
[Available from Historic. This is popularly known and remembered as *The Ed Sullivan Show*, but it officially changed its title from *Toast Of The Town* to *The Ed Sullivan Show* only on 18 September 1955. The above artists all appeared before that title change took place. See also *The Ed Sullivan Show* for artists appearing after the name change occured.]

Today Show, The [M] & [C].
US CBS TV broadcasts. 1960–78
Chuck Berry/Sam Chatmon/Jimmy Dawkins/ Willie Dixon/Helen Humes/Alberta Hunter/ Memphis Slim/James Son Thomas

Tom Coppin Productions [C].
Directed by Ken Kerbow. 1987
Tom [Tomcat] Courtney

Tom Jones Show [C].
UK BBC TV broadcast. 1972
Little Richard

Tonight {UK} [M].
UK BBC TV news magazine. 1963–65
Jesse Fuller/Muddy Waters/Big Joe Williams/ Sonny Boy Williamson/Jimmy Witherspoon
[All these artists were interviewed by Cliff Michelmore, the resident host of this programme.]

Tonight {USA} [M].
US NBC TV broadcasts. Host Steve Allen. 1954–57
Fats Domino/Mahalia Jackson/Jimmy Rushing/ Treniers

Tonight Show Starring Johnny Carson, The [M] & [C].
US NBC TV broadcasts. 1962–92
Chuck Berry/Ray Charles/Robert Cray/John Hurt/BB King/Furry Lewis/Little Richard/Esther Phillips/Joe Williams/Jimmy Witherspoon

Tonight Show with Jay Leno, The [C].
US NBC TV broadcast. 1997
Little Richard

Tonight with Belafonte [M].
US TV broadcast. Origin unknown. 1959
Brownie McGhee/Sonny Terry

Too Close to Heaven Parts 1–3 [D] [C].
Directed by Alan Lewens. INTERNATIONAL BROADCASTING TRUST. 1995
J W Alexander/Antioch Baptist Church Congregation/Morgan Babb/Horace Boyer/Shirley Caesar/Dorothy Love Coates/Fairfield Four/First Cosmopolitan Church Male Voice Choir/Flat Rock Baptist Church Congregation/Dorothy Ford/Clarence Fountain/Reverend Jessie Jackson/Elder Anderson Johnson/Joe Ligon/Bishop Dready & Mother Manning/Gatemouth Moore/Art Rupe**/Ira Tucker/Albertina Walker
[Art Rupe will be found in the index to non-performing interviewees. Available from International Broadcasting Trust.]

Toot that Trumpet [M].
Soundies Corporation. 1947
Delta Rhythm Boys/Louis Jordan
[also material by Apus & Estrellita and Dewey Brown.]

Top Man [F] [M].
Directed by Bernard W Burton. UNIVERSAL. 1943
Jimmy Rushing

Top of the Pops [M].
UK BBC TV broadcast. 1964
John Lee Hooker

Topanga Blues Festival [C].
Directed by Candace Jones-Sutton. AMERICAN CABLESYSTEMS, Marina del Rey, California. 1988
Cash McCall/Willie Dixon/Pinetop Perkins/Snooky Pryor/Otis Rush/Valerie Wellington

Toughing it Out [C].
US TV Broadcast. Origin unknown. 1976
Larry Johnson

Tribute to Muddy Waters, A [C].
US PBS TV broadcast. 1997
Bo Diddley/Buddy Guy/Johnny Johnson/Keb' Mo'/Robert Lockwood/Big Bill Morganfield/Pinetop Perkins/Mem Shannon/Koko Taylor

True Believers: The Story of Rounder Records [D] [C].
Directed by Robert Mugge. MUG-SHOT PRODUCTIONS. 1994
Beau Joque/Little Jimmy King/Irma Thomas
[Available from Mug-Shot Productions.]

Tube, The [C].
UK Channel 4 TV broadcasts. 1984
Bo Diddley/Robert Cray/BB King/Little Richard

TV AM [C].
UK ITV broadcast. 1985
Little Richard

TV Gospel Time [M].
Directed and produced by Howard Schwartz. US syndicated TV broadcasts. AMHURST PRODUCTIONS. 1962–66
Robert Anderson/Inez Andrews/Angelic Choir of Newark, New Jersey/Barrett Sisters/Bethel Baptist Choir/Bible Way Joybell Choir of Washington DC/Alex Bradford/Robert J Bradley/Emily Bram/Ruth Brown/Thomas Brown/Carolyn Bush/Calvin And the Majestics/Camp Meeting Gospel Chorus/Deloris Barrett Campbell/Cannon Temple Church of God in Christ Choir/Caravans/Cedar Street Baptist Church of Columbus, Ohio/Celestial Choir of Washington Temple/Celestial Echoes/Challengers/Reverend Julius Cheeks/Chicago Community Choir/Church Ushers Chorus/Reverend James Cleveland/Francis Cole/Combined Harvest and Christian Tabernacle Choirs/Consolers/Edna Gallmon Cooke/Cornerstone Baptist Choir/Ethel Davenport/Davis Sisters/Frank Davis/Archie Dennis/Dixie Hummingbirds/Doswell Temple Church of God in Christ Choir/Doylettes/Drinkard Singers/Echoneers Young People's Choir/Alma Ellison/Lorraine Ellison Singers/Pauline Ellison/Five Blind Boys of Alabama/Five Blind Boys of Mississippi/Lorenzo Fuller/Golden Leaf Baptist Church Choir/Gospel All-Stars/Gospel Clefs/

Gospel Clouds Of Joy/Gospel Harmonettes/Gospel Light and Glory Choruses/Gospel Seekers/Gospel Redeemers/Gospel Starlettes/Gospelaires/Bessie Griffin/Harmonizing Four/Goldia Haynes/Highway Q C's/Robert Hills/Rose Hines/Imperial Gospel Singers/Inspiring Voices of Evangel Temple/Abner Jay/Bettty Johnson/Myrtle Johnson/Kingdom Center Angelic Choir of Jacksonville, Florida/Marie Knight/Georgia Lewis/Nathaniel Lewis Singers/James Lowe/Loving Sisters/Marshall Heights Angels of Baltimore/Sallie Martin/Brother Joe May/Meditation Singers/Mighty Clouds of Joy/Alfred Miller/Mitchell Gospel Choral Ensemble/Mount Carmel Baptist Church Choir/Mount Olive Baptist Church Choir/Mount Sinai Gospel Chorus/Charles Neal/New Hope Choir of Newark, New Jersey/New Metropolitan Gospel Choir/New Salem Baptist Choir/New York State Choir/Nightingales/North Indiana State Church of God in Christ Choir/Dorothy Norwood/O'Neal Twins/Olivet Institutional Baptist Church Choir/Omega Baptist Church Radio Choir/Patterson Singers/PeeDee Choral Ensemble/Pentecostal Gospel Choir Of Memphis/Pentecostal Temple Church of God in Christ Choir/Pilgrim Jubilees/Pleasant Green Baptist Church Choir/Raymond Raspberry Singers/Refreshing Spring Church Choir/Refuge Temple Choir/Jessie Mae Renfro/Richburg Singers/Rising Echoes/Robert-ettes/Roberts Sisters/Reverend Cleophus Robinson/Helen Robinson Youth Chorus/Royal Travellers/St Mary's Church Choir/St Paul's Disciple Choir/St Timothy Male Chorus/Sanctuary Choir/Selah Jubilee Singers/Shady Grove Travellers/Shiloh Baptist Church Choir/Shiloh Christian Community Church Choir/Singing Angels/Carrie Smith/Columbus Smith/Soul Stirrers/Stars of Faith/Stevens Singers/Princess Stewart/Charles Story/Swanee Quintet/Charles Taylor/Tears of Music/Temple Radio Combined Choirs/Rosetta Tharpe/Jessie Mae Thomas/Thompson Community Singers/Three Gospel Professors/Trinity Baptist Church Radio Choir/Trumpeteers/Emma Tucker/Twilight Gospel Singers/Virginia Choir Ensemble/Voices of Faith/Voices Of Shiloh/Voices Of Southern/Marie Walker/Ernestine Washington/Washington Gospel Chorus/Washington Temple Angelic Choir/Washington Temple Celestial Chorus/Washington Templettes/Clifton West/Spencer Wiggins/Marion Williams/Reverend Ruben Willingham/James Wyns/Zion Baptist Church Female Chorus of Jacksonville

[Available from Historic. A total of 63 programmes were made. It has not been possible to trace the details of #46 or #62.]

Twenty Four Hours [C].
UK BBC TV news magazine. 1971
Jack Dupree

Two Black Churches [D] [M].
Directed by William Ferris. CENTRE FOR SOUTHERN CULTURE. 1977
Bishop A Coward/Reverend Isaac Thomas

Two Gun Man from Harlem [F] [M]#.
Produced by Richard C Kahn. MERIT PICTURES. Distributed by Sack Amusement Enterprises. 1938
Cats And The Fiddle/Four Tones

U2: Rattle and Hum
1988
BB King/Satan and Adam

Upbeat [M].
US TV broadcast. Origin unknown. 1968-69
Chuck Berry/Albert King/BB King/Taj Mahal

Uptown Jubilee
See *Sugar Hill Times.*

Van Morrison – Arena Special [D] [C].
UK BBC TV broadcast. 1991
John Lee Hooker

Vanishing Point [F] [C]#.
Directed by Richard Sarafian. 20th CENTURY FOX. 1971
Big Mama Thornton

Velvet Vampire [F] [C]#.
Directed by Stephanie Rothman. NEW WORLD. 1971
Johnny Shines

Virginia Graham Show, The [C].
US TV broadcast. Origin unknown. 1971
BB King/Brownie McGhee/Sonny Terry

Visage des PTT [F].
Origin unknown. 1964
Memphis Slim

Visions [C].
US TV broadcast. Origin unknown. 1978
Robert Shaw
[Shaw reportedly appears in an episode of the above entitled *Charlie Smith And The Fritter Tree*.]

Vitaphone [FS][M].
1928
Pullman Porter's Quartette
[Available from Historic.]

Voodoo Drums [F] [M].
LOUIS WEISS PRODUCTIONS.
1934
Alberta Perkins

W W & the Dixie Dancekings [F] [C].
Directed by John G Avildsen. 20th CENTURY FOX. 1975
Furry Lewis

Walking Hills, The [F] [M].
Directed by John Sturges. COLUMBIA. 1949
Josh White

Walking to New Orleans [C].
UK Channel 4 TV broadcast. 1985
Fats Domino

Warnung vor Einer Heiligen Nutte [C].
European TV broadcast. Origin unknown. 1970
Ray Charles

Wattstax [D] [C].
Directed by Mel Stuart. COLUMBIA. 1972
Reverend Jesse Jackson/Albert King/Little Milton/Rufus Thomas/Aaron Willis

Way to Escape the Ghetto, A
See *Out Of The Blacks, Into The Blues*.

Weequahic Park Love Festival [M].
US TV broadcast. Origin unknown. 1969
Bobby Bland

We Have Come for Your Daughters
See *Medicine Ball Caravan*.

We've Come a Long Way [F] [M].
Produced by Elder Solomon Lightfoot Michaux.
1943
contents unknown

We've Got the Devil on the Run [F] [M].
Produced by Elder Solomon Lightfoot Michaux.
NEGRO MARCHES ON CORPORATION.
1934
contents unknown

Well Spent Life, A [D] [C].
Directed by Les Blank. FLOWER FILMS. 1970
Mance Lipscomb/Rev. E S Wheeler

WETA-TV [D] [C].
Directed by David Grubin. Title unknown. 1988
John Cephas/John Jackson/Phil Wiggins
This production also features Cajun, Native American and other ethnic musics.

What's My Line [C].
US syndicated TV broadcast. 1972
BB King

Wheatland Music Festival [C].
Origin unknown. Possibly US PBS TV. 1987
Dixie Hummingbirds/Brownie McGhee

When We Were Kings [D] [C]#.
Directed by Leon Gast. 1996
BB King

Wild Women Don't Have the Blues [D] [C].
Origin unknown. 1989
Blue Lu Barker/Mae Barnes/Ida Goodson/Sam Price/Koko Taylor/Valerie Wellington

Wired [C].
UK Channel 4 TV broadcast. 1988
Albert Collins, Robert Cray

Within Southern Louisiana [D] [C].
French TV broadcast. 1974
Clifton Chenier

Wolf [D] [C].
Directed by Leonard Sauer. WGBH-TV Boston.
1971
Howlin' Wolf/Hubert Sumlin/Sunnyland Slim

Woman's a Fool, A [F] [M].
ASTOR PICTURES. 1947
Ida Cox

Woody Guthrie – Hard Travelin' [D] [C]
Directed by Jim Brown. GINGER GROUP/HAROLD LEVENTHAL MANAGEMENT INC. 1984
Sonny Terry

Woody Woodbury Show, The [M].
US TV broadcast. Origin unknown. 1967
Josh White

World by Night [D] [C].
Directed by Luigi Vanzi. JULIA FILMS. 1959
Dixie Hummingbirds/Imperial Gospel Singers/Swanee Quintet
[This is the English-language version of *Il Mondo Di Notte*. The British Film Institute hold a copy of this film.]

World of Music [M].
US TV broadcast. Origin unknown. 1966
Brownie McGhee/Sonny Terry/Josh White

You Bet Your Life [M].
US NBC TV broadcast. c.1952–53
Gladys Bryant

You're Never Too Old [M].
US TV broadcast. Origin unknown. 1950s
Jesse Fuller

Zydeco [D] [C].
Directed by Stephen Duplantier. 1986
Bois-Sec Ardoin

Zydeco Gumbo [D] [C].
Directed by Dan Hildebrand. RHAPSODY FILMS. 1988
Boozoo Chavis/C J Chenier/Clifton Chenier/John Delafose/Ann Goodley/Little Jeff/Rockin' Sydney/Terence Simien/Zydeco Express/Zydeco Straits

Zydeco Nite 'N' Day [D] [C]
Directed by Robert Dowling. ISLAND VISUAL ARTS. 1991
Bois-Sec Ardoin/Buckwheat Zydeco/Boozoo Chavis/C J Chenier/Clifton Chenier/John Delafose/Canray Fontenot/Holy Ghost Church Choir/Rockin' Dopsie/Ambrose Sam/Sam Brothers Five/Terrence Simien/Nathan Williams/Zydeco Force
See also *Aly Meets The Cajuns*, *Cajun Country* [1] & [2], *Clifton Chenier – King Of The Zydeco*, *Hot Pepper*, *J'ai Eté Au Bal* and *The Kingdom Of Zydeco* for further examples of Zydeco.

2 Index of Accompanists

Accompanist	Accompanying
Abshire, Nathan	Rockin' Dopsie
Aces	– see Below, Fred; Myers, David; Myers, Louis
Addison, Ike	Wells, Junior
Allen, Colin	Guy, Buddy; James, Etta; King, Albert; Wallace, Sippie; Wells, Junior
Allen, Lee	Domino, Fats; Little Richard
Alexander, Frank	Taylor, Koko
Alexander, Ray	Witherspoon, Jimmy
Allison, Bernard	Allison, Luther
Allison, Ray	Muddy Waters
Alphabetical Four	Smith, Mamie
Amiyoshi, Sumito	Lockwood, Robert; Payne, Odie
Anderson, Alvin 'Little Pink'	Anderson, Pink
Anderson, Ernestine	Otis, Johnny
Anderson, Ike	Robinson, Fenton
Anderson, O C	Brooks, Lonnie
Andrews, Kenny	Jordan, Louis
Appice, Carmine	Bo Diddley
Ardoin, Black, Bud and Morris	Ardoin, Bois-Sec
Ardoin, Ronald	Ardoin, Bois-Sec
Armstrong, Howard	Bogan, Ted; Martin, Carl; Rachell, Yank; Robinson, Banjo Ikey
Armstrong, Tom	Armstrong, Howard; Bogan, Ted; Rachell, Yank; Robinson, Banjo Ikey
Arnold, Jerome	Hooker, John Lee; Horton, Walter; Reed, Jimmy; Taylor, Eddie; Walker, T-Bone
Asbury Dukes [G]	– see Southside Johnny
Austin, William	Jordan, Louis
Ayres, Mitchell [orch]	Larks; Williams, Joe
Bacon, Trevor	Tharpe, Rosetta
Bailey, Richard	Guy, Buddy
Baker, Mickey	Memphis Slim; Mickey & Sylvia
Balfa, Dewey	Rockin' Dopsie
Banks, L V	Davis, John Henry
Barber, Chris	Dupree, Jack; McGhee, Brownie; Terry, Sonny; Tharpe, Rosetta
Barnett, Ted	Tharpe, Rosetta
Barrelhouse [G]	Collins, Albert
Bartley, Dallas	Jordan, Louis
Basie, Count [orch]	Berry, Chuck; Humes, Helen; Rushing, Jimmy; Williams, Joe
Batiste, Milton	K-Doe, Ernie
Beausoleil[G]	Fontenot, Canray
Bell, Carey	Caston, 'Baby Doo'; Louisiana Red
Bell, Lurrie	Bell, Carey; Dixon, Willie; Evans, Margie
Bellson, Louis	Walker, T-Bone
Below, Fred	Aces; Arnold, Billy Boy; Berry, Chuck; Boyd, Eddie; Carter, Joe; Good Rockin' Charles; Guy, Buddy; Horton, Walter; Lenoir, J B; Lockwood, Robert; Muddy Waters; Robinson, Jimmy Lee; Sykes, Roosevelt; Taylor, Koko; Thornton, Big Mama; Turner,

3 Index of Directors and Producers

4 Useful Resources

ARCHIVE FILM & TV
21 Stephen Street
London W1
England
[fax] 0171 580 7503
[Commercial only; leasing of BBC programmes]
Contact: Simon Brown

ARCHIVE FILMS
[stock footage library]
In the UK:
4th floor
184 Drummond Street
London NW1 3HP
England
[ph] 0171 383 0033; [fax] 0171 383 2333
internet: http//www.archivefilm.com/
[Commercial only; stock footage available to producers and directors of film and TV programmes]
Contact: Mark Piper

In the USA:
530 West 25th St
NYC, NY 10001
[ph] 212 620 355; [fax] 212 645 2137

ARHOOLIE RECORDS
10341 San Pablo Ave
El Cerrito
CA 94530
USA
Contact: Chris Strachwitz

B.B.C.
see Archive Film & TV

BRITISH FILM INSTITUTE
{National Film and Televison Archive}
21 Stephen Street
London W1
England
[ph] 0171 255 1444; [fax] 0171 580 7503
[Public research facilities and commercial only leasing of selected material from film and television.]

CALIFORNIA NEWSREEL
149 9th Street
San Francisco
CA 94103
USA
[Commercial only; distributors of *Saturday Night, Sunday Morning*]

CANYON CINEMA
see Lynn Sachs.

CBS NEWS ARCHIVES
524 West 57th St
NYC
New York, 10019
USA
[ph] 212 925 2843
Contact: Sam Suratt
[Commercial only]

CENTRE FOR SOUTHERN FOLK CULTURE
209 Beale Street
Memphis,
Tennessee
USA
[ph] 901 525 3655
Contact: Judy Peiser

CONTEMPORARY FILMS
24 Southwood Lawn
London N6
[ph] 0181 340 5715
[Commercial only. Including Flower Films]

FERRUM COLLEGE
Ferrum,
Virginia, 24088
USA
Contact: Roddy Moore or Vaughan Webb
[Commercial only. *Black Musical Traditions In Virginia*]

FIRST RUN FEATURES [FRF]
153 Waverly Place
New York
NY 10014
[ph] 1 800 229 8575
[Home video sales including *Say Amen Somebody!*]

FLOWER FILMS
c/o Arhoolie Records
10341 San Pablo Ave
El Cerrito
CA 94530
USA
[ph] 510-525-0942; [fax] 510 525 1204
email: blankfilm@aol.com/
website: http//www.lesblank.com/
Contact: Les Blank
[Commercial leasing of Flower material and direct sales of Flower films on prerecorded videotapes]

GRANADA TELEVISION
Extract Sales
Quay Street
Manchester M60 9EA
England
[ph] 0161 827 2207; [fax] 0161 827 2006
email: export.sales@granadatv.co.uk
Contact: Sylvia Cowling
[Commercial only]

HISTORIC FILMS
12 Goodfriend Drive
East Hampton
NY 11937
USA
[ph] 516 329 9200; [fax] 516 329 9260
email: info@historicfilms.com/
Contact: Joe Lauro
[Large library of vintage music film available on a commercial only basis to producers and directors of film and TV programmes]

HOUSE OF MUSICAL TRADITIONS
7040 Carroll Avenue
Takoma Park
Maryland 20912
USA
[ph] 301 270 9090; [fax] 301 270 3010
1-800 540 3794
email: hmtrad@hmtrad.com
website: http//www.hmtrad.com/
[Walk-in store and retail mail order for Videos, books, CDs, tapes]

IBT – INTERNATIONAL BROADCASTING TRUST
2 Ferdinand Place
London NW1
England
[ph] 0171 482 2487; [fax] 0171 284 3374
Contact: Nicola Ebenau
[Commercial only. *Too Close Too Heaven*]

ICE – INTERNATIONAL CREATIVE EXCHANGE
3575 Cahuenga Blvd West
Hollywood, CA
90068
USA
[ph] 213 850 8080; [fax] 213 850 8082
Contact: Phillip G. Catherall
[Commercial only. Soundies]

JUBILEE SHOWCASE
see Sidney Ordower.

K-JAZZ
29 May Road
Rochester
Kent ME12HY
England
[ph] 01634 405698; [fax] 01634 403732
Contact: Maggie Kay
[Home videos. Send SAE for full catalogue]

MONTREUX JAZZ
Montreux
Switzerland
[ph] 41 21 963 2344; [fax] 41 21 963 3705
Contact: Francine Masson
[Commercial only]

MUG-SHOT PRODUCTIONS
1271 Nicole Lane
Secane, PA
19018
USA
[ph] 610 553 3133; [fax] 610 553 1189
Contact: Robert Mugge
[Commercial only]

MULTICULTURAL MEDIA
RR3, Box 6655
Granger Road
Barre, Vermont
05641
USA
[ph] 802 223 1294; [fax] 802 229 1834
email: mcm@multiculturalmedia.com/
website: http://www.worldmusicstore.com
[Retail mail order world music and dance videos, recordings, books, CD-Roms for school, university and library systems and for home consumption]

MUSIC SALES LTD
Newmarket Road
Bury St. Edmunds
Suffolk IP33 3YB
England
[ph] 01284 702600; [fax] 01284 768301
email: music@musicsales.co.uk
Contact: Ian Morgan
[Commercial distributors of Vestapol videos]

NATIONAL FILM AND TELEVISON ARCHIVE
see British Film Institute.

SIDNEY ORDOWER
Chicago, Illinois
USA
[ph] 312 939 4544
[Commercial only; *Jubilee Showcase*]

PHOENIX LEARNING GROUP
2349 Chafee Drive,
St. Louis, MO
63146-3306
USA
[ph] 314 569 0211; [fax] 314 569 2834
Contact: Michelle Neilson
[Commercial only; Phoenix also represent a wide selection of classic African-American titles including the Tyler, Texas collection.]

RAMBLIN' VIDEO
see Vestapol.

RED LICK RECORDS
Porthmadog
Gwynedd, LL49 9DJ
Wales,
UK
[ph] 01766 12151; [fax] 01766 51251
[Retail mail order (no callers); Stockists of Anxious, BMG, DCI, Homespun, Hot Licks, REH, Storyville, Vestapol and Yazoo videos[PAL format]. Also CDs, books, magazines. [Write, fax or call for catalogue.]

RHAPSODY FILMS
46–2 Beckett Hill Road
Lyme, CT 06371
USA
[ph] 860 434 3610; [fax] 860 434 6201
email: rhapsody@internetmci.com
[Mail order home videos]

RHINO DIRECT
PO Box 60008
Tampa
Florida
33660–0008
USA
[ph] 1 800 432 0020
[Mail order for Rhino videos. Also sound recordings.]

ROUNDER RECORDS
1 Camp Street
Cambridge, MA
02140
USA
[Mail order and distributors of Vestapol videos. Also sound recordings.]

NORBERT RUECKER
Postfach 14
D–61382 Schmitten
Germany
[Mail-order music videotapes specialist]

LYNN SACHS
Canyon Cinema,
2325 Third St South
San Francisco
CA 94107
USA
[Commercial only; Sermons And Sacred Pictures]

SEARCHLIGHT PRODUCTIONS
Oakland, California
USA
[ph] 510 845 4135
Contact: Ashley James
[Commercial only]

SHANACHIE ENTERTAINMENT
37 E Clinton St
Newton
NJ 07860
USA
Mail Order: 1-800 497 1043
email: shanach@haven.ios.com/
[Mail order for Shanachie & Yazoo videotapes, both PAL & NTSC. Also sound recordings.
For commercial work, including leasing and acquisitions, contact Sherwin Dunner]

SMITHSONIAN–FOLKWAYS RECORDINGS
Suite 444
414 Hungerford Drive
Rockville,
MD 20850
USA
[ph] 800 410 9815; [fax] 301 443 1819
[Mail order. Also sound recordings.]

STEFAN GROSSMAN'S GUITAR WORKSHOP
in the UK:
PO Box 88988
London SW15 3ZB
[ph] 0181 780 2283; [fax] 0181 780 5787
Contact: Louise

in the USA:
PO Box 802
Sparta
NJ 07871
[ph] 973 729 5544; [fax] 973 726 0568
website: www.guitarvideos.com
Contact: Stefan Grossman
[Wholesale and retail mail order distribution of Vestapol videos]

STORYVILLE PRODUCTIONS
Dortheavej 39
DK2400 Copenhagen NV
Denmark
Contact: Karl Emil Knudsen
[Mail order videos]

SUDWESTFUNK MEDIA GmbH
76522 Baden-Baden
Germany
[ph] 07221 92 2373; [fax] 07221 92 2094
[Commercial only; American Folk Blues Festival programmes 1962–67 & 1970, Gospel Festival 1965]

TAP PRODUCTIONS
252 W.85th Street, apt 80
New York, NY 10024
USA
Contact: George Nierenberg
[Commercial only; *Say Amen Somebody!*, *That Rhythm – Those Blues*]

TCB RELEASING
Stone House
Rudge, Frome
Somerset, BA11 2QQ
England
[ph] 01373 830769; [fax] 01373 831028
Contact: Angus Trowbridge
[Commercial only; Licensing blues films and videotapes to broadcast TV and the home-video media. See K-Jazz, Rhapsody, Storyville, Vestapol and Yazoo for home-video titles. Also representing Mug-Shot films.]

TELE-7-FILM
Katharinenthal 11
51467 Bergisch Gladbach
Germany
[ph] 02202 81522; [fax] 02202 85922
Contact: Dietrich Wawzyn
[Commercial only. The Dietrich Wawzyn film collection]

TIMELESS VIDEO INC.
PO Box 16354
North Hollyowood
CA 91615–6354
USA
[Mail order of videotapes in VHS-NTSC format]

VESTAPOL
see Stefan Grossman's Guitar Workshop

VIDEOPLUS DIRECT
PO Box 190
Peterborough
PE2 6UW
England
[ph] 01733232800; [fax] 01733 230618
[direct mail for a wide selection of pre-recorded PAL tapes]

VINTAGE JAZZ CLASSICS
Larrikin Records Pty
PO Box 162
Paddington, 2021
Australia
[Vintage Jazz Classics videotapes]

WTTW (Windows To The World Telecommunications, Inc.)
5400 North St.Louis Street
Chicago
Illinois
60625
USA
[ph] 773 509 5550; [fax] 773 509 5300
Contact: Christine Callozzo
[Commercial only; Soundstage]

YAZOO
see Shanachie Entertainment

5 Commercially Available Videotapes

[The titles listed here which are compilations from various sources, and which are not therefore found in the production index, are provided with alphabetical lists of artists so that the reader may easily cross-reference them. The information in parenthesis is the country or countries of origin followed by the decode system.]

ADLA [US: NTSC]
1270 *Alberta Hunter – Jazz At The Smithsonian*

ANXIOUS [UK: PAL]
4509929643 *Deep Blues*

ARHOOLIE [US: NTSC]
ARV40 *Clifton Chenier*
ARV402 *It's Got To Be Rough To Be Sweet*

ARISTA [UK/US: PAL/NTSC]
1003–3 *Rolling Stones Rock And Roll Circus*

ARROW [UK: PAL]
AV015 *Saturday Blues*

BAVARIA [German: PAL]
12177 *Jazz Is Trumpf* {Ruth Brown/ Clovers/Larry Darnell/Martha Davis/Delta Rhythm Boys/ Dinah Washington and jazz artists}

BLACAST [US: NTSC]
BC8035 *Paradise In Harlem*
VY328 *Bessie Smith – St. Louis Blues*

BLUES HOUSEPARTY [US: NTSC]
BH-01 *Blues Houseparty*

BMG [UK/US:PAL/NTSC]
791010 *BB King – Live in Africa*
791051 *Buddy Guy and Junior Wells at Montreux*
791146 *Chuck Berry; Rock and Roll Music* (1969)
791150 *Keep On Rockin'*
791151 *Blues Alive 1990*
80008–3 *Louis Jordan – Five Guys Named Moe* [NTSC only]
80046–3 *Pride And Joy – The Story Of Alligator Records* [NTSC only]
4321135013 *Muddy Waters – Live 1981*
BV43–2427–3 *Harlem Highlights* [NTSC only] {Louis Jordan and jazz artists}
un-numbered *True Believers: The Story Of Rounder Records* [NTSC only]
un-numbered *The Kingdom Of Zydeco* [NTSC only]
un-numbered *Deep Blues* [NTSC only]

CALIFORNIA NEWSREEL [US: NTSC]
01 *Saturday Night, Sunday Morning*
02 *Wild Womem Don't Have The Blues*

CASTLE HENDRING [UK: PAL]
2.053 *B B King Live at Nick's*
2.239 *Jazz On A Summer's Day*
6.086 *Blues Survivors*
20496 *Mahalia Jackson 1911–1972*
[# unknown] *John Lee Hooker – Soul Survivor*
[# unknown] *The Gospel at Colonus*

CHANNEL 5 [UK: PAL]
CFV10542 *Fabulous Forties: All The Gals!* [sic] {Dorothy Dandridge and jazz and popular artists}
CFV10552 *Fabulous Forties: Sentimental Journey* {Nat King Cole and jazz and popular artists}
082–258–3 *Zydeco Nite'N'Day*
082–368–3 *Buckwheat Zydeco – Taking It Home Live in Concert*

CHARLY [UK: PAL]

02 *88 Key Boogie* {Lynn Albritton/Dorothy Dandridge/Johnny & George/Mabel Lee/Meade Lux Lewis/Maurice Rocco/Deryck Sampson}
Rhythmania {Dorothy Dandridge/Mabel Lee and jazz and dance artists}
05 *Mo' Jive* {Dallas Bartley/Louis Jordan/Roy Milton/Skeets Tolbert/Vanita Smythe}
07 *Sweet Harmony* {Deep River Boys/Jubalaires and jazz artists}
Sound–1940 *Images Of An Era* {Louis Jordan/Meade Lux Lewis and jazz/pop artists}

CMV [UK: PAL]

491132 *The Search For Robert Johnson*

DCI (tutorial) [UK/US: PAL/NTSC]

21733 *BB King Bluesmaster Vol. 1*
21734 *BB King Bluesmaster Vol. 2*
21735 *BB King Bluesmaster Vol. 3*
22393 *BB King Blues Master Highlights*

FIL A FILM [French: SECAM]

2022 *Jazz In Provence*
Sammy Price {and jazz artists}
2023 *Jazz Festival* {Ruth Brown/Clovers/Larry Darnell/Delta Rhythm Boys/Larks/Amos Milburn/Dinah Washington and jazz artists}

FLOWER FILMS [US: NTSC]

1 *The Blues According To Lightnin' Hopkins*
2 *A Well Spent Life*
3 *Spend It All*
4 *Dry Wood*
5 *Hot Pepper*
6 *Always For Pleasure*
7 *J'ai Eté Au Bal*

FRF {First Run Features} [US: NTSC]

un-numbered *Say Amen, Somebody!*

GOLD STAR [UK: PAL]

BSG203 *Rock Rock Rock*

HBO [US: NTSC]

0337 *BB King – Live In Africa*

HOLLYWOOD SELECT [US: NTSC]

50463 *Louis Jordan: Reet-Petite And Gone*
50543 *The Blood Of Jesus*
97803 *Miracle In Harlem*

HOMESPUN (tutorial) [UK: PAL]

3727A *John Jackson – The Fingerpickin' Blues*

HOTLICKS (tutorial) [UK/US: PAL/NTSC]

3032A *Otis Rush; Mastering Chicago Blues Guitar*
22234 *Junior Wells Teaches Blues Harmonica*
22345 *Buddy Guy; Teaching The Blues*

INTERNATIONAL COLLECTION [UK: PAL]

INVC5006 *Fats Domino Live 1989*

ISLAND [US: NTSC]

083 258–3 *Zydeco Nite'N'Day*
4973 *Let The Good Times Roll*
[# unknown] *Etta James – Live at Montreux*

JAZZ & JAZZ [Italian: PAL]

VIDJAZZ–13 *The Blues* {Big Bill Broonzy/Bessie Smith/T-Bone Walker/Sonny Boy Williamson}
VIDJAZZ–20 *Classic Jazz* {Meade Lux Lewis/Joe Turner and jazz artists}

JAZZ AVERTY [French: SECAM]

665008 *Memphis Slim Vol. 2 1973*
665031 *Memphis Slim Vol. 1 1962–1973*
[these numbers are correct]

JAZZ CLASSICS [US: NTSC]

JCVC105 *Blues And Boogie* {Una Mae Carlisle/Nat King Cole/Louis Jordan/Meade Lux Lewis and jazz artists}
JCVC106 untitled {Nat King Cole/Delta Rhythm Boys and the Mills Brothers}
JCVC107 *Fats Waller and Friends* {Dusty Brooks/Dorothy Dandridge/Tiny Grimes/Mabel Lee and jazz artists}
JCVC108 *Bessie Smith and Friends* {Albert Ammons & Pete Johnson/Bessie Smith and jazz artists}

JCVC109 *Count Basie and Friends* {Delta Rhythm River Boys/Louis Jordan/Jimmy Rushing and jazz artists}
JCVC110 *Harlem Harmonies Vol. 1* {Nat King Cole/Tiny Grimes/Rosetta Tharpe/Skeets Tolbert and jazz artists}
JCVC111 *Harlem Harmonies Vol. 2* {Louis Jordan/Jimmy Rushing and jazz artists}
JCVC112 *The Duke Is Tops*
JCVC114 *Louis Jordan – Reet-Petite and Gone*
JCVC115 *Jiving In Be Bop*

JEZEBEL [US: NTSC]
un-numbered *International Sweethearts Of Rhythm*
[# unknown] *Tiny and Ruby: Hell Diving Women*

JVC [US: NTSC]
111 *Boogie Woogie Dream*
[This may also contain other material]
225 *African-American Secular Music*
226 *European And Other Secular Traditions*
[Both 225 and 226 are parts of the 6 volume set *Music And Dance Of The Americas*. The JVC catalogue also contains much other US and world folk music]

K-JAZZ [UK: PAL]
KJ004 *Chicago Blues*
KJ012 *Last of The Blue Devils*
KJ014 *Blues Like Showers Of Rain/John Henry Bones*
KJ019 *Out Of The Blacks Into The Blues Pt. 2 – A Way To Escape The Ghetto*
KJ020 *Out Of The Blacks Into The Blues Pt. 1 – Along The Old Man River*
[these numbers are correct]
KJ030 *Good Morning Blues*
KJ031 *Maxwell Street Blues*
KJ053 *Blues According To Lightnin' Hopkins/The Sun's Gonna Shine*
KJ054 *Always For Pleasure*
KJ055 *A Well Spent Life*
KJ066 *Hot Pepper*
KJ067 *Dry Wood*
KJ073 *Sippie Wallace – Sippie*
KJ075 *Big City Blues*
KJ076 *John Jackson – An American Songster*
KJ081 *Mississippi Delta Blues*
KJ084 *Piano Players Rarely Ever Play Together*
KJ096 *Roosevelt Sykes* [1961]/*Jay McShann* [1978]
KJ098 *Zydeco Gumbo*
KJ100 *Mark Naftalin's Blue Monday Party*
KJ143 *Muddy Waters – Maintenance Shop Blues 1981*
KJ145 *Albert King – Maintenance Shop Blues*
[Other K-Jazz releases are Jazz films and documentaries]

MAGNUM [UK: PAL]
MMGV035 *America's Music – The Blues – Vol. 1*
MMGV020 *Memphis Slim Live In Nice*
MMGV037 *America's Music – The Blues – Vol. 2*
7991 *Johnny Copeland – The Three Sides Of*

MCA [US: NTSC]
V10944 *Sweet Home Chicago* [2]

MERCURY FILMS [US: NTSC]
[# unknown] *Shirley Caesar – Hold My Mule*
[# unknown] *Reverend James Cleveland – Gospel In The Holy Land*

MMG [UK: PAL]
V–010 *Legends Of Rock & Roll* {Bo Diddley/Fats Domino/Johnny Otis and rock & roll artists}
V–012 *Classic Hits From The 50's and 60's* {Ivory Joe Hunter and rock & roll artists}
V–015 *The London Rock & Roll Show*

MPI HOME VIDEO [US: NTSC]
1397 *Mississippi Blues* (aka *Saturday Blues*)
6243 *Koko Taylor – Queen Of The Blues*

MULTICULTURAL MEDIA [US: NTSC]
1008 *Saturday Night, Sunday Morning*

NEW YORK VIDEO [US: NTSC]
16590 *Jazz On A Summer's Day*

OLD GOLD [UK: PAL]
0001 *Chuck Berry – Live At The Roxy*

PARKFIELD [UK: PAL]
MJK007 *Jumpin' Jive* {Lena Horne [with Ammons & Johnson]/Louis Jordan/Jimmy Rushing/Treniers and jazz artists}
MJK008 *Swingin' Rhythm* {Albert Ammons & Pete Johnson/Delta Rhythm Boys/Louis Jordan/ Treniers and jazz artists}
MJK0014 *Alberta Hunter at the Smithsonian*

PNV [unknown]
PNV1043 *Jazz From Kansas City*

PRAISE [US: NTSC]
3012 *Hallelujah* [1965 Gospel Festival in Germany]

PROSERPINE [French: SECAM]
611 *Legends Of Jazz Vol. 1* {Delta Rhythm Boys/Louis Jordan/ Jimmy Rushing/Treniers and jazz artists}
666 *Legends Of Jazz Vol. 2* {Albert Ammons & Pete Johnson/Delta Rhythm Boys/Louis Jordan/ Treniers and jazz artists}
811 *Boogie Woogie Dream* [This may also contain other material]

RAMBLIN' [US: NTSC]
804 *Elizabeth Cotten* [and Mike Seeger] *in Concert*

RED LIGHTNIN' [UK: PAL]
RLVD0083 *U P Wilson: The Blues Guitar Tornado*

REH (tutorial) [UK: PAL]
18446 *Albert Collins*

RHAPSODY [US: NTSC]
8013 *John Jackson – An American Songster*
8020 *Big City Blues*
8022 *Blues Like Showers Of Rain*
8037 *Big Joe Turner and the LA All Stars*
8039 *Last Of The Blue Devils*
8045 *Maxwell Street Blues*
8054 *Sippie*
8062 *Zydeco Gumbo*
9012 *Chicago Blues*
9030 *Gospel According To Al Green*
un-numbered *Mark Naftalin's Blue Monday Party starring John Lee Hooker*

RHINO [US: NTSC]
R3.1453 *Shindig – Legends of Rock and Roll* {Chuck Berry and Rock/ pop/soul artists}
R3.1991 *Messing With The Blues*
R3.2076 *Soundstage – New Orleans Swamp*
R3.2101 *Masters Of The Blues Vol. 1* {Big Bill Broonzy/Son House/ Leadbelly/Bessie Smith and others}
R3.2102 *Masters Of The Blues Vol. 2* {Buddy Guy/B.B. King/Muddy Waters and others
R3.2222 *Bo Diddley's 30th Anniversary*
R3.2284 *Thirty Three And A Third Revolutions Per Monkee*
R3.2313 *Festival Presents The Blues*
R3.2410 *Rock Baby Rock It!*
R3.90673 *BB King – Blues Master Highlights*
R3.90701 *Hullabaloo!* [8 video set] {Chuck Berry, Bessie Griffin and rock/ pop/soul artists}
R3.91226 *Blues Alive*

SAVOY [US: NTSC]
9500 *Down Memory Lane*

SHANACHIE [US: NTSC]
1401 *Reverend Pearly Brown/Big Boy Crudup*
1402 *The Landis Family – A Singing Stream*
1403 *And This Is Free*
1405 *Cajun Country*

STORYVILLE [Danish: PAL]
SV6000 *Harlem Roots Vol. 1* {Bull Moose Jackson/Jimmy Rushing/Rosetta Tharpe and jazz artists}
SV6001 *Harlem Roots Vol. 2* {Louis Jordan and jazz artists}
SV6002 *Harlem Roots Vol. 3* {Deep River Boys/Delta Rhythm Boys/ Jubalaires and jazz artists}

SV6003 *Harlem Roots Vol. 4* {Nat King Cole/Mabel Lee/Roy Milton/ Vanita Smythe/ Rosetta Tharpe and jazz artists}
SV6013 *Boogie Woogie* {Lynn Albritton/ Albert Ammons & Pete Johnson/ Martha Davis/Meade Lux Lewis/ Maurice Rocco and jazz artists}
SV6015 *All Girl Bands* {International Sweethearts Of Rhythm and jazz artists}
SV6016 *Harlem Roots – R&B* {Faye Adams/Jimmy Brown/Ruth Brown/Clovers/Martha Davis/ Larks/Amos Milburn/Joe Turner/ Dinah Washington}
SV6017 *Variety At The Apollo* {Delta Rhythm Boys/Dinah Washington and jazz artists}
SV6031 *Louis Jordan And His Tympany Band* {musical extracts from *Beware*, *Reet-Petite and Gone* and *Look-Out Sister*}
SV6032 *The Blues 1929–1963* {Big Bill Broonzy/Ida Cox/Mamie Smith/ Sonny Boy Williamson}
SV6035 *Jivin' In Be Bop*
SV6041 *Snooks Eaglin – 1985 in New Orleans*
SV6042 *Rockin' Dopsie 1984 in New Orleans*

SOUTHERN CULTURE CATALOGUE (Centre For The Study Of Southern Culture) [US: NTSC]

1025 *Black Delta Religion*
1055 *Delta Blues Festival 1985*
1056 *Delta Blues Singer – James 'Sonny Ford' Thomas*
1059 *Du Cote Du Memphis* [sic]
1066 *Fannie Bell Chapman – Gospel Singer*
1077 *Give My Poor Heart Ease*
1080 *Gospel In Gary*
1135 *Mississippi Delta Blues*
1136 *James Son Thomas – Mississippi Delta Blues*
1139 *Mose Vinson – Mr Boogie Woogie*
1143 *Move Of God*
1192 *Sonny Terry – Shoutin' The Blues*
1210 *They Sing Of Heaven*
1219 *Two Black Churches*

[Flower films are also available from this catalogue]

TIMELESS VIDEO [US: NTSC]

5044 *The Duke Is Tops*
5045 *Louis Jordan – Beware*
5048 *Paradise In Harlem*
5055 *Go Down Death*
5058 *Murder On Lenox Avenue*
5060 *Sunday Sinners*
5603 *Boarding House Blues*
9583 *Murder In Harlem*

VERVE [UK: PAL]

CFV10222 *Count Basie And Friends* {Delta Rhythm Boys/Louis Jordan/ Jimmy Rushing}

VESTAPOL [UK/US: PAL/NTSC]

(numbers in parenthesis are European catalogue numbers)

13001 *Cajun Visits/Les Blues De Balfa*
13002 *Legends Of Bottleneck Blues Guitar* [11233] {Jesse Fuller/Son House/Furry Lewis/Mance Lipscomb/Fred McDowell/ Johnny Shines}
13003 *Legends Of Country Blues Guitar Volume 1* [11231] {Big Bill Broonzy/Reverend Gary Davis/ Son House/Mississippi John Hurt/Mance Lipscomb/Brownie McGhee/Henry Townsend/Josh White/Robert Pete Williams}
13004 *Legends Of Traditional Fingerstyle Guitar* [11232] {Elizabeth Cotten/Reverend Gary Davis/Mance Lipscomb/Brownie McGhee/Josh White and white country artists}
13010 *Freddy King – In Concert 1970–75* [11234]
13011 *Mance Lipscomb In Concert 1969* [11282]
13014 *Freddy King – The Beat, 1966/ Sweden 1973* [11279]
13015 *Elizabeth Cotten* (& John Fahey) [11278]
13016 *Legends Of Country Blues Guitar Volume 2* [11283] {Sam Chatmon/Reverend Gary Davis/ Son House/Leadbelly/Houston Stackhouse/Bukka White/Big Joe Williams}
13019 *Elizabeth Cotten* [11280]
13022 *Lightnin' Hopkins – Rare Performances 1960–79* [11294]

13028 *Freddy King – Dallas, Texas – January 20th 1973* [11295]

13035 *John Lee Hooker – Rare Performances 1960–84* [11364]

13037 *Blues Up The Country* [11336] {Pink Anderson/Reverend Gary Davis/Jesse Fuller/John Jackson/ Furry Lewis/George & Ethel McCoy/Josh White/Robert Pete Williams}

13038 *Legends Of The Delta Blues* [11337] {John Lee Hooker/Son House/Johnny Shines/Bukka White}

13041 *Texas Blues Guitar* [11359] {Albert Collins/Lightnin' Hopkins/Freddie King/Mance Lipscomb}

13042 *A Musical Journey – The Films of Pete, Toshi and Dan Seeger, 1957–64* [11407] {Big Bill Broonzy/J C Burris/Benny Richardson/Sonny Terry, unidentified artists #26 and other, non-AAVM artists}

13049 *Devil Got My Woman – Blues At Newport, 1966* [11395] {Reverend Pearly Brown/Mable Hillery/Son House/Howlin' Wolf/ Skip James/Bukka White}

13050 *Delta Blues/Cajun Two-Step; Newport, 1966* {Bois-Sec Ardoin/Canray Fontenot/Son House/Skip James/Bukka White/ Ed & Lonnie Young}

13051 *Billy In The Low Ground; Newport, 1966* {Bois-Sec Ardoin}

13054 *John Lee Hooker & Friends 1984–92*

13056 *Brownie McGhee & Sonny Terry – Red River Blues 1948–74* [11424]

13057 *Sonny Terry – Whoopin' The Blues 1958–74*

13060 *Brownie McGhee – Born With The Blues 1966–72* [11426]

13072 *Freddie King – Live At The Sugarbowl*

13076 *Jazz Parades – Feet Don't Fail Me Now*

13077 *Cajun Country – Don't Drop The Potato*

13078 *The Land Where The Blues Began*

13079 *Appalachian Journey*

13080 *Dreams And Songs of the Noble Old*

[This catalogue also contains much other American and world folk music]

VIDEO IMAGES [UK/US: NTSC/PAL]

73R *Showtime At The Apollo Vol. 1* {Faye Adams/Clovers/Larry Darnell/Larks/Amos Milburn/ Dinah Washington and jazz artists}

74 *Showtime At The Apollo Vol. 2* {Jimmy Brown/Ruth Brown/ Martha Davis/Delta Rhythm Boys/Larks/Amos Milburn and jazz artists

328 *Black Jazz And Blues* {Louis Jordan and jazz artists}

511 *Those Singin' Swingin' Years*

517 *Paradise In Harlem*

934 *Louis Jordan: Reet-Petite And Gone*

VIDEOPLUS [UK: PAL]

[The following appear in the Videoplus catalogue, but have not currently been traced to their origin; the catalogue numbers shown are those allocated by Videoplus]

2546 *Buddy Guy – Real Deal*

5356 *Chuck Berry – Hail Hail Rock & Roll*

95583 *Saturday Night At Rockefellers*

VIEW VIDEO [Italian: PAL]

1313 *The Ladies Sing The Blues* {Ruth Brown/Ida Cox/Helen Humes/ Bessie Smith/Rosetta Tharpe/ Dinah Washington and jazz artists}

VINTAGE JAZZ CLASSICS [Australian/ US: PAL/NTSC]

VJC2002 {Bessie Smith and jazz artists} unknown title

VJC2003 *Those Singin' Swingin' Years*

VJC2004 *Louis Jordan: Five Guys Named Moe*

VIRGIN [UK: PAL]

VVD762 *Boogie Woogie* {see Storyville SV6013 for details}

VVD771 *Alberta Hunter – My Castle's Rockin'*

VVD865 *Harlem Roots Vol. 1* {see Storyville SV6000 for details}
VVD866 *Harlem Roots Vol. 2* {see Storyville SV6001 for details}
VVD867 *Harlem Roots Vol. 3* {see Storyville SV6002 for details}
VVD868 *Harlem Roots Vol. 4* {see Storyville SV6003 for details}

WARNER [UK: PAL]

8536–50187–3 *The Sound Of Jazz* {Jimmy Rushing and jazz artists}
9031–74506–3 *Vintage Collection Vol. 1* {Jimmy Rushing and jazz artists}

YAZOO [UK/USA: PAL/NTSC)

500 *Son House & Bukka White*
501 *Gary Davis & Sonny Terry*
502 *Mance Lipscomb & Lightnin' Hopkins*
503 *Jesse Fuller & Elizabeth Cotten*
504 *Big Joe Williams & Fred McDowell*
505 *Good Morning Blues* [NTSC only]
506 *Out Of The Blacks, Into The Blues Pt. 1* [NTSC only]
507 *Out Of The Blacks, Into The Blues Pt. 2* [NTSC only]
509 *Albert King – Maintenance Shop Blues* [NTSC only]
512 *Times Ain't Like They Used To Be 1929–51* {Elder Solomon Lightfoot Michaux/Uncle John Scruggs/Whistler & His Jug Band annd other non-AAVM artists}
513 *Roosevelt Sykes & Lightnin' Hopkins* [NTSC only]
514 *At The Jazz Band Ball* {Bessie Smith and vintage jazz performances}
518 *Big Bill Broonzy & Roosevelt Sykes* [1961] [NTSC only]
519 *John Lee Hooker & Furry Lewis* [NTSC only]
520 *The Dietrich Wawzyn Collection*

6 Commercially Available Laser Discs

IMAGE

ID74240HB	*BB King Live In Africa*
ID7913VP	*Koko Taylor – Let The Good Times Roll*
ID8480RH	*Messin' With The Blues*

MCA

16015	*The Jerk*

PIONEER

PA94537	*Sweet Home Chicago* [2]

POLYGRAM

081–333–1	*Jump The Blues Away*

SONY

RO194L	*BB King Live At Nick's*

WARNER HOME VIDEO

11745	*The Color Purple*

7 Non-performing Interviewees

Name	Subject	Source
Abner, Ewart	Vee Jay records	*Record Row*
Adams, Joe [disc jockey]	Being a disc jockey	*Remembering Black Music*
Albertson, Chris [Author]	Bessie Smith	*Wild Women Don't Have The Blues*
Allen, Bill 'Hoss'	Rhythm and blues	*Rock and Roll Part 1*
Alexander, J.W. [Soul Stirrers member and manager]	Sam Cooke and the Soul Stirrers	*Too Close To Heaven*
Allen, Hoss [Disc jockey]	The gospel industry Interviews and comments	*Here Comes Gospel* *The Beat*
Babb, Morgan [Lead singer of the gospel group The Radio Four]	The gospel industry and blues	*Too Close To Heaven*
Barber, Chris [Bandleader]	Big Bill Broonzy	*Rhythms Of The World*
Barker, Blue Lu	Her career	*Wild Women Don't Have The Blues*
Barnes, Mae	Her career	*Wild Women Don't Have The Blues*
Bartholomew, Dave	Fats Domino	*Rock and Roll Part 1*
Bessman, Bernard [Record producer]	John Lee Hooker	*John Lee Hooker*
Blackwell, Robert [Record producer]	Record production	*Remembering Black Music*
Butler, Jerry	Vee Jay records	*Record Row*
Chess, Marshall [Chess records executive]	Chicago blues Chess records Chess records	*Sweet Home Chicago* [2] *Record Row* *Rock and Roll Part 1*

Chess, Philip [Chess records executive]	Chicago blues Chess records Chess records	*Sweet Home Chicago* [2] *Record Row* *Rock and Roll Part 1*
Clapton, Eric [Musician]	Robert Johnson	*The Search For Robert Johnson*
Clark, Dave [Record promoter]	Early days of record promotion	*Remembering Black Music*
Clark, Wink [Friend of Johnson]	Robert Johnson	*The Search For Robert Johnson*
Crayton, Esther [Musician's spouse]	Her husband, Pee Wee Crayton	*Remembering Black Music*
DeJean, Lois [Church leader]	The spiritual life	*Going Places – New Orleans*
Edick, George [Promoter]	St. Louis R&B St. Louis R&B	*George Edick's Showtime* *St. Soul – Soul Of St. Louis R&B*
'Famous Coachman' [Disc jockey]	John Lee Hooker	*John Lee Hooker*
Gardner, Carl	The Coasters	*Rock and Roll Part 2*
Geddins, Bob [Record producer]	Being a record producer	*Long Train Running*
Joe Gibson [Disc jockey]	Being a disc jockey	*Remembering Black Music*
Greensmith, Bill [Blues historian and photographer]	Henry Townsend	*That's The Way I Do It*
Hall, René [Record producer]	Record production	*Remembering Black Music*
Hammond Jr, John [Musician]	Robert Johnson	*The Search For Robert Johnson*
Hancock, Hunter [Disc jockey]	Being a disc jockey	*Remembering Black Music*
Hooker, Zakiya [John Lee Hooker's daughter]	John Lee Hooker	*John Lee Hooker*
Iglauer, Bruce [President, Alligator Records]	Alligator records Alligator records and Chicago blues	*Big City Blues* *Pride And Joy*

Jagger, Mick [Musician]	Chicago blues	*Sweet Home Chicago*
Kappus, Michael [John Lee Hooker's manager]	John Lee Hooker	*John Lee Hooker*
Koester, Robert [President, Delmark Records]	Chicago blues Chicago blues John Lee Hooker	*Chicago Blues* *Pride And Joy* *John Lee Hooker*
Korner, Alexis [Musician]	General comments	*The Blues* [BBC]
Korner, Bobbie & Sappho [Korner family members]	Big Bill Broonzy	*Rhythms Of The World*
Leaner, Bill	United Record Distributors	*Record Row*
Leiber, Jerry	Rhythm and blues	*Rock and Roll Part 2*
Lomax, Alan [Folklorist]	General comments Blues history	*American Patchwork* *Land Where The Blues Began*
Long, Worth [Blues historian at the Smithsonian Institute, Washington DC]	Blues history	*Baton Rouge Blues*
Matassa, Cosimo	New Orleans	*Rock and Roll Part 1*
Maxwell, Beatrice [Sharecropper]	Sharecropping in Mississippi	*Land Where The Blues Began*
Miller, J D [Record producer]	Recording blues	*Baton Rouge Blues*
Moore, James [Record producer]	West Coast blues	*Long Train Running*
O'Neal, Jim [Blues historian]	John Lee Hooker	*John Lee Hooker*
Oliver, Paul [Blues historian]	Boogie piano West Coast blues	*Boogie Woogie* *Long Train Running*
Palmer, Earl	Fats Domino	*Rock and Roll Part 1*
Palmer, Robert [Music journalist and author]	Southern blues	*Deep Blues*
Phillips, Sam	Sun Records	*Rock and Roll Part 1*

Pierson, Leroy [Blues historian]	Henry Townsend	*That's The Way I Do It*
Powell, Willie Mae [Friend of Johnson]	Robert Johnson	*The Search for Robert Johnson*
'Queen' Elizabeth [Friend of Johnson]	Robert Johnson	*The Search for Robert Johnson*
Richards, Keith [Musician]	Robert Johnson Blues	*The Search for Robert Johnson* *Record Row*
Richardson, Nat	Robert Johnson	*The Search for Robert Johnson*
Rupe, Art [Record producer]	Gospel recording	*Too Close to Heaven*
Schwab, Abe [Retailer]	Retailing lucky charms and blues records	*Deep Blues*
Seeger, Peggy [Musician]	Big Bill Broonzy	*Rhythms Of The World*
Shurman, Dick [Music journalist and record producer]	Chicago blues	*Pride And Joy*
Smith, Lucius [Sharecropper and musician] [Smith was 92 years old at the time of this interview]	Sharecropping in Mississippi	*Land Where The Blues Began*
Spann, Purvis [Disc jockey] [unused in the final edit but apparently still extant]	Chicago blues	*Devil's Music/The Blues* [BBC]
Spitzer, Nick [Folklorist]	Blues in Lousiana	*Baton Rouge Blues*
Stoller, Mike	Rhythm and blues	*Rock and Roll Part 2*
Strachwitz, Chris [President, Arhoolie Records]	Founding Arhoolie records	*It's Got To Be Rough To Be Sweet*
Taylor, 'Pops' [Husband of Koko Taylor]	The blues	*Queen Of The Blues*
Tyler, Alvin 'Red'	Fats Domino	*Rock and Roll Part 1*
Wilcox, Bert [Promoter]	Big Bill Broonzy	*Rhythms Of The World*

Wilford-Smith, Francis [Artist, collector and author]	Boogie piano	*Boogie Woogie*
Williams, Dootsie [Record producer]	Record production	*Remembering Black Music*
Williams, Shannon [Disc jockey]	The gospel industry	*Here Comes Gospel*
Wright, Billy [Musician]	His friendship with Little Richard	*The Little Richard Story*

8 Soundtracks

Only material directly related to film or television performance is listed here. The title of the production from which the material is drawn is shown in parenthesis. No attempt has been made to document every single reissue. This list is intended only to offer guidance on the most readily available soundtracks.

Artist	Title	Label/Cat.#/Format
Berry, Chuck [*Sounds For Saturday*, 1972 BBC TV]	*625*	625 [un-numbered] {LP}
Broonzy, Big Bill [Pete Seeger film, 1957]	untitled	Blues Special 1{EP}
Burley, Dan [*Jivin' In Be Bop*]	*Southside Shake*	Wolf WBJCD008 {CD}
Green, Al [*Gospel According To Al Green*]	*Gospel According To Al Green*	BG9376{CD}
Guy, Buddy and Wells, Junior [Montreux, 1974]	*Drinkin' TNT*	Sequel NEXCD657 {CD}
Harris, Hi-Tide [*Leadbelly*]	*Leadbelly*	ABC LP 9022–939 {LP}
International Sweethearts Of Rhythm [Various films and soundies, although opinions differ as to which recordings come from soundtracks and which are studio recordings released on 78rpm]		Rosetta RR1312{LP}
Jackson, Mahalia [*Jazz On A Summer's Day*]	[unknown title]	Columbia CL1244 {LP}
Johnson, Pete [sic] [*Boogie Woogie Dream, Boogie Woogie on St. Louis Blues*]	*Radio Broadcasts, Film Soundtracks, Alternate Takes 1939–c.1947*	Document DOCD–1009 {CD}
Jordan, Louis [*Reet-Petite And Gone/Caldonia*]	*On Film Volume 1*	Krazy Kat 7414 {LP}
[*Look-Out Sister/Jumpin' With Jordan*]	*On Film Volume 2*	Krazy Kat 7415 {LP}
[Compilation from above named films]	*On Film 1942–48*	Krazy Kat 17{CD}
McDowell, Fred [Mayfair Hotel, London, 1969]	*Standing At The Burying Ground*	Sequel NEBCD851{CD}

Muddy Waters [Jazz-USA]	*At Newport*	Chess CHD31269 {CD}
{Numerous vinyl issues of the above also exist}		
[*Jazz At The Maltings*]	*Rare Live Recordings*	Black Bear LP902 {LP}
[Montreux, 1972]	*Hoochie Coochie Man*	LRC CD9050 {LP}
[Dortmund, 1976]	*Live 1976*	Corinne LP100 {LP}
[*The Last Waltz*. One song only.]	*The Last Waltz*	WB CD7599–27346–2 {CD}
Nighthawk, Robert [*And This Is Free*]	*Live On Maxwell St*	Rounder 2022 {CD/LP}
Smith, Bessie [*St. Louis Blues, 1929*]	*Vol. 4*	Columbia CK2K57546 {CD}
Smith, Mamie [*Jailhouse Blues/Paradise In Harlem*]	*Vol. 4* (1923–42)	Document DOCD–5360 {CD}
Spann, Otis [*Jazz USA*]	*Rarest Recordings*	JSP LP1070 {LP}
Taylor, Koko [Montreux 1972]	*Blues Avalanche*	Chess LP60015 {LP}
Terry, Sonny and McGhee, Brownie [*Book Of Numbers*]	*Book Of Numbers*	Brut 6002 {LP}
Tharpe, Rosetta [*Soundies*]	*Sister Rosetta Tharpe*	Document DOCD–5334 {CD}
[*L'Aventure Du Jazz*]	unknown title	Jazz Odyssey LP005 {LP}
Wells, Junior – see Guy, Buddy		
Various [*Pride And Joy – The Story Of Alligator Records*]	*Alligator Records 20th Anniversary Tour*	Alligator CD105/6 {2CD}
Various [Soundtrack of the German TV broadcast]	*American Folk Blues Festival 1962*	Rare Recordings 2 {LP}
Various [*Angel Heart*. Includes Brownie McGhee]	*Angel Heart*	Antilles NDLP91085 {LP}
Various [*Baby Doll*. Includes Smiley Lewis]	*Baby Doll*	Columbia CL958 {LP}
Various [*The Blues*, 1962]	*The Blues*	Asch A101{LP}

Various	*Chicago Blues: 19 Tracks from the film Chicago Blues*	Red Lightnin' 055 {LP} Castle CLACD425 {CD}

[*Chicago Blues*. Both the above issues include recordings not found in the film. Either they were not originally filmed, or they were and have subsequently been lost]

Various	*Conversation With The Blues*	Decca LK4664 {LP} {CD} accompanying book of the same name. Cambridge University Press, 1997

[Some material included in *Blues Like Showers Of Rain*]

Various	*The Color Purple*	Qwest 9 25356–1 {LP}

[*The Color Purple*. Includes John Lee Hooker, Sonny Terry]

Various	*Crossroads*	Warner Bros 9 25399–1 {LP}

[*Crossroads*. Includes Terry Evans, Bobby King and Sonny Terry]

Various	*Deep Blues*	Atlantic [US] 782450–2 {CD}

[*Deep Blues*]

Various	*The Devil's Music Vol. 1*	Red Lightnin' 033 {2LP}
Various	*The Devil's Music Vol. 2*	Red Lightnin' 038 {LP}

[*The Devil's Music* aka *The Blues*]

Various	*Gospel At Newport*	Vanguard VCD770142 {CD}

[Alan Lomax footage of the Dixie Hummingbirds, Original Gospel Harmonettes and Swan Silvertones]

Various	*Into The Night*	MCA 5561 {LP}

[*Into The Night*. One performance by B.B. King]

Various	*J'ai Eté Au Bal Vol. 1*	Arhoolie CD331 {CD}
Various	*J'ai Eté Au Bal Vol. 2*	Arhoolie CD332 {CD}

[*J'ai Et Au Bal*. These two CDs also include complete versions of all the soundtrack recordings, including vintage commercial material]

Various	*Louie Bluie*	Arhoolie 470 {CD}

[*Louie Bluie*. This album also contains material not used in the final edit of the film]

Various	*Mississippi Delta Blues Festival '79*	Delta Blues DBF 79 {LP}

Various	*Those Singin' Swingin' Years*	Sounds Great 8003 {LP}

[*Those Singin' Swingin' Years*]

Bibliography

Catalogues

The catalogues of the following companies have been referred to in the compilation of this books:

Laser Video File, Westwood, New Jersey: 1992–93

Laser Video Guide, Paramus, New Jersey: 1997

Red Lick, Porthmadog, Gwynedd, Wales, UK: 1990–97

Rhino Records, Miami, Florida: 1997–98

Vestapol Videos: 1995–97

Videoplus: 1996–97

Journals

Blues And Rhythm, eds: Paul Vernon, issues 1–19; Tony Burke, issues 20–present. Specifically issue 71: 'Louis Jordan On Film 'by Tony Burke and Howard Rye and issue 74 'Louis Jordan', additions and corrections by Howard Rye.

Blues Unlimited, eds: Simon A. Napier and Mike Ledbitter, Bexhill, England, 1963–72; Bill Greensmith, Cilla Huggins, Mike Rowe and Bez Turner, London, England, 1972–86.

Blues World, ed. Bob Groom, Knutsford, England, 1965–68.

Jazz Beat, London, England, 1963–66.

Jazz Journal, ed. Sinclair Traill, London, England, 1955–70.

Jazz Monthly, ed. Albert McCarthy, London, England, 1960–70.

Juke Blues, eds John Broven, Cilla Huggins, Bez Turner, 1985–90; John Broven, Cilla Huggins, 1990–92; Cilla Huggins, 1990–97, London, England.

Radio Times, London, England: 1950–90.

Sailor's Delight, ed./publisher, Paul Vernon, London, England: 1978–84.

TV Times, London, England: 1955–90.

Books

Bastin, Bruce (1986), *Never Sell A Copyright*, Chigwell, UK: Storyville Publications.

Brooks, Tim and Marsh, Earle (1995), *Complete Directory To Primetime Network And Cable TV Shows*, New York: Ballantine Books.

Clarke, Donald (1989), *Penguin Encyclopedia of Popular Music*, London: Penguin Books.

Connors, Martin and Craddock, Jim (eds) (1998), *Video Hound's Golden Movie Retriever*, London and New York: Visible Ink Press.

Dixon, Robert M.W. and Godrich, John (1982), *Blues And Gospel Records 1902–1942* (third edition), Chigwell, UK: Storyville Publications.

Dixon, Robert M.W., Godrich, John and Rye, Howard (1997), *Blues And Gospel Records 1890–1943* (fourth edition), London and New York: Oxford University Press.

Erlewine, Bogdanov, Koda and Woodstra (1996), *All Music Guide To The Blues*, San Francisco: Miller Freeman Books.

Halliwell, Leslie, *Filmgoer's Companion* (various editions).

Harris, Sheldon (1990), *Blues Who's Who*, New York: DaCapo Press.

Hayes, Cedric J. and Laughton, Robert (1992), *Gospel Records 1943–1970*, Vols 1–2, Record Information Services, England.

Jones, G. William (1991), *Black Cinema Treasures Lost And Found*, Dallas: University of North Texas Press.

Jepsen, Jorgen Grunnet, *Jazz Records 1943–1970* (various editions).

Kennedy, Peter (ed.) (1970), *Films on Traditional And Ethnic Music*, Paris: Unesco.

Kisch, John and Mapp, Edward (1992), *A Separate Cinema*, New York: Noonday Press.

Leadbitter, Mike and Slaven, Neil (1987–94), *Blues Records 1943–1970*, Vols 1–2, Record Information Services, London.

Lornell, Kip and Wolfe, Charles (1992), *The Life And Legend of Leadbelly*, New York: HarperCollins.

Meeker, David (1970 and 1982), *Jazz In The Movies*, London: British Film Institute.

Metfessel, Milton (1928), *Phonophotography In Folk Music*, Chapel Hill: University of North Carolina Press.

Nash, Jay Robert and Ross, Stanley Ralph (1981), *Motion Picture Catalogue* (12 volumes), Chicago: Cinebooks.

Oliver, Paul (1965), *Conversation With The Blues*, London: Cassell and revised (1997) Cambridge: Cambridge University Press.

Oliver, Paul (1970), *Story Of The Blues*, London: Penguin Books.

Rust, Brian (1980), *Jazz Records 1897–1942*, Chigwell, UK: Storyville Publications.

Sampson, Henry T. (1977), *Blacks In Black And White – A Source Book On Black Film*, Metuchan: Scarecrow Press.

Sansahl, Linda J. (1987), *Rock Films*, London and New York, Facts On File.

Smith, Chris (1996), *Hit The Right Lick – The Recordings Of Big Bill Broonzy*, Bedford: Blues and Rhythm.

Stratemann, Klaus (1981), *Negro Bands On Film 1928–1950*, Lübbecke: Verlag Uhle und Kleimann.

Thompson, Kristin and Bordwell, David (1994), *Film History – An Introduction*, New York: McGraw-Hill..

Time Out Film Guide (various editions), London: Penguin Books.

Tooze, Sandra B. (1997), *Muddy Waters The Mojo Man*, Toronto: ECW Press. See in particular the discography by Fred Rothwell and Phil Wight.